English Renaissance Literary Criticism

English Renaissance Literary Criticism

EDITED BY

BRIAN VICKERS

CLARENDON PRESS · OXFORD

OXFORD

UNIVERSITY PRESS

Great Clarendon Street, Oxford OX2 6DP

Oxford University Press is a department of the University of Oxford.
It furthers the University's objective of excellence in research, scholarship,
and education by publishing worldwide in

Oxford New York

Athens Auckland Bangkok Bogotá Buenos Aires Calcutta
Cape Town Chennai Dar es Salaam Delhi Florence Hong Kong Istanbul
Karachi Kuala Lumpur Madrid Melbourne Mexico City Mumbai
Nairobi Paris São Paulo Singapore Taipei Tokyo Toronto Warsaw
and associated companies in Berlin Ibadan

Oxford is a registered trade mark of Oxford University Press
in the UK and certain other countries

Published in the United States
by Oxford University Press Inc., New York

© Brian Vickers 1999

The moral rights of the author have been asserted
Database right Oxford University Press (maker)

First published 1999

British Library Cataloguing in Publication Data

Data available

Library of Congress Cataloging in Publication Data

Data available

ISBN 0-19-818679-7

1 3 5 7 9 10 8 6 4 2

Typeset by Best-set Typesetter Ltd., Hong Kong
Printed in Great Britain
on acid-free paper by
Biddle Ltd,
Guildford and King's Lynn

FOR

LEO SALINGAR

AND IN MEMORY OF

R. T. H. REDPATH

AND

W. G. INGRAM

PREFACE

THIS anthology is intended to make available again several major texts which have long been out of print; to introduce some unfamiliar texts, including one (John Ford's elegy on John Fletcher) which has never been published before; and to place other, familiar texts, in a newly defined historical context. It owes much to two earlier collections, G. Gregory Smith (ed.), *Elizabethan Critical Essays*, 2 vols. (Oxford, 1904), and Joel Spingarn (ed.), *Critical Essays of the Seventeenth Century*, 3 vols. (Oxford, 1908), which were pioneering in their day, but reflect an earlier phase in the understanding of literary criticism. The biggest difference between my collection and theirs reflects the vastly increased understanding we have gained over the last fifty years of the importance of rhetoric to both the creation and reception of literature. Writers of poetry, drama, even prose fiction, took account of the precepts of rhetoric while composing their works, as did readers and critics evaluating them. In effect we are dealing with a truly homogeneous culture, in which theory and practice interlocked. My introduction and commentary acknowledges this new appreciation, and breaks new ground by showing the extent to which writers of the English Renaissance drew on classical rhetoric both for literary theory and for practical criticism. The names of Quintilian, Cicero, Horace, and other classical authorities occur so frequently in the notes that one may sometimes wonder whether our writers ever had any new ideas of their own. The same comment could be made about Italian and French critics, of course, for Renaissance concepts of literature drew extensively on classical sources: what really matters is how writers applied them in creating and criticizing vernacular literature. My anthology differs from others in accepting that English criticism was largely prescriptive, and in following out the implications for literature of this emphasis on the practicalities of composition.

The other overlooked aspect of Renaissance literary criticism to emerge from my evaluation concerns literary theory. Contrary to the opinions of some modern scholars, writers in this period had a perfectly coherent theory of literature. It, too, derived from rhetoric, the branch known as epideictic, in which orators praised virtue and attacked vice. Transferred to a later cultural context, in which literature was written to be read in private or performed on stage, this ethical emphasis produced a new psychology of reading. The writer's goal was seen as being to praise virtue and detest vice with such vividness that the reader would be stimulated—'inflamed' is the term commonly used—to emulate it in his or her life. This theory of affective arousal, which gave literature a central place in individual education and the forming of a good society, can be found in many of the texts presented here, from treatises on education and the elite genre of epic down to the popular theatres, with their justification of drama against its critics. Also prescriptive, it looked for practical fulfilment in the lives of both writers and readers.

In selecting English criticism from the period 1530 to 1650 I have tried to reflect the range of genres that were practised then: Senecan tragedy (Alexander Neville), moralized history (William Baldwin), a wide range of Elizabethan and Jacobean drama (Whetstone, Shakespeare, Heywood, Massinger, Jonson), up to the new Italianate tragicomedy (John Fletcher). In poetry I include pastoral and allegory (E.K. and Edmund Spenser), religious lyric (Robert Southwell), Homeric translations (George Chapman), and Italian epic (George Gascoigne). I also document critical reactions to the new poetry of Donne (Thomas Carew), and to what we may still call Metaphysical poetry (Dudley North). The interplay between rhetoric and poetics, never separated in the Renaissance, is represented by the treatises of Puttenham and Hoskyns, while the place of rhetoric in literary theory is discussed by Francis Bacon and Ben Jonson. If Jonson dominates the Jacobean part of this collection, among the Elizabethans the supremacy of Sir Philip Sidney's *Apology for Poetry*, arguably the best single critical treatise of the whole European Renaissance, is acknowledged by its being included complete.

In preparing the text from a variety of sources, I owe many thanks to Dr Margrit Soland, my assistant for over a decade, who did much of the early scanning, converting the vagaries of Elizabethan printing into a legible form. Her successor Katherine Hahn has invested great energy and patience in ordering both text and notes into a coherent whole, ably assisted by Annette Baertschi, who further helped identify Greek and Latin quotations. Jeremy Maule gave me permission to use his transcription of John Ford's elegy to John Fletcher (which he had discovered in the William Andrews Clark Memorial Library, Los Angeles) just a week before his tragically premature death; the Library have added their permission. Three colleagues kindly answered some recondite queries: Michael J. B. Allen (Ficino), Luc Deitz (Scaliger), and Bob Sharples (Alexander of Aphrodisias).

For permission to use the painting 'Homage to a Poet', by Giorgione (School of), I thank the National Gallery, London. The Library of Trinity College Cambridge has kindly supplied a print of the illustration to October in Spenser's *Shepherd's Calendar*, and I thank the Master and Fellows for granting permission to use it. I am grateful to Paul Keegan for his interest and support. My editors at OUP, Sophie Goldsworthy and Matthew Hollis, have been helpful and supportive throughout, while Heather Watson's keen-eyed copy-editing has saved me from various errors and inconsistencies. I thank them all.

The dedication remembers my three teachers at Trinity College Cambridge, who, many years ago, put me on the right road in Renaissance studies.

Brian Vickers

CONTENTS

ABBREVIATIONS

CLASSICAL SOURCES

Generally I follow the conventional abbreviations as given in the *Oxford Classical Dictionary* (rev. edn. 1996). The most frequently recurring works are listed here.

Anon.:	*Rhet. Her.*	*Rhetorica ad Herennium*
Aristotle:	*De an.*	*De anima*
	Eth. Nic.	*Ethica Nicomachea*
	Metaph.	*Metaphysica*
	Poet.	*Poetica*
	Pol.	*Politica*
	Rh.	*Rhetorica*
Cicero:	*Arch.*	*Pro Archia poeta*
	Brut.	*Brutus*
	Cat.	*In Catilinam*
	De or.	*De oratore*
	Fin.	*De finibus*
	Inv. rhet.	*De inventione rhetorica*
	Off.	*De officiis*
	Orat.	*Orator*
	QFr.	*Epistulae ad Quintum fratrem*
	Tusc.	*Tusculanae disputationes*
Homer:	*Il.*	*Iliad*
	Od.	*Odyssey*
Horace:	*Ars P.*	*Ars poetica*
	Epist.	*Epistulae*
	Sat.	*Satirae*
Ovid:	*Am.*	*Amores*
	Ars am.	*Ars amatoria*
	Fast.	*Fasti*
	Met.	*Metamorphoses*
	Rem. am.	*Remedia amoris*
Plato:	*Grg.*	*Gorgias*
	Phdr.	*Phaedrus*
	Resp.	*Respublica*
Plutarch:	*Mor.*	*Moralia*
	Poetas	*Quomodo adulescens poetas audire debeat*

Quintilian:	*Inst.*	*Institutio oratoria*
Seneca (the Elder):	*Controv.*	*Controversiae*
Seneca (the Younger):	*Ep.*	*Epistulae morales*
Tacitus:	*Dial.*	*Dialogus de oratoribus*
Virgil:	*Aen.*	*Aeneid*
	Ecl.	*Eclogues*
	Georg.	*Georgics*
Xenophon:	*Cyr.*	*Cyropaedia*

MODERN SOURCES

ALC   *Ancient Literary Criticism*, ed. D. A. Russell and M.
      Winterbottom (Oxford, 1972)
CES   *Critical Essays of the Seventeenth Century*, ed. J. E. Spingarn,
      3 vols. (Oxford, 1908; 1957)
CWE   *Collected Works of Erasmus* (Toronto and Buffalo, 1974–)
ECE   *Elizabethan Critical Essays*, ed. G. Gregory Smith, 2 vols.
      (Oxford, 1904; 1964)
IDR   *In Defence of Rhetoric*, by Brian Vickers (Oxford, 1988; rev. edn.,
      1997)
LCPD *Literary Criticism: Plato to Dryden*, ed. Allan H. Gilbert (New
      York, 1940; Detroit, 1962)
TPR   *Traités de poétique et de rhétorique de la Renaissance*, ed. F. Goyet
      (Paris, 1990)

A NOTE ON THE TEXTS

SINCE this anthology of Renaissance literary criticism is intended for general readers as well as scholars, while titles are quoted in old spelling all other texts have been modernized in both spelling and punctuation. Greek quotations have been transliterated, and I have attempted to identify all biblical and foreign-language quotations, providing translations where necessary. Unless otherwise stated, I have used the translations found in the Loeb Classical Library (London and Cambridge, Mass.). For Plato I have used the translations by various hands in *Plato. The Collected Dialogues*, ed. Edith Hamilton and Huntingdon Cairns (New York, 1963), and for Aristotle I have preferred the *Complete Works* in the revised Oxford translation, ed. Jonathan Barnes, 2 vols. (Princeton, 1984). In identifying quotations I have benefited from the two pioneering collections of literary criticism in this period, by G. G. Smith and J. E. Spingarn (see Further Reading, §A), and from individual editions, as acknowledged.

Editorial insertions are placed within square brackets. Words marked with an asterisk appear in the Glossary: here I gladly acknowledge my debt both to the complete *Oxford English Dictionary*, 2nd edition, and to its splendid digest, the *New Shorter Oxford English Dictionary On Historical Principles*, ed. Lesley Brown, 2 vols. (Oxford, 1993).

INTRODUCTION

RENAISSANCE literary criticism—a term that covers both literary theory and practical criticism—differs from modern expectations in several respects, not at first sight visible.

Unlike our assumption that when critics discuss an existing work or works of literature they do so as readers addressing other readers in an essentially *descriptive* process, much Renaissance criticism is *prescriptive*, telling a budding writer how to go about his or her task.

Where we expect literary criticism to constitute a *poetics*, a reasoned account of how a work of literature exists as an autonomous artefact, independent of its effect on readers, the Renaissance understood literature as being essentially a form of *rhetoric*, with an explicit or implicit design on its readers, intended to arouse their feelings and direct them to some moral end.[1]

Where we tend to think that every literary work worthy of the name is unique, a testimony to its author's creative originality, Renaissance theorists expected that not just beginning writers but all authors would achieve *originality* through a process of *imitation*.

And whereas post-Romantic aesthetics have notoriously rejected all notion of rules for composition, Renaissance writers and critics gladly accepted that certain *criteria of correctness* applied to works of literature, especially to those representing human behaviour and speech.

Finally, where our critical activities emerge out of an open engagement with genres, traditions, or writers, free of any constraints other than those of time, energy, or the material working conditions needed for sustained thought, much Renaissance criticism constitutes a *defence of literature*, or an apology for a particular author or genre against its critics.

These are some of the main differences between modern approaches and the literary criticism produced in England between the 1530s and 1650s. But the same observations would apply to the

---

[1] For this modern distinction, not valid for the Renaissance, see Brian Vickers, 'Rhetoric and Poetics', in C. B. Schmitt and Q. Skinner (eds.), *The Cambridge History of Renaissance Philosophy* (Cambridge, 1988), pp. 715–45. The best bibliographies of the two subjects are those contained in D. Sedge (ed.), *The Cambridge Bibliography of English Literature, Third Edition, Vol. 2: 1500–1700* (Cambridge, forthcoming): 'Rhetoric' by Lawrence D. Green, and 'Literary Criticism' by Robert Cockcroft.

critical tradition which started in Italy and France half a century earlier than in England, and produced a larger body of work.[2] The Renaissance was a European phenomenon, but while the national cultures shared many assumptions and methods the forms and goals of criticism differed, reflecting different intellectual and social contexts. In England, for instance, we find a later phase of a major linguistic and cultural transition that had already taken place in Italy and France. In all three countries scholars dissatisfied with the dominance of the ancient tongues attempted to establish the vernacular languages as being just as worthy of serious attention as Greek or Latin, whether for creative literature or for literary criticism. In Italy some critics chose to write in Latin: Vida did so for his *De arte poetica* (1527), as did Antonio Minturno for his *De poeta* (1559), and Giovanni Viperano for his *De arte poetica* (1579). But critics and theorists increasingly preferred the vernacular: Gian Giorgio Trissino published a *Poetica* in Italian in 1529, as did Daniello in 1536, Minturno in 1564, Patrizzi in 1586, followed by at least a dozen more writers of note by the end of the sixteenth century. In France, with the exception of Julius Caesar Scaliger's encyclopedic (and highly derivative) *Poetices libri septem* (1561),[3] all the treatises on poetry were written in French. In England, two of the earliest essays were published in Latin, Henry Dethick's *Oratio in laudem poëseos* (*c.* 1572)—which is virtually identical with the *Oratio in laudem artis poeticae* ascribed to John Rainolds[4]—and Richard Wills, *De re poetica* (1573).[5] But thereafter, with the exception of some criticism addressed to the learned Latin drama, all crit-

---

[2] The pioneer study was by Joel E. Spingarn, *A History of Literary Criticism in the Renaissance* (New York, 1899; 4th edn., 1924; repr. 1963, with an introd. by Bernard Weinberg). The subject was revolutionized by the wide-ranging study of Bernard Weinberg, *A History of Literary Criticism in the Italian Renaissance*, 2 vols. (Chicago, 1961, 1974), hereafter cited as *History*. Weinberg also edited two immensely useful collections, *Critical Prefaces of the French Renaissance* (Evanston, Ill., 1950), and *Trattati di Poetica e Retorica del Cinquecento*, 4 vols. (Bari, 1970–4). Two other outstanding studies came from Baxter Hathaway, *The Age of Criticism: The Late Renaissance in Italy* (Ithaca, NY, 1962) and *Marvels and Commonplaces: Renaissance Literary Criticism* (New York, 1968).

[3] See the admirable edition, with German translation, by Luc Deitz, of the first four books of Scaliger's *Poetices libri septem*. *Sieben Bücher über die Dichtkunst*, 3 vols. (Stuttgart—Bad Cannstatt, 1994–5); and my review in *Bulletin of the Society for Renaissance Studies*, 13 (1995), 23–9.

[4] See J. W. Binns, *Intellectual Culture in Elizabethan and Jacobean England: The Latin Writings of the Age* (Leeds, 1990), pp. 146–8, 444–9, for Dethick's authorship, based on evidence unavailable to earlier scholars, William Ringler and Walter Allen, in their edition and translation of John Rainolds, *Oratio in laudem artis poeticae c.1572* (Princeton, 1940).

[5] See Richard Wills, *De re poetica*, ed. and tr. A. D. S. Fowler (Oxford, 1958).

ical writings were in the vernacular, coinciding with the remarkable flourishing of English poetry, drama, and prose under Elizabeth and James.

The fact that the battle for the vernacular was fought first in Italy, then in France, and subsequently in England[6] shows the cultural time-lag between these countries. England, isolated by sea, was additionally disadvantaged compared to other countries north of the Alps, so that the fruits of the Italian Renaissance reached there with much delay. Some Englishmen travelled to Italy in the fifteenth century, experiencing at first hand the new humanist curriculum,[7] with its recovery of classical texts and its new analytical techniques (all reading to be accompanied by note-taking; notes to be organized according to both subject-matter and style, including metaphors, similes, and other tropes and figures; material to be assembled with an eye to its reuse in one's own compositions). But whereas the Italian grammar schools had been transformed in the early fifteenth century by such brilliant scholar-teachers as Gasparino Barzizza and Vittorino da Feltre, it was not until 1516 that John Colet, aided by Erasmus, northern Europe's greatest educationalist, reformed the curriculum of St Paul's School, giving rise to a huge increase in grammar schools across England, which totalled some 360 by 1575. Their curricula, modelled either on St Paul's or on that of Eton, as adapted by Westminster, established an education in Latin which taught with great thoroughness the humanist techniques of analytical reading and graded composition.[8] The effect of this intense exposure to (predominantly) Latin literature, absorbed in the original language but regularly reprocessed in Latin and English compositions, was profound. Indeed, the remarkable flourishing of poetry, drama, and prose fiction between 1570 and 1630, written by the first generations of grammar school (and in some cases university) products, can be largely credited to this source. As one historian has said, 'without Erasmus, no Shakespeare'.[9]

[6] On the rise of the vernaculars, see R. Hall, *The Italian Questione della Lingua: An Interpretative Essay* (Chapel Hill, NC, 1942); A. Mazzocco, *Linguistic Theories in Dante and the Humanists* (Leiden, 1993); and R. F. Jones, *The Triumph of the English Language* (Stanford, Calif., 1953).

[7] See Roberto Weiss, *Humanism in England during the Fifteenth Century* (3rd edn., Oxford, 1967); and for an illuminating account of the analytical techniques of humanism, R. R. Bolgar, *The Classical Heritage and its Beneficiaries* (Cambridge, 1954).

[8] See T. W. Baldwin, *William Shakspere's Small Latine & Lesse Greeke*, 2 vols. (Urbana, Ill., 1944; 1966).

[9] Emrys Jones, *The Origins of Shakespeare* (Oxford, 1977), p. 13.

England was late in experiencing the impact of the Italian Renaissance, but it more than made up for it in the range and quality of literature which it produced. However, in some respects England never caught up with Italy, due to the great social and cultural differences between the two countries. Italy, more especially Tuscany, had had a major literature for over two centuries, from Dante, Boccaccio, and Petrarch to Ariosto, Tasso, Machiavelli, Guicciardini, and a host of lesser poets and prose writers, writing in a language which was still comprehensible to any literate person. The great changes in the English language in the course of the sixteenth century, and the sporadic printing of medieval literature, deprived our writers and critics of any meaningful sense of a literary tradition, as we can see from the vagueness of references to Chaucer, Lydgate, or Skelton.[10] An Elizabethan writer was likely to be much more familiar with Virgil or Plutarch than with predecessors writing in his own language before 1550.[11]

Italy had not only a longer literary tradition but a much more vigorous body of literary criticism. The *Divina Commedia* attracted many commentators from the fourteenth to the sixteenth centuries, and although the prose works of Petrarch suffered an eclipse in the Renaissance his poetry inspired innumerable Petrarchists and anti-Petrarchists. While much of the early commentary literature merely explains allusions or unusual grammatical forms, in the sixteenth century a rapid spread of critical debate focused on Dante, Ariosto, Tasso, and other contemporary writers, addressing a series of much wider issues of poetic form, genre, social and moral questions. The result was a large body of writing,[12] often polemical debate, unlike anything produced in England before the eighteenth century (if then). The production of literary criticism was stimulated by other institutions which flourished earlier and more widely in Italy than in England: in courts, universities, and academies, where scholars and

---

[10] The great exception to these perfunctory references to medieval poets is Shakespeare, who made a creative use of Chaucer throughout his long career. See A. Thompson, *Shakespeare's Chaucer: A Study in Literary Origins* (Liverpool, 1978).

[11] A similar phenomenon occurred in France, where Du Bellay and the Pléiade poets imitated classical and contemporary Italian poetic styles and forms, rejecting all the genres of medieval French poetry: cf. H. Weber, *La Création poétique au XVIe siècle en France*, 2 vols. (Paris, 1956), i. 116–18.

[12] Bernard Weinberg devotes seven long chapters to this 'practical criticism', from the 'Quarrel over Dante' to the similar disputes surrounding Speroni, Ariosto, Tasso, and Guarini: *History*, ii. 815–1112.

creative writers competed for attention and patronage. Another factor which helped Italian literary criticism to develop more fully and profoundly than English was the far more advanced state of philology and textual criticism in Italian schools and universities, and the parallel existence of printer-publishers who were among the leading European editors of classical texts. The first publication of the Greek rhetorical tradition from original texts (as opposed to medieval Arabic or Latin versions, often incomplete or altered) was the two-volume *Rhetores Graeci* published by Aldus Manutius at Venice in 1508–9, to be followed by many more editions and translations of the classics. The first printing of Aristotle's *Poetics* was in the Latin translation by Giorgio Valla (Venice, 1498), and its first appearance in Greek was due to Manutius in 1508, while the first translation of the *Poetics* into any vernacular was by Lodovico Castelvetro, *Poetica d'Aristotele Vulgarizzata, et Sposta* (Vienna, 1570)—that is, 'translated and explained'.

This combination of circumstances accounts for the large number of new works in poetics and rhetoric appearing in Italy, and for their highly professional nature. They are often very extensive: Minturno's *De poeta* (1559) runs to 568 pages, his *L'Arte poetica* (1563) to 456 pages; Castelvetro's translation and commentary on the *Poetics* (1570) takes up 385 pages; Julius Caesar Scaliger (of Italian origin, who adopted French nationality) published a *Poetice* in seven books, totalling 364 pages in double column. Scaliger's work, like that of several other scholars, digests and reprocesses a vast amount of Greek and Latin material, including some only recently known, and had pretensions of being encyclopedic. Such texts were for the use of scholars, professional classicists, or historians.

The educational revolution brought about by Erasmus and other humanists had an immediate effect on grammar schools, and certainly affected the curricula of Oxford and Cambridge colleges, which adopted the new humanist emphasis on rhetoric; but it produced few major classical scholars in England. Sir John Cheke was revered as a teacher of Greek at Cambridge in the 1540s, but he published little or no original scholarship, and it was not until Sir Henry Savile's great edition of Chrysostom (8 vols., 1610–12) that an English scholar produced anything ranking with the work of Erasmus, Estienne, or Lipsius. The absence in England of any tradition of literary discussion comparable to that found in Italian courts, universities, and academies meant that works of literary criticism, when produced, were addressed not to scholars but to general readers, and to practising writers. The rhetorical treatises of Wilson and Puttenham may include an obligatory section on the origins of rhetoric, or poetry (as does Sidney's *Defence of Poetry*), but they are by no means as comprehensive as their Italian counterparts, and they are written in English. Not intended as scholastic texts, they specifically address an ideal reader—a lawyer, parliamentary officer, courtier, or poet—who will be speaking and writing in the vernacular.

To specialists in the history and theory of literary criticism, the English treatises of the sixteenth and seventeenth centuries, with their modest scope and local audience, may seem disappointing. But from the standpoint of the poet and dramatist—which is the position consciously represented in this anthology—they were enormously useful, since they translated and re-synthesized a great deal of doctrine, either directly from the classical texts or from their imitators in the continental Renaissance. The teachings of antiquity were domesticated, placed in the context of English society and English literature. In his *Arte of Rhetorique* (1553, 1560), while drawing on Cicero's *De inventione rhetorica*, Thomas Wilson substituted for the Roman's account of *par* (equity) a discussion of commons, the undivided land belonging to a community, which raised analogous issues of rights and custom, and he inserted illustrative anecdotes from the English parliament. Similarly, the rhetorical treatises of Puttenham, Abraham Fraunce, Henry Peacham, and John Hoskyns are illustrated with examples taken from English poets or the English Bible. Thus, although vitally connected with the European Renaissance and the new humanism, English literary criticism was directed specifically at the situation of writers in the vernacular, who may have been producing the first English versions of a classical or Renaissance genre (Senecan tragedy, moralizing pastoral, ode, tragicomedy). Although less impressive as academic treatises, these English texts have the great virtue of being practical, guiding and stimulating the process by which our literature measured itself against its distinguished predecessors. An aggressive phrase that Ben Jonson used in paying tribute to both William Shakespeare and Francis Bacon, asserting their achievements against those of 'insolent Greece, or haughty Rome', well expresses this shared sense of having mastered a body of knowledge—techniques of composition, the rules of a genre, the proper attitude towards an audience—such that an English writer could now set up on his own. The practicality of English Renaissance criticism may be not a weakness but its strength.

DESCRIPTION AND PRESCRIPTION

Anyone looking to the English Renaissance for works of descriptive criticism—analyses of a literary work as an end in itself—will soon be disappointed. Isolated comments on particular features of a work can be found, such as those on Sidney's *Arcadia* by Gabriel Harvey (p. 333) or John Hoskyns (p. 398), but only as incidental to another purpose. The first work of literary criticism in English, George Gascoigne's *Certayne Notes of Instruction concerning the making of Verse or Ryme in English* (1575), is typical of many that followed, being a prescriptive treatise intended for 'the correction [education] of the laureate', giving the would-be poet a brief digest of the topics to be mastered: imitation and invention, decorum, prosody, verse-form, rhyme, rhetoric, the correct qualities of style, and the major poetic forms (pp. 162 ff.). The much larger *Arte of English Poesie* by George Puttenham (pp. 190 ff.), published in 1589 but conceived and partly written earlier, covers all these topics in greater detail and deals with many others, including such traditional concerns as the antiquity and importance of poetry, the relation between nature and art, decorum as not just a literary but also a social concept, and so on. The size of the treatise varies according to the author's knowledge or ambition, and the printer's optimism (or subsidy). But the orientation of these and other treatises excerpted in this anthology—Thomas Wilson's *The Arte of Rhetorique*, John Hoskyns's *Directions for Speech and Style* (*c*.1599), Thomas Campion's *Observations in the art of English Poesy* (1602)—was firmly directed towards an audience of budding writers. Indeed, the term 'art' corresponds to the Latin *ars* (and Greek *techne*), describing manuals teaching how a particular discipline is to be mastered, moving—usually rather quickly—from theory to practical examples. In the scenes which he contributed to *The Reign of King Edward III* (*c*.1592), Shakespeare included one in which the lovesick king asks his secretary to write a poem to his beloved, heaping up hyperbole himself while criticizing his employee's attempts, a demonstration of how (not) to write love poetry which pokes fun at the clichés of the genre, already mocked in Sidney's *Astrophil and Stella*.

The presence of so many 'how to write' manuals might suggest a curious imbalance within the literary public, as if writers formed an abundant category, while readers as such were hardly recognized. However, everything we know about the growth of a reading public in the sixteenth and seventeenth centuries points to the existence of an audience able to deal with long and at times complicated literary texts—witness the appetite for epic poetry in the period after 1550, from Homer and Virgil to Tasso and Ariosto, in the original languages and in translation, and the popularity of comparably long texts in prose (Heliodorus' *Aethiopian Story*, Sidney's *Arcadia*, Cervantes' *Don Quixote*). Such a readership was surely able to reflect on the issues involved in producing and absorbing imaginative literature. The phenomenon of the dominance of prescriptive over descriptive works points to some further characteristics of critical writing in this period which deserve exploring.

First, we should recognize that in classical antiquity the major forms of literary discussion were rhetorical treatises, practical guides to speaking in public, or works on poetry and drama which had a similarly prescriptive intent. Aristotle's *Poetics*, although it devotes much of its brief space to analysing Athenian tragedy, actually informs the budding dramatist on how to manage things like plot and characterization; his much longer *Rhetoric* shares the goal of training an orator with other more mundane treatises, while raising the whole discussion on to a higher plane. As D. A. Russell has written, all classical literary criticism is rhetorical, in that 'the address is always to potential practitioners, not merely to readers or connoisseurs. . . . Horace's *Ars poetica* assumes—whether as fact or as convenient fiction—that the two young Piso brothers are about to sit down and write plays.' And although the resulting documents may disappoint modern readers' expectations of what literary criticism should be, 'this material provides a special insight into the attitudes and presuppositions of the creative writers of antiquity. We seem to glimpse the inside of the workshop.'[13] Many of these treatises include examples of good or bad structure or style, which their authors analyse to bring out just how an orator or poet has succeeded or failed. Such specimens of practical criticism made it very clear to those who were readers rather than writers that creation and criticism were two poles of the same activity, to be judged according to similar principles. And even where readers of these works did not intend to become writers (which must

---

[13] D. A. Russell, *Criticism in Antiquity* (London and Berkeley, 1981), pp. 2–3, 5. See also the marvellously inclusive anthology edited by D. A. Russell and Michael Winterbottom, *Ancient Literary Criticism: The Principal Texts in New Translations* (Oxford, 1972), hereafter cited as *ALC*. For an up-to-date survey by various authors see G. A. Kennedy (ed.), *The Cambridge History of Literary Criticism, i: Classical Criticism* (Cambridge and New York, 1989; repr. 1993). Older studies worth consulting include J. F. D'Alton, *Roman Literary Theory and Criticism* (London, 1931; repr. New York, 1962).

be true of the majority of Renaissance readers), by being exposed to so much discussion of how a writer goes to work they could hardly avoid being alerted to all that this involved: from the choice of a genre, in full awareness of the (usually classical) models it exemplified, to the workings of decorum—the rendering of human behaviour and speaking voices appropriate to characters' age, sex, and situation in life—and all the variety and effectiveness to be sought for in language. If these treatises were intended to teach you to write, they also taught you how to read, and using the same criteria.

The closeness between criticism and creation in the English Renaissance can be seen from the number of writers in this anthology who were practising poets or dramatists. Of the thirty-one writers included, twenty published poetry—Surrey, Baldwin, Gascoigne, Spenser, Puttenham, Harington, Sidney, Shakespeare, Chapman, Southwell, Hoskyns, Campion, Daniel, Fletcher, North, Ford, Massinger, Drummond, Carew, Milton, while Neville and Hobbes translated classical texts into English verse; nine (Whetstone, Shakespeare, Chapman, Jonson, Daniel, Heywood, Fletcher, Massinger, Ford) wrote dramas for the public stage, while seven (Gascoigne, Bacon, Jonson, Chapman, Fletcher, Campion, Milton) wrote masques or 'devices' for the court and private patrons. The remaining four—Elyot, Wilson, Ascham, Harvey—wrote in prose, but were fully involved in advancing the cause of literature. When Puttenham passes judgement on Wyatt, Surrey, or Dyer, he does so as a practising poet, who admires some things but believes he could have done others better—as do Gascoigne, Campion, Jonson. It is perhaps only in this period that one poet-critic could write poems specially to exemplify classical metres, as Campion does in 'Go, numbers, boldly pass, stay not for aid | Of shifting rhyme' (p. 435) and 'Rose-cheeked Laura' (p. 438), or that another could contribute to a critical argument by writing a poem defending the vitality of a poetic resource against its detractors, as Jonson does in his 'Fit of Rhyme against Rhyme' (p. 454).

But the prescriptive tradition had other ends in view. It taught writers not only the technicalities of their craft, but also how to address their readers, and what attitudes to take up towards their material. Here both psychology and ethics were involved. The writer was supposed to arouse the reader's emotions by his representation of life, in particular by showing human goodness as admirable, evil as detestable. By so doing the writer would also help to 'form' or shape the reader's character, 'inflaming' him to emulate virtue. As the

following sections will show, the Renaissance had a perfectly coherent
theory of literature, covering the whole sequence of composition and
consumption, which we might call ethical-rhetorical. The main
justification for poetry and drama was that literature helped create a
good society.

POETICS AND RHETORIC

Modern critics sometimes complain about the 'confusion' of rhetoric
and poetics in the Renaissance; or in the Middle Ages; or in ancient
Rome. Such judgements are anachronistic, deriving from a post-
Romantic aesthetic which was unsympathetic to rhetoric, and which
failed to realize that literature in the 1830s—as in the 1930s, or
today—cannot ignore such traditional issues as imitation, choice of
genre, appealing to an audience, finding the appropriate language for
poetry, and so on. In fact, theories of art for art's sake, or of the
artwork as autonomous object, simultaneously independent of its
author or audience, seem unfeasible. In the Renaissance, as in other
periods, works of art were never seen as autotelic, self-ending, having
no intention of working on or changing their readers' perception of
reality or history. For both writer and reader literature was a mode of
communication using persuasion and proof, addressed to the intellect
and to the emotions, existing as a force for good or evil. Many of us
today would share that conception of literature; but few of us would
be likely to derive our concepts of literary creation and reception from
rhetoric.

The dominance of rhetoric in both phases is easily explained.[14]
Due to its enormous importance in Athenian public life, where
citizens taking part in political or legal affairs had to speak in their
own person to defend their rights, rhetoric became a highly developed
communication system. Inevitably, it was soon transferred to education, and rearranged into graded levels, from beginners to advanced
students. In Rome, where democracy was less highly developed
(disappearing altogether as the Republic gave way to the Empire),
rhetorical skills were no longer the province of every citizen but of
professional lawyers and full-time politicians. But the prestige of

---

[14] See G. A. Kennedy, *The Art of Persuasion in Greece* (Princeton, 1963); *The Art of
Rhetoric in the Roman World* (Princeton, 1972).

taking part in the *vita activa*, together with Roman practicality, meant that rhetoric became codified in increasingly systematic treatises and taught as a fundamental subject in schools. Many manuals have been lost, but those surviving constitute what is in effect the first, and for many centuries the only, fully-worked-out aesthetic system. Although language-based, the initial processes of rhetorical composition—*inventio*, or finding material; *dispositio*, putting it into the appropriate sequence; *elocutio*, clothing it in the most effective language—could easily be adapted for treatises on the other arts. Indeed, from the fifteenth century, with the pioneering works on painting and architecture by Leon Battista Alberti, down to the eighteenth century, with the works on musical rhetoric by Mattheson and Forkel, rhetoric provided its sister arts with the basic concepts and categories, and only very gradually did they evolve their own, non-verbally based languages.[15] Even the last two stages of composition, addressed specifically to the orator—*memoria* (the memorization of a written speech, using some technical aids), *actio* and *pronuntiatio* (gesture and vocal delivery)—could also be applied to music theory and practice. Rhetoric was a universal system for all modes of communication.

A glance at the notes to this edition will show that the works most frequently used by English writers on literature in the sixteenth and seventeenth centuries were the major rhetorical treatises of classical antiquity: Aristotle's *Rhetoric* (*c*.370 BC); the anonymous *Rhetorica ad Herennium* (*c*.80 BC), formerly ascribed to Cicero; Cicero's youthful *De inventione* (*c*.80 BC); his mature dialogue *De oratore* (55 BC), together with his final works, *Brutus*, 'On distinguished orators', and *Orator*, 'On the best style of discourse' (both written in 46 BC); and Quintilian's comprehensive treatise in twelve books, *Institutio oratoria* (AD 95). The most surprising omission for the modern reader is Aristotle's *Poetics*, which was only properly edited and translated (first into Latin, then into Italian) in the mid-sixteenth century, and was used virtually for the first time in English[16] by Sir Philip Sidney in his *Defence of*

---

[15] See Brian Vickers, *In Defence of Rhetoric* (Oxford, 1988; 3rd, corrected edn., 1997), ch. 7: 'Rhetoric and the Sister Arts' (pp. 340–74), hereafter cited as *IDR*; G. Le Coat, *The Rhetoric of the Arts* (Berne, Frankfurt, 1975); and John Neubauer, *The Emancipation of Music from Language: Departure from Mimesis in Eighteenth Century Aesthetics* (New Haven, 1986).

[16] On the slow reception of the *Poetics* see Weinberg, *History*, i, chs. 9–11 (pp. 349–563); E. N. Tigerstedt, 'Observations on the Reception of the Aristotelian *Poetics* in the Latin West', *Studies in the Renaissance*, 15 (1968), 7–24; and M. T. Herrick, *The Poetics of Aristotle in England* (New Haven, 1930). Ascham refers to the *Poetics* in 1570 (p. 152), as does Gabriel Harvey in the 1580s (p. 164 n. 10).

Poetry (written *c*.1579–80; not published until 1595). But everybody knew Horace's *Ars poetica* (*c*.14–8 BC), a vastly influential rhetoricized poetics which had fully absorbed Aristotle's teachings through various intermediaries, and which synthesized much Hellenistic doctrine on poetics and rhetoric into a deceptively unsystematic but actually comprehensive construct. Two smaller works also frequently cited by Renaissance critics are Cicero's speech *Pro Archia poeta* (62 BC), and Plutarch's essay *Quomodo adulescens poetas audire debeat* (*c*. AD 90), 'How a Young Man Should Hear the Poets' (*Moralia* 14 D ff.)—that is, 'read' or understand them.

The range of subjects covered by these treatises was immense, and not all of them could be applied to vernacular literary discussions. Most of the detailed lore concerning court-room practices, with all the complex analyses of the *status* or legal point at issue, was ignored by Renaissance theorists, as were the specific stylistic problems of Greek and Latin. But the rhetorical system, as simplified and systematized by educationalists such as Erasmus, Melanchthon, Vives, Susenbrotus, or Soarez, taught every child who attended grammar school in the sixteenth and seventeenth centuries—in other words, all educated people—the basic principles of organizing thought and intention into a coherent verbal form, to be varied according to communicative context and audience addressed.

If we review the main ways in which classical rhetoric affected Renaissance literary criticism, we must begin, surprisingly perhaps, with ethics. In Greek and Latin speech contexts, whether politics or law, many topics under discussion or dispute would involve ethical issues, and the budding speaker was expected to be competent in this, as in other areas of knowledge. Thomas Wilson's *Arte of Rhetorique*, the first complete treatment of the subject in English, follows its classical sources in providing brief discussions of the four virtues, prudence or wisdom, justice, fortitude or manhood, and temperance, before going into detail. Justice is said to comprise natural love, thankfulness, 'stoutness to withstand and revenge evil', reverence, truth; temperance includes honourableness, stoutness, sufferance, continuance, and so forth. In this way, while absorbing rhetoric all students would gain a basic knowledge of ethics, to be reinforced by later study of such key texts as Aristotle's *Nicomachean Ethics* and Cicero's *De officiis* ('Of duties').

But it was not enough for future writers just to know about ethics. The rhetorical tradition insisted that the orator, defined as *vir bonus dicendi peritus*, 'a good man skilled in speaking', should take up an ethically responsible position on every topic he handled. Aristotle was the first to identify the three basic rhetorical genres: the deliberative or political speech, which advises an assembly what action should be taken; the forensic or legal speech, which argues for the guilt or innocence of a person on trial; and the epideictic speech, which 'displays' the good or bad qualities of its subject, praising virtue with such warmth that listeners and readers would be moved to imitate it, deterring them from evil by presenting it in disgusting terms. Literary works could take over some of the system used to prepare speeches in the first two categories, such as the formal division of a speech into seven parts, as outlined by Thomas Wilson (p. 81), faithfully rendering his Latin sources. When Sidney came to write his *Defence of Poetry*, as K. O. Myrick showed, he cast it into this form, with clearly marked divisions and transitions.[17] While writers could use selected parts of political or legal oratory, they could draw directly on the topics and methods of epideictic rhetoric at any point in a lyric, drama, or prose work in order to praise virtuous and denounce vicious behaviour. In this collection I have included several examples of poems by poets about fellow-poets, self-contained works of epideictic rhetoric: Surrey's tribute to Wyatt (p. 70), Ben Jonson's memorial poem to Shakespeare, printed in the 1623 First Folio (p. 537), Thomas Carew's *Elegy* on Donne (p. 554), and John Ford's eulogy to Fletcher (p. 541).

The ethical instruction contained in rhetoric, and the corresponding duty to single out virtues for praise, encouraged an analytical approach to human behaviour which profoundly affected both writers and reader. Poets, dramatists, and prose writers assumed, as a matter of course, that their craft would include the adoption of an ethically responsive attitude to good and evil in life, and to the inevitable conflict between them. 'We do not require in [the poet] mere elocution', writes Jonson (adapting Quintilian's specifications for the complete orator), 'or an excellent faculty in verse; but the exact knowledge of all virtues, and their contraries; with ability to render the one loved, the other hated, by his proper embattling them' (p. 568). This concern to embody fully-realized images of virtue and vice in literature is clearly visible in two of the greatest Elizabethan works, Sidney's

---

[17] *Sir Philip Sidney as a Literary Craftsman* (Cambridge, Mass., 1935), ch. 2: 'The *Defence of Poesie* as a Classical Oration' (pp. 46–83). The divisions are marked in the two best modern editions, by Geoffrey Shepherd and Jan van Dorsten (see 'Further Reading'), and below.

Arcadia and Spenser's *Faerie Queene*. The letter that Spenser wrote
to Ralegh explaining his plan for that poem announces that he has
modelled himself on the great exemplars for epic—Homer, 'who
in the persons of Agamemnon and Ulysses hath ensampled a good
governor and virtuous man', Virgil, Ariosto, and Tasso—by making
his major characters the embodiment of virtues in the private and
public realm.

By ensample of which excellent poets I labour to portray in Arthur before he
was king the image of a brave knight perfected in the twelve private moral
virtues as Aristotle hath devised, the which is the purpose of these first twelve
books.   (p. 298)

Spenser only completed the first six books, dealing with the virtues of
Holiness, Temperance, Chastity, Friendship, Justice, and Courtesy.
Yet we see from them both the complexity and variety with which he
was able to turn ethical concerns into verse. Sidney never left any
account of his own writings, but the whole argument of his *Defence
of Poetry* rests on a conception of literature as imitating good and evil
behaviour in order to encourage the one and discourage the other,
and it is striking how often he recurs to his canon of heroes: Achilles,
Aeneas, Cyrus, Theagenes, Orlando, Rinaldo. Certainly Sidney's
readers understood *Arcadia* as a representation of heroic, admirable
behaviour and their embattled 'contraries' (in Jonson's formulation),
as we can see from the responses of his close contemporaries Gabriel
Harvey (p. 334), and John Hoskyns (pp. 421–2).

    This agreement between writers and readers over the representa-
tion of good and evil, with the strongly differentiated responses
involved—evil is never a matter of indifferent or neutral presentation—means that Renaissance literary theory and critical practice
were unified to a great degree, sharing a coherent set of beliefs and
expectations. Where post-Romantic aesthetics saw rhetoric as a sign
of insincerity or excess for which one ought to apologize, the main
strength of rhetoric as a communication or aesthetic system in the
Renaissance was its internal coherence, which could be applied in
many different ways. The writer's goal or intentionality, the means by
which he could achieve it, the way in which listeners or readers would
respond—all of these levels cohered, giving to works of literature (or
music, or painting, or architecture) a unity of purpose and effect
at every level, from their overall plan down to the smallest details of
language.

If we look at rhetoric's teachings on *elocutio*, or expressivity, we must see it not as some incomprehensible elaboration of verbal devices for their own sake (the usual cliché of those who have never bothered to understand it), but as the final stage of a single communicative act. As Aristotle wrote in his *Rhetoric*, 'of the three elements in speech-making—speaker, subject, and person addressed—it is the last one, the hearer, that determines the speech's end and object' (1. 1. 1358[a]36–8). Cicero, followed by most other writers on rhetoric in antiquity and in modern times, classified the orator or writer's intentions towards the speaker under three interrelated heads: *docere*, to teach or instruct; *delectare*, to please or interest; and *movere*, to move the emotions.[18] Originally *docere* implied simply informing the judge and jury, or a political assembly (often very large, made up of ordinary citizens lacking specialist knowledge), of the facts of the issue under debate, but it subsequently came to mean teaching morally informed lessons. *Delectare* involved attracting the hearers' or readers' attention, and maintaining it throughout the speech. *Movere* aroused their emotions—fear, anger, hate, gratitude, love—focusing them on behalf of the policy advocated, the person prosecuted or defended, the virtues or vices being described. The three aims could be separately prepared, but in the finished work they had to cohere, all resources directed to persuading the audience that the presentation was valid.

The impact of this triple goal (the 'affective triad', as rhetoricians sometimes call it) on literature and literary criticism was enormous. In his casual-seeming but quite inclusive *Ars poetica*, Horace had restated the triad in words which every practitioner, and many readers, knew by heart: 'Non satis est pulchra esse poemata: dulcia sunto | et quocumque volent animum auditoris agunto . . . | si vis me flere, dolendum est primum ipsi tibi' (99 ff.): 'It is not enough for poetry to be beautiful; it must also be pleasing and lead the hearer's mind wherever it will'—so uniting *delectare* and *movere*; 'If you want me to cry, mourn first yourself; *then* your misfortunes will hurt me, Telephus and Peleus' (*ALC*, p. 282). 'Aut prodesse volunt aut delectare poetae | aut simul et iucunda et idonea dicere vitae . . . | omne tulit punctum qui miscuit utile dulci, | lectorem delectando pariterque monendo' (333 f., 343 f.): 'Poets aim either to do good or to give pleasure—or, thirdly, to say things which are both pleasing and serviceable for

---

[18] Cf. *De or.* 2. 27. 115, *Orat.* 21. 69; *IDR*, pp. 72–80.

life . . . The man who combines pleasure with usefulness wins every suffrage, delighting the reader and also giving him advice' (*ALC*, pp. 288–9)—so combining *delectare* and *docere*.

Horace's rhetoricized poetics merely recognized a state of affairs existing already in Greek literature and taken over in Rome. From the time of Aristotle's pupil Theophrastus (*c*.372–288 BC), who recognized that both 'poetry and rhetoric are concerned with the audience', and with persuasion rather than facts,[19] it was accepted that the goals and methods of the orator (or prose-writer) and poet overlapped. One of the speakers in *De oratore* makes the often-quoted statement that 'the poet is a very near kinsman of the orator, rather more heavily fettered as regards rhythm, but with ampler freedom in his choice of words, while in the use of many sorts of ornament he is his ally and almost his counterpart' (1. 16. 70; cf. Gascoigne, p. 167, Sidney, pp. 387–8, Jonson, p. 587). Ovid, a brilliant pupil of two famous rhetoricians, wrote to another rhetorician, Cassius Salanus (tutor in oratory to Germanicus Caesar), proclaiming the identity of poetry and rhetoric:

> Our work, though different, still issues
> from a common source: we both pursue liberal arts.
> My business is with the thyrsus, yours with the laurel,
> yet both of us need that spark,
> and just as your eloquence lends my verses muscle,
> so I impart a lustre to your words.[20]

It follows that poets and dramatists had to appeal to their audience's emotions, and were duly evaluated as having done so adequately or not. This expectation can be seen in several of the writers represented here.

More strikingly, this essentially rhetorical concept formed the key element in Sidney's eclectic definition of poetry:

Poesy therefore is an art of imitation, for so Aristotle termeth it in his word *mimesis*, that is to say, a representing, counterfeiting, or figuring forth—to speak metaphorically, a speaking picture—with this end, to teach and delight.   (p. 345)

In that synthesis—of Aristotle on imitation, Simonides (as reported by Plutarch) on the link between poetry and painting, and the goals

---

[19] Tr. Russell, *Criticism in Antiquity*, 94, 203–4.
[20] *Ex Ponto* 2. 5. 65 ff.; tr. Peter Green in *Ovid. The Poems of Exile* (Harmondsworth, Middx., 1994), p. 142.

of classical rhetoric[21]—the first two parts of Sidney's definition are unexceptional, and not particularly helpful in the defence of poetry, or literature in general. But the third element turns out to be decisive, since with its help Sidney can defend not only the legitimacy of poetry as one of the human sciences but its actual superiority over its two chief rivals, history and philosophy. Unlike the historian, Sidney argues, whose representation of human affairs is limited by what actually happens, in all its incoherence, the poet can make fictions in which the events and feelings represented correspond to ideal forms, showing the world as it ought to be. And where the philosopher can teach how to live, his mode of presentation is dry, lacking the *delectare* of fiction, and having no power over his readers' feelings (*movere*). But poets, in making poetry by the imitation of life,

imitate, both to *delight* and *teach*; and *delight*, to *move* men to take that goodness in hand, which without *delight* they would fly from as a stranger; and *teach*, to make them know that goodness whereunto they are *moved*,

this 'being the noblest scope to which ever any learning was directed' (p. 346; my italics). Sidney has realized that the interdependence of these three concepts makes them a conceptual unity, accounting for the fundamentally ethical function of literature, which neither history nor philosophy can match. By uniting *movere* and *docere*, the poet

excelleth history, not only in furnishing the mind with knowledge, but in setting it forward to that which deserveth to be called and accounted good: which setting forward, and moving to well-doing, indeed setteth the laurel crown upon the poet as victorious, not only of the historian, but over the philosopher . . . (p. 357)

Sidney's *Defence* is tightly woven, announcing arguments briefly in one place to develop them more fully later, or lightly touching on a point already discussed in more detail. So here he boldly anticipates his matching attack on the philosopher, who may indeed 'teach more perfectly [completely] than the poet', but cannot move his listeners' feeling to embrace what is being taught:

And that moving is of a higher degree than teaching, it may by this appear, that it is well nigh both the cause and effect of teaching. For who will be

---

[21] Cf. *Poet.* 1. 447²13 ff.; Plutarch, *How the young man should study poetry* (*Mor.* 17F; cf. *Rhetorica ad Herennium* 4. 38. 39), for Simonides' 'oft-repeated saying that "poetry is articulate painting, and painting is inarticulate poetry"'; and, on the rhetorical triad *movere*, *docere*, and *delectare*, Wilson, pp. 77–8, 116–18.

taught, if he be not moved with desire to be taught? and what so much good doth that teaching bring forth (I speak still of moral doctrine) as that it moveth one to do that which it doth teach? For, as Aristotle saith, it is not *gnōsis* but *praxis* must be the fruit. And how *praxis* can be, without being moved to practise, it is no hard matter to consider.   (p. 357)

As Sidney formulates it, rhetorical *movere* brings about the crucial transition from theory to practice, from knowledge to action: 'in nature we know it is well to do well . . . But to be moved to do that which we know, or to be moved with desire to know, *hic opus, hic labor est*'. Other Renaissance theorists applied the rhetorical triad to their definitions of literature, and many understood *movere* to be their major goal. In the scene where King Edward III gives his secretary instructions on how to write a love poem, Shakespeare makes him evoke the power of poetry to depict and arouse grief:

> And when thou writest of tears, encouch the word
> Before and after with such sweet laments,
> That it may raise drops in a Tartar's eye,
> And make a flint-heart Scythian pitiful—
> For so much moving hath a poet's pen.
> Then, if thou be a poet, move thou so . . .   (p. 328)

The importance of *movere* in poetry, as in rhetoric, was explicitly recognized by Elyot (pp. 63–4), Wilson (pp. 77–8), Puttenham (pp. 196, 236), and implicitly accepted by many other writers, but only Sidney made it the hinge of an entire literary theory, in which *movere* is vital to the functioning of several major genres: Lyric (p. 364), Elegy (p. 361), Comedy (pp. 362–3), and above all Epic, for the 'Heroical poet, whose champions' include Achilles, Cyrus, Aeneas, Turnus, Tydeus, Rinaldo, is he 'who doth not only *teach* and *move* to a truth, but *teacheth* and *moveth* to the most high and excellent truth; who maketh magnanimity and justice shine through all misty fearfulness and foggy desires . . .' (pp. 364–5). Sidney's argument is so firm that he can lighten it with a joke—'for if it be, as I affirm, that no learning is so good as that which *teacheth* and *moveth* to virtue, and that none can both *teach* and *move* thereto so much as to Poetry, then is the conclusion manifest that ink and paper cannot be to a more profitable purpose employed' (p. 369). Yet this may not be a joke, but another instance of Sidney's use of play to make a serious point. What printed material, we can all ask ourselves, do we value more than literature?

Sidney's *Defence of Poetry* derives not only its key argument and its overall design from rhetoric. In addition, the persuasiveness of its presentation, at many levels of discourse, owes a great deal to the figures and tropes of rhetoric: metaphor, simile, all kinds of verbal repetition and variation. Sidney's greatest work, his twice-written and unfinished prose-romance, *The Countess of Pembroke's Arcadia*, furnished several Renaissance rhetoricians with illustrative material for their handbooks: Abraham Fraunce in *The Arcadian rhetorike: or the praecepts of rhetorike made plaine by examples, Greeke, Latin, English* (1588), and John Hoskyns in his *Directions for Speech and Style* (*c*.1599; p. 398). Sidney's *Defence* could also be put to the same purpose, replete as it is with figures of thought and word, a rhetorical poetics which, like Horace's *Ars poetica*, exemplifies the art that it recommends. Sidney was, with Shakespeare, the most gifted rhetorician of the Renaissance, but both writers brought to its highest point what was a standard education in self-expression. The power of persuasion was rated so highly, not least by rhetoricians and full-time writers— whether their work was written gentleman-like, for the private pleasure of their family and friends, or performed in the public theatres—that generations of students, who would occupy all walks of life (including preachers, soldiers, physicists, mathematicians), strove to master the whole of rhetoric. Their studies, pursued with rigour and enthusiasm by their teachers, included the many verbal devices known as 'figures', which use repetition and other ways of deploying words as physical units of meaning so as to attain maximum effect, or 'tropes', which seek the same goal of efficacy but 'turn' the sense or application to some unexpected areas, as in metaphor, irony, allegory.

Although rhetoric has had a great revival in critical esteem over the last fifty years, those who have only studied it superficially still tend to dismiss the figures and tropes as mere itemizations of linguistic effects, having no other point. But if it had been so much dead knowledge, writers like Shakespeare, Sidney, Marlowe, Spenser, Donne, Bacon, Herbert, Marvell, would hardly have devoted so much time and energy to mastering this system and using it in their writing to recreate a huge range of human feeling, with the goal of arousing corresponding feelings in their readers.[22] No adequate comparative

---

[22] See Vickers, *IDR*, ch. 6, 'The Expressive Function of Rhetorical Figures' (pp. 294–339).

studies have yet been made, but it is arguable that the English Renaissance both domesticated and energized the tropes and figures more
intensely than any other European literature. Certainly the Elizabethan pioneers, loyally echoing their Greek and Latin models, had
no doubt that a mastery of the figures and tropes was the essential prerequisite for any creative writer. In his *Notes of Instruction* for writing
English poetry (1575) George Gascoigne warned the budding poet
that 'what theme soever you do take in hand, if you . . . never study
for some depth of device in the invention, and some figures also in the
handling thereof, it will appear to the skilful reader but a tale of a tub'
(p. 163). These rhetorical devices, he goes on, are perfectly proper to
poetry: 'You may use the same figures or tropes in verse which are
used in prose, and in my judgment they serve more aptly and have
greater grace in verse than they have in prose' (p. 167)—so disagreeing with Cicero.

   In Italy and France by the mid-sixteenth century, rhetorics had been
provided in the vernacular, directed towards poetry as well as oratory.
The religious and political upheavals in England, up to the accession
of Queen Elizabeth, undoubtedly delayed the spread of humanist
ideas and techniques, but under her long and peaceful reign a veritable explosion of learning took place. The first fully rhetoricized
poetics of the English Renaissance, George Puttenham's *Arte of
English Poesie* (1589), was the work of a scholar and courtier having a
wide personal knowledge of European courts, familiar with contemporary writings in Latin and French, and convinced, like so many of
his generation, that the English language and literature were just as
capable of variety and excellence as any of the European vernaculars.
He devoted the third and longest book of his *Arte* to 'Ornament', a
word which (like *ornatus* in Latin), did not refer to merely superficial
display but to language being properly 'fitted out', ready for active
service. The title of its second chapter is 'How our writing and
speeches public ought to be figurative; and, if they be not, do greatly
disgrace the cause and purpose of the speaker and writer' (p. 221).
Given that the figures and tropes constituted an expressive arsenal
covering almost any eventuality of thought and feeling, for Puttenham
it would be 'an imperfection in man's utterance to have none use of
figure at all' (ibid.). It was self-evident to him that 'eloquence is of
great force', that it can be used by 'every man after his sort and calling',
and that poets must avail themselves of resources which are not
only pleasure-giving but 'inwardly working a stir to the mind'. The

language of 'the excellent poet', he declares, must be 'gallantly arrayed in all his colours which figure can set upon it'. Figurative speech he defines as a heightening of ordinary language, while 'figure itself is a certain *lively or good grace* set upon words, speeches, and sentences *to some purpose and not in vain*, giving them *ornament or efficacy* by many manner of alterations in shape, in sound, and also in sense . . .' (p. 236; my italics). The key paired concepts there are 'ornament or efficacy', the poet shaping language to have a specific effect on his readers.

Convinced of the need for poetic expression to be unified, like the whole system of rhetoric, Puttenham now embarks on an idiosyncratically named and classified exposition of some 121 figures and tropes (about half the total that Shakespeare knew),[23] giving in each case a definition, and one or more examples of the figure as used in poetry. Most of his verse quotations come from earlier Tudor poetry, especially that famous compilation *Tottel's Miscellany* (1557; nine editions by 1587), but he is sufficiently in touch with the new poetry of the 1570s and 1580s to include examples from poems circulating in manuscript by Sidney, Ralegh, Dyer, and others. It must be emphasized that these are not just quotations from poets, but quotations of contemporary English poets using specific rhetorical figures, the poets thus demonstrating their knowledge and application of the rhetoric-dominated culture being promoted by educationalists and literary theorists. The dominance of rhetoric as a communication system applicable to poetry, literary criticism, and the other arts, meant that it produced a unified and homogeneous culture. The fusion of rhetoric and poetics, like the ultimate identity between prescriptive and descriptive criticism already noticed, explains why literary creation and literary criticism in this period shared a common fund of concepts, categories, and evaluative terms. When G. Gregory Smith produced his pioneering collection of *Elizabethan Critical Essays* in 1904, he gave adequate excerpts from the earlier parts of Puttenham, but merely listed the names of all the figures and tropes treated, since the author 'seldom adds any matter of purely critical value' (*ECE* ii.167–72). By giving a generous selection from this sequence, I hope to show that the Renaissance made a far more coherent connection between creation and criticism than has yet been realized. We cannot understand the goals and preoccupations of writers in the sixteenth and seventeenth centuries without a knowledge of their use of

[23] See Sister Miriam Joseph, *Shakespeare's Use of the Arts of Language* (New York, 1947; 1966).

rhetoric. Sir John Harington, writing two years after the publication of Puttenham's *Arte*, said that in it 'as it were a whole receipt of poetry is described, with so many new named figures as would put me in great hope in this age to come would breed many excellent poets' (p. 305). Puttenham may be a symptom of the new appreciation of rhetoric rather than the cause of the remarkable burst of creative writing that England experienced between 1580 and 1630. But certainly much credit was due to the vernacular having absorbed those classical writings on rhetoric which constitute 'perhaps the most careful analysis of any expressive medium ever undertaken'.[24] Most modern critics have yet to acquire the basic knowledge of rhetoric that would allow them to identify the verbal devices used by Renaissance poets, the necessary first stage in evaluating how they have been used, according to the coherent rationale given by rhetoricians like Puttenham or Peacham ('for a figure is ever used to some purpose'). It is a rather striking demonstration of how the post-Romantic dismissal of rhetoric has conditioned readers not to notice rhetorical devices, that no editor of Shakespeare's *Sonnets* and very few critics have observed that they use many common figures and tropes, hundreds of times over.[25] We are still a long way from recovering this central element in Renaissance literature.

ORIGINALITY AND IMITATION

The absorption of rhetoric into English literary language until it became an entirely natural resource was due to the sustained imitation of classical models, a practice that aroused much discussion. In approaching the Renaissance debate over imitation we must be clear that this refers not to *mimesis*, literature as an 'imitation' or representation of the human world, a function of poetry and drama attacked by Plato in the *Republic* and legitimized by Aristotle in the *Poetics*. Rather, it refers to *imitatio*, the use of models in learning to write, from the elementary stages of language-learning to advanced composition. In the context of Renaissance schooling compositions were mainly in Latin, of course, but in the wider debate it was argued that the imitation of Greek and Latin models in the vernacular would

---

[24] E. H. Gombrich, *Art and Illusion* (London, 1960), p. 317.
[25] See Brian Vickers, 'Rhetoric and Feeling in Shakespeare's *Sonnets*', in K. Elam (ed.), *Shakespeare Today: Directions and Methods of Research* (Florence, 1984), pp. 53–98.

enrich modern languages, an argument that can be followed from Italy to France, and on to England in the late sixteenth century. And as for works of literature, a majority of theorists believed that modern writers could only achieve excellence by the creative imitation of some classical model.

The debate over *imitatio*, often bitterly contested, ran from Italy in the fifteenth century through the whole of Europe a century later.[26] Although it had specifically local resonances, this debate re-enacted the course of a similar debate in Latin literary theory. It was a matter of some embarrassment to Roman intellectuals that when their culture began to articulate itself it was confronted by the already existing achievements of Greek civilization in philosophy, the natural sciences, and literature, which had reached a degree of excellence and diversity that Rome in its infancy could in no way match. Roman writers and thinkers had no option but to imitate Greek models, domesticate them in a different language and social structure, gradually achieving their own voice. Virgil could never have created the *Aeneid* without the examples of Homer's *Iliad* and *Odyssey*; Plautus and Terence openly admitted their indebtedness to Greek comedy, as did Horace and his fellows to Greek lyric poets, Cicero and Quintilian to the Attic orators and rhetoricians.

The necessities of imitation soon produced an accompanying legit-imizing theory. In *De oratore* Cicero briefly raised some of the main issues: the need to choose carefully, find a good model to imitate, copying its excellences, not its faults, doing so 'by frequent and large practice, and if possible, by written composition' (2. 22. 90 ff.). Cicero recommended *imitatio*, but also recorded that there were many suc-cessful orators 'who copy no man, but gain their objects by natural aptitude, without resembling any model'. In his much fuller treatment Quintilian specified exactly which Greek and Roman authors were to be selected as models for language and thought, there being 'no doubt that in art [*ars* being the practical realization of theory] no small portion of our task lies in imitation, since, although invention came first and is all-important, it is expedient to imitate whatever has been invented with success' (*Institutes of Oratory* 10. 2. 1 ff.). Modern

---

[26] See Martin L. McLaughlin, *Literary Imitation in the Italian Renaissance: The Theory and Practice of Literary Imitation in Italy from Dante to Bembo* (Oxford, 1995), and my review, *Modern Language Review*, 93 (1998), 850–2. Other useful studies include G. W. Pigman III, 'Versions of Imitation in the Renaissance', *Renaissance Quarterly*, 33 (1980), 1–32, and H. Gmelin, 'Das Prinzip der Imitatio in den Romanischen Literaturen der Renaissance', *Romanische Forschungen*, 46 (1932), 83–360.

readers might see an antithesis there, between 'imitation' and 'invention', but in rhetorical theory *inventio* did not mean 'creation out of
nothing' (or whatever meaning we might attach to that word), but the
finding of appropriate arguments, words, and expressions, which
would often be gathered from the notebook where the orator had
recorded them.

For Quintilian 'imitation alone is not sufficient, for a sluggish
nature is only too ready to rest content with the inventions of others'
(10. 2. 4). But if used properly, *imitatio* has a highly positive effect,
since it leads writers on to do better than their predecessors, to 'add
[more] to the existing stock of knowledge', to discover and develop
their potential in a beneficent emulation: 'For the man whose aim is
to prove himself better than another, even if he does not surpass him,
may hope to equal him' (10. 2. 9 f.). Warning his readers that 'all imitation is artificial, and moulded to a purpose which was not that of the
original orator', Quintilian advises them to analyse and reproduce the
excellencies of the original in a new context, while avoiding its blem-
ishes (10. 2. 11 ff.). The 'complete orator' does not imitate one author
alone, or 'one particular style', since this would result in a narrow and
superficial collection of idiosyncrasies. Rather, intending to 'make
whatever is best in each individual author his own', he discovers all
the 'good qualities' of the originals and then 'adds his own, . . . makes
good deficiencies and cuts down whatever is redundant'. He must
always be aware that imitation 'should not be confined merely to
words', but should consider appropriateness, structure of argument,
emotional effect (10. 2. 27 f.).

Several Roman literary theorists discussed just how a writer should
'add his own', the most influential contribution coming from the Stoic
moralist Lucius Annaeus Seneca, in the 84th of his *Epistulae morales*.
Seneca urges writers to consider 'the example of the bees, who flit
about and cull the flowers that are suitable for producing honey, and
then arrange and assort in their cells all that they have brought in'.
Seneca is not sure whether the bees 'change that which they have gathered into [honey] by blending something therewith', some peculiar
substance by which pollen 'is transformed', perhaps by analogy with
'fermentation, whereby separate elements are united into one substance' (3–4). But he is convinced that writers 'ought to copy these
bees, and sift whatever we have gathered from a varied course of
reading, for such things are better preserved if they are kept separate'—advice which suggests the keeping of notebooks. Then, 'by

applying the supervising care with which our nature has endowed
us,—in other words, our natural gifts,—we should so blend those
several flavours into one delicious compound that, even though it
betrays its origin, yet it nevertheless is clearly a different thing from
that whence it came' (5). Switching his analogy, Seneca compares this
process to digestion, for 'the food we have eaten . . . passes into tissue
and blood only when it had been changed from its original form'.
Similarly with 'the food which nourishes our higher nature': 'whatever we have absorbed should not be allowed to remain unchanged, or
it will be no part of us. We must digest it; otherwise it will merely
enter the memory and not the reasoning power' (6). Some Roman theorists believed that the writer should openly allude to his model, but
Seneca prefers that the mind 'should hide away all the materials by
which it has been aided, and bring to light only what it has made of
them'. Even if the writer carries over some likeness to the original
which he admires, 'I would have you resemble him as a child resembles his father, and not as a picture resembles its original; for a picture
is a lifeless thing' (8 f.). In this process of fusing the several elements
into something that we 'make our own', it is sometimes impossible to
know 'who is being imitated, if the copy is a true one; for a true copy
stamps its own form upon all the features which it has drawn from
what we may call the original, in such a way that they are combined
into a unity' (8).

The organic, transforming or metabolizing power of *imitatio*, when
correctly practised, was expressed in slightly different terms by the
unknown author—usually called 'Longinus'—of the treatise *On Sublimity* (first century AD), one of the most intelligent works of literary
criticism ever produced, which was just beginning to be known in the
late sixteenth century. One of the 'roads to excellence' that he recommends the budding writer to follow is 'imitation and emulation of
the great prose writers of antiquity'. Such an encounter is in no way
a routine or mechanical one, but a creative stimulus. We should be
'inspired by the spirit of another', for 'from the great spirits of the
ancients an influence as though from the holy cave of the oracle passes
into the spirits of the emulators', who are inspired to a matching excellence. So, 'when we are toiling on something that requires excellence
of expression and greatness of thought, [we should] ask in our hearts
how Homer would have said it or how Plato or Demosthenes or
Thucydides, in his history, would have given it distinction. For these
great characters appearing to us as objects of emulation and standing

prominently before us will raise our souls to the pitch we have imagined'. This process is imitation, Longinus concludes, but not plagiarism: 'such a proceeding is not theft; it is like obtaining a pattern from
beautiful forms or images or other works of art'.[27]

Imitation, then, should spark off inspiration, initiating a process
of emulation which gives the writer not just a pattern but also the
incentive to create something of his own. In Renaissance England, as
in Italy and France, this enlightened concept of *imitatio* prevailed
with creative writers, although those nearer to the school situation
inevitably had a rather narrower view. Towards the beginning of his
Arte of Rhetorique Thomas Wilson takes it as self-evident that 'before
we use either to write or speak eloquently, we must dedicate our minds
wholly to follow the most wise and learned men', so that we can
become 'like them. For if they that walk much in the sun, and think
not of it, are yet for the most part sunburnt, . . . they which wittingly
and willingly travail to counterfeit others must needs take some colour
of them . . . according to the proverb, By companying with the wise,
a man shall learn wisdom' (p. 79). The first full discussion of *imitatio*
in English is found in Roger Ascham's book *The Schoolmaster* (1570).
After an impassioned plea that students should care not only for the
res or 'matter' of a literary work, but also its 'words', Ascham distinguishes two kinds of imitation, first the *mimesis* attacked by Plato, and
secondly *imitatio*, in which we 'follow, for learning of tongues and sciences [bodies of knowledge] the best authors. Here riseth amongst
proud and envious wits a great controversy, whether one or many are
to be followed, and if one, who is that one: Seneca, Cicero, Sallust, or
Caesar, and so forth, in Greek and Latin' (p. 143 below). Ascham's
answer to that question ignores the warnings of Quintilian, telling students that 'ye must follow choicely a few, and chiefly some one, and
that namely in our school of eloquence, either for pen or talk' (p. 150).
The 'some one' whom Ascham wants students to follow turns out to
be Cicero, who had been celebrated by Velleius Paterculus in the first
century AD as embodying 'the perfection of eloquence' (p. 154), so that
he can recommend students to 'form . . . your speech and writing to
that excellent perfectness which was only in Tully, or only in Tully's
time' (p. 156). Ascham even writes an affectionate epistle to 'my
master Tully, . . . whom above all other I like and love best', in which
he displays the *aemulatio* recommended by Roman literary theorists,

---

[27] I cite the excellent translation by Donald Russell in *ALC*, pp. 475–6.

proudly claiming that 'your excellent eloquence is as well liked and loved and as truly followed in England at this day, as it is now, or ever was since your own time, in any place of Italy . . .' (p. 161).

Ascham's recommendation of Cicero as the best author for Latin prose, together with his endorsement of Pietro Bembo's advocacy of the strict imitation of one model—Cicero—as against Gianfrancesco Pico's more open advice to choose the best of many, place him on the conservative side in the *imitatio* debate. This group encouraged the rise of Ciceronianism, a curious phase in literary history which saw writers obsessively imitating Cicero's vocabulary and tricks of style, using such resources as Marius Nizolius' *Thesaurus Ciceronianus* in order to write what they claimed to be the only authentic Latin. This movement violated several of the sensible rules laid down by the classical authorities, and indeed degenerated into a 'study of words, not matter', justly rebuked by Francis Bacon in 1605 (p. 459). But to Ascham's credit, he gave a clear outline of how *imitatio* should be used in studying authors, as by comparing a speech of Cicero modelled on Demosthenes with its original, to establish which elements Cicero retains; which he leaves out, and to what 'end and purpose'; what he adds; what he minimizes; what he rearranges; and finally, what 'he altereth and changeth, either in property of words, in form of sentence, in substance of the matter, or in one or other convenient circumstances of the author's present purpose' (p. 145). Ascham is surely right, that such a comparative analysis of Cicero and Demosthenes, Virgil and Homer, or Shakespeare and Ovid, can be enormously instructive as to the later author's intentions, attitudes, and ability to realize them.

Ascham wrote essentially for students of Latin, not for creative writers in their mother tongue. (It is noteworthy that his only comments on contemporary literature concern neo-Latin tragedies, and that his criticisms are mainly addressed to their failure to follow the strict rules of Latin metrics.) But for the poets and dramatists who had studied at the grammar schools proliferating across Britain the doctrine of *imitatio* perfectly applied to their attempts to write in English. In his *Defence of Poetry* Sir Philip Sidney expressed the fervent wish, exactly in the spirit of Quintilian and Seneca, that

the diligent imitators of Tully and Demosthenes (most worthy to be imitated) did not so much keep Nizolian paper-books of their figures and phrases, as by attentive translation (as it were) devour them whole, and make them wholly theirs. For now they cast sugar and spice upon every dish that is served to the table . . .   (p. 386)

that is, practise imitation on a superficial verbal level. In his notebook *Timber: or Discoveries made upon men and matter* (*c*.1615–35) Ben Jonson showed that he, too, knew the classical authorities:

The third requisite in our poet or maker is imitation, to be able to convert the substance or riches of another poet to his own use. To make choice of one excellent man above the rest, and so to follow him till he grow very he, or so like him as the copy may be mistaken for the principal.   (p. 585)

Jonson goes on to use both the digestive metaphor and the bee metaphor, both of which were used by many other writers in this period. They appear, appropriately enough, in *Palladis Tamia: Wit's Treasury* (1598) by Francis Meres, a catalogue of English writers juxtaposed with their classical equivalents which, as Don Cameron Allen showed, was lifted bodily from the popular *Officina* of J. Ravisius Textor.[28]

   Such borrowings raise the question of the point at which imitation becomes plagiarism. H. O. White, in his pioneering study[29] of this topic, showed that accusations of plagiarism were made in the Renaissance, as they had been in classical antiquity (Martial protested about the activities of the *plagiarius*—the word meant 'kidnapper'), and that there are well-documented cases in our period of literary theft by unscrupulous writers and publishers. But he also shows that most writers clearly distinguished between theft and imitation, and that they all accepted the classical concept of *imitatio* as leading to *aemulatio* and, in time, to originality. For Renaissance writers, like their Roman predecessors, 'the test of originality is the degree of reinterpretation, of individualized transformation achieved by the author' (White, p. 112; also p. 137). Italian, French, and English critics believed that good writing can only emerge out of creative imitation (pp. 20–3, 28 f., 93 f.), and that the writer who ignored all models in the hope of inventing something totally original would merely 'affect singularity' (pp. 140, 150). Joseph Hall, writing in 1608, typifies the majority attitude, describing himself as 'one . . . that, in worthy examples, holds imitation better than invention; I have trod in their paths,

---

[28] See *Francis Meres's Treatise 'Poetrie': A Critical Edition*, ed. D. C. Allen (Urbana, Ill., 1933).

[29] *Plagiarism and Imitation During the English Renaissance: A Study in Critical Distinctions* (Cambridge, Mass., 1935; New York, 1965, 1973).

but with an higher and wider step' (cit. pp. 124 f.). Hall adopts here Quintilian's frequently copied metaphor of following in another writer's footsteps (*Inst.* 10. 2. 10), and validates the classical theory of how imitation leads to emulation. Gabriel Harvey, who left copious notes in his books, annotated his Quintilian twice, in 1567 and 1579, commenting on the discussion of *imitatio* in book 10 that 'The better the author, the better the emulation required, and in addition the more diligent the emulation'. The writer's goal is to surpass his or her model, to be 'not similar, but equal, or even better', a goal that Harvey summed up in the Italian expression *piu oltra* (p. 93). It is thanks to Harvey that we know of Spenser's aim, in writing *The Faerie Queene*, to take part in an *aemulatio* with Ariosto. Some of Spenser's recent works, Harvey tells him, more closely rival Ariosto's, 'either for the fineness of plausible [pleasing] elocution or the rareness of poetical invention, than that the *Elvish Queene* doth to his *Orlando Furioso*; which, notwithstanding, you will needs seem to emulate, and hope to overgo, as you flatly professed yourself in one of your last letters' (*ECE* ii. 115–16). Pietro Bembo, the influential literary theorist, had made a 'tripartite division of the imitative process into imitating (*imitari*), catching up with (*assequi*), and overtaking (*praeterire*) the model'.[30]

As for plagiarism, some recent writers (misled by Foucault's claims that individuality was only discovered in the eighteenth century) have argued that Renaissance authors had no concept of their literary compositions as constituting personal property. It is true that a copyright law, in our sense, was not formulated until later, and that the legislation enforced by the Stationers Company tended to protect the rights of the printer or publisher rather than the author. But Elizabethan and Jacobean writers had a keen sense of their individual identity and of their moral rights to the works they had composed. For evidence of their disapproval of plagiarism we need look no further than the poetry of Donne and Jonson. In his Second Satire Donne surveys various perversions of poetry, such as using it to flatter noble lords, or writing verse just because everyone else does so. The plagiary is then described:

> But he is worst, who (beggarly) doth chaw
> Others' wits' fruits, and in his ravenous maw
> Rankly digested, doth those things out spew,

---

[30] McLaughlin, *Literary Imitation*, p. 264.

> As his own things; and they are his own, 'tis true,
> For if one eat my meat, though it be known
> The meat was mine, th'excrement is his own.   (25–30)[31]

That calculatedly disgusting analogy expresses an anger widely shared by writers who had been plagiarized. Ben Jonson addressed one of his Epigrams (no. 81, based on Martial, 1. 63) to 'Prowl the Plagiary', vowing never to show him any of his poetry again unless he had two witnesses present, for 'Thy wit lives by it, and belly too'.[32] Jonson was a professional writer, who earned his living by his pen; Donne came from a higher social class, and avoided publishing his own poetry lest he be accused of writing for money. But both could tell the difference between plagiarism and legitimate imitation.

The debate over *imitatio* was largely sustained by creative writers, confirming my earlier diagnosis that Renaissance literary theory was more concerned with prescriptive than with descriptive criticism, and that it finds its real reason for existence in the achievements of those writers. Not all of these discussions are of great interest today. Ascham, unsurprisingly, advocated the imitation of classical metrics, and was scathing about the 'Gothian' rhymes which, according to him, disfigured all vernacular poetry since Petrarch (p. 157). This classicism gave rise in the 1570s, first in Cambridge, then in London, to discussion and experimentation with classical metres by several poets (although they never formed 'a group'), including Sidney, Dyer, and Spenser, with polemical contributions from Harvey. Their scholarly information derived from a set of metrical rules drawn up by Thomas Drant, but despite Sidney's extraordinary versatility in all forms of metrical experiment he soon abandoned this form of writing. The gifted poet and musician Thomas Campion took it up a few years later, but the treatise that he wrote (pp. 428 ff.) shows the unreal, academic nature of the discussion, much of it based on William Lilly's Latin grammar, and it was ably refuted by Samuel Daniel (pp. 441 ff.). Ben Jonson told his Scottish host, William Drummond, that he disagreed with both parties, but his only extended comment is the brilliant 'Fit of Rhyme against Rhyme' (p. 454).

If we are to look for the justification of imitation in the imaginative literature of the Renaissance, we need look no further than Jonson and his great corrival, Shakespeare. Jonson belongs with the learned,

---

[31] Donne, *The Complete English Poems*, ed. A. J. Smith (Harmondsworth, 1971), p. 158.
[32] Jonson, *The Complete Poems*, ed. G. Parfitt (Harmondsworth, 1975), p. 60.

self-conscious writers, who expect their allusions to be noticed. The elder Seneca (*c*.50 BC–AD 40) in his *Suasoriae* (a work giving excerpts from speeches by various orators, with critical analyses), recorded that Ovid had 'very much liked' a Virgilian phrase,[33] and had reused it, 'something he had done with many other lines of Virgil—with no thought of plagiarism, but meaning that his piece of open borrowing should be noticed' (3. 7). In the same spirit, Jonson filled the margins of his Roman tragedy *Sejanus* with references to his classical sources, and Drummond records Jonson's proud boast that 'In *Sejanus* he hath translated a whole oration from Tacitus' (p. 535). E.K., the unidentified commentator on Spenser's *Shepheardes Calendar*, took pains to point out his friend's imitations from Theocritus, Virgil, Marot, or Mantuan, according to the best classical tradition. The modern reader who admires Jonson's tribute to 'Our Shakespeare' (p. 561), or his equally generous praise of Francis Bacon (p. 565), may be disconcerted to find that the critic has in fact translated verbatim whole sequences from the elder Seneca's *Controversiae*, merely adding the contemporary writers' names. Presumably, though, Jonson hoped that some of his readers would have enough knowledge of both ancient and modern literatures to recognize the allusions, and to see how uncannily well they fitted.

Shakespeare's method of imitation is quite different, and seems rather to fulfil the requirements of Seneca, Quintilian, and Longinus, that the writer should make the borrowing his own. Excellent modern studies have shown his free handling and re-creation of Roman comedy, and some useful work has been done on his use of Plutarch and Ovid.[34] But Shakespeare seldom draws attention to his imitations in the way that Jonson did, and it is arguable that he excelled his learned friend in the digesting and metabolizing of the borrowed material. As a practical contribution to this debate I have extended my selection from Thomas Wilson's *The Arte of Rhetorique* to include one of the several specimen compositions that he provides, in the spirit of the great educationalist Erasmus. Discussing the 'Oration

---

[33] See Seneca, *Controversiae and Suasoriae*, ed. and tr. M. Winterbottom, 2 vols. (London, 1974.), ii. 542–4. The phrase, 'plena deo' ('She's full of the god'), does not appear in surviving texts of Virgil, but Edward Norden suggested that it may have been used in an earlier version to describe the Sibyl (*Aen.* 6. 45 ff.).

[34] See e.g. Leo Salingar, *Shakespeare and the Traditions of Comedy* (Cambridge, 1974); R. S. Miola, *Shakespeare and Classical Tragedy: The Influence of Seneca* (Oxford, 1992), and *Shakespeare and Classical Comedy: The Influence of Plautus and Terence* (Oxford, 1994); J. Bate, *Shakespeare and Ovid* (Oxford, 1994).

Deliberative', whereby 'we do persuade or dissuade, entreat or rebuke, exhort or dehort . . . any man', our aim being 'either to advise our neighbour to that thing which we think most needful for him, or else to call him back from that folly which hindereth much his estimation', Wilson includes as an example the *Encomium Matrimonii*, or *An Epistle to Persuade Young Gentlemen to Marriage, Devised by Erasmus in the Behalf of his Friend*, given here complete (pp. 93 ff.). The significance of this *Epistle* is that it provided the 'source material' for the first seventeen of Shakespeare's *Sonnets*.[35] The argument of Erasmus' letter overlaps with that of the 'procreation sequence' at several points. Shakespeare, like Erasmus, urges the addressee to marry and beget a son (typically enough, for Renaissance patrilineal beliefs), presenting this as an admirable choice in life, worthy of praise (*laus*), its opposite deserving the blame or *vituperatio* which formed the other branch of epideictic rhetoric. The two compositons differ in several ways, of course, beginning with their scale: Shakespeare's sonnets total 238 lines of verse, Erasmus' Epistle some 800 lines of prose. To argue his case, Erasmus draws on a wide range of historical and biblical examples; Shakespeare cites no proper names, and makes no definite allusions to any other text. But if Shakespeare's scope seems smaller, inevitably more compressed, it also includes several ideas not touched on by Erasmus.

The theme, as Shakespeare formulates it, appears at the outset:

> From fairest creatures we desire increase
> That thereby beauty's rose might never die.   (1. 1–2)

Where Erasmus, like other moralists, urges that all men have a duty to procreate, the person imagined as writing Shakespeare's sonnets urges this young man to beget a child because of his great beauty. His is an 'unused beauty' (4. 13), with its 'lovely gaze' (5. 2) and visage in 'fresh repair' (3. 3), constituting 'the world's fresh ornament' (1. 9). The young man to whom Erasmus writes is 'of lusty years and very comely for your personage' (p. 115), which gives him favourable marriage prospects but is not in itself an argument to marry. The young man to whom these sonnets are addressed, by contrast, has a 'fresh

---

[35] See H. E. Rollins (ed.), *The Sonnets*, 2 vols. (New York, 1944), i. 7, ii. 192, and K. M. Wilson, *Shakespeare's Sugared Sonnets* (London, 1974), pp. 146–67. I cite the New Cambridge edition by G. B. Evans (1996). In her New Arden edition (1998) Katherine Duncan-Jones does not discuss this point.

blood' and 'sweet semblance' (13. 4) which set him apart absolutely from

> those whom Nature hath not made for store,
> Harsh, featureless, and rude . . .   (11. 9–10)

who may 'barrenly perish', without regret. He has other qualities, 'wisdom, beauty' (11. 5), 'truth and beauty' (14. 11—that is, constancy), but it is principally 'the beauty of your eyes' (17. 5) that moves the speaker to urge him to beget a child, for 'truth and beauty shall together thrive | If from thyself to store thou wouldst convert'. If not,

> Thy end is truth's and beauty's doom and date.   (14. 11–14)

This emphasis on the young man's beauty expresses, no doubt, the speaker's great admiration and desire that such beauty will continue to exist—

> Make thee another self for love of me,
> That beauty still may live in thine or thee.   (10. 13–14)

But if that were the main argument in this sequence it would risk arousing the young man's vanity, to be told that his beauty were the only reason for having to procreate. For the poet then to accuse him of self-centredness would hardly be just.

If the emphasis on beauty[36] is unique to Shakespeare, the other arguments his speaker deploys have a wider application, as in Erasmus' epistle. The main argument of that letter is the biblical one, God's injunction that 'men should [not] live single, but that they should increase, be multiplied, and fill the earth' (p. 95). Frequently repeated, this idea takes both a positive form, as in the validation of 'carnal copulation' (p. 100) as mankind's sole 'way of increasing issue, that through labour of both the husband and wife mankind might still [always] be kept from destruction' (p. 113), and a negative, deterrent one:

Let it be forbidden that man and woman shall not come together, and within few years all mankind must needs decay forever . . . Take away marriage, and how many shall remain after a hundred years . . . ?   (p. 112)

---

[36] The word recurs 20 times in the first 17 sonnets, and only 71 times in the remaining 137—often in generalized contexts, not referring to the addressee.

Shakespeare takes over this argument with little adaptation, inter-
equating 'wisdom, beauty, and increase', and setting them over against
'folly, age, and cold decay':

> If all were minded so, the times should cease,
> And threescore year would make the world away.   (11. 7–8)

Shakespeare was also impressed by the recurrence in Wilson's
translation of the word 'decay'[37] to describe the consequences of procreation dying out:

But assured destruction must needs follow, except men through the benefit
of marriage supply issue, the which through mortality do from time to time
decay.   (p. 97)

For there is nothing so natural, not only unto mankind but also unto all other
living creatures, as . . . to keep their own kind from decay and through
increase of issue to make their whole kind immortal.   (p. 100)

. . . through marriage all things are and do still continue, and without the
same all things do decay and come to nought.   (ibid.)

. . . he is counted no good gardener that being content with things present
doth diligently prune his old trees, and hath no regard either to imp or graff
young sets because the selfsame orchard (though it be never so well trimmed)
must needs decay in time . . .   (p. 102)

. . . it lieth in your hands to keep that house from decay whereof you lineally
descended . . . seeing there is none other of your name and stock but yourself alone to continue the posterity.   (p. 105)

Shakespeare echoes this final passage by juxtaposing honour and
decay in Sonnet 13, to rebuke the young man for not preparing
'Against this coming end' by producing some 'sweet issue' for his
'sweet form':

> Who lets so fair a house fall to decay,
> Which husbandry in honour might uphold
> Against the stormy gusts of winter's day
> And barren rage of death's eternal cold?
>   O none but unthrifts: dear my love, you know
>   You had a father, let your son say so.   (13. 3, 8–14)

That couplet echoes several passages where Erasmus asks

What is more right or more meet than to give that unto the posterity, the
which we have received of our ancestors? . . . What is more unthankful than

---

[37] This word occurs 4 times in the first 17 sonnets, 5 times in the remaining 137.

to deny that unto younglings, the which (if thou hadst not received of thine elders) thou couldst not have been the man living able to have denied it unto them? (p. 94)

In that sonnet Shakespeare describes men who do not preserve their house by procreation as 'unthrifts', an economic metaphor developed in Sonnet 4:

> Unthrifty loveliness, why dost thou spend
> Upon thyself thy beauty's legacy? . . .
> Profitless usurer, why dost thou use
> So great a sum of sums, yet canst not live?
> For having traffic with thyself alone,
> Thou of thyself thy sweet self dost deceive.   (4. 1–10)

So Erasmus had used biblical precedent to set matrimony far above the single life, and to endorse the law of Moses for punishing 'the barrenness of married folk . . . because that they, like unprofitable persons, and living only to themselves, did not increase the world with any issue' (p. 97). This argument expresses the Renaissance belief in the superiority of the *vita activa*, where people took part in society for their mutual benefit, as against the solitary life, guilty of *philautia* or self-love.[38] Another form of selfishness condemned by the Bible, Erasmus notes, was the sin of Onan, 'that (being commanded to marry with the wife of his dead brother) did cast his seed upon the ground lest any issue should be had . . .' (p. 106), and some readers believe that in such phrases as 'having traffic with thyself alone' the speaker accused the young man of that practice. Certainly the couplet ending Sonnet 9

> No love toward others in that bosom sits
> That on himself such murd'rous shame commits   (9. 13–14)

either implies that sin, or echoes Erasmus' amplification of the evils of a single life:

You shall be compted a parricide or a murderer of your stock, that whereas you may by honest marriage increase your posterity, you suffer it to decay forever through your willful single life.   (pp. 113–14)

---

[38] In *All's Well that Ends Well* the clown describes 'self-love' as 'the most inhibited sin in the canon' (1. 1. 144–5), and in *Twelfth Night* Malvolio is accused of that vice (1. 5. 90). In Rabelais, as in Erasmus' *Praise of Folly*, Philautia is personified as a destructive vice; see also Harington, p. 320.

In that passage Wilson's translation of Erasmus used both 'decay' and (for the second time) 'posterity',[39] recalling Sonnet 3:

> For where is she so fair whose uneared womb
> Disdains the tillage of thy husbandry?
> Or who is he so fond will be the tomb
> Of his self-love to stop posterity?[40]

Shakespeare was able to compress many levels of meaning into a single quatrain, fusing together in the briefest form the passage from Erasmus just cited together with a later one, in which he expansively enlarges on the parallel between 'husbandry' in farming and in marriage:

If a man had land that were very fat and fertile, and suffered the same for lack of manuring forever to wax barren, should he not . . . be punished by the laws, considering it is for the commonweal's behoof that every man should well and truly husband his own? If that man be punished who little heedeth the maintenance of his tillage . . . what punishment is he worthy to suffer that refuseth to plough that land which being tilled yieldeth children?

Especially considering that ploughing land involves 'painful toiling . . . but in getting children there is pleasure which, being ordained as a ready reward for painstaking, asketh a short travail for all the tillage' (p. 106).

The speed with which Shakespeare shifts from theme to theme, obliquely handling a major argument, lightly touching another only to return to it with more insistence, shows how the humanist practice of *imitatio* gives a writer both the ground bass and the material for variation. The words 'single' and 'husband', which recur so often in Wilson's translation of Erasmus, are brought together completely unpredictably in Sonnet 8 ('Music to hear . . .'), the elaborate working-out of a musical analogy in which the unmarried young man is rebuked by 'the true concord of well-tunèd sounds, | By unions married', on the acoustic plane, which

---

[39] Cf. also: 'what could death do if thou shouldst depart, | Leaving thee living in posterity?' (6. 11–12).

[40] In his notes G. B. Evans suggests a parallel here with Erasmus' rebuke to the young man for not making proper use of his semen: 'The selfsame thing that either withered and drieth away in thy body or else putrifieth within thee, and so hurteth greatly thy health, yea, that selfsame which falleth from thee in thy sleep, would have been a man, if thou thyself hadst been a man' (p. 106).

> sweetly chide thee, who confounds
> In singleness the parts that thou shouldst bear;
> Mark how one string, sweet husband to another,
> Strikes each in each by mutual ordering;
> Resembling sire, and child, and happy mother,

who 'all in one' remind him: 'Thou single will prove none' (8. 4–14)—or, as Erasmus puts it, 'come to nought' (p. 100). At times Shakespeare follows his model closely, as when Erasmus describes the benefit of having children, adding great enjoyment to this life:

What a joy shall this be unto you, when your most fair wife shall make you a father in bringing forth a fair child unto you, where you shall have a pretty little boy running up and down your house, such a one as shall express your look and your wife's look, such a one as shall call you 'Dad' with his sweet lisping words? (p. 109)

Children are also a promise of immortality, a way of overcoming death by the flourishing of youth:

For so long as they shall live, you shall need never be thought dead yourself . . . Old age cometh upon us all, will we or nill we, and this way nature provided for us, that we should wax young again in our children and nephews. For what man can be grieved that he is old, when he seeth his own countenance which he had being a child to appear lively in his son? Death is ordained for all mankind, and yet by this means only nature by her providence mindeth unto us a certain immortality, while she increaseth one thing upon another, even as a young graff buddeth out when the old tree is cut down. (ibid.)

These passages were the direct inspiration for Sonnet 2, 'When forty winters shall besiege thy brow', where the young man's 'beauty' and 'lusty days' are foreseen as giving way to 'deep-sunken eyes', a process which cannot be stopped but could be redeemed,

> If thou couldst answer, 'This fair child of mine
> Shall sum my count, and make my old excuse',
> Proving his beauty by succession thine.
>   This were to be new made when thou art old,
>   And see thy blood warm when thou feel'st it cold. (2. 10–14)

Also, the threatening idea that the unmarried young man will vanish, leaving no trace behind, recurs in the couplet of Sonnet 7—'So thou

. . . | Unlooked on diest unless thou get a son' (7. 13–14)—to be set against the consoling alternative, which opens Sonnet 11:

> As fast as thou shalt wane, so fast thou grow'st
> In one of thine, from that which thou departest,
> And that fresh blood which youngly thou bestow'st
> Thou mayst call thine, when thou from youth convertest.   (11. 1–4)

Shakespeare is still writing within the Erasmian framework in the conclusion of Sonnet 12:

> And nothing 'gainst Time's scythe can make defence
> Save breed to brave him when he takes thee hence.   (12. 13–14)

But in following Erasmus Shakespeare adds something of his own. Where Erasmus had often referred to 'decay' as the chief harm to be overcome, Shakespeare adds Time, allegorizing the two forces in Sonnet 15. This poem uses another Erasmian analogy, noting how 'men as plants increase' but then 'decrease', and 'wear their brave state out of memory' (that is, as Evans glosses, 'wear away (in decay)', their prime of life only a memory):

> Then the conceit of this inconstant stay
> Sets you most rich in youth before my sight,
> Where wasteful Time debateth with Decay
> To change your day of youth to sullied night.

Just at this point Shakespeare reveals that the speaker, as a poet, has another weapon against mortality, besides procreation:

> And all in war with Time for love of you.
> As he takes from you, I ingraft you new.   (15. 9–14)

Erasmus had used the grafting metaphor for the process by which a child succeeds his father, 'even as a young graff buddeth out when the old tree is cut down': for Shakespeare it is a metaphor for the poet's power to bring immortality to his subject. The sonnet following takes up this power, again opposing it to both time and decay:

> But wherefore do not you a mightier way
> Make war upon this bloody tyrant Time,
> And fortify yourself in this decay
> With means more blessed than my barren rhyme?   (16. 1–4)

That self-depreciation is only momentary, making way for the argument that a child would be a 'more blessed' form of remembrance (16. 5–14), only for Sonnet 17 to collapse the opposition into union:

Who will believe my verse in time to come
If it were filled with your most high deserts?
    But were some child of yours alive that time
    You should live twice, in it and in my rhyme. (17. 1–2, 13–14)

The young man needs both marriage and poetry.

The references to time, and the immortality given by verse, derive, as has long been known, from Horace ('Exegi monumentum aere perennius', *Odes* 3. 30. 1 ff.) and Ovid, both for the notion of Time the destroyer ('Tempus edax rerum', *Met.* 15. 234 ff.) and for the permanence of poetry (*Met.* 15. 871 ff.). This book of the *Metamorphoses* also provided Shakespeare with several descriptions of the instability of human life as another argument to be used against the young man's self-sufficiency,[41] further evidence of how *imitatio* could be used as a spur to individual creativity. In this brief excursion I have kept in mind Ascham's practical outline of *imitatio* (p. 145), trying to see which elements Shakespeare retains, which he omits, and why, and above all which 'he altereth and changeth' in order to make the resulting work his own.

CRITERIA OF CORRECTNESS

Most literary discussion involves, at some point, an evaluation of the writer or work being read (the word *kritikos* in Greek means 'the man who is capable of judging'). In modern critical writing evaluative categories often involve such large and rather vaguely defined terms as 'imagination', 'originality', or 'truth to life', together with the traditional topics of characterization, plot, narrative. The rapid emergence and equally rapid obsolescence of some literary theories since the 1960s has meant that a bewildering variety of concepts and categories, new and old, now exist side by side, without any general consensus as to which should be used, and for what purpose. Renaissance critical theory was less diversified, and more coherent. The major evaluative criteria, once again, were taken over from classical rhetoric and initially applied to the basic situation of the orator or poet engaged in monologic discourse, first-person utterance addressed directly to an audience. Subsequently these criteria were transferred to the mimetic genres (drama, epic poetry, and prose fiction), being applied to the

[41] See Evans, pp. 119, 121, 125, 127.

imagined characters' speech and behaviour. Since the orator always faced a specific situation, a legal case in which he appeared either for the prosecution or the defence, or a political discussion in which his position was equally clear-cut, he had to get the subject-matter properly organized before he ever wrote a word of his speech. As D. A. Russell put it, 'a process of "invention" precedes the process of expression, and there is thus a sharp distinction between content (*to legomenon*) and verbal form (*lexis*). With some hazy and uncertain exceptions, ancient writers on poetry also adhered firmly to this distinction.'[42] Roman writers, and their Renaissance followers, endorsed the priority of the *res* or subject-matter over the *verba* in which it would finally be expressed, quoting Cato's reassuring advice that *rem tene, verba sequentur* ('look after the subject-matter and words will look after themselves'). Cicero, Horace, and Quintilian each echoed this advice in their own terms.[43] The further implication is that once the orator or poet has organized his subject-matter—which also involves considering what kind of audience he will address, what effect to arouse, and to what purpose—the words must then be chosen so as to achieve this complex goal, resulting in the theory of decorum, or appropriateness of language to subject-matter and intention.

Ancient rhetoric taught that the orator's language—and, by extension, whole compositions—ought to possess certain positive qualities, and to avoid their defects. In his *Rhetoric* Aristotle defined the four virtues of prose style: 'correctness' (by grammatical standards), 'clarity', 'dignity' (or 'expansiveness', the proper language for public address), and 'propriety' (3. 5–7. 1407^{a}6 ff.; *ALC*, pp. 142–6). His pupil, Theophrastus, remodelled the list to read: correctness, clarity, appropriateness, and 'ornament'. These terms were put into wider circulation by Cicero in his influential discussions, and spelled out in more detail by Quintilian.[44] Renaissance rhetoricians repeated this doctrine, adapting it to the vernaculars. Puttenham, for instance, laid down that the correct language for poetry was 'Southern English . . . the usual speech of the Court, and that of London and shires lying about London' within a sixty-mile radius (p. 226).

---

[42] *Criticism in Antiquity*, p. 4. On *decorum*, see also ibid., pp. 15, 42–3, 55–6, 115–16, 120, 129–30.
[43] See e.g. *De or.* 3. 21. 125 ('for a full supply of facts begets a full supply of words'); *Ars P.* 311 ('and when matter is in hand words will not be loath to follow'); *Inst.* 10. 1. 5 ('a copious supply of matter and words').
[44] See Cicero, *De or.* 3. 10. 37; *Rhet. Her.* 4. 12. 17; Quintilian, *Inst.* 11. 5. 1, 8. 1. 1–2.

Clarity was universally accepted as the prime virtue of language; as Aristotle put it, 'language to be good must be clear, as is proved by the fact that speech which fails to convey a plain meaning will fail to do just what speech has to do . . . clearness is secured by using the words . . . that are current and ordinary' (*Rh.* 3. 2. 1404^{b}1 ff.). For Cicero, 'because the subjects of the other arts are derived as a rule from hidden and remote sources, while the whole art of oratory lies open to the view, and is concerned in some measure with the common practice, custom, and speech of mankind, . . . in oratory the very cardinal sin is to depart from the language of everyday life, and the usage approved by the sense of the community' (*De oratore* 1. 3. 12). For classical and Renaissance theorists ambiguity was a vice of style, a sign of the poorly trained writer, or even of one who wants to deliberately mislead his hearers (*Rh.* 3. 2. 1404^{b}37). Demetrius, Cicero, and Quintilian agree that it should be avoided at all costs (*ALC*, pp. 207, 241, 376). As the early humanists recovered classical texts unknown to the Middle Ages, such as Cicero's rhetorical works and letters, they felt that the single most important quality of the correct Latin that they strove to produce was clarity.[45] Their English counterparts emphasized that the writer's first priority should be 'plainness', as Wilson called it, avoiding linguistic affectation or obscurity (p. 120), a preference for clarity or *perspicuitas* often repeated (Gascoigne, p. 167; Jonson, pp. 559, 575; North, p. 507; Hobbes, p. 615). So when George Chapman attempts to validate his preference for difficulty and obscurity in poetry (p. 392), he deliberately puts himself in a minority—or, as he would see it, an élite.

The most important of these virtues of style was appropriateness (*prepon*), or decorum. In his *Rhetoric* Aristotle sketched the multiple considerations that the orator must bear in mind:

Your language will be appropriate if it expresses emotion and character, and if it corresponds to its subject. 'Correspondence to subject' means that we must neither speak casually about weighty matters, nor solemnly about trivial ones . . .

When discussing human behaviour, such as that involved in a law-case, the orator must make the appropriate moral and emotional response:

you will employ the language of anger in speaking of outrage; the language of disgust and discreet reluctance to utter a word when speaking of impiety

[45] McLaughlin, *Literary Imitation*, pp. 69, 117, 154, 198.

or foulness; the language of exultation for a tale of glory, and that of hu-
miliation for a tale of pity; and so in all other cases.   (3. 7. 1408ᵃ10f.)

The third aspect of appropriateness, 'character', comes in whenever
the orator evokes a particular 'class of men' or 'type of disposition',
for each has 'its own appropriate way of letting the truth appear.
Under "class" I include differences of age, as boy, man, or old man;
of sex, as man or woman; of nationality, as Spartan or Thessalian.' By
'disposition' (*hexis*, or 'moral state') Aristotle means those influences
'which determine the character of a man's life', such as education, 'for
a rustic and an educated man will not say the same thing nor speak
in the same way' (1408ᵃ27 ff.). Language must be appropriate not only
to the orator's subject-matter, and to the emotions involved, but
also to the genre of oratory, for 'each kind of rhetoric has its own
appropriate style. The style of written prose is not that of spoken
orator, nor are those of political and forensic speaking the same'
(3. 12. 1413ᵇ2 ff.).

These positive injunctions for the speaker to observe appropriateness in language and the larger aspect of composition carried with
them a matching account of negative qualities; both positive and negative terms provide critics with criteria for evaluating writers and their
works. Metaphors and comparisons are a valuable resource for the
prose-writer, Aristotle says, but they 'must fairly correspond to the
thing signified: failing this, their inappropriateness will be conspicuous: the want of harmony between two things is emphasized by their
being placed side by side' (3. 2. 1405ᵃ10ff.). For Aristotle metaphor
has what we might call a zone of relevance, within which the mind
can perceive resemblances and make the needed 'transfer' of associations (the Latin for metaphor was *translatio*). So, 'in using metaphors
to give names to nameless things, we must draw them not from remote
but from kindred and similar things, so that the kinship is clearly perceived as soon as the words are said' (1405ᵃ35 ff.). Failure to observe
these criteria will produce faulty metaphors, one of the four types of
'frigidities in language' that Aristotle diagnoses (3. 3. 1405ᵇ34 ff.)—
the earliest recorded catalogue of stylistic faults. Prose-writers must
avoid inappropriate metaphors, whether vulgar or 'too lofty and
tragic', or simply 'far-fetched, for example Gorgias's phrase about
"pale and bloodless doings" or "You have sown shamefully and have
reaped badly". These are too poetic' (1406ᵇ6ff.; tr. Kennedy).

Aristotle's discussion of decorum in spoken oratory found its coun-

terpart in the Roman rhetorical texts, well known to Renaissance literary theorists, which include extended treatment of faults of style.[46]
More influential, however, since it made the transition from oratory
to poetry and drama, was Horace's detailed account of decorum in
the *Ars poetica*. The prescriptive nature of classical literary theory
accounts for the baldness with which Horace delivers his rulings about
the differences between literary genres and the styles appropriate to
each: 'a comic subject will not be set out in tragic verse . . . Everything
must keep the appropriate place to which it was allotted' (89 ff.; *ALC*,
p. 281). When the plot-situation demands it, however, comedy may
include anger, and tragic characters may 'lament in prosaic language,
when they . . . throw away their bombast and words half a yard
long [*sesquipedalia verba*], if they are anxious to touch the spectator's
heart with their complaint' (93 ff.; *ALC*, p. 282). Aristotle's precepts
concerning the orator's need to have his language display morally
appropriate reactions to the human behaviour described in court
are now adapted to the ways in which a dramatist represents his
characters:

Sad words suit a mournful countenance, threatening words an angry one;
sportive words are for the playful, serious for the grave. For nature first shapes
us within for any state of fortune—gives us pleasure or drives us to anger or
casts us down to the ground with grievous sorrow and pains us—and then
expresses the emotions through the medium of the tongue. If the words are
out of tune with the speaker's fortunes, the knights and infantry of Rome will
raise a cackle. (105 ff.; *ALC*, p. 282)

The audience in the Roman theatre, whether seated at the front (following the Roscian Law of 67 BC, Knights occupied the first fourteen
rows) or at the back, was evidently aware that language should be
appropriate to the characters' moral and emotional states, and to what
Aristotle described as 'class' and 'disposition': 'It will make a lot of
difference whether the speaker is a god or a hero, an old man of ripe
years or a hot youth, an influential matron or a hard-working nurse',
and so forth (114 ff.). The spiralling, unpredictable structure of the
Ars poetica allows Horace to return to one of these categories later, to
reiterate his point that

You must mark the manners of each time of life, and assign the appropriate
part to changing natures and ages . . . your character should always remain

[46] See e.g. Dio of Halicarnassus (*ALC*, p. 317); Longinus (*ALC*, pp. 463 ff.); Quintilian,
Inst. 8. 3. 44–61.

faithful to what is associated with his age and suits it.   (156ff., 170ff.; *ALC*, pp. 283f.)

The precepts of Aristotle, Horace, and the Roman rhetoricians concerning decorum reached Renaissance readers partly from those texts themselves, whether directly or through intermediaries, and partly from the grammatical and rhetorical commentaries attached to the comedies of Plautus and Terence, which formed the staple of elementary and intermediate education in Latin throughout all Renaissance schools.[47] The effects of this teaching can be seen first in the direct appropriation of material from classical rhetoric. In his pioneering *Arte of Rhetorique* Thomas Wilson's word for *decorum* is 'aptness', 'apt words' being those 'that properly agree unto that thing which they signify, and plainly express the nature of the same'. As always in this prescriptive form of criticism, the *res*—the poet or orator's choice of subject-matter, including his intention towards the audience—is prior. He must choose 'words most apt for their purpose. In weighty causes grave words are thought most needful, that the greatness of the matter may the rather appear in the vehemency of their talk'—*vehemens* being another category related to *movere*, arousing the audience's feelings to a high degree. Decorum not observed results in 'fondness [foolishness]' (p. 123). In *The Schoolmaster* (1570) Roger Ascham defined the various genres and urged that decorum (or 'propriety' as he calls it) applies at every stage of composition, 'in choice of words, in framing of sentences, in handling of arguments, and use of right form, figure, and number, proper and fit for every matter . . .' (p. 151), requirements spelled out in greater detail by George Puttenham (bk. 3, ch. 5: pp. 227ff.), who devotes two additional chapters to decorum.[48] Treating it first as a quality of speech, Puttenham proposes a psychological explanation for decorum in the working of the mind, which perceives 'sensible objects' and registers 'conformity, or proportion, or convenience' (or 'decency', or 'seemliness', all synonyms for *decorum*), then applies the same expectations to purely 'mental objects', following nature (p. 286). Puttenham, who had written a whole treatise *De decoro*, widens the discussion to consider the 'decency to be observed in every man's action and behaviour' (p. 289), moving literary criticism towards the conduct-book, it might

---

[47] See Madeleine Doran, *Endeavors of Art: A Study of Form in Elizabethan Drama* (Madison, 1954), pp. 16–17, 33–4, 148–71, 174–5, 234–5.

[48] See pp. 285ff., and, for the full text, *The Arte of English Poesie*, ed. G. D. Willcock and A. Walker (Cambridge, 1936; 1970), pp. 261–98.

seem—were it not that Renaissance theories of literature were from the first oriented towards ethics.

The effect of transferring the requirements of decorum to mimetic works, involving an imagined action and characters, can be seen in George Whetstone's difficulties with *Promos and Cassandra* (1578), which, the title-page announces, he has 'divided into two comical discourses' (p. 172). In the prefatory dedication Whetstone explains that, 'to make the actions appear more lively [life-like], I divided the whole history into two comedies—for that, decorum used, it would not be conveyed in one. The effects of both are good and bad: virtue intermixed with vice . . .'. Having fulfilled the criteria of decorum by separating out these two plot-strands, Whetstone virtuously criticizes the average English writer of comedies for being 'out of order. He first grounds his work on impossibilities, then in three hours runs he through the world, marries, gets children, makes children men', who conquer kingdoms and murder monsters. English dramatists commit further crimes against literary principles: 'they make a clown companion with a king . . . they use one order of speech for all persons— a gross indecorum . . .'. Like Aristotle, or Horace, Whetstone is quite happy with comic stereotypes: 'For, to work a comedy kindly'—that is, both 'naturally' and according to the appropriate literary 'kind' or genre—'grave old men should instruct, young men should show the imperfections of youth, strumpets should be lascivious, boys unhappy, and clowns should speak disorderly . . .' (p. 174). In perfect consistency with these principles, Sir John Harington can defend Ariosto from the charge of obscenity, pointing out that 'there is so meet a decorum in the persons of those that speak lasciviously' that a critic who objected would show his lack of judgement. Chaucer would be much more guilty of 'flat scurrility' in *The Miller's Tale* or *The Wife of Bath's Prologue and Tale*, 'in which only the decorum he keeps . . . excuseth it and makes it more tolerable' (p. 318).

For English critics the observation of decorum is a sign of literary excellence. E.K. praises 'the new poet', as he calls Spenser in *The Shepheardes Calender*, for 'his due observing of decorum everywhere, in personages, in seasons, in matters, in speech' (p. 176). But it is a quality more often found wanting, as we see from Gascoigne's warning that 'to intermingle merry jests in a serious matter is an indecorum' (p. 164), a criticism expressed at greater length in Sidney's attack on English writers for 'mingling comedy and tragedy' (pp. 360–1). A generation later John Fletcher could defend (p. 502) what Sidney called

'their mongrel tragi-comedy' (p. 383), but the classical principle that
these two genres should be kept separate was already well established,
as we can see from later seventeenth-century criticisms of Shakespeare's introduction of clowns into tragedy. This use of decorum as
a stick to beat unruly writers is found in many places, such as Puttenham's criticism of the early translators of Virgil for not using
language appropriate to the characters' dignity (p. 288). The most
articulate critic of indecorum was Ben Jonson, in several works
included here, attacking the improprieties of popular drama, including Shakespeare (p. 527), and singling out such varied writers as
Lucan, Guarini, and Sidney for not differentiating the speech of high-
born and low-born characters (p. 535)—criticism which hardly seems
applicable to Sidney's *Arcadia*. The demands of decorum are great,
as Puttenham saw, 'in so much as our speech asketh one manner of
"decency" in respect of the person who speaks; another, of his to
whom it is spoken; another, of whom we speak; another, to what we
speak, and in what place and time, and to what purpose' (p. 287). This
may seem an excessive demand, but the mature drama of Shakespeare
fulfils these criteria. They can all be observed in the language of
Hamlet, adapting itself chameleon-like to each situation and character confronted. Any competent analysis of that play would show how
his style differs according to whether he talks to Claudius, Gertrude,
Ophelia, Horatio, Polonius, Rosencrantz and Guildenstern, or the
gravediggers, and how it varies within his own soliloquies, according
to his moods (meditative, vindictive, conspiratorial) and the emotions
appropriate to each. If we recall the Renaissance concept of the artist
as a maker fashioning his work according to the principles of art we
will understand why Milton places towards the end of his ideal educational system the expectation that his pupils will have been properly trained to realize 'what decorum is, which is the grand
masterpiece to observe' (p. 605).

THE DEFENCE OF LITERATURE

Modern literary discussions address many issues, practical and theoretical, secure in the knowledge that literature is widely valued: by
ordinary readers, by educational institutions, and if not exactly
encouraged by Church or State, it is certainly not attacked in the West
by either religious or temporal powers. Occasionally critics such as
Matthew Arnold or F. R. Leavis may denounce philistinism, the

decline of taste, or the 'corrupt' London literary scene, but no one argues that literature itself is endangered.

In the fifteenth and sixteenth centuries, by contrast, many writers felt under real threat. As J. E. Spingarn wrote in his pioneering study (1899), 'the first problem of Renaissance criticism was the justification of imaginative literature'.[49] In the Middle Ages, the dominance of theology and the fact that much manuscript copying was in ecclesiastical hands, meant that only those works of literature were valued that had an explicitly moral and educational function, or could be given one retrospectively by allegorical interpretation. True, works of pure entertainment were written in the vernaculars, but they were not widely circulated outside noblemen's courts, and when they came to the notice of the Church fuelled further ecclesiastical disapproval of literature. Two outstanding early humanists confronted medieval enmity with well-argued defences, Giovanni Boccaccio in *De genealogia deorum* (*c*.1366), and Coluccio Salutati in *De laboribus Herculis* (*c*.1390).[50]

But as the humanists rediscovered and re-edited classical texts, the terms of the debate shifted. The Church continued to express distrust of literature, ecclesiastical censorship forming an important (if irregular) control over Elizabethan drama, both in performance and publication. To religious leaders theatres had always been suspect as places of public assembly where vice might flourish, and the Church Fathers (especially Tertullian in his *De spectaculis*) had produced violent diatribes against acting and actors, which were reused in the sixteenth century by rabid Puritans in their assault on the stage.[51] With the recovery of Greek and Roman texts, writers were provided with accurate texts of Plato's attacks on Homer and the tragedians, so often referred to by medieval moralists. But by the same post, as it were, they received several very competent defences of literature, by Aristotle in the *Poetics* and *Rhetoric*, by Cicero in his speech for Archias the poet, by Horace in the *Ars poetica*, by Plutarch in his essay 'How the young man should hear the poets'—that is, without incurring moral danger, and by the Stoic philosopher Strabo in his *Geography*. All these texts were well known to English writers, and references to them crop up frequently

---

[49] *A History of Literary Criticism in the Renaissance* (New York, 1899; 1924), p. 3.

[50] See e.g. C. C. Greenfield, *Humanist and Scholastic Poetics, 1250–1500* (Lewisburg and London, 1981).

[51] See e.g. Stephen Gosson, *The Schoole of Abuse* (1579), with Thomas Lodge's reply and the resulting controversy, as summarized by G. G. Smith, *ECE* i. 61–3; and J. A. Barish, *The Antitheatrical Prejudice* (Berkeley and London, 1981).

in the notes below. They could also draw on contemporary Italian and French treatises defending poetry, such as the *Poetica* of Daniello (1536), the *De poeta* of Minturno (1559), the *Poetices libri septem* of Scaliger (1561), Sébillet's *Art poétique français* (1548), Peletier's *Art poétique* (1555), and many more.

In these discussions the same basic arguments legitimizing poetry recur again and again. As Puttenham's opening chapter-titles sum it up: 'How poets were the first priests, the first prophets, the first legislators and politicians in the world'; 'How the poets were the first philosophers, the first astronomers and historiographers and orators and musicians of the world' (pp. 194, 195). Defenders reiterate that poetry is an ancient art, honoured by rulers and states (seven cities claimed the glory of having been Homer's birthplace). Plato's attacks are refuted over and over again, using the arguments of Aristotle or extending them. Plato, only allowing philosophy access to truth, had denied that either poetry or rhetoric had any access to knowledge, but peddled illusion and deceit. For Aristotle, however, it was a basic principle that 'all men desire to understand', and he declared poetic *mimesis*, since it worked at a higher level of generalization, to be 'more serious and philosophical' than history, say (*Poet.* 9. 1451^{b}6). Many later critics defended the poet as a teacher, and poetry as a source of knowledge, sometimes rather naively, as in Elyot's belief that students interested in hunting or agriculture will benefit from reading Virgil (p. 59). Francis Bacon offered a more thoughtful observation on the kind of knowledge to be found in poetry: 'for the expressing of affections, passions, corruptions, and customs we are beholding to poets more than to the philosophers' works' (p. 464).

But the most frequent basis for defending literature was its moral function. As we have seen, Sidney based his whole literary theory on how it uses *movere* and *delectare* in the service of *docere*. Much Renaissance literary theory is exemplary, expecting the poet to represent actions to be imitated or avoided. One historical virtue of poetry was that it preserves the memory of great actions for posterity. According to tradition, when Alexander the Great stood before the tomb of Achilles 'he exclaimed "Fortunate youth, to have found in Homer an herald of thy valour!"—Well might he exclaim', Cicero commented, 'for had the *Iliad* never existed, the same mound which covered Achilles' bones would also have overwhelmed his memory' (*Pro Archia* 10. 24). In two of his Odes, often quoted, Horace made the same point. In 4. 8 he celebrated the power of poetry to immortalize bravery:

non incisa notis marmora publicis,
per quae spiritus et vita redit bonis
post mortem ducibus . . .
si chartae sileant quod bene feceris
mercedem tuleris   (13–15, 21–2)

'Not marble graven with public records, whereby breath and life
return to goodly heroes after death', nor other brave deeds could
throw such lustre on the elder Scipio as did the poetry of Ennius; 'nor
would you reap your due reward, should the parchment leave your
worthy deeds unheralded'.

dignum laude virum Musa vetat mori
caelo Musa beat.   (28–9)

'The Muse of poetry forbids the hero worthy of renown to perish'—
a verse quoted by Ford in his elegy on Fletcher (p. 545)—'The Muse
bestows the boon of heaven'. And in 4. 9 Horace varied the theme,
seeing the poet as the crucial recorder of virtuous deeds:

vixere fortes ante Agamemnona
multi; sed omnes illacrimabiles
        urgentur ignotique longa
        nocte, carent quia vate sacro:
paulum sepultat distat inertiae
celata virtus   (25–30)

'Many heroes lived before Agamemnon; but all are overwhelmed in
unending night, unwept, unknown, because they lack a sacred bard.
In the tomb, hidden worth differs little from cowardice.'

   To some modern readers Horace may seem a remote lyric poet, but
to the Renaissance he was a living presence, like all the great classics.
When Ben Jonson wanted to present Elizabeth, Countess of Rutland,
with a New Year's gift for 1600, he celebrated both her virtue and his
power as a poet to memorialize it by boldly appropriating lines from
both Odes:

It is the muse alone can raise to heaven,
And at her strong arms' end hold up, and even,
The souls she loves. Those other glorious notes
Inscribed in touch or marble, or the coats
Painted or carved upon our great men's tombs,
Or in their windows, do but prove the wombs
That bred them, graves. When they were born, they died,

That had no muse to make their fame abide.
How many equal with the Argive queen
Have beauty known, yet none so famous seen?
Achilles was not first that valiant was,
Or in an army's head that, locked in brass,
Gave killing strokes. There were brave men, before
Ajax, or Idomen, or all the store
That Homer brought to Troy; yet none so live;
Because they lacked the sacred pen, could give
Like life unto them. Who heaved Hercules
Unto the stars? Or the Tyndarides?
Who placèd Jason's Argo in the sky?
Or set bright Ariadne's crowns so high?
Who made a lamp of Berenice's hair?
Or lifted Cassiopea in her chair?
But only poets, rapt with rage divine?[52]

(That is another example of *imitatio* as defined by Ovid, in which the poet expects his borrowings to be recognized.)

The general effect of these arguments, in English as in the other Renaissance languages, was to consolidate an image of literature as essential to the functioning of civilized life, both as a record of virtuous action and as an incentive towards its emulation. A key intermediary stage in this theory concerned the emotional state in which people are most likely to emulate virtuous behaviour, one in which they are 'aroused' or 'inflamed' by its example, another version of *movere*, connected with the rhetoric of praise and blame.[53] In his defence of the Greek poet Archias' claim to Roman citizenship Cicero testified that, ever since his youth, 'the moral lessons derived from a wide reading' convinced him 'that nothing is to be greatly sought after in this life save glory and honour, and that in their quest' all pain and danger can be easily borne.

All literature, all philosophy, all history, abounds with incentives to noble action, incentives which would be buried in black darkness were the light of the written word not flashed upon them. How many pictures of high endeavour the great authors of Greece and Rome have drawn for our use, not only for our emulation! These I have held ever before my vision throughout my public career, and have guided the workings of my brain and my soul by meditating upon patterns of excellence.   (*Arch.* 6. 14)

---

[52] *Forest* 12, in *Ben Jonson. The Complete Poems*, ed. G. Parfitt, p. 112.
[53] See Brian Vickers, 'Epideictic and Epic in the Renaissance', *New Literary History*, 14 (1983), 497–537, at pp. 510–11.

Where Cicero expressed this conviction in autobiographical terms, Plutarch generalized it in the Preface to his *Life of Pericles* as a rule in life, attacking 'those who waste the curiosity and love of knowledge which belongs to human nature, by directing it to worthless, not to useful objects'. Since everyone can concentrate his mind on whatever subject he pleases,

we ought to seek virtue not merely in order to contemplate it, but that we may ourselves derive some benefit from so doing. Just as those colours whose blooming and pleasant hues refresh our sight are grateful to the eyes, so we ought by our studies to delight in that which is useful for our own lives; and this is to be found in the acts of good men, which when narrated incite us to imitate them. (1)

In Plutarch's theory of human nature, 'we both admire the deeds to which virtue incites, and long to emulate the doers of them'. By performing 'virtuous actions' we wish 'to benefit others . . . That which is in itself admirable kindles in us a desire of emulation, whether we see noble deeds presented before us, or read of them in history. It was with this purpose in mind that I have engaged in writing biography . . .' (2).

Writers in the English Renaissance wholeheartedly adopted this rationale for depicting virtue so as to encourage its emulation. In 1531 Sir Thomas Elyot recommended the poems of Homer as containing 'not only the documents martial and discipline of arms, but also incomparable wisdoms and instructions for politic governance of people, with the worthy commendation and laud of noble princes; wherewith the readers shall be so all inflamed that they most fervently shall desire and covet, by the imitation of their virtues, to acquire semblable glory' (pp. 57–8). Among Wyatt's virtues, itemized by Surrey in his elegy (1542), were

> A tongue that served in foreign realms his king;
> Whose courteous talk to virtue did inflame
> Each noble heart, a worthy guide to bring
> Our English youth by travail unto fame. (p. 71)

Sidney celebrated the poet's ability to deliver the 'idea or fore-conceit' of his work so effectively that it will work 'not only to make a Cyrus, which had been but a particular excellency as Nature might have done, but to bestow a Cyrus upon the world to make many Cyruses, if they will learn aright why and how that maker made him' (p. 344). The poet's creation will help to 'form' or 'inform' his readers, that is, 'fashion' or shape themselves in the image of heroic virtue. As Spenser planned the *Faerie Queene*, it was to be '*Disposed into twelve books, fashioning XII. moral vertues*', its goal being 'to fashion a gentleman or noble person in virtuous and gentle discipline' (p. 298). In the rhetoricized poetics of the Renaissance this notion had been taken over from the *ars rhetorica* or handbook tradition, but given an ethical purpose. Cicero writes in *De oratore* that 'our orator must be shaped [*conformandus*] in regard to both his words and thoughts in the same way as persons whose business is the handling of weapons are trained' (3. 52. 200), and in *Orator* records that he is 'delineating the perfect orator' (2. 7: 'in summo oratore fingendo'). Quintilian regularly uses the verb *formare* to describe the 'moulding' or 'shaping' of the would-be orator: 'I propose to mould [*formare*] the studies of my orator from infancy' (*Inst.* 1. Pr. 5); 'I have undertaken the task of moulding [*formare*] the ideal orator' (2. 15. 33). He refers to 'the orator whom I desire to form' (12. 1. 44), who must in turn 'form his character on the precepts of philosophy and the dictates of reason' (12. 2. 4)—a point at which we can trace the transition from rhetoric to ethics. Fully aware of the rhetorical tradition, Castiglione wrote of *Il Cortegiano* (1528) that the dialogue's goal was 'formar con parole un perfetto cortegiano' (1. 12). Although he knew all these texts, Spenser's probable source was Orazio Toscanella, who in the prefatory letter to his *Bellezze del Furioso di M. Lodovico Ariosto* (Venice, 1574), uttered the conventional view that the poet's function is to stimulate men to practise virtue and avoid vice. Homer, Virgil, and Ariosto all imparted moral instruction in the same way: they 'placed several virtues in several individuals, one virtue in one character, another virtue in another character, in order to fashion out of all the characters a well-rounded and perfect man ["per formare un huomo quadrato e perfetto"]. A well-rounded and perfect man is the one adorned with all virtues.'[54] Writers gladly accepted the task of shaping their readers. Sir John Harington defended poetry for its ability to 'soften and polish the hard and rough dispositions of men, and make them capable of virtue and good discipline' (p. 305); Gabriel Harvey praised the *Arcadia* to those readers who 'honour virtue and would enkindle a noble courage in your minds' (p. 334). Jonson, listing 'the offices [duties] and functions of

[54] Cf. D. L. Aguzzi's valuable unpublished dissertation, 'Allegory in the Heroic Poetry of the Renaissance', Ph.D. diss., Columbia Univ., NY, 1959 (Univ. Microfilms order no. Mic. 59-6993), p. 208.

poet', defines him as 'able to inform young men to all good disciplines, inflame grown men to all great virtues . . .' (p. 469). The same goal was ascribed to the popular theatre by Thomas Heywood and his associates:

> Brave men, brave acts, being bravely acted too,
> Makes, as men see things done, desire to do,

wrote Arthur Hopton (p. 477). 'So bewitching a thing is lively and well-spirited action', wrote Heywood, 'that it hath power to new-mould the hearts of the spectators and fashion them to the shape of any noble and notable attempt' (p. 487). Massinger, making a vigorous defence of drama in *The Roman Actor* (1626), wrote of its power

> to inflame
> The noble youth with an ambitious heart
> To endure the frosts of danger, nay of death,
> To be thought worthy the triumphal wreath
> By glorious undertakings . . .   (pp. 550–1)

The 'main skill and groundwork' of Milton's reform of education was to make his pupils 'inflamed with the study of learning and the admiration of virtue, stirred up with high hopes of living to be brave men and worthy patriots, dear to God and famous to all ages' (pp. 602–3). For Hobbes the purpose of epic was 'to exhibit a venerable and amiable image of heroic virtue', and 'to raise admiration, principally, for three virtues: valour, beauty, and love' (pp. 613, 619).

That writers as diverse as Sidney and Heywood, Milton and Hobbes, should celebrate the power of poetry and drama to arouse a love of virtue and a desire to emulate it is further proof that Renaissance literary theory was perfectly coherent, being based on the union of rhetoric and ethics. There were no purely aesthetic theories, no poetics addressed to the artwork as a formal entity detached from its intended effect on the reader. One classical work could have provided an aesthetic theory, at least in part, namely Aristotle's *Poetics*, which includes among its various approaches to poetry the important concept of the poem's necessary unity (*Poet.* 26. 1462^{b}3 ff.).[55] Renaissance critics did know of this concept, but they juxtaposed it with the matching claim of *varietas*, as urged by classical rhetoric.[56] And in general Aristotelian ideas became absorbed into

---

[55] See Russell, *Criticism in Antiquity*, pp. 32, 91–3.
[56] See Weinberg, *History* ii, index, pp. 1182–3, s.v. 'Unity', 'Variety'.

the dominant rhetoricized poetics, as represented by the fusion of Cicero and Horace.[57]

But while justifying literature as a moral rather than as an aesthetic phenomenon, classical and Renaissance defences did acknowledge its power to give delight. Some unorthodox theorists (such as Castelvetro) argued that the real function of literature was to give pleasure, but for most Renaissance critics the long-standing elevation of virtue (*arētē*, *virtus*), with the total incrimination of pleasure (*hedōnē*, *voluptas*), as seen in the writings of Plato, Cicero, Plutarch, Seneca, and many others, meant that pleasure was a dubious commodity, not to be invoked without special precautions. One classical precedent they could invoke was Cicero, whose defence of Archias included an eloquent justification for literature as essential to human health and happiness. Having argued that literary pursuits naturally praise virtue, and are mainly useful in encouraging *humanitas*, Cicero—exceptionally for him—temporarily granted the opposed claim of pleasure. Setting aside virtue for the moment, he writes,

Let us assume that entertainment [*delectatio*] is the sole end of reading; even so, I think you would hold that no mental employment is so broadening to the sympathies or so enlightening to the understanding. Other pursuits belong not to all times, all ages, all conditions; but this gives stimulus to our youth and diversion to our old age; this adds a charm to success, and offers a haven of consolation to failure. In the home it delights, in the world it hampers not. Through the night-watches, on all our journeying, and in our hours of country ease, it is our unfailing companion. (7. 16)

That passage may have been in Sir Philip Sidney's mind when he described how the poet approaches his reader 'not with obscure definitions', like the philosopher,

but he cometh to you with words set in delightful proportion, either accompanied with, or prepared for, the well-enchanting skill of music; and with a tale forsooth he cometh unto you, with a tale which holdeth children from play, and old men from the chimney corner. (p. 358)

And the apologists for the popular theatre invoked its power to entertain and refresh its audience (pp. 477–9).

---

[57] See Weinberg, *History* i. 111–55, 'The tradition of Horace's *Ars Poetica* II. The confusion with Aristotle'; M. T. Herrick, *The Fusion of Horatian and Aristotelian Criticism, 1531–1555* (Urbana, Ill., 1946); and Tigerstedt (op. cit., n. 16), who concludes that 'it seems more appropriate to say that Aristotle as well as Horace was read in the light of a common rhetorical tradition than to argue that Aristotle was interpreted through Horace' (p. 23).

Sidney's *Defence of Poetry* rehearses all the traditional arguments on behalf of literature, giving them many fresh emphases, and organizing the whole—thanks to the help of rhetoric—into the most unified, concise, and verbally brilliant treatise in Renaissance literary criticism. The only aspect which may arouse regret is that he chose to model it on the form of the 'Disputa delle Arti', the attempt of one art to assert its superiority over its rivals.[58] The inevitable consequence of this choice was that Sidney elevated poetry at the expense of history, downgrading a discipline that he otherwise admired. As for philosophy (here identified with ethics, as often in the Renaissance), we note that Sidney asserts the superiority of poetry not as an autonomous discipline differing from philosophy, but rather as pursuing the same goals as philosophy, only more effectively. To modern eyes it may seem as if poetry is reduced by being identified with practical ethics, intended to incite its audience to virtuous action. But to many Renaissance readers, and creators of imaginative literature, that was its greatest justification, as a form of engagement with life. They were all familiar with Sallust's celebration, at the beginning of his *Bellum Catilinae*, of the historian's role in celebrating 'the outstanding merit and glory of good men'. Such activity, Sallust wrote, may not be as beneficial to one's fellow-men as direct military or political engagement; but still, 'it is noble to serve the state by action, and even to use a gift of eloquence on its behalf is no mean thing. Peace, no less than war, offers men a chance of fame: they can win praise by describing the exploits as well as by achieving them. And although the narrator earns much less renown than the doer, the writing of history is . . . a peculiarly difficult task' (1. 3).[59] Or, in Jonson's incomparably terse digest,

> Although to write be lesser than to do,
> It is the next deed, and a great one too.[60]

---

[58] See e.g. E. Garin (ed.), *La Disputa delle Arti nel Quattrocento* (Florence, 1947).

[59] Sallust, *The Jugurthine War. The Conspiracy of Catiline*, tr. S. A. Handford (Harmondsworth, Middx., 1963), pp. 176–7.

[60] 'To Sir Henry Savile', *Epigrams* 95; ed. Parfitt, p. 67.

I

Sir Thomas Elyot,
The value of poetry in education (1531)

SIR THOMAS ELYOT (1490?–1546), author and public servant (clerk of assize, 1511–28; JP for Oxfordshire, 1522; clerk of the privy council, 1523–30; knighted, 1530; ambassador to Charles V, 1531–2; MP for Cambridge, 1542). A friend of Sir Thomas More, Elyot played an important role in introducing Italian humanist ideas and texts into England. At Oxford between 1516 and 1523, he studied philosophy and law, and was taught Greek and medicine by Thomas Linacre. His publications include a philosophical treatise, *Of the knowledge whiche Maketh a Wise Man* (1533); *The Doctrinal of Princes* (1534), a translation of Isocrates' *Ad Nicoclem*; an influential Latin–English dictionary (1538; known in subsequent editions as *Bibliotecae Eliotae, Eliotis librarie*); and *The castle of health* (1537; 17 edns. by 1610).

TEXT. From *The Boke named the Governour* (1531; 7 edns. by 1580); modern edn. by H. H. S. Croft, 2 vols. (London, 1883), with copious annotation. The first excerpt comes from bk. 1, ch. 10: 'What order should be in learning, and which authors should be first read'; the second from bk. 1, ch. 13: 'The second and third decay of learning among gentlemen'. This pioneering work discusses how the commonwealth should be governed, the knowledge proper to humanity—for 'what so perfectly expresseth a man as doctrine?' (Croft, i. 112), and the particular education necessary for administrators, ranging from a knowledge of literature to possession of the moral virtues (prudence, benevolence, justice, fortitude, temperance, etc.). For further commentary see S. E. Lehmberg, *Sir Thomas Elyot, Tudor Humanist* (Austin, Tex., 1960), and John M. Major, *Sir Thomas Elyot and Renaissance Humanism* (Lincoln, Nebr., 1964).

. . . I could rehearse divers other poets which for matter and eloquence be very necessary, but I fear me to be too long from noble Homer, from whom as from a fountain proceeded all eloquence and learning.[1] For in his books be contained, and most perfectly expressed, not only the documents* martial and discipline* of arms, but also incomparable wisdoms and instructions for politic governance of people, with the worthy commendation and laud of noble princes; wherewith the

---

[1] Quintilian, *Inst.* 10. 1. 46, 12. 11. 21.

readers shall be so all inflamed that they most fervently shall desire and covet, by the imitation of their virtues, to acquire semblable glory. For the which occasion Aristotle, most sharpest witted and excellent learned philosopher, as soon as he had received Alexander from King Philip his father, he before any other thing taught him the most noble works of Homer; wherein Alexander[2] found such sweetness and fruit that ever after he had Homer not only with him in all his journeys, but also laid him under his pillow when he went to rest, and often times would purposely wake some hours of the night, to take as it were his pastime with that most noble poet. For by the reading of his work called *Iliados*, where the assembly of the most noble Greeks against Troy is recited with their affairs, he gathered courage and strength against his enemies; wisdom and eloquence for consultations; and persuasions to his people and army.

And by the other work called *Odyssea*, which recounteth the sundry adventures of the wise Ulysses,[3] he, by the example of Ulysses apprehended many noble virtues, and also learned to escape the fraud and deceitful imaginations of sundry and subtle crafty wits. Also there shall he learn to ensearch and perceive the manners and conditions of them that be his familiars, sifting out (as I might say) the best from the worst, whereby he may surely commit his affairs, and trust to every person after his virtues. Therefore I now conclude that there is no lesson for a young gentleman to be compared with Homer, if he be plainly and substantially expounded and declared by the master.

Notwithstanding, forasmuch as the said works be very long, and do require therefore a great time to be all learned and conned,* some Latin author would be therewith mixed, and specially Virgil; which in his work called *Aeneidos* is most like to Homer, and almost the same Homer in Latin. Also, by the joining together of those authors the one shall be the better understood by the other. And verily (as I before said) none one author serveth to so divers wits as doth Virgil. For there is not that affect* or desire whereto any child's fantasy* is disposed but in some of Virgil's works may be found matter* thereto apt and propise.*

---

[2] Plutarch, *Alexander* 8; Quintus Curtius 1. 4. 6f.

[3] Cf. Horace's praise of Homer: 'Again, of the power of worth and wisdom he has set before us an instructive pattern in Ulysses, that tamer of Troy, who looked with discerning eyes upon the cities and manners of many men, and while for self and comrades he strove for a return across the broad seas, many hardships he endured, but could never be o'erwhelmed in the waves of adversity' (*Epist.* 1. 2. 17–22).

For what thing can be more familiar than his *Bucolics?* nor no work so nigh approacheth to the common dalliance and manners of children, and the pretty controversies of the simple shepherds therein contained wonderfully rejoiceth the child that heareth it well declared, as I know by mine own experience. In his *Georgics*, lord what pleasant variety there is, the divers grains, herbs, and flowers that be there described that, reading therein, it seemeth to a man to be in a delectable garden or paradise. What ploughman knoweth so much of husbandry* as there is expressed? Who, delighting in good horses, shall not be thereto more inflamed reading there of the breeding, choosing, and keeping of them? In the declaration whereof Virgil leaveth far behind him all breeders, hackneymen,* and skosers.* Is there any astronomer that more exactly setteth out the order and course of the celestial bodies, or that more truly doth divine in his prognostications of the times of the year, in their qualities, with the future estate of all things provided by husbandry, than Virgil doth recite in that work?

If the child have a delight in hunting, what pleasure shall he take of the fable of Aristaeus; semblably in the hunting[4] of Dido and Eneas, which is described most elegantly in his book of *Aeneidos*. If he have pleasure in wrestling, running, or other like exercise,[5] where shall he see any more pleasant esbastements* than that which was done by Euryalus and other Trojans which accompanied Aeneas? If he take solace in hearing minstrels, what minstrel may be compared to Iopas,[6] which sang before Dido and Aeneas? or to blind Demodocus,[7] that played and sang most sweetly at the dinner that the king Alcinous made to Ulysses; whose ditties and melody excelled as far the songs of our minstrels as Homer and Virgil excel all other poets.

If he be more desirous (as the most part of children be), to hear things marvellous and exquisite,* which hath in it a visage of some things incredible, whereat shall he more wonder than when he shall behold Aeneas follow Sibylla[8] into hell? What shall he more dread than the terrible visages of Cerberus, Gorgon, Megera, and other furies and monsters?[9] How shall he abhor tyranny, fraud, and avarice when he doth see the pain of Duke Theseus, Prometheus, Sisyphus, and such other, tormented for their dissolute and vicious lying?[10] How glad soon after shall he be when he shall behold in the pleasant fields of

---

[4] *Georg.* 4. 317–558; *Aen.* 4. 117 ff.   [5] *Aen.* 5. 291 ff.
[6] *Aen.* 1. 740 ff.; Quint. *Inst.* 1. 10. 10.   [7] *Od.* 8. 62 ff.   [8] *Aen.* 6. 42–55.
[9] *Aen.* 6. 417–23, 289; 12. 845–8.   [10] *Aen.* 6. 617; *Ecl.* 6. 42; *Aen.* 6. 616.

Elisius[11] the souls of noble princes and captains which, for their virtue and labours in advancing the public weals of their countries, do live eternally in pleasure inexplicable? And in the last books of *Aeneidos* shall he find matter to minister to him audacity, valiant courage, and policy to take and sustain noble enterprises,[12] if any shall be needful for the assailing of his enemies. Finally (as I have said) this noble Virgil, like to a good nurse, giveth to a child, if he will take it, everything apt for his wit and capacity: wherefore he is in the order of learning to be preferred before any other author Latin.

I would set next unto him two books of Ovid, the one called *Metamorphoses*, which is as much to say as changing of men into other figure or form; the other is entitled *De fastis*,[13] where the ceremonies of the gentiles,* and especially the Romans, be expressed, both right necessary for the understanding of other poets. But because there is little other learning in them concerning either virtuous manners or policy I suppose it were better that, as fables and ceremonies happen to come in a lesson it were declared abundantly by the master, than that in the said two books a long time should be spent and almost lost, which might be better employed on such authors that do minister both eloquence, civil policy, and exhortation to virtue. Wherefore in his place let us bring in Horace, in whom is contained much variety of learning and quickness of sentence.*

This poet may be enterlaced with the lesson of *Odissea* of Homer, wherein is declared the wonderful prudence and fortitude of Ulysses in his passage from Troy. And if the child were induced to make verses[14] by the imitation of Virgil and Homer, it should minister to him much delectation and courage to study. Nor the making of verses is not discommended in a nobleman, since the noble Augustus[15] and almost all the old emperors made books in verses.

The two noble poets Silius,[16] and Lucan,[17] be very expedient to be

---

[11] *Aen.* 6. 638 ff.

[12] e.g. *Aen.* 11. 502 ff., 511 ff.

[13] A poetical calendar of the Roman year, expounding the astronomical, historical, and religious associations of each month. Ovid completed only six of the projected twelve books.

[14] Latin verse composition was basic to the grammar school curriculum.

[15] Suetonius, *Octavius* 85.

[16] Silius Italicus (*c*. AD 26–101), author of *Punica*, the longest Latin poem, a historical epic on the Second Punic War.

[17] M. Annaeus Lucanus (AD 39–65), author of the epic poem describing the war between Caesar and Pompey, *Bellum civile*, much admired for its rhetoric and sensationalism: cf. pp. 531, 632.

learned: for the one setteth out the emulation in qualities and prowess of two noble and valiant captains, one enemy to the other. That is to say, Silius writeth of Scipio the Roman, and Hannibal duke of Cartaginensis; Lucan declareth a semblable matter but much more lamentable, for as much as the wars were civil and, as it were, in the bowels of the Romans, that is to say, under the standards of Julius Caesar and Pompey.

Hesiodus, in Greek, is more brief than Virgil where he writeth of husbandry, and doth not rise so high in philosophy; but is fuller of fables, and therefore is more illecebrous.*

And here I conclude to speak any more of poets necessary for the childhood of a gentleman: for as much as these, I doubt not, will suffice until he pass the age of eight years. In which time childhood declineth, and reason waxeth ripe and deprehendeth* things with a more constant judgment. Here I would* should be remembered that I require not that all these works should be thoroughly read of a child in this time, which were almost impossible. But I only desire that they have, in every of the said books, so much instruction that they may take thereby some profit. Then the child's courage, inflamed by the frequent reading of noble poets,[18] daily more and more desireth to have experience in those things that they so vehemently do commend, in them that they write of.

Leonidas,[19] the noble king of Spartans, being once demanded of what estimation in poetry Tyrtaeus (as he supposed) was, it is written that he answering said that for steering the minds of young men he was excellent, for as much as they, being moved with his verses, do run into the battle regarding no peril, as men all inflamed in martial courage.

And when a man is come to mature years, and that reason in him is confirmed with serious learning and long experience, then shall he, in reading tragedies, execrate and abhor the intolerable life of tyrants, and shall condemn the folly and dotage expressed by poets lascivious. . . .

Now some man will require me to show mine opinion, if it be necessary that gentlemen should after the age of fourteen years continue in study. And to be plain and true therein: I dare affirm that if the

---

[18] The marginal note reads: 'Poets defended and praised'.
[19] Plutarch, *Cleomenes* 2; Horace, *Ars P.* 401 ff.

elegant speaking of Latin be not added to other doctrine, little fruit may come of the tongue, since Latin is but a natural speech, and the fruit of speech is wise sentence,* which is gathered and made of sundry learnings. And who that hath nothing but language only, may be no more praised than a popinjay,* a pie,* or a stare* when they speak featly.* There be many nowadays in famous schools and universities which be so much given to the study of tongues only, that when they write epistles they seem to the reader that, like to a trumpet, they make a sound without any purpose, whereunto men do hearken more for the noise than for any delectation that thereby is moved. Wherefore they be much abused that suppose eloquence to be only in words or colours of rhetoric, for as Tully[20] saith, what is so furious or mad a thing as a vain sound of words, of the best sort and most ornate, containing neither cunning* nor sentence?

WHAT ELOQUENCE IS

Undoubtedly very eloquence is in every tongue, where any matter or act done or to be done is expressed in words clean, propise,* ornate, and comely; whereof sentences[21] be so aptly compact that they by a virtue inexplicable do draw unto them the minds and consent of the hearers, they being therewith either persuaded, moved, or to delectation included.

Also every man is not an orator that can write an epistle or a flattering oration in Latin, whereof the last (as God help me) is too much used. For a right orator may not be without a much better furniture,* Tully[22] saying that to him belongeth the explicating or unfolding of sentence* with a great estimation, in giving counsel concerning matters of great importance; also to him appertaineth the stirring and quickening[23] of people languishing or despairing, and to moderate them that be rash and unbridled. Wherefore noble authors do affirm that in the first infancy of the world, men wandering like beasts in woods and on mountains, regarding neither the religion due unto God

---

[20] Cicero, *De or.* 1. 12. 50f.

[21] Elyot runs together Quintilian's list of the four virtues of style: correctness, lucidity, elegance, and appropriateness (*Inst.* 1. 5. 1, 8. 1. 1), with Cicero's definition of the orator's three duties: *docere, movere, delectare.* Cf. *Brut.* 185, 276; *De or.* 2. 29. 128f.; and Thomas Wilson, pp. 77, 120.

[22] Cicero, *De or.* 2. 9.

[23] These were traditional powers ascribed to *movere*: cf. e.g. Cicero, *Brut.* 23. 89, 49. 187, 54. 198–9; *Orat.* 28. 97, 36. 126–7. See *IDR*, pp. 74–7.

nor the office pertaining unto man, ordered all thing by bodily strength, until Mercurius (as Plato[24] supposeth), or some other man helped by sapience and eloquence, by some apt or proper oration assembled them together, and persuaded to them what commodity* was in mutual conversation and honest manners.

But yet Cornelius Tacitus[25] describeth an orator to be of more excellent qualities, saying that an orator is he that can or may speak or reason in every question sufficiently, elegantly; and to persuade properly, according to the dignity of the thing that is spoken of, the opportunity of time, and pleasure of them that be hearers. Tully[26] before him affirmed that a man may not be an orator heaped with praise but if he have gotten the knowledge of all things and arts of greatest importance. And how shall an orator speak of that thing that he hath not learned? And because there may be nothing but it may happen to come in praise or dispraise, in consultation or judgement, in accusation or defence, therefore an orator by others' instruction perfectly furnished may in every matter and learning commend or dispraise, exhort or dissuade, accuse or defend[27] eloquently, as occasion happeneth. Wherefore inasmuch as in an orator is required to be a heap* of all manner of learning—which of some is called the world of science,* of other the circle of doctrine, which is in one word of Greek *encyclopedia*[28]—therefore at this day may be found but a very few orators. For they that come in message from princes be for honour named new orators if they be in any degree of worship, only poor men having equal or more of learning being called messengers. Also they which do only teach rhetoric—which is the science whereby is taught an artificial form of speaking wherein is the power to persuade, move,

---

[24] *Protagoras* 322a ff. This claim for the civilizing power of oratory was also formulated by Plato's great rival, the Sophist Isocrates, in *Nicocles* 5 ff. (= *Antidosis* 253 ff.), passages appropriated by Roman rhetoricians: Cicero, *Inv. Rhet.* 1. 2. 2–1. 4. 5, *De or.* 1. 8. 32–3, and Quintilian, *Inst.* 2. 16. 9–17, etc. Cf. *IDR*, pp. 9–11. This tradition was widely disseminated in Renaissance rhetoric: see e.g. Thomas Wilson's reformulation of it in Christian terms, pp. 73–6.

[25] *Dial.* 30.

[26] Cicero, *De or.* 1. 6. 20, 1. 18. 80, 1. 48. 209 ff. (a much debated issue).

[27] Elyot summarizes the traditional division (originating in Aristotle, *Rh.* 1. 1358ª36–1358ᵇ28) of speeches into three kinds: epideictic—involving the praise of virtue and dispraise of vice; deliberative or political—concerning the expediency or harmfulness of a course of future action; and forensic or judicial—concerning the justice or injustice of some past action. Cf. *IDR*, pp. 20–2, and Wilson, p. 82.

[28] This modern formation (found in Budé, *Institution du Prince*, 1519), combines two separate words in Greek, *enkyklios* and *paideia*, a 'circle of learning'. Quintilian applies it to the orator's necessary breadth of education: *Inst.* 1. 10. 1.

and delight[29]—or by that science only do speak or write without any adminiculation* of other sciences ought to be named rhetoricians, declamators, artificial speakers (named in Greek *logodedali*),[30] or any other name than orators.

Semblably* they that make verses, expressing thereby none other learning but the craft of versifying, be not of ancient writers named poets, but only called versifiers.[31] For the name of a poet, whereat now (specially in this realm) men have such indignation that they use only poets and poetry in the contempt of eloquence, was in ancient time in high estimation, in so much that all wisdom was supposed to be therein included, and poetry was the first philosophy[32] that ever was known. Whereby men from their childhood were brought to the reason how to live well, learning thereby not only manners and natural affections, but also the wonderful works of nature, mixing serious matter with things that were pleasant—as it shall be manifest to them that shall be so fortunate to read the noble works of Plato and Aristotle, wherein he shall find the authority of poets frequently alleged.* Yea, and that more is: in poets was supposed to be science mystical and inspired; and therefore in Latin they were called *vates*, which word signifieth as much as prophets. And therefore Tully in his *Tusculan Questions* supposeth that a poet cannot abundantly express verses sufficient and complete, or that his eloquence may flow without labour words well sounding and plenteous, without celestial instinction. Which is also by Plato[33] ratified.

[29] Repeating the affective triad (n. 21): cf. also *De or.* 2. 27–115, *Orat.* 21. 69, *Inst.* 12. 10. 58 f., and Wilson, p. 77.

[30] This phrase was used by Plato in his attack on rhetoric (*Phdr.* 266–7), but taken over without any derogatory implications by Cicero, *Orat.* 12. 39, and Quintilian, *Inst.* 3. 1. 11.

[31] Quintilian's judgement on Cornelius Severus (*Inst.* 10. 1. 89); cf. also Sidney, p. 347, and Drummond, p. 53.

[32] The ultimate source for this didactic conception of poetry ('primary philosophy') may be the Stoic writer Strabo's *Geography* (c. AD 17) 1. 2. 3, which begins by defending poetry in general, and Homer in particular, against those who claim it offers mere entertainment, not instruction. 'The ancients held a different view. They regarded poetry as a sort of primary philosophy, which was supposed to introduce us to life from our childhood, and teach us about character, emotion, and action in a pleasurable way. My own school, the Stoics, actually said that only the wise man could be a poet. This is why Greek communities give children their first education through poetry, not for simple "entertainment" of course, but for moral improvement' (*ALC*, p. 300). On the poets as first philosophers, cf. Puttenham, p. 197, and Sidney, p. 539; on the necessity for the poet to be a good man, cf. Jonson, p. 469, and Milton, p. 598.

[33] The concept of the poet as *vates*, inspired like a prophet, appears first—but intended as a criticism of the irrational nature of poetic inspiration—in Plato's *Ion* 533 ff. (*ALC*,

But since we be now occupied in the defence of poets, it shall not be incongruent* to our matter to show what profit may be taken by the diligent reading of ancient poets, contrary to the false opinion that now reigneth of them that suppose that in the works of poets is contained nothing but bawdry (such is their foul word of reproach) and unprofitable leasings.* But first I will interpret some verses of Horace, wherein he expresseth the office* of poets; and after will I resort to a more plain demonstration of some wisdoms and counsels contained in some verses of poets. Horace[34] in his second book of *Epistles* saith in this wise, or much like:

> The poet fashioneth by some pleasant mean
> The speech of children tender and unsure,
> Pulling their ears from words unclean,
> Giving to them precepts that are pure,
> Rebuking envy and wrath if it dure.
> Things well done he can by example commend.
> The needy and sick he doth also his cure
> To recomfort, if aught he can amend.

But they which be ignorant in poets will perchance object, as is their manner, against these verses, saying that in Terence and other that were writers of comedies—also Ovid, Catullus, Martial, and all that rout of lascivious poets that wrote epistles and ditties of love, some called in Latin *elegiae* and some *epigrammata*—is nothing contained but incitation to lechery.[35] First, comedies, which they suppose to be a doctrinal of ribaldry, they be undoubtedly a picture or as it were a mirror of man's life. Wherein evil is not taught but discovered, to the intent that men beholding the promptness of youth unto vice, the snares of harlots and bawds laid for young minds, the deceit of servants, the chances of fortune contrary to men's expectation—they being thereof warned—prepare themself to resist or prevent* occasion. Semblably remembering the wisdoms, advertisements,*

pp. 42–5). It was taken over (without any pejorative connotations) by Cicero in his influential dialogue on philosophical themes, *Tusculanae disputationes* (1. 26. 64) and in *De or.* 2. 46. 194. See also Puttenham, p. 195, and Sidney, pp. 341, 346.

[34] *Epist.* 2. 1. 126–31.

[35] This accusation of the immorality of poetry and drama persisted throughout this period, and was intensified in the Puritans' attack on the stage. For the counter-arguments, of the ethical effect of drama, see Neville (p. 125), Whetstone (p. 172), Harington (p. 312), Sidney (p. 362), Heywood (p. 474), Jonson (p. 469), and Massinger (p. 546).

counsels, dissuasion from vice, and other profitable sentences* most
eloquently and familiarly showed in those comedies, undoubtedly
there shall be no little fruit out of them gathered. And if the vices in
them expressed should be cause that minds of the readers should be
corrupted, then by the same argument not only interludes in English,
but also sermons wherein some vice is declared, should be to the
beholders and hearers like occasion to increase sinners. And that by
comedies good counsel is ministered, it appeareth by the sentence of
Parmeno in the second comedy of Terence:[36]

> In this thing I triumph in mine own conceit,
> That I have founden for all young men the way
> How they of harlots shall know the deceit—
> Their wits, their manners—that thereby they may
> Them perpetually hate. For so much as they
> Out of their own houses be fresh and delicate,
> Feeding curiously; at home all the day
> Living beggarly, in most wretched estate.

There be many more words spoken which I purposely omit to translate, notwithstanding the substance of the whole sentence is herein
comprised.

But now to come to other poets, what may be better said than is
written by Plautus[37] in his first comedy?

> Verily virtue doth all things excel
> For if liberty, health, living, and substance,
> Our country, our parents and children do well,
> It happeneth by virtue she doth all advance.
> Virtue hath all things under governance.
> And in whom of virtue is founden great plenty,
> Anything that is good may never be dainty.

Also Ovid,[38] that seemeth to be most of all poets lascivious, in his
most wanton* books hath right commendable and noble sentences, as
for proof thereof I will recite some that I have taken at adventure:

---

[36] *Eunuchus* 5. 4. 8–18.
[37] *Amphitruo* 2. 2. 17–21.
[38] *Rem. am.* 131–6. The conclusion to this passage—'Fac monitis fugias otia prima
meis'—was much quoted in the moralizing literature against idleness: cf. Brian Vickers,
'Leisure and Idleness in the Renaissance: The Ambivalence of *otium*', *Renaissance Studies*,
4 (1990), 1–37, 107–54.

Time is in medicine if it shall profit.
Wine given out of time may be annoyance.
A man shall irritate vice if he prohibit
When time is not meet unto his utterance.
Therefore, if thou yet by counsel art recuperable,
Flee thou from idleness, and alway be stable.

Martial,[39] which for his dissolute writing is most seldom read of men of much gravity, hath notwithstanding many commendable sentences and right wise counsels, as among diverse I will rehearse one which is first come to my remembrance:

If thou wilt eschew bitter adventure,
And avoid the gnawing of a pensiful* heart,
Set in no one person all wholly thy pleasure:
The less joy shalt thou have, but the less shalt thou smart.

I could recite a great number of semblable good sentences out of these and other wanton poets, who in the Latin do express them incomparably with more grace and delectation to the reader than our English tongue may yet comprehend.

Wherefore since good and wise matter[40] may be picked out of these poets, it were no reason, for some light* matter that is in their verses, to abandon therefore all their works, no more than it were to forbear or prohibit a man to come into a fair garden lest the redolent savours of sweet herbs and flowers shall move him to wanton courage,* or lest in gathering good and wholesome herbs he may happen to be stung with a nettle. No wise man entereth into a garden but he soon espieth good herbs from nettles, and treadeth the nettles under his feet whiles he gathereth good herbs. Whereby he taketh no damage; or if he be stung, he maketh light of it, and shortly forgetteth it. Semblably if he do read wanton matter mixed with wisdom, he putteth the worst under foot, and sorteth out the best; or if his courage be stirred or provoked, he remembereth the little pleasure and great detriment* that should ensue of it, and, withdrawing his mind to some other study

---

[39] *Epigrams* 12. 34.

[40] This concept of the reader having to distinguish the wholesome from the unwholesome parts of literature was often expressed in the metaphor of a bee, also understood as standing for the poet making his selection of materials from existing poems. See Plutarch, *Poetas* 10. 28, 11. 30, 12. 32; *ECE* i. 79, 332, 312; St Basil, *Address to Young Men on reading Greek literature*, 4. 7–8 (in St Basil, *The Letters* (Loeb Library), 4. 391), and J. von Stackelberg, 'Das Bienengleichnis. Ein Beitrag zur Geschichte der literarischen *Imitatio*', *Romanische Forschungen*, 68 (1956), 271–93.

or exercise,* shortly forgetteth it. And therefore among the Jews, though it were prohibited to children until they came to ripe years to read the books of Genesis, of the Judges, *Cantica canticorum*, and some part of the book of Ezekiel[41] the prophet—for that in them was contained some matter which might happen to incense the young mind, wherein were sparks of carnal concupiscence—yet after certain years of men's ages, it was lawful for every man to read and diligently study those works. So although I do not approve the lesson of wanton poets to be taught unto all children, yet think I convenient* and necessary that, when the mind is become constant, and courage* is assuaged,* or that children of their natural disposition be shame-faced and continent, none ancient poet would be excluded from the lesson of such one as desireth to come to the perfection of wisdom.

But in defending of orators and poets, I had almost forgotten where I was. Verily there may no man be an excellent poet nor orator unless he have part of all other doctrine, specially of noble philosophy. And to say the truth, no man can apprehend the very delectation that is in the lesson of noble poets unless he have read very much and in diverse authors of diverse learnings. Wherefore as I late said, to the augmentation of understanding, called in Latin *intellectus et mens*, is required to be much reading and vigilant study in every science, specially of that part of philosophy named moral, which instructeth men in virtue and politic governance. Also no noble author, specially of them that wrote in Greek or Latin before twelve hundred years past, is not for any cause to be omitted. For therein I am of Quintilian's opinion,[42] that there is few or none ancient work that yieldeth not some fruit or commodity to the diligent readers. And it is a very gross or obstinate wit that, by reading much, is not somewhat amended. . . .

Finally, like as a delicate tree that cometh of a kernel, which, as soon as it burgeoneth out leaves, if it be plucked up or it be sufficiently rooted, and laid in a corner, it becometh dry or rotten, and no fruit cometh of it; if it be removed and set in another air or earth which is of contrary qualities where it was before, it either semblably* dieth, or beareth no fruit, or else the fruit that cometh of it loseth his verdure and taste, and finally his estimation—so the pure and excellent learning whereof I have spoken, though it be sown in a child never so timely, and springeth and burgeoneth never so pleasantly, if before it

---

[41] Croft (edn. cit. i. 130) cites Jerome's preface to his commentaries on Ezekiel (but this passage does not include Judges).

[42] *Inst.* 10. 1. 40.

take a deep root in the mind of the child it be laid aside, either by too much solace, or continual attendance in service, or else is translated to another study which is of a more gross or unpleasant quality, before it be confirmed or established by often reading or diligent exercise, in conclusion it vanisheth and cometh to nothing.

Henry Howard, Earl of Surrey,
Epitaph on Wyatt (1542)

HENRY HOWARD (1517–47), given the courtesy title Earl of Surrey in 1524, when his father Thomas Howard became the third Duke of Norfolk, was a courtier who achieved distinction as a soldier, but was executed for treason. His poetry appeared in the influential *Songs and Sonettes written by the ryght honorable Lorde Henry Haward, late Earle of Surrey, and other*, brought out by the printer Richard Tottel in 1557 and often reprinted: see the magnificent edition, *Tottel's Miscellany*, ed. H. E. Rollins, 2 vols. (Cambridge, Mass., 1928; rev. edn., 1965), also *The Arundel Harington Manuscript of Tudor Poetry*, ed. Ruth Hughey, 2 vols. (Columbus, Ohio, 1960).

TEXT. From *Poems*, ed. Emrys Jones (Oxford, 1964), to which I am also indebted for some of the annotation. Wyatt died in October 1542, and this poem (probably Surrey's first appearance in print) was originally part of an eight-page booklet, *An excellent Epitaffe of syr Thomas Wyat, With two other compendious dytties, wherin are touchyd, and set forth the state of mannes lyfe* (*c.*1542). In *Tottel's Miscellany* it is no. 31; nos. 29 and 263 are two further epitaphs by Surrey on Wyatt (ed. Jones, nos. 28–30).

> Wyatt resteth here, that quick* could never rest,[1]
>   Whose heavenly gifts, increased by disdain
> And virtue, sank the deeper in his breast,
>   Such profit he by envy could obtain.[2]
>
> A head, where wisdom mysteries did frame,[3]   5
>   Whose hammers[4] beat still in that lively brain

---

[1] This line translates an epitaph on the tomb in Milan of the soldier Jacopo Trivulzio (d. 1518): 'Hic mortuus requiescit semel, | qui vivus requievit nunquam'.

[2] 'His abilities were increased by the hostility of others'; in classical philosophy this was the proper response of virtue to malice.

[3] His intellect produced 'profound or pregnant thought' (Jones).

[4] The metaphor of the mind as a 'stithy' or forge, where ideas are 'wrought' or hammered into shape, was common in Renaissance poetry. Cf. Shakespeare, *Henry V*, 5 prol. 23: 'In the quick forge and working-house of thought'.

As on a stithy where that some work of fame
    Was daily wrought to turn to Britain's gain.

A visage stern and mild, where both did grow
    Vice to contemn, in virtue to rejoice;   10
Amid great storms whom grace assured so
    To live upright and smile at fortune's choice.[5]

A hand that taught what might be said in rhyme,
    That reft Chaucer the glory of his wit;
A mark the which, unparfited for time,[6]   15
    Some may approach but never none shall hit.

A tongue that served in foreign realms his king;
    Whose courteous talk to virtue did inflame
Each noble heart,[7] a worthy guide to bring
    Our English youth by travail unto fame.   20

An eye whose judgment none affect* could blind
    Friends to allure and foes to reconcile,
Whose piercing look did represent a mind
    With virtue fraught, reposed, void of guile.

A heart where dread was never so impressed   25
    To hide the thought that might the truth advance;[8]
In neither fortune loft nor yet repressed
    To swell in wealth or yield unto mischance.[9]

A valiant corps* where force and beauty met;
    Happy, alas, too happy but for foes;[10]   30
Lived, and ran the race that Nature set,
    Of manhood's shape where she the mould did lose.

But to the heavens that simple soul is fled,
    Which left with such as covet Christ to know

---

  [5] Uniting both Christian ('grace', in the Catholic sense of 'heavenly election') and classical remedies for dealing with fortune, good and bad.

  [6] His work unperfected, due to the shortness of life.

  [7] For literature as inflaming its readers with the desire to emulate virtuous deeds cf. Cicero, *Arch*. 6. 14, and the Introduction, pp. 9–10, 50–5.

  [8] The good counsellor speaks the truth, undeterred by threats or punishment.

  [9] Not moved by prosperity ('wealth') to proudly overweening behaviour, nor cast down by misfortune.

  [10] Surrey echoed this and the following line in his translation of Virgil's *Aeneid* 4. 873, 876: ed. Jones, p. 86.

Witness of faith that never shall be dead,[11]   35
Sent for our health, but not received so.

Thus for our guilt this jewel have we lost.
The earth his bones, the heavens possess his ghost.[12]

---

[11] Alluding to Wyatt's paraphrase of the Seven Penitential Psalms: Cf. the pseudo-Chaucerian *Flower and the Leaf*, l. 481: 'Victorious name which never may be dede'.

[12] Cf. Eccles. 12:7: 'Then shall the dust return to the earth as it was: and the spirit shall return unto God who gave it'.

Thomas Wilson,
An English rhetoric (1560)

THOMAS WILSON (1523?–81), was educated at Eton (under Nicholas Udall), King's College Cambridge, where his teachers included John Cheke and Roger Ascham, and (during his exile with other Protestants under Mary, from 1554 to 1560) at the Universities of Padua and Ferrara. Under Queen Elizabeth, Wilson began a career as a lawyer, was an MP for many years, served on two diplomatic missions to the Low Countries, and became a privy councillor and secretary of state. He played an important role in making humanist learning available to English readers lacking classical tongues. His digest of logic, the *Rule of Reason* (1551), the first vernacular treatise on logic, had three editions by 1553. He also published *The Three Orations of Demosthenes* (1570), the first English translations of that orator, and wrote a *Discourse upon Usury* (1572), denouncing it as evil.

TEXT. From *The Arte of Rhetorique, for the use of all soche as are studious in Eloquence, set forthe in Englishe, by Thomas Wilson. 1553. And now sette forthe again, with a Prologue to the Reader* (1560). This was the first treatise in English to present a unified treatment of rhetoric for the general reader; two earlier and less extensive compilations, by Leonard Cox in 1530, and Richard Sherry in 1550, were designed for grammar school use. The first edition appeared just after the accession of the Catholic Queen Mary, and was probably suppressed for its vigorously Protestant attitudes. Reissued in 1560, it proved deservedly popular, especially among law students, reaching an eighth edition by 1585. Modern editions: by Thomas J. Derrick (New York and London, 1982); by Peter E. Medine (University Park, Pa., 1994). I am indebted to these excellent scholarly editions for some of the following annotation. See also P. E. Medine, *Thomas Wilson* (Boston, Mass., 1986).

PREFACE

Eloquence First Given by God, and After Lost by Man, and Last Repaired by God Again

Man (in whom is poured the breath of life) was made at his first being an ever-living creature unto the likeness of God, endued with reason and appointed lord over all other things living. But after the fall of our first father, sin so crept in that our knowledge was much darkened, and by corruption of this our flesh man's reason and intendment* were both overwhelmed. At what time God, being sore grieved with the folly of one man, pitied of his mere goodness the whole state and posterity of mankind. And therefore (whereas through the wicked suggestion* of our ghostly enemy the joyful fruition of God's glory was altogether lost) it pleased our heavenly father to repair* mankind of his free mercy, and to grant an ever-living inheritance unto all such as would by constant faith seek earnestly thereafter.

Long it was ere that man knew himself, being destitute of God's grace, so that all things waxed savage: the earth untilled, society neglected, God's will not known, man against man, one against another, and all against order. Some lived by spoil; some like brute beasts grazed upon the ground; some went naked; some roamed like woodwoses;* none did anything by reason, but most did what they could by manhood.* None, almost, considered the ever-living God, but all lived most commonly after their own lust. By death they thought that all things ended; by life they looked for none other living. None remembered the true observation of wedlock; none tendered the education of their children; laws were not regarded; true dealing was not once used. For virtue, vice bare place; for right and equity, might used authority. And therefore, whereas man through reason might have used order, man through folly fell into error. And thus for lack of skill, and for want of grace, evil so prevailed that the devil was most esteemed, and God either almost unknown among them all or else nothing feared among so many. Therefore even now, when man was thus past all hope of amendment, God, still tendering his own workmanship, stirred up his faithful and elect* to persuade with reason all men to society. And gave his appointed ministers knowledge both to see the natures of men, and also granted them the gift of utterance, that they might with ease win folk at their will, and frame them by reason to all good order.

And therefore, whereas men lived brutishly in open fields—having neither house to shroud them in, nor attire to clothe their backs, nor yet any regard to seek their best avail—these appointed of God called them together by utterance of speech and persuaded with them what was good, what was bad, and what was gainful for mankind. And although at first the rude could hardly learn, and either for strangeness of the thing would not gladly receive the offer, or else for lack of knowledge could not perceive the goodness; yet being somewhat drawn and delighted with the pleasantness of reason and the sweetness of utterance, after a certain space they became through nurture and good advisement, of wild, sober; of cruel, gentle; of fools, wise; and of beasts, men. Such force hath the tongue, and such is the power of eloquence[1] and reason, that most men are forced even to yield in that which most standeth against their will. And therefore the poets do feign that Hercules,[2] being a man of great wisdom, had all men linked together by the ears in a chain, to draw them and lead them even as he lusted. For his wit was so great, his tongue so eloquent, and his experience such, that no one man was able to withstand his reason, but everyone was rather driven to do that which he would, and to will that which he did, agreeing to his advice both in word and work in all that ever they were able.

Neither can I see that men could have been brought by any other means to live together in fellowship of life, to maintain cities, to deal truly, and willingly to obey one another, if men at the first had not by art and eloquence persuaded that which they full oft found out by reason. For what man, I pray you, being better able to maintain himself by valiant courage than by living in base subjection, would not rather look to rule like a lord than to live like an underling, if by reason he were not persuaded that it behooveth every man to live in his own vocation, and not to seek any higher room than whereunto he was at the first appointed? Who would dig and delve from morn till evening? Who would travail and toil with the sweat of his brows? Yea, who would for his king's pleasure adventure and hazard his life, if wit had not so won men that they thought nothing more needful in this world, nor anything whereunto they were more bounden, than here to live in their duty, and to train their whole life according to their calling? Therefore, whereas men are in many things weak by nature, and subject to much infirmity, I think in this one point they pass all other creatures living: that they have the gift of speech and reason.

And among all others, I think him most worthy fame, and amongst men to be taken for half a god, that therein doth chiefly, and above all

---

[1] Wilson draws on the traditional praise of eloquence as the key civilizing factor in human development, first set out by Isocrates (*Nicocles* 5–9; *Panegyricus* 47–50), and taken over by Cicero (*Inv. rhet.* 1. 1. 1–1. 4. 5; *De or.* 1. 8. 30–5) and Quintilian (*Inst.* 2. 16. 15; 12. 11. 30).

[2] See Lucian, *Heracles* 3–6, and the emblem of the 'Gallic Hercules', who draws his hearers along by the chains of eloquence stretching from his mouth to their ears.

others, excel men wherein men do excel beasts.[3] For he that is among the reasonable of all most reasonable, and among the witty of all most witty, and among the eloquent of all most eloquent—him, think I, among all men not only to be taken for a singular man, but rather to be counted for half a god.[4] For in seeking the excellency hereof, the sooner he draweth to perfection, the nigher he cometh to God, who is the chief wisdom, and therefore called God because he is most wise, or rather wisdom itself.

Now then, seeing that God giveth his heavenly grace unto all such as call unto him with stretched hands and humble heart, never wanting to those that want not to themselves, I purpose by his grace and especial assistance to set forth precepts of eloquence, and to show what observation the wise have used in handling of their matters, that the unlearned, by seeing the practice of others may have some knowledge themselves, and learn by their neighbour's device what is necessary for themselves in their own case.

THE FIRST BOOK

What Is Rhetoric

Rhetoric is an art to set forth by utterance of words matter at large; or, as Cicero[5] doth say, it is a learned, or rather an artificial* declaration of the mind in the handling of any cause called in contention, that may through reason largely be discussed.

The Matter Whereupon an Orator Must Speak

An orator[6] must be able to speak fully of all those questions which by law and man's ordinance are enacted and appointed for the use and profit of man, such as are thought apt for the tongue to set forward. Now astronomy is rather learned by demonstration than taught by any great utterance. Arithmetic smally* needeth the use of eloquence, seeing it may be had wholly by numbering only. Geometry rather asketh a good square* than a clean-flowing tongue to set out the art. Therefore an orator's profession is to speak only of all such matters

---

[3] Cicero, *Inv. rhet.* 1. 4. 5; *De or.* 1. 8. 33; Quintilian, *Inst.* 2. 16. 17.
[4] Cicero, *De or.* 3. 14. 53.   [5] *Inv. rhet.* 1. 5. 6; *Rhet. Her.* 1. 2. 2.
[6] *Rhet. Her.* 1. 2. 2.

as may largely be expounded for man's behoof, and may with much grace be set out for all men to hear them . . .

The End of Rhetoric

Three things[7] are required of an orator:

1. To teach
2. To delight
3. And to persuade

First, therefore, an orator must labour to tell his tale that the hearers may well know what he meaneth, and understand him wholly; the which he shall with ease do if he utter his mind in plain words, such as are usually received, and tell it orderly, without going about the bush. That if he do not this, he shall never do the other. For what man can be delighted, or yet be persuaded, with the only hearing of those things which he knoweth not what they mean? The tongue is ordained to express the mind,[8] that one might understand another's meaning: now what availeth to speak when none can tell what the speaker meaneth? . . .

The next part that he hath to play is to cheer his guests, and to make them take pleasure with hearing of things wittily devised and pleasantly set forth. Therefore every orator should earnestly labour to file his tongue, that his words may slide with ease, and that in his deliverance he may have such grace as the sound of a lute, or any such instrument doth give. Then his sentences must be well framed, and his words aptly used, throughout the whole discourse of his oration.

Thirdly, such quickness of wit must be showed, and such pleasant saws* so well applied, that the ears may find much delight, whereof I will speak largely* when I shall entreat of moving laughter. And assuredly nothing is more needful than to quicken these heavy-loaden wits of ours, and much to cherish these our lumpish and unwieldy natures, for except men find delight, they will not long abide: delight them, and win them, weary them, and you lose them forever. And that

---

[7] The 'affective triad'—*docere, delectare, movere* (which Wilson, like many other rhetoricians, equates with persuasion)—was first formulated by Cicero (*Brut.* 49. 185, 80. 276; *Orat.* 20. 69; *De or.* 2. 28. 128–9), and taken over by Horace (*Ars P.* 99–105, 333–6), Quintilian (*Inst.* 3. 5. 2), and almost all Renaissance writers on rhetoric.

[8] This conception of language as a divine gift to enable human communication was widely shared in the Renaissance: cf. Sidney, p. 367; Hoskyns, p. 399; Jonson, p. 578.

is the reason that men commonly tarry the end of a merry play and cannot abide the half-hearing of a sour-checking sermon. Therefore even these ancient preachers must now and then play the fools in the pulpit to serve the tickle* ears of their fleeting* audience, or else they are like sometimes to preach to the bare walls, for though the spirit be apt and our will prone, yet our flesh is so heavy, and humours so over-whelm us, that we cannot without refreshing long abide to hear any one thing. Thus we see that to delight is needful, without the which weightier matters will not be heard at all: and therefore him can I thank, that both can and will ever mingle sweet among the sour . . .

Now when these two are done, he must persuade, and move the affections of his hearers in such wise that they shall be forced to yield unto his saying, whereof (because the matter is large, and may more aptly be declared when I shall speak of amplification) I will surcease to speak anything thereof at this time.

By What Means Eloquence Is Attained

First, needful it is that he which desireth to excel in this gift of oratory, and longeth to prove an eloquent man, must naturally have a wit* and an aptness thereunto; then must he to his book, and learn to be well stored with knowledge, that he may be able to minister matter for all causes necessary. The which when he hath got plentifully, he must use much exercise[9] both in writing and also in speaking. For though he have a wit and learning together, yet shall they both little avail without much practice. What maketh the lawyer to have such utterance? Practice. What maketh the preacher to speak so roundly?* Practice. Yea, what maketh women go so fast away with their words? Marry, practice, I warrant you. Therefore in all faculties diligent prac-tice and earnest exercise are the only things that make men prove excellent. Many men know the art very well, and be in all points thor-oughly grounded and acquainted with the precepts, and yet it is not their hap to prove eloquent. And the reason is that eloquence itself came not up first by the art, but the art rather was gathered upon elo-quence.[10] For wise men, seeing by much observation and diligent prac-tice the compass of divers causes, compiled thereupon precepts and lessons worthy to be known and learned of all men. Therefore before

---

[9] Wilson adapts the traditional emphasis on the qualities needed in training an orator: natural ability; art—that is, the theoretical knowledge of the principles of rhetoric; and prac-tice. Cf. *Rhet. Her.* 1. 2. 3; *Inv. rhet.* 1. 1. 2, *De or.* 1. 25. 113–15, 2. 22. 89–98; *Inst.* 3. 5. 1; Puttenham, pp. 223, 295; Sidney, p. 380; and Jonson, pp. 540, 583–6.

[10] *De or.* 1. 32. 146; *Inst.* 2. 17. 9–11; 3. 2. 3; *IDR*, pp. 1–3.

art was invented, eloquence was used and through practice made perfect, the which in all things is a sovereign* mean most highly to excel.

Now before we use either to write or speak eloquently, we must dedicate our minds wholly to follow the most wise and learned men,[11] and seek to fashion as well their speech and gesturing as their wit or inditing.* The which when we earnestly mind to do, we cannot but in time appear somewhat like them. For if they that walk much in the sun, and think not of it, are yet for the most part sunburnt,[12] it cannot be but that they which wittingly and willingly travail to counterfeit others must needs take some colour of them, and be like unto them in some one thing or other, according to the proverb, By companying with the wise, a man shall learn wisdom.

To What Purpose This Art Is Set Forth

To this purpose and for this use is the art compiled together by the learned and wise men: that those which are ignorant might judge of the learned, and labour (when time should require) to follow their works accordingly. Again, the art helpeth well to dispose and order matters of our own invention, the which we may follow as well in speaking as in writing. For though many by nature without art have proved worthy men, yet is art a surer guide than nature,[13] considering we see as lively by the art what we do as though we read a thing in writing, whereas nature's doings are not so open to all men. Again, those that have good wits by nature shall better increase them by art, and the blunt also shall be whetted through art, that want nature to help them forward.

Five Things to Be Considered in an Orator

Anyone that will largely handle any matter must fasten his mind first of all upon these five especial points[14] that follow, and learn them every one:

1. Invention of matter
2. Disposition of the same

[11] On the importance of imitating approved models cf. *Rhet. Her.* 1. 2. 3; *De or.* 2. 22. 90–6; *Inst.* 10. 2. 1–28; Ascham, p. 150; Sidney, p. 386; Jonson, p. 585.

[12] *De or.* 2.14.60; cf. E.K., p. 176.   [13] *De or.* 1. 25. 115.

[14] In this sequence Wilson follows closely the classical authorities on the five processes in rhetorical composition, *inventio, dispositio, elocutio, memoria* (orators were expected to learn their speeches by heart), and *actio* or *pronuntiatio* (delivery, gesture). Cf. *Rhet. Her.* 1. 2. 3; *Inv. rhet.* 1. 7. 9; *Inst.* 3. 3. 1–15.

3. Elocution
4. Memory
5. Utterance

The finding out of apt matter, called otherwise invention, is a searching out of things true or things likely, the which may reasonably set forth a matter and make it appear probable. The places of logic[15] give good occasion to find out plentiful matter. And therefore they that will prove any cause, and seek only to teach thereby the truth, must search out the places of logic, and no doubt they shall find much plenty.[16]

But what availeth much treasure and apt matter, if man cannot apply it to his purpose? Therefore in the second place is mentioned the settling or ordering of things invented for this purpose, called in Latin *dispositio*, the which is nothing else but an apt bestowing and orderly placing of things, declaring where every argument shall be set, and in what manner every reason shall be applied, for confirmation of the purpose.

But yet what helpeth it though we can find good reasons and know how to place them, if we have not apt words and picked* sentences to commend the whole matter? Therefore this point must needs follow: to beautify the cause, the which being called elocution, is an applying of apt words and sentences to the matter found out to confirm the cause. When all these are had together, it availeth little if man have no memory to contain them. The memory, therefore, must be cherished, the which is a fast holding both of matter and words couched together to confirm any cause.[17]

Be it now that one have all these four, yet if he want the fifth all the others do little profit. For though a man can find out good matter and good words, though he can handsomely set them together and carry them very well away in his mind, yet it is to no purpose if he have no utterance* when he should speak his mind and show men what he

---

[15] The commonplaces or categories into which discourse was divided. Wilson discussed them in *The Rule of Reason* (1553).

[16] Fullness of matter (*copia rerum*) and fullness of style (*copia verborum*), the two much desired qualities in the orator or writer. Cf. *De or.* 3. 31. 125; *Inst.* 10. 1. 5–6; and Erasmus' influential handbook, *De duplici copia verborum ac rerum commentarii duo* (1512; 4th enlarged edn., 1534).

[17] *Rhet. Her.* 1. 2. 3, *Inv. rhet.* 1. 9. The 'cause' is the legal case which the orator argues in court.

hath to say. Utterance, therefore, is a framing of the voice, countenance, and gesture, after a comely* manner.

Thus we see that every one of these must go together to make a perfect orator, and that the lack of one is a hindrance of the whole, and that as well all may be wanting as one, if we look to have an absolute* orator.

There Are Seven Parts[18] in Every Oration

1. The entrance or beginning
2. The narration
3. The proposition
4. The division or several parting of things
5. The confirmation
6. The confutation
7. The conclusion

The entrance, or beginning, is the former part of the oration, whereby the will of the standers-by or of the judge is sought for and required to hear the matter.

The narration is a plain and manifest pointing of the matter, and an evident setting-forth of all things that belong unto the same, with a brief rehearsal grounded upon some reason.

The proposition is a pithy sentence, comprehending in a small room the sum of the whole matter.

The division is an opening of things, wherein we agree and rest upon, and wherein we stick* and stand in traverse,* showing what we have to say in our own behalf.

The confirmation is a declaration of our own reasons with assured and constant proofs.

The confutation is a dissolving or wiping-away of all such reasons as make against us.

The conclusion is a clerkly* gathering of the matter spoken before and a lapping-up* of it altogether.

Now because in every one of these great heed ought to be had, and much art must be used, to content and like all parties, I purpose in

---

[18] Most authorities specify six parts: *exordium, narratio, partitio, confirmatio, confutatio, peroratio* (*Rhet. Her.* 1. 3. 4; *Inv. rhet.* 1. 14. 19–1. 56. 109; Cicero, *Partitiones oratoriae* 8. 27–17. 60). Wilson adds the *propositio*, as recommended by *Inst.* 4. 4. 1–3, Melanchthon, and other Renaissance authorities. For Sidney's use of this seven-part structure in his *Defence of Poetry* see p. 13.

the second book to set forth at large every one of these, that both we may know in all parts what to follow and what to eschew.

And first, when time shall be to talk of any matter, I would advise every man to consider the nature of the cause self, that the rather he might frame his whole oration thereafter . . .

There Are Three Kinds of Causes, or Orations, Which Serve for Every Matter

Nothing can be handled by this art but the same is contained within one of these three causes.[19] Either the matter consisteth in praise or dispraise of a thing; or else in consulting whether the cause be profitable or unprofitable; or lastly whether the matter be right or wrong. And yet this one thing is to be learned: that in every one of these three causes—these three several ends—may every of them be contained in any one of them. And therefore he that shall have cause to praise any one body shall have just cause to speak of justice, to entreat of profit, and jointly to talk of one thing with another. But because these three causes are commonly and for the most part sev-erally* parted, I will speak of them one after another, as they are set forth by wise men's judgments, and particularly declare their proper-ties all in order.

The oration demonstrative standeth either in praise or dispraise of some one man, or of some one thing, or of some one deed done.

The Kind Demonstrative, Wherein Chiefly It Is Occupied

There are divers things which are praised and dispraised, as men, countries, cities, places, beasts, hills, rivers, houses, castles, deeds done by worthy men, and policies invented by great warriors. But most commonly men are praised for divers respects before any of the other things are taken in hand.

Now in praising a noble personage, and in setting forth at large

[19] This classification of the three types of speech (the *genera causarum*) goes back to Aristotle, *Rh.* 1. 3. 1358ª36–1359ª5, and was taken over by Roman writers: *Rhet. Her.* 1. 2. 2; *Inv. rhet.* 1. 5. 7; *Part. or.* 69. 70; *Inst.* 3. 4. 1–16, 3. 7. 1–3. 9. 9. The demonstrative (or epideictic) oration praises virtue and attacks vice; the deliberative (or political) oration dis-cusses the expediency or harmfulness of a proposed course of action; and the forensic (or legal) oration evaluates the justice or injustice of some action performed.

his worthiness, Quintilian[20] giveth warning to use this threefolded order.

To observe things:	1. Before his life
	2. In his life
	3. After his death

Before a man's life are considered these places:

1. The realm	4. The parents
2. The shire	5. The ancestors
3. The town	

In a man's life praise must be parted threefold. That is to say, into the gifts of good things of the mind, the body, and of fortune. Now the gifts of the body and of fortune are not praiseworthy of their own nature, but even as they are used, either to or fro, so they are either praised or dispraised. Gifts of the mind deserve the whole trump* and sound commendation above all other, wherein we may use the rehearsal of virtues as they are in order, and beginning at his infancy tell all his doings till his last age.

The Places Whereof Are These:

The birth and infancy	Whether the person be a man or a woman
The childhood	The bringing-up, the nurturing, and the behaviour of his life
The stripling age or spring tide	To what study he taketh himself unto, what company he useth, how he liveth

Whereunto are referred these:

The man's state	Prowesses done either abroad or at home
The old age	His policies and witty devices in behalf of the public weal
The time of his departure or death	Things that have happened about his death . . .

If anyone shall have just cause to dispraise an evil man, he shall soon do it if he can praise a good man. For as Aristotle[21] doth say, of

[20] *Inst.* 3. 7. 10–17; also *Rhet. Her.* 3. 6. 10–3. 8. 15; *Inv. rhet.* 2. 59. 177. These 'places' or topics provide the structure for many biographies, from the classical period to the 18th cent.

[21] *Rh.* 1. 9. 1368ª33–7; Cicero, *De or.* 2. 85. 349.

contraries there is one and the same doctrine, and therefore he that can do the one shall soon be able to do the other.

An Oration Deliberative

An oration deliberative is a mean whereby we do persuade or dissuade, entreat or rebuke, exhort or dehort, commend or comfort any man. In this kind of oration, we do not purpose wholly to praise anybody, nor yet to determine any matter in controversy, but the whole compass of this cause is either to advise our neighbour to that thing which we think most needful for him, or else to call him back from that folly which hindereth much his estimation. As for example, if I would counsel my friend to travel beyond the seas for knowledge of the tongues and experience in foreign countries, I might resort to this kind of oration and find matter to confirm my cause plentifully. And the reasons which are commonly used to enlarge such matters are these that follow:

1.	The thing is honest	4.	Safe	7.	Lawful and meet
2.	Profitable	5.	Easy	8.	Praiseworthy
3.	Pleasant	6.	Hard	9.	Necessary

Now in speaking of honesty,[22] I may by division of the virtues make a large walk.* Again, look what laws, what customs, what worthy deeds or sayings have been used heretofore—all these might serve well for the confirmation of this matter; lastly, where honesty is called in to establish a cause, there is nature and God himself present, from whom cometh all goodness.

In the second place, where I spake of profit, this is to be learned: that under the same is comprehended the getting of gain and the eschewing of harm. Again, concerning profit (which also beareth the name of goodness), it partly pertaineth to the body, as beauty, strength, and health; partly to the mind, as the increase of wit, the getting of experience, and heaping together of much learning; and partly to fortune (as philosophers take it), whereby both wealth, honour, and friends are gotten. Thus he that divideth profit cannot want matter.

Thirdly, in declaring it is pleasant, I might heap together the variety of pleasures which come by travel: first, the sweetness of the tongue,

---

[22] Wilson's rendering of the Latin concept *honestum*, which we would translate as 'moral worth'. Cf. *Inv. rhet.* 2. 53. 159; *Rhet. Her.* 3. 2. 3.

the wholesomeness of the air in other countries; the goodly wits of the gentlemen; the strange and ancient buildings; the wonderful monuments; the great learned clerks* in all faculties; with divers other like and almost infinite pleasures.

The easiness of travel may thus be persuaded, if we show that free passage is by wholesome laws appointed for all strangers and wayfarers. And seeing this life is none other thing but a travel, and we as pilgrims wander from place to place, much fondness* it were to think that hard which nature hath made easy, yea, and pleasant also. None are more healthful, none more lusty,* none more merry, none more strong of body, than such as have travelled countries.

Marry, unto them that had rather sleep all day than wake one hour, choosing for any labour slothful idleness, thinking this life to be none other but a continual resting place—unto such, pardie,* it shall seem painful to abide any labour. To learn logic, to learn the law, to some it seemeth so hard that nothing can enter into their heads: and the reason is that they want* a will and an earnest mind to do their endeavour. For unto a willing heart nothing can be hard: lay load on such a man's back, and his good heart may sooner make his back to ache than his good will can grant to yield and refuse the weight. And now, where the sweet hath his sour joined with him, it shall be wisdom to speak somewhat of it, to mitigate the sourness thereof as much as may be possible . . .

To Advise One to Study the Laws of England

Again, when we see our friend inclined to any kind of learning, we must counsel him to take that way still, and by reason persuade him that it were the meetest way for him to do his country most good. As if he give his mind to the laws of the realm and find an aptness thereunto, we may advise him to continue in his good intent and by reason persuade him that it were most meet for him so to do.

And first we might show him that the study is honest and godly, considering it only followeth justice and is grounded wholly upon natural reason. Wherein we might take a large scope, if we would fully speak of all things that are comprehended under honesty. For he that will know what honesty is must have an understanding of all the virtues together.[23] And because the knowledge of them is most

[23] In the following section Wilson's digest of classical ethics derives largely from Cicero's exposition of the rules for deliberative oratory, *Inv. rhet.* 2. 52. 157–2. 54. 165. He may have also referred to the parallel sequence in the *Rhet. Her.* 3. 2. 3–3. 3. 5, and to Erasmus'

necessary, I will briefly set them forth. There are four especial and chief virtues,[24] under whom all others are comprehended:

1. Prudence or wisdom   3. Manhood
2. Justice   4. Temperance

Prudence, or wisdom (for I will here take them both for one), is a virtue that is occupied evermore in searching out the truth. Now we all love knowledge, and have a desire to pass* others therein, and think it shame to be ignorant: and by studying the law, the truth is gotten out; by knowing the truth, wisdom is attained. Wherefore in persuading one to study the law, you may show him that he shall get wisdom[25] thereby. Under this virtue are comprehended:

1. Memory
2. Understanding
3. Foresight

The memory calleth to accompt those things that were done heretofore, and by a former remembrance getteth an afterwit and learneth to avoid deceit.

Understanding seeth things presently done and perceiveth what is in them, weighing and debating them until his mind be fully contented.

Foresight is a gathering by conjectures what shall happen and an evident perceiving of things to come before they do come.

JUSTICE.[26] Justice is a virtue gathered by long space, giving everyone his own, minding in all things the common profit of our country, whereunto man is most bound and oweth his full obedience. Now nature first taught man to take this way, and would everyone so to do unto another as he would be done unto himself. For whereas rain watereth all in like, the sun shineth indifferently over all, the fruit of the earth increaseth egally, God warneth us[27] to bestow our good will after the same sort, doing as duty bindeth us and as necessity shall best require. Yea, God granteth his gifts diversely among men, because he would man should know and feel that man is born for man and that one hath need of another. And therefore, though nature hath not stirred some, yet through the experience that man hath concerning his

reworking of this material in *De conscribendis epistolis* (1522): cf. the excellent annotated translation by Charles Fantazzi, in *CWE*, vols. xxv–xxvi.

[24] *Inv. rhet.* 2. 53. 159: *prudentia, iustitia, fortitudo, temperantia.*
[25] Ibid. 2. 53. 160: *memoria, intelligentia, providentia.*
[26] Ibid. 2. 53. 160: *iustitia.*   [27] Matt. 5: 45.

commodity, many have turned the law of nature into an ordinary custom and followed the same as though they were bound to it by a law. Afterward, the wisdom of princes and the fear of God's threat, which was uttered by his word, forced men by a law both to allow things confirmed by nature and to bear with old custom, or else they should not only suffer in the body temporal punishment but also lose their souls forever.

Nature[28] is a right that fantasy hath not framed, but God hath graffed* and given man power thereunto, whereof these are derived:

1. Religion and acknowledging of God
2. Natural love to our children and others
3. Thankfulness to all men
4. Stoutness both to withstand and revenge
5. Reverence to the superior
6. Assured and constant truth in things

Religion is a humble worshipping of God, acknowledging him to be the creator of creatures and the only giver of all good things.

Natural love[29] is an inward goodwill that we bear to our parents, wife, children, or any others that be nigh of kin unto us, stirred thereunto not only by our flesh, thinking that like as we would love ourselves so we should love them, but also by a likeness of mind; and therefore generally we love all because all be like unto us, but yet we love them most that both in body and mind be most like unto us. And hereby it cometh that often we are liberal and bestow our goods upon the needy, remembering that they are all one flesh with us, and should not want when we have it, without our great rebuke and token of our most unkind dealing.

Thankfulness[30] is a requiting of love for love and will for will, showing to our friends the like goodness that we find in them, yea, striving to pass them in kindness, losing neither time nor tide to do them good.

Stoutness to withstand and revenge evil[31] is then used when either we are like to have harm and do withstand it, or else when we have suffered evil for the truth's sake and thereupon do revenge it, or rather punish the evil which is in the man.

---

[28] *Inv. rhet.* 2. 53. 161: *ius naturae, religio, pietas, gratia, vindicatio, observantia, veritas.*
[29] Ibid. 2. 53. 161: *pietas.*   [30] Ibid. 2. 53. 161: *gratia.*
[31] Ibid. 2. 53. 161: *vindicatio.* Discussions of Elizabethan revenge tragedy sometimes forget that in classical ethics to revenge evil is a virtue.

Reverence[32] is a humbleness in outward behaviour, when we do our duty to them that are our betters, or unto such as are called to serve the king in some great vocation.

Assured and constant truth[33] is when we do believe that those things which are, or have been, or hereafter are about to be, cannot otherwise be by any means possible.

That is right by custom[34] which long time hath confirmed, being partly grounded upon nature and partly upon reason, as where we are taught by nature to know the ever-living God and to worship him in spirit, we, turning nature's light into blind custom without God's will, have used at length to believe that he was really with us here in earth, and worshipped him not in spirit but in copes, in candlesticks, in bells, in tapers, and in censers, in crosses, in banners, in shaven crowns[35] and long gowns, and many good morrows else, devised only by the fantasy of man, without the express will of God. The which childish toys* time hath so long confirmed that the truth is scant able to try them out, our hearts be so hard and our wits be so far to seek.

Again, where we see by nature that everyone should deal truly, custom increaseth nature's will and maketh by ancient demesne* things to be justly observed[36] which nature hath appointed.

As:
1. Bargaining
2. Commons or equality
3. Judgment given[37]

Bargaining is when two have agreed for the sale of some one thing, the one will make his fellow to stand to the bargain, though it be to his neighbour's undoing, resting upon this point: that a bargain is a bargain and must stand without all exception, although nature requireth to have things done by conscience and would that bargaining should be builded upon justice, whereby an upright dealing and a charitable love is uttered amongst all men.

Commons,[38] or equality, is when the people by long time have a

---

[32] *Inv. rhet.* 2. 53. 161: *observantia.*
[33] Ibid. 2. 53. 161: *veritas.*   [34] Ibid. 2. 54. 162: *ius consuetudine.*
[35] This is one of the passages vigorously expressing Protestant attitudes which brought Wilson into conflict with the Catholic hierarchy under Queen Mary.
[36] *Inv. rhet.* 2. 54. 162.
[37] Ibid. 2. 54. 162: *pactum, par, indicatum.*
[38] As Medine notes (edn. cit., p. 257), 'for Cicero's reference to that part of law known as "equity" (*Inv. rhet.* 2. 54. 162), Wilson substitutes this allusion' to commons, that is, 'the undivided land belonging to the members of a local community as a whole' (*OED*). Many social thinkers in the 16th cent., from Sir Thomas More to Sir Francis Bacon, bitterly

ground, or any such thing among them, the which some of them will keep still for custom's sake, and not suffer it to be fenced and so turned to pasture, though they might gain ten times the value. But such stubbornness in keeping of commons for custom's sake is not standing with justice, because it is holden against all right.

Judgment given[39] is when a matter is confirmed by a parliament, or a law determined by a judge, unto the which many headstrong men will stand to die for it without sufferance of any alteration, not remembering the circumstance of things, and that time altereth good acts.

That is right[40] by a law, when the truth is uttered in writing and commanded to be kept even as it is set forth unto them.

FORTITUDE[41] or Manhood. Fortitude is a considerate hazarding upon danger, and a willing heart to take pains in behalf of the right. Now when can stoutness be better used than in just maintenance of the law and constant trying of the truth? Of this virtue there are four branches:[42]

1. Honourableness 3. Sufferance
2. Stoutness 4. Continuance

Honourableness is a noble ordering of weighty matters with a lusty heart, and a liberal using of his wealth to the increase of honour.

Stoutness is an assured trust in himself, when he mindeth the compass of most weighty matters, and a courageous defending of his cause.

Sufferance is a willing and a long bearing of trouble, and taking of pains for the maintenance of virtue and the wealth of his country.

Continuance is a steadfast and constant abiding in a purposed and well-advised matter, not yielding to any man in quarrel of the right.

TEMPERANCE.[43] Temperance is a measuring of affections according to the will of reason, and a subduing of lust unto the square of honesty. Yea, and what one thing doth sooner mitigate the immoderate passions of our nature than the perfect knowledge of right and

---

opposed the enclosure of common land to create private pasturage, but to no avail. Wilson asserts the primacy of law over custom.

[39] *Inv. rhet.* 2. 54. 162: *iudicatum.*   [40] Ibid. 2. 54. 162: *lege ius.*
[41] Ibid. 2. 54. 163: *fortitudo.*
[42] Ibid. 2. 54. 163–4: *magnificentia, fidentia, patientia, perseverantia.*
[43] Ibid. 2. 54. 164: *temperantia.*
[44] Ibid. 2. 54. 164: *continentia, clementia, modestia.*

wrong, and the just execution appointed by a law for assuaging the willful? Of this virtue there are three parts:[44]

1. Sobriety   3. Modesty
2. Gentleness

Sobriety is a bridling by discretion the willfulness of desire.

Gentleness is a calming of heat when we begin to rage, and a lowly behaviour in all our body.

Modesty is an honest shamefastness, whereby we keep a constant look and appear sober in all our outward doings. Now even as we should desire the use of all these virtues, so should we eschew not only the contraries hereunto, but also avoid all such evils as by any means do withdraw us from well-doing.

IT IS PROFITABLE.[45] After we have persuaded our friend that the law is honest, drawing our arguments from the heap of virtues, we must go further with him and bring him in good belief that it is very gainful. For many one seek not the knowledge of learning for the goodness' sake, but rather take pains for the gain which they see doth arise by it. Take away the hope of lucre, and you shall see few take any pains, no, not in the vineyard of the Lord.[46] For although none should follow any trade of life for the gain's sake, but even as he seeth it is most necessary for the advancement of God's glory, and not pass in what estimation things are had in this world; yet, because we are all so weak of wit in our tender years that we cannot weigh with ourselves what is best, and our body so nesh* that it looketh ever to be cherished, we take that which is most gainful for us, and forsake that altogether which we ought most to follow. So that for lack of honest means, and for want of good order, the best way is not used; neither is God's honour in our first years remembered. 'I had rather,' said one, 'make my child a cobbler than a preacher, a tankard-bearer than a scholar.

---

[45] Classical ethics, as summarized in Roman rhetorical treatises, distinguished between intrinsic and extrinsic values. The former constituted 'something which draws us to it by its intrinsic merit, not winning us by its own worth; to this class belong virtue, knowledge and truth'. The latter constituted 'something that is to be sought not because of its own merit and natural goodness, but because of some profit or advantage to be derived from it. Money is in this class.' A third category united the two: 'by its own merit and worth it entices us and leads us on, and also holds out to us a prospect of some advantage to induce us to seek it more eagerly. Examples are friendship and a good reputation' (*Inv. rhet.* 2. 52. 157). Although part of this tradition, Wilson uses the English background to describe the advantages of studying law, with some wry comments on how human litigiousness will always provide work for lawyers.

[46] Isaiah 5: 7.

For what shall my son seek for learning when he shall never get thereby any living? Set my son to that whereby he may get somewhat.' Do ye not see how everyone catcheth and pulleth from the Church what they can? I fear me one day they will pluck down Church and all. Call you this the Gospel, when men seek only to provide for their bellies and care not a groat though their souls go to hell? A patron of a benefice will have a poor ingram* soul to bear the name of a parson for twenty marks* or forty-one, and the patron himself will take up for his snapshare* as good as a hundred marks. Thus God is robbed, learning decayed, England dishonoured, and honesty not regarded. The old Romans, not yet knowing Christ, and yet being led by a reverent fear towards God, made this law: *Sacrum sacrove commendatum qui clepserit, rapseritve, parricida est*[47] ('He that shall closely steal, or forcibly take away that thing which is holy or given to the holy place, is a murderer of his country').

But what have I said? I have a greater matter in hand than whereof I was aware; my pen hath run overfar, when my leisure serveth not; nor yet my wit is able to talk this case in such wise as it should be and as the largeness thereof requireth. Therefore to my lawyer again, whom I doubt not to persuade but that he shall have the devil and all, if he learn apace,* and do as some have done before him. Therefore I will show how largely this profit extendeth, that I may have him the sooner to take this matter in hand. The law, therefore, not only bringeth much gain with it but also advanceth men both to worship, renown, and honour. All men shall seek his favour for his learning's sake; the best shall like his company for his calling; and his wealth with his skill shall be such that none shall be able to work him any wrong.

Some consider profit by these circumstances following:

1. To whom   3. Where
2. When   4. Wherefore

Neither can I use a better order than these circumstances minister unto me. To whom, therefore, is the law profitable? Marry, to them that be best learned, that have ready wits and will take pains. When is the law profitable? Assuredly both now and evermore, but especially in this age, where all men go together by the ears for this matter and that matter. Such alteration hath been heretofore, that hereafter needs must ensue much altercation. And where is all this ado? Even in little

---

[47] Cicero, *De legibus* 2. 9. 22.

England, or in Westminster Hall,[48] where never yet wanted business nor yet ever shall. Wherefore is the law profitable? Undoubtedly because no man could hold his own if there were not an order to stay us and a law to restrain us.

And I pray you, who getteth the money? The lawyers, no doubt. And were not land sometimes cheaper bought than got by the trial of a law? Do not men commonly for trifles fall out? Some, for lopping off a tree, spends all that ever they have; another, for a goose that grazeth upon his ground, tries the law so hard that he proves himself a gander. Now when men be so mad, is it not easy to get money among them? Undoubtedly the lawyer never dieth a beggar. And no marvel. For a hundred begs for him, and makes away all that they have, to get that of him, the which the oftener he bestoweth the more still he getteth. So that he gaineth always, as well by increase of learning as by storing his purse with money, whereas the others get a warm sun oftentimes and a flap with a foxtail[49] for all that ever they have spent. And why would they? Tush, if it were to do again, they would do it: therefore the lawyer can never want a living till the earth want men and all be void. . . .

| The law: | 1. Godly | 3. Necessary |
| | 2. Just | 4. Pleasant |

What needeth me to prove the law to be godly, just, or necessary, seeing it is grounded upon God's will, and all laws are made for the maintenance of justice? If we will not believe that it is necessary, let us have rebels again to disturb the realm.[50] Our nature is so fond that we know not the necessity of a thing till we find some lack of the same. Bows are not esteemed as they have been among us Englishmen, but if we were once well beaten by our enemies, we should soon know the want and with feeling the smart lament much our folly. Take away the law, and take away our lives, for nothing maintaineth our wealth, our health, and the safeguard of our bodies, but the law of a realm, whereby the wicked are condemned and the godly are defended.

[48] Little Britain is the name of a street near St Paul's Cathedral, which became a resort of booksellers between 1575 and 1720. Westminster Hall was the long-established main law-court in London, used for state trials, but also housing the courts of Common Pleas, King's Bench, Lord Chancellor's, etc.

[49] Two proverbial expressions: 'a warm sun' means 'undesirable results' (cf. *King Lear* 2. 2. 161 f.), and to 'flap with a foxtail' is to make a contemptuous dismissal.

[50] There were numerous uprisings in the 1530s and 1540s: in 1536–7, the Northern rebellion known as the Pilgrimage of Grace; in the spring of 1549, in Devon and Cornwall (the Western rebellion), followed in the summer by disturbances in Suffolk and Norfolk.

An Epistle to Persuade a Young Gentleman to Marriage,
Devised by Erasmus[51] *in the Behalf of His Friend*

'Albeit you are wise enough of yourself through that singular wisdom of yours, most loving cousin, and little needs the advice of other, yet either for that old friendship which hath been betwixt us and continued with our age even from our cradles, or for such your great good turns showed at all times towards me, or else for that fast kindred and alliance which is betwixt us, I thought myself thus much to owe unto you, if I would be such a one indeed as you ever have taken me—that is to say, a man both friendly and thankful—to tell you freely whatsoever I judged to appertain either to the safeguard or worship of you, or any of yours, and willingly to warn you of the same. We are better seen* oftentimes in other men's matters than we are in our own. I have felt often your advice in mine own affairs, and I have found it to be as fortunate unto me as it was friendly. Now if you will likewise in your own matters follow my counsel, I trust it shall so come to pass that neither I shall repent me for that I have given you counsel, nor yet you shall forthink* yourself that you have obeyed and followed mine advice.

'There was at supper with me the twelfth day of April when I lay in the country, Antonius Baldus, a man (as you know) that most earnestly tendereth your welfare, and one that hath been always of great acquaintance and familiarity with your son-in-law: a heavy feast we had, and full of much mourning. He told me greatly to both our heaviness that your mother, that most godly woman, was departed this life, and your sister, being overcome with sorrow and heaviness, had made herself a nun, so that in you only remaineth the hope of issue and maintenance of your stock. Whereupon your friends with one consent have offered you in marriage a gentlewoman of a good house and much wealth, fair of body, very well brought up, and such a one

---

[51] Erasmus composed this epistle, an *Encomium matrimonii*, as a model exercise for his pupil William Blount, and published it in 1518. When he issued his treatise on letter-writing, *De conscribendis epistolis* (1522), he included a revised and expanded version of it as a specimen of the *epistola suasoria*. From the outset Erasmus ran into trouble with theologians for making what they thought to be a veiled attack on ecclesiastical celibacy and monasticism. He defended himself first with an *Apologia* (1519), which argued that the treatise was merely a rhetorical exercise, but then with a full-scale treatise *Institutio christiani matrimonii* (1526), which reiterated his views on marriage. Erasmus' French translator was condemned for heresy and burned at the stake.

In annotating this epistle I have benefited both from Peter E. Medine's edition of Wilson's *Art of Rhetoric* and from Charles Fantazzi's edition and translation, cit. n. 23 above. On its significance as a source for Shakespeare's *Sonnets* 1–17 see the Introduction, pp. 31–9.

as loveth you with all her heart. But you (either for your late sorrows which you have in fresh remembrance, or else for religion's sake) have so purposed to live a single life, that neither can you for love of your stock, neither for desire of issue, nor yet for any entreaty that your friends can make, either by praying or by weeping, be brought to change your mind.

'And yet notwithstanding all this, if you will follow my counsel, you shall be of another mind, and leaving to live single, which both is barren and smally* agreeing with the state of man's nature, you shall give yourself wholly to most holy wedlock. And for this part I will neither wish that the love of your friends (which else ought to overcome your nature) nor yet mine authority that I have over you, should do me any good at all to compass this my request, if I shall not prove unto you by most plain reasons that it will be both much more honest, more profitable, and also more pleasant for you to marry than to live otherwise. Yea, what will you say, if I prove it also to be necessary[52] for you at this time to marry?

'And first of all, if honesty may move you in this matter (the which among all good men ought to be of much weight), what is more honest than matrimony, the which Christ himself did make honest when not only he vouchsafed to be at the marriage with his mother, but also did consecrate the marriage feast with the first miracle[53] that ever he did upon earth? What is more holy than matrimony, which the Creator of all things did institute, did fasten, and make holy, and nature itself did establish? What is more praiseworthy than that thing, the which whosoever shall dispraise is condemned straight for a heretic? Matrimony is even as honourable as the name of a heretic is thought shameful. What is more right or meet than to give that unto the posterity, the which we have received of our ancestors? What is more inconsiderate than under the desire of holiness to eschew that as unholy which God himself, the fountain and father of all holiness, would have to be counted as most holy? What is more unmanly than that man should go against the laws of mankind? What is more unthankful than to deny that unto younglings, the which (if thou hadst not received of thine elders) thou couldst not have been the man living, able to have denied it unto them?

'That if you would know who was the first founder of marriage,

---

[52] Erasmus sets out four of the topics used in suasory rhetoric: honesty, benefit, pleasure, necessity.

[53] John 2: 1–11.

you shall understand that it came up not by Lycurgus, nor yet by Moses, nor yet by Solon,[54] but it was first ordained and instituted by the chief founder of all things, commended by the same, made honourable and made holy by the same. For at the first when he made man of the earth, he did perceive that his life should be miserable and unsavoury, except he joined Eve as mate[55] unto him. Whereupon he did not make the wife upon the same clay whereof he made man, but he made her of Adam's ribs, to the end we might plainly understand that nothing ought to be more dear unto us than our wife, nothing more nigh unto us, nothing surer joined and (as a man would say) faster glued together. The selfsame God, after the general flood, being reconciled to mankind, is said to proclaim this law first of all, not that men should live single, but that they should increase, be multiplied,[56] and fill the earth. But how, I pray you, could this thing be, saving by marriage and lawful coming together? And first, lest we should allege here either the liberty of Moses' law, or else the necessity of that time, what other meaning else hath that common and commendable report of Christ in the Gospel: "For this cause," saith he, "shall man leave father and mother and cleave to his wife?"[57] And what is more holy than the reverence and love due unto parents? And yet the truth promised in matrimony is preferred before it. And by whose means? Marry, by God himself. At what time? Forsooth, not only among the Jews but also among the Christians. Men forsake father and mother and take themselves wholly to their wives. The son being past twenty years is free and at his liberty. Yea, the son being abdicated* becometh no son. But it is death only that parteth married folk, if yet death do part them.

'Now if the other sacraments (whereunto the Church of Christ chiefly leaneth) be reverently used, who doth not see that this sacrament should have the most reverence of all, the which was instituted of God, and that first and before all others. As for the others, they were instituted upon earth, this was ordained in paradise; the others were given for a remedy, this was appointed for the fellowship of felicity; the others were applied to man's nature after the fall, this only was given when man was in most perfect state. If we compt* those laws good that mortal men have enacted, shall not the law of matrimony be most holy, which we have received of Him by whom we have received life, the which law was then together enacted when man was

---

[54] Three famous lawgivers: Lycurgus for Sparta, Moses for Israel, Solon for Athens.
[55] Gen. 2: 18–23.   [56] Gen. 9: 1, 7.   [57] Matt. 19: 5; Mark 10: 7; Gen. 2: 24.

first created? And lastly, to strengthen this law with an example and deed done, Christ, being a young man (as the story reporteth), was called to a marriage and came thither willingly with his mother, and not only was he there present, but also he did honest* the feast with a wonderful marvel,[58] beginning first in none other place to work his wonders and to do his miracles.

'"Why then, I pray you," will one say, "how happeneth it that Christ forbare marriage?" As though, good sir, there are not many things in Christ at the which we ought rather to marvel than seek to follow. He was born and had no father; he came into this world without his mother's painful travail;* he came out of the grave when it was closed up—what is not in him above nature? Let these things be proper unto him. Let us, that live within the bounds of nature, reverence those things that are above nature, and follow such things as are within our reach, such as we are able to compass. "But yet," you say, "he would* be born of a virgin." Of a virgin I grant, but yet of a married virgin. A virgin being a mother did most become God, and being married she showed what was best for us to do. Virginity did become her, who being undefiled brought him forth by heavenly inspiration that was undefiled. And yet Joseph, being her husband, doth commend unto us the law of chaste wedlock.

'Yea, how could He better set out the society in wedlock than that, willing to declare the secret society of his divine nature with the body and soul of man, which is wonderful even to the heavenly angels, and to show his unspeakable and ever abiding love toward his church, he doth call himself the bridegroom and her the bride?[59] "Great is the sacrament of matrimony," said Paul, "betwixt Christ and his church."[60] If there had been under heaven any holier yoke, if there had been any more religious covenant than is matrimony, without doubt the example thereof had been used. But what like thing do you read in all Scripture of the single life? The Apostle Saint Paul,[61] in the thirteenth chapter of his Epistle to the Hebrews, calleth matrimony honourable among all men and a bed undefiled, and yet the single life is not so much as once named in the same place.

'Nay, they are not borne withal that live single, except they make some recompense with doing some greater thing. For else, if a man following the law of nature do labour to get children, he is ever to be preferred before him that liveth still unmarried for none other end but

---

[58] That is, turning water into wine (John 2: 1–11).
[59] Mark 2: 19; Hos. 2: 16–19; Rev. 21: 2, 9.   [60] Eph. 5: 32.   [61] Heb. 13: 4.

because he would be out of trouble and live more free. We do read that such as are in very deed chaste of their body and live a virgin's life have been praised;[62] but the single life was never praised of itself. Now again, the law of Moses[63] accurseth the barrenness of married folk, and we do read that some were excommunicated for the same purpose and banished from the altar. And wherefore, I pray you? Marry sir, because that they, like unprofitable persons, and living only to themselves, did not increase the world with any issue. In Deuteronomy[64] it was the chiefest token of God's blessings unto the Israelites that none should be barren among them, neither man nor yet woman. And Leah[65] is thought to be out of God's favour because she could not bring forth children. Yea, and in the Psalm of David, 128, it is compted one of the chiefest parts of bliss to be a fruitful woman. "Thy wife," saith the Psalm, "shall be plentiful like a vine, and thy children like the branches of olives round about thy table."[66] Then if the law do condemn and utterly disallow barren matrimony, it hath always much more condemned the single life of bachelors. If the fault of nature hath not escaped blame, the will of man can never want rebuke. If they are accursed that would have children and can get none, what deserve they which never travail to escape barrenness?

'The Hebrews had such a reverence to married folk that he which had married a wife, the same year should not be forced to go on warfare.[67] A city is like to fall in ruin, except there be watchmen to defend it with armour. But assured destruction must here needs follow, except men through the benefit of marriage supply issue, the which through mortality do from time to time decay.

'Over and besides this, the Romans[68] did lay a penalty upon their back that lived a single life; yea, they would not suffer them to bear any office in the commonweal. But they that had increased the world with issue had a reward by common assent, as men that had deserved well of their country. The old foreign laws did appoint penalties for such as lived single, the which although they were qualified* by Constantine the emperor in the favour of Christ's religion, yet these laws do declare how little it is for the commonweal's advancement, that either a city should be lessened for love of sole life, or else that

---

[62] Matt. 19: 10–12; 1 Cor. 7: 1–7, 32–40.
[63] Implied in Exod. 23: 26, Lev. 20: 21, 26: 9.   [64] 6: 3, 7: 14.
[65] A confusion of Leah with her sister Rachel: cf. Gen. 29: 31, 30: 1–2, 22–4.
[66] Ps. 128: 3.   [67] Deut. 20: 7, 24: 5.
[68] For the details of the Roman laws alluded to in the next two pages cf. Medine, edn. cit., pp. 258–9; Fantazzi, edn. cit., pp. 530–1.

the country should be filled full of bastards. And besides this, the
emperor Augustus, being a sore punisher of evil behaviour, examined
a soldier because he did not marry his wife according to the laws; the
which soldier had hardly escaped judgment, if he had not got three
children by her. And in this point do the laws of all emperors seem
favourable to married folk: that they abrogate such vows as were proclaimed to be kept and brought in by Miscella, and would that after
the penalty were remitted such covenants, being made against all right
and conscience, should also be taken of none effect and as void in the
law. Over and besides this, Ulpianus doth declare that the matter of
dowries was evermore and in all places the chiefest above all others,
the which should never have been so except there came to the
commonweal some especial profit by marriage.

'Marriage hath ever been reverenced, but fruitfulness of body hath
been much more, for so soon as one got the name of a father, there
descended not only unto him inheritance of land, but all bequests and
goods of such his friends as died intestate. The which thing appeareth
plain by the satire poet:[69]

> Through me thou art made an heir to have land;
> Thou hast all bequests, one with another;
> All goods and cattle are come to thy hand,
> Yea, goods intestate thou shalt have sure.

Now he that had three children was more favoured, for he was
exempted from all outward embassages. Again, he that had five children was discharged and free from all personal office, as to have the
governance or patronage of young gentlemen, the which in those days
was a great charge and full of pains without any profit at all. He that
had thirteen children was free by the emperor Julian's law not only
from being a man-at-arms or a captain over horsemen, but also from
all other offices in the commonweal.

'And the wise founders of all laws give good reason why such favour
was showed to married folk. For what is more blissful than to live ever?
Now whereas nature hath denied this, matrimony doth give it by a
certain sleight,* so much as may be. Who doth not desire to be
bruited* and live through fame among men hereafter? Now there is
no building of pillars, no erecting of arches, no blazing* of arms, that
doth more set forth a man's name than doth the increase of children.
Albinus obtained his purpose of the emperor Hadrian for none other

---

[69] Juvenal, *Satires* 9. 87–8.

desert of his but that he had begot a houseful of children. And therefore the emperor (to the hindrance of his treasure) suffered the children to enter wholly upon their father's possession, forasmuch as he
knew well that his realm was more strengthened with increase of children than with store of money. Again, all other laws are neither agreeing for all countries nor yet used at all times. Lycurgus made a law
that they which married not should be kept in summer from the sight
of stage plays and other wonderful shows, and in winter they should
go naked about the marketplace, and accursing themselves they should
confess openly that they had justly deserved such punishment because
they did not live according to the laws.

'And without any more ado, will ye know how much our old ancestors heretofore esteemed matrimony? Weigh well, and consider the
punishment for breaking of wedlock. The Greeks heretofore thought
it meet to punish the breach of matrimony with battle[70] that continued ten years. Yea moreover, not only by the Roman law but also by
the Hebrews[71] and strangers, advouterous* persons were punished
with death. If a thief paid four times the value of that which he took
away, he was delivered, but an advouterer's* offence was punished
with the sword. Among the Hebrews the people stoned the advouter-
ers[72] to death with their own hands, because they had broken that
without which the world could not continue. And yet they thought
not this sore law sufficient enough, but granted further to run him
through without law that was taken in advoutry; as who should say
they granted that to the grief* of married folk the which they would
hardly grant to him that stood in his own defence for safeguard of his
life, as though he offended more heinously that took a man's wife than
he did that took away a man's life. Assuredly wedlock must needs seem
to be a most holy thing, considering that being once broken it must
needs be purged with man's blood, the revenger whereof is not forced
to abide either law or judge; the which liberty is not granted any to
use upon him that hath killed either his father or his mother.

'But what do we with these laws written? This is the law of nature,
not written in the tables of brass but firmly printed in our minds, the
which law whosoever doth not obey, he is not worthy to be called a
man, much less shall he be compted a citizen. For if to live well (as
the Stoics[73] wittily* do dispute) is to follow the course of nature, what

---

[70] The Trojan war, fought over Paris' abduction of Helen, Menelaus' wife.
[71] Lev. 20: 10.   [72] Deut. 22: 22–7.
[73] Cicero, *Fin.* 3. 9. 31; Seneca, *Vita beata* 13. 1.

thing is so agreeing with nature as matrimony? For there is nothing
so natural, not only unto mankind but also unto all other living creatures, as it is for every one of them to keep their own kind from decay,
and through increase of issue to make their whole kind immortal. The
which thing (all men know) can never be done without wedlock and
carnal copulation. It were a foul thing that brute beasts should obey
the law of nature, and men like giants* should fight against nature.
Whose work if we would narrowly look upon, we shall perceive that
in all things here upon earth she would there should be a certain spice*
of marriage. I will not speak now of trees, wherein (as Pliny most certainly writeth) there is found marriage with some manifest difference
of both kinds, that except the husband tree do lean with his boughs
even as though he should desire copulation upon the woman trees
growing round about him, they would else altogether wax barren. The
same Pliny[74] also doth report that certain authors do think there is
both male and female in all things that the earth yieldeth. I will not
speak of precious stones, wherein the same author[75] affirmeth (and yet
not he only, neither) that there is both male and female among them.
And I pray you, hath not God so knit all things together with certain
links, that one ever seemeth to have need of another? What say you of
the sky or firmament that is ever stirring with continual moving? Doth
it not play the part of a husband while it puffeth up the earth, the
mother of all things, and maketh it fruitful with casting seed (as a man
would say) upon it.

'But I think it over tedious to run over all things. And to what end
are these things spoken? Marry, sir, because we might understand that
through marriage all things are and do still continue, and without the
same all things do decay and come to nought. The old ancient and
most wise poets do feign—who had ever a desire under the colour of
fables to set forth precepts of philosophy—that the giants,[76] which had
snakes' feet and were born of the earth, builded great hills that
mounted up to heaven, minding thereby to be at utter defiance with
God and all his angels. And what meaneth this fable? Marry, it
showeth unto us that certain fierce and savage men, such as were
unknown, could not abide wedlock for any world's good, and therefore they were stricken down headlong with lightning; that is to say,

---

[74] *Naturalis historia* 13. 7. 31, 35; 14. 3. 10.
[75] Ibid. 36. 47. 198, 37. 23. 86 ff., 37. 24. 90 ff.
[76] Ovid, *Met.* 1. 152, 183–4. In classical literature giants often represented rebellion
against the natural order.

they were utterly destroyed when they sought to eschew that whereby the weal and safeguard of all mankind only doth consist.

'Now again, the same poets do declare that Orpheus,[77] the musician and minstrel, did stir and make soft with his pleasant melody the most hard rocks and stones. And what is their meaning herein? Assuredly nothing else but that a wise and well-spoken man did call back hardhearted men, such as lived abroad like beasts, from open whoredom, and brought them to live after the most holy laws of matrimony. Thus we see plainly that such a one as hath no mind of marriage seemeth to be no man but rather a stone, an enemy to nature, a rebel to God himself, seeking through his own folly his last end and destruction.

'Well, let us go on still, seeing we are fallen into fables, that are not fables altogether. When the same Orpheus, in the midst of hell, forced Pluto himself and all the devils there to grant him leave to carry away his wife Eurydice,[78] what other thing do we think that the poets meant but only to set forth unto us the love in wedlock, the which even among the devils was compted good and godly? And this also makes well for the purpose, that in old time they made Jupiter Gamelius the god of marriage, and Juno Lucina lady midwife to help such women as laboured in childbed; being fondly* deceived and superstitiously erring in naming of the gods, and yet not missing the truth in declaring that matrimony is a holy thing, and meet for the worthiness thereof that the gods in heaven should have care over it.

'Among divers* countries and divers men, there have been divers laws and customs used. Yet was there never any country so savage, none so far from all humanity, where the name of wedlock was not counted holy and had in great reverence. This the Thracian, this the Sarmatian, this the Indian, this the Grecian, this the Latin, yea, "this the Britain that dwelleth in the furthest part of all the world"[79]—or if there be any that dwell beyond them—have ever counted to be most holy. And why so? Marry, because that thing must needs be common to all, which the common mother unto all hath graffed* in us all, and hath so thoroughly graffed the same in us that not only stockdoves and pigeons but also the most wild beasts have a natural feeling of this thing. For the lions are gentle against* the lioness. The tigers fight for safeguard of their young whelps. The ass runs through the hot fire (which is made to keep her away) for safeguard of her issue. And this

[77] Horace, *Ars P.* 398.   [78] Virgil, *Georg.* 4. 454–527; cf. Spenser, p. 184.
[79] Horace, *Odes* 1. 35. 29–30.

they call the law of nature, the which as it is of most strength and force, so it spreadeth abroad most largely. Therefore, as he is counted no good gardener that being content with things present doth diligently prune his old trees, and hath no regard either to imp* or graff young sets because the selfsame orchard (though it be never so well trimmed) must needs decay in time, and all the trees die within few years, so he is not to be counted half a diligent citizen that being content with the present multitude hath no regard to increase the number. Therefore there is no one man that ever hath been counted a worthy citizen who hath not laboured to get children and sought to bring them up in godliness.

'Among the Hebrews and the Persians he was most commended that had most wives, as though the country were most beholding to him that increased the same with the greatest number of children. Do you seek to be compted more holy than Abraham[80] himself? Well, he should never have been compted the father of many nations, and that through God's furtherance, if he had forborne the company of his wife. Do you look to be reckoned more devout than Jacob? He doubteth nothing to ransom Rachel[81] from her great bondage. Will you be taken for wiser than Solomon? And yet, I pray you, what a number of wives[82] kept he in one house? Will you be compted more chaste than Socrates, who is reported to bear* at home with Xanthippe, that very shrew,* and yet not so much therefore (as he is wont to jest according to his old manner) because he might learn patience at home, but also because he might not seem to come behind with his duty in doing the will of nature. For he, being a man (such a one as Apollo judged him by his oracle to be wise), did well perceive that he was got* for this cause, born for this cause, and therefore bound to yield so much unto nature.

'For if the old ancient philosophers have said well, if our divines have proved the thing not without reason, if it be used everywhere for a common proverb, and almost in every man's mouth, that neither God nor yet nature did ever make anything in vain,[83] why did he give

---

[80] Gen. 17: 1–8; 12: 2.

[81] As Medine notes, Wilson here mistranslates Erasmus: 'He, loving Rachel, did not hesitate to obtain her with such long servitude'. Jacob served his uncle Laban for seven years in order to win the hand of Rachel, but when he was given Leah instead, he served for another seven years; Gen. 29: 15–30.

[82] Kings 11: 1–3.

[83] It was a fundamental principle in Aristotelian philosophy that nature does nothing superfluous or in vain; cf. *De an.* 3. 12. 434ᵃ30 ff.; *De partibus animalium* 4. 12. 694ᵃ15, 4. 13. 695ᵇ19; *De generatione animalium* 2. 4. 739ᵇ20, 2. 5. 744ᵃ37.

us such members,* how happeneth we have such lust and such power to get issue, if the single life—and none other—be altogether praiseworthy? If one should bestow upon you a very good thing (as a bow, a coat, or a sword), all men would think you were not worthy to have the thing if either you could not, or you would not use it and occupy* it. And whereas all other things are ordained upon such great considerations, it is not like that nature slept or forgot herself when she made this one thing. And now here will some say that this foul and filthy desire, and stirring unto lust, came never in by nature but through sin, for whose words I pass* not a straw, seeing their sayings are as false as God is true. For I pray you, was not matrimony instituted—whose work cannot be done without these members—before there was any sin? And again, whence have all other brute beasts their provocations?* Of nature, or of sin? A man would think they had them of nature. But shall I tell you at a word: we make that filthy by our own imagination which of the own nature is good and godly. Or else, if we will examine matters not according to the opinion of men, but weigh them as they are of their own nature, how chanceth it that we think it less filthy to eat, to chew, to digest, to empty the body, and to sleep, than it is to use carnal copulation, such as is lawful and permitted? "Nay sir," you will say, "we must follow virtue rather than nature." A gentle dish! As though anything can be called virtue that is contrary unto nature. Assuredly there is nothing that can be perfectly got, either through labour or through learning, if man ground not his doings altogether upon nature.

'But you will live an Apostle's life, such as some of them did that lived single and exhorted others to the same kind of life. Tush, let them follow the Apostles that are Apostles indeed, whose office, seeing it is both to teach and bring up the people in God's doctrine, they are not able to discharge their duties both to their flock and to their wife and family. Although it is well known that some of the Apostles had wives, but be it that bishops live single—or grant we them to have no wives—what do you follow the profession of the Apostles, being one that is farthest in life from their vocation, being both a temporal man and one that liveth of* your own? They had this pardon granted them, to be clean void from marriage, to the end they might be at leisure to get unto Christ a more plentiful number of his children. Let this be the order of priests and monks, who belike have entered into the religion and rule of the Essenes[84] (such as among the Jews loathed

---

[84] An ascetic Jewish sect that held all goods in common, and sometimes abstained from marriage. Erasmus often used the term pejoratively, to refer to monks.

marriage), but your calling is another way. "Nay but," you will say, "Christ[85] himself hath compted them blessed which have gelded* themselves for the Kingdom of God." Sir, I am content to admit the authority, but thus I expound the meaning. First, I think that this doctrine of Christ did chiefly belong unto that time when it behooved them chiefly to be void of all cares and business of this world. They were fain to travel into all places, for the persecutors were ever ready to lay hands on them. But now the world is so, that a man can find in no place the uprightness of behaviour less stained than among married folk.

'Let the swarms of monks and nuns set forth their order never so much; let them boast and brag their bellies full of their ceremonies and church service, wherein they chiefly pass all others: yet is wedlock, being well and truly kept, a most holy kind of life. Again, would to God they were gelded in very deed, whatsoever they be, that colour* their naughty living with such a jolly name of gelding, living in much more filthy lust under the cloak and pretence of chastity. Neither can I report for very shame into how filthy offences they do often fall, that will not use that remedy which nature hath granted unto man. And last of all, where do you read that ever Christ commanded any man to live single and yet he doth openly forbid divorcement?[86] Then he doth not worst of all (in my judgment) for the commonweal of mankind that granteth liberty unto priests, yea, and monks also (if need be), to marry and to take them to their wives, namely seeing there is such an unreasonable number everywhere, among whom, I pray you, how many be there that live chaste? How much better were it to turn their concubines into wives, that whereas they have them now to their great shame with an unquiet conscience, they might have the other openly with good report, and get* children, and also bring them up godly, of whom they themselves not only might not be ashamed, but also might be counted honest men for them. And I think the bishops' officers would have procured* this matter long ago, if they had not found greater gains by priests' lemans* than they were like to have by priests' wives. "But virginity, forsooth, is a heavenly thing; it is an angel's life." I answer: "Wedlock is a manly thing, such as is meet for man." And I talk now as man unto man. I grant you that virginity is a thing praiseworthy, but so far I am content to speak in praise of it, if it be not so praised as though the just should altogether follow

---

[85] Matt. 19: 12.   [86] Matt. 19: 3–9.

it; for if men commonly should begin to like it, what thing could be invented more perilous to a commonweal[87] than virginity? Now be it that others deserve great praise for their maidenhead, you notwithstanding cannot want great rebuke, seeing it lieth in your hands to keep that house from decay whereof you lineally descended, and to continue still the name of your ancestors, who deserve most worthily to be known forever. And last of all, he deserveth as much praise as they which keep their maidenhood that keeps himself true to his wife, and marrieth rather for increase of children than to satisfy his lust. For if a brother be commanded to stir up seed[88] to his brother that dieth without issue, will you suffer the hope of all your stock to decay, namely seeing there is none other of your name and stock but yourself alone to continue the posterity?

'I know well enough that the ancient fathers have set forth in great volumes the praise of virginity, among whom Jerome[89] doth so take on, and praiseth it so much above the stars, that he fell in manner to deprave matrimony, and therefore was required of godly bishops to call back his words that he had spoken. But let us bear with such heat for that time's sake; I would wish now that they which exhort young folk everywhere, and without respect—such as yet know not themselves[90]—to live a single life and to profess virginity, that they would bestow the same labour in setting forth the description of chaste and pure wedlock. And yet those bodies that are in such great love with virginity are well contented that men should fight against the Turks, which in number are infinitely greater than we are. And now if these men think right in this behalf, it must needs be thought right good and godly to labour earnestly for children-getting, and to substitute youth from time to time for the maintenance of war. Except peradventure they think that guns, bills, pikes, and navies should be provided for battle, and that men stand in no stead at all with them. They also allow it well that we should kill miscreant and heathen parents, that the rather their children, not knowing of it, might be baptized and made Christians. Now if this be right and lawful, how much more gentleness were it to have children baptized being born in lawful marriage?

---

[87] Cf. *All's Well that Ends Well* 1. 1. 123 ff. Parolles: 'It is not politic in the commonwealth of nature to preserve virginity.'

[88] Deut. 25: 5–10.

[89] Many of the Church Fathers praised chastity; in *Adversus Jovinianum* Jerome went so far as to exalt virginity over marriage.

[90] Observing the classical injunction, 'Nosce teipsum' (know thyself) was thought to be a sign of mature judgement.

'There is no nation so savage, nor yet so hardhearted, within the whole world, but the same abhorreth murdering of infants and newborn babes. Kings also and head rulers do likewise punish most straitly* all such as seek means to be delivered before their time, or use physic* to wax* barren and never to bear children. What is the reason? Marry, they compt small difference betwixt him that killeth the child so soon as it beginneth to quicken, and the other that seeketh all means possible never to have any child at all. The selfsame thing that either withered and drieth away in thy body or else putrifieth within thee, and so hurteth greatly thy health, yea, that selfsame which falleth from thee in thy sleep, would have been a man, if thou thyself hadst been a man. The Hebrews abhor that man,[91] and wish him God's curse, that (being commanded to marry with the wife of his dead brother) did cast his seed upon the ground lest any issue should be had; and he was ever thought unworthy to live here upon earth that would not suffer that child to live which was quick in the mother's womb.

'But I pray you, how little do they swerve from this offence which bind themselves to live barren all the days of their life? Do they not seem to kill as many men as were like to have been born if they had bestowed their endeavours to have got children? Now I pray you, if a man had land that were very fat and fertile, and suffered the same for lack of manuring forever to wax barren, should he not, or were he not worthy to be punished by the laws, considering it is for the common-weal's behoof that every man should well and truly husband* his own? If that man be punished who little heedeth the maintenance of his tillage (the which although it be never so well manured, yet it yield-eth nothing else but wheat, barley, beans, and peas), what punishment is he worthy to suffer that refuseth to plough that land which being tilled yieldeth children? And for ploughing land, it is nothing else but painful toiling from time to time, but in getting children there is pleasure which, being ordained as a ready reward for painstaking, asketh a short travail for all the tillage.

'Therefore if the working of nature, if honesty, if virtue, if inward zeal, if godliness, if duty may move you, why can you not abide that which God hath ordained, nature hath established, reason doth counsel, God's word and man's word do commend, all laws do command, the consent of all nations doth allow, whereunto also the

---

[91] Onan; cf. Gen. 38: 9–10.

example of all good men doth exhort you? That if every honest man should desire many things that are most painful, for none other cause but only for that they are honest, no doubt but matrimony ought above all others most of all to be desired, as the which we may doubt whether it have more honesty in it or bring more delight and pleasure with it. For what can be more pleasant than to live with her with whom not only you shall be joined in fellowship of faithfulness and most hearty goodwill, but also you shall be coupled together most assuredly with the company of both your bodies?[92] If we compt* that great pleasure which we receive of the goodwill of our friends and acquaintance, how pleasant a thing is it above all others to have one with whom you may break the bottom of your heart,[93] with whom ye may talk as freely as with yourself, into whose trust you may safely commit yourself, such a one as thinketh all your goods to be her charge. Now what a heavenly bliss (trow* you) is the company of man and wife together, seeing that in all the world there can nothing be found either of greater weight and worthiness, or else of more strength and assurance. For with friends we join only with them in goodwill and faithfulness of mind, but with a wife we are matched together both in heart and mind, in body and soul, sealed together with the bond and league of a holy sacrament, and parting all the goods we have indifferently* betwixt us.

'Again, when others are matched together in friendship, do we not see what dissembling they use, what falsehood they practice, and what deceitful parts they play? Yea, even those whom we think to be our most assured friends, as swallows fly away when summer is past, so they hide their heads when fortune 'gins to fail. And oftimes when we get a new friend, we straight forsake our old. We hear tell of very few that have continued friends even till their last end. Whereas the faithfulness of a wife is not stained with deceit, nor dusked* with any dissembling, nor yet parted with any change of the world, but dissevered at last by death only, no not by death neither. She forsakes and sets light by father and mother, sister and brother, for your sake and for your love only. She only passeth* upon you, she puts her trust in you and leaneth wholly upon you, yea, she desires to die with you. Have you any worldly substance? You have one that will maintain it, you have one that will increase it. Have you none? You have a wife that will get it. If you live in prosperity, your joy is doubled; if the world

---

[92] Cf. Gen. 2: 24, Matt. 19: 5, 'thy twain shall be one flesh'.
[93] For this sequence in praise of a wife cf. *The Taming of the Shrew* 5. 2. 146 ff.

go not with you, you have a wife to put you in good comfort, to be at your commandment, and ready to serve your desire and to wish that such evil as hath happened unto you might chance unto herself.

'And do you think that any pleasure in all the world is able to be compared with such a goodly fellowship and familiar living together? If you keep home, your wife is at hand to keep your company, the rather that you might feel no weariness of living all alone; if you ride forth, you have a wife to bid you farewell with a kiss, longing much for you being from home and glad to bid you welcome at your next return. A sweet mate in your youth, a thankful comfort in your age. Every society or companying together is delightful and wished for by nature of all men, forasmuch as nature hath ordained us to be sociable, friendly, and loving together. Now how can this fellowship of man and wife be otherwise than most pleasant, where all things are common together betwixt them both? Now I think he is most worthy to be despised above all others that is born, as a man would say, for himself, that liveth to himself, that seeketh for himself, that spareth for himself, maketh cost only upon himself, that loveth no man, and no man loveth him. Would not a man think that such a monster were meet to be cast out of all men's company (with Timon[94] that careth for no man) into the midst of the sea? Neither do I here utter unto you those pleasures of the body, the which whereas nature hath made to be most pleasant unto man, yet these great-witted men rather hide them and dissemble them (I cannot tell how) than utterly contemn them. And yet what is he that is so sour of wit and so drooping of brain (I will not say blockheaded or insensate), that is not moved with such pleasure, namely if he may have his desire without offence either of God or man, and without hindrance of his estimation? Truly I would take such a one not to be a man but rather to be a very stone. Although this pleasure of the body is the least part of all those good things that are in wedlock.

'But be it that you pass* not upon this pleasure, and think it unworthy for man to use it, although indeed we deserve not the name of man without it, but compt it among the least and uttermost profits that wedlock hath, now I pray you, what can be more heartily desired than chaste love, what can be more holy, what can be more honest? And among all these pleasures you get unto you a jolly sort of kinsfolk, in whom you may take much delight. You have other parents,

---

[94] The Athenian misanthrope; cf. Shakespeare, *Timon of Athens*.

other brethren, sisters, and nephews. Nature indeed can give you but one father and one mother; by marriage you get unto you another father and another mother, who cannot choose but love you with all their hearts, as the which have put into your hands their own flesh and blood. Now again, what a joy shall this be unto you, when your most fair wife shall make you a father in bringing forth a fair child unto you, where you shall have a pretty little boy running up and down your house, such a one as shall express your look and your wife's look, such a one as shall call you "Dad" with his sweet lisping words?

'Now last of all, when you are thus linked in love, the same shall be so fastened and bound together, as though it were with the adamant* stone, that death itself can never be able to undo it. "Thrice happy are they," quod Horace,[95] "yea, more than thrice happy are they, whom these sure bands do hold; neither though they are by evil reporters* full oft set asunder, shall love be unloosed betwixt them two till death them both depart." You have them that shall comfort you in your latter days, that shall close up your eyes when God shall call you, that shall bury you and fulfill all things belonging to your funeral, by whom you shall seem to be newborn. For so long as they shall live, you shall need never be thought dead yourself. The goods and lands that you have got go not to other heirs than to your own. So that unto such as have fulfilled all things that belong unto man's life, death itself cannot seem bitter. Old age cometh upon us all, will we or nill we, and this way nature provided for us, that we should wax young again in our children and nephews. For what man can be grieved that he is old, when he seeth his own countenance which he had being a child to appear lively in his son? Death is ordained for all mankind, and yet by this means only nature by her providence mindeth* unto us a certain immortality, while she increaseth one thing upon another, even as a young graff* buddeth out when the old tree is cut down. Neither can he seem to die that, when God calleth him, leaveth a young child behind him.

'But I know well enough what you say to yourself all this while of my long talk. "Marriage is a happy thing if all things hap well: what and if one have a curst* wife? What if she be light?* What if his children be ungracious?" Thus I see you will remember all such men as by marriage have been undone. Well, go to it, tell as many as you can

<hr />

[95] *Odes* I. 13. 17–20.

and spare not: you shall find all these were the faults of the persons and not the faults of marriage. For believe me, none have evil wives but such as are evil men. And as for you, sir, you may choose a good wife if ye list. But what if she be crooked, and marred altogether, for lack of good ordering? A good honest wife may be made an evil woman by a naughty* husband, and an evil wife hath been made a good woman by an honest man. We cry out of wives untruly and accuse them without cause. There is no man (if you will believe me) that ever had an evil wife but through his own default. Now again, an honest father bringeth forth honest children, like unto himself. Although even these children, howsoever they are born, commonly become such men as their education and bringing up is. And as for jealousy, you shall not need to fear that fault at all. For none be troubled with such a disease but those only that are foolish lovers. Chaste, godly, and lawful love never knew what jealousy meant. What mean you to call to your mind and remember such sore tragedies and doleful dealings as have been betwixt man and wife? Such a woman being naught* of her body hath caused her husband to lose his head; another hath poisoned her goodman; the third, with her churlish dealing (which her husband could not bear), hath been his utter undoing and brought him to his end.

'But I pray you, sir, why do you not rather think upon Cornelia, wife unto Tiberius Gracchus? Why do ye not mind that most worthy wife of that most unworthy man Alcestis? Why remember ye not Julia, Pompey's wife, or Portia, Brutus's wife? And why not Artemisia, a woman most worthy ever to be remembered? Why not Hypsicratea, wife unto Mithridates, king of Pontus? Why do ye not call to remembrance the gentle nature of Tertia Aemilia? Why do ye not consider the faithfulness of Thuria? Why cometh not Lucretia and Lentula to your remembrance? And why not Arria?[96] Why not thousands other, whose chastity of life and faithfulness towards their husbands could not be changed, no not by death? "A good woman," you will say "is a rare bird,[97] and hard to be found in all the world." Well then, sir, imagine yourself worthy to have a rare wife, such as few men have. "A good woman," saith the Wiseman, "is a good portion."[98] Be you bold to hope for such a one as is worthy your manners. The chiefest point

---

[96] Erasmus lists many famous classical instances of outstandingly virtuous and devoted women. Similar lists were freely available in such compilations as Valerius Maximus, *Facta et dicta memorabilia* 4. 6.

[97] Horace, *Sat.* 2. 2. 26; Juvenal 6. 165.   [98] Prov. 12: 4, 18: 22, 31: 10–31.

standeth in this: what manner of woman you choose, how you use her, and how you order yourself towards her.

' "But liberty," you will say, "is much more pleasant, for whosoever is married weareth fetters upon his legs, or rather carrieth a clog,[99] the which he can never shake off till death part their yoke." To this I answer: I cannot see what pleasure a man shall have to live alone. For if liberty be delightful, I would think you should get a mate unto you with whom you should part* stakes and make her privy of all your joys. Neither can I see anything more free than is the servitude of these two, where the one is so much beholding and bound to the other that neither of them both would be loose, though they might. You are bound unto him whom you receive into your friendship, but in marriage neither party findeth fault that their liberty is taken away from them. Yet once again, you are sore afraid lest when your children are taken away by death you fall to mourning for want of issue. Well sir, if you fear lack of issue, you must marry a wife for the selfsame purpose, the which only shall be a mean that you shall not want issue.

'But what do you search so diligently, nay so carefully, all the incommodities of matrimony, as though single life had never any incommodity joined with it at all? As though there were any kind of life in all the world that is not subject to all evils that may happen. He must needs go out of this world that looks to live without feeling of any grief. And in comparison of that life which the saints of God shall have in heaven, this life of man is to be compted a death and not a life. But if you consider things within the compass of mankind, there is nothing either more safe, more quiet, more pleasant, more to be desired, or more happy, than is the married man's life. How many do you see that having once felt the sweetness of wedlock doth not desire eftsoons to enter into the same? My friend Mauricius,[100] whom you know to be a very wise man, did not he the next month after his wife died—whom he loved dearly—get him straight a new wife? Not that he was impatient of his lust and could not forbear any longer, but he said plainly it was no life for him to be without a wife, which should be with him as his yokefellow and companion in all things. And is not this the fourth wife that our friend Jovius hath married? And yet he so loved the others when they were on live that none was able to

[99] Cf. *All's Well that Ends Well* 2. 5. 53.
[100] Probably Sir Thomas More, who married Alice Middleton after a one-month widowhood.

comfort him in his heaviness, and now he hastened so much (when one was dead) to fill up and supply the void room of his chamber, as though he had loved the others very little.

'But what do we talk so much of the honesty and pleasure herein, seeing that not only profit doth advise us, but also need doth earnestly force us to seek marriage. Let it be forbidden that man and woman shall not come together, and within few years all mankind must needs decay forever. When Xerxes,[101] king of the Persians, beheld from a high place that great army of his, such as almost was incredible, some said he could not forbear weeping, considering of so many thousands there was not one like to be alive within seventy years after. Now why should not we consider the same of all mankind, which he meant only of his army? Take away marriage, and how many shall remain, after a hundred years, of so many realms, countries, kingdoms, cities, and all other assemblies that be of men throughout the whole world? On now, praise we a' God's name the single life above the nock,* the which is like forever to undo all mankind. What plague, what infection can either heaven or hell send more harmful unto mankind? What greater evil is to be feared by any flood? What could be looked for more sorrowful, although the flame of Phaeton[102] should set the world on fire again? And yet by such sore tempests many things have been saved harmless, but by the single life of man there can be nothing left at all. We see what a sort of diseases, what diversity of mishaps do night and day lie in wait to lessen the small number of mankind. How many doth the plague destroy, how many do the seas swallow, how many doth battle snatch up? For I will not speak of the daily dying that is in all places. Death taketh her flight everywhere round about;[103] she runneth over them; she catcheth them up; she hasteneth as much as she can possible to destroy all mankind: and now do we so highly commend single life and eschew marriage? Except haply we like the profession of the Essenes (of whom Josephus[104] speaketh that they will neither have wife nor servants) or the Dulopolitans,[105] called otherwise the rascals and slaves of cities, the which company of them is alway increased and continued by a sort of vagabond peasants that continue and be from time to time still together. Do we look that some Jupiter

---

[101] In 480 BC, when leading his army into Greece. Cf. Herodotus 7. 45–6.
[102] Cf. Ovid, *Met.* 2. 150–400.   [103] Horace, *Sat.* 2. 1. 58.
[104] In his *Bellum Judaicum* 2. 120–61.
[105] There was a city Dulopolis (Pliny, *Naturalis historia* 5. 29. 104) in Asia Minor, but this is probably a pun on the name's meaning, 'city of slaves'.

should give us that same gift, the which he is reported to have given unto bees,[106] that we should have issue without procreation, and gather with our mouths out of flowers the seed of our posterity? Or else do we desire that, like as the poets feign Minerva to be born out of Jupiter's head,[107] in like sort there should children leap out of our heads? Or last of all, do we look according as the old fables[108] have been, that men should be born out of the earth, out of rocks, out of stocks, stones, and old trees? Many things breed out of the earth without man's labour at all. Young shrubs grow and shoot up under the shadow of their grandsire trees. But nature would have man to use this one way of increasing issue, that through labour of both the husband and wife mankind might still be kept from destruction.

'But I promise you, if all men took after you and still forbare to marry, I cannot see but that these things which you wonder at and esteem so much could not have been at all. Do you yet esteem this single life so greatly? Or do we praise so much virginity above all other? Why man, there will be neither single men nor virgins alive if men leave to marry and mind not procreation! Why do you then prefer virginity so much, why set it you so high, if it be the undoing of all the whole world? It hath been much commended, but it was for that time and in a few. God[109] would have men to see as though it were a pattern, or rather a picture of that heavenly habitation where neither any shall be married, nor yet any shall give theirs to marriage. But when things be given for an example, a few may suffice, a number were to no purpose. For even as all grounds, though they be very fruitful, are not therefore turned into tillage for man's use and commodity, but part lieth fallow and is never manured, part is kept and cherished to like the eye and for man's pleasure: and yet in all this plenty of things, where so great store of land is, nature suffereth very little to wax barren. But now if none should be tilled, and ploughmen went to play, who seeth not but that we should all starve and be fain shortly to eat acorns? Even so, it is praiseworthy if a few live single, but if all should seek to live single; so many as be in this world, it were too great an inconvenience.

'Now again, be it that others deserve worthy praise that seek to live a virgin's life, yet it must needs be a great fault in you. Others shall be thought to seek a pureness of life; you shall be compted a parricide

---

[106] See Virgil, *Georg.* 4. 197–202.   [107] Cf. Hesiod, *Theogony* 924–6.
[108] Cf. Lucretius, *De rerum natura* 5. 805–17; Ovid, *Met.* 1. 348–415.
[109] Matt. 22: 30.

or a murderer of your stock, that whereas you may by honest marriage increase your posterity, you suffer it to decay forever through
your wilful single life. A man may, having a house full of children,
commend one to God to live a virgin all his life. The ploughman offer-
eth to God the tenths* of his own, and not his whole crop altogether
but you, sir, must remember that there is none left alive of all your
stock but yourself alone. And now it mattereth nothing whether you
kill or refuse to save that creature which you only might save, and that
with ease. But you will follow the example of your sister and live single
as she doth. And yet methinketh you should chiefly even for this selfsame cause be afraid to live single. For whereas there was hope of issue
heretofore in you both, now ye see there is no hope left but in you
only. Be it that your sister may be borne withal because she is a woman
and because of her years, for she, being but a girl and overcome with
sorrow for loss of her mother, took the wrong way. She cast herself
down headlong, and became a nun at the earnest suit either of foolish
women or else of doltish monks; but you, being much elder, must evermore remember that you are a man. She would need die together with
her ancestors; you must labour that your ancestors shall not die at all.
Your sister would not do her duty, but shrank away: think you now
with yourself that you have two offices to discharge. The daughters
of Lot[110] never stuck at the matter to have ado with their drunken
father, thinking it better with wicked whoredom and incest to provide
for their posterity than to suffer their stock to die forever. And will
not you with honest, godly, and chaste marriage (which shall be
without trouble and turn to your great pleasure) have a regard to your
posterity, most like else forever to decay?

'Therefore, let them on God's name follow the purpose of chaste
Hippolytus;[111] let them live a single life that either can be married men
and yet can get no children, or else such whose stock may be continued by means of other their kinsfolk, or at the least whose kindred is
such that it were better for the commonweal they were all dead than
that any of that name should be alive; or else such men as the ever-
living God of his most especial goodness hath chosen out of the whole
world to execute some heavenly office, whereof there is a marvelous
small number. But whereas you, according to the report of a physi-

---

[110] See Gen. 19: 30–8.
[111] Having dedicated himself to the chaste goddess Artemis, he rejected women; cf. Ovid,
Met. 15. 496–546, and Euripides, *Hippolytus.*

cian that neither is unlearned nor yet is any liar, are like to have many children hereafter; seeing also you are a man of great lands and revenues by your ancestors, the house whereof you came being both right honourable and right ancient, so that you could not suffer it to perish without your great offence and great harm to the commonweal; again, seeing you are of lusty years and very comely for your personage, and may have a maid to your wife such a one as none of your country hath known any to be more absolute for all things, coming of as noble a house as any of them, a chaste one, a sober one, a godly one, an excellent fair one, having with her a wonderful dowry; seeing also your friends desire you, your kinsfolk weep to win you, your cousins and alliance are earnest in hand with you, your country calls and cries upon you; the ashes of your ancestors from their graves make hearty suit unto you—do you yet hold back, do you still mind to live a single life? If a thing were asked you that were not half-honest, or the which you could not well compass, yet at the instance of your friends, or for the love of your kinsfolk, you would be overcome and yield to their requests. Then how much more reasonable were it that the weeping tears of your friends, the hearty goodwill of your country, the dear love of your elders, might win that thing at your hands unto the which both the law of God and man doth exhort you, nature pricketh you forward, reason leadeth you, honesty allureth you, so many commodities* call you, and last of all necessity itself doth constrain you.

'But here an end of all reasoning. For I trust you have now and a good while ago changed your mind through mine advice and taken yourself to better counsel.'

Of Exhortation

The places of exhorting and dehorting are the same which we use in persuading and dissuading, saving that he which useth persuasion seeketh by arguments to compass his device, he that labours to exhort doth stir affections.

Erasmus[112] showeth these to be the most especial places that do pertain unto exhortation:

1. Praise or commendation   3. Hope of victory
2. Expectation of all men   4. Hope of renown

[112] *De conscribendis epistolis*, ch. 26.

5. Fear of shame

6. Greatness of reward

7. Rehearsal of examples in all ages, and especially of things lately done . . .

Of Moving Pity, and Stirring Men to Show Mercy

Likewise we may exhort men to take pity of the fatherless, the widow and the oppressed innocent, if we set before their eyes the lamentable afflictions, the tyrannous wrongs, and the miserable calamities which these poor wretches do sustain. For if flesh and blood move us to love our children, our wives, and our kinsfolk, much more should the spirit of God and Christ's goodness towards man stir us to love our neighbours most entirely. These exhortations the preachers of God may most aptly use when they open his gospel to the people and have just cause to speak of such matters . . .

Of an Oration Judicial

The whole burden of weighty matters and the earnest trial of all controversies rest only upon judgment. Therefore when matters concerning land, goods, or life, or any such thing of like weight are called in question, we must ever have recourse to this kind of oration, and after just examining of our causes by the places thereof look for judgment[113] according to the law. . . .

THE SECOND BOOK

Of Moving Affections

Because the beauty of amplifying standeth most in apt moving of affections, it is needful to speak somewhat in this behalf, that the better it may be known what they are and how they may be used. Affections,[114] therefore, called passions, are none other thing but a stirring or forcing of the mind either to desire, or else to detest and loathe anything more vehemently than by nature we are commonly wont to do. We desire those things, we love them, and like them earnestly, that appear in our judgment to be godly; we hate and abhor those things that seem naught, ungodly, or harmful unto us. Neither only are we

---

[113] Cf. *Merchant of Venice* 4. 1.   [114] Quintilian, *Inst.* 6. 2. 7–24.

moved with those things which we think either hurtful or profitable for ourselves, but also we rejoice, we sorry, or we pity another
man's hap.* . . .

In moving affections and stirring the judges to be grieved, the
weight of the matter must be so set forth as though they saw it plain
before their eyes;[115] the report must be such and the offence made so
heinous, that the like hath not been seen heretofore, and all the circumstances must thus be heaped together: the naughtiness of his
nature that did the deed, the cruel ordering, the wicked dealing and
malicious handling, the time, the place; the manner of his doing, and
the wickedness of his will to have done more. The man that sustained
the wrong: how little he deserved, how well he was esteemed among
his neighbours, how small cause he gave him, how great lack men have
of him. 'Now if this be not reformed, no good man shall live safe: the
wicked will overflow[116] all the world, and best it were for safeguard to
be naught also, and to take part with them, for no good man shall go
quiet for them, if there be not speedy redress found and this fault punished to the example of all others.' . . .

Of Moving Pity

Now in moving pity and stirring men to mercy, the wrong done must
first be plainly told, or if the judges[117] have sustained the like extremity, the best were to will them to remember their own state, how they
have been abused in like manner, what wrongs they have suffered by
wicked doers, that by hearing their own they may the better hearken
to others.

Again, whereas all other miseries that befall unto man are grievous
to the ear, there is nothing more heinous than to hear that the most
honest men are soonest overthrown by them that are most wicked, and
virtue put to flight through the only might of vice. That if the like
hath not happened unto the hearers of this cause, yet it were meet to
show them that the like may happen, and so require them to give
judgment in this cause as they would do in their own, and remember
that harm may chance to everyone[118] that perhaps chanceth to anyone.
And no doubt every man remembering himself and his own case will
look well about him and give judgment according to right.

---

[115] *Rhet. Her.* 2. 30. 49; *Inv. rhet.* 1. 54. 104; *Inst.* 6. 2. 29–32.
[116] Cf. *King Lear* 3. 7. 99 ff.   [117] Cicero, *De or.* 2. 52. 211; *Inst.* 6. 1. 16.
[118] *Rhet. Her.* 2. 30. 48; *Inv. rhet.* 1. 53. 101.

Neither can any good be done at all when we have said all that ever we can, except we bring the same affections in our own heart,[119] the which we would the judges should bear towards our own matter. For how can he be grieved with the report of any heinous act, either in stomaching* the naughtiness of the deed, or in bewailing the miserable misfortune of the thing, or in fearing much the like evil hereafter, except the orator himself utter such passions outwardly, and from his heart fetch his complaints, in such sort that the matter may appear both more grievous to the ear and therewith so heinous that it requires earnestly a speedy reformation? There is no substance of itself that will take fire except ye put fire to it. Likewise, no man's nature is so apt straight to be heated except the orator himself be on fire and bring his heat with him. It is a common saying,[120] 'Nothing kindleth sooner than fire.' And therefore a fiery stomach causeth evermore a fiery tongue. And he that is heated with zeal and godliness shall set others on fire with like affection. No one man can better inveigh against vice than he can do which hateth vice with all his heart. Again, nothing moistureth sooner than water. Therefore a weeping eye causeth much moisture and provoketh tears. Neither is it any marvel, for such men both in their countenance, tongue, eyes, gesture, and in all their body else, declare an outward grief, and with words so vehemently and unfeignedly sets it forward, that they will force a man to be sorry with them and take part with their tears even against his will.[121] Notwithstanding, when such affections are moved, it were good not to stand long in them. For though a vehement talk may move tears, yet no art can long hold them. For as Cicero[122] doth say, 'Nothing drieth sooner than tears,' especially when we lament another man's cause and be sorry with him for his sake. . . .

THE THIRD BOOK

Of Apt Choosing and Framing of Words and Sentences Together, Called Elocution

And now we are come to that part of rhetoric the which above all others is most beautiful, whereby not only words are aptly used, but

[119] *De or.* 2. 55. 189; *Orat.* 132–3; *Inst.* 6. 2. 26; *Ars P.* 102 ff.
[120] *De or.* 2. 55. 190; *Inst.* 6. 2. 28.
[121] Cf. *Hamlet* 2. 2. 519 f., 560 ff.; *Julius Caesar* 3. 1. 280 ff., 3. 2. 169, 195.
[122] *Rhet. Her.* 2. 31. 50; *Inv. rhet.* 1. 55. 109; *Part. or.* 17. 57; *Inst.* 6. 1. 27.

also sentences are in right order framed. For whereas invention helpeth to find matter, and disposition serveth to place arguments, elocution getteth words to set forth invention, and with such beauty commendeth the matter that reason seemeth to be clad in purple, walking afore* both bare and naked. Therefore Tully[123] saith well: 'To find out reason and aptly to frame it is the part of a wise man, but to commend it by words and with gorgeous talk to tell our conceit, that is only proper to an orator.' Many are wise, but few have the gift to set forth their wisdom. Many can tell their mind in English, but few can use meet terms and apt order, such as all men should have and wise men will use, such as needs must be had when matters should be uttered. Now then, what is he at whom all men wonder and stand in amaze at the view of his wit? Whose doings are best esteemed? Whom do we most reverence and compt half a god among men?[124] Even such a one, assuredly, that can plainly, distinctly, plentifully, and aptly utter both words and matter, and in his talk can use such composition* that he may appear to keep a uniformity and (as I might say) a number in the uttering of his sentence.

Now an eloquent man[125] being smally learned can do much more good in persuading, by shift of words and meet placing of matter, than a great learned clerk shall be able with great store of learning, wanting words to set forth his meaning. Wherefore I much marvel that so many seek the only knowledge of things without any mind to commend or set forth their intendment,* seeing none can know either what they are or what they have without the gift of utterance. Yea, bring them to speak their mind and enter in talk with such as are said to be learned, and you shall find in them such lack of utterance that if you judge them by their tongue and expressing of their mind, you must needs say they have no learning. Wherein methinks they do like some rich snudges* that having great wealth go with their hose out at heels, their shoes out at toes, and their coats out at both elbows. For who can tell if such men are worth a groat, when their apparel is so homely and all their behaviour so base? I can call them by none other name but slovens, that may have good gear and neither can nor yet will once wear it cleanly.* What is a good thing to a man, if he neither know the use of it, nor yet, though he know it, is able at all to use it? If we think it comeliness and honesty to set forth the body with handsome

---

[123] Cicero, *De or.* 3. 26. 104.   [124] *De or.* 3. 14. 53.
[125] *De or.* 1. 15. 65; 3. 35. 142–3.

apparel, and think them worthy to have money that both can and will use it accordingly, I cannot otherwise see but that this part deserveth praise which standeth wholly in setting forth matter by apt words and sentences together, and beautifieth the tongue with great change of colours* and variety of figures.

Four Parts[126] *Belonging to Elocution*

1. Plainness   3. Composition
2. Aptness   4. Exornation

Among all other lessons, this should first be learned: that we never affect any strange inkhorn* terms but so speak as is commonly received, neither seeking to be overfine nor yet living overcareless, using our speech as most men do, and ordering our wits as the fewest have done. Some seek so far for outlandish English that they forget altogether their mother's language. And I dare swear this, if some of their mothers were alive, they were not able to tell what they say, and yet these fine English clerks will say they speak in their mother tongue, if a man should charge them for counterfeiting the king's English. Some far-journeyed gentlemen at their return home, like as they love to go in foreign apparel so they will powder their talk[127] with overseas language. He that cometh lately out of France will talk French English and never blush at the matter. Another chops in with English Italianated and applieth the Italian phrase to our English speaking, the which is as if an orator that professeth to utter his mind in plain Latin would needs speak poetry and far-fetched colours of strange antiquity. The lawyer will store his stomach with the prating of peddlers. The auditor, in making his account and reckoning, cometh in with 'sise sould,' and 'cater denere,' for 'six sous et quatre deniers'. The fine courtier will talk nothing but Chaucer. The mystical wise men and poetical clerks will speak nothing but quaint proverbs and blind allegories, delighting much in their own darkness, especially when none can tell what they do say. The unlearned or foolish fantastical* that smells but of learning—such fellows as have seen learned men in their

[126] The qualities of style that an orator must master: *Rhet. Her.* 4. 12. 17; *De or.* 3. 10. 37; *Inst.* 1. 5. 1, 8. 1. 1–2.

[127] Erasmus, in his *Moriae encomium* (tr. Chaloner, *The Praise of Follie*, 1549), satirized contemporary rhetoricians who tried 'to mingle their writings with words sought out of strange languages, as if it were a lovely thyng for them to poudre theyr bokes with ynkehorne terms'—that is, inappropriately learned language.

days—will so Latin their tongues that the simple cannot but wonder at their talk, and think surely they speak by some revelation. I know them that think rhetoric to stand wholly upon dark words, and he that can catch an inkhorn term by the tail, him they compt to be a fine Englishman and a good rhetorician. And the rather to set out this folly, I will add here such a letter as William Sommers[128] himself could not make a better for that purpose. Some will think, and swear it too, that there was never any such thing written. Well, I will not force any man to believe it, but I will say thus much, and abide by it too: the like have been made heretofore and praised above the moon.

A Letter Devised by a Lincolnshire Man for a Paid Benefice to a Gentleman That Then Waited upon the Lord Chancellor for the Time Being

'Pondering, expending, and revoluting with myself your ingent affability and ingenious capacity for mundane affairs, I cannot but celebrate and extol your magnifical dexterity above all others. For how could you have adepted such illustrate prerogative and dominical superiority, if the fecundity of your ingeny had not been so fertile and wonderful pregnant? Now, therefore, being accersited to such splendent renown and dignity splendidious, I doubt not but you will adjuvate such poor adnichilate orphans as whilom were condisciples with you, and of antique familiarity in Lincolnshire. Among whom I, being a scholastical panion, obtestate Your Sublimity to extol mine infirmity. There is a sacerdotal dignity in my native country contiguate to me where I now contemplate, which your worshipful benignity could soon impetrate for me, if it would like you to extend you schedules and collaud me in them to the right honourable lord chancellor, or rather archigrammatian of England. You know my literature, you know the pastoral promotion: I obtestate your clemency to invigilate thus much for me, according to my confidence, and as you know my condign merits for such a compendious living. But now I relinquish to fatigate your intelligence with any more frivolous verbosity, and therefore he that rules the climates be evermore your beautreux, your fortress, and your bulwark. Amen.

Dated at my dome, or rather mansion place, in Lincolnshire, the

---

[128] (d. 1560), the court fool of Henry VIII.

penult of the month sextile. *Anno millimo, quillimo, trillimo. Per me Johannes Octo.*'

What wise man reading this letter will not take him for a very calf that made it in good earnest, and thought by his inkpot terms to get a good parsonage? Doth wit rest in strange words, or else standeth it in wholesome matter and apt declaring of a man's mind? Do we not speak because we would have others to understand us? Or is not the tongue given for this end, that one might know what another meaneth? And what unlearned man can tell what half this letter signifieth? Therefore either we must make a difference of English, and say some is learned English and other some is rude English, or the one is court talk, the other is country speech; or else we must of necessity banish all such affected rhetoric and use altogether one manner of language . . .

Now whereas words be received, as well Greek as Latin, to set forth our meaning in the English tongue, either for lack of store* or else because we would enrich the language, it is well done to use them, and no man therein can be charged for any affectation when all others are agreed to follow the same way. There is no man aggrieved when he heareth 'letters patent,' and yet 'patent' is Latin and signifieth 'open' to all men. The 'Communion' is a 'fellowship' or a 'coming together,' rather Latin than English; the 'king's prerogative' declareth his power royal above all others: and yet I know no man grieved for these terms being used in their place, nor yet anyone suspected for affectation when such general words are spoken. The folly is espied when either we will use such words as few men do use, or use them out of place, when another might serve much better. Therefore to avoid such folly we may learn of that most excellent orator Tully,[129] who in his third book, where he speaketh of a perfect orator, declareth under the name of Crassus that for the choice of words four things should chiefly be observed. First, that such words as we use should be proper unto the tongue wherein we speak; again, that they be plain for all men to perceive; thirdly, that they be apt and meet, most properly to set out the matter; fourthly, that words translated from one signification to another—called of the Grecians tropes—be used to beautify the sentence, as precious stones are set in a ring to commend the gold.

---

[129] *De or.* 3. 10. 37, on the four virtues of style.

Aptness, What It Is

Such are thought apt words that properly agree unto that thing which they signify, and plainly express the nature of the same. Therefore they that have regard of their estimation do warely* speak and with choice utter words most apt for their purpose. In weighty causes grave words are thought most needful, that the greatness of the matter may the rather appear in the vehemency of their talk. So likewise of others, like order must be taken. Albeit some not only do not observe this kind of aptness, but also they fall into much fondness* by using words out of place and applying them to diverse matters without all discretion. As thus: an ignorant fellow, coming to a gentleman's place and seeing a great flock of sheep in his pasture, said to the owner of them: 'Now by my truth, sir, here is as goodly an audience of sheep as ever I saw in all my life'. Who will not take this fellow meeter to talk with sheep than to speak among men? Another, likewise, seeing a house fair builded, said to his fellow thus: 'Good lord, what a handsome phrase of building is this'. Thus are good words evil used when they are not well applied and spoken to good purpose. Therefore I wish that such untoward speaking may give us a good lesson to use our tongue warely, that our words and matter may still agree together.

OF EXORNATION. When we have learned apt words and usual phrases to set forth our meaning, and can orderly place them without offence to the ear, we may boldly commend and beautify our talk with divers goodly colours and delightful translations, that our speech may seem as bright and precious as a rich stone is fair and orient.

Exornation[130] is a gorgeous beautifying of the tongue with borrowed words and change of sentence, or speech with much variety. 'First, therefore,' as Tully[131] saith, 'an oration is made to seem right excellent by the kind self, by the colour and juice of speech.' There are three manner of styles or inditings: the great or mighty kind, when we use great words or vehement figures. The small kind, when we moderate our heat by meaner words, and use not the most stirring sentences. The low kind,[132] when we use no metaphors nor translated words, nor yet use any amplifications, but go plainly to

[130] *Rhet. Her.* 4. 12. 18.   [131] *De or.* 3. 25. 96.

[132] Although transmitting classical doctrine, Wilson here follows the terminology already used by Richard Sherry in his *Treatise of Schemes and Tropes* (1550). Cf. *Rhet. Her.* 4. 8. 11; *Orat.* 20. 69; *Inst.* 12. 10. 58.

work and speak altogether in common words. Now in all these three kinds, the oration is much commended and appeareth notable when we keep us still to that style which we first professed, and use such words as seem for that kind of writing most convenient. Yea, if we mind to increase or diminish, to be in a heat or to use moderation, to speak pleasantly or gravely, to be sharp or soft, to talk lordly or to speak finely, to wax ancient or familiar—which all are comprehended under one of the other three—we must ever make our words apt and agreeable to that kind of style which we first began to use. For as French hoods do not become lords, so Parliament robes are unfitting for ladies. Comeliness,* therefore, must ever be used, and all things observed that are most meet for every cause, if we look by attempts to have our desire.

4

Alexander Neville,
Tragedy and God's judgements (1563)

ALEXANDER NEVILLE (1544–1614) took his Cambridge BA in 1560, and
was secretary successively to three archbishops of Canterbury (Parker,
Grindal, and Whitgift). He also wrote several Latin theological treatises.

TEXT. *The Lamentable Tragedie of Oedipus the Sonne of Laius Kyng of Thebes
out of Seneca*, published on 28 April 1563, included (in a revised text) in
Thomas Newton (ed.), *Seneca his Tenne Tragedies Translated into Englysh*
(1581); repr. in 2 vols. (London, 1927), with an important preface by T. S.
Eliot, also published as 'Seneca in Elizabethan translation' in his *Selected
Essays* (London, 1932, etc.). Neville was one of several writers whose translation of Seneca influenced early English tragedy.

Behold here before thy face (good Reader) the most lamentable
tragedy of that most unfortunate Prince Oedipus, for thy profit
rudely* translated. Wonder not at the grossness of the style, neither
yet account the inventor's diligence disgraced by the translator's negligence; who, though that he hath sometimes boldly presumed to err
from his author, roving at random where he list, adding and sub-
tracting at pleasure, yet let not that engender disdainful suspicion
within thy learned breast.

Mark thou rather what is meant by the whole course of the history,
and frame thy life free from such mischiefs, wherewith the world at
this present is universally overwhelmed, the wrathful vengeance of
God provoked, the body plagued, the mind and conscience in midst
of deep devouring dangers most terribly assaulted—in such sort that
I abhor to write, and even at the thought thereof I tremble and quake
for very inward grief and fear of mind, assuredly persuading myself
that the right high and immortal God will never leave such horrible
and detestable crimes unpunished. As in this present tragedy, and so
forth in the process of the whole history, thou mayst right well perceive, wherein thou shalt see a very express and lively image of the
inconstant change of fickle fortune in the person of a Prince of passing
fame and renown, midst whole floods of earthly bliss, by mere

misfortune (nay rather by the deep hidden secret judgements of God)[1] piteously plunged in most extreme miseries. The whole realm for his sake in strangest guise grievously plagued; besides the apparent destruction of the nobility, the general death and spoil of the communalty, the miserable transformed face of the city, with an infinite number of mischiefs more which I pass over unrehearsed. Only wish I all men by this tragical history (for to that intent was it written) to beware of sin, the end whereof is shameful and miserable, as in the most unfortunate fall of this unhappy Prince right plainly appeareth. Who by inward grip of fearful consuming conscience wretchedly tormented, beholding the lamentable state of his vile infected realms, wasted by the burning rage of privy* spoiling* pestilence, finds himself in tract of time to be the only plague and misery of the almost quite destroyed city.

Whereupon calling together his priests and prophets, and asking counsel of the gods by them, for present remedy in those evils wherewith the realm was then universally overflown, answer was made that the plague should never cease till king Laius' death were thoroughly revenged, and the bloody murderer driven into perpetual exile. Which answer received, Oedipus, far more curious in bolting out* the truth than careful of his own estate, suddenly slides into an innumerable company of dreadful miseries. For as soon as he had once the perfect view of his own detestable deeds and wicked misdemeanour cast before his eyes, together with the unnatural killing of his father Laius, the incestuous marriage of his mother Jocasta, the preposterous* order of his ill misguided life, with a hundred more like mischiefs, which chaste and undefiled ears abhor to hear: fretting fury, common enemy and tormentor to corrupted consciences pricking him forward, all inflamed with frenzy and boiling in inward heat of vile infected mind, he rooteth out his wretched eyes unnaturally, bereaveth his mother her life[2] (though earnestly requested thereto) beastly, and in the end in most basest kind of slavery, banished, dieth miserably. Leaving behind him unto all posterities a dreadful example of God's horrible vengeance for sin.

---

[1] Neville imposes a Christian scheme on to Seneca's version of Sophocles, in which Oedipus' murder of the man who assaulted him (his own father, as he cannot know) is a coincidence, to which no design attaches. The fact that Oedipus acknowledges his responsibility for the deed by blinding himself is, rather, a triumphant demonstration of human ethics.

[2] But in Seneca (as in Sophocles) Jocasta kills herself.

Such like terrors as these requireth this our present age, wherein vice hath chiefest place, and virtue, put to flight, lies as an abject,* languishing in great extremity. For the which cause, so much the rather have I suffered this my base translated tragedy to be published, from his author in word and verse somewhat transformed, though in sense little altered, and yet oftentimes rudely increased with mine own simple invention; more rashly (I confess) than wisely, wishing to please all, to offend none. But whereas no man lives so uprightly whom slandering tongues leave undefamed, I refer myself to the judgement of the wisest, little esteeming the prejudicial mouths of such carping merchants which suffer no men's doings almost to escape undefiled. In fine, I beseech all together (if so it might be) to bear with my rudeness, and consider the grossness of our own country language, which can by no means aspire to the high lofty Latinist's style. Mine only intent was to exhort men to embrace virtue and shun vice, according to that of the right famous and excellent poet Virgil:[3]

Discite justitiam moniti, et non temnere divos.

This obtained, I hold myself thoroughly contented. In the mean season I end, wishing all men to shun sin, the plain (but most perilous) pathway to perfect infelicity.

---

[3] *Aen.* 6. 620, the warning given in Hades by Phlegyas: 'Be warned; learn ye to be just and not to slight the gods!'

5

William Baldwin,
Death of the poet Collingbourne (1563)

WILLIAM BALDWIN (*c*.1518–63?) worked from 1547 to 1553 as an assistant to the prominent Protestant publisher and printer Edward Whitchurch. His compilation of classical ethics, *A treatise of Morall Philosophie, contaynyng the sayinges of the wyse* (1547), had eighteen editions by 1640. He published a verse translation of *The Canticles or Balades of Salomon* (1549), in the wake of Calvin, and took holy orders in 1560. He helped prepare plays and pastimes for the courts of both Edward VI and Queen Mary, and supervised the publication of *The Mirror for Magistrates* between 1559 and 1563 (?), contributing numerous tragedies himself. Baldwin is also responsible for what has been called 'the first English novel', *Beware the Cat* (1570, 1584); ed. W. A. Ringler, Jr., and M. Flachmann (San Marino, Calif., 1988).

TEXT. From *A Mirror for Magistrates* (1559), second edition (1563). On the publishing history of this work see Lily B. Campbell (ed.), *The Mirror for Magistrates* (Cambridge, 1938; New York, 1960, 1970); for its impact on drama see Willard Farnham, *The Medieval Heritage of Elizabethan Tragedy* (Oxford, 1956). This famous collection of verse tragedies on English history was originally begun in 1555 as a continuation of Boccaccio's *De casibus virorum illustrium* (1364–74): in Lydgate's translation (1494), *The fall of Prynces*, that is, *The tragedies, gathered by Jhon Bochas, of all such Princes as fell from theyr estates throughe the mutability of Fortune since the creacion of Adam, until his time: wherin may be seen what vices bringe menne to destruccion, wyth notable warninges howe the like may be auoyded. Whereunto is added the fall of al such as since that time were notable in Englande: diligently collected out of the Chronicles.* This edition (by John Wayland) was suppressed by the Lord Chancellor in the reign of the Catholic Queen Mary, and only two title-pages and one leaf of text exist. Whatever the official objections had been, after Elizabeth's accession to the throne William Baldwin was able to issue this collection, which was continually expanded in subsequent editions, from nineteen tragedies (1559) to twenty-seven (1563; reprinted with corrections in 1571, 1574, 1575), with a further tragedy added in 1578 (the long-withheld account of Duke Humphrey of Gloucester). Meanwhile John Higgins had started a new collection, called *The First Parte of the Mirror for Magistrates* (1574, 1575, 1578), which was fused with Baldwin's collection in 1587, while Thomas Blenerhasset issued another supplementary work, *The Seconde part*

(1578), so that the work ultimately became a collective composition by a dozen or more writers. The moral-political didactic intent common to the whole enterprise is summed up in the title of the third edition: *A MYRROUR for Magistrates, Wherein may be seene by examples passed in this realme, with howe greueous plagues, vyces are punished in great princes and magistrates, and how frayle and unstable worldy prosperity is founde, where Fortune seemeth moste highly to favour* (1571).

In his Preface to the 1559 edition Baldwin records that he had procured the co-operation of seven gifted poets: George Ferrers, Thomas Chaloner, Thomas Phaer, Thomas Sackville, Thomas Churchyard, John Dolman, and Francis Seager. He also explained that he had copied the device of Boccaccio by acting as the interlocutor, so that in each tragedy 'the wretched princes compleyne unto me', while his collaborators 'tooke upon themselves every man for his parte to be sundrye personages, and in theyr behalfes to bewayle unto me theyr grevous chaunces, hevy destinies, and wofull misfortunes'. That is, each writer adopted the persona of the 'sundry Unfortunate Englishe men' whose fate they narrated. Baldwin then added prose passages to serve as an interlude between the verse tragedies, imagining all his contributors being present as an audience for each tale, and bringing out its significance.

William Collingbourne was executed in 1484 on the charge of treason (which accounts for his peculiarly gruesome execution). According to Baldwin's main source, Edward Hall's *Union of the Noble and Illustre Famelies of Lancastre and York* (1548), Richard III had him killed for writing a satirical couplet attacking himself and his three main counsellors:

> The Rat, the Catte, and Lovell our dogge
> Rule all Englande under the hogge.

As Hall explained, the three counsellors were 'the Lord Lovell, Sir Richard Radclyffe his myschevous mynion, and Sir Wylliam Catesby his secrete seducer . . . Meaning by the hogge, the dreadfull wilde bore whiche was the kynges cognisance [emblem]. But because the fyrste lyne ended in dogge, the metrician coulde not, observynge the regimentes of metre [i.e. rhyme], ende the second verse in Bore, but called the bore an hogge. This poeticall schoolemayster, corrector of breves and longes, caused Collyngborne to be abbreviate shorter by the hed, and too bee devyded into foure quarters': text in G. B. Churchill, *Richard III up to Shakespeare* (Berlin, 1900; Towota, NJ, 1976), p. 191.

Sir Richard Ratcliffe (d. 1485) carried out for Richard the execution of Rivers, Grey, and Vaughan, being rewarded with titles (Knight of the Garter, High Sheriff of Westmorland) and numerous lucrative offices and lands. William Catesby (d. 1485), a protégé of Hastings, from whose fall he benefited, was appointed Chancellor of the Exchequer in 1483, and Speaker of Richard's only parliament in 1484. He was captured at the Battle of Bosworth, 22 August 1485 (where Richard fell), and was executed three days later, leaving a remorseful will. The third counsellor, Francis, Viscount Lovell (1454–87?), called 'our dog' in allusion to his crest, was another loyal servant of the usurper, becoming Privy Councillor and Lord Chamberlain of the Household. He fought at Bosworth, but was pardoned by Henry VII, betraying that trust by taking part in two Yorkist insurrections in 1486–7.

Other historians, however, record that Collingbourne was executed not only for this rhyme but for other acts deemed treasonous by the tyrant. Robert Fabyan's *Chronicle* (1516), says that he 'was caste for sondry treasons' (Churchill, op. cit., p. 73), a judgement confirmed by Holinshed, who gives the full indictment, showing that the first charge was conspiracy to aid Richmond (the future Henry VII), the second the writing and publication of satiric verses (ibid., p. 219; followed by Stow, ibid., p. 227).

A MIRROR FOR MAGISTRATES

'How like you this,[1] my masters?' (quoth I). 'Very well', said one: 'The tragedy excelleth, the invention also of the *Induction*, and the descriptions are notable. But whereas he feigneth to talk with the princes in hell, that I am sure will be misliked, because it is most certain that some of their souls be in heaven. And although he herein do follow allowed* poets in their description of hell, yet it savoureth so much of purgatory, which the Papists have digged thereout, that the ignorant may thereby be deceived.

'Not a whit, I warrant you' (quoth I). 'For he meaneth not by his hell the place either of damned souls, or of such as lie for their fees,* but rather the grave, wherein the dead bodies of all sorts of people do rest till time of the resurrection. And in this sense is hell taken often in the scriptures, and in the writings of learned Christians. And so (as he himself hath told me) he meaneth, and so would have it taken.'

'Tush' (quoth another), 'what stand we here upon? It is a poesy and no divinity, and it is lawful for poets to feign[2] what they list, so it be appertinent to the matter. And therefore let it pass even in such sort

---

[1] The company has just heard Thomas Sackville's *Complaint of Henry, Duke of Buckingham*, with its famous *Induction*, depicting a journey to Hell, peopled by allegorical and historical figures (ed. Campbell, pp. 298–317).

[2] The traditional concept of 'poetic licence' (Cicero, *De or.* 3. 38. 153; Quintilian, *Inst.* 10. 5. 4; Horace, *Ars P.* 9 f.) becomes an organizing thread of Baldwin's verse narrative and of the prose discussions before and after.

as you have read it.' 'With a good will' (quoth I). 'But whereas you say a poet may feign what he list, indeed, methinks it should be so, and ought to be well taken of the hearers: but it hath not at all times been so allowed.' 'Ye say truth', quoth the reader, 'for here followeth in the story, that after the death of this duke, one called Collingbourne was cruelly put to death for making of rhyme.'

'I have his tragedy here' (quoth I). 'For the better perceiving whereof, you must imagine that you see him a marvellous well-favoured man, holding in his hand his own heart, newly ripped out of his breast, and smoking forth the lively spirit: and with his other hand beckoning to and fro, as it were to warn us to avoid; and with his faint tongue and voice saying as courageously as he may, these word that follow.'

HOW COLLINGBOURNE WAS CRUELLY EXECUTED FOR MAKING A FOOLISH RHYME

'Beware, take heed; take heed, beware! Beware   1
You poets, you that purpose to rehearse
By any art what tyrants' doings are.
Erinys'[3] rage is grown so fell and fierce
That vicious acts may not be touched* in verse.   5
The Muses' freedom, granted them of eld,
Is barred, sly reason's treasons high are held.

Be rough in rhyme, and then they say you rail,
Though Juvenal so be, that makes no matter.
With Jeremy you shall be had to jail,   10
Or forced with Martial,[4] Caesar's faults to flatter;
Clerks must be taught to claw* and not to clatter:*
Free Helicon, and frank* Parnassus' hills
Are helly haunts, and rank pernicious ills.

Touch covertly in terms, and then you taunt,   15
Though praised poets always did the like.
"Control us not![5] Else, traitor vile, avaunt,
What pass* we what the learned do mislike?

---

[3] The Erinyes were spirits of punishment avenging wrongs, especially those done to kindred.
[4] The satire of Juvenal (c. AD 50–127) was unconstrained. The biting satires of Martial (c. AD 40–104) coexisted with the poet's remarkable adulation of Domitian (emperor 81–96).
[5] The tyrants are imagined speaking, rejecting the poets' injunctions to obey morality.

Our sins we see, wherein to swarm* we seek.
We pass not what the people say or think.   20
Their shyttle* hate maketh none but cowards shrink."

"We know", say they, "the course of Fortune's wheel,
How constantly it whirleth still about,
Arrearing* now, while elder headlong reel,
How all the riders always hang in doubt.   25
But what for that? we count him but a lout
That sticks to mount, and basely like a beast
Lives temperately for fear of blockam* feast.

"Indeed we would of all be deemed gods,
Whatever we do; and therefore partly hate   30
Rude preachers that dare threaten us plagues and rods,
And blaze* the blots whereby we stain our state:
But nought we pass what any such do prate.
Of course* and office they must say their pleasure,
And we, of course, must hear and mend at leisure.   35

"But when these pelting* poets in their rhymes
Shall taunt, and jest, or paint our wicked works,
And cause the people know, and curse our crimes,
This ugly fault no tyrant lives but irks.
And therefore loath we taunters worse than Turks.   40
They mind thereby to make us know our miss
And so to amend, but they but dote in this.

"We know our faults as well as any other,
We also doubt* the dangers for them due.
Yet still we trust so right to guide the rudder   45
That 'scape we shall the surges that ensue.
We think we know more shifts than other knew;
In vain, therefore, for us are counsels writ:
We know our faults, and will not mend a whit."

These are the affections* of the wicked sort,   50
That press for honours, wealth, and pleasure vain.
Cease therefore, Baldwin, cease, I thee exhort,
Withdraw thy pen, for nothing shalt thou gain
Save hate, with loss of paper, ink and pain.
Few hate their sins, all hate to hear them touched,   55
How covertly soever they be couched.

Thy intent I know is godly, plain, and good,
To warn the wise, to fray the fond from ill;
But wicked worldlings are so witless wood,*
That to the worst they all things construe still.   60
With rigour oft they recompence good will.
They rack the words till time their sinews burst,
In doubtful senses straining still the worst.

A painful proof taught me the truth of this
Through tyrant's rage, and fortune's cruel turn: 65
They murdered me, for metering things amiss.
For wotst thou what? I am that Collingbourne
Which rhymed that which made full many mourn:
The cat, the rat, and Lovell our dog,
Do rule all England, under a hog.   70

Whereof the meaning was so plain and true
That every fool perceived it at first:
Most liked it, for most that most things knew,
In hugger mugger,* muttered what they durst.
The king himself of most was held accursed   75
Both for his own and for his fautor's* faults,
Of whom were three, the naughtiest* of all naughts.*

The chief was Catesby, whom I called a cat,
A crafty lawyer catching all he could.
The second Ratcliffe, whom I named a rat,   80
A cruel beast to gnaw on whom he should.
Lord Lovell barked and bit whom Richard would,
Whom therefore rightly I did term our dog,
Wherewith to rhyme I cleped* the King a hog.

Till he usurped the crown he gave the boar,   85
In which estate would God he had deceased.
Then had the realm not ruined so sore,
His nephew's reign should not so soon have ceased,
The noble blood had not been so decreased,
His rat, his cat, and bloodhound had not 'noyed   90
So many thousands as they have destroyed.

Their lawless dealings all men did lament,
And so did I, and therefore made the rhymes
To show my wit, how well I could invent,

To warn withal the careless of their crimes.   95
I thought the freedom of the ancient times
Stood still in force: *Ridentem dicere verum*
Quis vetat?[6] None, save climbers still *in ferum*.

Belike no tyrants were in Horace' days,
And therefore poets freely blamed vice.   100
Witness their satire sharp, and tragic plays,
With chiefest princes chiefly had in price:[7]
They name no man, they mix their gall with spice.
No more do I, I name no man outright,
But riddle-wise, I mean them as I might.   105

When bruit* had brought this to their guilty ears,
Who rudely named were noted in the rhyme,
They all conspired like most greedy bears
To charge me with most heinous traitorous crime;
And damned me the gallow tree to climb,   110
And strangled first in quarters to be cut,
Which should on high o'er London gates be put.

This wicked judgement vexed me so sore,
That I exclaimed against their tyranny.
Wherewith incensed, to make my pain the more,   115
They practised a shameful villany.
They cut me down alive, and cruelly
Ripped up my paunch* and bulk,* to make me smart,
And lingered long ere they took out my heart.

Here tyrant Richard played the eager hog,   120
His grashing* tusks my tender gristles shore.*
His bloodhound Lovell played the ravening dog,
His wolvish teeth my guiltless carcass tore.
His rat and cat did what they might, and more:
Cat Catesby clawed my guts to make me smart,   125
The rat Lord Ratcliffe gnawed me to the heart.

If Jews had killed the justest king alive,
If Turks had burnt up churches, Gods and all,
What greater pain could cruel hearts contrive
Than that I suffered for this trespass small?   130

---

[6] Horace, *Sat.* 1. 1. 24 f.: 'what harm can there be in presenting the truth with a laugh?'
[7] That is, 'satires and tragedies were then much valued by rulers'.

I am not prince nor peer, but yet my fall
Is worthy to be thought upon for this,
To see how cankered* tyrants' malice is.

  To teach also all subjects to take heed
They meddle not with magistrates' affairs,   135
But pray to God to mend them if it need;
To warn also all poets that be strayers,
To keep them close in compass of their chairs;
And when they touch things which they wish amended,
To sauce* them so that few need be offended.   140

  And so to mix their sharp rebukes with mirth
That they may pierce, not causing any pain
Save such as followeth every kindly* birth,
Requited straight with gladness of the gain.
A poet must be pleasant, not too plain,   145
No flatterer, no bolsterer* of vice,
But sound and sweet, in all things ware* and wise.

  The Greeks do paint a poet's office whole
In Pegasus, their feigned horse with wings,
Whom shaped so Medusa's blood did foal,   150
Who with his feet struck out the Muses' springs
From flinty rocks to Helicon[8] that clings;
And then flew up unto the starry sky,
And there abides among the heavens high.

  For he that shall a perfect poet be   155
Must first be bred out of Medusa's blood.
He must be chaste and virtuous[9] as was she,
Who to her power the Ocean god withstood.
To th'end also his doom be just and good,
He must (as she had) have one only eye,   160
Regard of truth that nought may lead awry.

  In courage eke he must be like a horse,
He may not fear to register the right.

---

[8] In Greek mythology, the dying Medusa (who had been loved by Poseidon), gave birth
to the winged horse, Pegasus, who subsequently carried the thunderbolt of Zeus. Helicon
is the largest mountain of Boeotia, traditionally the sanctuary of the Muses. Just below its
summit is the spring Hippocrene, struck by Pegasus' foot from the rock, which provides
the inspiration of poets. Cf. Ovid, *Met.* 5. 256–67.

[9] A restatement of the principle that the poet (like the orator) must himself be a good
man: cf. Elyot, p. 64, Jonson, p. 469, Milton, p. 598.

And that no power or fancy do him force,
No bit nor rein his tender jaws may twight,*   165
He must be armed with strength of wit and sprite*
To dash the rocks, dark causes and obscure,
Till he attain the springs of truth most pure.

His hooves must also pliant be and strong,
To rive* the rocks of lust and errors blind   170
In brainless heads, that always wander wrong:
These must he brise* with reasons plain and kind
Till springs of grace do gush out of the mind.
For till affections from the fond* be driven
In vain is truth told, or good counsel given.   175

Like Pegasus, a poet must have wings
To fly to heaven, there to feed and rest.
He must have knowledge of eternal things;
Almighty love must harbour in his breast.
With worldly cares he may not be oppressed,   180
The wings of skill and hope must heave him higher
Than all the joys which worldly wits desire.

He must be also nimble, free, and swift
To travel far to view the trades of men:
Great knowledge oft is gotten by the shift.*   185
Things notable he must be quick to pen,
Reproving vices sharply now and then.
He must be swift when touched tyrants chafe,
To gallop thence to keep his carcass safe.

These properties if I had well considered,   190
Especially that which I touchèd last,
With speedy flight my feet should have delivered
My feeble body from the stormy blast.
They should have caught me, ere I had been cast.*
But trusting vainly to the tyrant's grace   195
I never shrunk, nor changèd port or place.

I thought the poet's ancient liberties
Had been allowed plea at any bar.*
I had forgot how new-found tyrannies
With right and freedom were at open war,   200

That lust was law, that might did make and mar,
That with the lewd* save this no order was,
Sic volo, sic iubeo, stet pro ratione voluntas.[10]

Where this is law it booteth not to plead,
No privilege or liberties avail.   205
But with the learn'd whom law and wisdom lead,
Although through rashness poets hap to rail,
A plea of dotage* may all quarrels quail.
Their liberties, their writings to expound,
Doth quit them clear from faults by Momus[11] found.   210

This ancient freedom ought not be debarred*
From any wight* that speaketh aught, or writeth.
The author's meaning should of right be heard,
He knoweth best to what end he inditeth.*
Words sometime bear more than the heart behighteth.*   215
Admit therefore the author's exposition,
If plain, for truth: if forced, for his submission.

Of slanderers just laws require no more
Save to amend that seemed evil said,
Or to unsay the slanders said afore,   220
And ask forgiveness for the hasty braid.*
To heretics no greater pain is laid
Than to recant their errors or retract:
And worse than these can be no writer's act.

"Yes" (quoth the Cat), "thy railing words be treason,   225
And treason is far worse than heresy."
Then must it follow by this foolish reason
That kings be more than God in majesty,
And souls be less than bodies in degree.
For heretics both souls and God offend,   230
Traitors but seek to bring man's life to end.

I speak not this t' abase* the heinous fault
Of traitorous acts abhorred of God and man,

---

[10] Juvenal, *Satires* 6. 22: 'but this is my will and my command: let my will be voucher for the deed'.
[11] A type of the fault-finding critic, originally used by Callimachus as the mouthpiece of narrow-minded views.

But to make plain their judgement to be naught
That heresy for lesser sin do ban.*   235
I curse them both as deep as any can,
And always did. Yet through my foolish rhyme
They arraigned and stained me with that shameful crime.

    I never meant the king or council harm—
Unless to wish them safety were offence.   240
Against their power I never lifted arm,
Neither pen nor tongue for any ill pretence.
The rhyme I made, though rude, was sound in sense,
For they therein whom I so fondly named,
So ruled all that they were foul defamed.   245

    This was no treason but the very troth:
They ruled all, none could deny the same.
What was the cause then why they were so wroth
What, is it treason in a rhyming frame
To clip,* to stretch, to add or change a name?   250
And this reserved, there is no rhyme or reason
That any craft can clout* to seem a treason.

    For where I meant the king by name of Hog,
I only alluded to his badge, the Boar:
To Lovell's name I added more our Dog,   255
Because most dogs have borne that name of yore.
These metaphors I use with other more,
As Cat, and Rat, the half-names of the rest,
To hide the sense which they so wrongly wrest.

    I pray you now, what treason find you here?   260
"Enough: you rubbed the guilty on the gall,*
Both sense and names do note* them very near."
I grant that was the chief cause of my fall,
Yet can you find therein no treason at all.
There is no word against the prince or state,   265
Nor harm to them whom all the realm did hate.

    But since the guilty always are suspicious,
And dread the ruin that must sue by reason,
They cannot choose but count their council vicious
That note their faults, and therefore call it treason: 270
All grace and goodness with the lewd is geason.*

This is the cause why they good things detest,
Whereas the good take ill things to the best.

And therefore, Baldwin, boldly to the good
Rebuke thou vice, so shalt thou purchase thanks.   275
As for the bad, thou shalt but move his mood,
Though pleasantly thou touch his sinful pranks.
Warn poets, therefore, not to pass the banks
Of Helicon, but keep them in the streams,
So shall their freedom save them from extremes.'*   280

'God's blessing on his heart that made this' (said one), 'specially for reviving our ancient liberties. And I pray God it may take such place with the magistrates, that they may ratify our old freedom.' 'Amen' (quoth another), 'for that shall be a means both to stay and uphold themselves from falling; and also to preserve many kind, true, zealous, and well-meaning minds from slaughter and infamy. If King Richard and his counsellors had allowed, or at the least but winked at* some such wits, what great commodities* might they have taken thereby! First, they should have known what the people misliked and grudged* at (which no one of their flatterers either would or durst have told them), and so might have found means, either by amendment (which is best) or by some other policy to have stayed the people's grudge, the forerunner commonly of rulers' destructions. *Vox populi, vox dei*,[12] in this case is not so famous a proverb as true. The experience of all times doth approve it. They should also have been warned of their own sins, which call continually for God's vengeance, which never faileth to fall on their necks suddenly and horribly, unless it be stayed with hearty repentance.

These weighty commodities might they have taken by Collingbourne's vain rhyme. But as all things work to the best in them that be good,[13] so best things heap up mischief in the wicked, and all to hasten their utter destruction. For after this poor wretch's lamentable persecution (the common reward of best endeavours), straight followed the eternal destruction both of this tyrant and of his tormentors. Which I wish might be so set forth that they might be a warning forever to all in authority, to beware how they usurp or abuse their offices.'

---

[12] 'The voice of the people is the voice of God': Alcuin, Letter 164 in *Works* (1863), I. 438.   [13] Rom. 8: 28.

6

Roger Ascham,
On imitation (1570)

ROGER ASCHAM (1515/16–68) was educated at St John's College Cambridge, where he was taught by John Cheke (1514–57), the outstanding classicist and first Regius Professor of Greek. A Fellow of St John's from 1534 to 1548, Ascham was elected to a Readership in Greek, and in 1546 to the University Oratorship. In 1548 he became the private tutor of Princess Elizabeth, teaching her Greek (Sophocles, Isocrates, Demosthenes) in the mornings, Latin (Cicero, Livy) in the afternoons, together with Protestant theology. From 1550 to 1553 Ascham was secretary to the English ambassador to the Emperor Charles V, and from 1553 to his death in 1568 he was Latin Secretary, both to the Catholic Queen Mary and to the Protestant Queen Elizabeth, with whom he resumed studies in Latin and Greek, now more as an equal than a teacher. Ascham also published a book recommending archery, *Toxophilus, the Schole of Shootinge* (1545; repr. 1571, 1589), and *A Report of Germany* (1570).

TEXT. From *The Schoolmaster. Or plain and perfect way of teaching children, to understand, write, and speak the Latin tongue, but specially purposed for the private bringing-up of youth in gentlemen's and noblemen's houses, and commodious also for all such as have forgot the Latin tongue, and would, by themselves, without a schoolmaster, in short time, and with small pains, recover a sufficient ability to understand, write, and speak Latin* (London, 1570). Published posthumously, and unfinished, Ascham's teaching manual—designed for private Latin instruction and 'teach yourself' purposes—had five editions by 1589. Book One discusses 'The Bringing-up of Youth' in learning Latin, revealing the concerns of Renaissance educationalists (following Quintilian and Vives) to treat pupils in a humane manner, arousing a love of learning and virtue rather than drilling knowledge by rote and violence. Book Two, discussing 'The Ready Way to the Latin Tongue', follows Erasmus and other influential teachers (especially Johann Sturmius, the Strasbourg pedagogue with whom Ascham corresponded for many years) in emphasizing the need for students to write Latin daily, practising various ways of rehandling their classical models. Ascham outlines six (of which the extant text treats only the first five): *translatio linguarum* (where he recommends the technique of 'double translation', from Greek into Latin and back again into Greek), *paraphrasis, metaphrasis, epitome, imitatio*, and *declamatio*. I have chosen the section on *imitatio* since it addresses a key issue in Renaissance literary theory, learning to write by the imitation and emulation of models. It is noteworthy that Ascham treats the topic as an exercise in writing Latin, only: it does not occur to him that the same considerations apply to writers in the vernacular. As a Latinist, Ascham predictably disapproves of poets using accentual metres and rhyme, an issue still engaging English writers thirty years later: see Campion, p. 428. His conservative recommendation of Cicero as the main model for Latin prose, after over a century's controversies concerning the practice of *imitatio*, earned a rebuke from Francis Bacon: p. 459.

In annotating this text I have benefited from the edition by Lawrence V. Ryan (Ithaca, NY, 1967), author of the useful study, *Roger Ascham* (Stanford, Calif., 1963).

IMITATIO

Imitation is a faculty to express lively and perfectly that example which ye go about to follow. And of itself it is large and wide; for all the works of nature, in a manner, be examples for art to follow.

But to our purpose: all languages, both learned and mother tongues, be gotten, and gotten only by imitation. For as ye use to hear so ye learn to speak; if ye hear no other ye speak not yourself; and whom ye only hear of them ye only learn.

And therefore, if ye would speak as the best and wisest do ye must be conversant where the best and wisest are: but if you be born or brought up in a rude country, ye shall not choose but speak rudely.* The rudest man of all knoweth this to be true.

Yet nevertheless, the rudeness of common and mother tongues is no bar for wise speaking. For in the rudest country and most barbarous mother language many be found that can speak very wisely; but in the Greek and Latin tongue, the only two learned tongues which be kept not in common talk but in private books, we find always wisdom and eloquence, good matter and good utterance, never or seldom asunder.[1] For all such authors as be fullest of good matter and right judgment in doctrine be likewise always most proper in words, most apt in sentence, most plain and pure in uttering the same.

[1] For the paired concepts *sapientia et eloquentia*, 'wisdom and eloquence', cf. Cicero, *De or.* 1. 13. 58–14. 59, 2. 16. 67–8, 3. 5. 19–6. 24, 3. 19. 69–20. 76, 3. 22. 82, 3. 31. 122–5; *Orat.* 4. 14–5. 17, 21. 70 ('For after all the foundation of eloquence, as of everything else, is wisdom'), 32. 113–34. 120; *Brut.* 6. 23 (cit. Hoskyns, p. 399), 41. 152–3, 93. 322 (*eloquentiae philosophiam*). Ascham here draws on the ancient linguistic categories of 'matter' (*res*, thought or subject-matter) and 'words' (*verba*), in which priority was traditionally given to the thoughts expressed. He takes the orthodox position that if the subject-matter is not sound, then the language cannot possibly be good. Cf. *De or.* 3. 5. 19, 3. 31. 125.

And contrariwise, in those two tongues, all writers, either in religion or any sect of philosophy, whosoever be found fond* in judgment
of matter* be commonly found as rude in uttering their minds. For
Stoics, Anabaptists, and friars, with Epicures, libertines, and monks,[2]
being most like in learning and life, are no fonder and pernicious
in their opinions than they be rude and barbarous in their writings.
They be not wise therefore, that say 'What care I for man's words
and utterance, if his matter and reasons be good?' Such men say so,
not so much of ignorance as either of some singular pride in themselves, or some special malice of others, or for some private and partial
matter, either in religion or other kind of learning. For good and
choice meats be no more requisite for healthy bodies than proper and
apt words be for good matters, and also plain and sensible utterance
for the best and deepest reasons; in which two points standeth perfect eloquence, one of the fairest and rarest gifts that God doth give
to man.

Ye know not what hurt ye do to learning, that care not for words,
but for matter;[3] and so make a divorce betwixt the tongue and the
heart. For mark all ages, look upon the whole course of both the Greek
and Latin tongues, and ye shall surely find that when apt and good
words began to be neglected, and properties* of those two tongues to
be confounded,* then also began ill deeds to spring; strange manners
to oppress good orders; new and fond opinions to strive with old and
true doctrine, first in philosophy, and after in religion; right judgment
of all things to be perverted; and so virtue, with learning, is condemned, and study left off. Of ill thoughts cometh perverse judgment;
of ill deeds springeth lewd* talk. Which four misorders, as they mar
man's life, so destroy they good learning withal.

But behold the goodness of God's providence for learning: all old
authors and sects of philosophy, which were fondest in opinion and

---

[2] A typical list of *bêtes noires* to a Protestant humanist. The Stoics and Epicureans, leading
schools of philosophy in late antiquity, were pre-Christian; the Epicureans were also hedon-
ists (in a philosophical sense), and can thus be lumped with Catholic monks and friars, regularly abused as idle; the Anabaptists were a radical German sect who offended both
Protestants and Catholics.

[3] Echoing Cicero's complaint that whereas the Sophists had taught both philosophy
(*res*) and rhetoric (*verba*), Socrates 'separated the science of wise thinking from that of
elegant speaking, though in reality they are closely linked together', so creating 'the
undoubtedly absurd and unprofitable and reprehensible severance between the tongue and
the brain, leading to our having one set of professors to teach us to think and another to
teach us to speak' (*De or.* 3. 16. 6of.). But Ascham's setting *verba* above *res* defies the accepted
priority.

rudest in utterance, as Stoics and Epicures, first condemned of wise men, and after forgotten of all men, be so consumed by times as they be now not only out of use but also out of memory of man. Which thing I surely think will shortly chance to the whole doctrine, and all the books of fantastical* Anabaptists and friars, and of the beastly libertines and monks.

Again, behold on the other side how God's wisdom hath wrought, that of the Academici and Peripatetici,[4] those that were wisest in judgment of matters and purest in uttering their minds, the first and chiefest that wrote most and best in either tongue (as Plato and Aristotle in Greek, Tully in Latin), be so either wholly or sufficiently left unto us as I never knew yet scholar that gave himself to like and love and follow chiefly those three authors, but he proved both learned, wise, and also an honest man. If he joined withal the true doctrine of God's holy Bible, without the which the other three be but fine edge tools in a fool's or madman's hand.[5]

But to return to imitation again: there be three kinds of it in matters of learning.

The whole doctrine of comedies and tragedies is a perfect imitation, or fair lively painted picture of the life of every degree of man. Of this imitation writeth Plato at large, in *III. de Republica*;[6] but it doth not much belong at this time to our purpose.

The second kind of imitation is to follow, for learning of tongues and sciences, the best authors. Here riseth amongst proud and envious wits* a great controversy, whether one or many are to be followed; and if one, who is that one: Seneca, Cicero, Sallust, or Caesar, and so forth, in Greek and Latin.

The third kind of imitation belongeth to the second; as, when you be determined* whether you will follow one or more, to know perfectly, and which way, to follow that one; in what place, by what mean and order; by what tools and instruments ye shall do it; by what skill and judgment ye shall truly discern whether ye follow rightly or no.

---

[4] The two chief philosophical schools of 4th-cent. Athens and later, those trained in Plato's Academy or in Aristotle's Lyceum (where he taught while walking in a *peripatos* or covered walk).

[5] Perhaps alluding to Cicero's remark on the dangers of teaching rhetoric to immoral people: 'if we bestow fluency of speech on persons devoid of those virtues [integrity, wisdom], we shall not have made orators of them but shall have put weapons into the hands of madmen' (*De or.* 3. 14. 55).

[6] 394b–398b (*ALC*, pp. 61–6). Aristotle's *Poetics* validated *mimēsis* against Plato.

This *imitatio* is *dissimilis materiei similis tractatio*; and also, *similis materiei dissimilis tractatio*:[7] as, Virgil followed Homer, but the argument to the one was Ulysses, to the other, Aeneas. Tully persecuted Antony with the same weapons of eloquence that Demosthenes used before against Philip.

Horace followeth Pindar, but either of them his own argument and person: as the one Hiero king of Sicily, the other Augustus the emperor; and yet both for like respects, that is, for their courageous stoutness in war and just government in peace.

One of the best arguments for right imitation we lack, and that is Menander; whom our Terence (as the matter required), in like argument, in the same persons, with equal eloquence, foot by foot did follow.

Some pieces remain, like broken jewels, whereby men may rightly esteem and justly lament the loss of the whole.

Erasmus,[8] the ornament of learning in our time, doth wish that some man of learning and diligence would take the like pains in Demosthenes and Tully that Macrobius hath done in Homer and Virgil: that is, to write out and join together where the one doth imitate the other. Erasmus's wish is good; but surely it is not good enough. For Macrobius[9] gatherings for the *Aeneis* out of Homer, and Eobanus Hessus'[10] more diligent gatherings for the

---

[7] 'Similar treatment of dissimilar matter'; 'dissimilar treatment of similar matter'.

[8] In his *Epistolae*, no. 1708 (*CWE*, vol. xii); and in the preface to his Demosthenes.

[9] Ambrosius Theodosius Macrobius (fl. *c*. AD 400), in his *Saturnalia*, a symposium in seven books imagined as taking place during the three days of the Roman feast. The participants devote two mornings to the discussion of Virgil, who is praised as the complete poet (1. 24; 5. 1), and whose imitations of Homer are expounded in great detail (5. 2–5. 16), including the evaluation of those points in which the Roman poet excelled the Greek (5. 11), equalled (5. 12), or was inferior to him (5. 13), and where he imitated Homer's faults (5. 14). Macrobius then discusses Virgil's imitation of other Greek (5. 18–19) and of older Latin poets, Ennius, Catullus, and Lucretius (6. 1–3). His intention being 'to show how Virgil profited from his reading of the ancients, and how he gathered from their work the flowers and ornaments with which he embellished his poems', Macrobius recognizes that he might 'be giving ignorant or malicious readers the occasion of accusing this great poet of plagiarism, without recognizing that the fruit of reading is to be able to emulate what one finds good in other writers, and to appropriate for oneself what one most admires in them' (6. 1. 2). The was the practice of the most distinguished Greek and Roman poets, Macrobius asserts, quoting the explicit statement of Lucius Africanus (b. *c*.150 BC), the prolific composer of *comoediae togatae*, that he had freely borrowed material from Greek and Latin writers wherever it suited him. Virgil did the same, and often his borrowings have a greater effect than the original (6. 1. 4–7). See Macrobe, *Les Saturnales*, ed. and tr. H. Bornecque and F. Richard, 2 vols. (Paris, 1937). On the classical conception of *imitatio* see the Introduction, pp. 22–39.

[10] Helius Eobanus Hessus (1488–1540), translator of Theocritus, published a commen-

Bucolics out of Theocritus, as they be not fully taken out of the whole heap, as they should be, but even as though they had not sought for them of purpose but found them scattered here and there by chance in their way; even so, only to point out, and nakedly to join together their sentences, with no further declaring the manner and way how the one doth follow the other, were but a cold help to the increase of learning.

But if a man would take this pain also, when he hath laid two places of Homer and Virgil, or of Demosthenes and Tully together, to teach plainly withal after this sort:

1. Tully retaineth thus much of the matter, these sentences, these words.
2. This and that he leaveth out; which he doth wittily,* to this end and purpose.
3. This he addeth here.
4. This he diminisheth there.
5. This he ordereth thus, with placing that here, not there.
6. This he altereth and changeth, either in property* of words, in form of sentence, in substance of the matter, or in one or other convenient* circumstance of the author's present purpose.

In these few rude English words are wrapped up all the necessary tools and instruments wherewith true imitation is rightly wrought withal in any tongue. Which tools, I openly confess, be not of mine own forging but partly left unto me by the cunningest master, and one of the worthiest gentlemen, that ever England bred, Sir John Cheke, partly borrowed by me out of the shop of the dearest friend I have out of England, Joannes Sturmius.[11] And therefore I am the bolder to borrow of him and here to leave them to other, and namely to my children. Which tools, if it please God that another day they may be able to use rightly, as I do wish and daily pray they may do, I shall be more glad than if I were able to leave them a great quantity of land.

This foresaid order and doctrine of imitation would bring forth more learning and breed up truer judgment than any other exercise

tary on Virgil's *Eclogues* (Hagenau, 1529) in which he demonstrated the Latin poet's debts to the Greek.

[11] Sturmius (1507–89) was rector of the gymnasium (and later, the academy) of Strasbourg, and author of many educational treatises and works on rhetoric, including a 9-volume edition of Cicero (1557) and a dialogue on Cicero's *Partitiones oratoriae* (1539). Ascham corresponded with him for eighteen years.

that can be used; but not for young beginners, because they shall not be able to consider duly thereof. And truly it may be a shame to good students, who having so fair examples to follow as Plato and Tully, do not use so wise ways in following them for the obtaining of wisdom and learning, as rude ignorant artificers do for gaining a small commodity. For surely the meanest painter useth more wit, better art, greater diligence in his shop in following the picture of any mean man's face, than commonly the best students do even in the university for the attaining of learning itself.

Some ignorant, unlearned, and idle student, or some busy looker upon this little poor book, that hath neither will to do good himself nor skill to judge right of others, but can lustily condemn, by pride and ignorance, all painful* diligence and right order in study, will perchance say that I am too precise, too curious* in marking and piddling thus about the imitation of others; and that the old and worthy authors did never busy their heads and wits in following so precisely either the matter what other men wrote, or else the manner how other men wrote. They will say it were a plain slavery, and injury too, to shackle and tie a good wit, and hinder the course of a man's good nature with such bonds of servitude in following others. Except such men think themselves wiser than Cicero[12] for teaching of eloquence, they must be content to turn a new leaf. . . .

Concerning imitation, many learned men have written with much diversity for the matter, and therefore with great contrariety and some stomach* amongst themselves. I have read as many as I could get, diligently; and what I think of every one of them I will freely say my mind. With which freedom I trust good men will bear, because it shall tend to neither spiteful nor harmful controversy.

In Tully it is well touched, shortly taught, not fully declared by Antonius in *II. De oratore*; and afterward in *Oratore ad Brutum*,[13] for the liking and misliking of Isocrates. . . .

Dionysius Halicarnassaeus *Peri mimēseōs*[14] I fear, is lost; which

[12] Ascham now quotes various passages in which Cicero alludes to his own imitations of Aristotle (*Epistulae ad familiares.* 1. 9. 23; *Epistulae ad Atticum* 4. 16) and Plato (*De or.* 1. 7. 28; *Att.* 4. 16).

[13] *De or.* 2. 21. 89–2. 23. 98; *Orat.* 12. 40–2, 51. 172–53. 176.

[14] This work, *De imitatione et oratoria et historica*, which has survived in fragments, was Quintilian's source for *Inst.* 10. 1–2: cf. D. A. Russell, '*De imitatione*', in D. West and T. Woodman (eds.), *Creative Imitation and Latin Literature* (Cambridge, 1979), pp. 1–16.

author, next Aristotle, Plato, and Tully, of all others that write of eloquence, by the judgment of them that be best learned deserveth the next praise and place.

Quintilian writeth of it shortly and coldly for the matter, yet hotly and spitefully enough against the imitation of Tully.[15]

Erasmus,[16] being more occupied in spying other men's faults than declaring his own advice, is mistaken of many, to the great hurt of study, for his authority's sake. For he writeth rightly, rightly understanded, he and Longolius only differing in this: that the one seemeth to give overmuch, the other overlittle, to him whom they both best loved and chiefly allowed* of all other.

Budaeus[17] in his *Commentaries* roughly and obscurely after his kind of writing, and for the matter carried somewhat out of the way in overmuch misliking the imitation of Tully.

Philip Melanchthon,[18] learnedly and truly.

Camerarius,[19] largely, with a learned judgment, but somewhat confusedly and with overrough a style.

Sambucus,[20] largely, with a right judgment, but somewhat a crooked style.

Other have written also, as Cortesius to Politian, and that very well;

[15] *Inst.* 10. 2. 24–6. In fact Quintilian does recommend imitating Cicero, but urges that other models should also be used.
[16] In his *Dialogus cui titulus Ciceronianus: sive de optimo genere dicendi* (Paris, 1528), Erasmus evidently aroused the anger of Ascham by criticizing the excesses of those contemporaries who imitated Cicero too slavishly, including the Belgian humanist Christophe de Longeuil, responsible for a commentary on Cicero's *Rhetoric* (1541) and an edition of the *Letters to Atticus* (1549). On this whole issue see Izora Scott, *Controversies over the Imitation of Cicero in the Renaissance* (New York, 1910; Davis, Calif., 1991), which includes a translation of Erasmus' *Ciceronianus* (pp. 19–130). This dialogue is also available in an excellent annotated translation by Betty I. Knott, *CWE*, vol. xxviii.
[17] Guillaume Budé (1467–1540), the great French humanist, discussed imitation in his *Commentarii linguae Grecae* (Paris, 1529), also criticizing (to Ascham's displeasure) the excessive imitation of Cicero.
[18] Melanchthon (1497–1560), the influential German educationalist, nicknamed the 'Praeceptor Germaniae', discussed imitation in his *Elementorum rhetorices libri duo* (Wittenberg, 1539).
[19] Joachim Camerarius (1500–74), another prolific humanist educationalist, who edited Aesop, Cicero, Macrobius, Plautus, and Terence, discussed imitation in his *Elementa rhetoricae* (Basel, 1551).
[20] Joannes Sambucus (d. 1584), published *De imitatione a Cicerone petenda libri III* (Padua, 1559), often reprinted with a variant title (*De Imitatione Ciceroniana, Dialogi Tres*). He also produced an edition of Plautus, a commentary on Cicero, and an annotated paraphrase of Horace's *Ars poetica*.

Bembus[21] *ad Picum*, a great deal better; but Joannes Sturmius,[22] *De nobilitate literata, et De amissa dicendi ratione*, far best of all, in mine opinion, that ever took this matter in hand. For all the rest declare chiefly this point, whether one, or many, or all, are to be followed: but Sturmius only hath most learnedly declared who is to be followed; what is to be followed; and the best point of all, by what way and order true imitation is rightly to be exercised. And although Sturmius herein doth far pass all other, yet hath he not so fully and perfectly done it as I do wish he had, and as I know he could. For though he hath done it perfectly for precept, yet hath he not done it perfectly enough for example. Which he did, neither for lack of skill nor by negligence, but of purpose, contented with one or two examples; because he was minded in those two books to write of it both shortly, and also had to touch other matters.

Bartholomaeus Riccius[23] Ferrariensis also hath written learnedly, diligently, and very largely of this matter. . . . He writeth the better in mine opinion, because his whole doctrine, judgment, and order seemeth to be borrowed out of Joannes Sturmius's books. He addeth also examples, the best kind of teaching; wherein he doth well but not well enough; indeed he committeth no fault, but yet deserveth small praise. He is content with the mean, and followeth not the best; as a man that would feed upon acorns, when he may eat as good cheap* the finest wheat bread.

He teacheth, for example, where, and how, two or three Italian poets do follow Virgil; and how Virgil himself, in the story of Dido, doth wholly imitate Catullus[24] in the like matter of Ariadne. Wherein I like better his diligence and order of teaching than his judgment in choice of examples for imitation. But if he had done thus: if he had declared where, and how, how oft, and how many ways, Virgil doth follow

---

[21] Paolo Cortesi (1465–1510), Bishop of Urbino, a staunch Ciceronian, whose letter to Angelo Poliziano (1454–94), of which Ascham approves, was heavily criticized in Erasmus' *Ciceronianus*. The letter by the even more dedicated Ciceronian, Pietro Bembo (1470–1547), *De imitatione sermonis*, with the reply by Giovanni Francesco Pico della Mirandola (1470–1533), formed an equally famous controversy: cf. Martin McLaughlin, *Literary Imitation in the Italian Renaissance* (Oxford, 1995), pp. 249–78—the best modern account of *imitatio*.

[22] *De amissa dicendi ratione et quomodo ea recuperanda sit* (Strasbourg, 1538; enlarged, 1543); *Nobilitas literata ad Werteros fratres* (Strasbourg, 1549), English translation by T. Browne as *A ritch storehouse or treasurie . . . called Nobilitas literata* (London, 1570).

[23] Bartolomeo Ricci, *De imitatione libri tres* (Venice, 1545). He also compiled a Latin lexicon, *Apparatus Latinae Locutionis* (1533).

[24] *Aen.* 4. 1 ff.; Catullus 64. 50 ff.

Homer—as for example, the coming of Ulysses to Alcinoüs and Calypso, with the coming of Aeneas[25] to Carthage and Dido; likewise the games,[26] running, wrestling, and shooting that Achilles maketh in Homer, with the selfsame games that Aeneas maketh in Virgil; the harness of Achilles with the harness[27] of Aeneas, and the manner of making of them both by Vulcan; the notable combat[28] betwixt Achilles and Hector, with as notable a combat betwixt Aeneas and Turnus; the going down to hell[29] of Ulysses in Homer, with the going down to hell of Aeneas in Virgil; and other places infinite more, as similitudes, narrations, messages, descriptions of persons, places, battles, tempests, shipwrecks, and common places for divers purposes, which be as precisely taken out of Homer as ever did painter in London follow the picture of any fair personage. And when these places had been gathered together by this way of diligence, then to have conferred them together by this order of teaching, as diligently to mark what is kept and used in either author, in words, in sentences, in matter; what is added; what is left out; what ordered otherwise, either *praeponendo, interponendo*, or *postponendo*;[30] and what is altered for any respect, in word, phrase, sentence, figure, reason, argument, or by any way of circumstance. If Riccius had done this, he had not only been well liked for his diligence in teaching, but also justly commended for his right judgment in right choice of examples for the best imitation. . . .

Therefore, in perusing thus so many divers books for imitation, it came into my head that a very profitable book might be made *De imitatione*, after another sort than ever yet was attempted of that matter, containing a certain few fit precepts, unto the which should be gathered and applied plenty of examples out of the choicest authors of both the tongues. . . .

A book thus wholly filled with examples of imitation, first out of Tully, compared with Plato, Xenophon, Isocrates, Demosthenes, and Aristotle; then out of Virgil and Horace, with Homer and Pindar; next out of Seneca, with Sophocles and Euripides: lastly out of Livy, with Thucydides, Polybius, and Halicarnassaeus, gathered with good diligence and compared with right order, as I have expressed before, were

---

[25] But in book 5 of the *Odyssey* the hero is already at Calypso's Grotto. Ascham probably meant Odysseus' welcome by Alcinoüs and Arete, *Od.* 7. 81 ff.: cf. *Aen.* 1. 441 ff.

[26] *Il.* 23. 257 ff.; *Aen.* 5. 42 ff.   [27] *Il.* 18. 369 ff.; *Aen.* 8. 370 ff.

[28] *Il.* 22. 131 ff.; *Aen.* 12. 681 ff.   [29] *Od.* 11. 1 ff.; *Aen.* 6. 236 ff.

[30] 'By placing before, between, or after'.

another manner of work for all kind of learning, and namely for eloquence than be those cold gatherings of Macrobius, Hessus, Perion-
ius, Stephanus, and Victorius;[31] which may be used (as I said before)
in this case, as porters and carriers, deserving like praise as such men
do wages; but only Sturmius is he out of whom the true survey and
whole workmanship is specially to be learned.

I trust, this my writing shall give some good student occasion to
take some piece in hand of this work of imitation. . . .

Now to return to that question, whether one, a few, many, or all[32] are
to be followed? My answer shall be short: all, for him that is desirous
to know all; yea, the worst of all, as questionists,* and all the barbarous
nation of schoolmen,* help for one or other consideration. But in
every separate kind of learning and study by itself ye must follow
choicely a few, and chiefly some one, and that namely in our school of
eloquence, either for pen or talk. And as in portraiture and painting
wise men choose not that workman that can only make a fair hand or
a well-fashioned leg, but such a one as can furnish up fully all the features of the whole body of a man, woman, and child; and withal is
able too, by good skill, to give to every one of these three in their
proper kind the right form, the true figure, the natural colour that is
fit and due to the dignity of a man, to the beauty of a woman, to the
sweetness of a young babe: even likewise do we seek such one in our
school to follow, who is able always in all matters to teach plainly, to
delight pleasantly, and to carry away by force of wise talk[33] all that shall
hear or read him; and is so excellent indeed as wit is able, or wish can
hope, to attain unto; and this not only to serve in the Latin or Greek
tongue but also in our own English language. But yet, because the
providence of God hath left unto us in no other tongue, save only in
the Greek and Latin tongue, the true precepts and perfect examples
of eloquence; therefore must we seek in the authors only of those two

---

[31] Joachim Perion, *Ex Platonis Timaeo particula, Cicero de universitate libro respondens*
(Paris, 1540); Henri Estienne (Stephanus), *Ciceronianum Lexicon Graecolatinum* (Paris,
1557); Pietro Vettori, the elder (1499–1585), *Variarum Lectionum libri XXV* (Florence,
1553): by 1582 expanded to thirty-eight books.
[32] This was a stock issue in the *imitatio* debates. For the (sensible) classical position, that
imitation should not be restricted to one model, see Cicero, *De or.* 2. 22. 90 ff.; Seneca, *Ep.*
84; Quintilian, *Inst.* 10. 2. 1–28. Fanatical Renaissance Ciceronians, however, limited
approved Latin style to only those words used by Cicero.
[33] Ascham alludes to the orator's duties, the three *officia oratoris* first formulated by
Cicero: *docere, delectare, movere.*

tongues the true pattern of eloquence, if in any other mother tongue we look to attain either to perfect utterance of it ourselves or skilful judgment of it in others.

And now to know what author doth meddle only with some one piece and member of eloquence, and who doth perfectly make up the whole body, I will declare, as I can call to remembrance the goodly talk that I have had oftentimes of the true difference of authors, with that gentleman of worthy memory, my dearest friend and teacher of all the little poor learning I have, Sir John Cheke.

The true difference of authors is best known *per diversa genera dicendi*[34] that every one used; and therefore here I will divide *genus dicendi*, not into these three, *tenue, mediocre, et grande*,[35] but as the matter of every author requireth; as,

In genus	*Poeticum,*
	Historicum,
	Philosophicum,
	Oratorium.

These differ one from another in choice of words, in framing of sentences, in handling of arguments, and use of right form, figure, and number, proper and fit for every matter; and every one of these is diverse also in itself, as the first,

Poeticum, in	*Comicum,*
	Tragicum,
	Epicum,
	Melicum.[36]

And here, whosoever hath been diligent to read advisedly over Terence, Seneca, Virgil, Horace, or else Aristophanes, Sophocles, Homer, and Pindar, and shall diligently mark the difference they use in propriety of words, in form of sentence, in handling of their matter, he shall easily perceive what is fit, and decorum in every one, to the true use of perfect imitation.

When Mr. Watson,[37] in St John's College at Cambridge, wrote his excellent tragedy of *Absalom*, Mr. Cheke, he and I, for that part of

---

[34] 'Through the different kinds of discourse'.

[35] Ascham rejects the classification of genres according to the traditional three levels of style, high, medium, and low (cf. *IDR*, pp. 80–2) for one based on subject-matter; although he continues to apply the concept of decorum, the differences in style—'choice of words' (*electio verborum*), 'framing of sentences' (*compositio*), and so on—appropriate to each genre.

[36] Lyric poetry.

[37] Thomas Watson (1513–84), Master of St John's and Bishop of Lincoln. For a

true imitation, had many pleasant talks together, in comparing the precepts of Aristotle and Horace *de Arte Poetica* with the examples of Euripides, Sophocles, and Seneca. Few men in writing of tragedies in our days have shot at this mark. Some in England, more in France, Germany, and Italy also have written tragedies in our time; of the which not one, I am sure, is able to abide the true touch of Aristotle's precepts and Euripides' examples save only two, that ever I saw, Mr. Watson's *Absalom*, and Georgius Buchananus' *Iephthes*.[38] One man[39] in Cambridge, well liked of many, but best liked of himself, was many times bold and busy to bring matters upon stages which he called tragedies. In one, whereby he looked to win his spurs, and whereat many ignorant fellows fast clapped their hands, he began the *protasis* with *trochaiis octonariis*, which kind of verse, as it is but seldom and rare in tragedies, so is it never used save only *in epitasi*[40] when the tragedy is highest and hottest and full of greatest troubles. I remember full well what Master Watson merely* said unto me of his blindness and boldness in that behalf, although otherwise there passed much friendship between them. Master Watson had another manner care of perfection, with fear and reverence of the judgment of the best learned; who to this day would never suffer yet his *Absalom* to go abroad, and that only because *in locis paribus*[41] *anapaestus* is twice or thrice used instead of *iambus*. A small fault, and such one as perchance would never be marked, no, neither in Italy nor France. This I write not so much to note the first or praise the last as to leave in memory of writing for good example to posterity what perfection in my time was most diligently sought for in like manner, in all kind of learning, in that most worthy College of St John's in Cambridge.

Historicum, in
          Diaria,
          Annales,
          Commentarios,
          Justam Historiam.

For what propriety in words, simplicity in sentences, plainness and

commented edition of his play *Absalom* (*c*.1535) see J. H. Smith, *A Humanist's "Trew Imitation": Thomas Watson's Absalom* (Urbana, Ill., 1964).

[38] The *Tragoediae Iephthes* of George Buchanan (1506–81), written *c*.1554, was published in 1566.

[39] Possibly John Christopherson, afterwards Bishop of Chichester.

[40] That is, in the play's opening part he used a verse consisting of four double trochees, which was supposed to be used in the later part (*epitasis*), where the plot thickens, and the climax approaches.

[41] 'In similar places'.

light, is comely for these kinds, Caesar and Livy, for the two last, are perfect examples of imitation. And for the two first, the old patterns be lost; and as for some that be present, and of late time, they be fitter to be read once for some pleasure, than oft to be perused for any good imitation of them.

Philosophicum, in   Sermonem: as *Officia Ciceronis, et Ethica Aristotelis.*
                     Contentionem:[42] as the Dialogues of Plato, Xenophon, and Cicero.

Of which kind of learning and right imitation thereof Carolus Sigonius[43] hath written of late both learnedly and eloquently, but best of all, my friend Joannes Sturmius in his commentaries upon *Gorgias*[44] *Platonis*; which book I have in writing, and is not yet set out in print.

Oratorium, in   *Humile,*
                      Mediocre,
                      Sublime.

Examples of these three in the Greek tongue be plentiful and perfect, as Lysias, Isocrates, and Demosthenes; and all three in only Demosthenes, in divers orations, as *Contra Olympiodorum*, *In Leptinem*, and *Pro Ctesiphonte*. And true it is, that Hermogenes[45] writeth of Demosthenes, 'That all forms of eloquence be perfect* in him.' In Cicero's Orations *Medium et Sublime* be most excellently handled; but *Humile*, in his Orations, is seldom seen. Yet, nevertheless, in other books, as in some part of his *Offices*, and specially *In partitionibus*, he is comparable *in hoc humili et disciplinabili genere*[46] even with the best that ever wrote in Greek. But of Cicero more fully in fitter place.

And thus the true difference of styles in every author, and every kind of learning, may easily be known by this division . . . Which I thought in this place to touch only, not to prosecute at large; because,

[42] Ascham divides philosophy into monological 'discourse', as in the two key works of classical ethics, Cicero's *De officiis* ('Of duties') and Aristotle's *Nicomachean Ethics*; and 'debate', as in the dialogues of Plato, Xenophon (*The Apology of Socrates, Memorabilia*, and *Symposium*), and Cicero.

[43] Carlo Sigonio (1524–84), author of *De dialogo liber* (Padua, 1561), and other learned works, who ruined his scholarly reputation by publishing a forgery which he claimed as genuine Cicero.

[44] In 1547 Ascham procured notes of Sturmius' lectures on the *Gorgias*, which were never printed.

[45] *Peri ideōn* 215–16 (*ALC*, pp. 562–3). Sturmius published at least six works of commentary on Hermogenes.

[46] In *De partitione oratoria* Cicero is comparable 'in this plain and instructional style'.

God willing, in the Latin tongue I will fully handle it in my book *De imitatione*.[47]

Now to touch more particularly which of those authors that be now most commonly in men's hands will soon afford you some piece of eloquence, and what manner a piece of eloquence; and what is to be liked and followed, and what to be misliked and eschewed in them; and how some again will furnish you fully withal, rightly and wisely considered, somewhat I will write, as I have heard Sir John Cheke many times say.

The Latin tongue, concerning any part of pureness of it, from the spring to the decay of the same, did not endure much longer than is the life of a well-aged man; scarce one hundred years, from the time of the last Scipio Africanus and Laelius to the empire of Augustus. And it is notable that Velleius Paterculus[48] writeth of Tully, 'how that the perfection of eloquence did so remain only in him and in his time, as before him were few which might much delight a man, or after him any worthy admiration, but such as Tully might have seen, and such as might have seen Tully.' And good cause why: for no perfection is durable. Increase hath a time, and decay likewise, but all perfect ripeness remaineth but a moment; as is plainly seen in fruits, plums, and cherries; but more sensibly* in flowers, as roses and such like; and yet as truly in all greater matters. For what naturally can go no higher must naturally yield and stoop again.

Of this short time of any pureness of the Latin tongue, for the first forty years of it, and all the time before, we have no piece of learning left save Plautus and Terence, with a little rude unperfect pamphlet of the elder Cato. And as for Plautus, except the schoolmaster be able to make wise and wary choice, first in propriety of words, then in framing of phrases and sentences, and chiefly in choice of honesty of matter, your scholar were better to play than learn all that is in him. But surely, if judgment for the tongue and direction for the manners be wisely joined with the diligent reading of Plautus, then truly Plautus, for that pureness of the Latin tongue in Rome, when Rome did most flourish in well doing and so thereby in well speaking[49] also, is such a plentiful storehouse for common eloquence in mean matters

[47] Ascham never wrote such a treatise, but he discussed *imitatio* in a long Latin epistle to Sturmius (*c*. Dec. 1564), printed in J. A. Giles, *The Whole Works of Roger Ascham*, 3 vols. in 4 (London, 1864–5), ii. 174–91, and quoted in summary, *ECE* i. 347–9.

[48] *Historiae Romanae libri duo* 1. 17. 3.

[49] Ascham again correlates *res* and *verba*: he believes that 'well doing', *bene vivere*, automatically leads to 'well speaking', *bene dicere*.

and all private men's affairs as the Latin tongue, for that respect, hath not the like again. When I remember the worthy time of Rome wherein Plautus did live, I must needs honour the talk of that time, which we see Plautus doth use.

Terence is also a storehouse of the same tongue for another time, following soon after; and although he be not so full and plentiful as Plautus is, for multitude of matters and diversity of words; yet his words be chosen so purely, placed so orderly, and all his stuff so neatly packed up and wittily compassed* in every place, as by all wise men's judgment, he is counted the cunninger* workman, and to have his shop, for the room that is in it, more finely appointed and trimlier ordered than Plautus's is.

Three things chiefly, both in Plautus and Terence, are to be specially considered: the matter,* the utterance, the words, the metre. The matter in both is altogether within the compass of the meanest men's manners, and doth not stretch to any thing of any great weight at all, but standeth chiefly in uttering the thoughts and conditions of hard fathers, foolish mothers, unthrifty young men, crafty servants, subtle bawds, and wily harlots; and so is much spent in finding out fine fetches* and packing up pelting* matters, such as in London commonly come to the hearing of the masters of Bridewell.[50] Here is base stuff for that scholar that should become hereafter either a good minister in religion, or a civil gentleman in service of his prince and country (except the preacher do know such matters to confute them), when ignorance surely in all such things were better for a civil gentleman than knowledge. And thus for matter both Plautus and Terence be like mean* painters, that work by halves, and be cunning only in making the worst part of the picture; as if one were skilful in painting the body of a naked person from the navel downward, but nothing else.

For word and speech Plautus is more plentiful, and Terence more pure and proper. And for one respect Terence is to be embraced above all that ever wrote in this kind of argument, because it is well known by good record of learning, and that by Cicero's own witness,[51] that

---

[50] Bridewell, near Blackfriars Bridge, one of Henry VIII's palaces: but Edward VI 'Gave this . . . Palace in old Times, | For a chastising House of vagrant Crimes', with a whipping-post where floggings were administered publicly.

[51] Cicero (*Att.* 7. 3. 10) merely says that 'they used to ascribe his plays to Laelius'. Similarly Quintilian (*Inst.* 10. 1. 99) records a tradition that 'they used to credit' the plays to Scipio Africanus.

some comedies bearing Terence's name were written by worthy Scipio and wise Laelius, and namely *Heautontimorumenos* and *Adelphi*. And therefore, as oft as I read those comedies so oft doth sound in mine ear the pure fine talk of Rome, which was used by the flower of the worthiest nobility that ever Rome bred. Let the wisest man, and best learned that liveth read advisedly over the first scene of *Heautontimorumenos* and the first scene of *Adelphi*, and let him considerately judge whether it is the talk of a servile stranger born, or rather even that mild eloquent wise speech which Cicero in *Brutus*[52] doth so lively express in Laelius. And yet nevertheless, in all this good propriety of words and pureness of phrases which be in Terence, you must not follow him always in placing of them; because for the metre sake some words in him sometime be driven awry, which require a straighter placing in plain prose, if you will form, as I would ye should do, your speech and writing to that excellent perfectness which was only in Tully, or only in Tully's time.

The metre and verse of Plautus and Terence be very mean, and not to be followed; which is not their reproach, but the fault of the time wherein they wrote, when no kind of poetry in the Latin tongue was brought to perfection, as doth well appear in the fragments of Ennius, Caecilius, and others, and evidently in Plautus and Terence, if these in Latin be compared with right skill with Homer, Euripides, Aristophanes, and others in Greek of like sort. Cicero[53] himself doth complain of this imperfectness, but more plainly Quintilian,[54] saying *In comedia maxime claudicamus, et Vix levem consequimur umbram*: and most earnestly of all, Horace[55] *in Arte Poetica*. Which he doth namely *propter carmen Iambicum*, and referreth all good students herein to the imitation of the Greek tongue, saying,

> *vos exemplaria Graeca*
> *nocturna versate manu, versate diurna.*

This matter maketh me gladly remember my sweet time spent at Cambridge, and the pleasant talk which I had oft with Mr. Cheke and Mr. Watson of this fault, not only in the old Latin poets, but also in our new English rhymers at this day. They wished, as Virgil and Horace were not wedded to follow the faults of former fathers (a

---

[52] *Brut.* 20. 83–22. 88.
[53] *Brut.* 18. 71–19. 74.
[54] *Inst.* 10. 1. 99 f.: 'In comedy we limp badly . . . we scarcely attain a faint shadow' of Greek comedy.
[55] *Ars P.* 268–9: 'Study Greek models night and day' (*ALC*, p. 286).

shrewd* marriage in greater matters) but by right imitation of the perfect Grecians had brought poetry to perfectness also in the Latin tongue, that we Englishmen likewise would acknowledge and understand rightfully our rude beggarly rhyming, brought first into Italy by Goths and Huns,[56] when all good verses, and all good learning too were destroyed by them; and after carried into France and Germany, and at last received into England by men of excellent wit indeed but of small learning and less judgment in that behalf.

But now, when men know the difference and have the examples both of the best and of the worst, surely to follow rather the Goths in rhyming than the Greeks in true versifying were even to eat acorns with swine, when we may freely eat wheat bread amongst men. Indeed Chaucer, Thomas Norton[57] of Bristol, my Lord of Surrey, Master Wyatt, Thomas Phaer,[58] and other gentlemen in translating Ovid, Palingenius,[59] and Seneca, have gone as far to their great praise as the copy they followed could carry them. But if such good wits and forward diligence had been directed to follow the best examples, and not have been carried by time and custom to content themselves with that barbarous and rude rhyming, amongst their other worthy praises which they have justly deserved this had not been the least, to be counted amongst men of learning and skill, more like unto the Grecians than unto the Gothians in handling of their verse.

Indeed our English tongue, having in use chiefly words of one syllable, which commonly be long, doth not well receive the nature of *carmen heroicum*.[60] Because *Dactylus*, the aptest foot for that verse, containing one long and two short, is seldom therefore found in English, and doth also rather stumble than stand upon monosyllables. Quintilian,[61] in his learned chapter *De compositione*, giveth this lesson *de monosyllabis* before me, and in the same place doth justly inveigh against all rhyming; that if there be any who be angry with me for misliking of rhyming they may be angry for company too with Quintilian also,

[56] Ascham's disapproval of rhyme as 'Gothian' or Gothic (medieval barbarians) is typical of orthodox classicists. See also Campion, p. 428, and Daniel, p. 441.

[57] This Norton (fl. 1477), who wrote *The Ordinal of Alchemy* and other alchemical tracts in verse, is not to be confused with Sackville's collaborator.

[58] On Phaer (1510?–60), translator of Virgil, see Harvey, p. 170 n. 37, and Puttenham, p. 211.

[59] Marcellus Palingenius Stellatus, or Pietro Angelo Manzolli (1480?–1550), whose didactic astrological poem, *Zodiacus Vitae* (Venice 1531), was immensely popular in the 16th cent. Barnaby Googe's translation of it appeared in 1560–5.

[60] Latin epics were written in dactylic metre.

[61] *Inst.* 9. 4. 42: but only objecting to the overuse of rhyme (*similiter cadens*) in prose, not in poetry (an anachronistic reference).

for the same thing. And yet Quintilian had not so just cause to mislike
of it then, as men have at this day.

And although *carmen hexametrum* doth rather trot and hobble than
run smoothly in our English tongue, yet I am sure our English tongue
will receive *carmen iambicum*[62] as naturally as either Greek or Latin.
But for ignorance men cannot like, and for idleness men will not labour
to come to any perfectness at all. For as the worthy poets in Athens
and Rome were more careful to satisfy the judgment of one learned
than rash in pleasing the humour of a rude multitude, even so, if men
in England now had the like reverend regard to learning, skill, and
judgment, and durst not presume to write except they came with the
like learning, and also did use like diligence in searching out not only
just measure in every metre (as every ignorant person may easily do)
but also true quantity in every foot and syllable (as only the learned
shall be able to do, and as the Greeks and Romans were wont to do),
surely then rash ignorant heads, which now can easily reckon up fourteen syllables and easily stumble on every rhyme, either durst not, for
lack of such learning, or else would not, in avoiding such labour, be
so busy as every where they be, and shops in London should not be
so full of lewd and rude rhymes as commonly they are. But now the
ripest of tongue be readiest to write. And many daily in setting out
books and ballads make great show of blossoms and buds, in whom is
neither root of learning nor fruit of wisdom at all.

Some, that make Chaucer in English, and Petrarch in Italian, their
gods in verses, and yet be not able to make true difference what is a
fault and what is a just praise in those two worthy wits, will much
mislike this my writing. But such men be even like followers of
Chaucer and Petrarch, as one here in England did follow Sir Thomas
More; who, being most unlike unto him in wit and learning, nevertheless in wearing his gown awry upon the one shoulder, as Sir
Thomas More was wont to do, would needs be counted like unto him.

This misliking of rhyming beginneth not now of any new-fangle
singularity,* but hath been long misliked of many, and that of men of
greatest learning and deepest judgment. And such that defend it do so
either for lack of knowledge what is best, or else of very envy that any
should perform that in learning whereunto they (as I said before) either
for ignorance cannot, or for idleness will not labour to attain unto.

[62] Hexameter verse (the norm for classical epic) has never really been domesticated in
English, although several 16th-cent. poets attempted it; iambic, however, was early found
to be adaptable to the English accentual system.

And you that praise this rhyming because you neither have reason why to like it, nor can show learning to defend it, yet I will help you with the authority of the oldest and learnedest time. In Greece, when poetry was even at the highest pitch of perfectness, one Simmias Rhodius,[63] of a certain singularity, wrote a book in rhyming Greek verses, naming it '*Oon*', containing the fable how Jupiter in likeness of a swan begat that egg upon Leda, whereof came Castor, Pollux, and fair Helena. This book was so liked that it had few to read it but none to follow it, but was presently condemned, and soon after both author and book so forgotten by men and consumed by time as scarce the name of either is kept in memory of learning. And the like folly was never followed of any, many hundred years after, until the Huns and Goths, and other barbarous nations of ignorance and rude singularity did revive the same folly again.

The noble lord Thomas earl of Surrey, first of all Englishmen in translating the fourth book of Virgil, and Gonsalvo Perez,[64] that excellent learned man and secretary to king Philip of Spain, in translating the Ulysses of Homer out of Greek into Spanish, have both by good judgment avoided the fault of rhyming; yet neither of them hath fully hit perfect and true versifying. Indeed, they observe just number and even feet—but here is the fault, that their feet be feet without joints; that is to say, not distinct by true quantity of syllables; and so such feet be but numb feet, and be even as unfit for a verse to turn and run roundly withal as feet of brass or wood be unwieldly to go well withal. And as a foot of wood is a plain show of a manifest maim, even so feet in our English versifying without quantity and joints be sure signs that the verse is either born deformed, unnatural, or lame; and so very unseemly to look upon, except to men that be goggle-eyed themselves.

The spying of this fault now is not the curiosity* of English eyes but even the good judgment also of the best that write in these days in Italy; and namely of that worthy Senese Felice Figliucci,[65] who, writing upon Aristotle's *Ethics* so excellently in Italian as never did yet

---

[63] Simmias' poem was included in *The Greek Anthology* (15. 27): see Anthony Holden's excellent translation in *Greek Pastoral Poetry. Theocritus, Bion, Moschus. The Pattern Poems* (Penguin, Harmondsworth, 1974), p. 200. However, neither in rhyme nor about Leda, it is a *technopaegnion* or 'pattern poem', visually representing its subject-matter.

[64] Surrey's *Certaine Books of Virgil's Aeneis* appeared in 1557; Perez had earlier published *La Odisea de Homero* (Antwerp, 1553).

[65] Figliucci (from Siena), in his *De la filosofia morale libri dieci. Sopra li dieci dell'Ethica d'Aristotile* (Rome, 1551), included several translations into unrhymed Italian metres, with a commentary claiming authenticity for this practice.

any one in mine opinion either in Greek or Latin, amongst other things doth most earnestly inveigh against the rude rhyming of verses in that tongue. And whensoever he expresseth Aristotle's precepts with any example out of Homer or Euripides, he translateth them not after the rhymes of Petrarch but into such kind of perfect* verse, with like feet and quantity of syllables as he found them before in the Greek tongue, exhorting earnestly all the Italian nation to leave off their rude barbarousness in rhyming, and follow diligently the excellent Greek and Latin examples in true versifying.

And you, that be able to understand no more than ye find in the Italian tongue, and never went further than the school of Petrarch and Ariosto abroad, or else of Chaucer at home; though you have pleasure to wander blindly still in your foul wrong way, envy not others that seek, as wise men have done before them, the fairest and rightest way. Or else, beside the just reproach of malice, wise men shall truly judge that you do so, as I have said and say yet again unto you, because either for idleness you will not, or for ignorance ye cannot come by no better yourself.

And therefore, even as Virgil and Horace deserve most worthy praise, that they spying the unperfectness in Ennius and Plautus, by true imitation of Homer and Euripides brought poetry to the same perfectness in Latin as it was in Greek; even so those that by the same way would benefit their tongue and country deserve rather thanks than dispraise in that behalf.

And I rejoice that even poor England prevented* Italy, first, in spying out, then, in seeking to amend, this fault in learning.

And here for my pleasure I purpose a little, by the way, to play and sport with my master Tully, from whom commonly I am never wont to dissent. He himself, for this point of learning, in his verses doth halt* a little, by his leave. He could not deny it if he were alive, nor those defend him now that love him best. This fault I lay to his charge because once it pleased him, though somewhat merrily, yet overuncourteously, to rail upon poor England, objecting both extreme beggary and mere barbarousness unto it, writing thus unto his friend Atticus: 'There is not one scruple of silver in that whole isle, or anyone that knoweth either learning or letter.'[66]

But now, Master Cicero, blessed be God and his son Jesu Christ whom you never knew, except it were as it pleased him to lighten you

[66] *Att.* 4. 27.

by some shadow, as covertly in one place ye confess, saying, *Veritatis tantum umbram confectamur*,[67] as your master Plato did before you; blessed be God, I say, that sixteen hundred year after you were dead and gone it may truly be said that for silver there is more comely plate in one city of England than is in four of the proudest cities in all Italy, and take Rome for one of them. And for learning, beside the knowledge of all learned tongues and liberal sciences, even your own books, Cicero, be as well read, and your excellent eloquence is as well liked and loved and as truly followed in England at this day, as it is now, or ever was since your own time, in any place of Italy, either at Arpinum, where ye were born, or else at Rome, where ye were brought up. And a little to brag with you, Cicero, where you yourself, by your leave, halted in some point of learning in your own tongue, many in England at this day go straight up, both in true skill and right doing therein.

This I write, not to reprehend Tully, whom above all other I like and love best, but to excuse Terence because in his time, and a good while after, poetry was never perfected in Latin until by true imitation of the Grecians it was at length brought to perfection; and also thereby to exhort the goodly wits of England which, apt by nature, and willing by desire, give themselves to poetry, that they, rightly understanding the barbarous bringing-in of rhymes, would labour, as Virgil and Horace did in Latin, to make perfect also this point of learning in our English tongue. . . .

---

[67] *Off.* 3. 17. 69: 'We have obtained only a shadow of the truth'. However, Cicero was referring not to Christ (!) but to mankind's failure to find the 'image of true law and genuine Justice'. For Plato's image of the cave cf. *Resp.* 7. 515c ff.

7

George Gascoigne,
A primer of English poetry (1575)

GEORGE GASCOIGNE (1542–77), poet and soldier (his motto was *Tam Marti quam Mercurio*), was probably educated at Trinity College Cambridge, and at Gray's Inn (he was elected 'ancient' *c.*1557). He was MP for Bedford, 1557–9, and for Midhurst, 1572. In 1572 he went to Holland to avoid his creditors, fighting as a mercenary soldier, 1572–5, and being captured by the Spaniards. In 1575 he published his *Posies*, a collection of works including *Jocasta*, the second earliest English tragedy in blank verse. His numerous other works include a 'tragicall comedie', *The Glasse of Government* (1575), *The Adventures of Master F. J.* (first version in a *Hundred Sundry Flowers*, 1573; second version in *Posies*), *The Steele Glas* (1576), and the *Whole Woorkes* (1587). See J. W. Cunliffe (ed.), *The Posies* (Cambridge, 1907) and *The Glasse of Government* and other works (Cambridge, 1910).

TEXT. *Certayne notes of Instruction concerning the making of verse or ryme in English*, in *The Posies of George Gascoigne, Esquire, corrected, perfected, and augmented by the author* (1575). This is the earliest literary critical essay in English. In annotating it I have benefited from G. G. Smith, who reproduces (*ECE* i. 358–62) some manuscript notes from the Bodleian copy of *Posies* in the hands of Gabriel Harvey and another, unidentified reader.

The first and most necessary point that ever I found meet to be considered in making of a delectable poem is this, to ground it upon some fine invention.[1] For it is not enough to roll in pleasant words, nor yet to thunder in 'Rym, Ram, Ruff' by letter (quoth my master Chaucer),[2] nor yet to abound in apt vocables or epithets, unless the invention have

---

[1] The first stage in composition, according to rhetorical theory, was *inventio*, collecting material suitable to the proposed subject, either of your own notions or from others' work. Smith cites Ronsard, *Abrégé de l'art poétique françois* (1565): 'Tu auras en premier lieu les conceptions hautes, grandes, belles, et non traînantes à terre. Car le principal poinct est l'invention, laquelle vient tant de la bonne nature, que par la leçon des bons et anciens autheurs'.

[2] Prologue to *The Parson's Tale*, 42 f.: 'But trusteth wel, I am a Southern man, | I kan not geste "rum, ram, ruf"', by lettre': an apology for not attempting to write in alliterative verse, which in Chaucer's time was mainly written in the Northern and West Midland dialects. The nonsense-words 'rum-ram-ruf' parody the consonantal repetition so marked in alliterative verse.

in it also *aliquid salis*.[3] By this *aliquid salis* I mean some good and fine device, showing the quick capacity* of a writer: and where I say some 'good and fine invention' I mean that I would have it both fine and good. For many inventions are so superfine that they are *vix** good. And, again, many inventions are good, and yet not finely handled. And for a general forewarning: what theme soever you do take in hand, if you do handle it but *tanquam in oratione perpetua*,[4] and never study for some depth of device in the invention, and some figures also in the handling thereof, it will appear to the skilful reader but a tale of a tub.[5] To deliver unto you general examples it were almost impossible, since the occasions of inventions are (as it were) infinite; nevertheless, take in worth mine opinion, and perceive my further meaning in these few points.

If I should undertake to write in praise of a gentlewoman, I would neither praise her crystal eye, nor her cherry lip, etc. For these things are *trita et obvia*.[6] But I would either find some supernatural cause whereby my pen might walk in the superlative degree, or else I would undertake to answer for any imperfection that she hath, and thereupon raise the praise of her commendation. Likewise, if I should disclose my pretence in love, I would either make a strange discourse of some intolerable passion, or find occasion to plead by the example of some history, or discover my disquiet in shadows *per allegoriam*,[7] or use the covertest mean that I could to avoid the uncomely customs of common writers. Thus much I adventure to deliver unto you upon the rule of invention, which of all other rules is most to be marked, and hardest to be prescribed in certain and infallible rules; nevertheless, to conclude therein, I would have you stand most upon the excellency of your invention, and stick not to study deeply for some fine device. For, that being found, pleasant words will follow well enough and fast enough.[8]

2. Your invention being once devised, take heed that neither

---

[3] 'A pinch of salt'. In the elaborate narrative framework surrounding his *Adventures of Master F. J.* Gascoigne pretends to retain that work from a friend's collection of 'divers discourses and verses', which were mostly 'barreyne; but that (in my judgement) had in it *Aliquid salis*': *Posies*, ed. Cunliffe, pp. 490–1.

[4] 'As if in continuous prose': merely reproducing the given outline, without deepening the invention or using appropriate rhetorical figures.

[5] Some commonplace matter.   [6] 'Trite and obvious'.

[7] 'Revealing my feelings indirectly, by using allegory'.

[8] Rephrasing the ancient rhetorical principle, attributed to Cato the Elder, that if the subject-matter (or *res*) has been properly put together, the words will follow naturally: 'Rem tene, verba sequentur' (C. Julius Victor, *Ars rhetorica* 1).

pleasure of rhyme nor variety of device do carry you from it: for as to use obscure and dark phrases in a pleasant sonnet is nothing delectable, so to intermingle merry jests in a serious matter is an *indecorum*.

3. I will next advise you that you hold the just measure wherewith you begin your verse.[9] I will not deny but this may seem a preposterous* order; but, because I covet rather to satisfy you particularly than to undertake a general tradition,* I will not so much stand upon the manner as the matter[10] of my precepts. I say then, remember to hold the same measure wherewith you begin, whether it be in a verse of six syllables, eight, ten, twelve, etc.; and though this precept might seem ridiculous unto you, since every young scholar can conceive that he ought to continue in the same measure wherewith he beginneth, yet do I see and read many men's poems nowadays, which beginning with the measure of twelve in the first line, and fourteen in the second (which is the common kind of verse), they will yet (by that time they have passed over a few verses) fall into fourteen and fourteen, *et sic de similibus*,[11] the which is either forgetfulness or carelessness.

4. And in your verses remember to place every word in his natural *emphasis* or sound, that is to say, in such wise, and with such length or shortness, elevation or depression of syllables, as it is commonly pronounced or used. To express the same we have three manner of accents, *gravis, levis, et circumflexa*, the which I would English thus: the long accent, the short accent, and that which is indifferent. The grave accent is marked by this character \, the light accent is noted thus ⁄, and the circumflex or indifferent is thus signified ~. The grave accent is drawn out or elevated, and maketh that syllable long whereupon it is placed; the light accent is depressed or snatched up, and maketh that syllable short upon the which it lighteth; the circumflex accent is indifferent, sometimes short, sometimes long, sometimes depressed and sometimes elevated. For example of the emphasis or natural sound of words, this word *treasure* has the grave accent upon the first syllable; whereas if it should be written in this sort *treasúre*, now were the second syllable long, and that were clean contrary to the common use wherewith it is pronounced.

---

[9] Harvey adds the marginal note: 'The difference of the last verse from the rest in every stanza, a grace in *The Fairie Queene*'. The first eight lines of Spenser's stanza are decasyllabic, the last is a hexameter.

[10] Harvey comments: 'His aptest partition had been into precepts of Invention/Elocution, and the several rules of both, to be sorted and marshalled in their proper places. He doth prettily well; but might easily have done much better, both in the one and in the other, especially by the direction of Horace's and Aristotle's *Ars Poetica*'.

[11] 'And so of the same'. Harvey comments: 'An error (if an error) in some few Eclogues of Sir Philip Sidney'.

For further explanation hereof, note you that commonly nowadays in English rhymes (for I dare not call them English verses)[12] we use none other order but a foot of two syllables,[13] whereof the first is depressed or made short, and the second is elevated or made long; and that sound or scanning[14] continueth throughout the verse. We have used in times past other kinds of metres, as for example this following:

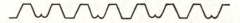

No wight in this world, that wealth can attain,
Unless he believe, that all is but vain.

Also our father Chaucer hath used the same liberty in feet and measures that the Latinists do use: and whosoever do peruse and well consider his works, he shall find that although his lines are not always of one selfsame number of syllables, yet, being read by one that hath understanding, the longest verse, and that which hath most syllables in it, will fall (to the ear)[15] correspondent unto that which hath fewest syllables in it; and likewise that which hath in it fewest syllables shall be found yet to consist of words that have such natural sound, as may seem equal in length to a verse which hath many more syllables of lighter accents. And surely I can lament that we are fallen into such a plain and simple manner of writing that there is none other foot used but one; whereby our poems may justly be called 'rhythms', and cannot by any right challenge the name of a verse.[16]

But since it is so, let us take the ford as we find it, and let me set down unto you such rules or precepts that even in this plain foot of two syllables you wrest no word from his natural and usual sound. I do not mean hereby that you may use none other words but of two syllables, for therein you may use discretion according to occasion of matter; but my meaning is, that all the words in your verse be so placed as the first syllable may sound short or be depressed, the second long

---

[12] For the distinction between 'rhyme' and 'verse' cf. Puttenham, pp. 215–6, Sidney, p. 388, and Jonson, p. 585.

[13] Harvey notes: 'The only verse *in esse*' (that is, 'in existence', opposed to *in posse*, 'in potentiality').

[14] Harvey comments: 'The reason of many a good verse marred in Sir Philip Sidney, Master Spenser, Master Fraunce, and in a manner all our excellent poets; in such words as heaven, evil, divel, and the like, made disyllables, contrary to their natural pronunciation'.

[15] Harvey notes: 'So Master Spenser, and Sir Philip, for the most part'. The other annotator writes: 'Our poems only rhymes, and not verses'.

[16] On 'rhythms' as opposed to 'verses', cf. Puttenham, p. 215.

or elevated, the third short, the fourth long, the fifth short, etc. For example of my meaning in this point mark these two verses:

I understand your meaning by your eye.
Your meaning I understand by your eye.

In these two verses there seemeth no difference at all, since the one hath the very selfsame words that the other hath, and yet the latter verse is neither true nor pleasant, and the first verse may pass the musters. The fault of the latter verse is that this word 'understand' is therein so placed as the grave accent falleth upon 'der', and thereby maketh 'der' in this word 'understand' to be elevated; which is contrary to the natural or usual pronunciation, for we say 'understand', and not 'understand'.

5. Here, by the way, I think it not amiss to forewarn you that you thrust as few words of many syllables[17] into your verse as may be: and hereunto I might allege many reasons. First, the most ancient English words are of one syllable, so that the more monosyllables that you use the truer Englishman you shall seem, and the less you shall smell of the inkhorn.* Also, words of many syllables do cloy a verse and make it unpleasant, whereas words of one syllable will more easily fall to be short or long as occasion requireth, or will be adapted to become circumflex or of an indifferent sound.

6. I would exhort you also to beware of rhyme without reason. My meaning is hereby that your rhyme lead you not from your first invention, for many writers, when they have laid the platform of their invention, are yet drawn sometimes (by rhyme) to forget it or at least to alter it, as when they cannot readily find out a word which may rhyme to the first (and yet continue their determinate* invention) they do then either botch it up with a word that will rhyme (how small reason soever it carry with it), or else they alter their first word and so percase* decline or trouble their former invention. But do you always hold your first determined invention, and do rather search the bottom of your brains for apt words than change good reason for rumbling rhyme.

7. To help you a little with rhyme (which is also a plain young scholar's lesson), work thus: when you have set down your first verse,

---

[17] The unidentified annotator protests: '*Non placet*. A greater grace and majesty in longer words, so they be current English. Monosyllables are good to make up a hobbling and huddling verse.'

take the last word thereof and count over all the words of the selfsame sound by order of the alphabet. As, for example, the last word of your first line is 'care', to rhyme therewith you have 'bare', 'clare', 'dare', 'fare', 'gare', 'hare', and 'share', 'mare', 'snare', 'rare', 'stare', and 'ware', etc. Of all these take that which best may serve your purpose, carrying reason with rhyme: and if none of them will serve so, then alter the last word of your former verse; but yet do not willingly alter the meaning of your invention.

8. You may use the same figures or tropes in verse which are used in prose,[18] and in my judgement they serve more aptly and have greater grace in verse than they have in prose. But yet therein remember this old adage, *Ne quid nimis,*[19] as many writers which do not know the use of any other figure than that which is expressed in repetition of sundry words beginning all with one letter,[20] the which (being modestly used) lendeth good grace to a verse, but they do so hunt a letter to death that they make it *Crambe,* and *Crambe bis positum mors est:*[21] therefore *Ne quid nimis.*

9. Also, as much as may be, eschew strange words, or *obsoleta et inusitata,*[22] unless the theme do give just occasion. Marry, in some places a strange word[23] doth draw attentive reading, but yet I would have you therein to use discretion.

10. And as much as you may, frame your style to *perspicuity*[24] and to be sensible,* for the haughty* obscure verse doth not much delight, and the verse that is too easy is like a tale of a roasted horse. But let your poem be such as may both delight and draw attentive reading, and therewithal may deliver such matter as be worth the marking.[25]

11. You shall do very well to use your verse after the English

[18] On the equal validity of rhetorical figures in prose and verse cf. Cicero, *De or.* 1. 16. 70. The anonymous annotator: 'Tropes and figures lend an especial grace to a verse'.

[19] A saying attributed to Bias: 'In nothing excess': cf. Puttenham, p. 233.

[20] On the excessive use of alliteration cf. also E.K., p. 179, and Sidney, p. 385.

[21] A popular proverb to describe monotonous repetition, deriving from the Greek saying, *Dis krambe thanatos* and Juvenal's mockery of the rhetoric-master's unchanging routine, *occidit miseros crambe repetito magistros*: 'Served up again and again, the cabbage is the death of the unhappy master' (*Satires* 7. 154). The English equivalent is 'Cabbage twice cooked (sodden) is death'.

[22] 'Obsolete and out of use'.

[23] Harvey comments: 'Spenser hath revived uncouth, whilom, of yore, for thy'. Cf. *The Shepheardes Calender,* pp. 176–7.

[24] On clarity or lucidity as a stylistic virtue cf. *De or.* 3. 10. 37 f., *Inst.* 1. 5. 1, 8. 1. 1 ff., North, p. 507, Jonson, pp. 559, 575, and Hobbes, p. 615.

[25] So fulfilling the rhetorician's goals of *delectare* and *docere.*

phrase, and not after the manner of other languages. The Latinists do commonly set the adjective after the substantive:[26] as, for example, *femina pulchra*, *aedes altae*, etc.; but if we should say in English 'a woman fair', 'a house high', etc., it would have but small grace, for we say 'a good man', and not 'a man good', etc. And yet I will not altogether forbid it you, for in some places it may be borne, but not so hardly* as some use it which write thus:

> Now let us go to Temple ours.
> I will go visit mother mine, etc.

Surely I smile at the simplicity* of such devisers, which might as well have said it in plain English phrase, and yet have better pleased all ears, than they satisfy their own fancies by such *superfinesse*. Therefore, even as I have advised you to place all words in their natural or most common and usual pronunciation, so would I wish you to frame all sentences in their mother phrase and proper *Idiōma*; and yet sometimes (as I have said before) the contrary may be borne, but that is rather where rhyme enforceth, or *per licentiam Poëticam*,[27] than it is otherwise lawful or commendable.

12. This poetical licence is a shrewd* fellow, and covereth many faults in a verse. It maketh words longer, shorter,[28] of more syllables, of fewer, newer, older, truer, falser; and, to conclude, it turkeneth* all things at pleasure, for example, 'ydone' for 'done', 'adown' for 'down', 'o'ercome' for 'overcome', 'ta'en' for 'taken', 'power' for 'powre', 'heaven' for 'heav'n', 'thews' for 'good parts' or 'good qualities', and a number of other, which were but tedious and needless to rehearse, since your own judgement and reading will soon make you espy such advantages.

13. There are also certain pauses or rests in a verse, which may be called *Caesures*, whereof I would be loath to stand long, since it is at discretion* of the writer, and they have been first devised (as should seem) by the musicians. But yet thus much I will adventure to write,

[26] Harvey demurs: 'And yet we use to say, "He is of the blood royal", and not "he is of the royal blood"; "he is heir apparent to the crown", and not "He is apparent heir to the crown"; "Rhyme royal" in *regula* 13 et 14, not "royal rhyme".'

[27] 'By poetic licence'. The poet's freedom, among other things, to depart from normal usage in order to follow the exigencies of verse-form was an ancient principle: cf. *De or.* 3. 38. 153, *Inst.* 10. 5. 4, and Horace, *Ars P.* 9–10.

[28] Harvey comments: 'All these in Spenser and many like; but with discretion, & tolerably, though sometimes not greatly commendably'.

that in mine opinion in a verse of eight syllables the pause will stand best in the midst; in a verse of ten it will best be placed at the end of the first four syllables;[29] in a verse of twelve, in the midst; in verses of twelve in the first and fourteen in the second, we place the pause commonly in the midst of the first, and at the end of the first eight syllables in the second.[30] In Rhyme royal it is at the writer's discretion, and forceth not where the pause be until the end of the line.

14. And here, because I have named Rhyme royal, I will tell you also mine opinion as well of that as of the names which other rhymes have commonly borne heretofore. Rhyme royal[31] is a verse of ten syllables; and seven such verses make a staff,* whereof the first and third lines do answer (across) in like terminations and rhyme; the second, fourth, and fifth do likewise answer each other in terminations, and the two last do combine and shut up the sentence. This hath been called Rhyme royal, and surely it is a royal kind of verse, serving best for grave discourses.

There is also another kind, called Ballad, and thereof are sundry sorts. For a man may write ballad in a staff of six lines, every line containing eight or six syllables, whereof the first and third, second and fourth do rhyme across, and the fifth and sixth do rhyme together in conclusion. You may write also your ballad of ten syllables, rhyming as before is declared; but these two were wont to be most commonly used in ballad, which proper name was (I think) derived of this word in Italian, *ballare*, which signifieth 'to dance'. And indeed those kinds of rhymes serve best for dances or light matters.

Then have you also a rondelet,[32] the which doth always end with one selfsame foot or repetition, and was thereof (in my judgement) called a rondelet. This may consist of such measure as best liketh the writer.

Then have you Sonnets: some think that all poems (being short) may be called Sonnets, as indeed it is a diminutive word derived of

---

[29] Ronsard makes a similar point in his *Abrégé*. In late 16th-cent. verse the medial pause usually followed the fourth syllable, but poets after 1600 tended to place it later in the line: cf. Ants Oras, *Pause-Patterns in Elizabethan and Jacobean Drama* (Gainesville, Fl., 1960).

[30] Harvey notes: 'A special note in Sir Philip's *Apology for Poetry*'; cf. p. 389.

[31] That is, a stanza ('staff') of seven pentameter lines, rhyming *ababbcc*, so called from its use by James I of Scotland, in *The Kingis Quair* (1423); also used in Shakespeare, *The Rape of Lucrece* (1593). Harvey comments: 'Rhyme royal still carrieth the credit for a gallant & stately verse'.

[32] A lyric form of varying lengths, of which the first line is repeated either as the refrain or as the last line.

sonare,[33] but yet I can best allow to call those Sonnets which are of fourteen lines, every line containing ten syllables. The first twelve do rhyme in staves of four lines by cross metre, and the last two rhyming together do conclude the whole.

There are Dizaines, and Sixaines, which are often of ten lines, and of six lines, commonly used by the French, which some English writers do also term by the name of Sonnets. Then is there an old kind of Rhyme called 'Verlays', derived (as I have read) of this word *Verd*, which betokeneth 'green', and *Lay*,[34] which betokeneth a 'song', as if you would say 'green songs'. But I must tell you by the way that I never read any verse which I saw by authority called *Verlay* but one, and that was a long discourse in verses of ten syllables, whereof the four first did rhyme across, and the fifth did answer to the first and third, breaking off there, and so going on to another termination. Of this I could show example of imitation in mine own verses[35] written to the right honourable the Lord Grey of Wilton upon my journey into Holland, etc. There are also certain poems devised of ten syllables, whereof the first answereth in termination with the fourth, and the second and third answer each other: these are more used by other nations than by us, neither can I tell readily what name to give them. And the commonest sort of verse which we use nowadays (*viz.* the long verse of twelve and fourteen syllables) I know not certainly how to name it, unless I should say that it doth consist of poulters' measure,[36] which giveth twelve for one dozen and fourteen for another. But let this suffice (if it be not too much) for the sundry sorts of verses which we use nowadays.[37]

15. In all these sorts of verses, whensoever you undertake to write, avoid prolixity and tediousness, and ever, as near as you can, do finish

---

[33] This etymology is correct. Sir Thomas Wyatt wrote sonnets after his return from Italy in 1527, mostly in the rhyme-scheme *abab abab cdd cee*. The Earl of Surrey fixed the Elizabethan form, which emphasizes the final couplet: *abab cdcd efef gg* (or *effe gg*). The genre was revived in 1573, with Gascoigne himself as one of its exponents.

[34] This etymology is wrong. The older French form *vireli* (or *virelay*) involves the repetition of rhymes (and sometimes whole lines) from stanza to stanza.

[35] In 'Gascoigne's journey into Hollande', *The Posies*, edn. cit., pp. 354–63. Harvey notes: 'Sir Philip useth this kind often: as in *Astrophil, Arcadia*'.

[36] Poulterers offered customers buying eggs an inducement to purchase more, giving twelve for the first dozen, fourteen for the second. In the late 16th cent. this verse form (a couplet consisting of one line of twelve, the other of fourteen syllables) was displaced by blank verse, and soon became matter for parody. See John Thompson, *The Founding of English Metre* (London, 1966).

[37] Harvey comments: 'Master Phaer's Virgil in a brave long verse, stately and flowing: the King of our English metricians'. On Phaer cf. Ascham, p. 157, and Puttenham, p. 211.

the sentence and meaning at the end of every staff where you write
staves, and at the end of every two lines where you write by couples
or poulters' measure. For I see many writers which draw their sentences in length, and make an end at latter Lammas:[38] for, commonly,
before they end, the reader hath forgotten where he began. But do you
(if you will follow my advice) eschew prolixity and knit up your sentences as compendiously as you may, since brevity (so that it be not
drowned in obscurity) is most commendable.[39]

16. I had forgotten a notable kind of rhyme, called 'riding rhyme',[40]
and that is such as our Master and Father Chaucer used in his *Canterbury Tales*, and in diverse other delectable and light enterprises.
But, though it come to my remembrance somewhat out of order, it
shall not yet come altogether out of time, for I will now tell you a
conceit* which I had before forgotten to write: you may see (by the
way) that I hold a preposterous* order in my traditions* but, as I said
before, I write moved by good will, and not to show my skill. Then to
return to my matter, as this 'riding rhyme' serveth most aptly to write
a merry tale, so Rhyme royal is fittest for a grave discourse. Ballads
are best of matters of love, and Rondelets most apt for the beating or
handling of an adage or common proverb. Sonnets serve as well in
matters of love as of discourse; Dizaines and Sixaines for short Fantasies; Verlays for an effectual* proposition,* although by the name
you might otherwise judge of Verlays; and the long verse of twelve
and fourteen syllables, although it be nowadays used in all themes, yet
in my judgement it would serve best[41] for Psalms and Hymns.

I would stand longer in these traditions, were it not that I doubt
mine own ignorance; but, as I said before, I know that I write to my
friend, and, affying* myself thereupon, I make an end.

---

[38] In the early English Church Lammas, 1 Aug., was a harvest festival. But the jocular
expression, 'Latter Lamas', meant 'a day that will never come'.

[39] Harvey adds: '*Gaudent brevitate moderni*. Spenser doth sometimes otherwise, and commendably, as the matter leadeth, the verse floweth, or other circumstances will bear it out'.

[40] Gascoigne does not in fact define 'riding rhyme', a term used for the 'heroic' or decasyllabic couplet (usually in iambic metre), according to some authorities, because Chaucer
used it for *The Canterbury Tales*, told by pilgrims while riding to the Shrine at Canterbury;
others think it refers rather to the line's ambling movement than to the rhyme. Cf. Puttenham, p. 211.

[41] Harvey adds: 'Or some heroical discourse, or stately argument'.

8

George Whetstone,
The morality of comedy (1578)

GEORGE WHETSTONE (1544?–87?), author and soldier, served in the Low
Countries against the Spaniards in 1572–4 and 1585–6, taking part in the
action at Zutphen; in 1578–9 he sailed in Sir Humphrey Gilbert's New-
foundland voyage. A friend of Gascoigne, he wrote commendatory verses to
his *Posies* (1575) and a *Remembraunce* on his death (1577). His publications
include several obituary panegyrics; *An Heptameron of Civill Discourses*
(1582, prose tales adapted from Giraldi Cinthio); and two accounts of conspiracies against Queen Elizabeth.

TEXT. From *The right Excellent and famous Historye, of Promos and Cassandra: Devided into two Commicall Discourses. In the fyrste parte is showne, the
unsufferable abuse, of a lewde Magistrate: The vertuous behaviours of a chaste
Ladye: The uncontrowled leawdenes of a favoured Curtisan. And the undeserved
estimation of a pernicious Parasyte. In the second part is discoursed, the perfect
magnanimitye of a noble Kinge, in checking Vice and favouring Vertue: Wherein
is showne, the Ruyne and overthrowe, of dishonest practises: with the advaunce-
ment of upright dealing* (London, 1578). This play, in rhymed versed, never
acted, was based either on the Latin tragedy *Philanira* by Claude Rouillet
(1556), or on the eighty-fifth tale of Cinthio's *Heccatomitthi* (1565), and provided the main source for Shakespeare's *Measure for Measure*. See G.
Bullough (ed.), *Narrative and Dramatic Sources of Shakespeare, ii: The Comedies, 1597–1603* (London, 1958), pp. 399–514.

[DEDICATION TO WILLIAM FLEETWOODE,
RECORDER OF LONDON]

Sir, desirous to acquit your tried friendship with some token of good
will, of late I perused diverse of my imperfect works, fully minded to
bestow on you the travail of some of my forepassed time. But, resolved
to accompany the adventurous Captain Sir Humfrey Gilbert[1] in his
honourable voyage, I found my leisure too little to correct the errors
in my said works. So that, enforced, I left them dispersed among my

---

[1] Gilbert (1539?–83), the navigator, was stepbrother of Sir Walter Ralegh.

learned friends, at their leisure to polish if I failed to return; spoiling by this means my study of his necessary furniture.* Among other unregarded papers I found this discourse of *Promos and Cassandra*; which for the rareness and the needful knowledge of the necessary matter contained therein, to make the actions appear more lively, I divided the whole history into two comedies—for that, decorum used, it would not be conveyed in one. The effects of both are good and bad: virtue intermixed with vice, unlawful desires, if it were possible, quenched with chaste denials: all needful actions (I think) for public view. For by the reward of the good, the good are encouraged in well doing, and with the scourge of the lewd,* the lewd are feared from evil attempts: maintaining this my opinion with Plato's authority.[2] Naughtiness comes of the corruption of nature, and not by reading or hearing the lives of the good or lewd (for such publication is necessary), but goodness, says he, is beautified by either action. And to these ends Menander, Plautus, and Terence, themselves many years since entombed, by their comedies in honour live at this day.

The ancient Romans held these shows of such price that they not only allowed the public exercise of them, but the grave senators themselves countenanced* the actors with their presence: who from these trifles won morality, as the bee sucks honey from weeds.[3] But the advised devices of ancient poets, discredited with trifles of young, unadvised, and rash-witted writers, has brought this commendable exercise in mislike. For at this day the Italian is so lascivious in his comedies that honest hearers are grieved at his actions; the Frenchman and Spaniard follows the Italian's humour; the German is too holy, for he presents on every common stage what preachers should pronounce in pulpits. The Englishman in this quality is most vain, indiscreet,* and out of order. He first grounds his work on impossibilities;[4] then in three hours' runs he through the world, marries, gets children, makes children men, men to conquer kingdoms, murder monsters; [he] bringeth gods from heaven, and fetcheth devils from hell. And, that which is worst, their ground is not so imperfect as their working indiscreet: not weighing, so the people laugh, though they

---

[2] A vague statement which apparently ignores the fact that Plato wanted poetry and drama banned from his ideal state, except for texts praising the gods or virtuous men.

[3] This important metaphor for the process by which the reader should select the wholesome parts of literary texts and ignore the immoral ones goes back to classical antiquity. See Elyot, p. 67, and Heywood, p. 478.

[4] Cf. Sidney, pp. 381–2, and Jonson, p. 527, for similar catalogues of improbabilities in contemporary drama.

laugh them, for their follies, to scorn. Many times, to make mirth, they make a clown companion with a king; in their grave counsels they allow the advice of fools. Yea, they use one order of speech for all persons—a gross indecorum,[5] for a crow will ill counterfeit the nightingale's sweet voice: even so, affected speech does misbecome a clown. For, to work a comedy kindly,[6] grave old men should instruct, young men should show the imperfections of youth, strumpets should be lascivious, boys unhappy, and clowns should speak disorderly: intermingling all these actions in such sort as the grave matter may instruct and the pleasant delight; for without this change the attention would be small, and the liking less.

But leave I this rehearsal of the use and abuse of comedies, lest that I check that in others which I cannot amend in myself. But this I am assured, what actions soever pass in this history, either merry or mournful, grave or lascivious, the conclusion shows the confusion of vice and the cherishing of virtue. And since the end tends to this good, although the work, because of evil handling, be unworthy your learned censure,* allow (I beseech you) of my good will, until leisure serves me to perfect some labour of more worth. No more, but that almighty God be your protector, and preserve me from danger in this voyage, the 29 of July, 1578.

[5] On decorum see also Sidney, p. 383, and Puttenham, pp. 228–30.

[6] That is, according to 'kind' or genre, obeying the principle of decorum, and achieving the traditional goals of *docere* and *delectare*. The moral function of comedy was asserted by the early commentators on Terence, such as Aelius Donatus and Evanthius, to whom were ascribed the influential essay 'De tragoedia et comoedia' printed in many early editions of Terence; cf. the translation by O. B. Hardison, Jr., in A. Preminger *et al.* (eds.), *Classical and Medieval Literary Criticism* (New York, 1974), pp. 299–309; M. T. Herrick, *Comic Theory in the Sixteenth Century* (Urbana, Ill., 1950), pp. 57–60, and M. Doran, *Endeavors of Art: A Study of Form in Elizabethan Drama* (Madison, 1954), pp. 105 ff.

Edmund Spenser and E.K.,
Pastoral poetry revived and explained (1579)

EDMUND SPENSER (1552?–99), son of a clothmaker, was educated at the Merchant Taylor's School in London, under Richard Mulcaster (a noted humanist scholar whose other pupils included Thomas Kyd, Lancelot Andrewes, and Thomas Lodge), and Pembroke Hall Cambridge (between 1569 and 1576). In 1579 he obtained through the influence of his college friend, Gabriel Harvey, a place in Leicester's household, and became acquainted with Sir Philip Sidney, experimenting (together with Edward Dyer and Thomas Drant) in writing English verse in classical metres.

E.K., the author of the Preface and Glosses, has not been surely identified. Some scholars identify him as E[dmundus] K[alendarius], i.e. 'Edmund [Spenser] the calendar-maker': cf. R. Rainbuss, *Spenser's Secret Career* (Cambridge, 1993). Others believe that he was either Spenser's Cambridge contemporary, Edward Kirke (1553–1613) of Pembroke, or even Gabriel Harvey. His annotations are printed in italics.

TEXT. From *The Shepheardes Calender. Conteyning twelve Aeglogues proportionable to the twelve moneths* (1579). Modern editions: William A. Oram, *et al.* (eds.), *The Yale Edition of the Shorter Poems of Edmund Spenser* (New Haven and London, 1989); Douglas Brooks-Davies (ed.), *Edmund Spenser: Selected Shorter Poems* (London and New York, 1995): I am indebted to them both for some of the following notes.

THE SHEPHERD'S CALENDAR

E.K., EPISTLE TO GABRIEL HARVEY

'Uncouth unkissed', said the old famous poet Chaucer,[1] whom for his excellency and wonderful skill in making,* his scholar Lydgate (a worthy scholar of so excellent a master), calleth 'the loadstar of our language';[2] and whom our Colin Clout[3] in his Eclogue calleth 'Tityrus the god of shepherds', comparing him to the worthiness of the Roman

---

[1] Chaucer, *Troilus and Criseyde* 809: 'Unknowne, unkist'.
[2] Lydgate, *Fall of Princes*, prol. l. 52.
[3] Spenser himself, as identified in the argument to 'January'.

Tityrus,[4] Virgil. Which proverb, mine own good friend Master Harvey, as in that good old poet it served well Pandar's purpose, for the bolstering of his bawdy brocage,* so very well taketh place in this our new poet, who for that he is uncouth (as said Chaucer) is unkissed and unknown to most men, is regarded but of few. But I doubt not, so soon as his name shall come into the knowledge of men, and his worthiness be sounded in the trump* of fame, but that he shall be not only kissed but also beloved of all, embraced of the most, and wondered at of the best. No less, I think, deserveth his wittiness* in devising, his pithiness in uttering, his complaints of love so lovely, his discourses of pleasure so pleasantly, his pastoral rudeness,* his moral wiseness, his due observing of decorum everywhere: in personages, in seasons, in matter, in speech, and generally in all seemly* simplicity* of handling his matter and framing his words (the which, of many things which in him be strange, I know will seem the strangest, the words themselves being so ancient,[5] the knitting of them so short and intricate, and the whole period and compass of speech so delightsome for the roundness* and so grave for the strangeness).

And first of the words to speak: I grant they be something hard, and of most men unused, yet both English, and also used of most excellent authors and most famous poets. In whom, when as this our poet hath been much travailed* and thoroughly read, how could it be (as that worthy orator[6] said) but that walking in the sun, although for other cause he walked, yet needs he mought* be sunburnt; and having the sound of those ancient poets still ringing in his ears, he mought needs in singing hit out some of their tunes. But whether he useth them by such casualty* and custom, or of set purpose and choice (as thinking them fittest for such rustical rudeness of shepherds, either for that their rough sound would make his rhymes more ragged and rustical, or else because such old and obsolete words are most used of country folk), sure I think—and think I think not amiss—that they bring great grace and, as one would say, authority to the verse.

For albeit amongst many other faults it specially be objected of Valla[7] against Livy, and of other against Sallust,[8] that with over-much

---

[4] Tityrus was Virgil's *persona* in the *Eclogues*.

[5] For criticism of Spenser's archaisms see Sidney, p. 380, and Jonson, pp. 573, 575–6.

[6] Cicero, *De or.* 2. 14. 60. Cf. Wilson, p. 79.

[7] Lorenzo Valla, a 15th-cent. Italian humanist noted for fiercely upholding standards of correct classical Latin, criticized Livy for lapsing into Paduan dialect; cf. *Inst.* 1. 5. 56; 8. 1. 3.

[8] In *The Schoolmaster* (1570) Roger Ascham had criticized this Roman historian for indulging in archaicism.

study they affect* antiquity, as coveting thereby credence and honour of elder years; yet I am of opinion (and eke* the best-learned are of the like) that those ancient solemn words are a great ornament both in the one and in the other; the one labouring to set forth in his work an eternal image of antiquity, and the other carefully discoursing matters of gravity and importance. For if my memory fail not, Tully[9] in that book wherein he endeavoureth to set forth the pattern of a perfect orator, saith that ofttimes an ancient word maketh the style seem grave and as it were reverend; no otherwise than we honour and reverence grey hairs, for a certain religious* regard which we have of old age.

Yet neither everywhere must old words be stuffed in, nor the common dialect and manner of speaking so corrupted thereby, that as in old buildings it seem disorderly and ruinous. But all,* as in most exquisite pictures they use to blaze* and portrait* not only the dainty lineaments of beauty, but also round about it to shadow* the rude thickets and craggy cliffs, that by the baseness of such parts more excellency may accrue to the principal; for ofttimes we find ourselves, I know not how, singularly delighted with the show of such natural rudeness, and take great pleasure in that disorderly order. Even so do those rough and harsh terms enlumine, and make more clearly to appear the brightness of brave* and glorious words. So oftentimes a discord in music maketh a comely concordance;[10] so great delight took the worthy poet Alcaeus[11] to behold a blemish in the joint of a well-shaped body. But if any will rashly blame such his purpose in choice of old and unwonted words, him may I more justly blame and condemn, or* of witless headiness* in judging, or of heedless hardiness* in condemning; for, not marking the compass of his bent, he will judge of the length of his cast.[12] For in my opinion it is one special praise—of many which are due to this poet—that he hath laboured to restore, as to their rightful heritage, such good and natural English words as have been long time out of use and almost clear disherited.

---

[9] In *De or.* 3. 58. 153 and *Orat.* 23. 80 Cicero defends the use of older words as adding dignity.

[10] The fashionable notion of *discordia concors*, resulting in a pleasing harmony. E.K. also invokes the new aesthetic notion of 'I know not how', 'je ne sais quoi', found in contemporary French sources, such as Du Bellay's *La Deffence et Illustration de la Langue Francoyse* (1549), and which was to become important in the 17th and 18th cents.

[11] This reference to Alcaeus (a Greek lyric poet, 7th cent. BC) comes from Cicero, *De natura deorum* 1. 28. 79.

[12] A metaphor from archery: 'not noting the bow's elevation (and hence, intended flight), a critic will not appreciate the archer's efforts'.

Which is the only cause that our mother tongue (which truly of itself
is both full enough for prose and stately enough for verse) hath long
time been counted most bare and barren of both. Which default, when
as some endeavoured to salve and recure, they patched up the holes
with pieces and rags of other languages—borrowing here of the
French, there of the Italian, everywhere of the Latin—not weighing
how ill those tongues accord with themselves, but much worse with
ours; so now they have made our English tongue a gallimaufry or
hodgepodge of all other speeches. Other some (not so well seen in the
English tongue as perhaps in other languages) if them happen to hear
an old word, albeit very natural and significant, cry out straight away
that we speak no English but gibberish—or rather, such as in old time
Evander's mother[13] spoke. Whose first shame is that they are not
ashamed in their own mother tongue strangers to be counted, and
aliens.

The second shame, no less than the first, that what so they understand not they straight away deem to be senseless, and not at all to be
understood (much like to the mole in Aesop's fable, that being blind
herself would in no wise be persuaded that any beast could see). The
last, more shameful than both, that of their own country and natural
speech (which together with their nurse's milk they sucked) they have
so base regard and bastard judgement that they will not only themselves not labour to garnish and beautify it, but also repine that of
other it should be embellished. Like to the dog in the manger, that
himself can eat no hay and yet barketh at the hungry bullock that so
fain would feed; whose currish kind, though cannot be kept from
barking, yet I con* them thank that they refrain from biting.

Now for the knitting of sentences[14] (which they call the joints and
members thereof) and for all the compass* of the speech, it is round*
without roughness and learned without hardness; such indeed as may
be perceived of the least, understood of the most, but judged only of
the learned. For what in most English writers useth to be loose and
as it were ungirt,* in this author is well grounded, finely framed, and

---

[13] According to Virgil (*Aen.* 8. 51–4), Evander and his mother had emigrated to Italy
from the rustic Arcadia, speaking an archaic dialect. The call to rediscover linguistic tradition was common throughout Europe, in the attempt to establish the vernaculars, against
Greek and Latin, as languages worthy of serious attention.

[14] *Compositio*, the 'artistic structure' or 'arrangement' of words and phrases, was an
important aspect of classical and Renaissance linguistic theory. See Quintilian, *Inst.* 9. 4. 1,
passim; Aldo Scaglione, *The Classical Theory of Composition from its Origins to the Present:
A Historical Survey* (Chapel Hill, NC, 1972).

strongly trussed up together. In regard whereof I scorn and spew out the rakehelly* rout of our ragged rhymers (for so themselves use to hunt the letter),[15] which without learning boast, without judgement jangle, without reason rage and foam, as if some instinct of poetical spirit had newly ravished them above the meanness of common capacity. And being in the midst of all their bravery,* suddenly (either for want of matter, or of rhyme, or having forgotten their former conceit)* they seem to be so pained and travailed in their remembrance as it were a woman in childbirth, or as that same Pythia when the trance came upon her.

Os rabidum fera corda domans,[16] etc.

Natheless, let them in God's name feed on their own folly, so they seek not to darken the beams of others' glory.

As for Colin, under whose person the author's self is shadowed, how far he is from such vaunted titles and glorious shows, both himself showeth, where he saith 'Of Muses, Hobbin, I con no skill', and, 'Enough is me to paint out my unrest',[17] etc. And also appeareth by the baseness of the name, wherein (it seemeth) he chose rather to unfold great matter of argument covertly[18] than professing it, not suffice thereto accordingly. Which moved him rather in eclogues than otherwise to write, doubting perhaps his ability, which he little needed; or minding to furnish our tongue with this kind, wherein it faulteth; or following the example of the best and most ancient poets, which devised this kind of writing, being both so base for the matter and homely for the manner, at the first to try their abilities; and as young birds, that be newly crept out of the nest, by little first to prove their tender wings before they make a greater flight. So flew Theocritus[19]

---

[15] Excessive use of alliteration: see E.K.'s note *n*, p. 188, and Sidney, p. 385.

[16] Virgil, *Aen.* 6. 80: 'governing her raving month and wild heart'—a description of the Cumaean Sibyl, whom Aeneas compelled to prophesy.

[17] See the 'June' eclogue, ll. 65, 79.

[18] In *The Arte of English Poesie* (1589), George Puttenham argued that poets wrote pastoral poetry 'not of purpose to counterfait or represent the rusticall manner of loves and communication: but under the vailes of homely persons, and in rude speeches, to insinuate and glaunce at greater matters, and such as perchance had not bene safe to have beene disclosed in any other sort, which may be perceived by the *Eclogues* of Virgil, in which are treated by figure matter of greater importance than the loves of Tityrus and Corydon. These eclogues came after to containe and enforme morall discipline, for the amendment of man's behaviour, as be those of Mantuan and other moderne poets'; ed. Willcock and Walker (Cambridge, 1936, 1970), pp. 38–9.

[19] The Greek poet Theocritus (*c.*310–250 BC), whose thirty *Idylls* are the founding texts of pastoral poetry.

(as you may perceive he was already full fledged). So flew Virgil,[20] as not yet well feeling his wings. So flew Mantuan,[21] as being not full summed.* So Petrarch; so Boccaccio; so Marot, Sannazaro,[22] and also divers other excellent both Italian and French poets, whose footing this author everywhere followeth; yet so as few (but they be well scented) can trace him out. So, finally, flieth this our new poet, as a bird whose principals* be scarce grown out, but yet as that in time shall be able to keep wing with the best.

Now, as touching the general drift and purpose of his eclogues, I mind not to say much, himself labouring to conceal it. Only this appeareth, that his unstaid* youth had long wandered in the common labyrinth of love, in which time to mitigate and allay the heat of his passion, or else to warn (as he saith) the young shepherds (*scilicet** his equals and companions) of his unfortunate folly, he compiled these twelve eclogues which, for that they be proportioned to the state of the twelve months, he termeth the *Shepherds' Calendar*, applying an old name[23] to a new work.

Hereunto have I added a certain gloss or *scholion* for the exposition of old words and harder phrases; which manner of glossing and commenting, well I wote,* will seem strange and rare in our tongue. Yet for so much as I knew many excellent and proper* devices both in words and matter would pass in the speedy course of reading (either as unknown, or as not marked),* and that in this kind, as in other, we might be equal to the learned of other nations, I thought good to take the pains upon me (the rather for that, by means of some familiar acquaintance, I was made privy to his counsel and secret meaning in them, as also in sundry other works of his). Which, albeit I know he nothing so much hateth as to promulgate, yet thus much have I adventured upon his friendship (himself being for long time far estranged),*

---

[20] Virgil's *Eclogues*, which frequently imitate Theocritus, were his first compositions.

[21] Baptista Spagnuoli (1448–1516), nicknamed Mantuan after his birthplace, famous for his satirical and moral eclogues (1498). The Latin text was frequently published in England (some 23 editions between 1523 and 1638); an English translation by George Turberville appeared in 1567.

[22] These were the leading Renaissance pastoral poets, in Latin: Francesco Petrarca (1304–74), with his twelve political-satirical eclogues; Giovanni Boccaccio (1313–75), with his sixteen allegorical eclogues; and in the vernacular: Clément Marot (1496–1544) wrote four in French (two of which are imitated by Spenser in 'November' and 'December'); Jacopo Sannazaro (1456–1530) wrote the prose and verse pastoral novel *Arcadia* in Italian, and in Latin the *Eclogae Piscatoriae*, with fishermen substituted for shepherds.

[23] *The Calendar of Shepherds*, an almanac of astrological and miscellaneous lore (translated from the French), had at least 7 editions between 1503 and 1559.

hoping that this will the rather occasion him to put forth divers other excellent works of his which sleep in silence, as his *Dreams*, his *Legends*, his *Court of Cupid*,[24] and sundry others; whose commendations to set out were very vain, the things (though worthy of many) yet being known to few.

These my present pains, if to any they be pleasurable or profitable, be you judge, mine own good Master Harvey, to whom I have, both in respect of your worthiness generally and otherwise upon some particular and special considerations, vowed this my labour, and the maidenhead of this our common friend's poetry, himself having already in the beginning dedicated it to the noble and worthy gentleman, the right worshipful Master Philip Sidney, a special favourer and maintainer of all kind of learning. Whose cause I pray you, Sir, if envy shall stir up any wrongful accusation, defend with your mighty rhetoric and other your rare gifts of learning (as you can)* and shield with your good will (as you ought), against the malice and outrage of so many enemies as I know will be set on fire with the sparks of his kindled glory. . . .

The General Argument of the Whole Book

Little, I hope, needeth me at large to discourse the first original of eclogues, having already touched the same. But for the word eclogues (I know), is unknown to most, and also mistaken of some the best learned (as they think), I will say somewhat thereof, being not at all impertinent to my present purpose.

They were first of the Greeks (the inventors of them), called *aeglogai*, as it were *aigon* or *aigonomon logoi*, that is, 'goatherds' tales'.[25] For, although in Virgil and others the speakers be most* shepherds and goatherds, yet Theocritus (in whom is more ground of authority than in Virgil, this specially from that deriving, as from the first head and wellspring, the whole invention of his eclogues) maketh goatherds the persons and authors of his tales. . . .

These twelve eclogues, everywhere answering* to the seasons of the twelve months, may be well divided into three forms or ranks. For either they be *plaintive* (as the first, the sixth, the eleventh, and the

---

[24] None of these works survive (if they ever existed).

[25] The word 'eclogue' actually means 'a selection' (Greek: *eklegein*, to choose). The false etymology (*aix*=goat), deriving from an early life of Virgil, was accepted by Petrarch, and widely disseminated in the Renaissance.

twelfth); or *recreative* (such as all those be which conceive matter of love, or commendation of special personages); or *moral*, which for the most part be mixed with some satirical bitterness (namely the second, of reverence due to old age; the fifth, of coloured* deceit; the seventh and ninth, of dissolute shepherds and pastors; the tenth, of contempt of poetry and pleasant wits). And to this division may everything herein be reasonably applied, a few only except, whose special purpose and meaning I am not privy to. And thus much generally of these twelve eclogues. . . .

EDMUND SPENSER, *OCTOBER*

Argument[26]

In Cuddy is set out the perfect* pattern of a poet, which finding no maintenance of his state and studies, complaineth of the contempt of poetry,[a] and the causes thereof, specially having been in all ages, and

---

[26] The 'Argument', like the glosses, and perhaps the illustrations, are probably the joint efforts of both Spenser and E.K. In the woodcut the aged Piers, as Virgil, crowned with laurel, offers Cuddy the oaten reeds symbolizing pastoral poetry.

[a] *This eclogue is made in imitation of Theocritus his sixteenth* Idyllion, *wherein he reproved*

even amongst the most barbarous, always of singular account and honour, and being indeed so worthy and commendable an art; or rather no art, but a divine gift and heavenly instinct* not to be gotten by labour and learning, but adorned with both: and poured into the wit by a certain *enthusiasmos*[27] and celestial inspiration, as the author hereof elsewhere at large discourseth in his book called *The English Poet*;[28] which book being lately come to my hands, I mind also by God's grace upon further advisement to publish.

Piers.

Cuddy, for shame hold up thy heavy head,
And let us cast with what delight to chase,*
And weary this long ling'ring Phoebus' race.*
Whilom thou wont the shepherd's lads to lead
In rhymes, in riddles, and in bidding base:*
Now they in thee, and thou in sleep, art dead.

Cuddy.

Piers, I have piped erst* so long with pain
That all mine oaten reeds been rent and wore,
And my poor Muse hath spent her spared store;
Yet little good hath got, and much less gain.
Such pleasance* makes the grasshopper[29] so poor,
And ligge so laid, when winter doth her strain.*

The dapper* ditties that I wont devise
To feed youth's fancy, and the flocking fry,[b]

the tyrant *Hiero of Syracuse* for his niggardice towards poets, in whom is the power to make men immortal for their good deeds, or shameful for their naughty life. And the like also is in Mantuan.[30] The style hereof (as also that in Theocritus) is more lofty than the rest, and applied to the height of poetical wit.

[b] Fry *is a bold metaphor, forced from the spawning fishes, for the multitude of young fish be called the* fry.

[27] The Greek term, like the English, refers to divine possession, an attribute assigned to the poet by Plato in *Ion*: cf. Thomas Sébillet, *Art poétique français* (1550), in *TPR*, pp. 52, 156 (citing the dictionary by Calepinus (1540): *Enthusiasmus, afflatus poetici furoris, divinus*), Puttenham, p. 192, and Sidney, p. 341.

[28] This book is lost (if it ever existed).

[29] Alluding to Aesop's fable of the provident ant and improvident grasshopper, who 'lies so faint and feeble' in winter, not having stored any food.

[30] In fact, Spenser does not imitate Theocritus 16, but rather follows Mantuan's fifth eclogue (for the first eighty lines of his poem), in which Candidus, a needy poet, requests help from Silvanus, a niggardly connoisseur of poetry, but only receives a lecture.

Delighten much—what I the bett' for-thy?[31]
They han* the pleasure, I a slender prize.
I beat the bush, the birds to them do fly:
What good thereof to Cuddy can arise?

Piers.

Cuddy, the praise is better than the prize,
The glory eke much greater than the gain.[32]
O what an honour is it, to restrain[c]
The lust of lawless youth with good advice,
Or prick them forth with pleasance[33] of thy vein,
Whereto thou list their trained wills entice.[34]

Soon as thou 'ginst to set thy notes in frame,
O how the rural routs* to thee do cleave!
Seemeth thou dost their soul of sense bereave,
All as the shepherd[d] that did fetch his dame
From Pluto's baleful bow'r withouten leave:
His music's might the hellish hound did tame.[35]

---

[c] *This place seemeth to conspire* with Plato,*[36] *who in his first book* De legibus *saith that the first invention of poetry was of very virtuous intent. For at what time an infinite number of youth usually came to their great solemn feasts called* Panegyrica *(which they used every five years to hold), some learned man, being more able than the rest for special gifts of wit and music, would take upon him to sing fine verses to the people in praise either of virtue, or of victory, or of immortality, or such like. At whose wonderful gift all men being astonished and, as it were, ravished with delight, thinking (as it was indeed) that he was inspired from above, called him* vatem. *Which kind of men afterwards framing their verses to lighter music (as of music be many kinds, some sadder, some lighter, some martial, some heroical, and so diversely eke affect the minds of men) found out lighter matter of poesy also (some playing with love, some scorning at men's fashions, some poured out in pleasures), and so were called* poets *or* makers.

[d] *Orpheus, of whom is said that by his excellent skill in music and poetry, he recovered his wife* Eurydice *from hell.*

[31] 'How am I the better?'

[32] It was a commonplace in Renaissance ethics that fame, or glory, was the proper recognition for virtue, far above material reward.

[33] The familiar injunction from Cicero and Horace, that the duty of the orator/poet is to blend *docere* and *delectare*, making moral instruction pleasant to receive by the use of narrative and literary resources.

[34] The 'Gallic Hercules', an emblem for the power of rhetoric, shows the god drawing listeners along by means of the chains of eloquence linking his mouth and their ears ('their trained wills'). Cf. Wilson, p. 75; Puttenham, p. 224.

[35] Orpheus' music calmed Cerberus, the three-headed dog guarding the entrance to the underworld.

[36] Not book 1 of Plato's *Laws*, but perhaps 8. 829b ff., on how the state should organize regular festivals at which citizens can compose panegyrics. Elsewhere (e.g. *Laws* 3. 682a, 4. 719c) Plato repeats his identification of poetry and inspiration.

Cuddy.

So praisen babes the peacock's spotted train,
And wondren at bright Argus' blazing eye.
But who rewards him ere the more for-thy,*
Or feeds him once the fuller by a grain?
Sike* praise is smoke, that sheddeth* in the sky,
Sike words bene wind, and wasten soon in vain.

Piers.

Abandon then the base and viler clown:
Lift up thyself out of the lowly dust
And sing of bloody Mars,[37] of wars, of jousts.
Turn thee to those that wield* the awe-full crown,
To doubted* knights, whose woundless armour rusts,[38]
And helms unbruised waxen daily brown.

There may thy Muse display[e] her flutt'ring wing
And stretch herself at large from east to west:
Whether thou list in fair Elisa rest,*
Or, if thee please, in bigger notes to sing,
Advance* the worthy whom she loveth best,
That first the white bear to the stake[39] did bring.

And when the stubborn stroke of stronger stounds*
Has somewhat slacked the tenor* of thy string,
Of love and lustihead tho* mayst thou sing,
And carol loud, and lead the miller's round,*
All* were Elisa one of th'ilk same ring:*
So mought our Cuddy's name to heaven sound.

Cuddy.

Indeed the Romish Tityrus,[f] I hear,

---

[e] *A poetical metaphor: whereof the meaning is, that if the poet list* show his skill in matter of more dignity than is the homely eclogue, good occasion is him offered of higher vein and more heroical argument, in the person of our most gracious sovereign, whom (as before) he calleth Elisa. Or if the matter of knighthood and chivalry please him better, that there be many noble and valiant men that are both worthy of his pain in their deserved praises, and also favourers of his skill and faculty.*

[f] *Well known to be Virgil, who by Maecenas's means was brought into the favour of the Emperor Augustus, and by him moved to write in loftier kind than he erst had done.*

[37] An injunction to abandon pastoral, the poetry of rustics, for epic, whose subject is war.
[38] Referring to the long peace under Queen Elizabeth, when her soldiers' unwounded armour rusted and their 'unbruised' helmets were unpolished.
[39] Robert Dudley, the Earl of Leicester (and Sidney's uncle), whose crest was a bear chained to an uprooted tree stump.

Through his Maecenas[40] left his oaten reed
(Whereon[g] he erst had taught his flocks to feed,
And laboured* lands to yield the timely ear),*
And eft* did sing of wars and deadly dread,
So as the heavens did quake his verse to hear.

But ah, Maecenas is yclad in clay,
And great Augustus long ago is dead;
And all the worthies liggen* wrapped in lead
That matter made for poets on to play:
For ever[h] who, in derring-do* were dread,*
The lofty verse of him was loved aye.

[g] *In these three verses are the three several works of Virgil intended: for in 'teaching his flocks to feed' is meant his* Eclogues; *in 'labouring of lands' is his* Georgics; *in 'singing of wars and deadly dread' is his divine* Aeneis *figured.*

[h] *He showeth the cause why poets were wont be had in such honour of noblemen: that is, that by them their worthiness and valour should, through their famous poesies, be commended to all posterities. Wherefore it is said that Achilles had never been so famous as he is but for Homer's immortal verses, which is the only advantage which he had of Hector. And also that Alexander the Great, coming to his tomb in Sigeus, with natural tears blessed him that ever was his hap* to be honoured with so excellent a poet's work, as so renowned and ennobled only by his means; which, being declared in a most eloquent oration of Tully's, is of* Petrarch[41] *no less worthily set forth in a sonnet:*

> Giunto Alexandro a la famosa tomba
> Del fero Achille sospirando disse:
> O fortunato che si chiara tromba.
> Trovasti, etc.

And that such account hath been always made of poets, as well showeth this, that the worthy Scipio, in all his wars against Carthage and Numantia, had evermore in his company (and that in a most familiar sort) the good old poet Ennius;[42] *as also that Alexander, destroying Thebes, when he was informed that the famous lyric poet Pindarus was born in that city, not only commanded straitly* that no man should, upon pain of death, do any violence to that house by fire or otherwise, but also specially spared most, and some highly rewarded, that were of his kin. So favoured he the only name of a poet; which praise otherwise was in the same man no less famous that, when he came to ransacking of King Darius's coffers (whom he lately had overthrown), he found in a little coffer of silver the two books of Homer's works, as laid up there for special jewels and riches; which he, taking thence, put one of them daily in his bosom, and the other every night laid under his pillow.[43] Such honour have poets always found in the sight of princes and noblemen; which this author here very well showeth, as elsewhere more notably.*

[40] Patron of Virgil, Horace, and others, and viceregent to Augustus Caesar at the battle of Actium.

[41] Cf. Cicero, *Arch.* 10. 24, which is echoed by Petrarch in *Rime* 187: 'When Alexander came to the famous tomb of the fierce Achilles, he sighing said: "O fortunate one, who found so clear a trumpet, one who wrote such high things of you!"' (tr. R. M. Durling).

[42] Cicero, *Arch.* 9. 22.

[43] This famous anecdote is recorded in Plutarch's 'Life' of Alexander 11. 4–6, 26. 1–4; and in Pliny, *Naturalis historia* 7. 29. 108–9.

But after[i] Virtue* 'gan for age to stoop,
And mighty manhood brought a-bed of ease,
The vaunting poets found nought worth a pease*
To put in press among the learned troop:[44]
Tho 'gan the streams of flowing wits* to cease,
And sun-bright Honour penned in shameful coop.[45]

And if that any buds of Poesy
Yet of the old stock 'gan to shoot again,
Or* it men's follies mote be forced to feign*
And roll with rest in rhymes of ribaldry;
Or as it sprung, it wither must again:
Tom Piper[j] makes us better melody.

Piers.

O peerless Poesy, where is then thy place?
If nor in princes' palace thou do sit
(And yet is princes' palace the most fit),
Ne breast of baser birth doth thee embrace,
Then make thee wings of thine aspiring wit,
And, whence thou cam'st, fly back to heaven apace.*

Cuddy.

Ah, Percy, it is all too weak and wan
So high to soar, and make so large a flight—
Her pieced pinions[k] bene not so in plight,*
For Colin fits* such famous flight to scan:*
He (were he not with love so ill bedight)
Would mount as high, and sing as sweet, as swan.[l]

---

[i] *He showeth the cause of contempt of poetry to be idleness and baseness of mind.*

[j] *An ironical* sarcasmus, *spoken in derision of these rude wits which make more account of a rhyming ribald than of skill grounded upon learning and judgement.*

[k] *Unperfect skill: spoken with humble modesty.*[46]

[l] *The comparison seemeth to be strange, for the swan hath ever won small commendation for her sweet singing. But it is said of the learned that the swan, a little before her death, singeth most pleasantly, as prophesying by a secret instinct her near destiny; as well saith the poet elsewhere in one of his sonnets:*[47]

> *The silver swan doth sing before her dying day*
> *As she that feels the deep delight that is in death, etc.*

[44] *Virtus* gave way to *otium* (idleness), and poets could find no worthwhile subject with which to emulate the learned poets of antiquity; or: 'gain the respect of learned commentators', such as E.K.

[45] 'Shut up in sloth, as in a coop or cage' (E.K.).

[46] The 'modesty topos' of classical rhetoric, in which the orator disclaims skill (usually before demonstrating it).

[47] This sonnet by Spenser is lost. For the swan and death see e.g. Virgil, *Ecl.* 8. 55–6.

Piers.

Ah fon,* for Love doth teach him climb so high,
And lifts him up out of the loathsome mire:
Such immortal mirror[m] as he doth admire
Would raise one's mind above the starry sky,
And cause a caitiff* courage to aspire,
For lofty Love[n] doth loath a lowly eye.

Cuddy.

All otherwise the state of poet stands,
For lordly Love is such a tyrant fell*
That, where he rules, all power he doth expel.
The vaunted* verse a vacant head demands,[o]
Ne wont with crabbed care* the Muses dwell.
Unwisely weaves, that takes two webs in hand.
Whoever casts* to compass* weighty prize,
And thinks to throw out thund'ring words of threat,
Let pour in lavish cups[p], and thrifty bits of meat;[48]
For Bacchus'[49] fruit is friend to Phoebus wise.
And when with wine the brain begins to sweat,
The numbers* flow as fast as spring doth rise.

---

[m] *Beauty, which is an excellent object of poetical spirits, as appeareth by the worthy Petrarch's*[50] *saying:*
> Fiorir faceva il mio debile ingegno
> A la sua ombra, et crescer ne gli affanni.

[n] *I think this playing with the letter to be rather a fault than a figure, as well in our English tongue, as it hath been always in the Latin, called* cacozelon.[51]

[o] *Imitateth Mantuan's saying:* vacuum curis divina cerebrum | Poscit.[52]

[p] *Resembleth that common verse:* Faecundi calices quem non fecere disertum.[53]

[48] This means either 'drink lavishly but eat sparingly', or 'eat proper food; of good quality'.

[49] Bacchus, god of wine, provides one form of inspiration; Phoebus Apollo, god of poetry and leader of the Muses, provides another. Ben Jonson had memorized these lines: cf. Drummond's testimony, p. 531.

[50] *Rime* 60: 'The noble tree [the laurel, Laura] that I have strongly loved for many years, ... made my weak wit flower in its shade and grow in my troubles' (tr. R. M. Durling). Piers argues the Neoplatonic conception of love as the ascent from the flesh to the soul, from earthly to heavenly beauty (the 'immortal mirror' being the reflection of the immortal world, which will raise our contemplation above the fixed stars and towards God). Cuddy counters with the physical power of love, rooted in the senses, and affected by wine.

[51] E.K.'s learning goes astray here: the Latin term *cacozelia* actually refers not to excessive alliteration but to verbal affectation, the unjustified use of 'high-sounding words' (*Inst.* 2. 3. 9), or to 'fonde [foolish] affectation', which tries 'to coin fine words out of the Latin, and to use new-fangled speeches . . .' (Puttenham, pp. 281–2).

[52] 'Divine [poetry] requires a brain free from worries.' This line does not occur in Mantuan, but similar expressions can be found in Juvenal, *Satires* 7. 59–66 and Ovid, *Heroides* 15. 14.

[53] Horace, *Epist.* 1. 519: 'Who is the man whom brimming cups have failed to make eloquent?'

Thou kenst not, Percy, how the rhyme should rage:*
O, if my temples[q] were distained with wine
And girt in girlonds of wild ivy[r] twine,
How I could rear the Muse[54] on stately stage,
And teach her tread aloft in buskin fine,[s]
With quaint* Bellona[55] in her equipage!*

But ah, my courage cools ere it be warm,
For-thy, content us in this humble shade,
Where no such troublous tides han* us assayed,
Here we our slender pipes may safely charm.[t]

Piers.
And when my goats shall han their bellies laid,
Cuddy shall have a kid to store* his farm.

Cuddy's Emblem[56]
Agitante[u] calescimus illo,[57]
etc.

[q] *He seemeth here to be ravished with a poetical fury;*[58] *for (if one rightly mark) the numbers rise so full, and the verse groweth so big, that it seemeth he hath forgot the meanness of shepherd's state and style.*

[r] *For it is dedicated to Bacchus, and therefore it is said that the Maenads (that is, Bacchus' frantic priests) used in their sacrifice to carry thyrsos, which were pointed staves or javelins wrapped about with ivy.*

[s] *It was the manner of poets and players in tragedies to wear buskins, as also in comedies to use stocks and light shoes; so that the* buskin *in poetry is used for tragical matter, as it said in Virgil:* Solo Sophocleo tua carmina digna cothurno; *and the like in Horace:* Magnum loqui, nitique cothurno.[59]

[t] *Temper and order; for charms were wont to be made by verses, as Ovid*[60] *saith:* Aut si carminibus.

[u] *Hereby is meant, as also in the whole course of this eclogue, that poetry is a divine instinct and unnatural rage, passing the reach of common reason. Whom Piers answereth* epiphonematicos,[61] *as admiring the excellency of the skill whereof in Cuddie he had already had a taste.*

[54] The Muse of tragedy is Melpomene.

[55] Bellona, goddess of war, appropriate to epic or tragic, not to pastoral poetry. But in the next stanza Cuddy's emotion ('courage') subsides, and he rejects the 'tides' or seasons of war for the safety of the countryside, where goats can give birth ('their bellies laid') in peace.

[56] But no emblem appears at the end of this eclogue.

[57] Cf. Plato, *Ion* 534a, as referred to by Elyot, p. 64, Sidney, p. 376, and Chapman, p. 523.

[58] Ovid, *Fast.* 6.5 ff., a passage in which Ovid reports the conflicting explanations for the name of the sixth month: '[I'll sing the truth, but some will say I lied, and think that no deities were ever seen by mortal. (*Est Deus in nobis:*) There is a god within us.] It is when he stirs us that our bosom warms; it is his impulse that sows the seeds of inspiration. I have a peculiar right to see the faces of the gods, whether because I am a bard [*vates*], or because I sing of sacred things' (tr. J. G. Frazer).

[59] Virgil, *Ecl.* 8. 10; Horace, *Ars P.* 280.

[60] E.K. may be recalling Ovid, *Am.* 3. 7. 27–30, on charms, but he seems to quote *Aen.* 4. 487: 'haec se carminibus', 'by her charms'.

[61] By way of the rhetorical figure *epiphonema*, a pithy summing-up ending a discourse; cf. Puttenham, pp. 264–5.

George Puttenham,
English poetics and rhetoric (1589)

GEORGE PUTTENHAM (*c.*1528–90) was the son of Robert Puttenham and Margery Elyot, sister to Sir Thomas Elyot. Elyot dedicated to her his treatise on *The Education or bringing up of children, translated oute of Plutarche* (London, *c.*1533), urging her 'to folowe the intent of Plutarche in bryinginge & inducing my litle nephewes [George and Richard] into the trayne and rule of vertue, whereby they shall fynally attayne to honour . . . and moste specially to the high pleasure of God, commoditye and profite of theyr countray'. George matriculated at Christ's College Cambridge, in November 1546, but left Cambridge without taking a degree (not deemed necessary for gentlemen). In August 1556 he entered the Middle Temple, and spent some time in the 1560s in Flanders and at various European courts. He was well connected by birth and marriage, being related to Edward Dyer and the Earl of Oxford, with friends at court and in government circles. In the 1570s he got into trouble with the authorities on various charges of conspiracy, outspoken criticism of Leicester and other councillors, and unpaid debts. But in 1584 the Queen granted him £1,000 for his 'good, true, faithful, and acceptable service'. Puttenham left in manuscript a treatise probably commissioned by the Queen (seven MS copies survive), *A Justification of Queene Elizabeth in Relacion to the affaire of Mary Queene of Scottes* (Camden Society Papers, 1867, pp. 65–134); and a collection of poems (*c.*1579–82) in praise of Queen Elizabeth, *Partheniades*, ed. W. R. Morfill in *Ballads from MSS* (London, 1873), 2. 72–91. Among the numerous other works he claimed to have written were *De Decoro*, a treatise on decorum; another on the *Originals and Pedigree of the English Tongue*; *Elpine* (1546; an eclogue to Edward VI), *Ginecocratia*, an academic comedy; and *Isle of Great Britain*, an Arthurian romance in verse.

TEXT. *The Arte of English Poesie. Contrived into three Bookes: The first of Poets and Poesie, the second of Proportion, the third of Ornament*, was published anonymously in 1589 by Richard Field, who also published Harington's translation of *Orlando Furioso* in 1591. (In a manuscript note Harington asked the printer to print all the prose passages in that work 'in the same printe that Putnams book ys': ed. McNulty, p. 557.) Although appearing half-way through Elizabeth's reign, much of the *Arte* was written earlier, and in temperament it belongs to the mid-Tudor period: the most frequently cited text is the *Songes and Sonettes*, otherwise known as *Tottel's Miscellany*, which first appeared in 1557. Ben Jonson's reference to the *Arte* as 'done 20 years since' (p. 535) may well imply that a first draught had existed as early as 1569; if so, it was partly revised in the mid-1580s to include references to *The Shepheardes Calendar* (1579), and quotations from manuscript poems of Dyer, Sidney, Ralegh and Oxford. All these matters were clarified by Gladys Willcock and Alice Walker in their excellent edition, *The Arte of English Poesie* (Cambridge, 1936, 1970), a milestone in the history of English literary criticism, referred to in the following notes as *WW*. I have also learned something from S. J. Doherty's critical edition of the *Arte* (Harvard University Ph.D. thesis, 1983; University Microfilms order no. 8322476). Neither edition goes into detail concerning the sources for Puttenham's account of rhetorical figures in book 3. According to La Rue van Hook ('Greek Rhetorical Terminology in Puttenham's *The Art of English Poesie*', *Transactions of the American Philological Association*, 45 (1914), 111–28), Puttenham derived his knowledge from Quintilian (who frequently gives the Greek name for specific figures) and the anonymous *Rhetorica ad Herennium*. However, I believe that Puttenham's main source was the popular handbook by Joannes Susenbrotus, *Epitome Troporum ac Schematum* (c.1541), which I cite in the outstanding edition by Joseph Xavier Brennan (University of Illinois Ph.D. thesis, 1953; UMI order no. 6921).

THE FIRST BOOK: OF POETS AND POESY

Chapter I
What a poet and poesy is,[1] *and who may be worthily said the most excellent poet of our time*

A poet is as much to say as a maker. And our English name well conforms with the Greek word, for of *poiein*, to make, they call a maker *poeta*. Such as (by way of resemblance and reverently) we may say of God; who without any travail* to his divine imagination made all the world of nought, nor also by any pattern or mould, as the Platonics

---

[1] Puttenham's discussion draws on various continental treatises, including Thomas Sébillet, *Art poétique français* (1548); Jacques Peletier, *Art poétique* (1555): cf. *TPR*, pp. 51–62 for Sébillet (ch. 1: 'De l'antiquité de la Poésie, et de son excellence'; ch. 2: 'Qu'est-ce que le Français doit appeler Rime?'; ch. 3: 'De l'invention, première partie de Poésie', etc.), and pp. 240 ff. for Peletier (ch. 1: 'De l'antiquité et de l'excellence de la Poésie', etc.). Other possible sources are Joachim Du Bellay, *La Deffence et Illustration de la Langue Francoyse* (1549); Antonio Minturno, *De poeta* (1555); Scaliger, *Poetices libri septem* (1561); and Sidney's *Defence of Poetry*, which was evidently circulating in manuscript, since Harington used it in 1591: see p. 305.

with their Ideas[2] do fantastically suppose. Even so the very poet makes and contrives out of his own brain both the verse and matter of his poem, and not by any foreign copy or example, as doth the translator, who therefore may well be said a versifier, but not a poet. The premises considered, it giveth to the name and profession no small dignity and preeminence, above all other artificers, scientific or mechanical. And nevertheless, without any repugnancy* at all, a poet may in some sort be said a follower or imitator, because he can express the true and lively of every thing is set before him, and which he taketh in hand to describe: and so in that respect is both a maker and a counterfeiter: and poesy an art not only of making, but also of imitation. And this science in his perfection cannot grow but by some divine instinct— the Platonics call it *furor*; or by excellency of nature and complexion;* or by great subtlety of the spirits* and wit; or by much experience and observation of the world, and course of kind;* or, peradventure, by all or most part of them. Otherwise, how was it possible that Homer,[3] being but a poor private man, and, as some say, in his later age blind, should so exactly set forth and describe, as if he had been a most excellent captain or general, the order and array of battles, the conduct of whole armies, the sieges and assaults of cities and towns? Or, as some great prince's majordomo* and perfect surveyor in court, the order, sumptuousness, and magnificence of royal banquets, feasts, weddings, and interviews? Or, as a politician very prudent and much inured* with the private and public affairs, so gravely examine the laws and ordinances civil, or so profoundly discourse in matters of estate and forms of all political regiment? Finally, how could he so naturally paint out the speeches, countenance, and manners of princely persons and private, to wit, the wrath of Achilles, the magnanimity of Agamemnon, the prudence of Menelaus, the prowess of Hector, the majesty of king Priamus, the gravity of Nestor, the policies and eloquence of Ulysses, the calamities of the distressed Queens, and valiance of all the captains and adventurous knights in those lamentable wars of Troy? It is therefore of poets thus to be conceived, that if they be able to devise and make all these things of themselves, without any subject of verity, that they be (by manner of speech) as creating gods. If they do it by instinct divine or natural, then surely much favoured from

---

[2] On the Platonic notion of *idea* cf. Sidney, p. 344. But Sidney rejects the Platonic *furor* as a prerequisite for poetic creation (p. 376).

[3] Praise of Homer as the founder of poetry was an ancient tradition, and is often found in England after Elyot's *The Governor* (p. 57); cf. Chapman, p. 517.

above; if by their experience, then no doubt very wise men; if by any precedent or pattern laid before them, then truly the most excellent imitators and counterfeiters of all others.

But you (madam)[4] my most honoured and gracious, if I should seem to offer you this my device for a discipline* and not a delight, I might well be reputed of all others the most arrogant and injurious, yourself being already, of any that I know in our time, the most excellent poet; forsooth, by your princely purse, favours, and countenance, making in manner what ye list, the poor man rich, the lewd* well learned, the coward courageous, and vile both noble and valiant. Then for imitation no less, your person as a most cunning counterfeiter lively representing Venus in countenance, in life Diana, Pallas for government, and Juno in all honour and regal magnificence.

Chapter II
That there may be an art of our English Poesy, as well as there is of the Latin and Greek

Then as there was no art in the world till by experience found out, so if Poesy be now an art, and of all antiquity hath been among the Greeks and Latins, and yet were none until by studious persons fashioned and reduced* into a method of rules and precepts, then no doubt may there be the like with us. And if the art of Poesy be but a skill appertaining to utterance, why may not the same be with us as well as with them, our language being no less copious, pithy, and significative[5] than theirs, our conceits the same, and our wits no less apt to devise and imitate than theirs were? If again art be but a certain order of rules prescribed by reason, and gathered by experience, why should not poesy be a vulgar* art with us as well as with the Greeks and Latins, our language admitting no fewer rules and nice* diversities* than theirs? But peradventure more by a peculiar* which our speech hath in many things differing from theirs; and yet, in the general points* of that art, allowed to go in common with them. So as if one point, perchance, which is their feet whereupon their measures[6] stand, and indeed is all the beauty of their poesy, and which feet

---

[4] Puttenham's treatise is dedicated to Queen Elizabeth, who was much admired as a poet: cf. L. Bradner (ed.), *The Poems of Queen Elizabeth I* (Providence, RI, 1964).

[5] For other assertions of the value of English as a literary language see Sidney, pp. 389–90, and R. F. Jones, *The Triumph of the English Language* (Stanford, Calif., 1953).

[6] Greek and Latin prosody was based on the quantity or length of syllables, not possible in English verse, which bases metre on accent, but does have the added resource of rhyme. Cf. Ascham, p. 157; Sidney, p. 388; Campion, p. 428; and Daniel, p. 441.

we have not, nor as yet never went about to frame (the nature of our language and words not permitting it), we have instead thereof twenty other curious* points in that skill more than they ever had, by reason of our rhyme and tunable* concords or symphony,* which they never observed. Poesy therefore may be an art in our vulgar, and that very methodical and commendable.

Chapter III
How poets were the first priests, the first prophets, the first legislators and politicians in the world

The profession and use of poesy is most ancient from the beginning, and not, as many erroneously suppose, after, but before any civil society[7] was among men. For it is written that poesy was the original cause and occasion of their first assemblies, when before the people remained in the woods and mountains, vagrant and dispersed like the wild beasts, lawless and naked, or very ill clad, and of all good and necessary provision for harbour or sustenance utterly unfurnished, so as they little differed for their manner of life from the very brute beasts of the field. Whereupon it is feigned* that Amphion and Orpheus, two poets of the first ages, one of them, to wit Amphion, built up cities, and reared walls with the stones that came in heaps to the sound of his harp, figuring* thereby the mollifying of hard and stony hearts by his sweet and eloquent persuasion. And Orpheus assembled the wild beasts to come in herds to hearken to his music, and by that means made them tame, implying thereby, how by his discreet and whole-some lessons uttered in harmony and with melodious instruments he brought the rude and savage people to a more civil and orderly life; nothing, as it seemeth, more prevailing or fit to redress and edify the cruel and sturdy courage of man than it. And as these two poets, and Linus before them, and Musaeus also and Hesiod, in Greece and Arcadia, so by all likelihood had more poets done in other places and in other ages before them, though there be no remembrance left of them by reason of the records by some accident of time perished and failing. Poets therefore are of great antiquity.

Then forasmuch as they were the first that intended* to the obser-vation of nature and her works, and specially of the celestial courses,

---

[7] On the role of poetry—or, in other versions, oratory—in making civil society possible, see Horace, *Ars P.* 391–407 (*ALC*, pp. 289–90); Sébillet and Peletier (*TPR*); Wilson, pp. 73–5; Sidney, p. 338.

by reason of the continual motion of the heavens, searching after the first mover, and from thence by degrees coming to know and consider of the substances separate and abstract, which we call the divine intelligences or good angels (*daimones*), they were the first that instituted sacrifices of placation, with invocations and worship to them, as to gods; and invented and established all the rest of the observances and ceremonies of religion, and so were the first priests and ministers of the holy mysteries.[8] And because for the better execution of that high charge and function it behoved them to live chaste and in all holiness of life, and in continual study and contemplation, they became by instinct divine, and by deep meditation, and much abstinence (the same assubtiling* and refining their spirits) to be made apt to receive visions, both waking and sleeping, which made them utter prophecies and foretell things to come. So also were they the first prophets or seers, *videntes*,[9] for so the scripture termeth them in Latin after the Hebrew word, and all the oracles and answers of the gods were given in metre or verse, and published to the people by their direction. And for that they were aged and grave men, and of much wisdom and experience in the affairs of the world, they were the first lawmakers to the people, and the first politicians, devising all expedient means for the establishment of commonwealth, to hold and contain the people in order and duty by force and virtue of good and wholesome laws, made for the preservation of the public peace and tranquillity; the same peradventure not purposely intended, but greatly furthered by the awe of their gods and such scruple of conscience as the terrors of their late invented religion had led them into.

Chapter IV
How poets were the first philosophers, the first astronomers, and historiographers, and orators, and musicians of the world

Utterance also and language is given by nature to man for persuasion of others and aid of themselves, I mean the first ability to speak. For speech itself is artificial* and made by man, and the more pleasing it

---

[8] Like Peletier (*TPR*, pp. 240, 325), Puttenham draws here on the popular work by Polydore Virgil, *De inventoribus rerum* (1499; enlarged 1521; English tr. by T. Langley, 1546), which records that poets first offered verses to pagan spirits whom they mistook for gods.

[9] It seems that the word *videntes* is not in the Vulgate, and is used in only one Renaissance Bible, the Douai version, in the gloss commenting on Exod. 7: 11, 'Then Pharaoh also called the wise men and the sorcerers'. (I owe this information to Mr Arend Küster of Chadwyck–Healey Ltd.)

is, the more it prevaileth[10] to such purpose as it is intended for. But speech by metre is a kind of utterance more cleanly couched and more delicate* to the ear than prose is, because it is more current* and slipper* upon the tongue, and withal tunable and melodious, as a kind of music, and therefore may be termed a musical speech or utterance, which cannot but please the hearer very well. Another cause is, for that is briefer and more compendious, and easier to bear away and be retained in memory, than that which is contained in multitude of words and full of tedious ambage* and long periods. It is, beside, a manner of utterance more eloquent and rhetorical than the ordinary prose which we use in our daily talk, because it is decked and set out with all manner of fresh colours* and figures, which maketh that it sooner inveigleth the judgment of man, and carrieth his opinion this way and that, whither soever the heart by impression of the ear shall be most affectionately bent and directed.[11] The utterance in prose is not of so great efficacy, because not only it is daily used, and by that occasion the ear is overglutted with it, but is also not so voluble* and slipper upon the tongue, being wide and loose, and nothing numerous,* nor contrived into measures and sounded with so gallant and harmonical accents, nor, in fine, allowed that figurative conveyance* nor so great licence in choice of words and phrases as metre is. So as the poets were also from the beginning the best persuaders, and their eloquence the first rhetoric of the world, even so it became that the high mysteries of the gods should be revealed and taught by a manner of utterance and language of extraordinary phrase,* and brief and compendious, and above all others sweet and civil, as the metrical is.

The same also was meetest to register the lives and noble gests* of princes, and of the great monarchs of the world, and all other the memorable accidents of time: so as the poet was also the first historiographer. Then, forasmuch as they were the first observers of all natural causes and effects in the things generable and corruptible,[12] and from thence mounted up to search after the celestial courses and influences, and yet penetrated further to know the divine essences and substances separate, as is said before, they were the first astronomers and philosophers and metaphysics.* Finally, because they

---

[10] On the power of persuasion cf. Wilson, pp. 75, 78; Sidney, pp. 386–7; Bacon, pp. 466–8.

[11] The 'colours' of rhetoric are various persuasive devices. On the irresistible force of rhetoric cf. Cicero, *De or*. 1. 8. 30, and *IDR*, pp. 75–80.

[12] According to Aristotle, all things beneath the moon are subject to both growth and decay.

did altogether endeavour themselves to reduce* the life of man to a certain method of good manners, and made the first differences between virtue and vice, and then tempered* all these knowledges and skills with the exercise of a delectable music by melodious instruments, which withall served them to delight their hearers, and to call the people together by admiration* to a plausible* and virtuous conversation,* therefore were they the first philosophers ethic, and the first artificial musicians of the world. Such was Linus, Orpheus, Amphion, and Musaeus, the most ancient Poets and philosophers of whom there is left any memory by the profane writers. King David also and Solomon his son and many other of the holy prophets wrote in metres, and used to sing them to the harp, although to many of us, ignorant of the Hebrew language and phrase, and not observing it, the same seem but a prose. It cannot be therefore that any scorn or indignity should justly be offered to so noble, profitable, ancient, and divine a science as Poesy is.

Chapter V
How the wild and savage people used a natural poesy in versicle* and rhyme as our vulgar is

And the Greek and Latin poesy was by verse numerous and metrical, running upon pleasant feet, sometimes swift, sometimes slow (their words very aptly serving that purpose), but without any rhyme or tunable concord in the end of their verses, as we and all other nations now use. But the Hebrews and Chaldees, who were more ancient than the Greeks, did not only use a metrical poesy, but also with the same a manner of rhyme,[13] as hath been of late observed by learned men. Whereby it appeareth that our vulgar rhyming poesy[14] was common to all the nations of the world besides, whom the Latins and Greeks in special called barbarous. So as it was, notwithstanding, the first and most ancient poesy, and the most universal; which two points do otherwise give to all human inventions and affairs no small credit. This is proved by certificate of merchants and travellers, who by late navigations have surveyed the whole world, and discovered large countries and strange peoples wild and savage, affirming that the American,* the Perusine,* and the very* cannibal do sing, and also

---

[13] This is in fact a misunderstanding of Hebrew verse.
[14] That is, English vernacular poetry using rhyme; I emend the 1589 text, which reads 'running poesy'.

say their highest and holiest matters in certain rhyming versicles, and not in prose, which proves also that our manner of vulgar poesy is more ancient than the artificial* of the Greeks and Latins, ours coming by instinct of nature, which was before art or observation, and used with the savage and uncivil, who were before all science or civility, even as the naked by priority of time is before the clothed, and the ignorant before the learned. The natural poesy therefore, being aided and amended by art, and not utterly altered or obscured, but some sign left of it (as the Greeks and Latins have left none), is no less to be allowed and commended than theirs. . . .

Chapter VIII
In what reputation poesy and poets were in old time with princes and otherwise generally, and how they be now become contemptible,[15] and for what causes

For the respects aforesaid, in all former ages and in the most civil countries and commonwealths, good poets and poesy were highly esteemed and much favoured of the greatest princes. For proof whereof we read how much Amyntas, king of Macedonia, made of the tragical poet Euripides; and the Athenians of Sophocles; in what price the noble poems of Homer were held with Alexander the great, in so much as every night they were laid under his pillow, and by day were carried in the rich jewel coffer of Darius lately before vanquished by him in battle. And not only Homer, the father and prince of the poets, was so honoured by him, but for his sake all other meaner poets, in so much as Cherillus,[16] one no very great good poet, had for every verse well made a Phillips noble of gold, amounting in value to an angel* English, and so for every hundreth verses (which a cleanly pen could speedily dispatch) he had a hundred angels. And since Alexander the great, how Theocritus the Greek poet was favoured by Ptolemy, king of Egypt, and Queen Berenice, his wife; Ennius likewise by Scipio, prince of the Romans; Virgil also by the Emperor Augustus.

---

[15] Laments for the decline of patronage were common among poets and writers of this period (as in Sidney, pp. 377–8), but are not borne out by the historical evidence. Cf. Phoebe Sheavyn, *The Literary Profession in the Elizabethan Age* (1909; rev. edn. by J. W. Saunders, Manchester, 1967).

[16] Cf. Horace, *Epist.* 2. 1. 233: 'The great king Alexander gave his favour to the notorious Choerilus, who repaid the royal gifts of gold pieces in verses ill-born and inelegant' (*ALC*, p. 278; also p. 289).

And in later times, how much were Jean de Meung and Guillaume de Lorris made of by the French kings; and Geoffrey Chaucer, father of our English Poets, by Richard the Second, who, as it was supposed, gave him the manor of new Holme in Oxfordshire; and Gower to Henry the Fourth; and Harding to Edward the Fourth. Also, how Francis the French king made Sangelais, Salmonius Macrinus, and Clement Marot of his privy chamber for their excellent skill in vulgar and Latin poesy; and King Henry the Eighth, her Majesty's father, for a few Psalms of David turned into English metre by Sternhold, made him groom of his privy chamber and gave him many other good gifts. And one Gray,[17] what good estimation did he grow unto with the same king Henry, and afterward with the Duke of Somerset, Protector, for making certain merry ballads, whereof one chiefly was 'The hunt is up, the hunt is up'? And Queen Mary, his daughter, for one *Epithalamie* or nuptial song made by Vargas, a Spanish Poet, at her marriage with king Philip in Winchester, gave him during his life two hundred crowns' pension.

Nor this reputation was given them in ancient times altogether in respect that poesy was a delicate* art, and the poets themselves cunning* prince-pleasers, but for that also they were thought for their universal knowledge to be very sufficient men for the greatest charges in their commonwealths, were it for counsel or for conduct; whereby no man need to doubt but that both skills may very well concur and be most excellent in one person. For we find that Julius Caesar, the first Emperor and a most noble captain, was not only the most eloquent orator of his time, but also a very good poet, though none of his doings therein be now extant. And Quintus Catullus, a good poet, and Cornelius Gallus, treasurer of Egypt; and Horace, the most delicate of all the Roman lyrics,* was thought meet and by many letters of great instance provoked to be secretary of estate to Augustus the Emperor, which nevertheless he refused for his unhealthfulness' sake, and, being a quiet-minded man and nothing ambitious of glory, *non voluit accedere ad Rempublicam*,[18] as it is reported. And Ennius the Latin Poet was not, as some perchance think, only favoured by Scipio the African for his good making of verses, but used as his familiar* and counsellor in the wars for his

---

[17] Thomas Sternhold, with others, produced *The Whole Book of Psalms* (1562), which included translations into English ballad stanza from the French versions by Marot and Beza. William Gray (d. 1551) wrote several birthday poems to Somerset.

[18] 'He did not want to take part in politics': Cicero, *De republica* 1. 5. 9. 1.

great knowledge and amiable conversation. And long before that, Antimenides and other Greek Poets, as Aristotle[19] reports in his *Politics*, had charge in the wars. And Tyrtaeus the poet, being also a lame man and halting upon one leg, was chosen by the oracle of the gods from the Athenians to be general of the Lacedemonians' army, not for his poetry, but for his wisdom and grave persuasions and subtle stratagems, whereby he had the victory over his enemies. So as the poets seemed to have skill not only in the subtleties of their art but also to be meet* for all manner of functions civil and martial, even as they found favour of the times they lived in, insomuch as their credit and estimation generally was not small.

But in these days, although some learned princes may take delight in them, yet universally it is not so. For as well poets as poesy are despised, and the name become of honourable infamous, subject to scorn and derision, and rather a reproach than a praise to any that useth it: for commonly who so is studious in the art or shows himself excellent in it, they call him in disdain a 'fantastical';* and a light-headed or fantastical man (by conversion) they call a poet. And this proceeds through the barbarous ignorance of the time, and pride of many gentlemen and others, whose gross heads not being brought up or acquainted with any excellent art, nor able to contrive or in manner conceive any matter of subtlety in any business or science, they do deride and scorn it in all others as superfluous knowledges and vain sciences, and whatsoever device be of rare invention they term it 'fantastical', construing it to the worst side: and among men such as be modest and grave, and of little conversation, nor delighted in the busy life and vain ridiculous actions of the popular, they call him in scorn a 'philosopher' or 'poet', as much to say as a fantastical man, very injuriously (God wot), and to the manifestation of their own ignorance, not making difference betwixt terms. For as the evil and vicious disposition of the brain[20] hinders the sound judgment and discourse of man with busy and disordered fantasies,* for which cause the Greeks call him

---

[19] *Pol.* 3. 14. 1285ᵃ35 ff.; Aristotle also mentions Antimenides' brother, the poet Alcaeus, and his banquet odes.

[20] Puttenham draws on Renaissance psychology and its belief that the mental processes—perception, imagination ('fantasy'), memory—existed within the brain in separate ventricles. The imagination, the faculty of making mental images, was held to be essential to the brain's functioning, but was also feared as being able to create images that it had not perceived. See E. Ruth Harvey, *The Inward Wits: Psychological Theory in the Middle Ages and the Renaissance* (London, 1975).

phantastikos,[21] so is that part, being well affected,* not only nothing disorderly or confused with any monstrous imaginations or conceits, but very formal, and in his much multiformity uniform, that is, well proportioned, and so passing clear, that by it, as by a glass or mirror, are represented unto the soul all manner of beautiful visions, whereby the inventive part of the mind is so much helped as without it no man could devise any new or rare thing. And where it is not excellent in his kind, there could be no politic captain, nor any witty* engineer or cunning artificer, nor yet any law-maker or counsellor of deep discourse, yea, the prince of philosophers sticks not to say *animam non intellegere absque phantasmate*;[22] which text to another purpose Alexander Aphrodisiensis[23] well noteth, as learned men know.

And this fantasy* may be resembled to a glass,* as hath been said, whereof there be many tempers* and manner of makings, as the perspectives* do acknowledge, for some be false glasses and show things otherwise than they be indeed, and others right,* as they be indeed, neither fairer nor fouler, nor greater nor smaller. There be again of these glasses that show things exceeding fair and comely; others that show figures very monstrous and ill-favoured. Even so is the fantastical part of man (if it be not disordered) a representer of the best, most comely, and beautiful images or apparances of things to the soul and according to their very truth. If otherwise, then doth it breed chimeras and monsters in man's imaginations, and not only in his imaginations, but also in all his ordinary actions and life which ensues. Wherefore such persons as be illuminated with the brightest irradiations of knowledge and of the verity and due proportion of things, they are called by the learned men not *phantastici* but *euphantasiōtoi*;[24] and of this sort of fantasy are all good poets, notable captains stratagematic,* all cunning artificers and engineers, all legislators, politicians, and

---

[21] Cf. Sidney, p. 371, on the pejorative associations of this term, and Bacon, pp. 466–7, for a more favourable view of the imagination.

[22] Aristotle, *De an.* 3. 7. 431ᵃ15 ff.: 'the soul never thinks without an image'; and *De memoria* 1. 450ᵃ1: 'Without an image thinking is impossible'.

[23] Alexander of Aphrodisias (fl. early 3rd cent. AD), a distinguished philosopher and commentator on Aristotle, who was notorious in the Renaissance for denying the immortality of any part of the individual soul, even the intellect. See his *De anima* 12. 19–24, ed. P. Accattino and P. L. Donini (Rome, 1996), pp. 125, 279, commenting on Aristotle's discussion (*De an.* 1. 1. 403ᵃ8–12) of whether the faculties of the soul (intellect, imagination) can exist without the body.

[24] Not 'subject to fantasy' in the pejorative sense, but 'having strong imagination'. Cf. M. W. Bundy, 'Invention and Imagination in the Renaissance', *Journal of English and Germanic Philology*, 29 (1930), 535–45.

counsellors of estate, in whose exercises the inventive part is most employed, and is to the sound and true judgment of man most needful. This diversity in the terms perchance every man hath not noted, and thus much be said in defence of the poets' honour, to the end no noble and generous mind be discomforted in the study thereof. . . .

But what of all this? Princes may give a good poet such convenient countenance* and also benefit as are due to an excellent artificer, though they neither kiss nor coax them, and the discreet poet looks for no such extraordinary favours, and as well doth he honour by his pen the just, liberal, or magnanimous prince, as the valiant, amiable or beautiful, though they be every one of them the good gifts of God. So it seems not altogether the scorn and ordinary disgrace offered unto poets at these days is cause why few gentlemen do delight in the art, but for that liberality is come to fail in princes, who for their largesse were wont to be accounted the only patrons of learning, and first founders* of all excellent artificers. Besides it is not perceived that princes themselves do take any pleasure in this science, by whose example the subject is commonly led and allured to all delights and exercises, be they good or bad, according to the grave saying of the historian. *Rex multitudinem religione implevit, quae semper regenti simi-lis est.*[25]

And peradventure in this iron and malicious age of ours Princes are less delighted in it, being over-earnestly bent and affected to the affairs of empire and ambition, whereby they are as it were enforced to endeavour themselves to arms and practices of hostility, or to intend* to the right policing of their states, and have not one hour to bestow upon any other civil or delectable art of natural or moral doctrine, nor scarce any leisure to think one good thought in perfect and godly con-templation, whereby their troubled minds might be moderated and brought to tranquillity. So as it is hard to find in these days of noble-men or gentlemen any good mathematician, or excellent musician, or notable philosopher, or else a cunning poet, because we find few great princes much delighted in the same studies. Now also of such among the nobility or gentry as be very well seen* in many laudable sciences, and especially in making or poesy, it is so come to pass that they have no courage to write; and, if they have, yet are they loath to be known [for] their skill. So as I know very many notable gentlemen in the court

---

[25] 'The king imbued the people with awe, which is always a constant of kingship'.

that have written commendably, and suppressed it again, or else suffered it to be published without their own names to it: as if it were a discredit for a gentleman[26] to seem learned and to show himself amorous of any good art. In other ages it was not so, for we read that Kings and Princes have written great volumes and published them under their own regal titles. . . .

Since therefore so many noble Emperors, Kings, and Princes have been studious of poesy and other civil arts, and not ashamed to bewray* their skills in the same, let none other meaner person despise learning, nor (whether it be in prose or in poesy, if they themselves be able to write, or have written any thing well or of rare invention) be any whit squeamish to let it be published under their names, for reason serves it, and modesty doth not repugn.*

Chapter IX
How poesy should not be employed upon vain conceits, or vicious, or infamous

Wherefore, the nobility and dignity of the art considered as well by universality as antiquity, and the natural excellence of itself, poesy ought not to be abased and employed upon any unworthy matter and subject, nor used to vain purposes; which nevertheless is daily seen, and that is to utter conceits* infamous and vicious, or ridiculous and foolish, or of no good example and doctrine. Albeit in merry matters (not unhonest) being used for man's solace and recreation it may be well allowed; for, as I said before, poesy is a pleasant manner of utterance, varying from the ordinary of purpose to refresh the mind by the ear's delight. Poesy also is not only laudable, because I said it was a metrical speech used by the first men, but because it is a metrical speech corrected and reformed by discreet judgments, and with no less cunning and curiosity than the Greek and Latin poesy, and by art beautified and adorned, and brought far from the primitive rudeness of the first inventors.

Otherwise it may be said to me that Adam and Eve's aprons were the gayest* garments because they were the first, and the shepherd's

[26] Members of the gentry and nobility in this period, who scorned to appear in print on the same level as commoners writing for money, usually allowed their work to circulate in manuscript, so that they could control its readership. Cf. J. W. Saunders, 'The Stigma of Print: A Note on the Social Bases of Tudor Poetry', *Essays in Criticism*, 1 (1951), 139–64, including material not repeated in Saunders, *The Profession of English Letters* (London, 1964).

tent or pavilion* the best housing, because it was the most ancient and most universal; which I would not have so taken, for it is not my meaning. But that Art and cunning* concurring with nature, antiquity, and universality, in things indifferent* and not evil, do make them more laudable. And right so our vulgar rhyming poesy, being by good wits brought to that perfection, we see is worthily to be preferred before any other manner of utterance in prose, for such use and to such purpose as it is ordained, and shall hereafter be set down more particularly.

Chapter X
The subject or matter of poesy

Having sufficiently said of the dignity of poets and poesy, now it is time to speak of the matter or subject of poesy, which to mine intent* is whatsoever witty* and delicate conceit* of man meet or worthy to be put in written verse, for any necessary use of the present time, or good instruction of the posterity. But the chief and principal is: the laud, honour, and glory of the immortal gods (I speak now in phrase of the gentiles);* secondly, the worthy gests* of noble princes, the memorial and registry of all great fortunes, the praise of virtue and reproof of vice, the instruction of moral doctrines, the revealing* of sciences natural and other profitable arts, the redress of boisterous* and sturdy courages by persuasion, the consolation and repose of temperate minds; finally, the common solace of mankind in all his travails and cares of this transitory life. And in this last sort, being used for recreation only, may allowably bear matter not always of the gravest or of any great commodity* or profit, but rather in some sort vain, dissolute, or wanton, so it be not very scandalous and of evil example. . . .

Chapter XXII
In what form of poesy the amorous affections and allurements
were uttered

The first founder of all good affections is honest love, as the mother of all the vicious is hatred. It was not therefore without reason that so commendable, yea honourable a thing as love well meant, were it in princely estate or private, might in all civil commonwealths be uttered in good form and order as other laudable things are. And because love is of all other human affections the most puissant and passionate, and most general to all sorts and ages of men and women, so as whether it be of the young or old, or wise or holy, or high estate or low, none ever could truly brag of any exemption in that case: it requireth a form of poesy[27] variable, inconstant, affected, curious, and most witty of any others, whereof the joys were to be uttered in one sort, the sorrows in another, and, by the many forms of poesy, the many moods and pangs of lovers thoroughly to be discovered; the poor souls sometimes praying, beseeching, sometimes honouring, advancing, praising, another while railing, reviling, and cursing; then sorrowing, weeping, lamenting, in the end laughing, rejoycing, and solacing the beloved again, with a thousand delicate devices, odes, songs, elegies, ballads, sonnets, and other ditties, moving one way and another to great compassion.

Chapter XXIII
The form of poetical rejoicings

Pleasure is the chief part of man's felicity in this world, and also, as our theologians say, in the world to come. Therefore, while we may (yea always, if it could be), to rejoice and take our pleasures in virtuous and honest sort, it is not only allowable but also necessary and very natural to man. And many be the joys and consolations of the heart, but none greater than such as he may utter and discover* by some convenient means: even as to suppress and hide a man's mirth, and not to have therein a partaker, or at least wise a witness, is no little grief and infelicity. Therefore nature and civility have ordained, besides the private solaces, public rejoicings for the comfort and recreation of many. And they be of diverse sorts and upon diverse occasions grown. One and the chief was for the public peace of a country, the greatest of any other civil good; and wherein your Majesty (my most gracious sovereign) have shown yourself to all the world, for this one and thirty years space of your glorious reign, above all other princes of Christendom, not only fortunate, but also most sufficient, virtuous, and worthy of empire. Another is for just and honourable victory achieved against the foreign enemy. A third at solemn feasts and pomps of coronations and instalments of honourable orders. Another for jollity at weddings and marriages. Another at the births of princes' children. Another for private entertainments in court, or other secret disports* in chamber, and such solitary places.

---

[27] Cf. Scaliger, *Poetice* 1. 44, 'Lyrica'.

And as these rejoicings tend to divers effects, so do they also carry diverse forms and nominations; for those of victory and peace are called *triumphal*, whereof we ourselves have heretofore given some example by our triumphals,[28] written in honour of her Majesty's long peace. And they were used by the ancients in like manner as we do our general processions or litanies, with banquets and bonfires and all manner of joys. Those that were to honour the persons of great Princes or to solemnise the pomps of any instalment* were called *encomia*; we may call them carols* of honour. Those to celebrate marriages were called songs nuptial or *epithalamies*, but in a certain mystical sense, as shall be said hereafter. Others for magnificence at the nativities of princes' children, or by custom used yearly upon the same days, are called songs natal, or *genethliaca*. Others for secret recreation and pastime in chambers with company or alone were the ordinary musics amorous, such as might be sung with voice or to the lute, cithaeron or harp, or danced by measures, as the Italian pavan and galliard are at these days in princes' courts and other places of honourable or civil assembly; and of all these we will speak in order and very briefly.

Chapter XXIV
The form of poetical lamentations

Lamenting is altogether contrary to rejoicing; every man saith so, and yet is it a piece of joy to be able to lament with ease, and freely to pour forth a man's inward sorrows and the griefs wherewith his mind is surcharged.[29] This was a very necessary device of the poet and a fine, besides his poetry to play also the physician, and not only by applying a medicine to the ordinary sickness of mankind, but by making the very grief itself (in part) cure of the disease.[30] Now are the causes of man's sorrows many: the death of his parents, friends, allies, and children (though many of the barbarous nations do rejoice at their burials and sorrow at their births), the overthrows and discomforts in battle, the subversions of towns and cities, the desolations of countries, the loss of goods and worldly promotions, honour and good

---

[28] Puttenham refers three times to these poems, which are lost, although many poems and collections in praise of Elizabeth have survived.

[29] Cf. Scaliger, *Poetice* 3. 122: 'consolatio est oratio reducans maerentis animum ad tranquillitatem'.

[30] To cure grief as if it were a disease was the aim of many texts in the *consolatio* tradition, the most famous being Cicero's *Tusculan Disputations*.

renown; finally, the travails and torments of love forlorn or ill-bestowed, either by disgrace, denial, delay, and twenty other ways that well-experienced lovers could recite.

Such of these griefs as might be refrained or holpen by wisdom and the parties' own good endeavour, the poet gave none order to sorrow them. For first, as to the good renown, it is lost for the more part by some default of the owner, and may be by his well-doings recovered again. And if it be unjustly taken away, as by untrue and famous libels, the offender's recantation may suffice for his amends: so did the poet Stesichorus, as it is written of him in his *Palinode* upon the dispraise of Helena, and recovered his eyesight. Also, for worldly goods, they come and go, as things not long proprietary to anybody, and are not yet subject unto fortune's dominion, so but that we ourselves are in great part accessary to our own losses and hindrances by oversight and misguiding of ourselves and our things; therefore, why should we bewail our such voluntary detriment? But death, the irrecoverable loss, death, the doleful departure of friends, that can never be recontinued by any other meeting or new acquaintance—besides our uncertainty and suspicion of their estates and welfare in the places of their new abode—seemeth to carry a reasonable pretext* of just sorrow. Likewise, the great overthrows in battle and desolations of countries by wars, as well for the loss of many lives and much liberty, as for that it toucheth the whole state, and every private man hath his portion in the damage. Finally, for love, there is no frailty in flesh and blood so excusable as it, no comfort or discomfort greater than the good and bad success thereof, nothing more natural to man, nothing of more force to vanquish his will and to inveigle his judgment.

Therefore of death and burials, of the adversities by wars, and of true love lost or ill-bestowed are the only sorrows that the noble poets sought by their art to remove or appease, not with any medicament of a contrary temper, as the Galenists use to cure *contraria contrariis*, but as the Paracelsians,[31] who cure *similia similibus*, making one dolour to expel another, and, in this case, one short sorrowing the remedy[32] of a long and grievous sorrow. And the lamenting of deaths was chiefly

---

[31] Galenic medicine used a variety of remedies which were not necessarily 'opposite' in kind to the complaint; but Paracelsian physicians did base much of their system on the doctrine of signatures, those apparent similarities between various levels of the creation, so using a yellow plant to cure jaundice, for instance. Shakespeare refers to this difference between the two medical schools in *All's Well that Ends Well* 2. 3. 11.

[32] Cicero, *Tusc.* 3. 21. 75.

at the very burials of the dead, also at months' minds[33] and longer times, by custom continued yearly, when as they used many offices of service and love towards the dead, and thereupon are called obsequies in our vulgar; which was done not only by cladding the mourners their friends and servants in black vestures, of shape doleful and sad, but also by woeful countenances and voices, and besides by poetical mournings in verse. Such funeral songs were called *epicedia* if they were sung by many, and *monodia* if they were uttered by one alone, and this was used at the interment of Princes and others of great account, and it was reckoned a great civility to use such ceremonies, as at this day is also in some country used. In Rome they accustomed to make orations funeral and commendatory of the dead parties in the public place called *Pro rostris*; and our theologians instead thereof use to make sermons, both teaching the people some good learning and also saying well of the departed. Those songs of the dolorous discomfits in battle and other desolations in war, or of towns saccaged* and subverted,* were sung by the remnant of the army overthrown, with great shrikings* and outcries, holding the wrong end of their weapon upwards in sign of sorrow and despair. The cities also made general mournings and offered sacrifices with poetical songs to appease the wrath of the martial gods and goddesses. The third sorrowing was of loves, by long lamentation in *elegie*:[34] so was their song called, and it was in a piteous manner of metre, placing a limping *pentameter* after a lusty *hexameter*, which made it go dolorously, more than any other metre. . . .

Chapter XXX
Of short epigrams called posies*

There be also other like epigrams that were sent usually for New year's gifts, or to be printed or put upon their banqueting dishes of sugar plate or of marchpanes,* and such other dainty meats as by the courtesy and custom every guest might carry from a common feast home with him to his own house, and were made for the nonce. They were called *nenia* or *apophoreta*,[35] and never contained above one verse, or two at the most, but the shorter the better; we call them posies, and do paint them nowadays upon the back sides of our fruit trenchers*

---

[33] Remembrances of the dead a month after their death.

[34] On elegy as a verse form cf. Campion, p. 437.

[35] But although *apophoreta* were presents given to guests, especially at the time of the Saturnalia, a *nenia* was a funeral song or dirge (*Inst.* 8. 2. 8; Scaliger, *Poetice* 1. 50).

of wood, or use them as devices in rings and arms and about such courtly purposes.

So have we remembered and set forth to your Majesty very briefly all the commended forms of the ancient poesy, which we in our vulgar makings do imitate and use under these common names: interlude, song, ballad, carol, and ditty;* borrowing them also from the French, all saving this word 'song' which is our natural Saxon English word; the rest, such as time and usurpation by custom have allowed us out of the primitive Greek and Latin, as comedy, tragedy, ode, epitaph, elegy, epigram, and other more. And we have purposely omitted all nice* or scholastical* curiosities* not meet for your Majesty's contemplation in this our vulgar art, and what we have written of the ancient forms of poems we have taken from the best clerks writing in the same art.

The part that next followeth, to wit of proportion, because the Greeks nor Latins never had it in use nor made any observation, no more than we do of their feet, we may truly affirm to have been the first devisers thereof ourselves, as *autodidaktoi*,* and not to have borrowed it of any other by learning or imitation, and thereby trusting to be held the more excusable if anything in this our labours happen either to mislike or to come short of the author's purpose, because commonly the first attempt in any art or engine* artificial is amendable, and in time by often experiences reformed. And so no doubt may this device of ours be, by others that shall take the pen in hand after us.

Chapter XXXI
Who in any age have been the most commended writers in our English poesy, and the author's censure given upon them

It appeareth by sundry records of books both printed and written that many of our countrymen have painfully* travailed in this part. Of whose works some appear to be but bare translations, other some matters of their own invention and very commendable, whereof some recital shall be made[36] in this place, to the intent chiefly that their names should not be defrauded of such honour as seemeth due to them, for having by their thankful studies so much beautified our English tongue as at this day it will be found our nation is in nothing

---

[36] Puttenham (following the example of Italian and French treatises) gives the first systematic historical outline of English poetry, which was frequently imitated.

inferior to the French or Italian for copy* of language, subtlety of device,* good method and proportion in any form of poem, but that they may compare with the most, and perchance pass a great many of them. And I will not reach above the time of King Edward the Third and Richard the Second for any that wrote in English metre, because before their times, by reason of the late Norman conquest, which had brought into this realm much alteration both of our language and laws, and therewithall a certain martial barbarousness, whereby the study of all good learning was so much decayed as long time after no man or very few intended to write in any laudable science.* So as beyond that time there is little or nothing worth commendation to be found written in this art.

And those of the first age were Chaucer and Gower, both of them, as I suppose, knights. After whom followed John Lydgate, the monk of Bury, and that nameless, who wrote the satire called *Piers Plowman*; next him followed Harding, the chronicler; then, in King Henry the Eighth's time, Skelton (I wot not for what great worthiness) surnamed the Poet Laureate. In the latter end of the same king's reign sprang up a new company of courtly makers, of whom Sir Thomas Wyatt the elder and Henry, Earl of Surrey were the two chieftains, who having travelled into Italy, and there tasted the sweet and stately measures and style of the Italian poesy, as novices newly crept out of the schools of Dante, Ariosto, and Petrarch, they greatly polished our rude and homely manner of vulgar poesy from that it had been before, and for that cause may justly be said the first reformers of our English metre and style. In the same time, or not long after, was the Lord Thomas Vaux, a man of much facility in vulgar makings.

Afterward, in King Edward the sixth's time, came to be in reputation for the same faculty* Thomas Sternhold, who first translated into English certain Psalms of David, and John Heywood, the epigrammatist, who for the mirth and quickness of his conceits, more than for any good learning was in him, came to be well benefited by the king. But the principal man in this profession at the same time was Master Edward Ferrers,[37] a man of no less mirth and felicity* that way, but of much more skill and magnificence in his metre, and therefore wrote for the most part to the stage, in tragedy and sometimes in comedy or interlude, wherein he gave the king so much good recreation as he had

---

[37] An error for George Ferrers (*c.*1500–79), poet and politician, who acted as 'Master of the King's Pastimes' in 1551–2 for Edward VI, and contributed both to the *Mirror for Magistrates* (1559) and *The Princely Pleasures* at Kenilworth (1575).

thereby many good rewards. In Queen Mary's time flourished above any other Doctor Phaer, one that was well learned and excellently well translated into English verse heroical certain books of Virgil's *Aeneid*. Since him followed Master Arthur Golding, who with no less commendation turned into English metre the *Metamorphoses* of Ovid, and that other Doctor,[38] who made the supplement to those books of Virgil's *Aeneid* which Master Phaer left undone.

And in her Majesty's time that now is, are sprung up another crew of courtly makers, noblemen and gentlemen of her Majesty's own servants, who have written excellently well, as it would appear if their doings could be found out and made public with the rest. Of which number is first that noble gentleman Edward Earl of Oxford, Thomas Lord of Buckhurst, when he was young; Henry Lord Paget, Sir Philip Sidney, Sir Walter Raleigh, Master Edward Dyer, Master Fulke Greville, Gascoigne, Breton, Turberville, and a great many other learned gentlemen, whose names I do not omit for envy, but to avoid tediousness, and who have deserved no little commendation.

But of them all particularly, this is mine opinion, that Chaucer, with Gower, Lydgate, and Harding, for their antiquity ought to have the first place, and Chaucer, as the most renowned of them all, for the much learning appeareth to be in him above any of the rest. And though many of his books be but bare translations out of the Latin and French, yet are they well handled, as his books of *Troilus and Criseyde*, and the *Roman of the Rose*, whereof he translated but one half, the device was Jean de Meung's, a French poet. The *Canterbury Tales* were Chaucer's own invention, as I suppose, and where he showeth more the natural of his pleasant wit than in any other of his works. His similitudes, comparisons, and all other descriptions are such as cannot be amended. His metre heroical of *Troilus and Criseyde* is very grave and stately, keeping the staff of seven and the verse[39] of ten; his other verses of the *Canterbury Tales* be but riding rhyme, nevertheless very well becoming the matter of that pleasant pilgrimage, in which every man's part is played with much decency.*

Gower, saving for his good and grave moralities,* had nothing in him highly to be commended, for his verse was homely and without good measure, his words strained much deal* out of the French

---

[38] Phaer's *Aeneid* translation was completed by Thomas Twyne, who issued bks. 10–12 in 1573.

[39] That is, a 'staff' or stanza of seven lines, each of which has ten syllables. On Chaucer's 'riding rhyme' cf. Gascoigne, p. 171 n. 40.

writers, his rhyme wrested,* and in his inventions small subtlety. The applications of his moralities are the best in him, and yet those many times very grossly* bestowed; neither doth the substance of his works sufficiently answer the subtlety of his titles. Lydgate, a translator only, and no deviser of that which he wrote, but one that wrote in good verse. Harding, a poet epic or historical, handled himself well according to the time and manner of his subject. He that wrote the satire of *Piers Plowman* seemed to have been a malcontent of that time, and therefore bent himself wholly to tax* the disorders of that age, and specially the pride of the Roman* clergy, of whose fall he seemeth to be a very true prophet. His verse is but loose metre, and his terms* hard and obscure, so as in them is little pleasure to be taken. Skelton, a sharp satirist, but with more railing and scoffery than became a poet laureate. Such among the Greeks were called *pantomimi*;[40] with us buffoons, altogether applying their wits to scurrilities and other ridiculous matters. Henry Earl of Surrey and Sir Thomas Wyatt, between whom I find very little difference, I repute them (as before) for the two chief lanterns of light to all others that have since employed their pens upon English poesy. Their conceits were lofty, their styles stately, their conveyance* cleanly, their terms proper, their metre sweet and well proportioned, in all imitating very naturally and studiously their master Francis Petrarcha. The Lord Vaux his commendation lieth chiefly in the facility of his metre, and the aptness of his descriptions such as he taketh upon him to make, namely in sundry of his songs, wherein he showeth the counterfeit* action very lively and pleasantly.

Of the latter sort I think thus. That for tragedy, the Lord of Buckhurst and Master Edward Ferrers, for such doings as I have seen of theirs, do deserve the highest price; the Earl of Oxford, and Master Edwards of her Majesty's Chapel, for comedy and interlude. For eclogue and pastoral poesy, Sir Philip Sidney and Master Chaloner, and that other gentleman who wrote the late *Shepherd's Calendar*. For ditty and amorous ode I find Sir Walter Raleigh's vein* most lofty, insolent,* and passionate. Master Edward Dyer, for elegy most sweet, solemn, and of high conceit. Gascoigne, for a good metre and for a plentiful vein. Phaer and Golding, for a learned and well corrected verse, specially in translation clear and very faithfully answering their

---

[40] Cf. Scaliger, *Poetice* 1. 10, on the poetry of ridicule.

authors' intent. Others have also written with much facility, but more commendably perchance if they had not written so much, nor so popularly. But last in recital and first in degree is the Queen our sovereign Lady, whose learned, delicate, noble muse easily surmounteth all the rest that have written before her time or since, for sense, sweetness and subtlety, be it in ode, elegy, epigram, or any other kind of poem heroic or lyric, wherein it shall please her Majesty to employ her pen, even by as much odds as her own excellent estate and degree exceedeth all the rest of her most humble vassals.

THE SECOND BOOK: OF PROPORTION POETICAL

Chapter I
Of proportion poetical

It is said by such as profess the mathematical sciences, that all things stand by proportion, and that without it nothing could stand to be good or beautiful. The doctors of our theology to the same effect, but in other terms, say that God made the world by number, measure, and weight;[41] some for weight say tune, and peradventure better. For weight is a kind of measure or of much convenience* with it; and therefore in their descriptions be always coupled together *statica* et *metrica*, weight and measures. Hereupon it seemeth the philosopher gathers* a triple proportion, to wit, the arithmetical, the geometrical, and the musical.[42] And by one of these three is every other proportion guided of the things that have conveniency* by relation, as the visible by light, colour, and shadow; the audible by stirs,* times, and accents; the odorable by smells of sundry temperaments;* the tastable by savours to the rate;* the tangible by his objects in this or that regard. Of all which we leave to speak, returning to our poetical proportion, which holdeth of* the musical, because, as we said before, poesy is a skill to speak and write harmonically: and verses or rhyme be a kind of musical utterance, by reason of a certain congruity in sounds pleasing the ear, though not perchance so exquisitely as the

---

[41] Cf. the Wisdom of Solomon 11: 21, celebrating the divine creation: 'thou hast ordered all things by measure and number and weight'. On the importance of this verse in medieval and later biblical interpretation cf. E. R. Curtius, *European Literature and the Latin Middle Ages*, tr. W. R. Trask (New York, 1953), excursus xv, 'Numerical Composition' (pp. 501–9).

[42] Cf. Scaliger, *Poetice* 2. 2: 'De pede, metro, rhythmo', for this distinction between measures which are musical, arithmetical, or geometrical.

harmonical consents* of the artificial* music, consisting in strained* tunes, as is the vocal music, or that of melodious instruments, as lutes, harps, regals,* recorders, and such like. And this our proportion poetical resteth in five points: staff, measure, concord, situation,* and figure, all which shall be spoken of in their places.

Chapter II
Of proportion in staff

Staff in our vulgar poesy I know not why it should be so called, unless it be for that we understand it for a bearer or supporter of a song or ballad, not unlike the old weak body that is stayed up by his staff, and were not otherwise able to walk or to stand upright. The Italian called it *stanza*, as if we should say a resting place. And if we consider well the form of this poetical staff, we shall find it to be a certain number of verses allowed to go altogether and join without any intermission, and do or should finish up all the sentences of the same with a full period, unless it be in some special cases, and there to stay till another staff follow of like sort. And the shortest staff containeth not under four verses, nor the longest above ten; if it pass that number it is rather a whole ditty* than properly a staff. Also, for the more part the staves stand rather upon the even number of verses than the odd, though there be of both sorts.

The first proportion, then, of a staff is by quatrain or four verses. The second of five verses, and is seldom used. The third by sixaine or six verses, and is not only most usual, but also very pleasant to the ear. The fourth is in seven verses, and is the chief of our ancient proportions used by any rhymer writing anything of historical or grave poem, as ye may see in Chaucer and Lydgate, the one writing the loves of *Troilus and Criseyde*, the other of the fall of princes: both by them translated, not devised. The fifth proportion is of eight verses very stately and heroic, and which I like better than that of seven, because it receiveth better band.* The sixth is of nine verses, rare but very grave. The seventh proportion is of ten verses, very stately, but in many men's opinion too long; nevertheless of very good grace and much gravity. Of eleven and twelve I find none ordinary staves used in any vulgar language, neither doth it serve well to continue any historical report and ballad or other song, but is a ditty of itself, and no staff; yet some modern writers have used it, but very seldom. Then last of all have ye a proportion to be used in the number of your staves, as to a carol and a ballad, to a song, and a round,[43] or virelay.[44] For to an historical poem no certain number is limited, but as the matter* falls out. Also, a distich or couple of verses is not to be accounted a staff, but serves for a continuance, as we see in elegy, epitaph, epigram, or such metres, of plain concord, not harmonically intertangled as some other songs of more delicate music be. . . .

Chapter III
Of proportion in measure

Metre and measure is all one,* for what the Greekes called *metron*, the Latins call *mensura*, and is but the quantity of a verse, either long or short. This quantity with them consisteth in the number of their feet; and with us in the number of syllables which are comprehended* in every verse, not regarding his feet—otherwise than that we allow, in scanning our verse, two syllables to make one short portion (suppose it a foot) in every verse. And after that sort ye may say we have feet in our vulgar rhymes, but that is improperly; for a foot by his sense natural is a member of office and function, and serveth to three purposes, that is to say, to go, to run, and to stand still; so as he must be sometimes swift, sometimes slow, sometime unegally* marching, or peradventure steady. . . .

Chapter VI
Of proportion in concord, called symphony or rhyme

Because we use the word rhyme (though by manner of abusion),* yet to help that fault[45] again we apply it in our vulgar poesy another way very commendably and curiously. For wanting the currentness* of the Greek and Latin feet, instead thereof we make in the ends of our verses a certain tunable sound; which anon after with another verse reasonably distant we accord together in the last fall or cadence, the ear taking pleasure to hear the like tune reported,* and to feel his

---

[43] The rondeau (from Old French) was originally a poem in three stanzas, with thirteen or fifteen lines, usually octosyllabic, of which the opening words became the refrain. It was popular in 16th-cent. France.

[44] A Provençal verse-form, usually consisting of short-lined stanzas with two rhymes, variously arranged.

[45] In 16th-cent. English, as in French, the words for 'rhyme' and 'rhythm' were both derived from the Latin *rhythmus*, and their spelling was often confused. Following either Sébillet (*TPR*, pp. 54–6) or Du Bellay (*Deffence*, bk. 2, ch. 8), Puttenham explains the confusion at some length: cf. *WW*, pp. 76–8; *ECE* i. 267 (Webbe); and Scaliger, *Poetice* 2. 2.

return. And for this purpose serve the monosyllables of our English Saxons excellently well, because they do naturally and indifferently* receive any accent, and in them, if they finish the verse, resteth the shrill* accent of necessity,* and so doth it not in the last of every bisyllable, nor of every polysyllable word.

But to the purpose: 'rhyme' is a borrowed word from the Greeks by the Latins and French, from them by us Anglo-Saxons, and by abusion as hath been said, and therefore it shall not do amiss to tell what this *rithmos* was with the Greeks, for what is it with us hath been already said. There is an accountable* number which we call arithmetical (*arithmos*) as one, two, three. There is also a musical or audible number, fashioned by stirring of tunes and their sundry times in the utterance of our words, as when the voice goeth high or low, or sharp or flat, or swift or slow: and this is called *rithmos* or numerosity,[46] that is to say, a certain flowing utterance by slipper* words and syllables, such as the tongue easily utters, and the ear with pleasure receiveth. And which flowing of words, with much volubility smoothly proceeding from the mouth, is in some sort harmonical and breedeth to the ear a great compassion.*

This point grew by the smooth and delicate running of their feet, which we have not in our vulgar, though we use as much as may be the most flowing words and slipper syllables that we can pick out. Yet do not we call that by the name of rhyme, as the Greeks did, but do give the name of rhyme only to our concords, or tunable* consents in the latter end of our verses, and which concords the Greeks nor Latins never used in their poesy, till by the barbarous soldiers out of the camp* it was brought into the Court, and thence to the school,* as hath been before remembered. And yet the Greeks and Latins both used a manner of speech by clauses of like termination, which they called *homoioteleuton*,[47] and was the nearest that they approached to our rhyme, but is not our right concord. So as we in abusing this term (rhyme) be nevertheless excusable, applying it to another point in poesy no less curious than their *rithme* or numerosity, which indeed passed the whole verse throughout, whereas our concords keep but the latter end of every verse, or perchance the middle and the end in metres that be long. . . .

---

[46] Cf. Gascoigne, p. 165, and Scaliger, *Poetice* 2. 2.

[47] For this figure, in which successive phrases or clauses end with a word having identical termination (otherwise known as *similiter desinens*) cf. Sidney, p. 386, Campion, p. 431, and Scaliger, *Poetice* 4. 41.

Chapter IX
How the good maker will not wrench his word to help his rhyme, either
by falsifying his accent,* or by untrue orthography

Now there cannot be in a maker a fouler fault than to falsify his accent
to serve his cadence,* or by untrue orthography to wrench his words
to help his rhyme, for it is a sign that such a maker is not copious* in
his own language, or (as they are wont to say) not half his craft's
master. As, for example, if one should rhyme to this word 'restore',
he may not match him with 'door' or 'poor', for neither of both are
of like terminant,* either by good orthography or in natural sound;
therefore such rhyme is strained; so is it to this word 'ram' to say
'came', or to 'bean', 'den', for they sound not nor be written alike; and
many other like cadences which were superfluous to recite, and are
usual with rude rhymers who observe not precisely the rules of
prosody. Nevertheless in all such cases, if necessity constrained, it is
somewhat more tolerable to help the rhyme by false orthography than
to leave an unpleasant dissonance to the ear by keeping true orthography and losing the rhyme. As, for example, it is better to rhyme
'dore' with 'restore' than in his truer orthography, which is 'door', and
to this word 'desire' to say 'fier' than 'fire', though it be otherwise
better written 'fire'. For since the chief grace of our vulgar poesy consisteth in the symphony,* as hath been already said, our maker must
not be too licentious* in his concords, but see that they go even, just,
and melodious in the ear, and right so in the numerosity or currentness of the whole body of his verse, and in every other of his proportions. For a licentious maker is in truth but a bungler and not a
poet. Such men were in effect the most part of all your old rhymers,
and specially Gower, who to make up his rhyme would for the most
part write his terminant syllable with false orthography, and many
times not stick to put in a plain French word for an English. And so,
by your leave, do many of our common rhymers at this day, as he that
by all likelihood having no word at hand to rhyme to this word 'joy',
he made his other verse end in 'Roy', saying very impudently thus:

> O mighty Lord of love, dame Venus' only joy,
> Who art the highest God of any heavenly Roy.[48]

Which word was never yet received in our language for an English

---

[48] George Turberville, 'The Lover to Cupid for Mercie', in *Epitaphes, Epigrams, Songs and Sonets* (1567); see again, p. 282.

word. Such extreme licentiousness is utterly to be banished from our school, and better it might have been borne with in old rhyming writers, because they lived in a barbarous age, and were grave moral men but very homely poets, such also as made most of their works by translation out of the Latin and French tongue, and few or none of their own engine,* as may easily be known to them that list* to look upon the poems of both languages.

Finally, as ye may rhyme with words of all sorts, be they of many syllables or few, so nevertheless is there a choice by which to make your cadence (before remembered) most commendable. For some words of exceeding great length, which have been fetched from the Latin inkhorn* or borrowed of strangers, the use of them in rhyme is nothing pleasant, saving perchance to the common people, who rejoice much to be at plays and interludes, and, besides their natural ignorance, have at all such times their ears so attentive to the matter, and their eyes upon the shows of the stage, that they take little heed to the cunning* of the rhyme, and therefore be as well satisfied with that which is gross* as with any other finer and more delicate.

Chapter X
Of concord in long and short measures, and by near or far distances, and which of them is most commendable

But this ye must observe withal, that, because your concords contain the chief part of music in your metre, their distances[49] may not be too wide or far asunder, lest the ear should lose the tune and be defrauded of his delight. And whensoever ye see any maker use large and extraordinary distances, ye must think he doth intend to show himself more artificial than popular; and yet therein is not to be discommended, for respects* that shall be remembered in some other place of this book.

Note also that rhyme or concord is not commendably used both in the end and middle of a verse, unless it be in toys* and trifling poesies, for it showeth a certain lightness either of the matter or of the maker's head, albeit these common rhymers use it much. For, as I said before, like as the symphony in a verse of great length is, as it were, lost by looking after him, and yet may the metre be very grave and stately, so on the other side doth the over-busy and too speedy return of one manner of tune too much annoy and, as it were, glut the ear. Unless

---

[49] That is, the number of lines between the rhymes.

it be in small and popular musics sung by these *cantabanqui** upon benches and barrels' heads, where they have none other audience than boys or country fellows that pass by them in the street; or else by blind harpers or such like tavern minstrels that give a fit* of mirth for a groat,* and their matters being for the most part stories of old time, as *The Tale of Sir Topas*, the reports* of *Bevis of Southampton*, *Guy of Warwick*, *Adam Bell*, and *Clym of the Clough*, and such other old romances or historical rhymes, made purposely for recreation of the common people at Christmas dinners and bridals, and in taverns and alehouses, and such other places of base resort. Also they be used in carols and rounds and such light or lascivious poems, which are commonly more commodiously uttered by these buffoons or vices in plays than by any other person. Such were the rhymes of Skelton, usurping the name of a Poet Laureate, being indeed but a rude* railing* rhymer and all his doings ridiculous. He used both short distances and short measures, pleasing only the popular ear; in our courtly maker we banish them utterly.

Chapter XI
Of proportion by situation[50]

This proportion consisteth in placing of every verse in a staff or ditty by such reasonable distances as may best serve the ear for delight, and also to show the poet's art and variety of music. And the proportion is double: one by marshalling the metres, and limiting their distances, having regard to the rhyme or concord how they go and return; another by placing every verse, having a regard to his measure and quantity only, and not to his concord. As, to set one short metre to three long, or four short and two long, or a short measure and a long, or of diverse lengths with relation one to another, which manner of situation, even without respect of the rhyme, doth alter the nature of the poesy, and make it either lighter or graver, or more merry, or mournful, and many ways passionate to the ear and heart of the hearer; seeming for this point that our maker by his measures and concords of sundry proportions doth counterfeit the harmonical tunes of the vocal and instrumental musics. As the Dorian, because his falls, sallies, and compass be diverse from those of the Phrygian, the

---

[50] That is, the disposition of rhyme-schemes within a stanza. Puttenham illustrates these graphically: cf. *WW*, pp. 85–90.

Phrygian likewise from the Lydian, and all three from the Aeolian,
Myolidian, and Ionian,[51] mounting and falling from note to note such
as be to them peculiar,* and with more or less leisure or precipitation.
Even so, by diversity of placing and situation of your measures and
concords, a short with a long, and by narrow or wide distances, or
thicker or thinner bestowing of them, your proportions differ, and
breedeth a variable and strange harmony not only in the ear, but also
in the conceit of them that hear it. . . .

THE THIRD BOOK: OF ORNAMENT

Chapter I
Of ornament poetical

As, no doubt, the good proportion of anything doth greatly adorn and
commend it, and right so our late remembered proportions do to our
vulgar poesy, so is there yet requisite to the perfection of this art
another manner of exornation,* which resteth in the fashioning of our
maker's language and style, to such purpose as it may delight and
allure as well the mind as the ear of the hearers with a certain novelty
and strange manner of conveyance,[52] disguising it no little from the
ordinary and accustomed; nevertheless, making it nothing the more
unseemly or misbecoming, but rather decenter and more agreeable to
any civil ear and understanding. And as we see in these great madams
of honour, be they for personage or otherwise never so comely and
beautiful, yet if they want their courtly habiliments or at leastwise
such other apparel as custom and civility have ordained to cover their
naked bodies, would be half ashamed or greatly out of countenance
to be seen in that sort, and perchance do then think themselves more
amiable in every man's eye when they be in their richest attire, suppose
of silks or tissues and costly embroideries, than when they go in cloth
or in any other plain and simple apparel; even so cannot our vulgar
poesy show itself either gallant or gorgeous if any limb be left naked
and bare and not clad in his kindly* clothes and colours,* such as may
convey them somewhat out of sight, that is from the common course
of ordinary speech and capacity of the vulgar judgment, and yet being

[51] Renaissance critics continued to discuss the various 'modes' classified in Greek music
theory, even though they were unable to recreate them aurally.
[52] Puttenham summarizes Quintilian's definition of figurative speech: *Inst.* 9. 1. 14.

artificially* handled must needs yield it much more beauty and commendation.

This ornament we speak of is given to it by figures and figurative speeches, which be the flowers, as it were, and colours that a poet setteth upon his language of art, as the embroiderer doth his stone* and pearl or passements* of gold upon the stuff of a princely garment, or as the excellent painter bestoweth the rich orient colours upon his table of portrait. So, nevertheless as if the same colours in our art of poesy (as well as in those other mechanical arts) be not well tempered,* or not well laid, or be used in excess, or never so little disordered or misplaced, they not only give it no manner of grace at all, but rather do disfigure the stuff and spoil the whole workmanship, taking away all beauty and good liking from it. No less than if the crimson taint which should be laid upon a lady's lips, or right in the centre of her cheeks, should by some oversight or mishap be applied to her forehead or chin, it would make (ye would say) but a very ridiculous beauty; wherefore the chief praise and cunning of our poet is in the discreet* using of his figures, as the skilful painter's is in the good conveyance of his colours and shadowing* traits* of his pencil, with a delectable variety, by all measure and just proportion, and in places most aptly to be bestowed.

Chapter 11
*How our writing and speeches public ought to be figurative;
and, if they be not, do greatly disgrace the cause and purpose of the
speaker and writer*

But as it hath been always reputed a great fault to use figurative speeches foolishly and indiscreetly, so is it esteemed no less an imperfection in man's utterance to have none use of figure at all, specially in our writing and speeches public, making them but as our ordinary talk, than which nothing can be more unsavoury and far from all civility.[53] I remember in the first year of Queen Mary's reign a knight of Yorkshire[54] was chosen speaker of the Parliament, a good gentleman and wise in the affairs of his shire and not unlearned in the laws of

---

[53] By 'civility' Puttenham implies the whole range of behaviour expected from a responsible member of society. Cf. the treatise by Stefano Guazzo, *La civile conversazione* (1574)—where 'conversation' means 'social intercourse'—tr. G. Petty in 1581, completed by B. Young in 1586.

[54] Perhaps Sir Thomas Gargrave of York; but he was the first Speaker in Elizabeth's reign (1558), not Mary's.

the realm, but as well for some lack of his teeth as for want of language nothing well spoken, which at that time and business was most behoveful for him to have been. This man, after he had made his oration to the Queen, which ye know is of course* to be done at the first assembly of both houses, a bencher of the Temple both well learned and very eloquent, returning from the Parliament house, asked another gentleman, his friend, how he liked M. Speaker's oration. 'Marry,' quoth the other, 'methinks I heard not a better alehouse tale told this seven years.' This happened because the good old Knight made no difference between an oration or public speech, to be delivered to the ear of a Prince's Majesty and state of a realm, than he would have done of an ordinary tale to be told at his table in the country, wherein all men know the odds* is very great. And though grave and wise counsellors in their consultations do not use much superfluous eloquence, and also in their judicial hearings do much mislike all scholastical* rhetorics, yet in such a case as it may be (and as this Parliament was), if the Lord Chancellor of England or Archbishop of Canterbury himself were to speak, he ought to do it cunningly* and eloquently, which cannot be without the use of figures; and nevertheless none impeachment* or blemish to the gravity of their persons or of the cause. Wherein I report* me to them that knew Sir Nicholas Bacon, Lord Keeper of the great Seal, or the now Lord Treasurer[55] of England, and have been conversant with their speeches made in the Parliament house and Star Chamber. From whose lips I have seen to proceed more grave and natural eloquence than from all the orators of Oxford or Cambridge; but all is as it is handled, and maketh no matter whether the same eloquence be natural to them or artificial* (though I think rather natural), yet were they known to be learned and not unskilful of the art when they were younger men.

And as learning and art teacheth a scholar to speak, so doth it also teach a counsellor, and as well an old man as a young, and a man in authority as well as a private person, and a pleader* as well as a preacher, every man after his sort and calling as best becometh. And that speech which becometh one doth not become another. For manners of speeches, some serve to work in excess, some in medioc-

---

[55] Sir Nicholas Bacon (1509–79), a distinguished humanist and counsellor, who was Lord Keeper to Elizabeth for over twenty years, and father of Francis Bacon (see p. 457). The Lord High Treasurer from 1572 to 1598 was William Cecil, Baron Burghley (1520–98), educated at Grantham School and St John's College Cambridge (1535–41), where he studied Greek with Sir John Cheke (with whom he was also related by marriage).

rity; some to grave purposes, some to light; some to be short and brief, some to be long; some to stir up affections, some to pacify and appease them. And these common despisers of good utterance, which resteth altogether in figurative speeches, being well used (whether it come by nature, or by art, or by exercise), they be but certain gross ignorants, of whom it is truly spoken, *scientia non habet inimicum nisi ignoran-tem.*[56] I have come to the Lord Keeper Sir Nicholas Bacon, and found him sitting in his gallery alone with the works of Quintilian before him; indeed he was a most eloquent man, and of rare learning and wisdom as ever I knew England to breed, and one that joyed as much in learned men and men of good wits. . . .

And because I am so far waded* into this discourse of eloquence and figurative speeches, I will tell you what happened on a time, myself being present, when certain Doctors of the civil law were heard in a litigious cause betwixt a man and his wife, before a great magistrate who (as they can tell that knew him) was a man very well learned and grave, but somewhat sour, and of no plausible* utterance. The gen-tleman's chance was to say, 'my Lord, the simple woman is not so much to blame as her lewd abettors, who by violent persuasions have led her into this wilfulness.' Quoth the judge, 'what need such elo-quent terms in this place?' The gentleman replied, 'doth your Lord-ship mislike the term *violent*, and methinks I speak it to great purpose, for I am sure she would never have done it but by force of persuasion, and if persuasions were not very violent to the mind of man it could not have wrought so strange an effect as we read that it did once in Egypt'—and would have told the whole tale at large if the magistrate had not passed it over very pleasantly. Now to tell you the whole matter as the gentleman intended, thus it was. There came into Egypt a notable orator, whose name was Hegesias,[57] who inveighed so much against the incommodities of this transitory life, and so highly com-mended death, the dispatcher of all evils, as a great number of his hearers destroyed themselves, some with weapon, some with poison, others by drowning and hanging themselves, to be rid out of this vale of misery. Insomuch as it was feared lest many more of the people would have miscarried by occasion of his persuasions, if King Ptolemy had not made a public proclamation that the orator should avoid* the country, and no more be allowed to speak in any matter. Whether now

[56] 'Knowledge has no enemy save the ignorant': a common saying of obscure origin. Cf. Harington, p. 303. For the triad *ars, imitatio, exercitatio*, cf. p. 295.
[57] Cicero, *Tusc.* 1. 34. 83.

persuasions may not be said violent and forcible, to simple minds in
special, I refer it to all men's judgments that hear the story. At least
ways, I find this opinion confirmed by a pretty device or emblem that
Lucianus[58] allegeth he saw in the portrait of Hercules within the city
of Marseilles in Provence, where they had figured a lusty old man with
a long chain tied by one end at his tongue, by the other end at the
people's ears, who stood afar off and seemed to be drawn to him by
the force of that chain fastened to his tongue, as who would say, by
force of his persuasions. And to show more plainly that eloquence is
of great force and not (as many men think amiss) the property and
gift of young men only, but rather of old men, and a thing which better
becometh hoary hairs than beardless boys, they seem to ground it
upon this reason. Age (say they and most truly) brings experience,
experience bringeth wisdom; long life yields long use and much exercise of speech; exercise and custom with wisdom make an assured and
voluble* utterance. So is it that old men more than any other sort speak
most gravely, wisely, assuredly, and plausibly, which parts are all that
can be required in perfect eloquence. And so in all deliberations of
importance, where counsellors are allowed freely to opine and show
their conceits, good persuasion is no less requisite than speech itself;
for in great purposes to speak and not to be able or likely to persuade
is a vain thing. Now let us return back to say more of this poetical
ornament.

Chapter III
How ornament poetical is of two sorts, according to the double virtue and efficacy of figures

This ornament then is of two sorts, one to satisfy and delight the ear
only by a goodly outward show set upon the matter, with words and
speeches smoothly and tunably running; another by certain intendments* or sense of such words and speeches inwardly working a stir
to the mind. That first quality the Greeks called *enargeia*, of this word
argos, because it giveth a glorious lustre and light. This latter they
called *energeia*,[59] of *ergon*, because it wrought with a strong and vir-

---

[58] Lucian, *Heracles* 1. This account inspired the iconographical figure known as
'Hercules Gallicus', a popular Renaissance illustration of the power of eloquence.

[59] Puttenham misunderstands *enargeia*, which 'does not refer to the titillation of the
ear through pleasing and ornamental figures, but to vividness of style (graphic, vivid
representation), whereby an event or situation is luminously revealed to the mind's eye
of the hearer or reader. *Enargeia* is a conspicuous characteristic of the style of Lysias, who

tuous operation. And figure breedeth them both, some serving to give gloss* only to a language, some to give it efficacy* by sense; and so by that means some of them serve the ear only, some serve the conceit only and not the ear. There be of them also that serve both turns, as common servitors appointed for the one and the other purpose, which shall be hereafter spoken of in place. But because we have alleged before that ornament is but the good, or rather beautiful habit* of language or style, and figurative speeches the instrument wherewith we burnish our language, fashioning it to this or that measure and proportion, whence finally resulteth a long and continual phrase or manner of writing or speech, which we call by the name of 'style': we will first speak of language; then of style; lastly of figure, and declare their virtue and differences, and also their use and best application, and what portion in exornation every of them bringeth to the beautifying of this art.

Chapter IV
Of language

Speech is not natural to man, saving for his only ability to speak, and that he is by kind* apt to utter all his conceits with sounds and voices diversified many manner of ways, by means of the many and fit instruments he hath by nature to that purpose, as: a broad and voluble* tongue, thin and movable lips, teeth even and not shagged, thick ranged, a round vaulted palate, and a long throat; besides an excellent capacity of wit that maketh him more disciplinable* and imitative than any other creature. Then, as to the form and action of his speech, it cometh to him by art and teaching, and by use or exercise. But after a speech is fully fashioned to the common understanding, and accepted by consent of a whole country and nation, it is called a language, and receiveth none allowed alteration but by extraordinary occasions, by little and little, as it were insensibly, bringing in of many corruptions that creep along with the time. Of all which matters we

used figures sparingly' (van Hook, op. cit., p. 113). Quintilian (*Inst.* 8. 3. 89) defines *energeia* as 'vigour . . . which derives its name from action and [ensures] that nothing that we say is tame'. *Enargeia* (Lat. *illustratio, evidentia*), by contrast, 'makes us seem not so much to narrate as to exhibit the actual scene, while our emotions will be no less actively stirred than if we were present at the actual occurence' (6. 2. 32). This 'vivid illustration' presents the facts at issue to the judge 'clearly and vividly', so that they are 'displayed in their living truth to the eyes of the mind' (8. 2. 61–2). Scaliger discusses *energeia* (*Poetice* 2. 6), calling it '*Efficacia*'. The two figures are often confused by Renaissance and modern critics.

have more largely spoken in our books of the originals and pedigree of the English tongue.[60]

Then, when I say language, I mean the speech wherein the poet or maker writeth, be it Greek or Latin, or as our case is the vulgar English, and when it is peculiar unto a country it is called the mother speech of that people. The Greeks term it *idiōma*:[61] so is ours at this day the Norman English. Before the Conquest of the Normans it was the Anglo-Saxon, and before that the British, which, as some will, is at this day the Welsh, or as others affirm the Cornish. I for my part think neither of both, as they be now spoken and pronounced. This part in our maker or poet must be heedily* looked unto, that it be natural, pure, and the most usual of all his country; and for the same purpose rather that which is spoken in the kings' court, or in the good towns and cities within the land, than in the marches* and frontiers, or in port towns, where strangers haunt for traffic* sake, or yet in universities, where scholars use much peevish* affectation of words out of the primitive languages, or finally, in any uplandish* village or corner of a realm, where is no resort but of poor rustical or uncivil people. Neither shall he follow the speech of a craftsman or carter, or other of the inferior sort, though he be inhabitant or bred in the best town and city in this realm, for such persons do abuse good speeches by strange accents or ill-shapen sounds and false orthography. But he shall follow generally the better brought up sort, such as the Greeks call *charientes*,[62] men civil and graciously behavioured and bred. Our maker therefore at these days shall not follow *Piers Plowman* nor Gower nor Lydgate nor yet Chaucer, for their language is now out of use with us; neither shall he take the terms of Northernmen, such as they use in daily talk, whether they be noblemen or gentlemen or of their best clerks,* all is a matter; nor in effect any speech used beyond the river of Trent, though no man can deny but that theirs is the purer English Saxon at this day, yet it is not so courtly nor so current as our Southern English is; no more is the far Western man's speech. Ye shall therefore take the usual speech of the court, and that of London and the shires lying about London within sixty miles, and not much above. I say not this but that in every shire of England there be gentlemen

---

[60] This lost work would have been in line with the many Renaissance treatises justifying the vernacular languages, a movement which spread from Italy to France to England.

[61] Cf. Gascoigne, p. 168.

[62] Plato, *Resp.* 452b, and Aristotle, *Pol.* 2. 7. 1266[b]37 ff.; both use the term in contrast to the *hoi polloi*.

and others that speak, but specially write as good Southern as we of Middlesex or Surrey do, but not the common people of every shire, to whom the gentlemen and also their learned clerks do for the most part condescend;* but herein we are already ruled by the English dictionaries and other books written by learned men, and therefore it needeth none other direction in that behalf. Albeit peradventure some small admonition be not impertinent, for we find in our English writers many words and speeches amendable,* and ye shall see in some, many inkhorn terms so ill-affected brought in by men of learning, as preachers and schoolmasters, and many strange terms of other languages by secretaries and merchants and travellers, and many dark* words and not usual nor well sounding, though they be daily spoken in court. Wherefore great heed must be taken by our maker in this point that his choice be good. . . .

Chapter V
Of style

Style is a constant and continual phrase or tenor* of speaking and writing, extending to the whole tale or process* of the poem or history, and not properly to any piece or member of a tale, but is, of words, speeches, and sentences together, a certain contrived form and quality, many times natural to the writer,[63] many times his peculiar by election* and art, and such as either he keepeth by skill or holdeth on by ignorance, and will not or peradventure cannot easily alter into any other. So we say that Cicero's style and Sallust's were not one,* nor Caesar's and Livy's, nor Homer's and Hesiod's, nor Herodotus' and Thucydides', nor Euripides' and Aristophanes', nor Erasmus' and Budaeus' styles. And because this continual course and manner of writing or speech showeth the matter and disposition of the writer's mind more than one or few words or sentences can show, therefore there be that have called style the image of man, *mentis character.* For man is but his mind, and as his mind is tempered* and qualified* so are his speeches and language at large; and his inward conceits be the mettle of his mind, and his manner of utterance the very warp and woof of his conceits, more plain, or busy and intricate, or otherwise affected after the rate.* Most men say that not any one point in all physiognomy is so certain as to judge a man's manners by his eye; but

---

[63] See Scaliger's long discussion of style, *Poetice* 4. 1: 'Character', and Horace, *Ars P.* 89 ff., 156 ff.

more assuredly in mine opinion, by his daily manner of speech and ordinary writing. For if the man be grave, his speech and style is grave; if light-headed, his style and language also light. If the mind be haughty and hot, the speech and style is also vehement and stirring; if it be cold and temperate, the style is also very modest; if it be humble, or base and meek, so is also the language and style. And yet peradventure not altogether so, but that every man's style is for the most part according to the matter and subject of the writer, or so ought to be, and conformable thereunto. Then again may it be said as well, that men do choose their subjects according to the mettle of their minds, and therefore a high-minded man chooseth him high and lofty matter to write of; the base courage, matter base and low; the mean and modest mind, mean and moderate matters after the rate.

Howsoever it be, we find that under these three principal complexions* (if I may with leave so term them), high, mean, and base style[64] there be contained many other humours or qualities of style, as the plain and obscure, the rough and smooth, the facile and hard, the plentiful and barren, the rude and eloquent, the strong and feeble, the vehement and cold styles, all which in their evil are to be reformed, and the good to be kept and used. But generally, to have the style decent* and comely it behoveth the maker or poet to follow the nature of his subject: that is, if his matter be high and lofty that the style be so too; if mean, the style also to be mean; if base, the style humble and base accordingly; and they that do otherwise use it, applying to mean matter high and lofty style, and to high matters style either mean or base, and to the base matters the mean or high style, do utterly disgrace their poesy, and show themselves nothing skilful in their art, nor having regard to the decency,* which is the chief praise of any writer. Therefore, to rid all lovers of learning from that error, I will, as near as I can, set down which matters be high and lofty, which be but mean, and which be low and base, to the intent the styles may be fashioned to the matters, and keep their *decorum* and good proportion in every respect.

I am not ignorant that many good clerks be contrary to mine opinion, and say that the lofty style may be decently used in a mean and base subject, and contrariwise, which I do in part acknowledge, but with a reasonable qualification. For Homer hath so used it in his trifling work of *Batrachomyomachia*, that is in his treatise of the war

---

[64] This classification of the three styles and their respective subject-matters was common to many rhetoric books: cf. *IDR*, pp. 80–2.

betwixt the frogs and the mice; Virgil also in his *Bucolics*, and in his *Georgics*, whereof the one is counted mean, the other base, that is the husbandman's* discourses and the shepherd's. But hereunto serveth a reason in my simple conceit: for first to that trifling poem of Homer, though the frog and the mouse be but little and ridiculous beasts, yet to treat of war is a high subject, and a thing in every respect terrible and dangerous to them that it alights on; and therefore of learned duty asketh martial grandiloquence, if it be set forth in his kind and nature of war, even betwixt the basest creatures that can be imagined. So also is the ant or pismire, and they be but little creeping things, not perfect* beasts, but insects, or worms. Yet, in describing their nature and instinct, and their manner of life approaching to the form of a commonwealth,[65] and their properties not unlike to the virtues of most excellent governors and captains, it asketh a more majesty of speech than would the description of another beast's life or nature, and perchance of many matters pertaining unto the baser sort of men, because it resembleth the history of a civil regiment,* and of them all the chief and most principal, which is monarchy. So also in his *Bucolics*, which are but pastoral speeches and the basest of any other poem in their own proper nature, Virgil used a somewhat swelling style when he came to insinuate* the birth of Marcellus,[66] heir apparent to the Emperor Augustus as child to his sister, aspiring by hope and greatness of the house to the succession of the Empire, and establishment thereof in that family. Whereupon Virgil could do no less than to use such manner of style, whatsoever condition the poem were of, and this was decent,* and no fault or blemish to confound* the tenors* of the styles for that cause. But now, when I remember me again that this *Eclogue* (for I have read it somewhere) was conceived by Octavian the Emperor to be written to the honour of Pollio, a citizen of Rome and of no great nobility, the same was misliked again as an implicative,* nothing decent nor proportionable* to Pollio his fortunes and calling, in which respect I might say likewise the style was not to be such as if it had been for the Emperor's own honour and those of the blood imperial, than which subject there could not be among the Roman writers a higher nor graver to treat upon.

So can I not be removed from mine opinion, but still methinks that in all decency the style ought to conform with the nature of the subject, otherwise if a writer will seem to observe no *decorum* at all,

[65] See the famous account of the bees' society in Virgil, *Georg.* 4.
[66] Virgil, *Ecl.* 4.

nor pass* how he fashion his tale to his matter,* who doubteth but he may in the lightest cause speak like a Pope, and in the gravest matters prate like a parrot, and find words and phrases enough to serve both turns, and neither of them commendably. For neither is all that may be written of Kings and Princes such as ought to keep a high style, nor all that may be written upon a shepherd to keep the low, but according to the matter reported, if that be of high or base nature; for every petty pleasure and vain delight of a king are not to be accounted high matter for the height of his estate, but mean and perchance very base and vile. Nor so a poet or historiographer[67] could decently* with a high style report the vanities of Nero, the ribaldries of Caligula, the idleness of Domitian, and the riots of Heliogabalus; but well the magnanimity and honourable ambition of Caesar, the prosperities of Augustus, the gravity of Tiberius, the bounty of Trajan, the wisdom of Aurelius, and generally all that which concerned the highest honours of Emperors, their birth, alliances, government, exploits in war and peace, and other public affairs. For they be matter stately and high, and require a style to be lift up and advanced by choice of words, phrases, sentences, and figures, high, lofty, eloquent, and magnific* in proportion. So be the mean matters to be carried with all words and speeches of smoothness and pleasant moderation; and finally the base things to be holden within their tether by a low, mild, and simple manner of utterance, creeping rather than climbing, and marching rather than mounting upwards with the wings of the stately subjects and style.

Chapter VI
Of the high, low, and mean subject

The matters therefore that concern the gods and divine things are highest of all other to be couched in writing; next to them the noble gests and great fortunes of Princes, and the notable accidents* of time, as the greatest affairs of war and peace. These be all high subjects, and therefore are delivered over to the poets hymnic and historical, who be occupied either in divine lauds or in heroical reports. The mean matters be those that concern mean men, their life and business, as lawyers, gentlemen, and merchants, good householders and honest citizens, and which sound* neither to matters of state nor of war, nor leagues, nor great alliances, but smatch* all the common conversation, as of the civiller and better sort of men. The base and low matters be

---

[67] Lucian, 'How to write history' (*ALC*, pp. 536–47).

the doings of the common artificer, servingman, yeoman, groom, husbandman, day-labourer, sailor, shepherd, swineherd, and such like of homely calling, degree, and bringing up. So that in every of the said three degrees not the selfsame virtues be equally to be praised, nor the same vices equally to be dispraised, nor their loves, marriages, quarrels, contracts, and other behaviours be like high, nor do require to be set forth with the like style, but every one in his degree and decency. Which made that all hymns and histories and tragedies were written in the high style, all comedies and interludes and other common poesies of loves and such like in the mean style, all eclogues and pastoral poems in the low and base style; otherwise they had been utterly disproportioned.

Likewise, for the same cause some phrases and figures be only peculiar to the high style, some to the base or mean, some common to all three, as shall be declared more at large hereafter when we come to speak of figure and phrase. Also some words and speeches and sentences do become the high style that do not become the other two, and contrariwise, as shall be said when we talk of words and sentences. Finally, some kind of measure* and concord* do not beseem the high style that well become the mean and low, as we have said speaking of concord and measure. But generally the high style is disgraced, and made foolish and ridiculous by all words affected, counterfeit, and puffed up, as it were a windball* carrying more countenance than matter, and cannot be better resembled than to these midsummer pageants in London, where, to make the people wonder, are set forth great and ugly giants marching as if they were alive, and armed at all points; but within they are stuffed full of brown paper and tow,* which the shrewd* boys underpeering do guilefully discover and turn to a great derision. Also, all dark* and unaccustomed words, or rustical and homely, and sentences that hold too much of the merry and light,* or infamous and unshamefaced, are to be accounted of the same sort, for such speeches become not Princes nor great estates, nor them that write of their doings, to utter or report and intermingle with the grave and weighty matters.[68]

Chapter VII
Of figures and figurative speeches

As figures be the instruments of ornament in every language, so be they also in a sort abuses or rather trespasses in speech,[69] because they

---

[68] Cf. Whetstone, p. 174.   [69] Quintilian, *Inst.* 9. 1. 11 ff., 9. 3. 3, etc.

pass the ordinary limits of common utterance, and be occupied of purpose to deceive the ear and also the mind, drawing it from plainness and simplicity to a certain doubleness, whereby our talk is the more guileful and abusing.* For what else is your *metaphor* but an inversion* of sense by transport;* your *allegory*[70] by a duplicity of meaning or dissimulation under covert and dark intendments; onewhile speaking obscurely and in riddle called *enigma*; anotherwhile by common proverb or adage called *paroemia*; then by merry scoff called *ironia*; then by bitter taunt called *sarcasmus*; then by *periphrasis* or circumlocution, when all might be said in a word or two; then by incredible comparison giving credit, as by your *hyperbole*; and many other ways seeking to inveigle* and appassionate* the mind. Which thing made the grave judges Areopagites[71] (as I find written) to forbid all manner of figurative speeches to be used before them in their consistory of justice, as mere illusions to the mind, and wresters of upright judgment, saying that to allow such manner of foreign and coloured talk to make the judges affectioned were all one* as if the carpenter before he began to square his timber would make his squire* crooked; insomuch as the straight and upright mind of a judge is the very rule of justice, till it be perverted by affection.*

This no doubt is true and was by them gravely considered. But in this case, because our maker or poet is appointed not for a judge, but rather for a pleader, and that of pleasant and lovely causes and nothing perilous, such as be those for the trial of life, limb, or livelihood; and before judges neither sour nor severe, but in the ear of princely dames, young ladies, gentlewomen, and courtiers, being all for the most part either meek of nature or of pleasant humour; and that all his abuses* tend but to dispose the hearers to mirth and solace* by pleasant conveyance* and efficacy of speech, they are not in truth to be accounted vices, but for virtues in the poetical science very commendable. On the other side, such trespasses in speech (whereof there be many) as give dolour and disliking to the ear and mind by any foul indecency or disproportion of sound, situation, or sense, they be called and not without cause, the vicious parts or rather heresies* of language. Wherefore, the matter resteth much in the definition and acceptance

---

[70] Quintilian, *Inst.* 9. 1. 3.

[71] Cf. Aristotle, *Rht.* 1. 1. 1354ᵃ15 ff. (and Lucian, *Anarchasis* 19): yet this merely states that 'The arousing of prejudice, pity, anger, and similar emotions has nothing to do with the essential facts' and should be proscribed in 'the rules for trials'; for this reason 'the court of the Areopagus . . . forbid talk about non-essentials'. It is doubtful whether such a ban was ever observed.

of this word *decorum*, for whatsoever is so cannot justly be misliked. In which respect it may come to pass that what the grammarian setteth down for a viciosity* in speech may become a virtue and no vice; contrariwise, his commended figure may fall into a reproachful fault. The best and most assured remedy whereof is generally to follow the saying of Bias: *ne quid nimis.*[72] So as in keeping measure, and not exceeding nor showing any defect in the use of his figures, he cannot lightly do amiss, if he have besides (as that must needs be) a special regard to all circumstances* of the person, place, time, cause, and purpose he hath in hand; which being well observed, it easily avoideth all the recited* inconveniences, and maketh now and then very vice go for a formal* virtue in the exercise of this art.

Chapter VIII
Six points set down by our learned forefathers for a general regiment of all good utterance, be it by mouth or by writing

But before there had been yet any precise observation made of figurative speeches, the first learned artificers of language considered that the beauty and good grace of utterance rested in no many points, and whatsoever transgressed those limits they counted it for vicious;* and thereupon did set down a manner of regiment in all speech generally to be observed, consisting in six points.[73] First, they said that there ought to be kept a decent proportion in our writings and speech, which they termed *analogia*. Secondly, that it ought to be voluble* upon the tongue, and tunable* to the ear, which they called *taxis*. Thirdly, that it were not tediously long, but brief and compendious as the matter might bear, which they called *syntomia*. Fourthly, that it should carry an orderly and good construction, which they called *synthesis*. Fifthly, that it should be a sound, proper, and natural speech, which they called *kyriologia*. Sixthly, that it should be lively and stirring, which they called *tropos*. So as it appeareth by this order of theirs that no vice could be committed in speech, keeping within the bounds of that restraint. But, sir, all this being by them very well conceived, there remained a greater difficulty to know what this proportion, volubility, good construction, and the rest were, otherwise we could not be ever the more relieved.* It was therefore of necessity that a more curious* and particular

---

[72] 'Nothing to excess'. According to Erasmus (*Adagia* 1. 6. 96), more than twenty classical writers used this saying in one form or another.

[73] Puttenham synthesizes several ancient rhetorical texts (details in *ECE* ii. 419 f.).

description should be made of every manner of speech, either trans-gressing or agreeing with their said general prescript. Whereupon it came to pass that all the commendable parts of speech were set forth by the name of figures, and all the illaudable parts under the name of vices or viciosities, of both which it shall be spoken in their places.

Chapter IX
*How the Greeks first, and afterward the Latins, invented new names for every figure, which this author is also enforced to do in his vulgar**

The Greeks were a happy people for the freedom and liberty of their language, because it was allowed them to invent any new name that they listed,* and to piece many words together to make of them one entire, much more significative than the single word. So among other things did they to their figurative speeches devise certain names. The Latins came somewhat behind them in that point, and for want of con-venient single words to express that which the Greeks could do by cobbling many words together, they were fain to use the Greeks' still, till after many years that the learned orators and good grammarians among the Romans, as Cicero, Varro, Quintilian,[74] and others, strained themselves to give the Greek words Latin names, and yet nothing so apt and fitty.* The same course are we driven to follow in this descrip-tion, since we are enforced to cull out for the use of our poet or maker all the most commendable figures. Now to make them known (as behoveth), either we must do it by the original Greek name, or by the Latin, or by our own. But when I consider to what sort of readers I write, and how ill-faring the Greek term would sound in the English ear; then also how short the Latins come to express many of the Greek originals; finally, how well our language serveth to supply the full signification of them both, I have thought it no less lawful, yea per-adventure, under licence of the learned, more laudable to use our own natural, if they be well chosen and of proper signification, than to borrow theirs. So shall not our English poets, though they be to seek of the Greek and Latin languages, lament for lack of knowledge sufficient to the purpose of this art.

And in case any of these new English names given by me to any figure shall happen to offend, I pray that the learned will bear with me and to think the strangeness thereof proceeds but of novelty and

---

[74] Cf. Quintilian, *Inst.* 1. 5. 70; 8. 3. 30.

disacquaintance with our ears, which in process of time and by custom will frame very well. And such others as are not learned in the primitive languages, if they happen to hit upon any new name of mine, so ridiculous in their opinion as may move them to laughter, let such persons yet assure themselves that such names go as near as may be to their originals, or else serve better to the purpose of the figure than the very original, reserving always that such new name should not be unpleasant in our vulgar nor harsh upon the tongue. And where it shall happen otherwise, that it may please the reader to think that hardly any other name in our English could be found to serve the turn better. Again, if to avoid the hazard of this blame I should have kept the Greek or Latin, still it would have appeared a little too scholastical for our makers,* and a piece of work more fit for clerks* than for courtiers, for whose instruction this travail is taken. And if I should have left out both the Greek and Latin name, and put in none of our own neither, well perchance might the rule of the figure have been set down, but no convenient name to hold him in memory. It was therefore expedient we devised for every figure of importance his vulgar name, and to join the Greek or Latin original with them; after that sort much better satisfying as well the vulgar as the learned learner, and also the author's own purpose, which is to make of a rude rhymer a learned and a courtly poet.

Chapter X
A division of figures, and how they serve in exornation of language

And because our chief purpose herein is for the learning of ladies and young gentlewomen, or idle* courtiers, desirous to become skilful in their own mother tongue, and for their private recreation to make now and then ditties* of pleasure, thinking for our part none other science so fit for them and the place as that which teacheth *beau semblant*,* the chief profession as well of courting* as of poesy; since to such manner of minds nothing is more cumbersome than tedious doctrines and scholarly methods of discipline, we have in our own conceit devised a new and strange* model of this art, fitter to please the court than the school, and yet not unnecessary for all such as be willing themselves to become good makers in the vulgar, or to be able to judge of other men's makings. Wherefore, intending to follow the course which we have begun, thus we say that, though the language of our poet or maker be pure and cleanly (and not disgraced by such vicious parts as have been before remembered in the chapter of language),[75] be sufficiently pleasing and commendable for the ordinary use of speech; yet is not the same so well appointed for all purposes of the excellent poet as when it is gallantly arrayed in all his colours which figure can set upon it. Therefore we are now further to determine of figures and figurative speeches.

Figurative speech is a novelty of language evidently (and yet not absurdly) estranged from the ordinary habit and manner of our daily talk and writing; and figure itself is a certain lively or good grace set upon words, speeches, and sentences to some purpose and not in vain, giving them ornament or efficacy by many manner of alterations in shape, in sound, and also in sense, sometimes by way of surplusage, sometimes by defect, sometimes by disorder or mutation, and also by putting into our speeches more pith and substance, subtlety, quickness, efficacy, or moderation, in this or that sort tuning and tempering them, by amplification, abridgement, opening, closing, enforcing, meekening,* or otherwise disposing them to the best purpose.[76] Whereupon the learned clerks who have written methodically of this art in the two master languages, Greek and Latin, have sorted all their figures into three ranks,[77] and the first they bestowed upon the poet only, the second upon the poet and orator indifferently,* the third upon the orator alone. And that first sort of figures doth serve the ear only and may be therefore called 'auricular'. Your second serves the conceit* only and not the ear, and may be called 'sensable', not sensible* nor yet sententious. Your third sort serves as well the ear as the conceit, and may be called 'sententious figures', because not only they properly appertain to full sentences,* for beautifying them with a current and pleasant numerosity,* but also giving them efficacy and enlarging the whole matter besides with copious amplifications.

---

[75] See above, p. 235.

[76] This compendious definition combines many elements, from Quintilian (*Inst.* 9.1–9.3) to Henry Peacham, *The Garden of Eloquence* (1577).

[77] In the Greek and Roman tradition rhetorical devices are divided into *tropi* (tropes), which involve a 'turning' or change of meaning, as in metaphor, irony, allegory, etc. (cf. *Inst.* 8. 6. 1–76), and *figurae* (figures), which involve the redisposition of words to form new patterns, or new 'gestures', as Quintilian puts it (9. 1. 10–14). Figures were then subdivided into figures of thought (*figurae sententiarum*) and figures of language (*figurae verborum*): cf. *Inst.* 9. 1. 15–18. Puttenham's idiosyncratic classification blurs this scheme: his 'sensable' figures are largely tropes; his 'sententious' figures are a mixture of figures of thought and figures of language; while his 'auricular' figures form a heterogeneous category.

I doubt not but some busy* carpers will scorn at my new devised terms 'auricular' and 'sensable', saying that I might with better warrant have used in their steads these words 'orthographical' or 'syntactical',[78] which the learned grammarians left ready made to our hands, and do import* as much as the other that I have brought. Which thing peradventure I deny not in part, and nevertheless for some causes thought them not so necessary; but with these manner of men I do willingly bear, in respect of their laudable endeavour to allow* antiquity and flee innovation. With like benevolence I trust they will bear with me, writing in the vulgar speech and seeking by my novelties to satisfy not the school but the court. Whereas they know very well, all old things soon wax stale and loathsome, and the new devices are ever dainty* and delicate; the vulgar instruction requiring also vulgar and communicable terms, not clerkly or uncouth, as are all these of the Greek and Latin languages primitively received, unless they be qualified* or by much use and custom allowed and our ears made acquainted with them.

Thus then I say that 'auricular' figures be those which work alteration in the ear by sound, accent, time, and slipper* volubility* in utterance, such as for that respect was called by the ancients numerosity* of speech. And not only the whole body of a tale in a poem or history may be made in such sort pleasant and agreeable to the ear, but also every clause by itself, and every single word carried in a clause, may have their pleasant sweetness apart. And so long as this quality extendeth but to the outward tuning of the speech, reaching no higher than the ear, and forcing* the mind little or nothing, it is that virtue which the Greeks call *enargeia*, and is the office of the 'auricular' figures to perform. Therefore, as the members of language at large are whole sentences, and sentences are compact* of clauses, and clauses of words, and every word of letters and syllables, so is the alteration (be it but of a syllable or letter) much material* to the sound and sweetness of utterance. Wherefore beginning first at the smallest alterations, which rest in letters and syllables, the first sort of our figures 'auricular' we do appoint to single words as they lie in language; the second to clauses of speech; the third to perfect* sentences and to the whole mass or body of the tale, be it poem or history, written or reported. . . .

---

[78] Henry Peacham had divided figures into 'Tropes and Schemes, Grammatical, Orthographical, Syntactical': *The Garden of Eloquence* (1577), sig. B₁r.

Chapter XII
Of auricular figures pertaining to clauses of speech, and by them working
no little alteration to the ear

As your single words may be many ways transfigured to make the
metre or verse more tunable and melodious, so also may your whole
and entire clauses be in such sort contrived by the order of their construction as the ear may receive a certain recreation, although the mind
for any novelty of sense be little or nothing affected. And therefore all
your figures of grammatical construction, I account them but merely
auricular in that they reach no further than the ear. To which there
will appear some sweet or unsavoury point to offer you dolour or
delight, either by some evident defect, or surplusage, or disorder, or
immutation* in the same speeches notable, altering either the congruity grammatical, or the sense, or both.

ECLIPSIS;[79] *or, the figure of default.*

And first of those that work by defect, if but one word or some little
portion of speech be wanting, it may be supplied by ordinary understanding and virtue of the figure *eclipsis*, as to say, 'so early a man?',
for 'are ye so early a man?'; 'he is to be entreated', for 'he is easy to
be entreated'; 'I thank God I am to live like a gentleman', for 'I am
able to live . . .'.

APOSIOPESIS;[80] *or, the figure of silence.*

Ye have another auricular figure of defect, and [that] is when we
begin to speak a thing and break off in the middle way, as if either it
needed no further to be spoken of, or that we were ashamed, or afraid
to speak it out. It is also sometimes done by way of threatening, and
to show a moderation of anger. The Greeks call him *aposiopesis*; I, 'the
figure of silence' or 'of interruption', indifferently.

If we do interrupt our speech for fear, this may be an example,
where as one durst not make the true report as it was, but stayed half
way for fear of offence, thus:

> He said you were, I dare not tell you plain:
> For words once out, never return again.[81]

---

[79] Susenbrotus, *Epitome Troporum ac Schematum* (hereafter cited as Susenb.), tr. Brennan,
p. 25, with similar examples.

[80] *Inst.* 9. 2. 54; Susenb., pp. 25–6. Puttenham's account of its application ('for fantastical heads') is narrower than that given by Peacham and other rhetoricians: cf. *IDR*,
pp. 317–18, 330–7.

[81] Horace, *Ars P.* 390: *nescit vox missa reverti*, 'the word once sent forth can never come
back'.

If it be for shame, or that the speaker suppose it would be indecent to tell all, then thus (as he that said to his sweetheart, whom he checked for secretly whispering with a suspected person):

> And did ye not come by his chamber door?
> And tell him that—go to, I say no more.

If it be for anger, or by way of menace, or to show a moderation of wrath, as the grave and discreeter sort of men do, then thus,

> If I take you with such another cast
> I swear by God—but let this be the last.

Thinking to have said further, viz., 'I will punish you'.

If it be for none of all these causes, but upon some sudden occasion that moves a man to break off his tale, then thus:

> He told me all at large—lo yonder is the man,
> Let himself tell the tale that best tell can.

This figure is fit for fantastical* heads and such as be sudden or lack memory. I know one of good learning that greatly blemisheth his discretion* with this manner of speech: for if he be in the gravest matter of the world talking, he will upon the sudden, for the flying of a bird overthwart the way, or some other such slight cause, interrupt his tale and never return to it again.

PROLEPSIS;[82] *or, the propounder.*

Ye have yet another manner of speech purporting at the first blush a defect which afterward is supplied. The Greeks call him *prolepsis*, we, 'the propounder', or 'the explainer' . . . By this manner of speech our maker sets down before all the matter by a brief proposition, and afterward explains it by a division more particularly . . .

Chapter XIII
Of your figures auricular working by disorder

HYPERBATON;[83] *or, the trespasser.*

To all their speeches which wrought by disorder the Greeks gave a general name, *hyperbaton*, as much to say as 'the trespasser'. And because such disorder may be committed many ways it receiveth sundry particulars under him, whereof some are only proper to the

---

[82] Susenb., pp. 28–9.
[83] *Inst.* 8. 6. 62 f.; Longinus, *On Sublimity*, ch. 22 (*ALC*, pp. 484–5); Susenb., p. 31.

Greeks and Latins and not to us; other some ordinary in our manner of speeches, but so foul and intolerable as I will not seem to place them among the figures, but do range them as they deserve, among the vicious or faulty speeches.

PARENTHESIS;[84] *or, the insertor.*

Your first figure of tolerable disorder is *parenthesis*, or, by an English name, 'the insertor', and is when ye will seem for larger information, or some other purpose, to piece* or graft in the midst of your tale an unnecessary parcel of speech, which nevertheless may be thence without any detriment to the rest. The figure is so common that it needeth none example; nevertheless, because we are to teach ladies and gentlewomen to know their school points and terms appertaining to the art, we may not refuse to yield examples even in the plainest cases, as that of master Dyer's,[85] very aptly:

> But now my Dear (for so my love makes me to call you still)
> That love I say, that luckless love, that works me all this ill.

. . . But you must not use such insertions often nor too thick, nor those that be very long as this of ours, for it will breed great confusion to have the tale so much interrupted.

HYSTERON PROTERON;[86] *or, the preposterous.**

Ye have another manner of disordered speech, when ye misplace your words or clauses and set that before which should be behind, *ed è converso.* We call it in English proverb, 'the cart before the horse', the Greeks call it *hysteron proteron.* We name it 'the preposterous', and if it be not too much used is tolerable enough, and many times scarce perceivable, unless the sense be thereby made very absurd; as he that described his manner of departure from his mistress, said thus, not much to be misliked:

> I kissed her cherry lip and took my leave

for 'I took my leave and kissed her'. And yet I cannot well say whether a man use to kiss before he take his leave, or take his leave before he kiss, or that it be all one business. It seems the taking leave is by using

[84] *Inst.* 9. 3. 23; Scaliger, *Poet.* 4. 38; Susenb., p. 33 ('when some mediate idea interrupts the continuation of a discourse').

[85] From the poem beginning 'Before I dy, faire dame' (BL, Harl. MS 7392); cf. B. Wagner, 'New Poems by Sir Edward Dyer', *Review of English Studies*, 44 (1935), 467–8.

[86] Related to *anastrophe* (*Inst.* 8. 6. 5; Susenb., p. 31), this term seems to be later than the classical tradition: cf. Susenb., pp. 32–3, who quotes Antonio Mancinelli, *Carmen de Figuris* (1493 etc.) and gives the Latin equivalent, *praeposteratio.*

some speech, entreating licence of departure; the kiss a knitting up of the farewell, and as it were a testimonial of the licence, without which here in England one may not presume of courtesy to depart. Let young courtiers decide this controversy. . . .

Chapter XV
Of auricular figures working by exchange

ENALLAGE;[87] *or, the figure of exchange.*

Your figures that work auricularly by exchange were more observable to the Greeks and Latins, for the braveness* of their language over that ours is, and for the multiplicity of their grammatical accidents* or verbal affects,* as I may term them, that is to say, their diverse cases, moods, tenses, genders, with variable terminations. By reason whereof they changed not the very word, but kept the word and changed the shape of him only, using one case for another, or tense, or person, or gender, or number, or mood. We, having no such variety of accidents, have little or no use of this figure. They called it *enallage*.

HYPALLAGE;[88] *or, the changeling.**

But another sort of exchange which they had, and very pretty, we do likewise use, not changing one word for another by their accidents or cases, as the *enallage*; nor by the places, as 'the preposterous'; but changing their true construction and application, whereby the sense is quite perverted and made very absurd. As, he that should say, for 'tell me truth and lie not', 'lie me truth and tell not'; for 'come dine with me and stay not', 'come stay with me and dine not'. . . .

Chapter XVII
Of the figures which we call sensible, because they alter and affect the mind by alteration of sense; and first in single words

The ear having received his due satisfaction by the auricular figures, now must the mind also be served with his natural delight, by figures sensible: such as by alteration of intendments* affect the courage,* and give a good liking to the conceit.* And first, single words have their sense and understanding altered and figured many ways, to wit, by transport,* abuse,* cross-naming, new naming, change of name. This will seem very dark to you, unless it be otherwise explained more particularly: and first of 'transport'.

---

[87] *Inst.* 9. 3. 6 ff.   [88] *Inst.* 8. 6. 23; Susenb., p. 34.

METAPHORA;[89] *or, the figure of transport.*

There is a kind of wresting of a single word from his own right*
signification to another not of natural, but yet of some affinity or convenience* with it: as to say, 'I cannot digest your unkind words', for
'I cannot take them in good part'; or as the man of law said, 'I feel you
not', for 'I understand not your case', because he had not his fee in
his hand. Or as another said to a mouthy advocate, 'why barkest thou
at me so sore?' Or to call the top of a tree or of a hill, 'the crown' of
a tree or of a hill: for indeed 'crown' is the highest ornament of a
prince's head, made like a close garland, or else the top of a man's
head, where the hair winds about. And because such [a] term is not
applied naturally to a tree or to a hill, but is transported from a man's
head to a hill or tree, therefore it is called by *metaphora*, or 'the figure
of transport'.

And three causes moves us to use this figure; one for necessity or
want of a better word, thus:

> As the dry ground that thirsts after a shower
> Seems to rejoice when it is well i-wet,
> And speedily brings forth both grass and flower,
> If lack of sun or season do not let.[90]

Here for want of an apter and more natural word to declare the dry
temper of the earth, it is said to thirst and to rejoice, which is only
proper to living creatures. And yet being so inverted, doth not so much
swerve from the true sense, but that every man can easily conceive the
meaning thereof.

Again, we use it for pleasure and ornament of our speech, as thus
in an *Epitaph* of our own making to the honourable memory of a dear
friend, Sir John Throckmorton, knight, Justice of Chester, and a man
of many commendable virtues:

> Whom virtue reared, envy hath overthrown
> And lodged full low, under this marble stone:
> Nay never were his values so well known
> Whilst he lived here, as now that he is gone.

Here these words, 'reared', 'overthrown', and 'lodged', are inverted,*
and metaphorically applied, not upon necessity but for ornament only;
afterward again in these verses:

---

[89] *Inst.* 8. 6. 4–19; Lat. *translatio*; Susenb., p. 7.   [90] Versified from *Inst.* 8. 6. 6.

> No sun by day that ever saw him rest,
> Free from the toils of his so busy charge;
> No night that harbour'd rancour in his breast,
> Nor merry mood made reason run at large.

In these verses the inversion or metaphor lieth in these words, 'saw', 'harbour'd', 'run', which naturally are applied to living things and not to insensible: as, the 'sun', or the 'night'. And yet they approach so near, and so conveniently,* as the speech is thereby made more commendable. Again, in more verses of the same *Epitaph*, thus:

> His head a source of gravity and sense,
> His memory a shop of civil art;
> His tongue a stream of sugared eloquence,
> Wisdom and meekness lay mingled in his heart.

In which verses ye see that these words, 'source', 'shop', 'flood', 'sugared', are inverted from their own signification to another, not altogether so natural but of much affinity with it.

Then also do we [use] it sometimes to enforce a sense and make the word more significative, as thus:

> I burn in love, I freeze in deadly hate,
> I swim in hope, and sink in deep despair.[91]

These examples I have the willinger given you to set forth the nature and use of your figure metaphor, which of any other being choicely made, is the most commendable and most common.

CATACHRESIS;[92] *or, the figure of abuse.*

But if for lack of natural and proper term or word we take another, neither natural nor proper, and do untruly apply it to the thing which we would seem to express, and without any just inconvenience,* it is not then spoken by this figure *metaphora*, or of 'inversion' as before,

---

[91] These verses are typical of the use by Petrarch and his imitators of the figure *oxymoron* or *synoeciosis* (cf. p. 415), the 'union of contraries', to describe the effects of love. Puttenham seems to have run together phrases in common use, as in Surrey, 'Description of the fickle affections panges and sleightes of love' (*Tottel's Miscellany*, no. 4): 'In standyng nere my fire I know how that I freze; Farre off I burne, in both I wast, and so my life I leze'; or George Gascoigne, 'Don Bartholomewes Dolorous discourses': 'I freeze in hope, yet burne in haste of heate' (in *The Posies* (1575), ed. J. W. Cunliffe (Cambridge, 1907), p. 115); or Thomas Churchyard, 'Churchyardes Choise' (1579): 'O deadly hope, and grounde of deepe despaire'; or Nicholas Breton, 'A Dolorous discourse': 'To swim and sinke, to burne and be a-colde, | To hope and feare, to sigh and yet to sing'.

[92] *Inst.* 8. 6. 34 f.; *Rhet. Her.* 4. 45; Susenb., p. 11 (Lat. *abusio*; 'the adaptation of a proximate term to objects without a name . . . occurs when a name is completely lacking').

but by plain abuse:* as he that bade his man go into his library and get him his bow and arrows, for indeed there was never a book there to be found; or as one should in reproach say to a poor man, 'thou rascal knave', where 'rascal' is properly the hunter's term given to young deer, lean and out of season, and not to people; or as one said very prettily in this verse:

I lent my love to loss, and gaged my life in vain.[93]

Whereas this word 'lent' is properly [used] of money or some such other thing as men do commonly borrow for use, to be repaid again, and being applied to love is utterly abused; and yet very commendably spoken, by virtue of this figure. For he that loveth and is not beloved again, hath no less wrong than he that lendeth and is never repaid.

METONYMIA;[94] or, the misnamer.

Now doth this understanding or secret conceit reach many times to the only nomination of persons or things in their names, as of men, or mountains, seas, countries and such like, in which respect the wrong naming, or otherwise naming of them than is due carrieth not only an alteration of sense but a necessity of intendment figuratively: as when we call love by the name of Venus, fleshly lust by the name of Cupid, because they were supposed by the ancient poets to be authors and kindlers of love and lust; Vulcan for fire, Ceres for bread, Bacchus for wine by the same reason. . . .

These and such other speeches, where ye take the name of the author for the thing itself, or the thing containing for that which is contained, and in many other cases do as it were wrong name the person or the thing, so nevertheless as it may be understood, it is by the figure *metonymia*, or 'misnamer'. . . .

EPITHETON;[95] or, the qualifier, otherwise the figure of attribution.

Your *epitheton* or 'qualifier', whereof we spake before, placing him among the figures auricular, now because he serves also to alter and enforce* the sense, we will say somewhat more of him in this place. And do conclude that he must be apt and proper for the thing he is added unto, and not disagreeble or repugnant, as one that said, 'dark disdain',[96] and 'miserable pride', very absurdly, for disdain or dis-

---

[93] Anonymous poem, 'The lover refused lamenteth his estate', in *Tottel's Miscellany* (1557), no. 195, l. l.

[94] *Inst.* 8. 6. 23–7, and Susenb., pp. 8–9; examples common to both.

[95] *Inst.* 8. 6. 40–3; Susenb., p. 39.   [96] Gascoigne, *Posies*, ed. cit., p. 458.

dained things cannot be said dark, but rather bright and clear, because they be beholden and much looked upon; and pride is rather envied than pitied or miserable, unless it be in Christian charity, which helpeth not the term in this case. Some of our vulgar writers take great pleasure in giving epithets, and do it almost to every word which may receive them, and should not be so, yea though they were never so proper and apt, for sometimes words suffered to go single do give greater sense and grace than words qualified* by attributions do. . . .

EMPHASIS;[97] *or, the re-enforcer*.

And one notable means to affect the mind is to enforce the sense of any thing by a word of more than ordinary efficacy, [which] nevertheless is not apparent, but as it were secretly implied; as he that said thus of a fair lady:

> O rare beauty, o grace, and courtesy.

And by a very evil man, thus:

> O sin itself, not wretch, but wretchedness.

Whereas if he had said thus, 'O gracious, courteous and beautiful woman'; and 'O sinful and wretched man', it had been all to one effect, yet not with such force and efficacy, to speak by the denominative as by the thing itself.

LITOTES;[98] *or, the moderator*.

As by the former figure we use to enforce our sense, so by another we temper our sense with words of such moderation as in appearance it abateth it, but not in deed; and is by the figure *litotes*, which therefore I call 'the moderator'. And [it] becomes us many times better to speak in that sort qualified than if we spoke it by more forcible terms; and nevertheless is equipollent in sense, thus:

> I know you hate me not, nor wish me any ill.[99]

Meaning indeed that he loved him very well and dearly; and yet the words do not express so much, though they purport so much. Or if you would say, 'I am not ignorant', for 'I know well enough'; 'such a man is no fool', meaning indeed that he is a very wise man.

---

[97] *Inst.* 8. 3. 83; Susenb., pp. 44–5 ('secondly, Emphasis occurs when something is signified which is not stated . . .').

[98] This figure was defined late in the classical tradition, in the commentaries of Servius on Virgil and Donatus on Terence (both 4th cent. AD). Susenbrotus cites Servius' definition, 'when we attenuate our words for the sake of avoiding arrogance' (p. 41).

[99] Virgil, *Ecl.* 74 'Quid prodest, quod me ipse animo non spernis . . .' .

PARADIASTOLE;[100] *or, the curry-favell.**

But if such moderation of words tend to flattery, or soothing, or excusing, it is by the figure *paradiastole*, which therefore nothing improperly we call 'the curry-favell', as when we make the best of a bad thing, or turn a signification to the more plausible sense, as to call an unthrift, a liberal gentleman; the foolish-hardy, valiant or courageous; the niggard, thrifty; a great riot or outrage, a youthful prank and such like terms, moderating and abating the force of the matter by craft, and for a pleasing purpose. . . .

MEIOSIS;[101] *or, the disabler.*

But if you diminish and abase a thing by way of spite or malice, as it were to deprave* it, such speech is by the figure *meiosis*, or 'the disabler', spoken of hereafter in the place of sententious figures.

> A great mountain as big as a molehill,
> A heavy burden *perdy*, as a pound of feathers!

TAPINOSIS;[102] *or, the abaser.*

But if ye abase your thing or matter by ignorance or error in the choice of your word, then is it by vicious manner of speech called *tapinosis*, whereof ye shall have examples in the chapter of vices hereafter following.

SYNECDOCHE;[103] *or, the figure of quick conceit.*

Then again, if we use such a word (as many times we do) by which we drive the hearer to conceive more, or less, or beyond, or otherwise than the letter expresseth, and it be not by virtue of the former figures *metaphora*, and 'abaser' and the rest, the Greeks then call it *synecdoche*, the Latins *sub intellectio* or understanding. For by part we are enforced to understand the whole, by the whole part, by many things one thing, by one many, by a thing precedent a thing consequent, and generally one thing out of another by manner of contrariety to the word which is spoken, *aliud ex alio*. Which because it seemeth to ask a good, quick, and pregnant* capacity,* and is not for an ordinary or dull wit so to do, I chose to call him the figure not only 'of conceit' after the Greek original, but also 'of quick conceit'. As for example we will give none

---

[100] *Inst.* 9. 2. 92; Susenb., pp. 45–6 ('when we palliate our own or other people's faults by some flattering explanation . . . when we call a prodigal man liberal, a rash person brave, an avaricious person frugal . . .'). *Paradiastole* has a long and complex history: cf. Quentin Skinner, *Reason and Rhetoric in the Philosophy of Hobbes* (Cambridge, 1996), pp. 142–80.

[101] *Inst.* 8. 3. 50; Susenb., p. 75 ('when we are eager to drag the character or cause of an adversary down into contempt').

[102] *Inst.* 8. 3. 48; Susenb., p. 35.　　　[103] *Inst.* 8. 6. 19–22; Susenb., pp. 7–8.

because we will speak of him again in another place, where he is ranged among the figures sensable appertaining to clauses.

Chapter XVIII
Of sensable figures altering and affecting the mind by alteration of sense or intendments in whole clauses or speeches

As by the last remembered figures the sense of single words is altered, so by these that follow is that of whole and entire speech; and first by the courtly figure *allegoria*, which is when we speak one thing and think another, and that our words and our meanings meet not. The use of this figure is so large, and his virtue of so great efficacy, as it is supposed no man can pleasantly utter and persuade without it, but in effect is sure never or very seldom to thrive and prosper in the world that cannot skilfully put in ure.* Insomuch as not only every common courtier, but also the gravest counsellor, yea and the most noble and wisest Prince of them all are many times enforced to use it, by example (say they) of the great Emperor, who had it usually in his mouth to say, *Qui nescit dissimulare nescit regnare.*[104] Of this figure therefore, which for his duplicity we call the figure of 'false semblant' or 'dissimulation', we will speak first, as of the chief ringleader and captain of all other figures, either in the poetical or oratory science.

ALLEGORIA;[105] *or, the figure of false semblant.*

And ye shall know that we may dissemble, I mean speak otherwise than we think, in earnest as well as in sport; under covert and dark* terms, and in learned and apparent* speeches; in short sentences, and by long ambage* and circumstance of words; and finally, as well when we lie as when we tell truth. To be short, every speech wrested from his own natural signification to another not altogether so natural is a kind of dissimulation, because the words bear contrary countenance to the intent. But properly, and in his principal virtue, allegory is when we do speak in sense translative, and wrested from the own signification, nevertheless applied to another not altogether contrary but having much convenience with it, as before we said of the metaphor. As, for example, if we should call the commonwealth a ship, the prince a pilot, the counsellors mariners, the storms wars, the calm and haven peace, this is spoken all in allegory. And because such

---

[104] 'Who cannot dissimulate cannot rule'; the maxim of Louis XI of France.
[105] *Inst.* 8. 6. 44–53, including the comparison of the commonwealth to a ship, taken from Horace, *Odes* 1. 14; repeated by Susenb., pp. 12–13.

inversion of sense in one single word is by the figure *metaphora*, of whom we spoke before, and this manner of inversion extending to whole and large speeches, it maketh the figure *allegory* to be called a long and perpetual metaphor. A nobleman, after a whole year's absence from his lady, sent to know how she did, and whether she remained affected toward him as she was when he left her:

> Lovely lady, I long full sore to hear
> If ye remain the same I left you the last year.

To whom she answered in *allegory* other two verses:

> My loving lord, I will well that ye wist,
> The thread is spun that never shall untwist.

Meaning that her love was so steadfast and constant toward him, as no time or occasion could alter it.

Virgil, in his shepherdly poems called *Eclogues*, used as rustical but fit allegory for the purpose thus:

> *Claudite iam rivos pueri sat prata biberunt.*[106]

Which I English thus:

Stop up your streams (my lads), the meads have drunk their fill.

As much to say, 'leave off now, ye have talked of the matter enough'. For the shepherd's guise in many places is by opening certain sluices to water their pastures, so as when they are wet enough they shut them again; this application is full allegoric.

Ye have another manner of allegory not full, but mixed, as he that wrote thus:

> The clouds of care have covered all my cost,
> The storms of life do threaten to appear:
> The waves of woe, wherein my ship is tossed,
> Have broke the banks where lay my life so dear.
> Chips of ill chance are fallen amidst my choice,
> To mar the mind that meant for to rejoice.[107]

I call him not a full allegory, but mixed, because he discovers withal what the 'cloud', 'storm', 'wave', and the rest are, which in a full alle-

---

[106] *Ecl.* 3. 111.
[107] Gascoigne, 'Preface' to *The Adventures of Master F. J.*, in *The Posies* (1575), ed. Cunliffe, p. 400.

gory should not be discovered but left at large to the reader's judgement and conjecture.

We dissemble again under covert and dark speeches when we speak by way of riddle (ENIGMA),[108] of which the sense can hardly be picked out but by the parties' own assoil;* as he that said:

> It is my mother, well I wot,
> And yet the daughter that I begot.

Meaning by it the ice, which is made of frozen water, the same being molten by the sun or fire makes water again.

My mother had an old woman in her nursery, who in the winter nights would put us forth many pretty riddles, whereof this is one:

> I have a thing and rough it is,
> And in the midst a hole, I wis:*
> There came a young man with his gin,*
> And he put it a handful in.

The good old gentlewoman would tell us that were children how it was meant by a furred glove; some other naughty body would peradventure have construed it not half so mannerly. The riddle is pretty but that it holds too much of the *cachemphaton*[109] or foul speech, and may be drawn to a reprobate sense. . . .

IRONIA;[110] *or, the dry mock.*

Ye do likewise dissemble when ye speak in derision or mockery, and that may be many ways: as sometimes in sport, sometimes in earnest, and privily, and apertly,* and pleasantly, and bitterly. But first by the figure *ironia*, which we call 'the dry mock', as he that said to a bragging ruffian that threatened he would kill and slay, 'no doubt you are a good man of your hands'; or, as it was said by a French king to one that prayed his reward, showing how he had been cut in the face at a certain battle fought in his service: 'ye may see', quoth the king, 'what it is to run away and look backwards'. . . .

CHARIENTISMUS;[111] *or, the privy* nip.*

---

[108] *Inst.* 8. 6. 52–3; Susenb., p. 14, with the example from Mancinellus: '"My mother bore me; soon she shall be born from me". For from water snow is born, and is resolved back into water.'

[109] Language to which perverted usage has given an obscene meaning; cf. n. 212 below.

[110] *Inst.* 8. 6. 54–5, 9. 2. 44–5; Susenb., pp. 14–15.

[111] This figure is a later addition to the rhetoric handbooks, as in Julius Rufinianus (4th cent. AD), *De figuris sententiarum et elocutionis liber.* Cf. Susenb., p. 17: 'where we desire to assuage by words someone who has been aroused and perturbed by wrath. So much for the species of *allegory*'.

Or when ye give a mock under smooth and lowly words, as he that heard one call him all to nought and say, 'thou art sure to be hanged ere thou die'; quoth the other very soberly, 'Sir, I know your mastership speaks but in jest'. The Greeks call it *charientismus*, we may call it 'the privy nip', or a mild and appeasing mockery. All these be soldiers to the figure *allegoria*, and fight under the banner of dissimulation.

HYPERBOLE;[112] *or, the over-reacher, otherwise called the loud liar.*

Nevertheless ye have yet two or three other figures that smatch* a spice of the same 'false semblant', but in another sort and manner of phrase; whereof one is when we speak in the superlative and beyond the limits of credit, that is by the figure which the Greeks call *hyperbole*, the Latins *dementiens*, or the 'lying figure'. I for his immoderate excess call him 'the over-reacher', right with his original, or 'loud liar', and methinks not amiss. Now when I speak that which neither I myself think to be true, nor would have any other body believe, it must needs be a great dissimulation, because I mean nothing less than that I speak. And this manner of speech is used when either we would greatly advance, or greatly abase the reputation of any thing or person, and must be used very discreetly, or else it will seem odious. For although a praise or other report may be allowed beyond credit it may not be beyond all measure, specially in the proseman; as he that was speaker in a Parliament of King Henry the Eighth's reign, in his oration (which, ye know, is of ordinary to be made before the Prince at the first assembly of both houses), would seem to praise his Majesty thus: 'What should I go about to recite your Majesty's innumerable virtues, even as much as if I took upon me to number the stars of the sky, or to tell the sands of the sea.' This *hyperbole* was both *ultra fidem* and also *ultra modum*,[113] and therefore of a grave and wise counsellor made the speaker to be accounted a gross flattering fool. Peradventure if he had used it thus it had been better—and nevertheless a lie too, but a more moderate lie and no less to the purpose of the king's commendation—thus: 'I am not able with any words sufficiently to express your Majesty's regal virtues. Your kingly merits, also, towards us your people and realm are so exceeding many as your praises therefore are infinite, your honour and renown everlasting.' And yet all this, if we shall measure it by the rule of exact verity, is but an untruth, yet a more cleanly commendation than was master speaker's.

---

[112] *Inst.* 8. 6. 67–76; Susenb., pp. 17–19 ('for the sake of exaggeration or minimization').
[113] 'Beyond belief'; 'beyond propriety'.

Nevertheless, as I said before, if we fall apraising, specially of our mistress's virtue, beauty, or other good parts, we be allowed now and then to over-reach a little by way of comparison, as he that said thus in praise of his lady:

> Give place ye lovers here before,
> That spent your boasts and brags in vain:
> My Lady's beauty passeth more
> The best of yours, I dare well say[ne],
> Than doth the sun the candle light,
> Or brightest day the darkest night . . .[114]

PERIPHRASIS;[115] *or, the figure of ambage.**

Then have ye the figure *periphrasis*, holding somewhat of the dissembler, by reason of a secret intent not appearing by the words; as when we go about the bush, and will not in one or a few words express that thing which we desire to have known, but do choose rather to do it by many words. . . . It is one of the gallantest figures among the poets, so it be used discreetly and in his right kind. But many of these makers, that be not half their craft's masters, do very often abuse it, and also many ways. For if the thing or person they go about to describe by circumstance be by the writers' improvidence otherwise bewrayed,* it loseth the grace of a figure; as he that said:

> The tenth of March, when Aries received
> Dan Phoebus' rays into his horned head.[116]

Intending to describe the spring of the year, which every man knoweth of himself, hearing the day of March named. The verses be very good, the figure nought worth, if it were meant in *periphrasis* for the matter. That is, the season of the year, which should have been covertly disclosed by ambage, was by and by blabbed out by naming the day of the month, and so the purpose of the figure disappointed. Peradventure it had been better to have said thus:

> The month and day when Aries received
> Dan Phoebus' rays into his horned head.

For now there remaineth for the reader somewhat to study and guess

---

[114] Surrey, 'A praise of his love', in *Tottel's Miscellany* (1557), no. 20, ll. 1–6.
[115] *Inst.* 8. 6. 59–61; Susenb., pp. 39–41 ('very frequent in the works of poets').
[116] Gascoigne, 'The Lady Being Wounded', in *The Posies* (1575), ed. Cunliffe, p. 333.

upon, and yet the spring time to the learned judgement sufficiently expressed.

The noble Earl of Surrey wrote thus:

> In winter's just return, when Boreas 'gan his reign,
> And every tree unclothed him fast, as nature taught them plain.[117]

I would fain learn of some good maker whether the Earl spoke this in figure of *periphrasis*, or not. For mine own opinion, I think that if he meant to describe the winter season he would not have disclosed it so broadly as to say winter at the first word, for that had been against the rules of art and without any good judgement, which in so learned and excellent a personage we ought not to suspect; we say therefore, that for winter it is no *periphrasis* but language at large. We say, for all that, having regard to the second verse that followeth, it is a *periphrasis*, seeming that thereby he intended to show in what part of the winter his loves gave him anguish. That is, in the time which we call the fall of the leaf, which begins in the month of October, and stands very well with the figure to be uttered in that sort, notwithstanding winter be named before, for winter hath many parts: such namely as do not shake off the leaf, nor unclothe the trees as here is mentioned. Thus may ye judge as I do, that this noble Earl wrote excellently well and to purpose.

Moreover, when a maker will seem to use circumlocution to set forth anything pleasantly and figuratively, yet no less plain to a ripe reader than if it were named expressly, and when all is done, no man can perceive it to be the thing intended, this is a foul oversight in any writer. As did a good fellow, who, weening to show his cunning, would needs by periphrase express the realm of Scotland in no less than eight verses, and when he had said all, no man could imagine it to be spoken of Scotland, and did, besides many other faults in his verse, so deadly belie* the matter by his description as it would pity any good maker to hear it. . . .

Chapter XIX
Of figures sententious, otherwise called rhetorical

Now if our presupposal be true, that the poet is of all other the most ancient orator, as he that by good and pleasant persuasions first reduced* the wild and beastly people into public societies and civility

---

[117] 'Complaint of a dying lover', in *Tottel's Miscellany* (1557), no. 18, ll. 1–2.

of life, insinuating unto them under fictions, with sweet and coloured speeches, many wholesome lessons and doctrines, then no doubt there is nothing so fit for him as to be furnished with all the figures that be rhetorical, and such as do most beautify language with eloquence and sententiousness.* Therefore, since we have already allowed to our maker his 'auricular' figures, and also his 'sensable', by which all the words and clauses of his metres are made as well tunable to the ear as stirring to the mind, we are now by order to bestow upon him those other figures which may execute both offices, and all at once to beautify and give sense and sententiousness to the whole language at large. So as if we should entreat our maker to play also the orator, and whether it be to plead, or to praise, or to advise, that in all three cases he may utter and also persuade both copiously and vehemently.

And your figures rhetorical, besides their remembered ordinary virtues—that is, sententiousness and copious amplification, or enlargement of language—do also contain a certain sweet and melodious manner of speech, in which respect they may, after a sort, be said 'auricular', because the ear is no less ravished with their current* tune than the mind is with their sententiousness. For the ear is properly but an instrument of conveyance for the mind, to apprehend the sense by the sound. And our speech is made melodious or harmonical not only by strained* tunes, as those of music, but also by choice of smooth words. And thus, or thus, marshalling them in their comeliest construction and order, and as well by sometimes sparing, sometimes spending them more or less liberally, and carrying or transporting of them farther off or nearer, setting them with sundry relations* and variable forms in the ministry* and use of words, do breed no little alteration in man. For to say truly, what else is man but his mind? Which, whosoever have skill to compass and make yielding and flexible, what may not he command the body to perform? He, therefore, that hath vanquished the mind of man hath made the greatest and most glorious conquest. But the mind is not assailable unless it be by sensible* approaches, whereof the audible is of greatest force for instruction or discipline, the visible for apprehension of exterior knowledges, as the philosopher[118] saith. Therefore, the well tuning of your words and clauses to the delight of the ear maketh your information no less plausible to the mind than to the ear; no, though you filled them with never so much sense and sententiousness.

---

[118] Cf. Aristotle, *De sensu* 1. 437ª5 ff., and Sidney, p. 351.

Then also must the whole tale (if it tend to persuasion) bear his just and reasonable measure, being rather with the largest than with the scarcest. For, like as one or two drops of water pierce not the flint stone, but many and often droppings do, so cannot a few words (be they never so pithy or sententious) in all cases and to all manner of minds, make so deep an impression as a more multitude of words to the purpose discreetly,* and without superfluity uttered: the mind being no less vanquished with large load of speech than the limbs are with heavy burden. Sweetness of speech, sentence, and amplification* are therefore necessary to an excellent orator and poet, ne* may in no wise be spared from any of them.

And first of all others, your figure that worketh by iteration or repetition of one word or clause doth much alter and affect the ear and also the mind of the hearer, and therefore is counted a very brave figure both with the poets and rhetoricians; and this repetition may be in seven sorts.

ANAPHORA;[119] *or, the figure of report.**

Repetition in the first degree we call the figure of 'report', according to the Greek original, and is when we make one word begin and, as they are wont to say, lead the dance to many verses in suit,* as thus:

> To think on death it is a misery,
> To think on life it is a vanity;
> To think on the world, verily it is
> To think that here man hath no perfect bliss.

And this, written by Sir Walter Raleigh[120] of his greatest mistress, in most excellent verses:

> In vain mine eyes, in vain you waste your tears,
> In vain my sighs, the smokes of my despairs:
> In vain you search the earth and heavens above,
> In vain ye seek, for fortune keeps my love. . . .

ANTISTROPHE;[121] *or, the counter-turn.*

Ye have another sort of repetition, quite contrary to the former,

---

[119] *Inst.* 9. 3. 30; *Rhet. Her.* 4. 13. 19 (which calls it *repetitio*); Susenb., pp. 47–8.
[120] From an otherwise lost poem: see *The Poems of Sir Walter Ralegh*, ed. A. Latham (London, 1951), no. 6.
[121] *Inst.* 9. 3. 30–1; *Rhet. Her.* 4. 13. 19; Susenb., p. 50 (Lat. *conversio*). This figure is usually called *epistrophe*.

when ye make one word finish many verses in suit, and, that which is harder, to finish many clauses in the midst of your verses or ditty (for to make them finish the verse, in our vulgar, it should hinder the rhyme). And because I do find few of our English makers use this figure, I have set you down two little ditties which our selves in our younger years played upon the *antistrophe*, for so is the figure's name in Greek. . . .

The second upon the merits of Christ's passion toward mankind, thus:

> Our Christ, the son of God, chief author of all good,
> Was he, by his allmight that first created man;
> And with the costly price of his most precious blood,
> He that redeemed man; and by his instance wan*
> Grace in the sight of God, his only father dear,
> And reconciled man; and to make man his peer
> Made himself very man. Brief, to conclude the case,
> This Christ both God and man, he all and only is;
> The man brings man to God and to all heaven's bliss.

The Greeks call this figure *antistrophe*, the Latins, *conversio*. I, following the original, call him 'the counter-turn', because he turns counter in the midst of every metre.

Anadiplosis;[122] *or, the redouble.*

Ye have another sort of repetition when with the word by which you finish your verse, ye begin the next verse with the same, as thus:

> Comfort it is for man to have a wife,
> Wife chaste, and wise, and lowly all her life.

Or thus:

> Your beauty was the cause of my first love,
> Love while I live, that I may sore repent.

The Greeks call this figure *anadiplosis*, I call him 'the redouble' as the original bears.

Epanalepsis;[123] *or, the echo sound; otherwise, the slow return.*

Ye have another sort of repetition when ye make one word both

---

[122] *Inst.* 9. 3. 44, which cites Cicero, *Cat.* 1. 1. 2 (cf. Sidney, p. 386); Susenb., pp. 49–50 (Lat. *reduplicatio*).

[123] *Inst.* 8. 3. 50–1 (tautology); 9. 3. 34; Susenb., p. 48.

begin and end your verse, which therefore I call 'the slow return', otherwise 'the echo sound', as thus:

> Much must he be beloved, that loveth much.
> Fear many must he needs, whom many fear.[124]

Unless I called him 'the echo sound' I could not tell what name to give him, unless it were 'the slow return'.

EPIZEUXIS;[125] *or, the underlay,** or cuckoo-spell.**

Ye have another sort of repetition when in one verse, or clause of a verse, ye iterate one word without any intermission, as thus:

> It was Maryne, Maryne that wrought mine woe.

And this, bemoaning the departure of a dear friend:

> The chiefest staff of mine assured stay,
> With no small grief is gone, is gone away.

And that of Sir Walter Raleigh's,[126] very sweet:

> With wisdom's eyes had but blind fortune seen,
> Then had my love, my love for ever been.

The Greeks call him *epizeuxis*, the Latins *subiunctio*; we may call him 'the underlay'. Methinks if we regard his manner of iteration, and would depart from the original, we might very properly in our vulgar, and for pleasure call him 'the cuckoo-spell'. For right as the cuckoo repeats his lay, which is but one manner of note, and doth not insert any other tune betwixt, and sometimes for haste stammers out two or three of them one immediately after another, as 'cuck, cuck, cuckoo', so doth the figure *epizeuxis* in the former verses, 'Maryne, Maryne', without any intermission at all.

PLOKE;[127] *or, the doubler.*

Yet have ye one sort of repetition, which we call 'the doubler', and is as the next before, a speedy iteration of one word, but with some little intermission by inserting one or two words between. As, in a most excellent ditty written by Sir Walter Raleigh,[128] these two closing verses:

---

[124] Macrobius, *Saturnalia* 2. 7. 4, ascribes to Laberius this saying, 'Many he needs must fear, whom many fear'.

[125] *Inst.* 9. 3. 28; Susenb., p. 49 (Lat. *subiunctio*).

[126] Otherwise unknown: *Poems*, ed. Latham, no. 7.

[127] *Inst.* 9. 3. 28–9; Susenb., p. 51 (Lat. *duplicatio*).

[128] The concluding couplet of 'Calling to minde mine eie long went about', printed in *The Phoenix Nest* (1593); *Poems*, ed. Latham, no. 9.

> Yet when I saw myself to you was true,
> I loved myself, because my self loved you.

Now also be there many other sorts of repetition, if a man would use them, but are nothing commendable, and therefore are not observed in good poesy. As a vulgar rhymer, who doubled one word in the end of every verse, thus:

> adieu, adieu,
> my face, my face.

And another that did the like in the beginning of his verse, thus:

> To love him and love him, as sinners should do.

These repetitions be not figurative but fantastical,* for a figure is ever used to a purpose, either of beauty or of efficacy. And these last recited be to no purpose, for neither can ye say that it urges affection, nor that it beautifieth or enforceth the sense, nor hath any other subtlety in it, and therefore is a very foolish impertinency* of speech, and not a figure. . . .

TRADUCTIO;[129] *or, the translater*.

Then have ye a figure which the Latins call *traductio*, and I 'the translater': which is when ye turn and translate a word into many sundry shapes, as the tailor doth his garment, and after that sort do play with him in your ditty, as thus:

> Who lives in love his life is full of fears,
> To lose his love, livel[ih]ood or liberty.
> But lively sprites that young and reckless be,
> Think that there is no living like to theirs.

Or as one who much gloried in his own wit, whom Persius taxed in a verse very pithily and pleasantly, thus:

> *Scire tuum nihil est nisi te scire, hoc sciat alter.*[130]

Which I have turned into English, not so briefly but more at large, of purpose the better to declare the nature of the figure, as thus:

> Thou weeneth thy wit nought worth if other weet it not
> As well as thou thyself. But one thing well I wot:

---

[129] *Inst.* 9. 3. 42 including the quotation from Persius; repeated by Susenb., p. 52 (who gives the Latin term *traductio*). This figure is better known by the Greek term, *polyptoton*.

[130] *Sat.* 1. 27; 'Is all your knowledge to go so utterly for nothing unless other people know that you possess it?'

Who so in earnest weens, he doth in mine advice
Show himself witless, or more witty than wise.

Here ye see how in the former rhyme this word 'life' is translated into
'live, living, lively, livelihood'; and in the latter rhyme this word 'wit'
is translated into 'weet, ween, wot, witless, witty' and 'wise', which
come all from one original.

ANTHYPOPHORA;[131] *or, figure of response.*

Ye have a figurative speech which the Greeks call *anthypophora*. I
name him 'the response', and is when we will seem to ask a question
to the intent we will answer it ourselves; and is a figure of argument
and also of amplification. Of argument, because proponing such
matter as our adversary might object and then to answer it ourselves,
we do unfurnish and prevent* him of such help as he would otherwise have used for himself. Then, because such objection and answer
spend much language, it serves as well to amplify and enlarge our tale.
Thus, for example:

Wily worldling, come tell me, I thee pray,
Wherein hopest thou, that makes thee so to swell?
Riches? Alack, it tarries not a day,
But where fortune, the fickle, list to dwell.
In thy children? How hardly shalt thou find
Them all at once good, and thrifty, and kind.
Thy wife? O fair but frail metal to trust.
Servants? What, thieves? What, treachorous and unjust?
Honour, perchance? It rests in other men.
Glory? A smoke. But wherein hopest thou then?
In God's justice? And by what merit, tell?
In his mercy? O now thou speakest well,
But thy lewd life hath lost his love and grace,
Daunting all hope, to put despair in place.

We read that Crates the philosopher cynic, in respect of the manifold discommodities of man's life, held opinion that it was best for
man never to have been born or soon after to die (*Optimum non nasci*

---

[131] *Inst.* 9. 2. 15, 9. 3. 87; Susenb., pp. 59–60 ('the admission of some opposing argument,
the granting of some troublesome and unfavourable point').

vel citò mori),[132] of whom certain verses are left written in Greek which I have Englished, thus:

What life is thee liefest? The needy is full of woe and awe,
The wealthy full of brawl and brabbles of the law.
To be a married man? How much art thou beguiled,
Seeking thy rest by cark,* for household, wife, and child.
To till it is a toil, to graze home, honest gain,
But such as gotten is with great hazard and pain.
The sailor of his ship, the merchant of his ware,
The soldier in arms, how full of dread and care!
A shrewd* wife brings thee bate;* wive not, and never thrive;
Children a charge, childless the greatest lack alive.
Youth witless is, and frail, age sickly and forlorn;
Then better to die soon, or never to be born.

Metrodorus the philosopher Stoic was of a contrary opinion, reversing all the former suppositions against Crates, thus:

What life list ye to lead? In good city and town
Is won both wit and wealth; court gets us great renown;
Country keeps us in heal,* and quietness of mind,
Where wholesome airs, and exercise, and pretty sports we find.
Traffic* it turns to gain, by land and eke* by seas;
The land-born lives safe, the foreign at his ease;
Householder hath his home, the rogue roams with delight,
And makes more merry meals than doth the lordly wight.
Wed and thou hast a bed of solace and of joy;
Wed not and have a bed of rest without annoy.
The settled love is safe, sweet is the love at large;
Children they are a store, no children are no charge;
Lusty and gay is youth, old age honoured and wise;
Then not to die, or be unborn, is best in mine advice.

---

[132] This saying, 'Not to be born is best', forms the subject of a well-known essay by Erasmus, *Adagia* 2. 3. 49 (*CWE* xxxiii. 160–2, 393–4). In it Erasmus translates into Latin the two famous complementary epigrams ascribed to Poseidippos (*c*.310–260 BC) and to Metrodorus, found in the *Anthologia Palatina* (9. 359–60), and (with the ascription to Crates) in the *Anthologia Planudea* (ed. Aldus, 1503). These matching poems were imitated in the Renaissance (as by the Scottish humanist George Buchanan, in his Latin *Epigrams*), and translated, as by Nicolas Grimald in *Tottel's Miscellany* (1557; nos. 151–2), a version known to Puttenham. Francis Bacon made an English verse translation of the first poem, 'The world's a bubble', *c*.1597–8: cf. B. Vickers (ed.), *Francis Bacon* (Oxford 1996), p. 332.

Edward Earl of Oxford,[133] a most noble and learned gentleman, made in this figure of response an emblem of desire, otherwise called *Cupid*, which for his excellency and wit, I set down some part of the verses, for example:

> When wert thou born, desire?
> In pomp and prime of May,
> By whom, sweet boy, wert thou begot?
> By good conceit, men say.
> Tell me, who was thy nurse?
> Fresh youth in sugared joy.
> What was thy meat and daily food?
> Sad sighs with great annoy.
> What hadst thou then to drink?
> Unfeigned lovers' tears.
> What cradle wert thou rocked in?
> In hope devoid of fears. . . .

CLIMAX;[134] *or, the marching figure.*

Ye have a figure which, as well by his Greek and Latin originals, and also by allusion to the manner of a man's gait or going, may be called 'the marching figure', for after the first step all the rest proceed by double the space; and so in our speech one word proceeds double to the first that was spoken, and goeth as it were by strides or paces. It may as well be called 'the climbing figure', for *climax* is as much to say as a ladder, as in . . . Jean de Meung, the French poet:

> Peace makes plenty, plenty makes pride,
> Pride breeds quarrel, and quarrel brings war.
> War brings spoil,* and spoil poverty,
> Poverty patience, and patience peace:
> So peace brings war, and war brings peace.[135]

ANTIMETABOLE;[136] *or, the counter-change.*

Ye have a figure which takes a couple of words, to play with in a

---

[133] Edward de Vere, 'When Wert Thou Borne Desire', in *Brittons Bowre of Delights* (1591), no. 40.

[134] *Inst.* 9. 3. 54–7; Susenb., pp. 77–8 (Lat. *gradatio*).

[135] This paradox circulated in England from the 15th cent. onwards (*WW*, p. 332). In his 'Dulce Bellum Inexpertis', Gascoigne described it as one of the 'old sayde sawes': *Posies*, ed. Cunliffe, p. 142.

[136] *Inst.* 9. 3. 85, including the illustrative example, 'Non, ut edam, vivo: sed, ut vivam, edo'; repeated in Susenb., pp. 78–9.

verse, and by making them to change and shift one into other's place they do very prettily exchange and shift the sense, as thus:

> We dwell not here to build us bowers,
> And halls for pleasure and good cheer:
> But halls we build for us and ours,
> To dwell in them whilst we are here.

Meaning that we dwell not here to build, but we build to dwell; as 'we live not to eat, but eat to live'; or thus:

> We wish not peace to maintain cruel war,
> But we make war to maintain us in peace.

Or thus:

> If poesy be, as some have said,
> A speaking picture to the eye:
> Then is a picture not denied
> To be a mute poesy.[137]

Or as the philosopher Musonius[138] wrote:

> With pleasure if we work unhonestly and ill,
> The pleasure passeth, the bad bideth still:
> Well if we work with travail and with pains,
> The pain passeth and still the good remains. . . .

ANTITHETON;[139] *or, the rencounter.**

Ye have another figure very pleasant and fit for amplification, which to answer the Greek term, we may call 'the encounter'. But following the Latin name, by reason of his contentious nature we may call him 'the quarreller', for so be all such persons as delight in taking the contrary part of whatsoever shall be spoken. When I was a scholar in Oxford they called every such one '*Iohannes ad oppositum*'.

---

[137] Puttenham versifies, either from *Rhet. Her.* 4. 28. 39: 'Poema loquens pictura, pictura tacitum poema debet esse', or (more likely) from Susenb., p. 78, who writes 'si poema loquens pictura est . . .'.

[138] See *Tottel's Miscellany*, no. 134 for Nicholas Grimald's versification of 'Musonius the Philosopher's Saying' (ed. H. E. Rollins (Cambridge, Mass., 1928), i. 97–8 and ii. 229). The ultimate source is Aulus Gellius, *Noctes Atticae* 16. 1, recording this 'true and brilliant saying' of Musonius: 'If you accomplish anything noble with toil, the toil passes, but the noble deed endures. If you do anything shameful with pleasure, the pleasure passes, but the shame endures', adding a similar saying by Marcus Cato.

[139] *Inst.* 9. 3. 81–6; Susenb., pp. 69–70 ('when we amplify by means of contraries') (Lat. *contentio, contrapositum*).

> Good have I done you much, harm did I never none,
> Ready to joy your gains, your losses to bemoan.
> Why therefore should you grudge so sore at my welfare,
> Who only bred your bliss, and never caused your care?

Or as it is in these two verses, where one speaking of Cupid's bow, deciphered thereby the nature of sensual love, whose beginning is more pleasant than the end, thus allegorically and by *antitheton*:

> His bent* is sweet, his loose* is somewhat sour,
> In joy begun, ends oft in woeful hour.[140]

Master Dyer,[141] in this quarrelling figure:

> Nor love hath now the force on me which it once had,
> Your frowns can neither make me mourn, nor favours make me glad.

Isocrates the Greek orator was a little too full of this figure, and so was the Spaniard[142] that wrote the life of Marcus Aurelius. And many of our modern writers in vulgar use it in excess and incur the vice of fond* affectation; otherwise the figure is very commendable. . . .

EROTEMA;[143] *or, the questioner*.

There is a kind of figurative speech when we ask many questions and look for none answer, speaking indeed by interrogation, which we might as well say by affirmation. This figure I call 'the questioner' or 'inquisitive', as when Medea,[144] excusing her great cruelty used in the murder of her own children which she had by Jason, said:

> Was I able to make them, I pray you, tell,
> And am I not able to mar them all as well? . . .

ECPHONESIS;[145] *or, the outcry*.

The figure of exclamation, I call him 'the outcry', because it utters our mind by all such words as do show any extreme passion, whether it be by way of exclamation or crying out, admiration or wondering,

---

[140] *Rhet. Her.* 4. 15. 21 (referring to flattery); repeated by Susenb., p. 69.

[141] 'But this and then no more', ll. 19–20.

[142] Antonio de Guevara (1490–1545), Spanish writer, whose *Libreo aureo* or *Golden Book of Marcus Aurelius*, a compilation of largely apocryphal anecdotes concerning the famous philosopher, had a vast popularity in the Renaissance.

[143] *Inst.* 9. 2. 6–12; Susenb., pp. 56–7 (Lat. *interrogatio*).

[144] From Ovid's lost play on Medea; cit. *Inst.* 8. 5. 6, and Susenb., p. 57.

[145] *Inst.* 9. 2. 26–7; Susenb., pp. 60–1 ('whenever emotion breaks forth with violence') (Lat. *exclamatio*).

imprecation or cursing, obtestation* or taking God and the world to witness, or any such like as declare an impotent affection; as Chaucer[146] of the Lady Criseyde by exclamation:

> O sop of sorrow sunken into care,
> O caitiff Cresseid, for now and evermare.

Or as Gascoigne[147] wrote, very passionately and well to purpose:

> Ay me, the days that I in dole consume,
> Alas, the nights which witness well mine woe!
> O wrongful world, which mak'st my fancy fume,
> Fie, fickle fortune, fie, fie, thou art my foe!
> Out and alas! So froward* is my chance,
> No nights nor days nor worlds can me advance. . . .

BRACHYLOGIA;[148] *or, the cut comma.*

We use sometimes to proceed all by single words, without any close or coupling, saving that a little pause or comma is given to every word. This figure for pleasure may be called in our vulgar 'the cut comma', for that there cannot be a shorter division than at every word's end. The Greeks in their language call it short language, as thus:

> Envy, malice, flattery, disdain,
> Avarice, deceit, falsehood, filthy gain.[149]

If this loose language be used, not in single words but in long clauses, it is called *asyndeton*, and in both cases we utter in that fashion when either we be earnest, or would seem to make haste.

PARISON;[150] *or, the figure of even.*

Ye have another figure, which we may call 'the figure of even', because it goeth by clauses of equal quantity, and not very long, but

---

[146] In fact, these lines are from Robert Henryson, *The Testament of Cresseid* (late 15th cent., but were included in the 1532 and subsequent editions of Chaucer's *Works* as if forming the sixth book of *Troilus and Criseyde*); in G. G. Smith (ed.), *Poems of Robert Henryson* (London, 1914), ii. 407–8.

[147] 'The Fruite of Fetters', in *The Posies* (1575), ed. Cunliffe, p. 367.

[148] *Inst.* 8. 3. 82, 9. 3. 50; *Rhet. Her.* 4. 19. 26; Susenb., pp. 52–3 ('when a sentence has been sharply pruned and single words are separated only by pauses . . . Poets call it *asyndeton*') (Lat. *articulus*).

[149] Cf. Romans 1: 29; cit. Susenb. (p. 69) as an example of *synathroismos* or *congeries*.

[150] *Inst.* 9. 3. 76; *Rhet. Her.* 4. 19. 26, 4. 20. 27; Susenb., p. 53 ('this scheme involves units of discourse composed of an equal or almost equal number of syllables . . . Those examples are especially esteemed which consist in three parts . . . The grace of this scheme is lost if the parts be too long . . .') (Lat. *compar*).

yet not so short as the cut comma; and they give good grace to a ditty, but specially to a prose. In this figure we once wrote, in a melancholic humour, these verses:

> The good is geason,* and short is his abode,
> The bad bides long, and easy to be found:
> Our life is loathsome, our sins a heavy load,
> Conscience a cursed judge, remorse a privy goad.
> Disease, age and death still in our ear they round,
> That hence we must, the sickly and the sound:
> Treading the steps that our forefathers trod,
> Rich, poor, holy, wise, all flesh it goes to ground.

In a prose there should not be used at once of such even clauses past three or four at the most . . .

EPIPHONEMA;[151] *or, the surclose.**

Our poet in his short ditties, but specially playing the epigrammatist, will use to conclude and shut up his epigram with a verse or two, spoken in such sort as it may seem a manner of allowance* to all his premisses, and that with a joyful approbation, which the Latins call *acclamatio.* We therefore call this figure 'the surclose' or 'consenting close', as Virgil,[152] when he had largely spoken of Prince Aeneas his success and fortunes, concluded with this close:

> *Tantae molis erat Romanam condere gentem.*

In English thus:

> So huge a piece of work it was and so high,
> To rear the house of Roman progeny.

Sir Philip Sidney[153] very prettily closed up a ditty in this sort:

> What medicine then can such disease remove,
> Where love breeds hate, and hate engenders love . . .

Lucretius Carus,[154] the philosopher and poet, inveighing sore against the abuses of the superstitious religion of the gentiles, and recounting the wicked fact* of king Agamemnon in sacrificing his only daugh-

---

[151] *Inst.* 8. 5. 11, including the Virgil quotation repeated in Susenb., p. 92.
[152] *Aen.* 1. 33.
[153] The closing couplet of a poem from the *Old Arcadia*, 'The Love which is imprinted in my soul'; *The Poems of Sir Philip Sidney*, ed. W. A. Ringler, Jr. (Oxford, 1962), p. 85.
[154] *De rerum natura* 1. 101.

ter Iphigeneia, being a young damsel of excellent beauty, to the intent
to please the wrathful gods, hinderers of his navigation; after he had
said all, closed it up in this one verse, spoken in *epiphonema*:

> *Tantum religio potuit suadere malorum.*

In English thus:

> Lo what an outrage could cause to be done,
> The peevish scruple of blind religion.

AUXESIS;[155] *or, the advancer.*

It happens many times that to urge and enforce the matter we speak
of, we go still mounting by degrees and increasing our speech with
words or with sentences of more weight one than another, and [it] is
a figure of great both efficacy and ornament. As he that, declaring the
great calamity of an unfortunate* prince, said thus:

> He lost besides his children and his wife,
> His realm, renown, liege liberty and life.

By which it appeareth that to any noble Prince the loss of his estate
ought not to be so grievous as of his honour, nor any of them both
like to the lack of his liberty, but that life is the dearest detriment* of
any other. We call this figure by the Greek original 'the advancer' or
'figure of increase', because every word that is spoken is one of more
weight than another.

MEIOSIS;[156] *or, the disabler.*

After 'the advancer' followeth 'the abaser', working by words and
sentences of extenuation* or diminution, whereupon we call him 'the
disabler' or 'figure of extenuation'. And this extenuation is used to
diverse purposes, sometimes for modesty's sake, and to avoid the
opinion of arrogance, speaking of ourselves or of ours; as he that disabled himself to his mistress, thus:

> Not all the skill I have to speak or do,
> Which little is, God wot (set love apart),

---

[155] *Inst.* 8. 4. 3–9; Susenb., pp. 68–9 ('Style may be heightened . . . if one progresses continually from one grave term to another more grave') (Lat. *incrementum*).

[156] *Inst.* 8. 3. 50–1; Susenb., pp. 75–7 ('when we depreciate ourselves and our affairs with
modesty and discretion . . . in order to avoid arrogance and animosity; also . . . to drag the
character or cause of an adversary down into contempt. We use it, finally, when we desire
to diminish and remove the difficulty of doing anything . . . Thus Hannibal depreciated the
difficulty of the Alps and the extremely arduous journey ahead . . .') (Lat. *extenuatio*).

> Livelihood nor life, and put them both thereto,
> Can counterpoise the due of your desert.

It may be also done for despite, to bring our adversaries in contempt, as he that said [of] one (commended for a very brave soldier) disabling* him scornfully, thus:

> A jolly man (forsooth) and fit for the war,
> Good at hand-grips, better to fight afar;
> Whom bright weapon in show, as it is said,
> Yea his own shade, hath often made afraid.

The subtlety of the scoff lieth in these Latin words, *eminus et cominus pugnare.*[157]

Also, we use this kind of extenuation when we take in hand to comfort or cheer any perilous enterprise, making a great matter seem small, and of little difficulty; and [it] is much used by captains when they (to give courage to their soldiers) will seem to disable the persons of their enemies, and abase their forces, and make light of everything that might be a discouragement to the attempt; as Hannibal did in his oration to his soldiers, when they should come to pass the Alps to enter Italy, and for sharpness of the weather, and steepness of the mountains, their hearts began to fail them.

We use it again to excuse a fault, and to make an offence seem less than it is, by giving a term more favourable, and of less vehemence than the truth requires; as, to say of a great robbery, that it was but a pilfry matter; of an arrant ruffian, that he is a tall fellow of his hands; of a prodigal fool, that he is a kind-hearted man; of a notorious unthrift, a lusty youth; and such like phrases of extenuation, which fall more aptly to the office of the figure *curry favell*, before remembered. . . .

EPANODOS;[158] *or, the figure of retire.*

This figure of retire holds part with the propounder, of which we spoke before (*prolepsis*), because of the resumption* of a former proposition uttered in generality to explain the same better by a particular division. But their difference is, in that the propounder resumes but the matter only, this 'retire' resumes both the matter and the terms, and is therefore accounted one of the figures of repetition, and in that respect may be called by his original Greek name 'the

---

[157] Unidentified.   [158] *Inst.* 9. 3. 35–7; Susenb., p. 79 (Lat. *regressio*).

resound' or 'the retire', for this word *hodos* serves both senses, resound and retire. The use of this figure is seen in this ditty following:

> Love, hope, and death do stir in me much strife,
> As never man but I lead such a life:
> For burning love doth wound my heart to death,
> And when death comes at call of inward grief,
> Cold lingering hope doth feed my fainting breath
> Against my will, and yields my wound relief;
> So that I live, but yet my life is such
> As never death could grieve me half so much.[159]

DIALYSIS;[160] *or, the dismemberer.*

Then have ye a manner of speech, not so figurative as fit for argumentation, and worketh not unlike the *dilemma* of the logicians, because he proposes two or more matters entirely, and doth as it were set down the whole tale or reckoning of an argument, and then clear every part by itself; as thus:

> It cannot be but niggardship or need
> Made him attempt this foul and wicked deed;
> Niggardship not, for always he was free,
> Nor need, for who doth not his riches see?[161]

Or as one that entreated for a fair young maid who was taken by the watch in London and carried to Bridewell to be punished:

> Now gentle sirs, let this young maid alone,
> For either she hath grace or else she hath none:
> If she have grace she may in time repent,
> If she have none, what boots her punishment? . . .[162]

MERISMUS;[163] *or, the distributor.*

Then have ye a figure very meet for orators or eloquent persuaders, such as our maker or poet must in some cases show himself to be, and is when we may conveniently utter a matter in one entire speech or proposition, and will rather do it piecemeal and by distribution of every part, for amplification's sake. As for example, he that might say,

---

[159] Gascoigne, 'Love, Hope and Death', in *The Posies* (1575), ed. Cunliffe, p. 394.
[160] *Inst.* 9. 2. 105; *Rhet. Her.* 4. 39. 51, 4. 40. 52; Susenb., p. 33 (Lat. *divisio*).
[161] A versification of *Rhet. Her.* 4. 38. 50.
[162] Cf. *Rhet. Her.* 4. 40. 52.
[163] *Inst.* 9. 2. 2; Scaliger, *Poet.* 3. 69 (Lat. *distributio*).

'a house was outrageously plucked down' will not be satisfied so to say, but rather will speak it in this sort: 'they first undermined the ground-sills, they beat down the walls, they unfloored the lofts, they untiled it and pulled down the roof'. For so indeed is a house pulled down by circumstances,* which this figure of distribution doth set forth every one apart, and therefore I name him 'the distributor', according to his original.

As wrote the Tuscan poet, in a sonnet which Sir Thomas Wyatt[164] translated with very good grace, thus:

> Set me whereas the sun doth parch the green,
> Or where his beams do not dissolve the ice;
> In temperate heat where he is felt and seen,
> In presence pressed of people mad or wise;
> Set me in high or yet in low degree,
> In longest night or in the shortest day,
> In clearest sky, or where clouds thickest be,
> In lusty youth or when my hairs are grey,
> Set me in heaven, in earth, or else in hell,
> In hill, or dale, or in the foaming flood;
> Thrall or at large, alive where so I dwell,
> Sick or in health, in evil fame or good:
> Hers will I be, and only with this thought
> Content myself, although my chance be naught.

All which might have been said in these two verses:

> Set me wheresoever ye will,
> I am and will be yours still. . . .

This figure serves for amplification,* and also for ornament, and to enforce persuasion mightily. Sir Geoffrey Chaucer,[165] father of our English poets, hath these verses following, in the distributor:

> When faith fails in prieste's saws,
> And Lords' hests are holden for laws,
> And robbery is taken for purchase,
> And lechery for solace

---

[164] In fact Surrey, 'Vow to love faithfully howsoever he be rewarded' (translating Petrarch, *Rime* 145: 'Pommi ove 'l sole occide i fiori et l'erba') in *Tottel's Miscellany* (1557), no. 12.

[165] From an apocryphal poem included in the early Chaucer canon. Shakespeare echoed it (perhaps via Puttenham) for the Fool's prophecy in *King Lear* 3. 2. 80–95.

> Then shall the realm of Albion
> Be brought to great confusion.

Where he might have said as much in these words: 'when vice abounds, and virtue decayeth in Albion, then' etc.

EPIMONE;[166] *or, the love-burden.*

The Greek poets who made musical ditties to be sung to the lute or harp, did use to link their staves together with one verse running throughout the whole song by equal distance, and was, for the most part, the first verse of the staff, which kept so good sense and conformity with the whole as his often repetition did give it greater grace. They called such linking verse *epimone*, the Latins *versus intercalaris*, and we may term him 'the love-burden', following the original; or if it please you 'the long repeat'. In one respect, because that one verse alone beareth the whole burden* of the song, according to the original; in another respect, for that it comes by large distances to be often repeated, as in this ditty made by the noble knight Sir Philip Sidney:[167]

> My true love hath my heart and I have his,
> By just exchange one for another given;
> I hold his dear, and mine he cannot miss,
> There never was a better bargain driven.
> My true love hath my heart and I have his.
> His heart in me keeps him and me in one,
> My heart in him his thoughts and senses guides;
> He loves my heart, for once it was his own,
> I cherish his because in me it bides.
> My true love hath my heart, and I have his . . .

PARAMOLOGIA;[168] *or, the figure of admittance.*

The good orator useth a manner of speech in his persuasion,

---

[166] In Greek rhetoric this figure describes 'a dwelling on a point or argument (in sense, not words) whether by iteration or elaboration' (van Hook, op. cit., pp. 119–20); cf. Longinus, *On Sublimity*, ch. 12 (*ALC*, pp. 474). But Puttenham draws on Susenbrotus, who defines *epimone* as 'when the same verse or sentiment is inserted very often in a poem or oration. Mancinellus: "When an idea is often repeated we have *Epimone*. Intercalary verses also produce this scheme, as the line 'Begin with me, my flute, a song of Maenalus' in Virgil" [*Ecl.* 8. 22, 25 etc.]. This scheme appears quite frequently in the Psalms of David, in testimony to the burning affection of his heart.'

[167] From the *Old Arcadia*; *Poems*, ed. Ringler, pp. 75–6 (but the original has no refrain; the opening line is repeated once only, at the end of the sonnet).

[168] *Inst.* 9. 2. 17; Susenb., pp. 81–2 ('when we concede many issues to an adversary but introduce one point, nevertheless, which demolishes all the concessions made before') (Lat. *confessio*).

[which] is when all that should seem to make against him being spoken by the other side, he will first admit it, and in the end avoid* all for his better advantage. And this figure is much used by our English pleaders in the Star Chamber and Chancery, which they call 'to confess and avoid', if it be in case of crime or injury, and is a very good way. For when the matter is so plain that it cannot be denied or traversed, it is good that it be justified by confessal and avoidance. I call it 'the figure of admittance'. As we once wrote to the reproof of a lady's, fair but cruelty:

> I know your wit, I know your pleasant tongue,
> Your some sweet smiles, your some but lovely lowers:*
> A beauty to enamour old and young.
> Those chaste desires, that noble mind of yours,
> And that chief part whence all your honour springs,
> A grace to entertain the greatest kings.
> All this I know: but sin it is to see
> So fair parts spilt by too much cruelty.

AITIOLOGIA;[169] *or, the reason-renderer, or the tell-cause.*

In many cases we are driven for better persuasion to tell the cause that moves us to say thus or thus; or else when we would fortify our allegations by rendering reasons to every one, this assignation of cause the Greeks called *aitiologia*, which, if we might without scorn of a new invented term call 'tell-cause', it were right according to the Greek original. . . . And this manner of speech is always contemned with these words: 'for', 'because', and such other confirmatives. The Latins having no fit name to give it in one single word, gave it no name at all, but by circumlocution. We also call him 'the reason-renderer', and leave the right English word ('tell-cause'), much better answering the Greek original. Aristotle was most excellent in use of this figure, for he never proposes any allegation, or makes any surmise, but he yields a reason or cause to fortify and prove it, which gives it great credit. For example ye may take these verses, first pointing, then confirming by similitudes:

> When fortune shall have spat out all her gall
> I trust good luck shall be to me allowed,

---

[169] *Inst.* 9. 2. 17; Susenb., p. 81 ('when we suggest at once the reason for some proposition') (Lat. *causa*).

> For I have seen a ship in haven fall,
> After the storm had broke both mast and shroud.[170]

And this:

> Good is the thing that moves us to desire,
> That is to joy the beauty we behold:
> Else were we lovers as in an endless fire,
> Always burning and ever chill a-cold. . . .

HORISMOS;[171] *or, the definer of difference.*

The logician useth a definition to express the truth or nature of everything by his true kind and difference; as to say, wisdom is a prudent and witty foresight and consideration of human or worldly actions, with their events. This definition is logical. The orator useth another manner of definition, thus: 'Is this wisdom? No, it is a certain subtle knavish crafty wit. It is no industry as ye call it, but a certain busy* brainsickness, for industry is a lively and unwearied search and occupation in honest things, eagerness is an appetite in base and small matters . . .'.

PARALEPSIS;[172] *or, the passager.*

It is also very many times used for a good policy in pleading or persuasion, to make wise as if we set but light of the matter, and that therefore we do pass it over lightly – when indeed we do then intend most effectually* and despitefully* (if it be invective) to remember it. It is also when we will not seem to know a thing, and yet we know it well enough, and may be likened to the manner of women who, as the common saying is, 'will say nay and take it':

> I hold my peace, and will not say, for shame,
> The much untruth of that uncivil dame;
> For if I should her colours kindly* blaze
> It would so make the chaste ears amaze, etc. . . .

---

[170] Wyatt, 'The lover hopeth of better chance', in *Tottel's Miscellany* (1557), no. 72.

[171] *Rhet. Her.* 4. 25. 35; Susenb., pp. 82–3 ('not every definition is a scheme, but that definition which dialecticians call *katadiaphoran* nearly always is when a difference in words is sought for. For example: "That is not frugality but avarice, since frugality is . . . whereas avarice is . . ."') (Lat. *definitio*).

[172] *Rhet. Her.* 4. 27. 37; *Inst.* 9. 2. 75; Susenb., pp. 79–80 ('when we pretend that we are omitting, or don't know, or don't wish to say, what we then proceed to say in particular') (Lat. *occupatio*). Cf. *Richard III*, 3.7.51: 'Play the maid's part, still answer nay, and take it'.

EXPEDITIO;[173] *or, the speedy dispatcher.*

Occasion offers many times that our maker as an orator, or persuader, or pleader should go roundly* to work, and by a quick and
swift argument despatch his persuasion; and as they are wont to say,
not to stand all day trifling to no purpose, but to rid it out of the way
quickly. This is done by a manner of speech both figurative and argu-
mentative, when we do briefly set down all our best reasons serving
the purpose, and reject all of them saving one, which we accept to
satisfy the cause. . . .

Though we might call this figure [*COMPARATIO*] very well and properly 'the paragon',[174] yet dare I not so to do for fear of the courtiers'
envy, who will have no man use that term but after a courtly manner,
that is, in praising of horses, hawks, hounds, pearls, diamonds, rubies,
emeralds, and other precious stones, specially of fair women whose
excellence is discovered* by paragonizing or setting one to another,
which moved the zealous poet, speaking of the maiden Queen, to call
her the paragon of queens. This considered, I will let our figure enjoy
his best beknown name, and call him still in all ordinary cases 'the
figure of comparison'. As when a man will seem to make things appear
good or bad, or better or worse, or more or less excellent, either upon
spite or for pleasure, or any other good affection, then he sets the less
by the greater, or the greater to the less, the equal to his equal, and by
such confronting of them together drives out the true odds that is

---

[173] *Rhet. Her.* 4. 29. 40; Susenb., p. 94 ('when several methods are enumerated . . . and
all are dismissed save one, to which we then turn our attention').

[174] As Frank Whigham has observed ('A Lacuna in Puttenham's *Arte of English Poesie*',
English Language Notes, 22 (1984), 20–2), there seems to be a gap in the text here, since the
previous figure discussed, *expeditio*, 'the speedy dispatcher', has nothing to do with *paragon*
or any other form of comparison. The text also lacks the usual marginal note calling attention to each figure as it is introduced; nor does *paragon* appear in the concluding chart of
figures (*WW*, pp. 311–13), all of which points to the inadvertent omission of a preceding
paragraph introducing *paragon*. I suggest that Puttenham's coinage refers to the figure *comparatio* (*Inst.* 9. 2. 100; 8–4–9; Scaliger, *Poetice* 3. 50: under *tractatio*), and that he drew on
Susenbrotus, who wrote that '*comparison* comes about by way of parallel instance when we
represent some case as a comparable example, so that what we are amplifying may appear
to either approach it, or parallel it, or even surpass it' (p. 70). It is a figure 'in which we
amplify from minor matters, for if these be great in the opinion of everyone, then what we
wish to amplify must necessarily appear even greater by comparison. It also occurs when
. . . we compare, or even prefer, the lesser to the greater, the more easy to the more difficult,
or the unworthy to the much more unworthy, not so much for the sake of proving something as for the sake of ornament.' He adds that one can also use it to compare persons, as:
'By the judgment of all, the most praiseworthy ruler was Trajan, and more praiseworthy
yet was the philosoper-emperor, Marcus Aurelius; but our emperor Charlemagne surpasses
both of these by far' (p. 72). Puttenham's account includes all these details. Cf. also Hoskyns,
p. 411.

betwixt them, and makes it better appear. As when we sang of our sovereign Lady thus, in the twentieth *Partheniade*:

> As falcon fares to buzzard's flight,
> As eagle's eyes to owlet's sight,
> As fierce saker* to coward kite,
> As brightest noon to darkest night,
> As summer sun exceedeth far
> The moon and every other star:
> So far my Princess' praise doth pass
> The famoust Queen that ever was . . .[175]

GNOME;[176] *or, the director.**

In weighty causes and for great purposes, wise persuaders use grave and weighty speeches, specially in matters of advice or counsel. For which purpose there is a manner of speech to allege texts or authorites of witty sentence, such as smatch* moral doctrine and teach wisdom and good behaviour. By the Greek original we call him 'the director', by the Latin he is called *sententia*; we may call him 'the sage sayer', thus:

> Nature bids us as a loving mother
> To love ourselves first, and next to love another.[177]

> The Prince that covets all to know and see
> Had need full mild and patient to be.[178]

> Nothing sticks faster by us, as appears,
> Than that which we learn in our tender years . . .[179]

Heed must be taken that such rules or sentences be choicely made and not often used, lest excess breed loathsomeness.

SYNATHROISMOS;[180] *or, the heaping figure.*

---

[175] Puttenham, *Partheniades*, no. 16. See headnote and *WW*, pp. xxxiff. For a scathing (but not unfounded) contemporary evaluation see Harington, p. 305.

[176] *Inst.* 8. 5. 3; Susenb., pp. 90–1 ('what points out to us with proper brevity what must be done in life, or what ought to be done . . . take care that these sentences be not excessively crowded . . .') (Lat. *sententia*).

[177] Terence, *Andria* 2. 5. 426–7; perhaps via Erasmus, *Adagia* 1. 3. 91. But cf. Susenb., p. 91: 'All prefer to be better to themselves than to others'.

[178] Quintilian (8. 5. 3) attributes this saying to Domitius Afer.

[179] Erasmus, *Adagia* 2. 4. 20; but cf. Susenb., p. 91: 'Nothing sticks more tenaciously than what we learn as boys'.

[180] *Inst.* 8. 4. 27; Susenb., p. 69 ('an enumeration of words signifying various things . . . various concepts are piled up confusedly without any orderly progression') (Lat. *congeries*).

Art and good policy* moves us many times to be earnest in our speech, and then we lay on such load, and so go to it by heaps, as if we would win the game by multitude of words and speeches, not all of one but of diverse matter and sense. For which cause the Latins called it *congeries*, and we 'the heaping figure', as he that said:

> To muse in mind how fair, how wise, how good,
> How brave, how free, how courteous and how true
> My lady is, doth but inflame my blood.[181]

Or thus:

> I deem, I dream, I do, I taste, I touch
> Nothing at all but smells of perfect bliss.[182]

And thus by master Edward Dyer,[183] vehement, swift, and passionately:

> But if my faith my hope, my love my true intent,
> My liberty, my service vowed, my time and all be spent,
> In vain, etc.

But if such earnest and hasty heaping up of speeches be made by way of recapitulation, which commonly is in the end of every long tale and oration, because the speaker seems to make collection* of all the former material points, to bind them as it were in a bundle, and lay them forth to enforce the cause and renew the hearer's memory, then ye may give him more properly the name of 'the collector', or 'recapitulator', and serveth to very great purpose. . . .

APOSTROPHE;[184] *or, the turn-tale.*

Many times when we have run a long race in our tale spoken to the hearers, we do suddenly fly out, and either speak or exclaim at some other person or thing. And therefore the Greeks call such figure (as we do) 'the turn-way' or 'turn-tale', and breedeth by such exchange a certain recreation to the hearers' minds; as this used by a lover to his unkind mistress:

---

[181] Gascoigne, 'Dan Bartholomew his Second Triumphe', in *The Posies* (1575), ed. Cunliffe, p. 104.

[182] *Ibid.* 103.

[183] This poem, beginning 'But this and then no more' (BL, MS Harl. 7392), is now attributed to Sir Arthur Gorges.

[184] *Inst.* 9. 2. 38–9; Susenb., p. 65 ('it conduces wonderfully to the excitement of the emotions') (Lat. *aversio*).

And as for you (fair one) say now by proof ye find
That rigour* and ingratitude soon kill a gentle mind.[185]

HYPOTYPOSIS;[186] *or, the counterfeit representation.*

The matter and occasion leadeth us many times to describe and set
forth many things in such sort as it should appear they were truly
before our eyes, though they were not present; which to do it requireth
cunning, for nothing can be kindly* counterfeit or represented in his
absence but by great discretion* in the doer. And if the things we covet
to describe be not natural or not veritable, then yet the same asketh
more cunning to do it, because to feign a thing that never was nor is
like to be, proceedeth of a greater wit and sharper invention than to
describe things that be true.

PROSOPOGRAPHIA.[187]

And these be things that a poet or maker is wont to describe sometimes as true or natural, and sometimes to feign as artificial and not
true, *viz.* the visage, speech and countenance of any person absent or
dead, and this kind of representation is called 'the counterfeit countenance'. As Homer doth in his *Iliad,* diverse personages, namely
Achilles and Thersites, according to the truth and not by fiction; and
as our poet Chaucer doth in his *Canterbury Tales* set forth the Sum-
moner, Pardoner, Manciple, and the rest of the pilgrims, most naturally and pleasantly.

PROSOPOPOEIA;[188] *or, the counterfeit impersonation.*

But if ye will feign any person with such features, qualities and conditions, or if ye will attribute any human quality, as reason or speech,
to dumb creatures or other insensible things, and do study (as one may
say) to give them a human person, it is not *prosopographia*, but
prosopopoeia, because it is by way of fiction. And no prettier examples
can be given to you thereof than in the *Roman of the Rose*, translated
out of French by Chaucer, describing the persons of avarice, envy, old
age, and many others, whereby much morality is taught.

[185] [Gorges], 'But this and then no more', 29–30.
[186] *Inst.* 9. 2. 40; *Rhet. Her.* 4. 55. 68; Susenb., p. 83 ('when a person, place, time or anything else must be expressed verbally in such a way . . . that it seems to be perceived . . . as
though one were personally present . . .') (Lat. *demonstratio*).
[187] *Rhet. Her.* 4. 49. 63; Susenb., p. 83 ('when either a real or fictional person is described,
as though by a picture, and is placed before our eyes, in the physical form, the attire, the
character, and other characteristics') (Lat. *effictio*).
[188] *Inst.* 9. 2. 29–37; Scaliger, *Poetice* 3. 47; Susenb., pp. 83–4 ('when we create for something mute and deprived of sense, a personality suitable to it. Of this mode are the
personification of Folly in Erasmus . . .') (Lat. *fictio personae*).

CHRONOGRAPHIA;[189] *or, the counterfeit time.*

So if we describe the time or season of the year, as winter, summer, harvest, day, midnight, noon, evening, or such like, we call such description 'the counterfeit time', *cronographia*; examples are everywhere to be found.

TOPOGRAPHIA;[190] *or, the counterfeit place.*

And if this description be of any true place, city, castle, hill, valley or sea, and such like, we call it the counterfeit place, *topographia*; or if ye feign places untrue, as heaven, hell, paradise, the house of fame, the palace of the sun, the den of sleep, and such like which ye shall see in poets . . .

HOMOEOSIS;[191] *or, resemblance.*

As well to a good maker and poet as to an excellent persuader in prose, the figure of 'similitude' is very necessary, by which we not only beautify our tale, but also very much enforce and enlarge it. I say enforce because no one thing more prevaileth with all ordinary judgements than persuasion by similitude. Now because there are sundry sorts of them, which also do work after diverse fashions in the hearers' conceits, I will set them all forth by a triple division, exempting the general 'similitude' as their common ancestor, and I will call him by the name of 'resemblance' without any addition. From which I derive three other sorts, and give everyone his particular name, as: 'resemblance by portrait or imagery', which the Greeks call *icon*; 'resemblance moral or mystical', which they call *parabole*; and 'resemblance by example', which they call *paradigma*.

And first we will speak of the general resemblance, or bare similitude, which may be thus spoken:

---

[189] Susenb., pp. 85–6: 'a straightforward description coloured by the circumstances of the time. . . . Sometimes it is used merely for the sake of giving delight, such as when poets describe the day, night, dawn, or twilight.'

[190] *Inst.* 9. 2. 44; Susenb., p. 85: 'whenever the whole aspect of a place is so depicted that one seems to be looking at it, such as descriptions of a city, mountain region, river, port . . . *Topothesia* is the fictitious and simulated description of a location that is nowhere on earth. Examples of this are the abode of Sleep, the house of fame, and the kingdom of the sun in Ovid. . . .' (cf. *Met.* 11. 593; 12. 43; 2. 1) (Lat. *locus*).

[191] *Inst.* 8. 3. 72 ff.; *Rhet. Her.* 4. 45. 594–59. 62; Susenb., pp. 95–7: 'when some comparable feature is transferred from one thing to something different; or when one thing is compared to another on the basis of some similarity. Mancinellus: "Homoeosis occurs whenever a comparison is made. Its species are *icon, parable*, and *paradigm*." . . . It lends to discourse much brilliance and dignity, but it also contributes much to demonstration.'

But as the wat'ry showers delay the raging wind,
So doth good hope clean put away despair out of my mind.[192]

And in this other, likening the forlorn lover to a stricken deer:

Then as the stricken deer withdraws himself alone,
So do I seek some secret place where I may make my moan.[193]

And in this of ours[194] where we liken glory to a shadow:

As the shadow (his nature being such)
Followeth the body, whether it will or no,
So doth glory, refuse it ne'er so much,
Wait on virtue, be it in weal or woe.
And even as the shadow in his kind,
What time it bears the carcass* company,
Goeth oft before, and often comes behind:
So doth renown, that raiseth us so high,
Come to us quick, sometime not till we die.
But the glory that grow'th not over fast
Is ever great, and likely long to last . . .

ICON;[195] *or, resemblance by imagery.*

But when we liken a human person to another in countenance, stature, speech or other quality, it is not called 'bare resemblance', but 'resemblance by imagery or portrait', alluding to the painter's term, who yieldeth to the eye a visible representation of the thing he describes and painteth in his table.* . . .

And this manner of resemblance is not only performed by likening of lively creatures one to another, but also of any other natural thing bearing a proportion or similitude; as, to liken yellow to gold, white to silver, red to the rose, soft to silk, hard to the stone, and such like. Sir Philip Sidney[196] in the decription of his mistress excellently well

---

[192] Surrey, 'Against him that had slaundered a gentlewoman with him selfe', in *Tottel's Miscellany* (1557), no. 245, ll. 47–8.

[193] Surrey, ibid. 21–2.

[194] Versified from Seneca, *Ep.* 79. 13, via Erasmus, *Parabolae*: cf. *CWE* xxiii. 213, ll. 23–4.

[195] Susenb., p. 97: 'When an image is expressed of either persons or things; or it is a comparison of one form with another, by reason of some likeness; or it is a statement demonstrating the similarity of bodies or natures. Of bodies: "Head and shoulders like to a god's . . .". *Image* . . . is derived only from the form of an animated being; it makes for either the amplification of pictorial representation of a thing, and for clearness, gravity, and beauty of style.'

[196] Probably the poem 'What toong can her perfections tell', from the *Old Arcadia* (62); *Poems*, ed. Ringler, p. 85.

handled this figure of resemblance by imagery, as we may see in his book of *Arcadia*; and ye may see the like of our doings, in a *Partheniade*[197] written of our sovereign Lady, wherein we resemble every part of her body to some natural thing of excellent perfection in his kind, as of her forehead, brows and hair, thus:

> Of silver was her forehead high,
> Her brows two bows of ebony,
> Her tresses trussed were to behold
> Frizzled* and fine as fringe of gold.

And of her lips:

> Two lips wrought out of ruby rock,
> Like leaves to shut and to unlock,
> As portal door in princes' chamber;
> A golden tongue in mouth of amber.

And of her eyes:

> Her eyes, God wot what stuff they are,
> I durst be sworn each is a star,
> As clear and bright as wont to guide
> The pilot in his winter tide.

And of her breasts:

> Her bosom sleek as Paris plaster
> Held up two balls of alabaster,
> Each bias* was a little cherry,
> Or else I think a strawberry.

And all the rest that followeth, which may suffice to exemplify your figure of *icon*, or resemblance by imagery and portrait. . . .

PARABOLE;[198] *or, resemblance mystical.**

But whensoever by your similitude ye will seem to teach any morality or good lesson by speeches mystical and dark, or far-fetched, under a sense metaphorical applying one natural thing to another, or one case to another, inferring by them a like consequence in other cases, the Greeks call it *parabole*, which term is also by custom accepted of us. Nevertheless we may call him in English 'the resemblance mystical',

---

[197] Puttenham, *Partheniades*, no. 7.
[198] *Inst.* 5. 11. 23, 8. 3. 77; Susenb., pp. 97–8: 'a comparison which foreshadows the truth . . . Many such comparisons are found in the Gospel.'

as when we liken a young child to a green twig, which ye may easily bend every way ye list; or an old man who laboureth with continual infirmities, to a dry and dricksy* oak. Such parables were all the preachings of Christ in the gospel, as those of the wise and foolish virgins, of the evil steward, of the labourers in the vineyard, and a number more. And they may be feigned, as well as true; as those fables of Aesop, and other apologues[199] invented for doctrine's sake by wise and grave men.

PARADIGMA;[200] *or, resemblance by example.*

Finally, if in matter of counsel or persuasion we will seem to liken one case to another, such as pass ordinarily in man's affairs, and do compare the past with the present, gathering probability of like success to come in the things we have presently in hand; or if ye will draw the judgements precedent and authorized by antiquity as verit-able, and peradventure feigned and imagined for some purpose, into similitude or dissimilitude with our present actions and affairs, it is called 'resemblance by example'. As if one should say thus, 'Alexander the Great in his expedition to Asia did thus, so did Han-nibal coming into Spain, so did Caesar in Egypt, therefore all great captains and generals ought to do it' . . .

Chapter XX
The last and principal figure of our poetical ornament

EXERGASIA;[201] *or, the gorgeous.*

For the glorious lustre it setteth upon our speech and language, the Greeks call it *exergasia*, the Latin *expolitio*, a term transferred from these polishers of marble or porphyrite, who after it is rough-hewn and reduced* to that fashion they will, do set upon it a goodly glass, so smooth and clear as ye may see your face in it; or otherwise, as it fareth by the bare and naked body, which being attired in rich and gor-geous apparel seemeth to the common usage of the eye much more comely and beautiful than the natural. So doth this figure, which

---

[199] Moral fables, especially with animals or inanimate things as characters.

[200] *Inst.* 5. 11. 1; Susenb., pp. 98–9: 'the narration of an example exhorting and dissuad-ing. . . . Those examples move most powerfully which are ancient, illustrious.'

[201] Puttenham is mistaken: '*exergasia* does not refer primarily to figurative embellishment, but to careful literary workmanship in general, and to the thorough treatment of a subject' (van Hook, p. 120). Cf. *Inst.* 8. 3. 88: 'finish, which produces completeness of effect', and Dionysius Halicarnassus on Isocrates (*ALC*, pp. 308–9). Susenb. (pp. 86–7) treats it as a figure of repetition and variation, 'when we repeat something and amplify it continually by other words, units of discourse, ideas and figures'.

therefore I call 'the gorgeous', polish our speech, and as it were attire it with copious and pleasant amplifications, and much variety of sentences all running upon one point and to one intent. So as I doubt whether I may term it a figure, or rather a mass of many figurative speeches, applied to the beautifying of our tale or argument. . . .

Chapter XXI
Of the vices or deformities in speech and writing principally noted by ancient poets

It hath been said before how by ignorance of the maker a good figure may become a vice, and by his good discretion a vicious speech go for a virtue in the poetical science. This saying is to be explained and qualified, for some manner of speeches are always intolerable, and such as cannot be used with any decency* but are ever indecent,* namely barbarousness, incongruity, ill-disposition, fond affectation, rusticity, and all extreme darkness, such as it is not possible for a man to understand the matter without an interpreter. All which parts are generally to be banished out of every language, unless it may appear that the maker or poet do it for the nonce,* as it was reported by the philosopher Heraclitus[202] that he wrote in obscure and dark terms, of purpose not to be understood, whence he merited the nickname Scotinus. Otherwise I see not but the rest of the common faults may be borne with sometimes, or pass without any great reproof, not being used overmuch or out of season as I said before. So as every surplusage, or preposterous* placing, or undue iteration, or dark word, or doubtful speech are not so narrowly to be looked upon in a large poem, nor specially in the pretty poesies and devices of ladies and gentlewomen makers, whom we would not have too precise* poets lest with their shrewd* wits, when they were married, they might become a little too fantastical* wives. Nevertheless, because we seem to promise an art which doth not justly admit any wilful error in the teacher, and to the end we may not be carped at by these methodical men that we have omitted any necessary point in this business to be regarded, I will speak somewhat touching these viciosities of language particularly and briefly, leaving no little to the grammarians[203] for maintenance of the scholastical war and altercations. We, for our part, condescending in

---

[202] Heraclitus of Ephesus (6th cent. BC), an important but difficult philosopher, nicknamed *o skoteinos*; in Latin, *obscurus* (Cicero, *Fin.* 2. 5. 15).

[203] This discussion of faults of style follows both *Rhet. Her.* 4. 12. 17 and *Inst.* 8. 1. 2, 8. 3. 44–60 in stating that such faults also concern the grammarian.

this device of ours to the appetite of princely personages and other so tender and queasy complexions in Court, as are annoyed with nothing more than long lessons and overmuch good order.

Chapter XXII
Some vices in speeches and writing are always intolerable, some others now and then borne withall by licence of approved authors and custom

BARBARISMUS;[204] *or, foreign speech.*

The foulest vice in language is to speak barbarously. This term grew by the great pride of the Greeks and Latins, when they were dominators of the world, reckoning no language so sweet and civil as their own and that all nations beside themselves were rude and uncivil, which they called barbarous. So as when any strange word not of the natural Greek or Latin was spoken, in the old time they called it 'barbarism', or when any of their own natural words were sounded and pronounced with strange and ill-shapen accents, or written by wrong orthography, as he that would say with us in England, a 'dousand' for a 'thousand', 'isterday', for 'yesterday', as commonly the Dutch and French people do, they said it was barbarously spoken. The Italian at this day, by like arrogance, calleth the Frenchman, Spaniard, Dutch, English, and all other breed behither* their mountains Apennines, '*Tramontani*', as who would say 'barbarous'. . . .

SOLECISMUS;[205] *or, incongruity.*

Your next intolerable vice is *solecismus* or incongruity, as when we speak false English, that is by misusing the grammatical rules to be observed in cases, genders, tenses and such like. Every poor scholar knows the fault, and calls it 'the breaking of Priscian's head',[206] for he was among the Latins a principal grammarian.

CACOZELIA;[207] *or, fond affectation.*

Ye have another intolerable ill manner of speech, which by the Greeks' original we may call 'fond affectation', and is when we affect new words and phrases other than the good speakers and writers in any language, or than custom hath allowed. [It] is the common fault of young scholars, not half well studied before they come from the university or schools, and when they come to their friends or happen to get some benefice or other promotion in their countries,* will seem to coin fine words out of the Latin, and to use new-fangled

---

[204] *Rhet. Her.* 4. 12. 17.
[205] Ibid.   [206] Cf. *Love's Labour's Lost* 5. 1. 28 f.   [207] *Inst.* 8. 3. 59.

speeches, thereby to show themselves among the ignorant the better learned.

SORAISMUS;[208] *or, the mingle-mangle.*

Another of your intolerable vices is that which the Greeks call *soraismus*, and we may call 'the mingle mangle', as when we make our speech or writings of sundry languages, using some Italian word, or French, or Spanish, or Dutch, or Scottish, not for the nonce or for any purpose (which were in part excusable) but ignorantly and affectedly. As one that said, using this French word 'roy' to make rhyme with another verse, thus:

> O mighty Lord of love, dame Venus' only joy,
> Whose princely power exceeds each other heavenly roy.[209]

The verse is good but the term peevishly* affected.

Another[210] of reasonable good facility in translation, finding certain of the hymns of Pindar's and of Anacreon's odes, and other lyrics among the Greeks very well translated by Ronsard the French poet, and applied to the honour of a great prince in France, comes our minion* and translates the same out of French into English, and applieth them to the honour of a great nobleman in England (wherein I commend his reverent mind and duty), but doth so impudently rob the French poet both of his praise, and also of his French terms, that I cannot so much pity him as be angry with him for his injurious dealing, our said maker not being ashamed to use these French words 'freddon', 'egar', 'superbous', 'filanding', 'celest', 'calabrois', 'thebanois' and a number of others for English words, which have no manner of conformity with our language, either by custom or derivation, which may make them tolerable. And in the end (which is worst of all) makes his vaunt that never English finger but his hath touched Pindar's string—which was nevertheless word by word as Ronsard had said before, by like braggery. These be his verses:

> And of an ingenious invention, infanted with pleasant travail.

Whereas the French word is '*enfante*', as much to say 'born as a child'. In another verse he saith:

---

[208] *Inst.* 8. 3. 59, under the name *sardismos.*

[209] George Turberville, 'The Lover to Cupid for Mercy', in *Epitaphes, Epigrams, Songs and Sonets* (1567); cf. p. 217.

[210] Thomas Soowthern, in *Pandora, the musyque of the beautie of his mistresse Diana* (1584); the dedicatory ode to the Earl of Oxford is based on Ronsard's dedication of his *Odes* to Henry II of France.

> I will freddon in thine honour.

for 'I will shake or quiver my fingers', for so in French is 'freddon'; and in another verse:

> But if I will thus like Pindar,
> In many discourses egar.

This word '*egar*' is as much to say as to 'wander or stray out of the way', which in our English is not received, nor these words '*calabrois*', '*thebanois*', but rather 'Calabrian', 'Theban', 'filanding sisters', for the 'spinning sisters'. This man deserves to be indited of petty larceny for pilfering other men's devices from them and converting them to his own use, for indeed as I would wish every inventor which is the very poet to receive the praises of his invention, so would I not have a translator be ashamed to be acknown of his translation.

CACOSYNTHETON;[211] *or, the misplacer.*

Another of your intolerable vices is ill disposition or placing of your words in a clause or sentence. As when you will place your adjective after your substantive, thus: 'maiden fair', 'widow rich', 'priest holy', and such like, which though the Latins did admit, yet our English did not; as one that said ridiculously:

> In my years lusty, many a deed doughty did I.

All these remembered faults be intolerable and ever indecent.

CACEMPHATON;[212] *or, the figure of foul speech.*

Now have ye other vicious manners of speech, but sometimes and in some cases tolerable, and chiefly to the intent to move laughter and to make sport, or to give it some pretty strange grace. [It] is when we use such words as may be drawn to a foul and unshameful sense, as one that would say to a young woman, 'I pray you let me jape with you', which indeed is no more but 'let me sport with you'. Yea, and though it were not altogether so directly spoken, the very sounding of the word were not commendable, as he that in the presence of ladies would use this common proverb,

---

[211] *Inst.* 8. 3. 59; Susenb., p. 36 ('defective composition of words . . . awkward conjunction of words').

[212] *Inst.* 8. 3. 44–7; Susenb., p. 36—who, however, avoids the standard Roman connotation of 'language to which perverted usage has given an obscene meaning' (*Inst.*), treating it simply as 'a rude and awkward composition of words'.

> Jape with me but hurt me not,
> Board with me but shame me not.

For it may be taken in another perverser* sense by that sort of persons that hear it, in whose ears no such matter ought almost to be called in memory. This vice is called by the Greeks *cacemphaton*; we call it 'the unshameful', or 'figure of foul speech', which our courtly maker shall in any case shun, lest of a poet he become a buffoon or railing companion; the Latins called him *scurra*. . . .

HYSTERON PROTERON;[213] *or, the preposterous.*

Your misplacing and preposterous placing is not all one* in behaviour of language, for the misplacing is always intolerable, but the preposterous is a pardonable fault and many times gives a pretty grace unto the speech. We call it by a common saying, 'to set the cart before the horse', and it may be done either by a single word or by a clause of speech. By a single word thus:

> And if I not perform, God let me never thrive.[214]

for 'perform not'. And this vice is sometimes tolerable enough, but if the word carry any notable sense it is a vice not tolerable. As he that said, praising a woman for her red lips, thus:

> A coral lip of hue.[215]

which is no good speech, because either he should have said no more but 'a coral lip', which had been enough to declare the redness, or else he should have said 'a lip of coral hue' and not 'a coral lip of hue'. Now if this disorder be in a whole clause which carrieth more sentence than a word, it is then worst of all. . . .

AMPHIBOLOGIA;[216] *or, the ambiguous.*

Then have ye one other vicious speech, with which we will finish this chapter, and is when we speak or write doubtfully, and that the sense may be taken two ways, such ambiguous terms they call *amphibologia*. We call it 'the ambiguous', or 'figure of sense uncertain', as if one should say 'Thomas Taylor saw William Tyler drunk', it is indif-

---

[213] Susenb., pp. 32–3: 'in Latin *praeposteratio*; occurs when what is designed for the second place occupies the first in the order of a sentence; or it occurs when anything is narrated in a reverse order . . . [with] a veritable change of the meaning'.

[214] Gascoigne, from *The Adventures of Master F. J.*, in *The Posies* (1575), ed. Cunliffe, p. 414.

[215] Turberville, *Epitaphes*, etc. (1567).

[216] *Inst.* 3. 6. 43, 7. 9. 1–15, 9. 4. 32; *Rhet. Her.* 4. 53–67.

ferent to think either the one or the other drunk. Thus said a gentleman in our vulgar prettily, notwithstanding because he did it not
ignorantly, but for the nonce:

> I sat by my Lady soundly sleeping,
> My mistress lay by me bitterly weeping.

No man can tell by this whether the mistress or the man slept or wept.
These doubtful speeches were used much in the old times by their
false prophets, as appeareth by the oracles of Delphos and of the
Sybils' prophecies, devised by the religious persons of those days to
abuse the superstitious people, and to encumber their busy brains with
vain hope or vain fear.

Lucian,[217] the merry Greek, reciteth a great number of them,
devised by a cozening companion, one Alexander, to get himself the
name and reputation of the god Aesculapius. And in effect all our old
British and Saxon prophecies be of the same sort, that, turn them on
which side ye will the matter of them may be verified; nevertheless,
carrieth generally such force in the heads of fond* people that by the
comfort of those blind prophecies many insurrections and rebellions
have been stirred up in this realm, as that of Jack Straw and Jack Cade,
in Richard the Second's time, and in our time by a seditious fellow in
Norfolk calling himself Captain Ket,[218] and others in other places of
the realm led altogether by certain prophetical rhymes, which might
be construed two or three ways, as well as to that one whereunto the
rebels applied it. Our maker shall therefore avoid all such ambiguous
speeches, unless it be when he doth it for the nonce and for some
purpose.

Chapter XXIII
What it is that generally makes our speech well pleasing and commendable; and of that which the Latins call decorum[219]

In all things to use decency,* is it only that giveth every thing his good
grace, and without which nothing in man's speech could seem good
or gracious. In so much as many times it makes a beautiful figure fall
into a deformity, and on the other side a vicious speech seem pleasant
and beautiful. This decency is therefore the line and level* for all good
makers to do their business by. But herein resteth the difficulty, to

---

[217] *Alexander* 10, 22, 32, 49.   [218] These rebellions took place in 1450 and 1549.
[219] Puttenham probably draws here on his (lost) treatise *De Decoro* (see p. 290).

know what this good grace is, and wherein it consisteth, for peradventure it be easier to conceive than to express. We will therefore
examine it to the bottom and say that every thing which pleaseth the
mind or senses, and the mind by the senses as by means instrumental, doth it for some amiable point or quality that is in it, which
draweth them to a good liking and contentment with their proper
objects. But that cannot be if they discover any ill-favouredness* or
disproportion to the parts apprehensive,* as for example, when a
sound is either too loud, or too low, or otherwise confused, the ear is
ill-affected. So is the eye, if the colour be sad,* or not luminous* and
recreative,* or the shape of a membered body without his due measures and symmetry; and the like of every other sense in his proper
function. These excesses or defects, or confusions and disorders in the
sensible objects, are deformities and unseemly to the sense. In like sort
the mind, for the things that be his mental objects, hath his good
graces and his bad, whereof the one contents him wondrous well, the
other displeaseth him continually, no more nor no less than ye see the
discords of music do to a well tuned ear. The Greeks call this good
grace of everything in his kind, *to prepon*, the Latins *decorum*, we in
our vulgar call it by a scholastical* term, 'decency'. Our own Saxon
English term is 'seemliness', that is to say, for his good shape and outer
appearance well pleasing the eye. We call it also 'comeliness',* for the
delight it bringeth coming towards us, and to that purpose may be
called 'pleasant approach'. So as every way seeking to express this
prepon of the Greeks, and *decorum* of the Latins, we are fain in our
vulgar tongue to borrow the term which our eye, only for his noble
prerogative over all the rest of the senses, doth usurp and to apply the
same to all good, comely, pleasant and honest things, even to the spiritual objects of the mind, which stand no less in the due proportion
of reason and discourse than any other material thing doth in his sensible* beauty, proportion and comeliness.

Now because this comeliness resteth in the good conformity of
many things and their sundry circumstances* with respect one to
another, so as there be found a just correspondence between them by
this or that relation, the Greeks call it *analogie*, or a convenient proportion. This lovely conformity, or proportion, or convenience*
between the sense and the sensible hath nature herself first most carefully observed in all her own works, then also by kind* graft it in the
appetites of every creature, working by intelligence to covet and desire
and in their actions to imitate and perform, and of man chiefly before

any other creature, as well in his speeches as in every other part of his behaviour. And this in generality and by an usual term is that which the Latins call *decorum*. So, albeit we before alleged that all our figures be but transgressions of our daily speech, yet if they fall out decently to the good liking of the mind or ear, and to the beautifying of the matter or language, all is well; if indecently, and to the ears and minds misliking (be the figure of itself never so commendable) all is amiss. The election* is the writers', the judgement is the world's, as theirs to whom the reading appertaineth.

But since the actions of man with their circumstances be infinite, and the world likewise replenished with many judgements, it may be a question who shall have the determination of such controversy as may arise, whether this or that action or speech be decent or indecent. And verily, it seems to go all by discretion, not perchance of every one, but by a learned and experienced discretion.* For otherwise* seems the *decorum* to a weak and ignorant judgement than it doth to one of better knowledge and experience, which showeth that it resteth in the discerning part of the mind. So as he who can make the best and most differences of things, by reasonable and witty* distinction, is to be the fittest judge or sentencer of 'decency'. Such, generally, is the discreetest man, particularly in any art the most skilful and discreetest, and in all other things for the more part those that be of much observation and greatest experience.

The case then standing, that discretion must chiefly guide all those businesses, since there be sundry sorts of discretion all unlike, even as there be men of action or art, I see no way so fit to enable a man truly to estimate of 'decency' as example, by whose verity we may deem the differences of things and their proportions, and by particular discussions come at length to sentence* of it generally, and also in our behaviours, the more easily to put it in execution. But by reason of the sundry circumstances that man's affairs are as it were wrapped in, this 'decency' comes to be very much alterable and subject to variety, in so much as our speech asketh one manner of 'decency', in respect of the person who speaks; another, of his to whom it is spoken; another, of whom we speak; another, of what we speak, and in what place and time, and to what purpose. And as it is of speech, so of all other our behaviours. We will therefore set you down some few examples of every circumstance, how it alters the decency of speech or action, and by these shall ye be able to gather a number more, to confirm and establish your judgement by a perfect discretion.

This decency, so far forth as appertaineth to the consideration of our art, resteth in writing, speech and behaviour. But because writing is no more than the image of character or speech, they shall go together in these our observations. . . .

And there is a measure to be used in man's speech or tale, so as it be neither for shortness too dark, nor for length too tedious. Which made Cleomenes,[220] king of the Lacedemonians, give this unpleasant answer to the ambassadors of the Samians, who had told him a long message from their city, and desired to know his pleasure in it. 'My masters', saith he, 'the first part of your tale was so long that I remember it not, which made that the second I understood not; and as for the third part, I do nothing well allow* of.' Great princes and grave counsellors who have little spare leisure to hearken, would have speeches used to them such as be short and sweet. . . .

And yet, in speaking or writing of a prince's affairs and fortunes there is a certain *decorum*, that we may not use the same terms in their business as we might very well do in a meaner person's, the case being all one, such reverence is due to their estates. As for example, if an historiographer shall write of an Emperor or King, how such a day he joined battle with his enemy, and being overlaid* 'ran out of the field, and took his heels', or 'put spur to his horse and fled as fast as he could', the terms be not decent; but of a mean soldier or captain it were not indecently spoken. And as one[221] who, translating certain books of Virgil's *Aeneid* into English metre, said that Aeneas was fain to 'trudge' out of Troy, which term became better to be spoken of a beggar or of a rogue, or a lackey: for so we use to say to such manner of people, 'be trudging hence'.

Another Englishing this word of Virgil, '*fato profugus*',[222] called Aeneas, 'by fate a fugitive',[223] which was indecently spoken, and not to the author's intent in the same word: for whom he studied by all means to advance above all other men of the world for virtue and magnanimity, he meant not to make him a fugitive. But by occasion of his great distresses, and of the hardness of his destinies, he would have it appear that Aeneas was enforced to flee out of Troy, and for many years to be a roamer and a wanderer about the world both by land and sea, '*fato profugus*', and never to find any resting place till he came into

---

[220] Plutarch, *Sayings of the Spartans* (*Mor.* 223D).
[221] Richard Stanyhurst's version of the *Aeneis* (1582), 1. 7: 'Lyke wandring pilgrim too famosed Italie trudging'.
[222] *Aen.* 1. 2.   [223] Gavin Douglas was guilty of this fault, in his *Eneados* (1553).

Italy. So as ye may evidently perceive in this term 'fugitive', a notable indignity offered to that princely person, and by the other word ('a wanderer') none indignity at all, but rather a term of much love and commiseration.

The same translator,[224] when he came to these words,

> [*quidve dolens regina deum*] *tot volvere casus*
> *insignem pietate virum, tot adire labores*
> *impulerit*[225]

he turned* it thus: 'what moved Juno to tug so great a captain as Aeneas?' Which word 'tug', spoken in this case, is so indecent as none other could have been devised, and took his first original from the cart, because it signifieth the pull or draught of the oxen or horses. And therefore the leathers that bear the chief stress of the draught, the carters call them tugs, and so we use to say that shrewd boys 'tug' each other by the ears, for 'pull'. . . .

It were too busy a piece of work for me to tell you of all the parts of decency and indecency which have been observed in the speeches of man and in his writings, and this that I tell you is rather to solace your ears with pretty conceits, after a sort of long scholastical precepts (which may happen have doubled* them), rather than for any other purpose of institution or doctrine, which to any courtier of experience is not necessary in this behalf. And as they appear by the former examples to rest in our speech and writing, so do the same by like proportion consist in the whole behaviour of man, and that which he doth well and commendably is ever decent, and the contrary indecent, not in every man's judgement always one, but after their several discretion and by circumstance diversely, as by the next chapter shall be showed.

Chapter XXIV
Of decency in behaviour, which also belongs to the consideration of the poet or maker

And there is a decency to be observed in every man's action and behaviour as well as in his speech and writing, which some peradventure would think impertinent to be treated of in this book, where we do

---

[224] This was in fact Stanyhurst's rendering, in his *Aeneis* (1582), of l. 11: 'Wyth sharp sundrye perils too tugge so famus a captayne'.

[225] *Aen.* i. 9–11.

but inform the commendable fashions of language and style. But that is otherwise, for the good maker or poet who is, in decent speech and good terms, to describe all things, and with praise or dispraise to report every misbehaviour, ought to know the comeliness of an action as well as of a word, and thereby to direct himself both in praise and persuasion or any other point that pertains to the orator's art. Wherefore some examples we will set down of this manner of decency in behaviour, leaving you for the rest to our book which we have written *De Decoro*, where ye shall see both parts handled more exactly. And this decency of man's behaviour, as well as of his speech, must also be deemed by discretion, in which regard the thing that may well become one man to do may not become another; and that which is seemly to be done in this place is not so seemly in that, and at such a time decent, but at another time indecent, and in such a case and for such a purpose, and to this and that end, and by this and that event, perusing all the circumstances with like consideration. . . .

To tell you the decencies of a number of other behaviours, one might do it to please you with pretty reports,* but to the skilfull courtiers it shall be nothing necessary, for they know all by experience without learning. Yet some few remembrances we will make you of the most material, which ourselves have observed, and so make an end. . . .

And with these examples I think sufficient to leave, giving you information of this one point, that all your figures poetical or rhetorical are but observations of strange speeches, and such as without any art at all we should use, and commonly do, even by very nature without discipline. But more or less aptly and decently, or scarcely, or abundantly, or of this or that kind of figure, and one of us more than another, according to the disposition of our nature, constitution of the heart, and facility of each man's utterance. So as we may conclude, that nature herself suggesteth the figure in this or that form, but art aideth the judgement of his use and application. Which gives me occasion finally, and for a full conclusion to this whole treatise, to inform you in the next chapter how art should be used in all respects, and specially in this behalf of language; and when the natural is more commendable than the artificial,* and contrariwise.

Chapter XXV
That the good poet or maker ought to dissemble his art; and in what cases the artificial is more commended than the natural, and contrariwise

And now, most excellent Queen, having largely said of poets and poesy, and about what matters they be employed; then of all the commended forms of poems; thirdly of metrical proportions, such as do appertain to our vulgar art; and last of all set forth the poetical ornament, consisting chiefly in the beauty and gallantness* of his language and style, and so have apparelled him to our seeming in all his gorgeous habiliments; and pulling him first from the cart to the school, and from thence to the court, and preferred* him to your Majesty's service, in that place of great honour and magnificence to give entertainment to princes, ladies of honour, gentlewomen and gentlemen, and by his many moods* of skill, to serve the many humours of men thither haunting and resorting, some by way of solace, some of serious advice, and in matters as well profitable as pleasant and honest, we have in our humble conceit sufficiently performed our promise or rather duty to your Majesty in the description of this art. So always, as we leave him not unfurnished of one piece that best beseems that place of any other, and may serve as a principal good lesson for all good makers to bear continually in mind in the usage of this science: which is, that being now lately become a courtier he show not himself a craftsman, and merit to be disgraded and with scorn sent back again to the shop, or other place of his first faculty and calling, but that so wisely and discreetly he behave himself as he may worthily retain the credit of his place, and profession of a very courtier, which is in plain terms, cunningly to be able to dissemble. But (if it please your Majesty) may it not seem enough for a courtier to know how to wear a feather and set his cap a flaunt, his chain *en écharpe*, a straight buskin *all'inglese*, a loose *allo Turquesque*, the cape *alla Spagniola*, the breech *à la Française*, and by twenty manner of new fashioned garments to disguise his body and his face with as many countenances, whereof it seems there be many that make a very art, and study who can show himself most fine, I will not say most foolish and ridiculous! Or perhaps, rather, that he could dissemble his conceits* as well as his countenances, so as he never speak as he thinks, or think as he speaks, and that in any matter of importance his words and his meaning very seldom meet. For so, as I remember, it was concluded by us setting forth the figure *allegoria*, which therefore not impertinently we call 'the Courtier', or 'figure of faire semblant'. Or is it not, perchance, more requisite our courtly poet do dissemble not only his countenances and conceits but also all his ordinary actions and behaviour, or the most part of them, whereby the better to win his purposes and good advantages? . . .

These and many such like disguisings do we find in man's behaviour, and specially in the courtiers of foreign countries, where in my youth I was brought up, and very well observed their manner of life and conversation (for of mine own country I have not made so great experience). Which parts, nevertheless, we allow not now in our English maker, because we have given him the name of an honest man and not of an hypocrite. And therefore, leaving these manner of dissimulations to all base-minded men and of vile nature or mystery,* we do allow our courtly poet to be a dissembler only in the subtleties of his art: that is, when he is most artificial so to disguise and cloak it as it may not appear, nor seem to proceed from him by any study or trade of rules, but to be his natural;[226] nor so evidently to be descried as every lad that reads him shall say he is a good scholar, but will rather have him to know his art well, and little to use it.

And yet peradventure in all points it may not be so taken, but in such only as may discover his grossness or his ignorance by some scholarly affectation, which thing is very irksome to all men of good training, and specially to courtiers. And yet for all that our maker may not be in all cases restrained, but that he may both use and also manifest his art to his great praise, and need no more be ashamed thereof than a shoemaker to have made a cleanly shoe, or a carpenter to have built a fair house. Therefore, to discuss and make this point somewhat clearer, to wit, where art ought to appear and where not, and when the natural is more commendable than the artificial in any human action or workmanship, we will examine it further by this distinction.

In some cases, we say, art is an aid and coadjutor to nature,[227] and a furtherer of her actions to good effect, or peradventure a mean to supply her wants, by reinforcing the causes wherein she is impotent and defective; as doth the art of physic by helping the natural concoction, retention, distribution, expulsion, and other virtues in a weak and unhealthy body. Or as the good gardener seasons his soil by sundry sorts of compost . . . and waters his plants, and weeds his herbs and flowers, and prunes his branches, and unleaves his boughs to let in the sun, and twenty other ways cherisheth them and cureth their infirmities, and so makes that never or very seldom any of them miscarry, but bring forth their flowers and fruits in season. And in both

---

[226] Cf. Sidney, p. 387; the ancient injunction, ars est celare artem, 'the art is to conceal art'; and Castiglione's discussion of *sprezzatura* ('dissembling of abilities') in *Il Cortegiano* (bk. 1, chs. 26–7).

[227] For some of Aristotle's utterances on art imitating nature cf. *Physica* 2. 8. 199ª15 ff., *Meteorologica* 4. 3. 381ᵇ4 ff.; *De caelo* 5. 396ᵇ11 ff.; *Metaph.* 7. 7. 1032ª11 ff.

these cases it is no small praise for the physician and gardener to be called good and cunning artificers.

In another respect art is not only an aid and coadjutor to nature in all her actions, but an alterer of them, and in some sort a surmounter* of her skill, so as by means of it her own effects shall appear more beautiful, or strange and miraculous, as in both cases before remembered. The physician by the cordials* he will give his patient, shall be able not only to restore the decayed spirits of man and render him health, but also to prolong the term of his life many years over and above the stint of his first and natural constitution. And the gardener by his art will not only make a herb, or flower, or fruit, come forth in his season without impediment, but also will embellish the same in virtue, shape, odour and taste, that nature of herself would never have done. As, to make the single gilliflower, or marigold, or daisy, double; and the white rose, red, yellow, or carnation; a bitter melon, sweet; a sweet apple, sour; a plum or cherry without a stone; a pear without core or kernel; a gourd or cucumber like to a horn, or any other figure he will: any of which things nature could not do without man's help and art.[228] These actions also are most singular, when they be most artificial.

In another respect, we say, art is neither an aider nor a surmounter, but only a bare* imitator of nature's works, following and counterfeiting her actions and effects, as the marmoset* doth many countenances and gestures of man. Of which sort are the arts of painting and carving, whereof one represents the natural by light, colour and shadow in the superficial* or flat, the other in a body massive expressing the full and empty, even, extent,* rebated,* hollow, or whatsoever other figure and passion* of quantity. So also the alchemist counterfeits gold, silver, and all other metals, the lapidary, pearls and precious stones by glass and other substances, falsified and sophisticated by art. These men also be praised for their craft, and their credit is nothing impaired to say that their conclusions and effects are very artificial.

Finally, in another respect art is, as it were, an encounterer* and contrary to nature, producing effects neither like to hers, nor by participation with her operations, nor by imitation of her patterns, but makes things and produceth effects altogether strange and diverse, and

---

[228] Cf. *The Winter's Tale* 4. 4. 79 ff.: Shakespeare recalls several parts of Puttenham's discussion.

of such form and quality (nature always supplying stuff)[229] as she
never would nor could have done of herself, as the carpenter that
builds a house, the joiner that makes a table or a bedstead, the tailor
a garment, the smith a lock or a key, and a number of like. In which
case the workman gaineth reputation by his art, and praise when it is
best expressed, and most apparent, and most studiously. Man also, in
all his actions that be not altogether natural, but are gotten by study
and discipline or exercise, as to dance by measures, to sing by note, to
play on the lute, and such like, it is a praise to be said an artificial
dancer, singer, and player on instruments, because they be not exactly
known or done but by rules and precepts, or teaching of schoolmasters. But in such actions as be so natural and proper to man as he
may become excellent therein without any art or imitation at all
(custom and exercise excepted, which are requisite to every action not
numbered among the vital or animal), and wherein nature should seem
to do amiss, and man suffer reproach to be found destitute of them:
in those to show himself rather artificial than natural were no less to
be laughed at than for one that can see well enough to use a pair of
spectacles, or not to hear but by a trunk* put to his ear, nor feel without
a pair of annealed* gloves. Which things indeed help an infirm sense
but annoy the perfect, and therefore showing a disability natural, move
rather to scorn than commendation, and to pity sooner than to praise.

But what else is language and utterance, and discourse and persuasion, and argument in man, than the virtues of a well-constituted body
and mind, little less natural than his very sensual* actions, saving that
the one is perfected by nature at once, the other not without exercise
and iteration? Peradventure, also, it will be granted that a man sees
better and discerns more brimly* his colours, and hears and feels more
exactly by use, and often hearing and feeling and seeing; and though
it be better to see with spectacles than not to see at all, yet is their
praise not equal, nor in any man's judgement comparable. No more is
that which a poet makes by art and precepts rather than by natural
instinct, and that which he doth by long meditation rather than by a
sudden inspiration, or with great pleasure and facility than hardly*
(and as they are wont to say) in spite of nature or Minerva,[230] than
which nothing can be more irksome or ridiculous.

---

[229] The common Aristotelian distinction between form and matter ('stuff' rendering the
Greek term *hyle*).
[230] Cf. Horace, *Ars P.* 385: 'Tu nihil invita dices faciesve Minerva', 'But you will say
nothing and do nothing against Minerva's will'. Cicero takes the phrase *invita Minerva* to
mean 'in direct opposition to one's natural genius' (*Off.* 1. 31. 110).

And yet I am not ignorant that there be arts and methods both to speak and to persuade, and also to dispute, and by which the natural is in some sort relieved,* as the eye by his spectacle—I say relieved in his imperfection, but not made more perfect than the natural. In which respect I call those arts of grammar, logic, and rhetoric not bare imitations, as the painter or carver's craft and work in a foreign subject, *viz.* a lively portrait in his table or wood, but by long and studious observation rather a repetition or reminiscence natural, reduced* into perfection, and made prompt by use and exercise.[231] And so, whatsoever a man speaks or persuades he doth it not by imitation artificially, but by observation naturally (though one follow another), because it is both the same and the like that nature doth suggest. But if a popinjay speak, she doth it by imitation of man's voice, artificially and not naturally, being the like but not the same that nature doth suggest to man.

But now, because our maker or poet is to play many parts and not one alone, as first to devise his plot or subject, then to fashion his poem, thirdly to use his metrical proportions, and last of all to utter with pleasure and delight, which rests in his manner of language and style, as hath been said, whereof the many moods* and strange phrases are called figures, it is not altogether with him as with the craftsman, nor altogether otherwise than with the craftsman. For in that he useth his metrical proportions by appointed and harmonical measures and distances, he is like the carpenter or joiner, for, borrowing their timber and stuff of nature, they appoint and order it by art otherwise than nature would do, and work effects in appearance contrary to hers. Also, in that which the poet speaks or reports of another man's tale or doings, as Homer of Priamus or Ulysses, he is as the painter or carver, that work by imitation and representation in a foreign subject. In that he speaks figuratively, or argues subtly, or persuades copiously and vehemently, he doth as the cunning gardener that, using nature as a coadjutor, furthers her conclusions and many times makes her effects more absolute* and strange.*

But for that in our maker or poet which rests only in device, and issues from an excellent sharp and quick invention, holpen by a clear and bright fantasy and imagination, he is not as the painter, to counterfeit the natural by the like effects and not the same; nor as the gardener, aiding nature to work both the same and the like; nor as the carpenter, to work effects utterly unlike but even as nature herself,

---

[231] Cf. the basic triad by which orators were promised mastery of persuasion: 'art, imitation, exercise' (*Rhet. Her.* 1. 2. 3).

working by her own peculiar virtue and proper instinct, and not by example or meditation or exercise, as all other artificers do, is then most admired when he is most natural and least artificial. And in the feast of his language and utterance, because they hold as well of nature to be suggested and uttered as by art to be polished and reformed. Therefore shall our poet receive praise for both, but more by knowing of his art than by unseasonable using it, and be more commended for his natural eloquence than for his artificial, and more for his artificial well dissembled than for the same overmuch affected, and grossly or indiscreetly bewrayed,* as many makers and orators do.

Edmund Spenser,
Allegory and the chivalric epic (1590)

EDMUND SPENSER (see p. 175 for his earlier career). After the *Shepheardes Calendar* was published and well received, Spenser began work on *The Faerie Queene*. But in 1580 he was appointed secretary to Lord Grey de Wilton, Lord Deputy for Ireland, remaining in Ireland (with visits to London in 1589–91 and 1596 to oversee publication of his epic) until 1598, when his castle at Kilcolman was burned in an insurrection, and he returned to London. According to some traditions Spenser died in 1599 'for lack of bread', but other evidence lists payments made to him by the crown. He was buried in Westminster Abbey, as Camden records, 'near to Chaucer, at the charge of the Earl of Essex, his hearse being attended by poets, and mournful elegies and poems, with the pens that wrote them, thrown into the tomb'.

TEXT. From *The Faerie Queene. Disposed into twelve books, fashioning XII. moral vertues* (London, 1590), which ends with 'A letter of the Author's, expounding his whole intention in the course of this work, which for that it giveth great light to the reader, for the better understanding is hereunto annexed'.

First mentioned in 1580, in his *Letters* to and from Harvey, Spenser had completed the first three books of *The Faerie Queene* by 1589, showing them to Ralegh on his visit to Ireland. The dedicatory letter is dated 23 January 1589 (i.e. 1590 New Style). Books 4 to 6 were published in 1596; the fragmentary Book 7 ('Of Mutabilitie') in 1609, in the first Folio edition of the complete text.

[LETTER TO SIR WALTER RALEGH, PREFIXED TO *THE FAERIE QUEENE*]

Sir, knowing how doubtfully all allegories may be construed, and this book of mine, which I have entitled *The Faerie Queene*, being a continued allegory,[1] or dark conceit, I have thought good as well for avoiding of jealous* opinions and misconstructions, as also for your better light in reading thereof (being so by you commanded), to discover* unto you the general intention and meaning which in the whole

---

[1] In classical rhetoric allegory was often defined as 'a continued metaphor' (*Inst.* 9. 2. 46), followed by several English Renaissance rhetoricians, Erasmus, Puttenham (p. 247), Peacham, Fenner, Day. On the dangers of allegory being misinterpreted cf. Baldwin, p. 138.

course thereof I have fashioned, without expressing of any particular purposes or by-accidents* therein occasioned. The general end therefore of all the book is to fashion[2] a gentleman or noble person in virtuous and gentle discipline. Which, for that I conceived should be most plausible* and pleasing, being coloured with an historical fiction, the which the most part of men delight to read, rather for variety of matter than for profit of the example: I chose the history of King Arthur as most fit for the excellency of his person, being made famous by many men's former works, and also furthest from the danger of envy and suspicion of present time. In which I have followed all the antique poets historical: first Homer, who in the persons of Agamemnon and Ulysses has exampled a good governor and a virtuous man, the one in his *Iliad*, the other in his *Odyssey*; then Virgil, whose like intention was to do in the person of Aeneas. After him Ariosto comprised them both in his Orlando; and lately Tasso dissevered them again, and formed both parts in two persons, namely that part which they in philosophy call ethics, or virtues of a private man, coloured in his Rinaldo; the other, named politics, in his Goffredo.[3] By example of which excellent poets, I labour to portrait in Arthur, before he was king, the image of a brave knight, perfected* in the twelve private moral virtues, as Aristotle[4] has devised, the which is the purpose of these first twelve books. Which, if I find to be well accepted, I may be perhaps encouraged to frame the other part of politic virtues in his person after that he came to be king.

[2] For the significance of literature being to 'fashion' or 'form' its readers see the Introduction, pp. 50–3.

[3] Lodovico Ariosto's *Orlando Furioso* (1516) was reissued in 1542 with an apparatus of allegorical explanations, repeated in one form or another in over a hundred subsequent editions; cf. Harington, p. 302. Torquato Tasso published in 1562 *Rinaldo*, a *romanzo* in twelve books; the 1583 edition added an allegory written by Tasso himself, which describes Rinaldo as having learned ethical behaviour through his love for a beautiful and virtuous woman, exemplifying such virtues as prudence, friendship, chastity, and courtesy. His *Gerusalemme liberata*—or *Goffredo*, as he originally planned to call it (1580 and following), aroused enthusiasm and censure in equal measure. In 1581 he included an attempted self-justification called 'The Allegory of the Poem', in which he states that allegory, being by definition obscure, needs to be explained. Tasso describes the *Odyssey* as illustrating the contemplative life, while the *Iliad* deals with the political life and the virtues appropriate to it; the *Aeneid* unites both private and political virtues. His *Gerusalemme* illustrates not the private life and ethical problems of an individual but political life, with Goffredo standing for the intellectual virtues which bring political happiness. Cf. D. L. Aguzzi, 'Allegory in the Herioic Poetry of the Renaissance', pp. 489–504, and J. Nohrnberg, *The Analogy of 'The Faerie Queene'* (Princeton, 1976), pp. 58–65.

[4] In the *Nicomachean Ethics*, as treated in medieval commentaries.

To some, I know, this method will seem displeasant, which had rather have good discipline delivered plainly in way of precepts, or sermoned at large, as they use, than thus cloudily enwrapped in allegorical devices. But such, me seems, should be satisfied with the use of these days, seeing all things accounted by their shows, and nothing esteemed of that is not delightful and pleasing to common sense. For this cause is Xenophon preferred before Plato,[5] for that the one, in the exquisite depth of his judgement, formed a commonwealth such as it should be, but the other, in the person of Cyrus and the Persians, fashioned a government such as might best be. So much more profitable and gracious is doctrine by example than by rule.[6] So have I laboured to do in the person of Arthur, whom I conceive after his long education by Timon (to whom he was by Merlin delivered to be brought up, so soon as he was born of the Lady Igrayne) to have seen in a dream or vision the Faery Queen. With whose excellent beauty ravished, he awaking resolved to seek her out, and so being by Merlin armed, and by Timon thoroughly instructed, he went to seek her forth in Faery land.

In that Faery Queen I mean glory in my general intention, but in my particular I conceive the most excellent and glorious person of our sovereign the Queen, and her kingdom in Faery land.[7] And yet, in some places else I do otherwise shadow* her. For considering she bears two persons, the one of a most royal Queen or Empress, the other of a most virtuous and beautiful lady, this latter part in some places I do express in Belphoebe, fashioning her name according to your own excellent conceit of Cynthia[8] (Phoebe and Cynthia being both names of Diana). So in the person of Prince Arthur I set forth magnificence in particular, which virtue for that (according to Aristotle[9] and the rest) it is the perfection of all the rest, and containeth in it them all, therefore in the whole course I mention the deeds of Arthur applicable to that virtue, which I write of in that book. But of the twelve other virtues, I make twelve other knights the patrons, for the more

[5] For the superiority of the *Cyropaedia* to the *Republic* cf. Sidney, pp. 347, 353–5.

[6] That is, by the rules or precepts of the philosophers; cf. Sidney, p. 351.

[7] The Faery Queen represents Elizabeth (often known as Gloriana), her Kingdom England.

[8] Alluding to Ralegh's great unfinished poem, *The Ocean to Cynthia*.

[9] In the *Nicomachean Ethics* 4. 1124ᵃ Aristotle in fact says that 'magnanimity'—greatness of spirit—'is a sort of crown of the virtues'; similarly in *Eudemian Ethics* 3. 1232ᵃ29 ff. he writes that magnanimity 'accompanies all the virtues'.

variety of the history. Of which these three books contain three: the first, of the knight of the Redcross, in whom I express Holiness; the second of Sir Guyon, in whom I set forth Temperance; the third of Britomartis a Lady knight, in whom I picture Chastity.

But because the beginning of the whole work seemeth abrupt and as depending upon other antecedents, it needs that ye know the occasion of these three knights' several adventures. For the method of a poet historical is not such as of an historiographer. For an historiographer discourseth of affairs orderly, as they were done, accounting as well the times as the actions. But a poet thrusts into the midst,[10] even where it most concerns him, and there recoursing* to the things fore past, and divining of things to come, makes a pleasing analysis of all. The beginning therefore of my history, if it were to be told by an historiographer, should be the twelfth book, which is the last, where I devise that the Faery Queen kept her annual feast twelve days, upon which twelve several days the occasions of the twelve several adventures happened, which, being undertaken by twelve several knights, are in these twelve books severally* handled and discoursed.

The first was this. In the beginning of the feast there presented himself a tall clownish young man,[11] who, falling before the Queen of Fairies desired a boon (as the manner then was) which during that feast she might not refuse: which was that he might have the achievement of any adventure which during that feast should happen. That being granted, he rested him on the floor, unfit through his rusticity for a better place. Soon after entered a fair lady in mourning weeds, riding on a white ass, with a dwarf behind her leading a warlike steed that bore the arms of a knight, and his spear in the dwarf's hand. She, falling before the Queen of Fairies, complained that her father and mother, an ancient King and Queen, had been by an huge dragon many years shut up in a brazen castle, who thence suffered them not to issue; and therefore besought the Faery Queen to assign her some one of her knights to take on him that exploit. Presently that clownish person upstarting, desired that adventure; whereat the Queen much wondering, and the Lady much gainsaying, yet he earnestly importuned his desire. In the end the Lady told him that unless that armour which she brought would serve him (that is, the armour of a Christian man specified by St Paul,[12] Ephesians) that he could not

---

[10] Cf. Horace, *Ars P.* 148 ff. (*ALC*, p. 283).
[11] Red Cross Knight is St George, who had been raised as a ploughman.
[12] Eph. 6: 11–17.

succeed in that enterprise. Which, being forthwith put upon him with due furnitures* thereunto, he seemed the goodliest man in all that company, and was well liked of the Lady. And eftsoons* taking on him knighthood, and mounting on that strange courser, he went forth with her on that adventure: where beginneth the first book, viz.

A gentle knight [was] pricking on the playne, etc.   [1. 1. 1]

The second day there came in a Palmer* bearing an infant with bloody hands, whose parents he complained to have been slain by an enchantress called Acrasia: and therefore craved of the Faery Queen to appoint him some knight to perform that adventure. Which, being assigned to Sir Guyon, he presently* went forth with that same Palmer: which is the beginning of the second book and the whole subject thereof.

The third day there came in a groom, who complained before the Faery Queen that a vile enchanter called Busirane had in hand a most fair lady called Amoretta, whom he kept in most grievous torment because she would not yield him the pleasure of her body. Whereupon Sir Scudamour, the lover of that lady, presently took on him that adventure. But being unable to perform it by reason of the hard enchantments, after long sorrow* in the end met with Britomartis, who succoured him, and rescued his love. But by occasion hereof many other adventures are intermedled, but rather as accidents* than intendments.* As, the love of Britomart, the overthrow of Marinell, the misery of Florimell, the virtuousness of Belphoebe, the lasciviousnes of Hellenora, and many the like.

Thus much, Sir, I have briefly overrun, to direct your understanding to the well-head of the history, that from thence gathering the whole intention of the conceit, ye may as in a handful grip all the discourse, which otherwise may haply seem tedious and confused. . . .

Sir John Harington,
An apology for Ariosto: poetry, epic,
morality (1591)

SIR JOHN HARINGTON (1561–1612), godson of Queen Elizabeth, was educated at Eton, King's College Cambridge, and Lincoln's Inn. A favoured courtier, compelled by the Queen to translate *Orlando Furioso* in 1596, he was banished from court for his scurrilous *Metamorphosis of Ajax* ('a-jakes', the newly-invented water-closet) and other satires. A close friend of Essex, he accompanied him to Ireland, and attempted to appease the Queen's anger against him. His collected *Epigrams* appeared in 1618, other letters and papers not until 1769, in *Nugae Antiquae*.

TEXT. From *Orlando Furioso in English Heroical Verse* (1591). 'A Preface or rather, a Briefe Apologie of Poetrie and of the Author and Translator of the Poem' is prefixed to the translation. Some of Harington's ideas, as he freely acknowledges, came from Sidney's *Defence of Poetry*, which he had read in manuscript. He also drew on the extensive Italian literature discussing Ariosto: see Bernard Weinberg, *A History of Literary Criticism in the Italian Renaissance*, 2 vols. (Chicago, 1961), chs. xix–xx, 'The Quarrel over Ariosto and Tasso' (ii. 954–1073). For the textual history of Harington's translation see the outstanding modern edition, *Ludovico Ariosto's Orlando Furioso translated into English Heroical Verse by Sir John Harington (1591)*, ed. Robert McNulty (Oxford, 1972). In annotating this selection I have benefited from O. B. Hardison, Jr. (ed.), *English Literary Criticism: The Renaissance* (New York, 1963).

The learned Plutarch[1] in his laconical apophthegms tells of a sophister that made a long and tedious oration in praise of Hercules, and expecting at the end thereof for some great thanks and applause of the hearers, a certain Lacedemonian demanded him who had dispraised Hercules? Methinks the like may be now said to me, taking upon me the defence of poesy, for surely if learning in general were of that account among us as it ought to be among all men, and is among wise men, then should this my apology of poesy (the very first nurse and ancient grandmother of all learning)[2] be as vain and superfluous

---

[1] *Apophthegmata regum et imperatorum* (*Moralia* 192 C).
[2] Cf. Strabo, cit. p. 64, n. 32, and Sidney, p. 338.

as was that sophister's, because it might then be answered and truly answered that no man disgraced it. But since we live in such a time in which nothing can escape the envious tooth and backbiting tongue of an impure mouth, and wherein every blind corner hath a squint-eyed Zoilus[3] that can look a right upon no man's doings (yea sure there be some that will not stick to call Hercules himself a dastard because, forsooth, he fought with a club and not at the rapier and dagger), therefore I think no man of judgement will judge this my labour needless in seeking to remove away those slanders that either the malice of those that love it not or the folly of those that understand it not hath devised against it, for indeed, as the old saying is, *Scientia non habet inimicum praeter ignorantem*:[4] 'knowledge hath no foe but the ignorant'.

THE DIVISION OF THIS APOLOGY INTO THREE PARTS

But now, because I make account I have to deal with three sundry kinds of reprovers, one of those that condemn all poetry, which (how strong head soever they have) I count but a very weak faction; another of those that allow* poetry, but not this particular poem, of which kind sure there cannot be many; a third of those that can bear with the art, and like of the work, but will find fault with my not well handling of it; which they may not only probably but I doubt too truly do, being a thing as commonly done as said, that 'where the hedge is lowest there doth every man go over'. Therefore against these three I must arm me with the best defensive weapons I can, and if I happen to give a blow now and then in mine own defence, and, as good fencers use to ward and strike at once, I must crave pardon of course, seeing our law allows that is done *se defendendo* and the law of nature teacheth *vim vi repellere*.[5]

OF POETRY

First therefore, of poetry itself, for those few that generally disallow* it might be sufficient to allege those many that generally approve it, of which I could bring in such an army, not of soldiers but of

---

[3] A Greek grammarian in the time of Philip of Macedon, notorious for his violent attack on Homer; the type of carping critic.

[4] An unascribed saying; it is also quoted by Puttenham, p. 223.

[5] 'In self-defence'; 'use force to repel force'.

famous Kings and captains, as not only the sight but the very sound of them were able to vanquish and dismay the small forces of our adversaries. For who would once dare to oppose himself against so many Alexanders, Caesars, Scipios[6] (to omit infinite other Princes both of former and later ages, and of foreign and nearer countries) that with favour, with study, with practice, with example, with honours, with gifts, with preferments, with great and magnificent cost, have encouraged and advanced poets and poetry? As witness the huge theatres and amphitheatres, monuments of stupendous charge, made only for tragedies and comedies, the works of poets to be represented on. But all these aids and defences I leave as superfluous, my cause I count so good and the evidence so open that I neither need to use the countenance of any great state to bolster it, nor the cunning of any subtle lawyer to enforce it. My meaning is, plainly and *bona fide*, confessing all the abuses that can truly be objected against some kind of poets, to show you what good use there is of poetry.

Neither do I suppose it to be greatly behoveful for this purpose to trouble you with the curious* definitions of a poet and poesy and with the subtle distinctions of their sundry kinds, nor to dispute how high and supernatural the name of a maker is, so christened in English by that unknown godfather[7] that this last year save one, viz. 1589, set forth a book called *The Arte of English Poesie*; and least of all do I purpose to bestow any long time to argue whether Plato, Xenophon, and Erasmus,[8] writing fictions and dialogues in prose, may justly be called poets, or whether Lucan,[9] writing a story in verse, be an historiographer, or whether Master Phaer[10] translating Virgil, Master Golding[11] translating Ovid's *Metamorphoses*, and myself in this work that you see be any more than versifiers, as the same *Ignoto* termeth all translators.[12] For as for all or the most part of such

---

[6] One of many borrowings from Sidney's *Defence of Poetry*; cf. p. 377.

[7] George Puttenham: see pp. 190 ff.

[8] Referring to Plato's philosophical works, all cast in dialogue form; Xenophon's *Cyropaedia*, an idealized biography of Cyrus the Elder, much admired in the Renaissance; Erasmus, *Praise of Folly*.

[9] The *Bellum civile* (sometimes called *Pharsalia*), an epic in ten books, written *c*. AD 62–3, recounting the war between Caesar and Pompey.

[10] Thomas Phaer (1510?–60), lawyer and physician, translated nine books of the *Aeneid* into English verse between 1555 and 1560. Thomas Twyne completed the translation in 1584.

[11] Arthur Golding (?1536–?1605) published his version in 1565–7.

[12] Cf. Puttenham, p. 192.

questions I will refer you to Sir Philip Sidney's *Apology*,[13] who doth handle them right learnedly, or to the forenamed treatise, where they are discoursed more largely, and where as it were a whole receit of poetry is prescribed, with so many new named figures[14] as would put me in great hope in this age to come would breed many excellent poets—save for one observation that I gather out of the very same book. For though the poor gentleman labours greatly to prove, or rather to make poetry an art, and reciteth (as you may see, in the plural number) some pluralities of patterns and parcels of his own poetry, with diverse pieces of *Partheniads*[15] and hymns in praise of the most praiseworthy, yet whatsoever he would prove by all these, sure in my poor opinion he doth prove nothing more plainly than that which Master Sidney[16] and all the learneder sort that have written of it do pronounce: namely, that it is a gift and not an art. I say he proveth it because making himself and many others so cunning in the art, yet he showeth himself so slender a gift in it, deserving to be commended as Martial[17] praiseth one that he compares to Tully:

> *carmina quod scribis, musis et Apolline nullo*
> *laudari debes, hoc Ciceronis habes.*

But to come to the purpose, and to speak after the phrase of the common sort, that term all that is written in verse poetry, and rather in scorn than in praise bestow the name of a poet on every base rhymer and ballad-maker: this I say of it, and I think I say truly, that there are many good lessons to be learned out of it, many good examples to be found in it, many good uses to be had of it; and that therefore it is not, nor ought not to be, despised by the wiser sort, but so to be studied and employed as was intended by the first writers and devisers thereof, which is to soften and polish the hard and rough dispositions of men, and make them capable of virtue and good discipline.

I cannot deny but to us that are Christians, in respect of the high end of all, which is the health of our souls, not only poetry but all other studies of philosophy are in a manner vain and superfluous; yea (as the

---

[13] Written *c.*1579–80, not published until 1595: see pp. 336 ff.

[14] Figures of rhetoric, an essential resource in Renaissance poetry: cf. Gascoigne, p. 163, Puttenham, pp. 221 ff, Hoskyns, p. 405, and Jonson, p. 574.

[15] See p. 273, n. 175.

[16] See Sidney, pp. 376, 379.

[17] *Epigrams* 2. 89: 'Your writing poems, aided by no Muse and no Apollo, must merit praise; this gift of yours was Cicero's'.

wise man[18] saith) 'whatsoever is under the sun is vanity of vanities and nothing but vanity'. But since we live with men and not with saints, and because few men can embrace this strict and stoical divinity; or rather indeed, for that the holy scriptures in which those high mysteries of our salvation are contained are a deep and profound study and not subject to every weak capacity, no nor to the highest wits and judgements, except they be first illuminate by God's spirit, or instructed by his teachers and preachers. Therefore we do first read some other authors, making them as it were a looking-glass to the eyes of our mind; and then, after we have gathered more strength, we enter into profounder studies of higher mysteries, having first as it were enabled our eyes, by long beholding the sun in a basin of water, at last to look upon the sun itself. So we read how that great Moses,[19] whose learning and sanctity is so renowned over all nations, was first instructed in the learning of the Egyptians before he came to that high contemplation of God and familiarity (as I may so term it) with God. So the notable Prophet Daniel[20] was brought up in the learning of the Chaldeans, and made that the first step of his higher vocation to be a Prophet.

If then we may by the example of two such special servants of God spend some of our young years in studies of humanity, what better and more meet study is there for a young man than poetry? Especially heroical poesy, that with her sweet stateliness[21] doth erect* the mind and lift it up to the consideration of the highest matters, and allureth them that of themselves would otherwise loathe them, to take and swallow and digest the wholesome precepts of philosophy, and many times even of the true divinity. Wherefore Plutarch,[22] having written a whole treatise of the praise of Homer's works, and another of reading poets, doth begin this latter with this comparison, that as men that are sickly and have weak stomachs or dainty tastes do many times think that flesh most delicate to eat that is not flesh, and those fishes that be not fish, so young men (saith he) do like best that philosophy that is not philosophy, or that is not delivered as philosophy; and such are the pleasant writings of learned poets that are the popular philosophers and the popular divines. Likewise Tasso in his excellent work of *Gerusalemme Liberata* likeneth poetry to the physic that men give

---

[18] Eccles. 1: 2.   [19] Cf. Exod. 2: 9 ff.

[20] Cf. Dan. 1: 4 ff., 17 ff.   [21] Cf. Puttenham, ed. Willcock and Walker, p. 41.

[22] The essay on Homer (*De Homero*) is now attributed to pseudo-Plutarch; the other essay Harington cites, *Quomodo adulescens poetas audire debeat*, is authentic. For the passage cited cf. *Moralia* 14 D–E.

unto little children when they are sick. His verse is this in Italian, speaking to God with a pretty *prosopopeia*:[23]

> *Sai che là corre il mondo, ove più versi*
> *di sue dolcezze il lusinghier Parnaso,*
> *e che 'l vero condito in molli versi*
> *i più schivi allettando ha persuaso;*
> *così a l'egro fanciul porgiamo aspersi*
> *di soavi licor gli orli del vaso:*
> *succhi amari ingannato intanto ei beve,*
> *e da l'inganno suo vita riceve.*[24]

Thou knowst, the wanton worldlings ever run
To sweet Parnassus' fruits, how otherwhile
The truth well saw'st with pleasant verse hath won
Most squeamish stomachs with the sugared style:
So the sick child that potions all doth shun
With comfits* and with sugar we beguile
And cause him take a wholesome sour receit:
He drinks and saves his life with such deceit.

This is, then, that honest fraud in which (as Plutarch saith) he that is deceived is wiser than he that is not deceived, and he that doth deceive is honester than he that doth not deceive.

FOUR OBJECTIONS AGAINST POETRY

But briefly to answer to the chief objections. Cornelius Agrippa,[25] a man of learning and authority not to be despised, maketh a bitter invective against poets and poesy, and the sum of his reproof of it is this (which is all that can with any probability be said against it): That it is a nurse of lies, a pleaser of fools, a breeder of dangerous errors, and an enticer to wantonness. I might here warn those that will urge this man's authority to the disgrace of poetry to take heed (of what calling soever they be) lest with the same weapon that they think to give poetry a blow they give themselves a maim.

---

[23] Cf. Puttenham's definition, p. 275, and Hoskyns, pp. 426–7.

[24] *Gerusalemme Liberata*, canto 1, stanza 3.

[25] Heinrich Cornelius Agrippa von Nettesheim (1486–1535), German occult philosopher, who wrote both a serious exposition, *De occulta philosophia* (1531–3), and the (deliberately paradoxical?) attack on all knowledge, *De vanitate et incertitudine scientarum* (1530); cf. the translation by James Sanford, *Of the Vanitie and Uncertaintie of Arts and Sciences* (1569, 1575), ch. 4, 'Of Poetrie'; ed. Catherine M. Dunn (Northridge, Calif., 1974), pp. 30–4.

For Agrippa taketh his pleasure of greater matters than poetry; I marvel how he durst do it, save that I see he has done it—he has spared neither mitres nor sceptres. The courts of Princes where virtue is rewarded, justice maintained, oppressions relieved, he calls them a college of giants, of tyrants, of oppressors. Warriors, the most noble sort of noble men, he termeth cursed, bloody, wicked, and sacrilegious persons. Noble men (and us poor gentlemen) that think to borrow praise of our ancestors' deserts and good fame, he affirmeth to be a race of the sturdier sort of knaves and licentious livers. Treasurers and other great officers of the commonwealth, with grave counsellors whose wise heads are the pillars of the state, he affirmeth generally to be robbers and peelers* of the realm, and privy traitors that sell their Princes' favours and rob well-deserving servitors of their reward.

I omit as his *peccadilia** how he nicknameth priests, saying for the most part they are hypocrites; lawyers, saying they are all thieves; physicians, saying they are many of them murderers; so as I think it were a good motion, and would easily pass by the consent of the three estates, that this man's authority should be utterly annihilated that dealeth so hardly and unjustly with all sorts of professions. But for the rejecting of his writings I refer it to others that have power to do it, and to condemn him for a general libeller; but for that he writeth against poetry, I mean to speak a word or two in refuting thereof.

And first for lying: I might, if I list,* excuse it by the rule of *poetica licentia*,[26] and claim a privilege given to poetry, whose art is but an imitation (as Aristotle[27] calleth it) and therefore are allowed to feign what they list, according to that old verse,

> *juridicis, Erebo, fisco, fas vivere rapto,*
> *militibus, medicis, tortori, occidere Ludo est:*
> *mentiri astronomis, pictoribus atque poetis.*[28]

Which, because I count it without reason, I will English without rhyme:

> Lawyers, Hell, and the Chequer are allowed to live on spoil;
> Soldiers, Physicians and hangmen make a sport of murder;
> Astronomers, Painters, and Poets may lie by authority.

[26] Cf. Baldwin, p. 130, Cicero, *De or.* 3. 38. 153, and Horace, *Ars P.* 9 f.
[27] *Poet.* 1. 1447ª3 ff.
[28] Untraced; a parodic extension of Horace, *Ars P.* 9 f.

Thus you see that poets may lie, if they list, *cum privilegio*;[29] but what if they lie least of all other men? What if they lie not at all? Then, I think, that great slander is very unjustly raised upon them. For in my opinion they are said properly to lie that affirm that to be true that is false, and how other arts can free themselves from this blame let them look that profess them. But poets, never affirming any for true but presenting them to us as fables and imitations, cannot lie[30] though they would; and because this objection of lies is the chiefest and that upon which the rest be grounded, I will stand the longer upon the clearing thereof.

The ancient poets have indeed wrapped as it were in their writings diverse and sundry meanings, which they call the senses or mysteries[31] thereof. First of all for the literal sense (as it were the utmost* bark or rind) they set down, in manner of an history, the acts and notable exploits of some persons worthy memory. Then in the same fiction, as a second rind and somewhat more fine, as it were, nearer to the pith and marrow, they place the moral sense, profitable for the active life of man, approving virtuous actions and condemning the contrary. Many times also under the selfsame words they comprehend some true understanding of natural philosophy; or sometimes of politic government, and now and then of divinity, and these same senses that comprehend so excellent knowledge we call the allegory, which Plutarch[32] defines to be when one thing is told and by that another is understood. Now let any man judge if it be a matter of mean art or wit to contain in one historical narration, either true or feigned, so many, so diverse, and so deep conceits. . . .

It sufficeth me therefore to note this, that the men of greatest learning and highest wit in the ancient times did of purpose conceal these deep mysteries of learning and, as it were, cover them with the veil of fables[33] and verse, for sundry causes. One cause was that they might not be rashly abused by profane wits, in whom science* is corrupted like good wine in a bad vessel. Another cause why they wrote in verse was

---

[29] 'With permission': the phrase printed in a book's preliminaries to verify that it had been licensed by the official authorities.

[30] Cf. Sidney, p. 370.

[31] Medieval allegorical interpretation distinguished four levels of meaning, as Harington defines them. Renaissance scholars (notably Erasmus) rejected this scheme, usually preserving only the moral sense.

[32] Plutarch, *Poetas* 19E.

[33] On such 'veiling' of knowledge cf. Spenser, p. 299, and Chapman, p. 393. Harington draws on Sidney, p. 390.

conservation of the memory of their precepts, as we see yet the general rules almost of every art, not so much as husbandry,* but they are oftener recited and better remembered in verse than in prose. Another and a principal cause of all is to be able with one kind of meat and one dish (as I may so call it) to feed diverse tastes. For the weaker capacities will feed themselves with the pleasantness of the history and sweetness of the verse, some that have stronger stomachs will as it were take a further taste of the moral sense, a third sort more high conceited than they will digest the allegory, so as indeed it hath been thought by men of very good judgement, such manner of poetical writing was an excellent way to preserve all kind of learning from that corruption which now it is come to since they left that mystical writing of verse. . . .

But, to go higher, did not our Saviour himself speak in parables?[34] as that divine parable of the sower, that comfortable parable of the prodigal son, that dreadful parable of Dives and Lazarus, though I know of this last many of the fathers hold it is a story indeed and no parable. But in the rest it is manifest that he that was all holiness, all wisdom, all truth, used parables and even such as discreet poets use, where a good and honest and wholesome allegory is hidden in a pleasant and pretty fiction.[35] And therefore, for that part of poetry of imitation, I think nobody will make any question but it is not only allowable but godly and commendable, if the poets' ill handling of it do not mar and pervert the good use of it.

TWO PARTS OF POETRY: IMITATION OR INVENTION, AND VERSE

The other part of poetry, which is verse, as it were the clothing or ornament of it, hath many good uses. Of the help of memory I spoke somewhat before, for the words being couched* together in due order, measure, and number, one doth as it were bring on another . . .

Another special grace in verse is the forcible manner of phrase, in which if it be well made it far excels loose speech or prose; a third is the pleasure and sweetness to the ear, which makes the discourse pleasant unto us oftentime when the matter itself is harsh and unacceptable. For mine own part I was never yet so good a husband* to take any delight to hear one of my ploughmen tell how an acre of wheat must be fallowed and twifallowed,* and how cold land should be

---

[34] Respectively, Matt. 13: 3–23 (cf. Mark 4: 3 ff., Luke 8: 5 ff.); Luke 15: 11–32; 16: 19–31.
[35] Cf. Sidney, p. 353.

burned and how fruitful land must be well harrowed; but when I hear
one read Virgil where he saith:

> Saepe etiam steriles incendere profuit agros
> atque levem stipulam crepitantibus urere flammis.
> sive inde occultas vires et pabula terrae
> pinguia concipiunt; sive illis omne per ignem
> excoquitur vitium atque exsudat inutilis humor,[36] etc.

And after:

> Multum adeo, rastris glebas qui frangit inertes
> vimineasque trahit crates, juvat arva.[37]

With many other lessons of homely husbandry but delivered in so
good verse that methinks all that while I could find in my heart to
drive the plough.

But now for the authority of verse: if it be not sufficient to say for
them that the greatest philosophers and gravest senators that ever
were have used them both in their speeches and in their writings; that
precepts of all arts have been delivered in them; that verse is as ancient
a writing as prose, and indeed more ancient in respect that the oldest
works extant be verse, as Orpheus, Linus, Hesiodus,[38] and others
beyond memory of man or mention almost of history; if none of these
will serve for credit of it, yet let this serve, that some part of the scripture was written in verse, as the Psalms of David and certain other
songs of Deborah, of Solomon, and others (which the learnedest
divines do affirm to be verse and find that they are in metre, though
the rule of the Hebrew verse they agree not on). Sufficeth it me only
to prove that by the authority of sacred scriptures, both parts of poesy,
invention or imitation and verse are allowable, and consequently that
great objection of lying is quite taken away and refuted.

Now the second objection is pleasing of fools. I have already shown
how it displeaseth not wise men; now if it have this virtue, to please

---

[36] Virgil, *Georg.* 1. 84 ff.: 'Often, too, it has been useful to fire barren fields, and burn the
light stubble in crackling flames; whether it be that the earth derives thence hidden strength
and rich nutriment, or that in the flame every taint is baked out and the useless moisture
sweats from it . . .'.

[37] Virgil, ibid. 94 ff.: 'Yea, and much service does he do the land who with the mattock
breaks up the sluggish clods, and drags over it wicker hurdles. . . .'

[38] This list of the first poets (or orators), common in antiquity (cf. e.g. Cicero, *Inv. rhet.*
1. 1. 2 ff.; Horace, *Ars P.* 391 ff.), recurs in Wilson, Lodge, Sidney, Puttenham, Webbe, and
other writers.

the fools and ignorant, I would think this an article of praise, not of rebuke. Wherefore I confess that it pleaseth fools, and so pleaseth them that if they mark it and observe it well, it will in time make them wise, for in verse is both goodness and sweetness, rhubarb and sugar candy, the pleasant and the profitable. Wherefore, as Horace saith, *Omne tulit punctum qui miscuit utile dulce*,[39] he that can mingle the sweet and the wholesome, the pleasant and the profitable, he is indeed an absolute good writer, and such be poets, if any be such. . . .

Now for the breeding of errors, which is the third objection: I see not why it should breed any, when none is bound to believe that they write, nor they look not to have their fictions believed in the literal sense. And therefore he that well examines whence errors spring shall find the writers of prose, and not of verse, the authors and maintainers of them; and this point I count so manifest as it needs no proof.

The last reproof is lightness* and wantonness.* This is indeed an objection of some importance since, as Sir Philip Sidney confesseth,[40] Cupido is crept even into the heroical poems, and consequently maketh that also subject to this reproof. I promised in the beginning not partially to praise poesy but plainly and honestly to confess that that might truly be objected against it, and if anything may be, sure it is this lasciviousness. Yet this I will say, that of all kind of poesy the heroical is least infected therewith. The other kinds I will rather excuse than defend, though of all the kinds of poesy it may be said where any scurrility and lewdness is found, there poetry does not abuse us but writers have abused poetry.[41]

And briefly to examine all the kinds. First, the tragical is merely* free from it, as representing only the cruel and lawless proceedings of princes, moving nothing but pity or detestation. The comical (whatsoever foolish playmakers make it offend in this kind) yet being rightly used, it represents them so as to make the vice scorned and not embraced. The satiric is merely free from it, as being wholly occupied in mannerly* and covertly reproving of all vices. The elegy is still mourning; as for the pastoral, with the sonnet or epigram, though many times they savour of wantonness and love and toying,* and now and then, breaking the rules of poetry go into plain scurrility, yet even the worst of them may be not ill applied and are, I must confess, too delightful. In so much as Martial saith:

---

[39] *Ars P.* 343.
[40] See p. 371. (Cupido is the Latin for 'desire'.)   [41] Cf. Sidney, p. 371.

laudant illa sed ista legunt.[42]

And in another place:

> *erubuit posuitque meum Lucrecia librum,*
> *sed coram Bruto; Brute, recede: leget.*[43]

Lucretia (by which he signifies any chaste matron) 'will blush and be ashamed to read a lascivious book, but how? not except Brutus be by'.—That is, if any grave man should see her read it; but if Brutus turn his back, she will to it again and read it all.

But to end this part of my apology, as I count and conclude heroical poesy allowable and to be read and studied without all exception, so I may as boldly say that tragedies well handled be a most worthy kind of poesy, that comedies may make men see and shame at their own faults, that the rest may be so written and so read as much pleasure and some profit may gathered out of them. And for my own part, as Scaliger writes of Virgil,[44] so I believe that the reading of a good heroical poem may make a man both wiser and honester. And for tragedies, to omit other famous tragedies, that that was played at Saint John's in Cambridge of *Richard the Third*[45] would move (I think) Phalaris the tyrant and terrify all tyrannous-minded men from following their foolish ambitious humours, seeing how his ambition made him kill his brother, his nephews, his wife, beside infinite others; and last of all, after a short and troublesome reign to end his miserable life and to have his body harried after his death. Then for comedies: how full of harmless mirth is our Cambridge *Pedantius?*[46] and the Oxford *Bellum Grammaticale?*[47] or to speak of a London comedy, how much good matter, yea and matter of state,* is there in that comedy called *The play of the Cards?*[48] in which it is shown how four parasitical knaves rob the four principal vocations of

---

[42] *Epigrams* 4. 49: 'those they praise, but they read the others'.

[43] Ibid. 11. 16: 'Lucretia blushed and laid down my volume; but Brutus was present. Brutus, go away: she will read it'.

[44] Cf. *Poetice* 3. 19 (ed. Deitz, ii. 242–3), and Sidney, p. 390.

[45] Thomas Legge's *Richardus Tertius*, acted at St John's College Cambridge, in Mar. 1580.

[46] A Latin satirical comedy by Edward Forsett acted at Trinity College Cambridge in Feb. 1581 and printed in 1631.

[47] *Bellum Grammaticale, sive Nominum Verborumque Discordia Civilis*, a Latin comedy by Leonard Hutton, was acted before Queen Elizabeth at Christ Church Oxford, on 24 Sept. 1592, and printed in 1635.

[48] The anonymous lost play, *A Game of the Cards*, acted by the Children of the Chapel at court on 26 Dec. 1582.

the realm, *videl.** the vocation of soldiers, scholars, merchants, and husbandmen. Of which comedy I cannot forget the saying of a notable wise counsellor,[49] that is now dead, who when some (to sing *Placebo*) advised that it should be forbidden because it was somewhat too plain, and indeed as the old saying is, 'sooth board is no board', yet he would have it allowed, adding it was fit that 'they which do that they should not, should hear that they would not'. Finally, if comedies may be so made as the beholders may be bettered by them, without all doubt all other sorts of poetry may bring their profit as they do bring delight; and if all, then much more the chief of all, which by all men's consent is the heroical. And thus much be said for poesy.

THE SECOND PART OF THIS APOLOGY

Now for this poem of *Orlando Furioso*, which as I have heard hath been disliked by some—though by few of any wit or judgement—it follows that I say somewhat in defence thereof; which I will do the more moderately and coldly by how much the pains I have taken in it (rising as you may see to a good volume) may make me seem a more partial praiser. Wherefore I will make choice of some other poem that is allowed and approved by all men, and a little compare them together. And what work can serve this turn so fitly as Virgil's *Aeneid*, whom above all other it seemeth my author doth follow, as appears both by his beginning and ending? The one begins:

> *Arma virumque cano*

The other:

> *Le donne, i cavallier, l'arme, gli amori,*
> *le cortesie, l'audaci imprese io canto.*[50]

Virgil ends with the death of Turnus:

> *vitaque cum gemitu fugit indignata sub umbras.*

Ariosto ends with the death of Rodomont:

---

[49] Sir Francis Walsingham (d. 1590); 'to sing *Placebo*': to be servile or time-serving (from the Vulgate version of Ps. 114, 'Placebo Domino . . .').

[50] 'Arms and the man I sing' (*Aen.* 1. 1); 'Of Dames, of Knights, of armes, of loves delight, | Of curtesies, of high attempts I speake' (*OF* 1. 1–2, tr. Harington).

> *bestemmiando fuggi l'alma sdegnosa,*
> *che fu sì altiera al mondo e sì orgogliosa.*[51]

Virgil extolleth Aeneas to please Augustus, of whose race he was thought to come. Ariosto praiseth Ruggiero to the honour of the house of Este.[52] Aeneas hath his Dido that retaineth him; Ruggiero hath his Alcina. Finally, lest I should note every part, there is nothing of any special observation in Virgil but my author hath with great felicity* imitated it, so as whosoever will allow Virgil must *ipso facto* (as they say) admit Ariosto. Now of what account Virgil is reckoned and worthily reckoned, for ancient times witnesseth Augustus Caesar's verse of him:

> *ergone supremis potuit vox improba verbis*
> *tam dirum mandare nefas?* etc.

Concluding thus:

> *laudetur, placeat, vigeat, relegatur, ametur.*[53]

This is a great praise coming from so great a Prince.

For later times, to omit Scaliger, whom I recited before, that affirmeth the reading of Virgil may make a man honest and virtuous, that excellent Italian poet Dante[54] professeth plainly that when he wandered out of the right way (meaning thereby when he lived fondly* and loosely),* Virgil was the first that made him look into himself and reclaim himself from that same dangerous and lewd course. But what need we further witness: do we not make our children read it commonly, before they can understand it, as a testimony that we do generally approve it? and yet we see old men study it as a proof that they do specially admire it, so as one writes very prettily that 'children do wade in Virgil and yet strong men do swim in it'.

---

[51] '[But the other's limbs grew slack and chill,] and with a moan passed indignant to the Shades below' (*Aen.* 12. 951–2); 'Sunk his disdainfull soule . . . | Blaspheming as it went and cursing lowd | That was on earth so loftie and so proud' (*OF* 46. 140; in Harington's version, stanza 123).

[52] The house of Este, one of the oldest and most illustrious families of Italy. Ludovico Ariosto (1474–1533), became a servant at the Ferrara court of the Cardinal Ippolito d'Este in 1503, and completed a first version of *Orlando Furioso* by 1516. When the cardinal left Italy in 1518, his brother, the Duke Alfonso, invited Ariosto to his service, treating him liberally, and being lauded in the poem's third, enlarged version (1532).

[53] 'And could a depraved voice recount such a dire crime in noble language? . . . May he be praised, may he please, may he flourish, be cherished and loved' (tr. Hardison). Verses attributed to Augustus Caesar in the *Scholastica in Virgilium*.

[54] *Inferno* 1.79 ff.

Now to apply this to the praise of mine author, as I said before so I say still, whatsoever is praiseworthy in Virgil is plentifully to be found in Ariosto; and some things that Virgil could not have, for the ignorance of the age he lived in, you find in my author sprinkled over all his work, as I will very briefly note and refer you for the rest to the book itself. The devout and Christian demeanour of Charlemagne in the 14th book, with his prayer:

> *non voglia tua bontà, pel mio fallire,*
> *che 'l tuo popul fedele abbia a patire,* etc.[55]

And in the beginning of the 17th book, that would beseem any pulpit:

> *Il giusto Dio, quando i peccati nostri.*[56]

But above all that in the 41st book, of the conversion of Ruggiero to the Christian religion where the Hermit speaketh to him, containing in effect a full instruction against presumption and despair,[57] which I have set down thus in English:

> Now (as I said) this wise that Hermit spoke
> And part doth comfort him and part doth check.*
> He blameth him that in that pleasant yoke
> He had so long deferred to put his neck
> But did to wrath his maker still provoke
> And did not come at his first call and beck
> But still did hide himself away from God
> Until he saw him coming with his rod.
>
> Then did he comfort him and make him know
> That grace is ne'er denied to such as ask,
> (As do the workmen in the Gospel show
> Receiving pay alike for diverse task).

And so after, concluding:

> How to Christ he must impute
> The pardon of his sins, yet near the later
> He told him he must be baptised in water.

---

[55] 'O Lord (said he) though I myself be nought, Let not my sinne, my wickednesse, and ill | Move thee thy faithfull peoples blood to spill' (*OF* 14. 69; in Harington, st. 59).

[56] 'The most just God, when once mans sins do grow | Beyond the bounds of pardon and of grace . . .' (*OF* 17. 1).

[57] *OF* 41. 55–8.

These and infinite places full of Christian exhortation, doctrine, and example I could quote out of the book save that I hasten to an end, and it would be needless to those that will not read them in the book itself and superfluous to those that will. But most manifest it is, and not to be denied, that in this point my author is to be preferred before all the ancient poets, in which are mentioned so many false gods and of them so many foul deeds, their contentions, their adulteries, their incest as were both obscene in recital and hurtful in example; though indeed those whom they termed gods were certain great princes that committed such enormous faults as great princes in late ages (that love still to be called gods of the earth) do often commit.

But now it may be, and is by some objected, that although he write Christianly in some places yet in other some he is too lascivious, as in that of the bawdy Friar, in Alcina's and Ruggiero's copulation, in Anselmus his Egyptian, in Richardetto his metamorphosis, in mine host's tale of Astolfo, and some few places beside. Alas, if this be a fault, pardon him this one fault, though I doubt too many of you (gentle readers) will be too exorable* in this point.—Yea methinks I see some of you searching already for these places of the book, and you are half offended that I have not made some directions that you might find out and read them immediately. But I beseech you stay a while, and as the Italian says *pian piano*, fair and softly, and take this caveat with you, to read them as my author meant them, to breed detestation and not delectation. Remember when you read of the old lecherous Friar that a fornicator is one of the things that God hateth. When you read of Alcina, think how Joseph[58] fled from his enticing mistress; when you light on Anselmus' tale, learn to loathe beastly covetousness; when on Richardetto, know that sweet meat will have sour sauce; when on mine host's tale (if you will follow my counsel) turn over the leaf and let it alone. Although even that lewd tale may bring some men profit, and I have heard that it is already (and perhaps not unfitly) termed the comfort of cuckolds. But as I say, if this be a fault, then Virgil committed the same fault in Dido and Aeneas' entertainment,* and if some will say he tells that mannerly and covertly, how will they excuse that where Vulcan was entreated by Venus to make an armour for Aeneas?

---

[58] For the story of Joseph and Potiphar's wife, see Genesis 39: 1.

> *Dixerat, et niveis hinc atque hinc diva lacertis*
> *cunctantem amplexu molli fovet. ille repente*
> *accepti solitam flammam, notusque medullas*
> *intravit calor.*[59]

And a little after:

> *ea verba locutus*
> *optatos dedit amplexus placidumque petivit*
> *coniugis infusus gremio per membra soporem.*[60]

I hope they that understand Latin will confess this is plain enough, and yet with modest words and no obscene phrase; and so I dare take upon me that in all Ariosto (and yet I think it is as much as three *Aeneids*) there is not a word of ribaldry or obscenity. Further, there is so meet a decorum in the persons of those that speak lasciviously as any of judgement must needs allow. And therefore, though I rather crave pardon than praise for him in this point, yet methinks I can smile at the finesse* of some that will condemn him and yet not only allow but admire our Chaucer, who both in words and sense incurreth more the reprehension of flat scurrility, as I could recite many places, not only in his Miller's tale, but in the good wife of Bath's tale and many more, in which only the decorum he keeps is that that excuseth it and maketh it more tolerable.

But now whereas some will say Ariosto wanteth art, reducing* all heroical poems unto the method of Homer and certain precepts of Aristotle: for Homer, I say that that which was commendable in him to write in that age, the times being changed, would be thought otherwise now, as we see both in phrase and in fashions the world grows more curious* each day than other. Ovid[61] gave precepts of making love, and one was that one should spill wine on the board and write his mistress' name therewith. This was a quaint cast* in that age, but he that should make love so now his love would mock him for his labour and count him but a slovenly suitor; and if it be thus changed since Ovid's time, much more since Homer's time. And yet for Ariosto's tales, that many think unartificially* brought in,

---

[59] *Aen.* 8. 387 ff.: 'She ceased, and, as he falters, throws her snowy arms round about him and fondles him in soft embrace. At once he caught the wonted flame; the familiar warmth passed into his marrow and ran through his melting frame . . .'.

[60] *Aen.* 8. 404 ff.: 'Thus speaking, he gave the desired embrace, and, sinking on the bosom of his spouse, wooed calm, slumber in every limb'.

[61] Ovid, *Ars am.* 1. 571 ff.; *Am.* 1. 4. 20; 2. 5. 17 f. Cf. Peter Green (ed. and tr.), Ovid, *The Erotic Poems* (Harmondsworth, Middx., 1980), pp. 90, 117, 183-4, 272, 356.

Homer himself hath the like, as in the *Iliad* the conference[62] of Glaucus with Diomedes upon some acts of Bellerophon, and in his *Odyssey* the discourse[63] of the hog with Ulysses. Further, for the name of the book which some carp at because he called it *Orlando Furioso* rather than *Ruggiero*, in that he may also be defended by example of Homer who, professing to write of Achilles, calleth his book *Iliad of Troy* and not *Achillide*. As for Aristotle's rules, I take it he hath followed them very strictly.

Briefly, Aristotle and the best censurers of poesy,[64] would have the *epopeia*, that is, the heroical poem, should ground on some history and take some short time in the same to beautify with his poetry. So doth my author take the story of K. Charles the great, doth not exceed a year or thereabout in his whole work. Secondly, they hold[65] that nothing should be feigned utterly incredible. And sure Ariosto neither in his enchantments exceedeth credit (for who knows not how strong the illusions of the devil are?), neither in the miracles that Astolfo, by the power of St. John is feigned to do, since the Church holdeth that Prophets both alive and dead have done mighty great miracles. Thirdly, they would have an heroical poem (as well as a tragedy) to be full of *peripeteia*,[66] which I interpret an agnition* of some unlooked-for fortune, either good or bad, and a sudden change thereof: of this, what store there be the reader shall quickly find. As for apt similitudes, for passions well expressed, of love, of pity, of hate, of wrath, a blind man may see, if he can but hear, that this work is full of them.

There follows only two reproofs, which I rather interpret two peculiar praises of this writer, above all that wrote before him in this kind. One, that he breaks off narrations very abruptly, so as indeed a loose unattentive reader will hardly carry away any part of the story. But this doubtless is a point of great art, to draw a man with a continual thirst to read out the whole work, and toward the end of the book to close up the diverse matters briefly and cleanly. If Sir Philip Sidney had counted this a fault, he would not have done so himself in his *Arcadia*. Another fault is that he speaketh so much in his own person by digression, which they say also is against the rules of poetry, because neither Homer nor Virgil did it. Methinks it is a sufficient

---

[62] *Il.* 6. 119–233.   [63] *Od.* 19. 386–468.

[64] As G. Gregory Smith pointed out (*ECE* ii. 424 f.), in this section Harington drew on Antonio Minturno's treatise, *De poeta libri sex* (1559).

[65] Cf. Aristotle, *Poet.* 23–24. 1459ᵃ16–1460ᵇ3.   [66] Ibid. 11. 1452ᵃ22 ff.

defence to say, Ariosto doth it. Sure I am, it is both delightful and very profitable, and an excellent breathing-place for the reader. And even as if a man walked in a fair long alley, to have a seat or resting place here and there is easy and commodious, but if at the same seat were planted some excellent tree, that not only with the shade should keep us from the heat but with some pleasant and right wholesome fruit should allay our thirst and comfort our stomach, we would think it for the time a little paradise. So are Ariosto's morals and pretty digressions sprinkled through his long work, to the no less pleasure than profit of the reader. And thus much be spoken for defence of mine author, which was the second part of my apology.

THE THIRD PART OF THE APOLOGY

Now remains the third part of it, in which I promised to speak somewhat for myself. Which part, though it have most need of an apology both large and substantial, yet I will run it over both shortly and slightly, because indeed the nature of the thing itself is such that the more one doth say the less he shall seem to say, and men are willinger to praise that in another man which himself shall debase,* than that which he shall seem to maintain. Certainly if I should confess or rather profess that my verse is unartificial, the style rude, the phrase barbarous, the metre unpleasant, many more would believe it to be so than would imagine that I thought them so. For this same *philautia*[67] or self-pleasing is so common a thing as the more a man protests himself to be free from it the more we will charge him with it. Wherefore let me take thus much upon me, that admit it have many of the forenamed imperfections, and many not named; yet as writing goes nowadays, it may pass among the rest. And as I have heard a friend of mine (one very judicious in the beauty of a woman) say of a lady whom he meant to praise that she had a low forehead, a great* nose, a wide mouth, a long visage, and yet all these put together she seemed to him a very well-favoured woman: so I hope, and I find already some of my partial friends, that what several imperfections soever they find in this

---

[67] *Philautia*, or self-love, a vice often attacked by classical philosophers and moralists (Plato, *Laws* 5. 731e; Aristotle, *Eth. Nic.* 9. 7. 1168ᵃ29, Horace, *Odes* 1. 18. 14), and their Renaissance successors. Erasmus discusses it in *Adagia* 1. 3. 92 (*Philautoi*, self-lovers), and in his satire *Moriae Encomium* made Philautia one of the companions of Folly. Cf. Introduction, p. 35.

translation, yet taking all together they allow it; or at least wise they read it, which is a great argument of their liking.

Sir Thomas More, a man of great wisdom and learning but yet a little inclined (as good wits are many times) to scoffing, when one had brought him a book of some shallow discourse and pressed him very hard to have his opinion of it, advised the party to put it into verse. The plain-meaning man in the best manner he could did so, and a twelve-month after at the least came with it to Sir Thomas who slightly perusing it gave it this *encomium*, that now there was rhyme in it but afore it had neither rhyme nor reason. If any man had meant to serve me so, yet I have prevented* him, for sure I am he shall find rhyme in mine, and if he be not void of reason, he shall find reason too. Though for the matter I can challenge no praise, having but borrowed it, and for the verse I do challenge none, being a thing that everybody that never scarce baited* their horse at the university take upon them to make. It is possible that if I would have employed that time that I have done upon this, upon some invention of mine own, I could have by this made it have risen to a just volume; and if I would have done as many spare not to do, flown very high with stolen feathers. But I had rather men should see and know that I borrow all than that I steal any, and I would wish to be called rather 'one of the not worst translators' than 'one of the meaner makers'. Especially since the Earl of Surrey and Sir Thomas Wyatt, that are yet called the first refiners of the English tongue, were both translators out of Italian.

Now for those that count it such a contemptible and trifling matter to translate, I will but say to them as M. Bartholomew Clarke, an excellent learned man and a right good translator, saith in a manner of a pretty challenge in his Preface (as I remember) upon *The Courtier*, which book he translated out of Italian into Latin:[68] 'You (saith he) that think it such a toy, lay aside my book and take my author in your hand and try a leaf or such a matter and compare it with mine.' If I should say so, there would be enough that would quickly put me down perhaps, but doubtless he might boldly say it, for I think none could have mended him. But as our English proverb[69] saith, 'many talk of

---

[68] Published in 1571.

[69] A proverb dating back to Chaucer, and included in Thomas Heywood's collection (1546). Cf. F. P. Wilson (ed.), *The Oxford Dictionary of English Proverbs* (Oxford, 1970), p. 761.

Robin Hood that never shot in his bow', and some correct *Magnificat* that know not *quid significat.*[70] For my part, I will thank them that will mend* anything that I have done amiss, nor I have no such great conceit of that I have done but that I think much in it is to be mended. And having dealt plainly with some of my plain-dealing friends to tell me frankly what they heard spoken of it (for indeed I suffered some part of the printed copies to go among my friends, and some more perhaps went against my will), I was told that these in effect were the faults were found with it.

FOUR FAULTS FOUND IN THIS WORK

Some grave men misliked that I should spend so much good time on such a trifling work as they deemed a poem to be. Some more nicely* found fault with so many two-syllabled and three-syllabled rhymes. Some (not undeservedly) reproved the fantasticalness* of my notes, in which they say I have strained myself to make mention of some of my kindred and friends that might very well be left out. And one fault more there is which I will tell myself, though many would never find it, and that is I have cut short some of his Cantos in leaving out many staves* of them, and sometimes put the matter of two or three staves into one.

To these reproofs I shall pray you, gentle and noble readers, with patience hear my defence, and then I will end. For the first reproof, either it is already excused or it will never be excused, for I have, I think, sufficiently proved both the art to be allowable and this work to be commendable. Yet I will tell you an accident* that happened unto myself. When I was entered a pretty way into the translation, about the seventh book, coming to write that where Melissa in the person of Rogero's tutor comes and reproves Rogero in the fourth staff:*

> What, was't for this that I in youth thee fed
> With marrow? etc.

And again:

> Is this a means or ready way you trow
> That other worthy men have trod before,
> A Caesar or a Scipio to grow?[71] etc.

---

[70] 'Set up as authorities on usage when they barely know Latin.'
[71] *OF* 7. 56–65 (in Harington's version, 49–54).

Straight I began to think that my tutor,[72] a grave and learned man and one of a very austere life, might say to me in the like sort: 'Was it for this that I read Aristotle and Plato to you and instructed you so carefully both in Greek and Latin, to have you now become a translator of Italian toys?' But while I thought thus, I was aware that it was no toy* that could put such an honest and serious consideration into my mind.

Now for them that find fault with polysyllable metre, methinks they are like those that blame men for putting sugar in their wine, and chide too bad about it and say 'they mar all', but yet end with 'God's blessing on their hearts'. For indeed, if I had known their diets I could have saved some of my cost, at least some of my pain. For when a verse ended with 'civility', I could easier after the ancient manner of rhyme have made 'see' or 'flee' or 'decree' to answer it, leaving the accent upon the last syllable, than hunt after three-syllabled words to answer it with 'facility', 'gentility', 'tranquillity', 'hostility', 'scurrillity', 'debility', 'agility', 'fragility', 'nobility', 'mobility', which who mislike may taste lamp oil[73] with their ears. And as for two-syllabled metres, they be so approved in other languages that the French call them the feminine rhyme, as the sweeter, and the one-syllable the masculine. But in a word to answer this and to make them forever hold their peaces of this point, Sir Philip Sidney not only useth them but affecteth* them: 'signify', 'dignify'; 'shamed is', 'named is', 'blamed is'; 'hide away', 'bide away'. Though if my many blotted papers that I have made in this kind might afford me authority to give a rule of it, I would say that to part them with a one-syllable metre between them would give it best grace. For as men use to sow with the hand and not with the whole sack, so I would have the ear fed but not cloyed with these pleasing and sweet-falling metres.

For the third reproof about the notes, sure they were a work (as I may so call it) of supererogation,* and I would wish sometimes they had been left out; and this rather if I be in such fair possibility to be thought a fool or fantastical* for my labour. True it is, I added some notes to the end of every canto, even as if some of my friends and myself reading it together (and so it fell out indeed many times) had after debated upon them what had been most worthy consideration in them, and so oftentimes immediately I set it down. And whereas

---

[72] 'Samuel Flemming of Kings Colledge in Cambridge' (marginal note).
[73] 'Lamp oil' is scholarly work done at night.

I make mention here and there of some of mine own friends and kin, I did it the rather because Plutarch[74] in one place, speaking of Homer, partly lamenteth and partly blameth him that writing so much as he did, yet in none of his works there was any mention made or so much as inkling to be gathered of what stock he was, of what kindred, of what town, nor—save for his language—of what country. Excuse me then if I, in a work that may perhaps last longer than a better thing, and, being not ashamed of my kindred, name them here and there to no man's offence, though I meant not to make everybody so far of my counsel why I did it, till I was told that some person of some reckoning noted me of a little vanity for it; and thus much for that point.

For my omitting and abbreviating some things, either in matters impertinent* to us or in some too tedious flatteries of persons that we never heard of, if I have done ill I crave pardon, for sure I did it for the best. But if any being studious of the Italian would for his better understanding compare them, the first six books, save a little of the third, will stand him in stead. But yet I would not have any man except* that I should observe his phrase so strictly as an interpreter, nor the matter so carefully as if it had been a story, in which to vary were as great a sin as it were simplicity* in this to go word for word.

But now to conclude, I shall pray you all that have troubled yourselves to read this my triple apology to accept my labours and to excuse my errors, if with no other thing, at least with the name of youth (which commonly hath need of excuses); and so, presuming this pardon to be granted, we shall part good friends. Only let me entreat you in reading the book ensuing not to do me that injury that a potter did to Ariosto.[75]

---

[74] Ps.-Plutarch, *De Homero*; Cicero, *Arch.* 8. 19.

[75] In the *Life of Ariosto* appended to his translation, Harington records the 'pretie tale' of how Ariosto treated a potter whom he heard singing a stanza from the *Orlando Furioso* 'so ill-favouredly' that the poet broke several of his pots with his walking-stick. When the potter complained, 'Varlet, quoth Ariosto, I am yet scarce even with thee for the wrong thou hast done me here afore my face, for I have broken but half a dozen base pots of thine that are not worth so many halfpence, but thou hast broken and mangled a fine stanza of mine worth a mark of gold' (ed. McNulty, pp. 575–6).

William Shakespeare,
How to write love poetry (*c.*1592)

WILLIAM SHAKESPEARE, born at Stratford-upon-Avon in 1564, presumably attended the local grammar school, since his knowledge of Latin literature, rhetoric, and composition techniques conforms in every respect to the standard grammar-school curriculum, as T. W. Baldwin definitively established.[1] The date when he began his career as an actor and playwright in London is not known, but most scholars argue for the early 1590s, when he was probably attached to the Earl of Pembroke's Men. From 1594 to the end of his career he was with the Lord Chamberlain's (after 1603, the King's) Men, the only dramatist who was simultaneously an actor, playwright, and 'sharer' or manager of a theatre. It was very common in this period for two or more dramatists to collaborate in writing a play, the task being divided up sometimes by Acts, sometimes (as here) by main plot/sub-plot. Although the identity of his collaborator(s) has not yet been established, we know that Shakespeare worked together with George Peele on *Titus Andronicus*, with Thomas Middleton on *Timon of Athens*, and with John Fletcher on *Henry VIII* and *The Two Noble Kinsmen*. See K. Muir, *Shakespeare as Collaborator* (London, 1960).

TEXT. From *The Raigne of King Edward the third* (1596), as edited by Edward Capell in *Prolusions; or, select pieces of Antient Poetry, II. Edward the third, a Play, thought to be writ by Shakespeare* (London, 1760), checked against the edition by George Melchiori in the New Cambridge Shakespeare (1998). Modern scholars assign to Shakespeare the three scenes involving the Countess of Salisbury, with whom the King falls in love (1. 2, 2. 1, 2. 2), and a later battle scene (4. 4). The play has been dated between 1590 and 1594, but as W. L. Godshalk has argued (*Notes and Queries*, 240 (1995), 299–300), the fact that Thomas Deloney's verse collection *The Garden of Good Will*, which includes the ballad 'Of King Edward the third, and the faire Countess of Salisbury', largely based on the play, was entered in the Stationer's Register on 5 March 1593, suggests a first performance in the winter of 1592–3.

The action takes place at the beginning of the Hundred Years War (1337–41), and is based on the Chronicles of Froissart and Holinshed, with the romantic sub-plot being taken from novel 46 in William Painter's

[1] *William Shakspere's Small Latine & Lesse Greeke*, 2 vols. (Urbana, Ill., 1944, 1966).

collection, *The Palace of Pleasure* (1566, 1575). England is in dispute with France when the Scots King breaks his truce, captures the border town of Berwick, and lays siege to the castle of Roxborough, 'where enclosed | The Countess of Salisbury is like to perish' (1. 1. 130–1). Daughter of the Earl of Warwick, the Countess is unprotected, her husband being a prisoner in Flanders, and King Edward sets off to 'repulse the traitorous Scots' (155). Falling in love with her at first sight (1. 2. 94 ff.), the King invokes the aid of his secretary, Lodowick, to woo her in verse, in the excerpt presented here (2. 1. 1–184): but the Countess remains loyal to her husband. Shakespeare mocks some of the current clichés in love poetry, as Sidney had already done in *Astrophel and Stella* (1591).

THE REIGN OF KING EDWARD THE THIRD

2. 1. ROXBOROUGH. GARDENS OF THE CASTLE

Enter LODOWICK

LODOWICK. I might perceive his eye in her eye lost,
   His ear to drink her sweet tongue's utterance,
   And changing passions, like inconstant clouds
   That rack[2] upon the carriage of the winds,
   Increase and die in his disturbèd cheeks.   5
   Lo, when she blushed, even then did he look pale,
   As if her cheeks by some enchanted power
   Attracted had the cherry blood from his;
   Anon, with reverent fear when she grew pale,
   His cheeks put on their scarlet ornaments,[3]   10
   But no more like her oriental* red
   Than brick to coral, or live things to dead.
   Why did he then thus counterfeit her looks?
   If she did blush, 'twas tender modest shame,
   Being in the sacred presence of a king.   15
   If he did blush, 'twas red immodest shame,
   To vail* his eyes amiss, being a king.
   If she looked pale, 'twas silly* woman's fear,
   To bear herself in presence of a king.

---

  [2] 'Drive before the wind'. I accept Melchiori's reading, from the second Quarto edition (1599). Capell followed Q1 (1596): 'rackt'.
  [3] Cf. Shakespeare, Sonnet 142. 5–6: '. . . not from those lips of thine, | That have profaned their scarlet ornaments'.

If he looked pale, it was with guilty fear,   20
To dote amiss, being a mighty king.
Then, Scottish wars, farewell; I fear 'twill prove
A lingering English siege of peevish* love.
—Here comes his highness, walking all alone   [*withdraws*
                    Enter KING EDWARD
KING EDWARD. She is grown more fairer far since I came
          hither   25
Her voice more silver every word than other,
Her wit more fluent. What a strange discourse
Unfolded she, of David and his Scots?
'Even thus', quoth she, 'he spake', and then spoke broad,[4]
With epithets and accents of the Scot,   30
But somewhat better than the Scot could speak.
'And thus' quoth she—and answered then herself—
For who could speak like her? But she herself
Breathes from the wall an angel's note from heaven
Of sweet defiance to her barbarous foes.   35
When she would talk of peace, methinks her tongue
Commanded war to prison; when of war,
It wakened Caesar from his Roman grave
To hear war beautified by her discourse.
Wisdom is foolishness but in her tongue,   40
Beauty a slander but in her fair face;
There is no summer but in her cheerful looks,
Nor frosty winter but in her disdain.
I cannot blame the Scots that did besiege her,
For she is all the treasure of our land,   45
But call them cowards that they ran away,
Having so rich and fair a cause to stay.
—Art thou there, Lodowick? Give me ink and paper.
LODOWICK. I will, my liege.
KING EDWARD. And bid the lords hold on their play at chess,   50
For we will walk and meditate alone.
LODOWICK. I will, my sovereign.   [*Exit*
KING EDWARD. This fellow is well read in poetry,
And hath a lusty and persuasive spirit;
I will acquaint him with my passion,   55

---

[4] The Countess was mocking the 'broad' Scottish dialect.

Which he shall shadow with a veil of lawn,[5]
Through which the queen of beauty's queen shall see
Herself the ground* of my infirmity.
                    Enter LODOWICK
Hast thou pen, ink, and paper ready, Lodowick?
LODOWICK. Ready, my liege.   60
KING EDWARD. Then in the summer arbour* sit by me,
Make it our council house or cabinet:
Since green our thoughts,[6] green be the conventicle
Where we will ease us by disburd'ning them.
Now, Lod'wick, invocate some golden Muse   65
To bring thee hither an enchanted pen
That may for sighs set down true sighs indeed,
Talking of grief, to make thee ready groan;
And when thou writest of tears, encouch the word
Before and after with such sweet laments   70
That it may raise drops in a Tartar's eye,
And make a flint-heart Scythian pitiful—[7]
For so much moving hath a poet's pen.
Then, if thou be a poet, move thou so,
And be enrichèd by thy sovereign's love.   75
For if the touch of sweet concordant strings
Could force attendance in the ears of hell,[8]
How much more shall the strains of poets' wit
Beguile and ravish soft and human minds?
LODOWICK. To whom, my lord, shall I direct my style?[9]   80
KING EDWARD. To one that shames the fair and sots* the
     wise,
Whose body as an abstract* or a brief
Contains each general virtue in the world.
'Better than beautiful', thou must begin,
Devise for fair a fairer word than fair,[10]   85

---

⁵ To 'shadow' is to depict in writing or drawing; 'lawn' was a fine, almost transparent linen fabric.
⁶ 'Green' here has the connotations of 'growing', 'hopeful'.
⁷ The Tartars and Scythians were proverbially cruel and hard-hearted in the Renaissance.
⁸ The fable of Orpheus winning back Eurydice from Hades by arousing 'attendance' (sympathy) with his music.
⁹ Both *stilus* (pen), and discourse, address.
¹⁰ Cf. Marlowe, *1 Tamburlaine*, 5. 1. 135–6: 'Ah fair Zenocrate, divine Zenocrate, | Fair is too foul an epitheit for thee'.

And every ornament that thou wouldst praise
Fly it a pitch above the soar of praise.[11]
For flattery fear thou not to be convicted,
For, were thy admiration* ten times more,
Ten times ten thousand more the worth exceeds   90
Of that thou art to praise, thy praise's worth.
Begin; I will to contemplate the while.
—Forget not to set down how passionate,
How heart-sick, and how full of languishment*
Her beauty makes me.
LODOWICK.   Write I to a woman?   95
KING EDWARD. What beauty else could triumph over me?
Or who but women do our love-lays* greet?
What, thinkst thou I did bid thee praise a horse?[12]
LODOWICK. Of what condition or estate she is
'Twere requisite that I should know, my lord.   100
KING EDWARD. Of such estate[13] that hers is as a throne,
And my estate the footstool where she treads;
Then mayst thou judge what her condition is
By the proportion of her mightiness.
Write on, while I peruse her in my thoughts.   105
[. . .][14]
Her voice to music or the nightingale:
To music every summer-leaping swain
Compares his sun-burnt lover when she speaks—
And why should I speak of the nightingale?   110
The nightingale sings of adulterate wrong,[15]
And that compare[16] is too satirical,

---

[11] The common falconry metaphor, for the highest point to which a falcon can fly, becomes the first of several hyperboles. The King, while mocking the absurdities of love poets, exemplifies some of them himself.

[12] Cf. *Henry V*, 3. 7. 39 ff., where the Dauphin records that he 'once wrote a sonnet in praise of his horse, beginning "Wonder of nature"', to which Orleans sarcastically comments: 'I have heard a sonnet begin so to one's mistress'.

[13] Punning on 'estate' as status, royal pomp, and 'state' or condition.

[14] Editors suggest that one or more lines are missing here, in which the King considers the comparisons he might use for his mistress's beauty.

[15] Philomela was transformed into a nightingale after Tereus raped her; cf. Ovid, *Met.* 6. 455 ff.; and Shakespeare, *Lucrece* 1079–80, 1127 ff.

[16] I accept Melchiori's conjecture, taking 'compare' as a noun meaning 'comparison'. Cf. Sonnet 21. 5: 'Making a complement of proud compare', and 35. 6: 'Authorising thy trespass with compare'.

For sin, though sin, would not be so esteemed,
But rather virtue sin, sin virtue deemed.
Her hair, far softer than the silkworm's twist,   115
Like to a flattering glass doth make more fair
The yellow amber.—'Like a flattering glass'
Comes in too soon, for, writing of her eyes,
I'll say that like a glass they catch the sun,
And thence the hot reflection doth rebound   120
Against my breast, and burns my heart within.
Ah, what a world of descant makes my soul
Upon this voluntary ground[17] of love!
—Come, Lod'wick, hast thou turned thy ink to gold?
If not, write but in letters capital   125
My mistress' name, and it will gild[18] thy paper.
Read, lord, read!
Fill thou the empty hollows of mine ears[19]
With the sweet hearing of thy poetry.
LODOWICK. I have not to a period[20] brought her praise.   130
KING EDWARD. Her praise is as my love, both infinite,
Which apprehend such violent extremes
That they disdain an ending period.
Her beauty hath no match but my affection;*
Hers more than most, mine most and more than more;   135
Hers more to praise than tell the sea by drops—
Nay, more than drop, the massy earth by sands,[21]
And sand by sand print them in memory.
Then wherefore talk'st thou of a period
To that which craves unended admiration?   140
Read, let us hear!
LODOWICK. 'More fair and chaste than is the queen[22] of
    shades'—
KING EDWARD. That line hath two faults, gross and palpable.

[17] A metaphor from music, the descant being the melodic variations composed over a constant rhythmic pattern, while a 'voluntary' is music added to a vocal or instrumental piece at the will of the performer.
[18] The 'capital letters' in illuminated manuscripts were decorated with gold leaf.
[19] Cf. *Romeo and Juliet* 3. 5. 3: 'the fearful hollow of thine ear'.
[20] Full-stop, completed utterance. In the following speech Edward rejects all idea of boundaries to his love.
[21] Conventional expressions for something unlimited, counting the drops of water in the sea, or the grains of sand.
[22] Diana, goddess of chastity and the moon.

Compar'st thou her to the pale queen of night
Who, being set in dark, seems therefore light?[23]   145
What is she, when the sun lifts up his head,
But like a fading taper, dim and dead?
My love shall brave* the eye of heaven at noon
And, being unmasked, outshine the golden sun!
LODOWICK. What is the other fault, my sovereign lord?   150
KING EDWARD. Read o'er the line again.
LODOWICK.   'More fair and chaste'—
KING EDWARD. I did not bid thee talk of chastity,
To ransack so the treasure of her mind,
For I had rather have her chased than chaste.[24]
Out with the moon line, I will none of it,   155
And let me have her likened to the sun.[25]
Say she hath thrice more splendour than the sun,
That her perfections emulates the sun,
That she breeds sweets as plenteous as the sun,
That she doth thaw cold winter like the sun,   160
That she doth cheer fresh summer like the sun,
That she doth dazzle gazers like the sun,
And in this application to the sun
Bid her be free and general as the sun,
Who smiles upon the basest weed that grows   165
As lovingly as on the fragrant rose.[26]
—Let's see what follows that same moonlight line.
LODOWICK. 'More fair and chaste than is the queen of
    shades,
More bold in constancy'—
KING EDWARD. In constancy than who?
LODOWICK.   —'than Judith was'.[27]   170
KING EDWARD. O monstrous line! Put in the next a sword

---

[23] Possibly punning on 'light', fickle, unsteady.

[24] The pun on 'chased' and 'chaste' recurs in *Lucrece* 1834–6.

[25] Nine successive lines ending with the same word, 'sun', exemplify the figure *epistrophe*: cf. Puttenham, pp. 254–5, Hoskyns, p. 406, and *Richard III*, 1. 1. 55–8. Cf. Sonnet 130: 'My mistress' eyes are nothing like the sun'.

[26] For these two metaphors cf. Sonnet 94. 12: 'The basest weed outbraves his dignity' and 95. 2: 'like a canker in the fragrant rose'. The concluding line from Sonnet 94, 'Lilies that fester smell far worse than weeds', recurs later in this scene (*Edward III*, 2. 1. 452). See *The Sonnets*, ed. G. B. Evans (Cambridge, 1996), p. 202.

[27] For Judith, the Jewish heroine who slew the Assyrian general Holofernes, see the Apocryphal book Judith 13: 6–8.

And I shall woo her to cut off my head!
Blot, blot, good Lod'wick! Let us hear the next.
LODOWICK. There's all that yet is done.
KING EDWARD. I thank thee then: thou hast done little ill—   175
But what is done is passing passing ill.[28]
No, let the captain talk of boist'rous war,
The prisoner of immurèd dark constraint;
The sick man best sets down the pangs of death,
The man that starves the sweetness of a feast,   180
The frozen soul the benefit of fire,
And every grief his happy opposite.
Love cannot sound well but in lovers' tongues.[29]
Give me the pen and paper, I will write.

---

[28] An apparent compliment that becomes a criticism: 'You have written little, but exceedingly badly'.
[29] Cf. *Romeo and Juliet* 2. 2. 165: 'How silver-sweet sound lovers' tongues'. The King
contradicts himself, first arguing that a passion is best 'set down' (expressed in writing) by
one who feels it (177–9, 183), then affirming the 'opposite' (180–2). Cf. Orsino, *Twelfth
Night* 2. 4. 32–5, 93–103.

14

Gabriel Harvey,
In praise of Sidney's *Arcadia* (1593)

GABRIEL HARVEY (*c*.1550–1630/1) was educated at Christ's College Cambridge (BA, 1570), and at Pembroke Hall (MA, 1573), where he became a Fellow and made the acquaintance of Spenser. Harvey moved to Trinity Hall in 1578, and was junior proctor in 1583. He became known for his lectures on rhetoric, publishing in 1577 two Latin orations, *Rhetor* and *Ciceronianus* (the latter ed. and tr. H. S. Wilson and C. A. Forbes (Lincoln, Nebr., 1945)). In 1586 he received an Oxford degree as Doctor of Civil and Canon Laws, leaving Cambridge a few years later to practise in the Court of Arches, London (the highest of the ecclesiastical courts). Having failed to make a career in London, in 1593 he returned home to Saffron Walden, where he lapsed into a long obscurity. In 1592–3 (and perhaps subsequently) he was involved in a long polemic with Robert Greene (1560?–92) and then with Thomas Nashe (1567–1601). See also G. C. Moore Smith (ed.), *Gabriel Harvey's Marginalia* (Stratford-upon-Avon, 1913); V. F. Stern, *Gabriel Harvey. His Life, Marginalia and Library* (Oxford, 1979).

TEXT. From *Pierce's Supererogation or a New Prayse of the Old Asse. A Preparative to certaine Discourses, intituled Nashes S. Fame* (London, 1593). This exuberant, tasteless, verbose pamphlet formed part of Harvey's long-winded quarrel with Nashe, which ended when the Bishop of London issued an order on 1 June 1599 stipulating that 'all Nashes and Doctor Harvyes bookes be taken wheresoever they maye be found and that none of their bookes bee ever printed hereafter'. Harvey seldom focuses on any topic for long, which makes this encomium to the *Arcadia* (published 1590) more noteworthy. Cf. also Hoskyns, p. 398.

What should I speak of the two brave knights, Musidorus and Pyrocles, combined in one excellent knight, Sir Philip Sidney, at the remembrance[1] of whose worthy and sweet virtues my heart melteth? Will you needs have a written *Palace of Pleasure*,[2] or rather a printed *Court of Honour*? Read *The Countess of Pembroke's Arcadia*, a gallant

---

[1] Sidney's premature death in 1586 produced a huge number of poetical tributes.
[2] William Painter's popular compilation of one hundred classical anecdotes and *novelle*, from Italian and French, *The Palace of Pleasure*, was published between 1566 and 1580.

legendary,* full of pleasurable accidents* and profitable discourses; for three things especially very notable—for amorous courting (he was young in years), for sage counselling (he was ripe in judgement), and for valorous fighting (his sovereign profession was arms); and delightful pastime by way of pastoral exercises may pass for the fourth. He that will love, let him learn to love of him that will teach him to live, and furnish him with many pithy and effectual instructions, delectably interlaced by way of proper descriptions of excellent personages and common narrations of other notable occurrences, in the vein of Sallust, Livy, Cornelius Tacitus, Justin, Eutropius,[3] Philip de Comines, Guicciardini, and the most sententious* historians that have powdered their style with the salt of discretion, and seasoned their judgement with the leaven of experience. There want not some subtle stratagems of importance, and some politic secrets of privity;* and he that would skilfully and bravely manage his weapon with a cunning fury may find lively precepts in the gallant examples of his valiantest duellists; especially of Palladius and Daiphantus, Zelmane and Amphialus, Phalantus and Amphialus, but chiefly of Argalus and Amphialus, Pyrocles and Anaxius, Musidorus and Amphialus, whose lusty combats may seem heroical monomachies.*

And that the valour of such redoubted men may appear the more conspicuous and admirable by comparison and interview* of their contraries, smile at the ridiculous encounters of Dametas and Dorus, of Dametas and Clinias; and ever when you think upon Dametas, remember the confuting champion, more surquidrous* than Anaxius, and more absurd than Dametas; and if I should always hereafter call him Dametas, I should fit him with a name as naturally proper unto him as his own. Gallant gentlemen, you that honour virtue and would enkindle a noble courage in your minds to every excellent purpose, if Homer be not at hand (whom I have often termed the prince of poets and the poet of princes), you may read his furious *Iliads* and cunning *Odysseys* in the brave adventures of Pyrocles and Musidorus; where Pyrocles playeth the doughty fighter, like Hector or Achilles, Musidorus the valiant captain, like Pandarus or Diomedes, both the famous errant knights, like Aeneas or Ulysses.

Lord, what would himself have proved *in fine*,[4] that was the gentle-

---

[3] This list of historians includes two unusual names: Justin Martyr (*c.* AD 100–*c.*156), author of an *Apologia* for Christianity, to whom several works were falsely attributed (see also p. 359, n. 69); and Eutropius (d. *c.* AD 370), secretary to the Emperor Constantine, who wrote a *Breviarium Historiae Romanae*, probably intended for use in schools.

[4] 'Finally; at last.'

man of courtesy, the esquire of industry, and the knight of valour at those years? Live ever sweet book, the silver image of his gentle wit, and the golden pillar of his noble courage, and ever notify unto the world, that your writer was the secretary of eloquence, the breath of the muses, the honey-bee of the daintiest flowers of wit and art, the pith of moral and intellectual virtues, the arm of Bellona in the field, the tongue of Suada[5] in the chamber, the spirit of practice *in esse*,[6] and the paragon of excellency in print. . . .

[5] Bellona was the Roman goddess of war; Suada (the Latin equivalent of Peitho) the goddess of Persuasion.
[6] 'In existence'—as opposed to *in posse*, in potentiality.

Sir Philip Sidney,
A defence of poetry (1595)

SIR PHILIP SIDNEY (1554–86), soldier, statesman, and poet; educated at Shrewsbury School (along with Fulke Greville, who subsequently wrote his biography), and Christ Church Oxford (between 1567 and 1571). He travelled extensively in Europe between 1572 and 1575, forming a significant friendship with the Dutch humanist Hubert Languet. In 1577 he was entrusted with diplomatic missions to the Elector Palatine and the Emperor Rudolf II (1577). He gained favour with Queen Elizabeth, but lost it for tactless behaviour. Together with Edward Dyer and Thomas Drant, he discussed and experimented with the use of classical metres in English verse, and became friends with Spenser, who dedicated *The Shepheardes Calendar* to him. He took part in military actions in the Low Countries in 1585–6, receiving a thigh wound at the battle of Zutphen on 22 Sept. 1586, which became infected and caused his untimely death. Over 200 poetic memorials to him appeared. In between his public activities he lived mostly at Wilton in Wiltshire, the house of his sister Mary Herbert, Countess of Pembroke, herself an accomplished poet. As befitted an aristocrat and non-professional writer, none of his works appeared publicly during his lifetime, and several were only published to discredit an illicit text, such as the unauthorized *Astrophel and Stella* (1591). Sidney's works are difficult to date, but it seems as if the first version of his great prose romance, *The Countess of Pembroke's Arcadia*, was written between 1577 and 1580; the unfinished revision (as *The New Arcadia*) between 1583 and 1585; *Astrophel and Stella* in 1581–2; and the *Defence of Poetry* in 1580–1.

TEXT. Two versions of Sidney's *Defence* were published in 1595: the first, by William Ponsonby, the established printer of Sidney's literary remains, as *The Defence of Poesie*; the second, by Henry Olney, as *An Apologie for Poetrie*. Ponsonby's text has the greater authority, but was carelessly printed. Olney's unauthorized version was edited and printed with great care, but was withdrawn once he discovered that Ponsonby had already registered his rights to the work; some composite copies exist. There are also two manuscript copies, one from Penshurst Place (the De L'Isle MS), which had belonged to Robert Sidney, and one in the Norfolk Record Office, Norwich. The most thorough evaluation of these four texts was made by Jan van Dorsten for his edition of the *Defence* in the *Miscellaneous Prose of Sir Philip Sidney*, ed. Katherine

Duncan-Jones and Jan van Dorsten (Oxford, 1973), with whose textual judgements I mostly concur. I have also benefited from the edition by Geoffrey
K. Shepherd, *An Apology for Poetry or The Defence of Poesy* (London, 1965;
Manchester, 1973), with remarkably full annotation, a mine of information
which everyone interested in Renaissance literary theory should use. These
editions are abbreviated in the following notes as *JVD*, *GKS*.

[EXORDIUM]

When the right virtuous Edward Wotton[1] and I were at the Emperor's
court together, we gave ourselves to learn horsemanship of John Pietro
Pugliano, one that with great commendation had the place of an
esquire in his stable. And he, according to the fertileness of the Italian
wit, did not only afford us the demonstration of his practice,* but
sought to enrich our minds with the contemplations* therein which
he thought most precious. But with none I remember mine ears were
at any time more loaden, than when (either angered with slow
payment, or moved with our learner-like admiration) he exercised his
speech in the praise of his faculty.* He said soldiers were the noblest
estate of mankind, and horsemen the noblest of soldiers. He said they
were the masters of war and ornaments of peace, speedy goers and
strong abiders, triumphers both in camps and courts. Nay, to so unbe-
lieved a point he proceeded, as that no earthly thing bred such wonder
to a prince as to be a good horseman. Skill of government was but
a *pedanteria* in comparison. Then would he add certain praises,
by telling what a peerless beast the horse was, the only serviceable
courtier without flattery, the beast of most beauty, faithfulness,
courage, and such more, that if I had not been a piece of a logician[2]
before I came to him, I think he would have persuaded me to have
wished myself a horse. But thus much at least with his no few words
he drave into me, that self-love is better than any gilding to make that
seem gorgeous wherein ourselves be parties.

Wherein, if Pugliano's strong affection* and weak arguments will
not satisfy you, I will give you a nearer example of myself, who (I know

[1] Edward Wotton (1548–1626), courtier and diplomat, accompanied Sidney to the court
of Emperor Maximilian II at Vienna in the winter of 1574–5.

[2] A characteristic use of the 'modesty topos'. Sidney was celebrated for his skill in logic
at Oxford, it being recorded in 1569 how another student was 'called to dispute extempore
. . . with the matchless Sir Philip Sidney [aged 15] in the presence of the Earls of Leicester [his uncle], Warwick and divers other great personages' (cit. *JVD*, pp. 191–2). Sidney
uses logical processes at various points in the *Defence*.

not by what mischance) in these my not old years and idlest times having slipped into the title of a poet, am provoked to say something unto you in the defence of that my unelected* vocation, which if I handle with more good will than good reasons, bear with me, since the scholar is to be pardoned that followeth the steps of his master. And yet I must say that, as I have more just cause to make a pitiful defence of poor poetry,[3] which from almost the highest estimation of learning is fallen to be the laughing-stock of children, so have I need to bring some more available* proofs, since the former is by no man barred of his deserved credit, the silly* latter hath had even the names of philosophers used to the defacing of it, with great danger of civil war among the Muses.

[NARRATION]

And first, truly, to all them that, professing learning, inveigh against poetry, may justly be objected that they go very near to ungratefulness, to seek to deface that which, in the noblest nations and languages that are known, hath been the first light-giver to ignorance,[4] and first nurse, whose milk by little and little enabled them to feed afterwards of tougher knowledges. And will they now play the hedgehog that, being received into the den, drave out his host? Or rather the vipers, that with their birth kill their parents?[5] Let learned Greece in any of his manifold sciences* be able to show me one book before Musaeus, Homer, and Hesiod, all three nothing else but poets. Nay, let any history be brought that can say any writers were there before them, if they were not men of the same skill, as Orpheus, Linus,[6] and some other are named, who, having been the first of that country that made pens deliverers* of their knowledge to the posterity, may justly challenge* to be called their fathers in learning: for not only in time they had this priority (although in itself antiquity be venerable) but went before them, as causes to draw with their charming sweetness

---

[3] To bemoan the low status of poetry, compared to its past prestige, was a commonplace among its defenders: cf. Elyot, p. 64, E.K., p. 182, and Puttenham, p. 198ff.

[4] For other arguments that poets were the first philosophers and teachers, cf. Strabo, cit. p. 64 n. 32, Cicero, *Tusc.* 1. 1. 3, Puttenham, p. 196; Harington, p. 302.

[5] For these traditional instances of ingratitude cf. the Aesopic fable of the snake and the hedgehog, and Pliny, *Naturalis historia* 10. 82.

[6] Lists of the first poets were common in Renaissance literary treatises: cf. Scaliger, *Poetice* 1. 2, Puttenham, p. 197. For the metaphor of 'milk' cf. 1 Cor. 3: 2, Heb. 5: 12–14, 1 Pet. 2: 2; taken up by Erasmus and many others.

the wild untamed wits to an admiration of knowledge. So, as Amphion was said to move stones with his poetry to build Thebes, and Orpheus[7] to be listened to by beasts—indeed stony and beastly people—so among the Romans were Livius Andronicus, and Ennius.[8] So in the Italian language the first that made it aspire to be a treasure-house of science were the poets Dante, Boccaccio, and Petrarch. So in our English were Gower and Chaucer, after whom, encouraged and delighted with their excellent fore-going,* others have followed, to beautify our mother tongue, as well in the same kind as in other arts.

This did so notably show itself, that the philosophers of Greece[9] durst not a long time appear to the world but under the masks of poets. So Thales, Empedocles, and Parmenides sang their natural philosophy in verses; so did Pythagoras and Phocylides their moral counsels; so did Tyrtaeus in war matters, and Solon in matters of policy: or rather they, being poets, did exercise their delightful vein in those points of highest knowledge, which before them lay hid to the world. For that wise Solon was directly a poet it is manifest, having written in verse the notable fable of the Atlantic Island, which was continued by Plato.

And truly even Plato, whosoever well considereth shall find that in the body of his work, though the inside and strength were philosophy, the skin as it were and beauty depended most of poetry:[10] for all standeth upon* dialogues wherein he feigneth many honest burgesses of Athens to speak of such matters, that, if they had been set on the rack, they would never have confessed them; besides his poetical describing the circumstances of their meetings, as the well ordering of a banquet, the delicacy* of a walk, with interlacing* mere tales, as Gyges' Ring,[11] and others, which who knoweth not to be flowers of poetry did never walk into Apollo's garden.

And even historiographers (although their lips sound of things

---

[7] Amphion and Orpheus as examples of the power of poetry and music were coupled by Horace, *Ars P.* 391–403, and by many subsequent writers.

[8] Livius Andronicus (d. 204 BC), and Ennius (239–169 BC), author of the *Annales*, a verse history of Rome, are types of 'fathers in learning'.

[9] Henry Estienne had recently published a pioneering collection of verse ascribed to Greek philosophers, *Poesis philosophica* (1573), which included in its preface a number of statements in praise of poetry, on which Sidney draws (cf. *JVD*, pp. 187–8).

[10] Ever since Quintilian (*Inst.* 5. 11. 39; 10. 1. 81) it had been common to note the paradox that Plato, who condemned poetry, was really a poet.

[11] Cf. Plato, *Resp.* 2. 359 d–360d; Cicero, *Off.* 3. 9. 38.

done, and verity be written in their foreheads) have been glad to borrow both fashion* and perchance weight of the poets. So Herodotus[12] entitled his history by the name of the nine Muses; and both he and all the rest that followed him either stole or usurped of poetry their passionate describing of passions, the many particularities of battles, which no man could affirm, or, if that be denied me, long orations put in the mouths of great kings and captains, which it is certain they never pronounced.

So that truly neither philosopher nor historiographer could at the first have entered into the gates of popular judgements, if they had not taken a great passport* of poetry, which in all nations at this day, where learning flourisheth not, is plain to be seen; in all which they have some feeling of poetry.[13]

In Turkey, besides their law-giving divines, they have no other writers but poets. In our neighbour country Ireland, where truly learning goeth very bare, yet are their poets held in a devout reverence. Even among the most barbarous and simple Indians where no writing is, yet have they their poets who make and sing songs, which they call *areytos*,[14] both of their ancestors' deeds and praises of their gods—a sufficient probability that, if ever learning come among them, it must be by having their hard dull wits softened and sharpened with the sweet delights of poetry; for until they find a pleasure in the exercises of the mind, great promises of much knowledge will little persuade them that know not the fruits of knowledge. In Wales, the true remnant of the ancient Britons, as there are good authorities to show the long time they had poets, which they called bards, so through all the conquests of Romans, Saxons, Danes, and Normans, some of whom did seek to ruin all memory of learning from among them, yet do their poets even to this day last; so as it is not more notable in soon beginning than in long continuing.

But since the authors of most of our sciences were the Romans, and before them the Greeks, let us a little stand upon their authorities, but* even so far as to see what names they have given unto this now scorned skill.

---

[12] Alexandrian scholars divided the *History* of Herodotus into nine books, each named after a Muse.

[13] For the love of poetry among even savage and uncultivated peoples cf. Cicero, *Arch.* 9. 18–19; Spenser, p. 183; Puttenham, pp. 197–8.

[14] A ceremonial ring-dance accompanied by song, praising the deeds of ancestors. Sidney draws here on contemporary histories of the West Indies: cf. *GKS*, p. 150.

Among the Romans a poet was called *vates*, which is as much as a diviner, foreseer, or prophet,[15] as by his conjoined words *vaticinium* and *vaticinari* is manifest: so heavenly a title did that excellent people bestow upon this heart-ravishing knowledge. And so far were they carried into the admiration thereof, that they thought in the chanceable hitting upon any such verses great foretokens of their following fortunes were placed. Whereupon grew the word of *sortes Virgilianae*, when by sudden opening Virgil's book they lighted upon any verse of his making (as it is reported by many): whereof the histories of the emperors' lives are full, as of Albinus, the governor of our island, who in his childhood met with this verse,

Arma amens capio; nec sat rationis in armis;[16]

and in his age performed it: which, although it were a very vain and godless superstition, as also it was to think spirits were commanded by such verses—whereupon this word charms, derived of *carmina*, cometh—so yet serveth it to show the great reverence those wits were held in. And altogether not without ground, since both the oracles of Delphos and Sibylla's prophecies were wholly delivered in verses. For that same exquisite observing of number* and measure* in the words, and that high flying liberty of conceit* proper to the poet, did seem to have some divine force in it.

And may not I presume a little further, to show the reasonableness of this word *vates*, and say that the holy David's Psalms are a divine poem? If I do, I shall not do it without the testimony of great learned men, both ancient and modern. But even the name of Psalms will speak for me, which being interpreted, is nothing but songs;[17] then, that it is fully written in metre, as all learned hebricians* agree, although the rules be not yet fully found; lastly and principally, his handling his prophecy, which is merely* poetical. For what else is the awaking his musical instruments, the often and free changing of

[15] For poetry as prophecy cf. Elyot, p. 64; Puttenham, p. 192; and Harington (following Sidney), *ECE*, ii. 205. Sidney, like Puttenham, avoids any implication of 'divine fury' (p. 376; but see p. 390); for them both, writing poetry is a rational activity, demanding knowledge, planning, and control.

[16] Virgil, *Aen.* 2. 314: 'Frantic I seize arms; yet little purpose is there in arms . . .'. Sidney takes the anecdote of Albinus (governor of Britain and Emperor in the late 2nd cent. AD) from *Sex scriptores historiae Augustae*. The *sortes Virgilianae*, opening Virgil at random and applying that passage to contemporary affairs, goes back to imperial Roman times.

[17] 'What else is a Psalm but a holy and spiritual kind of composition for singing?': preface to part III of the (Protestant) Latin Bible by Junius and Tremellius (cf. p. 345): cit. *GKS*, p. 151. Sidney and his sister Mary translated the Psalms into verse.

persons, his notable *prosopopoeias*,[18] when he maketh you, as it were, see God coming in His majesty, his telling of the beasts' joyfulness, and hills leaping, but a heavenly poesy,[19] wherein almost* he showeth himself a passionate lover of that unspeakable and everlasting beauty to be seen by the eyes of the mind, only cleared by faith? But truly now having named him, I fear me I seem to profane that holy name, applying it to poetry, which is among us thrown down to so ridiculous an estimation. But they that with quiet judgements will look a little deeper into it, shall find the end and working of it such as, being rightly applied, deserveth not to be scourged out of the church of God.

But now let us see how the Greeks named it, and how they deemed of it. The Greeks called him 'a poet', which name hath, as the most excellent, gone through other languages. It cometh of this word *poiein*, which is, 'to make':[20] wherein I know not whether by luck or wisdom, we Englishmen have met with the Greeks in calling him 'a maker': which name, how high and incomparable a title it is, I had rather were known by marking the scope of other sciences than by any partial allegation.[21]

There is no art delivered to mankind that hath not the works of nature[22] for his principal object, without which they could not consist, and on which they so depend, as they become actors and players, as it were, of what nature will have set forth. So doth the astronomer look upon the stars, and, by that he seeth, set down what order nature hath taken therein. So do the geometrician and arithmetician in their diverse sorts of quantities. So do the musicians in times[23] tell you which by nature agree, which not. The natural philosopher thereon hath his name, and the moral philosopher standeth upon the natural

---

[18] Cf. Ps. 114: 4, 'The mountains skipped like rams, and the little hills like lambs'. For these stylistic qualities, cf. Psalm 57: 9 for invocations; Ps. 2 for the interchange of voices; and Ps. 50 for other personages as speakers. For *prosopopoeia*, cf. Puttenham, p. 275.

[19] Sidney generally distinguishes between 'poesy', the poet's 'skill or craft of making', as Ben Jonson defined it (p. 582), and 'poetry', signifying the product of that art.

[20] Sidney draws on Scaliger, *Poetice* 1. 1; as does Puttenham, p. 191.

[21] 'I will show the excellence of poetry by comparing it to other disciplines rather than by a prejudiced assertion.' Professing impartiality is, of course, an ancient rhetorical ploy.

[22] For this fundamental Aristotelian principle cf. *Physica* 2. 2. 194ª12 ff.; Scaliger, *Poetice* 1. 1; Puttenham, p. 292.

[23] Both printed texts read 'times', that is, 'units of time (especially in music)'. Van Dorsten, however, prefers 'time', the reading of the De L'Isle MS. For this concept in Renaissance music theory, see (e.g.) Thomas Morley, *A Plain & Easy Introduction to Practical Music* (1597), ed. R. A. Harman and T. Dart (London, 1952; New York, 1973), pp. 22 ff.

virtues, vices, or passions of man; and 'follow Nature'[24] (saith he) 'therein, and thou shalt not err'. The lawyer saith what men have determined;* the historian what men have done. The grammarian speaketh only of the rules of speech; and the rhetorician and logician, considering what in nature will soonest prove and persuade, thereon give artificial* rules, which still are compassed within the circle of a question according to the proposed matter.[25] The physician weigheth the nature of man's body, and the nature of things helpful or hurtful unto it. And the metaphysic,* though it be in the second and abstract notions, and therefore be counted supernatural, yet doth he indeed build upon the depth of nature.[26]

Only the poet, disdaining to be tied to any such subjection, lifted up with the vigour of his own invention, doth grow in effect another nature,[27] in making things either better than nature bringeth forth, or, quite anew, forms such as never were in Nature, as the Heroes, Demigods, Cyclops, Chimeras, Furies, and such like: so as he goeth hand in hand with Nature, not enclosed within the narrow warrant of her gifts, but freely ranging only within the zodiac* of his own wit. Nature never set forth the earth in so rich tapestry as divers poets have done; neither with so pleasant rivers, fruitful trees, sweet-smelling flowers, nor whatsoever else may make the too much loved earth more lovely. Her world is brazen, the poets only deliver a golden.[28]

But let those things alone, and go to man—for whom as the other things are, so it seemeth in him her uttermost cunning is employed— and know whether she have brought forth so true a lover as Theagenes, so constant a friend as Pylades, so valiant a man as Orlando, so right a prince as Xenophon's Cyrus, so excellent a man every way as Virgil's Aeneas.[29]

---

[24] Cf. Cicero, *Off.* 1. 28. 10.

[25] These rules are limited according to the questions they address.

[26] That is, although these notions are 'extranatural', outside the physical world, metaphysics still derives its first principles from empirical reality, so in that sense also builds on nature.

[27] Sidney is still drawing on the opening chapter of Scaliger's *Poetice*, which argues that poetry embraces all the activities of philosophy and oratory, 'and as a result it is more outstanding than other arts because all other verbal arts reproduce things as they are, as a sort of picture for the ear, but the poet produces another nature altogether, and in this process even makes himself almost into another god' (tr. *GKS*, p. 155). *JVD* (pp. 189–90) sees here a Christian Platonist argument.

[28] Only poetry can create a golden world, that of ideal perfection, as opposed to the imperfections of reality.

[29] In classical and Renaissance literary theory writers were praised for creating heroic figures who exemplified particular virtues. Theagenes is the lover of Chariclea in the

Neither let this be jestingly conceived, because the works of the one be essential,* the other in imitation or fiction; for any understanding knoweth the skill of each artificer standeth in that *idea* or fore-conceit[30] of the work, and not in the work itself. And that the poet hath that *idea* is manifest, by delivering them forth in such excellency as he hath imagined them. Which delivering forth also is not wholly imaginative,* as we are wont to say by them that build castles in the air; but so far substantially it worketh, not only to make a Cyrus, which had been but a particular excellency as Nature might have done, but to bestow a Cyrus upon the world to make many Cyruses,[31] if they will learn aright why and how that maker made him.

Neither let it be deemed too saucy a comparison to balance the highest point of man's wit with the efficacy of nature; but rather give right honour to the heavenly Maker of that maker, who having made man to His own likeness, set him beyond and over all the works of that second nature: which in nothing he showeth so much as in poetry, when with the force of a divine breath he bringeth things forth—surpassing her doings with no small arguments to the credulous of that first accursed fall of Adam: since our erected wit maketh us know what perfection is, and yet our infected will[32] keepeth us from reaching unto it. But these arguments will by few be understood, and by fewer granted. This much (I hope) will be given me, that the Greeks with some probability of reason gave him the name above all names of learning.

Now let us go to a more ordinary opening* of him, that the truth may be the more palpable: and so I hope, though we get not so unmatched a praise as the etymology of his names will grant, yet his very description, which no man will deny, shall not justly be barred from a principal commendation.

Aethiopica, the Greek prose romance by Heliodorus (4th cent. AD), which was extremely popular in the Renaissance, and identified by John Hoskyns (p. 421) as one of Sidney's models for *Arcadia*. Pylades, in Greek tragedy, assists Orestes in avenging his father's murder. Orlando is the hero of a succession of Italian epics, culminating in Ariosto's *Orlando Furioso* (see Harington, p. 302). Cyrus (whom Sidney refers to eight times) is the hero of Xenophon's *Cyropaedia* (4th cent. BC), a fictionalized biography much admired in the Renaissance. Virgil's Aeneas was often taken as embodying all the virtues.

[30] In Platonic philosophy the idea is the abstract form preceding creation. Cf. (e.g.) *Phaedo* 73–8, *Timaeus* 30 ff., *Phdr.* 249c ff., *Symposium* 211.

[31] Readers of an exemplary fiction, such as the *Cyropaedia*, will be moved to emulate its hero's virtues in their own lives. Cf. Elyot, pp. 57–8, Spenser, pp. 298–9, Jonson, pp. 469–70, Milton, pp. 602–3, and Hobbes, pp. 618–19.

[32] Man walks upright ('erected') as God created him, but his will has become 'infected' or corrupted by the Fall. *GKS* (p. 159) cites relevant passages from Calvin.

[PROPOSITION]

Poesy therefore is an art of imitation, for so Aristotle termeth it in his word *mimēsis*, that is to say, a representing, counterfeiting, or figuring forth—to speak metaphorically, a speaking picture—with this end, to teach and delight.[33]

[DIVISION]

Of this have been three general kinds. The chief, both in antiquity and excellency, were they that did imitate the inconceivable excellencies of God. Such were David in his Psalms; Solomon in his Song of Songs, in his Ecclesiastes, and Proverbs; Moses and Deborah in their Hymns; and the writer of Job: which, beside other, the learned Emanuel Tremellius and Franciscus Junius[34] do entitle the poetical part of the Scripture. Against these none will speak that hath the Holy Ghost in due holy reverence. In this kind, though in a full wrong divinity, were Orpheus, Amphion, Homer in his Hymns, and many other, both Greeks and Romans. And this poesy must be used by whosoever will follow St. James's counsel[35] in singing psalms when they are merry, and I know is used with the fruit of comfort by some, when, in sorrowful pangs of their death-bringing sins, they find the consolation of the never-leaving goodness.

The second kind is of them that deal with matters philosophical: either moral, as Tyrtaeus, Phocylides, Cato; or natural, as Lucretius and Virgil's *Georgics*; or astronomical, as Manilius and Pontanus;[36] or historical, as Lucan: which who mislike, the fault is in their judgement quite out of taste, and not in the sweet food of sweetly uttered knowledge.

But because this second sort is wrapped within the fold of the

---

[33] Sidney's definition blends three elements: cf. Introduction, p. 16. Although he could have derived it from several sources, Sidney seems to draw on Scaliger, *Poetice* 1. 1; his following classification of the kinds of poetry comes from ibid. 1. 2.

[34] Tremellius (1510–80), a great Oriental scholar, worked with the French theologian Junius (1545–1602), to produce the influential Protestant Latin translation of the Bible, *Testamenta Veteris Biblia Sacra*, etc. (Frankfurt am Main, 1575–9; 18 editions in England between 1579 and 1640). Tremellius' New Testament, dedicated to Queen Elizabeth, had been published by Estienne in 1569.

[35] James 5: 13.

[36] Manilius (1st cent. AD) wrote *Astronomica*, a poem about the heavens; Giovanni Pontano (1426–1503) wrote a neo-Latin poem, *Urania*, on the stars, which Scaliger praised highly (*Poetice* 6. 4).

proposed subject, and takes not the free course of his own invention,[37] whether they properly be poets or no let grammarians dispute, and go to the third, indeed right* poets, of whom chiefly this question ariseth. Betwixt whom and these second is such a kind of difference as betwixt the meaner sort of painters, who counterfeit only such faces as are set before them, and the more excellent, who having no law but wit,* bestow that in colours upon you which is fittest for the eye to see:[38] as the constant though lamenting look of Lucretia, when she punished in herself another's fault; wherein he painteth not Lucretia whom he never saw, but painteth the outward beauty of such a virtue. For these third be they which most properly do imitate to teach and delight, and to imitate borrow nothing of what is, hath been, or shall be; but range, only reined with learned discretion,* into the divine consideration of what may be and should be.[39] These be they that, as the first and most noble sort may justly be termed *vates*, so these are waited* on in the excellentest languages and best understandings, with the foredescribed name of poets; for these indeed do merely make, to imitate, and imitate, both to delight and teach; and delight, to move[40] men to take that goodness in hand, which without delight they would fly as from a stranger; and teach, to make them know that goodness whereunto they are moved: which being the noblest scope* to which ever any learning was directed, yet want there not idle tongues to bark at them.

These be subdivided into sundry more special denominations.[41] The most notable be the Heroic, Lyric, Tragic, Comic, Satiric, Iambic, Elegiac, Pastoral, and certain others, some of these being termed according to the matter they deal with, some by the sorts of verses they liked best to write in; for indeed the greatest part of poets have apparelled their poetical inventions in that numbrous* kind of

[37] That is, both philosophical and historical poets are limited by their subject-matter and their aims; 'right' or true poets are free to invent their own material.

[38] Cf. Aristotle, *Poet.* 15. 1454^{b}8 ff., and *GKS*, pp. 48–50, 162.

[39] Cf. Aristotle, *Poet.* 9. 1451^{a}36 ff.

[40] Sidney reiterates the orator's three main tasks, *movere, docere, delectare*. A major part of his justification for poetry rests on its efficacy, conceived in the same terms as rhetoric, to persuade its readers to follow goodness and shun evil. Cf. also pp. 357–8, 361–6 for reiteration of this point.

[41] Sidney's eclectic list of the main literary genres follows classical models, such as Horace (*Ars P.* 70–98) and Quintilian (10. 1. 85–100), but adding pastoral, which was a new genre in the Renaissance (cf. Scaliger, *Poetice* 1. 4). He combines a classification by subject-matter with one from verse-form—hence 'iambic' as a kind (see pp. 361–2).

writing which is called verse—indeed but apparelled, verse being but an ornament and no cause to Poetry,[42] since there have been many most excellent poets that never versified, and now swarm many versifiers that need never answer to the name of poets. For Xenophon, who did imitate so excellently as to give us *effigiem justi imperii*, 'the portraiture of a just empire', under the name of Cyrus (as Cicero[43] saith of him), made therein an absolute* heroical poem. So did Heliodorus in his sugared* invention of that picture of love in Theagenes and Chariclea; and yet both these writ in prose: which I speak to show that it is not rhyming and versing that maketh a poet—no more than a long gown maketh an advocate, who though he pleaded in armour should be an advocate and no soldier. But it is that feigning notable images of virtues, vices, or what else, with that delightful teaching, which must be the right describing note* to know a poet by, although indeed the senate of poets hath chosen verse as their fittest raiment, meaning, as in matter they passed all in all,[44] so in manner to go beyond them: not speaking (table-talk fashion or like men in a dream) words as they chanceably fall from the mouth, but peising* each syllable of each word by just proportion according to the dignity of the subject.

Now therefore it shall not be amiss first to weigh this latter sort of poetry by his works, and then by his parts, and if in neither of these anatomies* he be condemnable, I hope we shall obtain a more favourable sentence.*

[CONFIRMATION OR PROOF]

This purifying of wit, this enriching of memory, enabling* of judgement, and enlarging of conceit,[45] which commonly we call learning, under what name soever it come forth, or to what immediate end soever it be directed, the final end is to lead and draw us to as high a

---

[42] Cf. Aristotle, *Poet.* 9. 1451ᵃ37 ff., and Elyot, p. 64.

[43] *QFr.* 1. 1. 8: 'The Cyrus by Xenophon is not drawn according to historical accuracy but in the likeness of a model ruler, in whom the writer associates supreme dignity with outstanding friendliness. In it nothing is omitted which has to do with the office of a loving and tempered ruler.' Cf. Spenser, p. 299.

[44] 'As they surpassed all others in all respects.'

[45] Sidney casually itemizes the mental faculties: 'wit', the intellect or understanding (*intellectus*), which presides over memory (the passive storing of knowledge), judgement (*ratio*, intellectual evaluation), and conceit (here, the activity of the mind in forming notions about things). Cf. *GKS*, p. 166, *JVD*, p. 192, and E. Ruth Harvey, *The Inward Wits: Psychological Theory in the Middle Ages and the Renaissance* (London, 1975).

perfection as our degenerate souls, made worse by their clayey lodg-ings,[46] can be capable of.

This, according to the inclination of the man, bred many formed impressions. For some that thought this felicity principally to be gotten by knowledge, and no knowledge to be so high and heavenly as acquaintance with the stars, gave themselves to astronomy; others, persuading themselves to be demi-gods if they knew the causes of things,[47] became natural and supernatural philosophers; some an admirable delight drew to music; and some the certainty of demon-stration to the mathematics. But all, one and other, having this scope— to know, and by knowledge to lift up the mind from the dungeon of the body to the enjoying his own divine essence.*

But when by the balance of experience it was found that the astronomer looking to the stars might fall into a ditch, that the inquir-ing philosopher might be blind in himself, and the mathematician[48] might draw forth a straight line with a crooked heart, then lo, did proof, the overruler of opinions, make manifest that all these are but serving sciences, which, as they have each a private end in themselves, so yet are they all directed to the highest end of the mistress-knowledge, by the Greeks called *architektonikē*, which stands (as I think) in the knowledge of a man's self, in the ethic and politic consideration, with the end of well-doing and not of well-knowing[49] only: even as the saddler's next* end is to make a good saddle, but his farther end to serve a nobler faculty, which is horsemanship; so the

---

[46] A Christian version of the Platonic idea (*Phaedo* 82–3) that philosophic knowledge will enable man to overcome imprisonment in the flesh; cf. Milton, p. 600.

[47] Cf. Virgil, *Georg.* 2. 490–2: 'Felix qui potuit rerum cognoscere causas': 'Blessed is he who has been able to win knowledge of the causes of things'.

[48] Cf. Plato, *Theaetetus* 174a for the often-repeated story of the astronomer Thales 'when he was looking up to study the stars and tumbled down a well', which Socrates cites to show that 'anyone who gives his life to philosophy is open to such mockery'; and Seneca, *Ep.* 88. 13: 'You know what a straight line is; but how does it benefit you if you do not know what is straight in this life of ours?'

[49] Sidney summarizes the argument of Aristotle, *Eth. Nic.* 1. 1. 1094ᵃ3–17, which dis-tinguishes the ends or goals of the 'master arts' ('the end of the medical art is health, that of shipbuilding a vessel, that of strategy victory') from the 'subordinate ends' ('as bridle-making and the other arts concerned with the equipment of horses fall under the art of riding, and this and every military action under strategy'), declaring the former more impor-tant. But Aristotle nowhere mentions poetry in this discussion, nor does he rank 'well-doing' above 'well-knowing': indeed, the concluding position of his treatise is that the philoso-pher's contemplative life is to be preferred before the politician's active life. Here, as else-where, Sidney adapts classical concepts and categories to different Renaissance priorities, notably the superiority of the *vita activa*, life directed towards the good of the whole com-munity, over contemplation, seen as self-directed.

horseman's to soldiery, and the soldier not only to have the skill, but to perform the practice of a soldier. So that, the ending end of all earthly learning being virtuous action, those skills, that most serve to bring forth that, have a most just title to be princes over all the rest.

Wherein if we can, show we the poet's nobleness, by setting him before his other competitors, among whom as principal challengers step forth the moral philosophers, whom, me thinketh, I see coming towards me with a sullen gravity, as though they could not abide vice by daylight, rudely clothed for to witness outwardly their contempt of outward things, with books in their hands against glory, whereto they set their names,[50] sophistically speaking against subtlety,* and angry with any man in whom they see the foul fault of anger. These men casting largesse as they go of definitions, divisions, and distinctions, with a scornful interrogative do soberly ask whether it be possible to find any path so ready to lead a man to virtue as that which teacheth what virtue is—and teacheth it not only by delivering forth his very being, his causes, and effects, but also by making known his enemy, vice, which must be destroyed, and his cumbersome* servant, passion, which must be mastered, by showing the generalities that containeth it, and the specialities* that are derived from it; lastly, by plain setting down, how it extendeth itself out of the limits of a man's own little world to the government of families, and maintaining of public societies.

The historian scarcely giveth leisure to the moralist to say so much, but that he, loaden with old mouse-eaten records,[51] authorising himself (for the most part) upon other histories, whose greatest authorities are built upon the notable foundation of hearsay; having much ado to accord* differing writers and to pick truth out of partiality; better acquainted with a thousand years ago than with the present age, and yet better knowing how this world goeth than how

---

[50] Cf. Cicero, *Tusc.* 1. 15. 34, and *Arch.* 11. 26: 'These same philosophers set their own names even upon the books in which they condemn the pursuit of glory'. The reproof was widely quoted, e.g. by Bacon, *Essay* 'Of Vain-Glory'. Sidney's mockery of moral philosophy (in defence of poetry) extends from the technicalities of argument, which he himself had mastered, to major treatises on society, such as Plato's *Republic*, which he otherwise admired.

[51] Sidney's mocking account of the deficiencies of history is not, of course, his considered judgement, which was otherwise favourable: see e.g. his letter of 15 Oct. 1580 to his younger brother Robert, on how to study history: *Works*, ed. A Feuillerat (Cambridge, 1912; 1963), iii. 130–2. This temporary devaluing of history is the inevitable consequence of his choosing the mode of epideictic rhetoric, in which he can praise poetry and dispraise the other arts. One piquant detail is that in praising poetry at the expense of history he picks up and reverses the arguments for the superiority of history used by Jacques Amyot in the preface to his translation of Plutarch's *Parallel Lives* (French edn., 1559; English tr., by Sir Thomas North, 1579).

his own wit runneth; curious for antiquities and inquisitive of novelties; a wonder to young folks and a tyrant in table talk, denieth, in a great chafe,* that any man for teaching of virtue, and virtuous actions is comparable to him. 'I am *testis temporum, lux veritatis, vita memoriae, magistra vitae, nuntia vetustatis.*[52] The philosopher', saith he, 'teacheth a disputative* virtue, but I do an active. His virtue is excellent in the dangerless Academy of Plato, but mine showeth forth her honourable face in the battles of Marathon, Pharsalia, Poitiers, and Agincourt. He teacheth virtue by certain abstract considerations, but I only bid you follow the footing of them that have gone before you. Old-aged experience goeth beyond the fine-witted philosopher, but I give the experience of many ages. Lastly, if he make the song-book, I put the learner's hand to the lute; and if he be the guide, I am the light.'

Then would he allege you innumerable examples, confirming story* by stories, how much the wisest senators and princes have been directed by the credit of history, as Brutus, Alphonsus of Aragon,[53] and who not, if need be? At length the long line of their disputation maketh a point* in this, that the one giveth the precept, and the other the example.[54]

Now whom shall we find (since the question standeth for the highest form in the school of learning) to be moderator?[55] Truly, as me seemeth, the poet; and if not a moderator, even the man that ought to carry the title from them both, and much more from all other serving sciences. Therefore compare we the poet with the historian and with the moral philosopher; and if he go beyond them both, no other human skill can match him. For as for the divine, with all reverence it is ever to be excepted, not only for having his scope as far beyond any of these as eternity exceedeth a moment, but even for passing each of these in themselves. And for the lawyer, though *Ius* be the daughter of justice, and justice the chief of virtues, yet because

---

[52] Cicero, *De or.* 2. 9. 36: 'History indeed is the witness of the ages, the light of truth, the life of memory, the governess of life, the herald of antiquity', a famous and much-quoted definition.

[53] In the preface to his Plutarch Amyot instances Alphonsus V of Aragon (1396–1458) as combining state duties with a love of history, having reportedly cured himself from sickness by reading about the deeds of Alexander the Great.

[54] This is one of Amyot's main claims for history's pre-eminence, which Sidney takes over only to subvert, here and later.

[55] That is, 'this question (or proposition) engages the top class' or highest form, and needs a skilled master to preside over the academic disputation. That Sidney would give this role to the poet, however, one of the parties to the dispute, is against all the rules.

he seeketh to make men good rather *formidine poenae* than *virtutis amore*;[56] or, to say righter, doth not endeavour to make men good, but that their evil hurt not others; having no care, so he be a good citizen, how bad a man he be: therefore as our wickedness maketh him necessary, and necessity maketh him honourable, so is he not in the deepest truth to stand in rank with these who all endeavour to take naughtiness* away and plant goodness even in the secretest cabinet* of our souls. And these four are all that any way deal in the consideration of men's manners,* which being the supreme knowledge, they that best breed it deserve the best commendation.

The philosopher therefore and the historian are they which would win the goal, the one by precept, the other by example. But both, not having both, do both halt.* For the philosopher, setting down with thorny argument the bare rule, is so hard of utterance and so misty to be conceived, that one that hath no other guide but him shall wade* in him till he be old before he shall find sufficient cause to be honest. For his knowledge standeth so upon the abstract and general, that happy is that man who may understand him, and more happy that can apply what he doth understand. On the other side, the historian, wanting* the precept, is so tied, not to what should be but to what is, to the particular truth of things and not to the general reason of things, that his example draweth no necessary consequence, and therefore a less fruitful doctrine.

Now doth the peerless poet perform both: for whatsoever the philosopher saith should be done, he giveth a perfect picture of it in some one by whom he presupposeth it was done, so as he coupleth the general notion with the particular example.[57] A perfect picture I say, for he yieldeth to the powers of the mind an image of that whereof the philosopher bestoweth but a wordish description, which doth neither strike, pierce, nor possess the sight of the soul[58] so much as that other doth. For as in outward things, to a man that had never seen an elephant or a rhinoceros, who should tell him most exquisitely* all their shapes, colour, bigness, and particular marks; or of a gorgeous

[56] Horace, *Epist.* 1. 16. 52–3: 'oderunt peccare boni virtutis amore: | tu nihil admittes in te formidine poenae' ('Good men hate to sin through love of virtue; but you will admit nothing in yourself from fear of punishment').

[57] Sidney's argument is tightly woven, picking up threads already established along with others yet to be fully introduced. This distinction between general and particular anticipates the later Aristotelian argument, p. 354 and n. 68.

[58] Many authorities made sight the most valuable of the senses: Plato, *Phdr.* 250d; Aristotle, *Metaph.* 1. 980ᵃ24 ff.; Horace, *Ars P.* 180–2; Cicero, *De or.* 3. 40. 160–1.

palace, an *architector*,* with declaring the full beauties might well make the hearer able to repeat, as it were by rote, all he had heard, yet should never satisfy his inward conceit with being witness to itself of a true lively knowledge; but the same man, as soon as he might see those beasts well painted, or that house well in model, should straightways grow, without need of any description, to a judicial* comprehending of them: so no doubt the philosopher with his learned definitions— be it of virtue or vices, matters of public policy or private government—replenisheth the memory with many infallible grounds of wisdom, which, notwithstanding, lie dark before the imaginative and judging power, if they be not illuminated or figured forth by the speaking picture[59] of poesy.

Tully[60] taketh much pains, and many times not without poetical helps, to make us know the force love of our country hath in us. Let us but hear old Anchises speaking in the midst of Troy's flames, or see Ulysses[61] in the fulness of all Calypso's delights bewail his absence from barren and beggarly Ithaca. Anger, the Stoics said, was a short madness: let but Sophocles bring you Ajax[62] on a stage, killing and whipping sheep and oxen, thinking them the army of Greeks, with their chieftains Agamemnon and Menelaus, and tell me if you have not a more familiar insight into anger than finding in the schoolmen his genus and difference. See whether wisdom and temperance in Ulysses and Diomedes, valour in Achilles, friendship in Nisus and Euryalus, even to an ignorant man carry not an apparent* shining;* and, contrarily, the remorse of conscience in Oedipus, the soon repenting pride of Agamemnon, the self-devouring cruelty in his father Atreus, the violence of ambition in the two Theban brothers, the sour-sweetness of revenge in Medea;[63] and, to fall lower, the Terentian Gnatho[64] and our Chaucer's Pandar so expressed that we now use their names to signify their trades; and finally, all virtues, vices, and passions so in their own natural states laid to the view, that we seem not to hear of them, but clearly to see through them.

---

[59] Cf. n. 33 above and Puttenham, p. 261.

[60] *Fin.* 3. 64; *De or.* 1. 44. 196; *Off.* 1. 17. 57 f., 1. 24. 83 f., etc.

[61] For Anchises, cf. *Aen.* 2. 638 ff.; for Ulysses, cf. *Od.* 5. 149 ff.

[62] Horace, *Epist.* 1. 2. 62: 'ira furor brevis est'; Seneca, *De ira,* 1. 1. However, in Sophocles' *Ajax* these effects of the hero's anger are not shown onstage.

[63] These characters are from Seneca's versions of Greek tragedy, *Oedipus, Agamemnon, Thyestes, Phoenissae* (on the brothers Eteocles and Polynices), and *Medea* (whose 'sour-sweet' revenge consisted of murdering her children in order to spite her unfaithful husband, Jason).

[64] In Terence, *Eunuchus*; often used as a type-name for a parasite.

But even in the most excellent determination* of goodness, what philosopher's counsel can so readily direct a prince, as the feigned Cyrus in Xenophon;[65] or a virtuous man in all fortunes, as Aeneas in Virgil; or a whole commonwealth, as the way of Sir Thomas More's *Utopia*? I say the way, because where Sir Thomas More erred, it was the fault of the man and not of the poet, for that way of patterning a commonwealth was most absolute,* though he perchance hath not so absolutely performed it. For the question is, whether the feigned image of poetry or the regular* instruction of philosophy hath the more force in teaching: wherein if the philosophers have more rightly showed themselves philosophers than the poets have obtained to the high top of their profession, as in truth,

> *mediocribus esse poetis,*
> *non dii, non homines, non concessere columnae;*[66]

it is, I say again, not the fault of the art, but that by few men that art can be accomplished.

Certainly, even our saviour Christ could as well have given the moral commonplaces of uncharitableness and humbleness as the divine narration of Dives and Lazarus; or of disobedience and mercy, as that heavenly discourse of the lost child and the gracious father;[67] but that His throughsearching wisdom knew the estate of Dives burning in hell, and of Lazarus being in Abraham's bosom, would more constantly (as it were) inhabit both the memory and judgement. Truly, for myself, meseems I see before my eyes the lost child's disdainful prodigality, turned to envy a swine's dinner: which by the learned divines are thought not historical acts,* but instructing parables.

For conclusion, I say the philosopher teacheth, but he teacheth obscurely, so as the learned only can understand him; that is to say, he teacheth them that are already taught. But the poet is the food for the tenderest stomachs, the poet is indeed the right popular philosopher, whereof Aesop's tales give good proof; whose pretty allegories, stealing under the formal* tales of beasts, make many, more beastly than beasts, begin to hear the sound of virtue from these dumb speakers.

But now may it be alleged that if this imagining of matters be so

---

[65] Cf. Spenser, p. 299.
[66] Horace, *Ars P.* 372–3: 'But neither men nor gods nor shop-fronts allow a poet to be mediocre' (*ALC*, p. 289).
[67] Respectively, Luke 16: 19–31, and 15: 11–32.

fit for the imagination, then must the historian needs surpass, who bringeth you images of true matters, such as indeed were done, and not such as fantastically or falsely may be suggested to have been done. Truly, Aristotle[68] himself, in his discourse of poesy, plainly determineth this question, saying that Poetry is *philosophōteron* and *spoudaioteron*, that is to say, it is more philosophical and more studiously serious than history. His reason is, because poesy dealeth with *katholou*, that is to say, with the universal consideration, and the history with *kathekaston*, the particular: 'now', saith he, 'the universal weighs what is fit to be said or done, either in likelihood or necessity (which the poesy considereth in his imposed names), and the particular only marks whether Alcibiades did, or suffered, this or that.' Thus far Aristotle: which reason of his (as all his) is most full of reason.

For indeed, if the question were whether it were better to have a particular act truly or falsely set down, there is no doubt which is to be chosen, no more than whether you had rather have Vespasian's picture right* as he was, or, at the painter's pleasure, nothing resembling. But if the question be for your own use and learning, whether it be better to have it set down as it should be, or as it was, then certainly is more doctrinable* the feigned Cyrus of Xenophon than the true Cyrus in Justin, and the feigned Aeneas in Virgil than the right Aeneas in Dares Phrygius:[69] as to a lady that desired to fashion her countenance to the best grace, a painter should more benefit her to portray a most sweet face, writing Canidia upon it, than to paint Canidia as she was, who, Horace[70] sweareth, was full ill favoured.

If the poet do his part aright, he will show you in Tantalus, Atreus, and such like, nothing that is not to be shunned; in Cyrus, Aeneas, Ulysses, each thing to be followed; where* the historian, bound to tell things as things were, cannot be liberal (without* he will be poetical) of a perfect pattern,[71] but, as in Alexander or Scipio himself, show doings, some to be liked, some to be misliked. And then how will you discern what to follow but by your own discretion, which you had

---

[68] *Poet.* 9. 1451^{b}4–11.

[69] The Christian writer Justin, in his *Histories* (English tr. by Arthur Golding, 1564), gives a brief account of Cyrus (bk. 1, chs. 4–8). Dares the Phrygian was the apocryphal author of a medieval history of the Trojan War.

[70] Horace, *Epodes* 5, gives a vivid account of the witch Canidia's attempts to regain her lost beauty.

[71] 'Does not have the freedom to create an idealizing fiction'.

without reading Quintus Curtius? And whereas a man may say, though in universal consideration of doctrine the poet prevaileth, yet that the history, in his saying such a thing was done, doth warrant a man more in that he shall follow[72]—the answer is manifest: that if he stand upon that *was*—as if he should argue, because it rained yesterday, therefore it should rain to-day—then indeed hath it some advantage to a gross conceit; but if he know an example only informs a conjectured likelihood, and so go by reason, the poet doth so far exceed him[73] as he is to frame his example to that which is most reasonable, be it in warlike, politic, or private matters; where the historian in his bare *was* hath many times that which we call fortune to overrule the best wisdom. Many times he must tell events whereof he can yield no cause; or, if he do, it must be poetically.

For that a feigned example hath as much force to teach as a true example (for as for to move, it is clear, since the feigned may be tuned to the highest key of passion),[74] let us take one example wherein an historian and a poet did concur. Herodotus and Justin[75] do both testify that Zopyrus, King Darius' faithful servant, seeing his master long resisted by the rebellious Babylonians, feigned himself in extreme disgrace of his king: for verifying of which, he caused his own nose and ears to be cut off, and so flying to the Babylonians, was received, and for his known valour so sure credited, that he did find means to deliver them over to Darius. Much like matter doth Livy record of Tarquinius and his son. Xenophon[76] excellently feigneth such another stratagem performed by Abradatas in Cyrus' behalf. Now would I fain know, if occasion be presented unto you to serve your prince by such an honest dissimulation, why you do not as well learn it of Xenophon's fiction as of the other's verity? And truly so much the better, as you shall save your nose by the bargain; for Abradatas did not counterfeit so far. So then the best of the historian is subject to the poet; for whatsoever action, or faction, whatsoever counsel, policy, or war stratagem the historian is bound to recite, that may the poet (if he list)* with his imitation make his own, beautifying it both for further teaching, and more delighting, as it please him: having all, from Dante's heaven to

---

[72] 'Is a better guarantee for those actions he should emulate'.

[73] That is, the historian.

[74] That is, given the function of *movere* in winning belief, presented with maximum intensity.

[75] Cf. Herodotus 3. 153–60; Justin 1. 10.

[76] Cf. Livy, *Histories* 1. 53–4; Xenophon, *Cyr.* 6. 1. 39 (but Sidney confuses the characters involved).

his hell, under the authority of his pen. Which if I be asked what poets have done so, as I might well name some, so yet say I and say again, I speak of the art, and not of the artificer.

Now, to* that which commonly is attributed to the praise of history, in respect of the notable learning is gotten by marking the success, as though therein a man should see virtue exalted and vice punished—truly that commendation is particular to poetry, and far off from history. For indeed poetry ever setteth virtue so out in her best colours, making fortune[77] her well-waiting handmaid, that one must needs be enamoured of her. Well may you see Ulysses in a storm, and in other hard plights; but they are but exercises of patience and magnanimity,* to make them shine the more in the near-following prosperity. And of the contrary part, if evil men come to the stage, they ever go out (as the tragedy writer[78] answered to one that misliked the show of such persons) so manacled as they little animate folks to follow them. But the history, being captived to the truth of a foolish world, is many times a terror from well-doing, and an encouragement to unbridled wickedness. For see we not valiant Miltiades rot in his fetters? the just Phocion and the accomplished Socrates put to death like traitors? the cruel Severus live prosperously? the excellent Severus miserably murdered? Sulla and Marius dying in their beds? Pompey and Cicero slain then when they would have thought exile a happiness? See we not virtuous Cato driven to kill himself, and rebel Caesar so advanced that his name yet, after 1600 years, lasteth in the highest honour? And mark but even Caesar's own words of the forenamed Sulla (who in that only did honestly, to put down his dishonest tyranny), *literas nescivit*,[79] as if want of learning caused him to do well. He meant it not by* poetry, which, not content with earthly plagues, deviseth new punishments in hell for tyrants, nor yet by philosophy, which teacheth *occidendos esse;*[80]

---

[77] A key issue in classical (e.g. Aristotle, *Eth. Nic.* 1. 10. 1100ᵇ1 ff.) and Renaissance ethics concerned the relations between *virtus*, innate goodness or strength, and *fatum* or *fortuna*. The virtuous person was supposed to derive from philosophy the inner strength needed to overcome adverse fortunes.

[78] Euripides, according to Plutarch (*Poetas* 4), 'said to those who railed at his Ixion as an impious and detestable character: "But I did not remove him from the stage until I had fastened him to the wheel"' (*Moralia*, 19 E).

[79] A much-quoted saying, 'Sullam nescisse literas, qui dictaturam deposuerit' (Suetonius, *Julius Caesar* 77): 'Sulla did not know how to read or write'—sc. 'the alphabet of politics'—'since he let others do all the dictating', with a pun on 'dictation'.

[80] Whether it was just to kill tyrants was a frequent topic in medieval and Renaissance political theory. For tyrants being punished in hell cf. *Od.* 11; *Aen.* 6; Dante, *Inferno* 12. 104 ff.

but no doubt by skill in history, for that indeed can afford your Cypselus, Periander, Phalaris, Dionysius,[81] and I know not how many more of the same kennel, that speed well enough in their abominable injustice of usurpation.

I conclude therefore, that he excelleth history, not only in furnishing the mind with knowledge, but in setting it forward[82] to that which deserveth to be called and accounted good: which setting forward, and moving to well-doing, indeed setteth the laurel crown upon the poet as victorious, not only of the historian, but over the philosopher, howsoever in teaching it may be questionable.*

For suppose it be granted (that which I suppose with great reason may be denied) that the philosopher, in respect of his methodical proceeding, doth teach more perfectly than the poet, yet do I think that no man is so much *philophilosophos*[83] as to compare the philosopher in moving with the poet.

And that moving is of a higher degree than teaching, it may by this appear, that it is well nigh both the cause and effect of teaching. For who will be taught, if he be not moved with desire to be taught? and what so much good doth that teaching bring forth (I speak still of moral doctrine) as that it moveth one to do that which it doth teach? For, as Aristotle[84] saith, it is not *gnōsis* but *praxis* must be the fruit. And how *praxis* can be, without being moved to practise, it is no hard matter to consider.

The philosopher showeth you the way, he informeth you of the particularities, as well of the tediousness of the way, as of the pleasant lodging you shall have when your journey is ended, as of the many by-turnings that may divert you from your way. But this is to no man but to him that will read him, and read him with attentive studious painfulness;* which constant desire whosoever hath in him, hath already passed half the hardness of the way, and therefore is beholding to the philosopher but for the other half. Nay truly, learned men have learnedly thought that where once reason hath so much overmastered passion as that the mind hath a free desire to do well, the inward light each mind hath in itself is as good as a philosopher's book; since in nature we know it is well to do well, and what is well and what

---

[81] Four tyrants who were successful, and unpunished.

[82] That is, 'he' (poetry) 'sets forward', moves or incites the reader's mind to the emulation of good deeds, a faculty denied to philosophy.

[83] 'Lover of the philosophers'.

[84] *Eth. Nic.* 1. 3. 1095ᵃ4: 'The end aimed at is not knowledge but action'.

is evil, although not in the words of art which philosophers bestow upon us; for out of natural conceit the philosophers drew it. But to be moved to do that which we know, or to be moved with desire to know, *hoc opus, hic labor est.*[85]

Now therein of all sciences (I speak still of human,[86] and according to the human conceit) is our poet the monarch. For he doth not only show the way, but giveth so sweet a prospect into the way, as will entice any man to enter into it. Nay, he doth, as if your journey should lie through a fair vineyard, at the very first give you a cluster of grapes, that full of that taste, you may long to pass further. He beginneth not with obscure definitions, which must blur the margent[87] with interpretations, and load the memory with doubtfulness;* but he cometh to you with words set in delightful proportion, either accompanied with, or prepared for, the well enchanting skill of music; and with a tale forsooth he cometh unto you, with a tale which holdeth children from play, and old men from the chimney corner. And, pretending no more, doth intend* the winning of the mind from wickedness to virtue,[88] even as the child is often brought to take most wholesome things by hiding them in such other as have a pleasant taste; which, if one should begin to tell them the nature of *aloes* or *rhabarbarum*[89] they should receive, would sooner take their physic* at their ears than at their mouth. So is it in men (most of which are childish in the best things, till they be cradled in their graves): glad they will be to hear the tales of Hercules, Achilles, Cyrus, Aeneas; and, hearing them, must needs hear the right description of wisdom, valour, and justice; which, if they had been barely, that is to say philosophically, set out, they would swear they be brought to school again.

That imitation whereof poetry is, hath the most conveniency* to Nature of all other, insomuch that, as Aristotle[90] saith, those things which in themselves are horrible, as cruel battles, unnatural monsters, are made in poetical imitation delightful. Truly, I have known men,

---

[85] Virgil, *Aen.* 6. 126 f.: ['Easy is the descent to Avernus; . . . but to recall thy steps and pass out to the upper air], this is the task, this the toil!'

[86] That is, avoiding theology.

[87] The margins of early printed books sometimes carried explanatory glosses.

[88] Cf. Spenser, p. 184, and n. 33.

[89] A long tradition deriving from rhetoric saw the delightful and enthralling stories in poetry (*delectare*), as a mode of conveying moral attitudes (*docere*), just as the physician gave bitter medicines a sweet coating. Cf. *LCPD* index, p. 695, s.v. 'Poetry, as pleasant medicine'.

[90] *Poet.* 4. 1448b9 ff.

that even with reading *Amadis de Gaule*[91] (which God knoweth wanteth much of a perfect poesy) have found their hearts moved to the exercise of courtesy, liberality, and especially courage. Who readeth Aeneas carrying old Anchises on his back, that wisheth not it were his fortune to perform so excellent an act? Whom doth not these words of Turnus move, the tale of Turnus having planted his image in the imagination?

> *[terga dabo et Turnum] fugientem haec terra videbit?*
> *usque adeone mori miserum est?*[92]

Where the philosophers, as they think scorn to delight, so must they be content little to move—saving wrangling whether *virtus* be the chief or the only good, whether the contemplative or the active life do excel—which Plato and Boethius[93] well knew, and therefore made mistress philosophy very often borrow the masking raiment of poesy. For even those hardhearted evil men who think virtue a school name, and know no other good but *indulgere genio*,[94] and therefore despise the austere admonitions of the philosopher, and feel not the inward reason they stand upon, yet will be content to be delighted—which is all the good-fellow* poet seemeth to promise—and so steal to see the form of goodness (which seen they cannot but love)[95] ere themselves be aware, as if they took a medicine of cherries.

Infinite proofs of the strange effects of this poetical invention might be alleged; only two shall serve, which are so often remembered as I think all men know them. The one of Menenius Agrippa,[96] who, when the whole people of Rome had resolutely divided themselves from the senate, with apparent show of utter ruin, though he were (for that time) an excellent orator, came not among them upon trust either of figurative speeches or cunning insinuations, and much less with far-fetched maxims of philosophy, which (especially if they were Platonic)

---

[91] A late medieval chivalric romance, added to by many Spanish authors, very popular in England following its French translation (1540), and partly imitated by Sidney in *Arcadia*.

[92] *Aen.* 12. 645–6: 'Shall I turn my back, and shall this land see Turnus in flight? Is death so sad?' The life and death of Turnus are narrated in the last six books of Virgil's epic.

[93] In *Consolations of Philosophy* 1. 1, Philosophy rejects verse produced by the muses of poetry, substituting her own more austere mode.

[94] Persius, *Sat.* 5. 151, 'Indulge genio, carpamus dulcia'. *Luxuria* exhorts men to indulge their own desires, for that is all life offers.

[95] Cf. Plato, *Phdr.* 250d for this idea, much repeated e.g. by Cicero, *Fin.* 2. 16. 52, *Off.* 1. 5. 15. Cf. also n. 122 below.

[96] Cf. Livy, *Histories* 2. 32; Plutarch, *Life of Coriolanus*; Quintilian, *Inst.* 5. 11. 1 (who uses it to illustrate the moving power of poetry).

they must have learned geometry[97] before they could well have conceived; but forsooth* he behaves himself like a homely and familiar
poet. He telleth them a tale, that there was a time when all the parts
of the body made a mutinous conspiracy against the belly, which they
thought devoured the fruits of each other's labour: they concluded
they would let so unprofitable a spender starve. In the end, to be short
(for the tale is notorious, and as notorious that it was a tale), with
punishing the belly they plagued themselves. This applied by him
wrought such effect in the people, as I never read that ever words
brought forth but then so sudden and so good an alteration; for upon
reasonable conditions a perfect reconcilement ensued. The other is of
Nathan[98] the prophet, who, when the holy David had so far forsaken
God as to confirm* adultery with murder, when he was to do the tenderest office of a friend, in laying his own shame before his eyes, sent
by God to call again so chosen a servant, how doth he it but by telling
of a man whose beloved lamb was ungratefully taken* from his
bosom?—the application most divinely true, but the discourse itself
feigned; which made David (I speak of the second and instrumental
cause) as in a glass see his own filthiness, as that heavenly psalm of
mercy[99] well testifieth.

By these, therefore, examples and reasons, I think it may be manifest that the poet, with that same hand of delight, doth draw the mind
more effectually than any other art doth. And so a conclusion not
unfitly ensueth: that, as virtue is the most excellent resting place for
all worldly learning to make his end of, so poetry, being the most familiar to teach it, and most princely to move towards it, in the most excellent work is the most excellent workman.

But I am content not only to decipher him by his works (although
works in commendation or dispraise must ever hold an high
authority), but more narrowly* will examine his parts; so that, as in
a man, though all together may carry a presence full of majesty
and beauty, perchance in some one defectuous piece we may find
blemish. Now in his parts, kinds, or species (as you list to term them),
it is to be noted that some poesies have coupled together two or
three kinds, as the tragical and comical, whereupon is risen the

---

[97] In *Resp.* 7 Plato made the study of proportion fundamental to the education of his guardians.

[98] Cf. 2 Sam. 12: 1–15.

[99] Psalm 51, a confession of sins. David is the 'second' cause, the first having been God, who moved him to repent.

tragi-comical.[100] Some, in the manner, have mingled prose and verse, as Sannazaro and Boethius. Some have mingled matters heroical and pastoral. But that cometh all to one in this question, for, if severed* they be good, the conjunction cannot be hurtful. Therefore, perchance forgetting some and leaving some as needless to be remembered, it shall not be amiss in a word to cite the special kinds, to see what faults may be found in the right use of them.

Is it then the Pastoral poem which is misliked? For perchance where the hedge is lowest they will soonest leap over. Is the poor pipe disdained, which sometime out of Meliboeus' mouth can show the misery of people under hard lords and ravening* soldiers? And again, by Tityrus,[101] what blessedness is derived to them that lie lowest from the goodness of them that sit highest; sometimes, under the pretty tales of wolves and sheep, can include the whole considerations of wrongdoing and patience;[102] sometimes show that contentions for trifles can get but a trifling victory: where perchance a man may see that even Alexander and Darius, when they strave who should be cock of this world's dunghill, the benefit they got was that the afterlivers may say,

> Haec memini et victum frustra contendere Thyrsin:
> ex illo Corydon, Corydon est tempore nobis.[103]

Or is it the lamenting Elegiac; which in a kind heart would move rather pity than blame, who bewails with the great philosopher Heraclitus the weakness of mankind and the wretchedness of the world; who surely is to be praised, either for compassionate accompanying just causes of lamentations, or for rightly painting out how weak be the passions of woefulness? Is it the bitter but wholesome Iambic,[104]

---

[100] Classical literature generally recognized only single genres, tragedy, epic, etc. The union of genres, as in tragicomedy or pastoral romance, came in the Renaissance. Cf. Shakespeare's mockery of Polonius' readiness to run all the genres together: 'tragical-comical-historical-pastoral' (Hamlet 2. 2. 396 ff.), and Fletcher, pp. 503–4.

[101] In Virgil's first Eclogue Meliboeus laments at having been dispossessed of his land and cattle, while Tityrus (Virgil himself) rejoices in the freedom and security he owes to Augustus Caesar.

[102] Many Renaissance poets, imitating Virgil's socio-political context, used pastoral as a means of satire and complaint. Cf. E.K. and Spenser, pp. 182 ff.

[103] The concluding lines to Virgil, Ecl. 7: 'This I remember, and how Thyrsis, vanquished, strove in vain. From that day it is Corydon, Corydon with us'. Alexander's victory over the Persian king in 330 BC is also now just a memory, a written record.

[104] From the Greek iambos, a lampoon poem in a metre based on speech rhythms, directly attacking faults, as opposed to satire's use of indirection and irony.

who rubs the galled* mind, in making shame the trumpet of villainy with bold and open crying out against naughtiness?* Or the Satiric, who

omne vafer vitium ridenti tangit amico;

who sportingly* never leaveth till he make a man laugh at folly, and at length ashamed to laugh at himself, which he cannot avoid, without avoiding the folly; who, while

circum praecordia ludit,[105]

giveth us to feel how many headaches a passionate life bringeth us to; how, when all is done,

est Ulubris, animus si nos non deficit aequus?[106]

No, perchance it is the Comic, whom naughty play-makers and stage-keepers have justly made odious. To the arguments of abuse I will answer after. Only thus much now is to be said, that the Comedy is an imitation of the common errors of our life,[107] which he representeth in the most ridiculous and scornful sort that may be, so as it is impossible that any beholder can be content to be such a one.

Now, as in geometry the oblique must be known as well as the right, and in arithmetic the odd as well as the even, so in the actions of our life who seeth not the filthiness of evil wanteth a great foil to perceive the beauty of virtue. This doth the Comedy handle so in our private and domestical matters, as with hearing it we get as it were an experience, what is to be looked for of a niggardly Demea, of a crafty Davus, of a flattering Gnatho, of a vainglorious Thraso;[108] and not only to know what effects are to be expected, but to know who be such, by the signifying badge[109] given them by the comedian. And little

[105] Persius, *Sat.* 1. 116–17: '[Horace,] sly dog, worming his way playfully into the vitals of his friend, touches up his every fault'.

[106] Horace, *Epist.* 1. 11. 30: 'it is at Ulubrae [a decaying town in the Pomptine marshes], if there fail you not a mind well balanced'. Sidney substitutes '*nos*' for Horace's '*te*'.

[107] Cf. Aristotle, *Poet.* 5. 1449ᵃ31 ff.: Comedy is 'an imitation of men worse than the average; worse, however, . . . as regards one particular kind [of fault], the ridiculous, which is a species of the ugly. The ridiculous may be defined as a mistake or deformity not productive of pain or harm to others'. For the moral function of comedy in representing vice, a stock principle in Renaissance literary theory, cf. Elyot, pp. 65–6, Whetstone, pp. 172–4, Jonson, p. 469, and Heywood, pp. 495–6.

[108] Characters in Terence; respectively: a miserly father, a tricky servant, a hanger-on or parasite, and a military braggart.

[109] That is, in order to display human follies the comic dramatist must use a 'signifying badge', a conventional representation through dress, looks, or behaviour.

reason hath any man to say that men learn the evil by seeing it so set out; since, as I said before, there is no man living but, by the force truth hath in nature, no sooner seeth these men play their parts, but wisheth them *in pistrinum*;[110] although perchance the sack of his own faults lie so hidden behind his back[111] that he seeth not himself dance the same measure; whereto yet nothing can more open his eyes than to see his own actions contemptibly set forth.

So that the right use of Comedy will (I think) by nobody be blamed, and much less of the high and excellent Tragedy, that openeth the greatest wounds, and showeth forth the ulcers that are covered with tissue; that maketh kings fear to be tyrants, and tyrants manifest their tyrannical humours; that, with stirring the affects* of admiration and commiseration,[112] teacheth the uncertainty of this world, and upon how weak foundations gilden roofs are builded; that maketh us know,

> *Qui sceptra duro saevus imperio regit,*
> *timet timentes; metus in auctorem redit.*[113]

But how much it can move, Plutarch[114] yieldeth a notable testimony of the abominable tyrant Alexander Pheraeus, from whose eyes a tragedy, well made and represented, drew abundance of tears, who without all pity had murdered infinite numbers, and some of his own blood; so as he that was not ashamed to make matters for tragedies, yet could not resist the sweet violence of a tragedy. And if it wrought no further good in him, it was that he, in despite of himself, withdrew himself from hearkening to that which might mollify his hardened heart. But it is not the Tragedy they do mislike; for it were too absurd to cast out so excellent a representation of whatsoever is most worthy to be learned.

---

[110] In Roman society, slaves were punished by having to work a mill operated by stamping and pounding.

[111] As in Aesop's fable (*Phaedrus* 4. 9) of the two sacks human beings carry: one on the back containing their own faults, visible to others but not themselves, and one on the front, containing other people's faults.

[112] Aristotle described tragedy as arousing the 'affects' or emotions of pity and fear (*Poet.* 6. 1449^{b}25 ff.). For fear Sidney substitutes 'admiration', wonder or amazement, a post-medieval concept. Cf. *ECE* i. 392–3; *LCPD*, pp. 459–61 and index, s.v. 'admiration'; M. T. Herrick, 'Some neglected sources of *admiratio*', *Modern Language Notes*, 62 (1947), 222–6, and J. V. Cunningham, *Woe or Wonder; the emotional effect of Shakespearean Tragedy* (Denver, 1951).

[113] Seneca, *Oedipus* 3. 705–6: 'Who harshly wields the sceptre with tyrannic sway, fears those who fear; terror recoils upon its author's head'.

[114] Plutarch, *Life of Pelopidas* 29: while watching a performance of Euripides' *The Trojan Women*, he wept at the sufferings of Hecuba and Andromache.

Is it the Lyric that most displeaseth? who with his tuned lyre and well-accorded voice, giveth praise, the reward of virtue, to virtuous acts; who gives moral precepts, and natural problems;[115] who sometimes raiseth up his voice to the height of the heavens, in singing the lauds of the immortal God.[116] Certainly, I must confess my own barbarousness,* I never heard the old song of Percy and Douglas[117] that I found not my heart moved more than with a trumpet; and yet is it sung but by some blind crowder,* with no rougher voice than rude style; which, being so evil apparelled in the dust and cobwebs of that uncivil age, what would it work, trimmed in the gorgeous eloquence of Pindar? In Hungary[118] I have seen it the manner at all feasts, and other such like meetings, to have songs of their ancestors' valour, which that right soldierlike nation think one of the chiefest kindlers of brave courage. The incomparable Lacedemonians[119] did not only carry that kind of music ever with them to the field, but even at home, as such songs were made, so were they all content to be singers of them; when the lusty men were to tell what they did, the old men what they had done, and the young what they would* do. And where a man may say that Pindar many times praiseth highly victories of small moment, rather matters of sport than virtue; as it may be answered, it was the fault of the poet, and not of the poetry, so indeed the chief fault was in the time and custom of the Greeks, who set those toys* at so high a price that Philip of Macedon reckoned a horserace won at Olympia among his three fearful felicities.[120] But as the unimitable Pindar often did, so is that kind most capable and most fit to awake the thoughts from the sleep of idleness, to embrace honourable enterprises.

There rests the Heroical, whose very name (I think) should daunt all backbiters; for by what conceit can a tongue be directed to speak evil of that which draweth with him no less champions than Achilles, Cyrus,

---

[115] Questions of natural philosophy.

[116] Sidney subsumes lyric under epideictic rhetoric, with the task of praising virtue and rousing readers to emulation: cf. Scaliger, *Poetice* 1. 44.

[117] Some version of the ballad of Chevy Chase, which Addison celebrated (recalling Sidney) in *Spectator*, 70 and 74.

[118] Sidney visited Hungary in the summer of 1573.

[119] Plutarch, *Lycurgus* 21, and in other places, records these rituals. The Spartans were much admired for their austerity and discipline.

[120] Plutarch, *Alexander* 3. These 'felicities' or successes were 'fearful', because too much good luck was considered ominous.

Aeneas, Turnus, Tydeus, Rinaldo?[121] who doth not only teach and move to a truth, but teacheth and moveth to the most high and excellent truth; who maketh magnanimity* and justice shine through all misty fearfulness and foggy desires; who, if the saying of Plato and Tully[122] be true, that who could see virtue would be wonderfully ravished with the love of her beauty—this man sets her out to make her more lovely in her holiday apparel, to the eye of any that will deign not to disdain until they understand. But if anything be already said in the defence of sweet poetry, all concurreth to the maintaining the Heroical, which is not only a kind, but the best and most accomplished kind of poetry. For as the image of each action stirreth and instructeth the mind, so the lofty image of such worthies most inflameth[123] the mind with desire to be worthy, and informs with counsel how to be worthy. Only let Aeneas be worn in the tablet* of your memory, how he governeth himself in the ruin of his country; in the preserving his old father, and carrying away his religious ceremonies;* in obeying the god's commandment to leave Dido, though not only all passionate kindness, but even the human consideration of virtuous gratefulness, would have craved other of him; how in storms, how in sports, how in war, how in peace, how a fugitive, how victorious, how besieged, how besieging, how to strangers, how to allies, how to enemies, how to his own; lastly, how in his inward self, and how in his outward government; and I think, in a mind not prejudiced with a prejudicating humour, he will be found in excellency fruitful, yea, even as Horace saith,

melius Chrysippo et Crantore.[124]

But truly I imagine it falleth out with these poet-whippers, as with some good women, who often are sick, but in faith they cannot tell where. So the name of poetry is odious to them, but neither his cause nor effects, neither the sum that contains him, nor the

---

[121] Epic was generally regarded in the Renaissance as the supreme literary form. Tydeus is a heroic figure in Statius, *Thebais*; Rinaldo is the name of a hero in both Ariosto and Tasso (where he is the captor of Jerusalem).

[122] Cf. n. 95 above.

[123] The verbs in this sentence repeat the key rhetorical terms *docere* ('instructeth', 'informs') and *movere* ('stirreth', 'inflameth'). The psychological model, of readers or hearers being irritated or provoked to emulate virtue, is widely shared in Renaissance literary theory: cf. Introduction, pp. 50–5.

[124] *Epist.* 1. 2. 3 f.: '[Homer] tells us what is fair, what is foul, what is helpful, what not, more plainly and better than Chrysippus or Crantor'. Chrysippus was an early Stoic philosopher, Crantor a Platonist.

particularities* descending from him, give any fast* handle to their carping dispraise.

Since then poetry is of all human learning the most ancient and of most fatherly antiquity, as from whence other learnings have taken their beginnings; since it is so universal that no learned nation doth despise it, nor no barbarous nation is without it; since both Roman and Greek gave such divine names unto it, the one of 'prophesying', the other of 'making', and that indeed that name of 'making' is fit for him, considering that where all other arts retain themselves within their subject, and receive, as it were, their being from it, the poet only bringeth his own stuff, and doth not learn a conceit out of a matter, but maketh matter for a conceit; since neither his description nor end containing any evil, the thing described cannot be evil; since his effects be so good as to teach goodness and to delight the learners of it; since therein (namely in moral doctrine, the chief of all knowledges) he doth not only far pass the historian, but, for instructing, is well nigh comparable to the philosopher, for moving, leaves him behind him; since the Holy Scripture (wherein there is no uncleanness) hath whole parts in it poetical, and that even our saviour Christ vouchsafed to use the flowers of it; since all his kinds are not only in their united forms but in their severed dissections* fully commendable; I think (and think I think rightly) the laurel crown appointed for triumphant captains doth worthily (of all other learnings) honour the poet's triumph.[125]

[REFUTATION]

But because we have ears as well as tongues, and that the lightest reasons that may be will seem to weigh greatly if nothing be put in the counterbalance, let us hear, and, as well as we can, ponder what objections be made against this art, which may be worthy either of yielding* or answering.

First, truly I note not only in these *misomousoi*, poet-haters, but in all that kind of people who seek a praise by dispraising others, that they do prodigally spend a great many wandering words in quips and scoffs, carping and taunting at each thing which, by stirring the spleen,* may stay the brain from a through-beholding* the worthiness of the subject. Those kind of objections, as they are full of a very

---

[125] The famous ceremony in 1341, awarding Petrarch a triumph on the Capitoline Hill in Rome, started a fashion for crowning poets with a laurel wreath.

idle easiness,* since there is nothing of so sacred a majesty but that an itching tongue may rub itself upon it, so deserve they no other answer, but, instead of laughing at the jest, to laugh at the jester. We know a playing wit can praise[126] the discretion of an ass, the comfortableness of being in debt, and the jolly commodities of being sick of the plague. So of the contrary side, if we will turn Ovid's verse,

Ut lateat virtus proximitate mali,[127]

that 'good lie hid in nearness of the evil', Agrippa will be as merry in showing the vanity of science as Erasmus was in the commending of folly. Neither shall any man or matter escape some touch of these smiling railers. But for Erasmus and Agrippa, they had another foundation than the superficial part would promise. Marry, these other pleasant faultfinders, who will correct the verb before they understand the noun, and confute others' knowledge before they confirm their own, I would have them only remember that scoffing cometh not of wisdom; so as the best title in true English they get with their merriments is to be called good fools, for so have our grave forefathers ever termed that humorous kind of jesters.

But that which giveth greatest scope to their scorning humour is rhyming and versing. It is already said (and, as I think, truly said) it is not rhyming and versing that maketh poesy. One may be a poet without versing, and a versifier without poetry. But yet presuppose it were inseparable (as indeed it seemeth Scaliger[128] judgeth) truly it were an inseparable commendation. For if *oratio* next to *ratio*, speech next to reason, be the greatest gift bestowed upon mortality,[129] that cannot be praiseless which doth most polish that blessing of speech; which considers each word, not only (as a man may say) by his most

---

[126] Paradoxical encomia were popular among Renaissance intellectuals and satirists. Heinrich Cornelius Agrippa praised 'the discretion of an ass', while Francesco Berni (1497–1535) eulogized both indebtedness and the plague.

[127] *Ars am.* 2. 661–2: 'Et lateat vitium proximitate boni', 'any fault may be concealed by being associated with a virtue': which Sidney parodies.

[128] In *Poetice* 1. 2 he argues that the poet is named not from making fables but from making verses, an anti-Aristotelian position which Sidney elsewhere rejects.

[129] This important conception of the gift of language as separating man from beast was known to Renaissance readers best of all from Cicero, *Off.* 1. 16. 50, where the first principle of existence that Nature has established for human society is 'the connection subsisting between all members of the human race; and that bond of connection is reason and speech', uniting us while distinguishing us from animals ('Eius autem vinculum est ratio et oratio . . .'); also Quintilian, *Inst.* 2. 16. 12–15; 12. 11. 30. It was widely repeated in the Renaissance: cf. Wilson, p. 77, Hoskyns, p. 391; Campion, p. 429, and Jonson, p. 578.

forcible quality, but by his best measured quantity,[130] carrying even in themselves a harmony—without,* perchance, number, measure, order, proportion be in our time grown odious. But lay aside the just praise it hath, by being the only fit speech for music (music, I say, the most divine striker of the senses), thus much is undoubtedly true, that if reading be foolish without remembering, memory being the only treasure of knowledge, those words which are fittest for memory are likewise most convenient for knowledge.

Now, that verse far exceedeth prose in the knitting up* of the memory, the reason is manifest: the words (besides their delight, which hath a great affinity to memory) being so set as one cannot be lost but the whole work fails; which accusing itself, calleth the remembrance back to itself, and so most strongly confirmeth it. Besides, one word so, as it were, begetting another, as, be it in rhyme or measured verse, by the former a man shall have a near guess to the follower. Lastly, even they that have taught the art of memory[131] have showed nothing so apt for it as a certain room divided into many places well and thoroughly known. Now, that hath the verse in effect perfectly, every word having his natural seat, which seat must needs make the word remembered. But what needeth more in a thing so known to all men? Who is it that ever was a scholar that doth not carry away some verses[132] of Virgil, Horace, or Cato, which in his youth he learned, and even to his old age serve him for hourly lessons? But the fitness it hath for memory[133] is notably proved by all delivery* of arts: wherein for the most part, from grammar to logic, mathematics, physic, and the rest, the rules chiefly necessary to be borne away are compiled in verses. So that verse being in itself sweet and orderly, and being best for memory, the only handle of knowledge, it must be in jest that any man can speak against it.

---

[130] That is, not only considering the forcefulness (as in rhetoric), but also its length, the quantities basic to classical metrics.

[131] The penultimate stage in literary composition, according to classical rhetoric, after *inventio, dispositio, elocutio,* and before *pronuntiatio* (cf. Wilson, pp. 79–81), was the art of *memoria* (since speeches were delivered from memory, not from written texts). The most popular memory-system was based on 'places' or *loci* (topics), which the orator could recall more easily if he imagined them to be distributed around a room. Cf. *Rhet. Her.* 3. 16–24.

[132] At this point the authorized printed text, Ponsonby's *Defence of Poesie,* inserts two verses which van Dorsten rejects as 'sophistications', '*Percontatorem fugito, nam garrulus idem est*' [Horace, *Epist.* 1. 18. 69: 'Avoid a questioner, for he is also a tattler'] and '*Dum tibi quisque placet, credula turba sumus*' [Ovid, *Rem. am.* 686: 'self-flatterers, a credulous lot are we'].

[133] On the popularity of verse as an aid to memorizing treatises in medicine and other subjects, cf. Puttenham, p. 196, Daniel, pp. 443–4.

Now then go we to the most important imputations laid to the poor poets.[134] For aught I can yet learn, they are these. First, that there being many other more fruitful knowledges, a man might better spend his time in them than in this. Secondly, that it is the mother of lies. Thirdly, that it is the nurse of abuse, infecting us with many pestilent desires, with a siren's sweetness drawing the mind to the serpent's tale of sinful fancies (and herein, especially, comedies give the largest field to ear, as Chaucer[135] saith); how both in other nations and in ours, before poets did soften us,[136] we were full of courage, given to martial exercises, the pillars of manlike liberty, and not lulled asleep in shady idleness with poets' pastimes. And lastly, and chiefly, they cry out with open mouth as if they overshot Robin Hood, that Plato banished them out of his commonwealth. Truly, this is much, if there be much truth in it.

First, to the first, that a man might better spend his time is a reason indeed; but it doth (as they say) but *petere principium*:[137] for if it be, as I affirm, that no learning is so good as that which teacheth and moveth to virtue, and that none can both teach and move thereto so much as Poetry, then is the conclusion manifest that ink and paper cannot be to a more profitable purpose employed. And certainly, though a man should grant their first assumption, it should follow (methinks) very unwillingly, that good is not good because better is better. But I still and utterly deny that there is sprung out of earth a more fruitful knowledge.

To the second therefore, that they should be the principal liars, I answer paradoxically, but truly,[138] I think truly, that of all writers under the sun the poet is the least liar, and, though he would, as a poet can scarcely be a liar. The astronomer, with his cousin the geometrician,

---

[134] Many of the traditional attacks on poetry had been answered by Boccaccio in *De genealogia deorum* 14. 2–20: cf. *Boccaccio on Poetry*, tr. C. Osgood (Princeton, 1930; Indianapolis, 1956), pp. 17–96. They had recently been restated by H. C. Agrippa in *Of the Vanitie and Uncertaintie of the Sciences* (tr. J. Sanford, 1569): see pp. 307–8 for Harington's summary and reply, and Elyot, pp. 61 ff. for an earlier defence. Full documentation in *GKS*, pp. 197–203.

[135] 'To plough': Cf. *Knight's Tale* 28: 'I have, God woot, a large feeld to eare', implying that the following story will be long.

[136] Cf. Spenser, p. 186. Virtue is corrupted or 'softened' by *otium*, idleness.

[137] 'To beg the question', an elementary error in reasoning.

[138] Cicero defends paradoxes as 'admirabilia contraque opinionem omnium' (*Paradoxa Stoicorum* 4: 'These doctrines are surprising, and they run counter to universal opinion'). Sidney's paradox, that only those who set out to affirm a truth can be called liars, derives from Agrippa, as do some of his examples (*JVD*, p. 202).

can hardly escape, when they take upon them to measure the height of the stars. How often, think you, do the physicians lie, when they aver things good for sicknesses, which afterwards send Charon a great number of souls drowned in a potion before they come to his ferry? And no less of the rest, which take upon them to affirm. Now for the poet, he nothing affirms, and therefore never lieth. For, as I take it, to lie is to affirm that to be true which is false; so as the other artists,* and especially the historian, affirming many things, can, in the cloudy* knowledge of mankind, hardly escape from many lies. But the poet (as I said before) never affirmeth. The poet never maketh any circles about your imagination, to conjure you to believe for true what he writes. He citeth not authorities of other histories, but even for his entry* calleth the sweet Muses to inspire into him a good invention; in truth, not labouring to tell you what is or is not, but what should or should not be. And therefore, though he recount things not true, yet because he telleth them not for true, he lieth not—without* we will say that Nathan lied in his speech before-alleged to David; which as a wicked man durst scarce say, so think I none so simple would say that Aesop lied in the tales of his beasts; for who thinks that Aesop writ it for actually true were well worthy to have his name chronicled among the beasts he writeth of. What child is there that, coming to a play, and seeing *Thebes* written in great letters upon an old door,[139] doth believe that it is Thebes? If then a man can arrive to that child's age, to know that the poets' persons and doings are but pictures what should be, and not stories what have been, they will never give the lie to things not affirmatively but allegorically and figuratively written. And therefore, as in history looking for truth, they may go away full fraught with falsehood, so in poesy looking but for fiction, they shall use the narration but as an imaginative ground-plot of a profitable invention.[140]

But hereto is replied, that the poets give names to men they write of, which argueth a conceit of an actual truth, and so, not being true, proves a falsehood. And doth the lawyer lie then, when under the names of 'John a Stile' and 'John a Noakes'[141] he puts his case? But that is easily answered. Their naming of men is but to make their

[139] In court and university plays (but not in the public theatre) doors were sometimes labelled to localize the action.

[140] 'An imaginary map, as it were, on which the "inventions" are "placed" in such a way that the reader may fetch them back for his own use' (*JVD*).

[141] Names used in fictitious legal actions.

picture the more lively, and not to build any history: painting men, they cannot leave men nameless. We see we cannot play at chess but that we must give names to our chessmen; and yet, methinks, he were a very partial champion of truth that would say we lied for giving a piece of wood the reverend title of a bishop. The poet nameth Cyrus and Aeneas no other way than to show what men of their fames, fortunes, and estates should do.

Their third is, how much it abuseth men's wit, training it to wanton sinfulness and lustful love: for indeed that is the principal, if not only abuse I can hear alleged. They say the comedies rather teach than reprehend amorous conceits. They say the lyric is larded with passionate sonnets, the elegiac weeps the want of his mistress,[142] and that even to the heroical Cupid hath ambitiously climbed. Alas, Love, I would thou couldst as well defend thyself as thou canst offend others. I would those on whom thou dost attend could either put thee away, or yield good reason why they keep thee. But grant love of beauty to be a beastly fault (although it be very hard, since only man, and no beast, hath that gift to discern beauty); grant that lovely name of Love to deserve all hateful reproaches (although even some of my masters the philosophers spent a good deal of their lamp-oil in setting forth the excellency of it); grant, I say, whatsoever they will have granted, that not only love, but lust, but vanity, but (if they list)* scurrility, possess many leaves of the poets' books; yet think I, when this is granted, they will find their sentence may with good manners put the last words foremost, and not say that poetry abuseth man's wit, but that man's wit abuseth poetry.

For I will not deny but that man's wit may make poesy, which should be *eikastikē* (which some learned have defined, 'figuring forth good things'), to be *phantastikē*[143] (which doth, contrariwise, infect the fancy with unworthy objects); as the painter, that should give to the

---

[142] When Sidney first mentioned the Elegy as a poetic form (p. 361 above) he limited it to poems of sorrow, concealing the fact that it was also the major form used by the Latin love poets Ovid, Tibullus, and Propertius. Humanists who defended the use of poetry in teaching recommended the teacher to make a careful selection from this 'rout of lascivious poets': cf. Elyot, pp. 65–8, and F. Watson (ed.), *Vives: On Education. A Translation of the* De Tradendis Disciplinis *of Juan Luis Vives* (Cambridge, 1913; Totowa, NJ, 1971), pp. 124–9, 135–6.

[143] These terms, *eikastikē* ('imitative') and *phantastikē* ('fanciful, imaginary'), were used by Plato in *Sophist* (235d–236c) to distinguish between the art of making likenesses, which he found acceptable, and that of making appearances or fanciful images, rejected as harmful (264c–266e). Plato's categories were taken up in 16th-cent. literary theory; Puttenham, pp. 200–1, defends 'the fantastical' in poetry.

eye either some excellent perspective, or some fine picture, fit for building or fortification, or containing in it some notable example, as Abraham sacrificing his son Isaac, Judith killing Holofernes, David fighting with Goliath, may leave those, and please an ill-pleased* eye with wanton shows of better hidden matters. But what, shall the abuse of a thing make the right use odious? Nay truly, though I yield that poesy may not only be abused, but that being abused, by the reason of his sweet charming force, it can do more hurt[144] than any other army of words, yet shall it be so far from concluding* that the abuse should give reproach to the abused, that contrariwise it is a good reason that whatsoever, being abused, doth most harm, being rightly used (and upon the right use each thing conceiveth his title),* doth most good.

Do we not see the skill of physic (the best rampire* to our often-assaulted bodies), being abused, teach poison, the most violent destroyer? Doth not knowledge of law, whose end is to even and right all things, being abused, grow the crooked fosterer of horrible injuries? Doth not (to go to the highest) God's word abused breed heresy, and His name abused become blasphemy? Truly a needle cannot do much hurt, and as truly (with leave of ladies be it spoken) it cannot do much good. With a sword thou mayest kill thy father, and with a sword thou mayest defend thy prince and country. So that, as in their calling poets fathers of lies they said nothing, so in this their argument of abuse they prove the commendation.

They allege herewith, that before poets began to be in price our nation had set their hearts' delight upon action, and not imagination, rather doing things worthy to be written, than writing things fit to be done. What that before-time was, I think scarcely Sphinx can tell, since no memory is so ancient that hath not the precedent of poetry. And certain it is that, in our plainest homeliness, yet never was the Albion nation without poetry. Marry, this argument, though it be

---

[144] Sidney's concession of the damaging power of any expressive medium when put to 'wrong' ends, recalls the Roman rhetoricians' naive belief that oratorical skills would never be misused. Cf. Cicero, *De or.* 3. 14. 55, and Quintilian, *Inst.* 12. 1. 1–2 (part of an unsatisfactory attempt to legitimize the orator as 'vir bonus dicendi peritus', 'a good man skilled in speaking', which even claims that no evil man could ever speak well). At the end of this rather sophistic sequence Sidney tries to rescue his position by invoking Aristotle's reply to Plato's charge that rhetoric lends itself to misuse: 'that is a charge which may be made in common against all good things except virtue, and above all against the things that are most useful, as strength, health, wealth, generalship. A man can confer the greatest of benefits by a right use of these, and inflict the greatest of injuries by using them wrongly' (*Rh.* 1. 1. 1355^{b}3–7). Cf. also Quintilian, *Inst.* 2. 16. 1–19.

levelled against poetry, yet is it indeed a chainshot* against all learning, or bookishness, as they commonly term it. Of such mind were
certain Goths, of whom it is written[145] that, having in the spoil of a
famous city taken a fair library, one hangman (belike fit to execute the
fruits of their wits who had murdered a great number of bodies),
would have set fire in it. 'No,' said another very gravely, 'take heed
what you do, for while they are busy about those toys,* we shall with
more leisure conquer their countries.'

This indeed is the ordinary doctrine of ignorance, and many words
sometimes I have heard spent in it; but because this reason is generally against all learning, as well as poetry, or rather, all learning but
poetry; because it were too large a digression to handle it, or at least
too superfluous (since it is manifest that all government of action is
to be gotten by knowledge, and knowledge best by gathering many
knowledges, which is reading), I only, with Horace, to him that is of
that opinion,

$$iubeo\ stultum\ esse\ libenter;^{146}$$

for as for poetry itself, it is the freest from this objection.

For poetry is the companion of camps. I dare undertake, Orlando
Furioso, or honest King Arthur, will never displease a soldier: but the
quiddity of *ens* and *prima materia*[147] will hardly agree with a corslet.*
And therefore, as I said in the beginning, even Turks and Tartars are
delighted with poets. Homer, a Greek, flourished before Greece flourished. And if to a slight conjecture a conjecture may be opposed, truly
it may seem, that as by him their learned men took almost their first
light of knowledge, so their active men received their first motions of
courage. Only Alexander's example may serve, who by Plutarch[148] is
accounted of such virtue that fortune was not his guide but his footstool; whose acts speak for him, though Plutarch did not,—indeed the
phoenix of warlike princes. This Alexander left his schoolmaster,
living Aristotle, behind him, but took dead Homer with him. He put

---

[145] By the continuator of Dio Cassius, *Roman Histories* 54. 17.

[146] Adapting Horace's line 'iubeas miserum esse libenter' (*Sat.* 1. 1. 63), to mean 'I bid
him cheerfully remain a fool'.

[147] 'Scholastic terms: *quiddity*, the essential nature, that which makes a thing what it is;
ens, being, pure existence; *prima materia*, first matter ... the mere possibility of being'
(*GKS*, p. 205).

[148] In his *Alexander* 7–8, as in other essays, Plutarch recorded the general's reverence for
Aristotle and Homer—he kept a copy of the *Iliad* under his pillow, next to his sword—in
terms often echoed by the defenders of poetry: cf. Elyot, p. 58, and E.K., p. 186, n. *h*.

the philosopher Callisthenes to death for his seeming philosophical, indeed mutinous stubbornness, but the chief thing he was ever heard to wish for was that Homer had been alive. He well found he received more bravery of mind by the pattern of Achilles than by hearing the definition of fortitude. And therefore, if Cato misliked Fulvius[149] for carrying Ennius with him to the field, it may be answered that if Cato misliked it, the noble Fulvius liked it, or else he had not done it: for it was not the excellent Cato Uticensis (whose authority I would much more have reverenced), but it was the former, in truth a bitter punisher of faults, but else a man that had never well sacrificed to the graces. He misliked and cried out against all Greek learning, and yet, being four score years old, began to learn it (belike* fearing that Pluto understood not Latin). Indeed, the Roman laws allowed no person to be carried to the wars but he that was in the soldiers' roll, and therefore, though Cato misliked his unmustered* person, he misliked not his work. And if he had, Scipio Nasica, judged by common consent the best Roman,[150] loved him. Both the other Scipio brothers, who had by their virtues no less surnames than of Asia and Afric, so loved him that they caused his body to be buried in their sepulture.[151] So as Cato's authority being but against his person, and that answered with so far greater than himself, is herein of no validity.

But now indeed my burden is great; now Plato's name is laid upon me, whom, I must confess, of all philosophers I have ever esteemed most worthy of reverence, and with good reason: since of all philosophers he is the most poetical. Yet if he will defile the fountain out of which his flowing streams have proceeded, let us boldly examine with what reasons he did it. First, truly a man might maliciously object that Plato, being a philosopher, was a natural enemy of poets.[152] For indeed, after the philosophers had picked out of the sweet mysteries of poetry the right discerning true points of knowledge, they forthwith, putting

---

[149] Cato the Censor (234–149 BC), celebrated for his strict virtue and opposition to 'bad influences' from Greece, nevertheless learned Greek late in life (Plutarch). M. Fulvius Nobilior, consul in 189 BC, was accompanied by the poet Ennius on his victorious campaign against the Aetolians. Cato Uticensis, the great-grandson of the censor, was famous as a model of superhuman republican virtue.

[150] Cf. Livy, *Hist.* 29. 14.

[151] But Cicero, *Arch.* 9. 22, merely says that a marble statue of Ennius was placed in the Scipios' tomb. Sidney's error probably derives from Boccaccio, *De genealogia deorum* 14. 4: *Boccaccio on Poetry*, tr. Osgood, pp. 27–8.

[152] Plato refers to the ancient quarrel between philosophy and poetry while justifying his decision to banish it from his ideal state: *Resp.* 10. 595–607, also 2. 376–3. 398 (*ALC*, pp. 50–74). Sidney now contradicts himself: cf. p. 339.

it in method, and making a school-art of that which the poets did only teach by a divine delightfulness, beginning to spurn at their guides, like ungrateful prentices, were not content to set up shop for themselves, but sought by all means to discredit their masters; which by the force of delight[153] being barred them, the less they could overthrow them, the more they hated them. For indeed, they found for Homer seven cities strave[154] who should have him for their citizen; where many cities banished philosophers as not fit members to live among them. For only repeating certain of Euripides' verses, many Athenians had their lives saved[155] of the Syracusans, where the Athenians themselves thought many philosophers unworthy to live. Certain poets, as Simonides and Pindar, had so prevailed with Hiero the First, that of a tyrant they made him a just king; where Plato could do so little with Dionysius, that he himself of a philosopher was made a slave. But who should do thus, I confess, should requite the objections made against poets with like cavillations against philosophers; as likewise one should do that should bid one read *Phaedrus* or *Symposium* in Plato, or the discourse of love in Plutarch, and see whether any poet do authorize abominable filthiness,[156] as they do. Again, a man might ask out of what commonwealth Plato doth banish them. In sooth, thence where he himself alloweth community of women. So as belike this banishment grew not for effeminate wantonness, since little should poetical sonnets be hurtful when a man might have what woman he listed. But I honour philosophical instructions, and bless the wits which bred them: so as they be not abused, which is likewise stretched to poetry.

St Paul himself (who yet, for the credit of poets, twice citeth two poets, and one of them by the name of 'their prophet'), setteth a watchword upon philosophy,[157]—indeed upon the abuse. So doth Plato upon the abuse, not upon poetry. Plato found fault that the poets of his time filled the world with wrong opinions of the gods, making

[153] As Sidney showed earlier (p. 357), philosophers may use *docere* ('philosophical instructions'), but they cannot use either *delectare* or *movere*.

[154] Cf. Cicero, *Arch.* 8. 19, a Renaissance commonplace.

[155] Recorded by Plutarch in *Nicias* 29.

[156] Sidney borrows this orthodox condemnation of what was seen as Greek homosexuality from Scaliger, *Poetice* 1. 2. Plato allowed 'community of women' in *Resp.* 5.

[157] Cf. Acts 17: 28 (which resembles utterances by Aratus and Cleanthes), Titus 1: 12 (referring to Epimenides of Crete as 'a prophet'), and 1 Cor. 15: 33 (a quotation from Menander), biblical passages often used to justify Christians acquiring pagan learning: cf. *GKS*, pp. 208–9. The 'watchword' or warning was Paul's injunction 'Beware lest any man spoil you through philosophy' (Col. 2: 8).

light tales of that unspotted essence, and therefore would not have the youth depraved* with such opinions. Herein may much be said; let this suffice: the poets did not induce* such opinions, but did imitate those opinions already induced. For all the Greek stories* can well testify that the very religion of that time stood upon many and many-fashioned gods, not taught so by poets, but followed according to their nature of imitation. Who list may read in Plutarch the discourses[158] of Isis and Osiris, of the cause why oracles ceased, of the divine providence, and see whether the theology of that nation stood not upon such dreams which the poets indeed superstitiously observed and truly (since they had not the light of Christ) did much better in it than the philosophers, who, shaking off superstition, brought in atheism. Plato therefore (whose authority I had much rather justly construe than unjustly resist) meant not in general of poets, in those words of which Julius Scaliger saith, *Qua authoritate barbari quidam atque hispidi abuti velint ad poetas e republica exigendos;*[159] but only meant to drive out those wrong opinions of the Deity (whereof now, without further law,* Christianity hath taken away all the hurtful belief), perchance (as he thought) nourished by the then esteemed poets. And a man need go no further than to Plato himself to know his meaning: who, in his dialogue called *Ion*,[160] giveth high and rightly divine commendation to poetry. So as Plato, banishing the abuse, not the thing—not banishing it, but giving due honour to it—shall be our patron and not our adversary. For indeed I had much rather (since truly I may do it) show their mistaking of Plato (under whose lion's skin they would make an ass-like braying[161] against Poesy) than go about to overthrow his authority; whom, the wiser a man is, the more just cause he shall find to have in admiration; especially since he attributeth unto Poesy more than myself do, namely, to be a very inspiring of a divine force, far above man's wit, as in the fore-named dialogue is apparent.

Of the other side, who would show the honours have been by the best sort of judgements granted them, a whole sea of examples

---

[158] See these three treatises in the *Moralia* (351 C ff., 409 E ff., 568 B ff.).

[159] *Poetice* 1. 2, discussing those divinely inspired, as Plato says, 'whose authority certain barbarous and uncouth men seek to use in order to expel poets from the republic'. Scaliger adds that Plato often draws on the poets he condemns.

[160] In this dialogue Socrates' ironic account of rhapsodic possession as a form of irrationality was taken literally in the Renaissance, as a praise of poetry. Cf. Elyot, p. 64; E.K., p. 183. Sidney, like Puttenham, denies that poetry depends on divine inspiration.

[161] Cf. Aesop's fable of the ass who crept into a lion's skin to seem like a lion.

would present themselves: Alexanders, Caesars, Scipios, all favourers of poets; Laelius, called the Roman Socrates,[162] himself a poet, so as part of *Heautontimorumenos* in Terence was supposed to be made by him; and even the Greek Socrates,[163] whom Apollo confirmed to be the only wise man, is said to have spent part of his old time in putting Aesop's fables into verses. And therefore, full evil should it become his scholar Plato to put such words in his master's mouth against poets. But what need more? Aristotle writes the *Art of Poesy*: and why, if it should not be written? Plutarch[164] teacheth the use to be gathered of them, and how, if they should not be read? And who reads Plutarch's either history or philosophy, shall find he trimmeth both their garments with guards* of poesy. But I list not to defend poesy with the help of his underling historiography. Let it suffice to have showed it is a fit soil for praise to dwell upon; and what dispraise may be set upon it is either easily overcome, or transformed into just commendation.

So that, since the excellencies of it may be so easily and so justly confirmed, and the low-creeping objections so soon trodden down: it not being an art of lies, but of true doctrine; not of effeminateness, but of notable stirring of courage; not of abusing man's wit, but of strengthening man's wit; not banished, but honoured by Plato; let us rather plant more laurels for to engarland the poets' heads (which honour of being laureate, as besides them only triumphant captains wear, is a sufficient authority to show the price they ought to be had in) than suffer the ill-favoured breath of such wrongspeakers once to blow upon the clear springs of poesy.

[DIGRESSION]

But since I have run so long a career in this matter, methinks, before I give my pen a full stop,[165] it shall be but a little more lost time to inquire why England (the mother of excellent minds) should be grown so hard a stepmother to poets, who certainly in wit ought to pass all others, since all only proceedeth from their wit, being

---

[162] By Cicero, *Off.* 1. 26. 90, who also records (*Att.* 8. 3, 10) the tradition that the plays of Terence were partly written by Laelius, a philosopher and literary patron. Cf. also Ascham, pp. 155–6.

[163] Cf. Plato, *Apologia* 21a, and *Phaedo* 60c–61b.

[164] The treatise *How the young man should study poetry* (*Mor.* 14E–37B). Plutarch, a Platonist, emulates Plato by frequently quoting poetry.

[165] That is, 'galloped for so long at full speed, before stopping'.

indeed makers of themselves, not takers of others. How can I but exclaim,

Musa, mihi causas memora, quo numine laeso?[166]

Sweet poesy, that hath anciently had kings, emperors,[167] senators, great captains, such as, besides a thousand others, David, Adrian, Sophocles, Germanicus, not only to favour poets, but to be poets; and of our nearer times can present for her patrons a Robert, king of Sicily, the great King Francis of France, King James of Scotland; such cardinals as Bembus and Bibbiena: such famous preachers and teachers as Beza and Melanchthon; so learned philosophers as Fracastorius and Scaliger; so great orators as Pontanus and Muretus; so piercing wits as George Buchanan; so grave counsellors as, besides many, but before all, that Hospital of France,[168] than whom (I think) that realm never brought forth a more accomplished judgement, more firmly builded upon virtue—I say these, with numbers of others, not only to read others' poesies, but to poetize for others' reading—that poesy, thus embraced in all other places, should only find in our time a hard welcome in England, I think the very earth lamenteth it, and therefore decketh our soil with fewer laurels than it was accustomed. For heretofore poets have in England also flourished, and, which is to be noted, even in those times when the trumpet of Mars did sound loudest. And now that an overfaint quietness should seem to strew the house for poets,[169] they are almost in as good reputation as the mountebanks at Venice. Truly even that, as of the one side it giveth great praise to poesy, which like Venus (but to better purpose) had rather be troubled in the net with Mars than enjoy the homely quiet of Vulcan;[170] so serves it for a piece of a reason why they are less grateful* to idle England, which now can scarce endure the pain of a pen.

Upon this necessarily followeth, that base men with servile wits undertake it, who think it enough if they can be rewarded of the printer. And so as Epaminondas[171] is said, with the honour of his

---

[166] Virgil, *Aen.* 1. 8: 'Tell me, O Muse, the cause; wherein thwarted in will or wherefore, angered . . .'.

[167] To justify poetry by listing the eminent men who had practised and encouraged it was Cicero's strategy in *Pro Archia poeta* 8. 1 ff., and was much copied in the Renaissance: cf. Elyot, pp. 58, 61; E.K., p. 186 n. *h*; Puttenham, pp. 198 ff.; and *GKS*, pp. 211–14.

[168] Michel de l'Hôpital (1503–73), Chancellor of France 1560–8, a patron of literature and a minor poet. For the other names listed here cf. *JVD*, pp. 204–5.

[169] 'Now that a prolonged peace seems to prepare a welcome to poets'.

[170] Cf. Homer, *Od.* 8. 266–367.

[171] Cf. Plutarch, *Precepts of statecraft* 15 (*Mor.* 811 B). Epaminondas said that 'not only does the office distinguish the man, but also the man the office'.

virtue to have made an office, by his exercising it, which before was contemptible, to become highly respected, so these men, no more but setting their names to it, by their own disgracefulness disgrace the most graceful poesy. For now, as if all the Muses were got with child to bring forth bastard poets, without any commission they do post over the banks of Helicon, till they make the readers more weary than post-horses;* while, in the meantime, they,

queis meliore luto finxit praecordia Titan,[172]

are better content to suppress the outflowings of their wit, than, by publishing them, to be accounted knights of the same order.[173] But I that, before ever I durst aspire unto the dignity, am admitted into the company of the paper-blurrers, do find the very true cause of our wanting estimation is want* of desert, taking upon us to be poets in despite of Pallas.[174]

Now, wherein we want desert were a thankworthy labour to express; but if I knew, I should have mended myself. But I, as I never desired the title, so have I neglected the means to come by it. Only, overmastered by some thoughts, I yielded an inky tribute[175] unto them. Marry, they that delight in poesy itself should seek to know what they do, and how they do; and especially look themselves in an unflattering glass of reason, if they be inclinable unto it. For poesy must not be drawn by the ears; it must be gently led, or rather it must lead; which was partly the cause that made the ancient-learned affirm it was a divine gift, and no human skill: since all other knowledges lie ready for any that hath strength of wit; a poet no industry can make, if his own genius be not carried into it; and therefore it is an old proverb, *orator fit, poeta nascitur.*[176]

---

[172] Juvenal, *Sat.* 14. 33–5: 'one whose soul the Titan [Prometheus] has fashioned with kindlier skill and of a finer clay'.

[173] Cf. Horace, *Ars P.* 383: '[the man who knows not how dares to frame verses. Why not? He is . . . free-born,] is rated at the fortune of a knight'.

[174] Cf. Horace, *Ars P.* 385, 'invita Minerva', that is, 'against Minerva's will', or lacking wisdom. Sidney's censure of English literature as deficient in both 'Art and Imitation' (pp. 380 ff.) is strangely academic, recalling the schoolmaster Ascham's disapproval of contemporary writers for not strictly following classical models and rules (pp. 156 ff).

[175] Sidney's self-deprecation reads oddly today, given that by this time he had probably written *Astrophil and Stella*, the most innovative collection of poems ever published in English, and the first version of *Arcadia*, a pastoral romance of brilliant narrative skill and considerable ethical depth.

[176] 'An orator is made, a poet born': a common saying first found in a 3rd-cent. commentary on Horace's *Ars poetica*.

Yet confess I always that as the fertilest ground must be manured,* so must the highest-flying wit have a Daedalus[177] to guide him. That Daedalus they say, both in this and in other, hath three wings to bear itself up into the air of due commendation: that is, Art, Imitation, and Exercise.[178] But these, neither artificial rules nor imitative patterns, we much cumber ourselves withal. Exercise indeed we do, but that very fore-backwardly: for where we should exercise to know, we exercise as having known; and so is our brain delivered of much matter which never was begotten by knowledge. For there being two principal parts—matter to be expressed by words[179] and words to express the matter—in neither we use Art or Imitation rightly. Our matter is *quodlibet** indeed, though wrongly performing Ovid's verse,

Quicquid conabor dicere, versus erit:[180]

never marshalling it into any assured rank, that almost the readers cannot tell where to find themselves.

Chaucer, undoubtedly, did excellently in his *Troilus and Criseyde*; of whom, truly, I know not whether to marvel more, either that he in that misty time could see so clearly, or that we in this clear age go so stumblingly after him. Yet had he great wants,* fit to be forgiven in so reverent an antiquity. I account the *Mirror of Magistrates* meetly* furnished of beautiful parts, and in the Earl of Surrey's lyrics many things tasting of a noble birth, and worthy of a noble mind. The *Shepherds' Calendar* hath much poetry in his eclogues, indeed worthy the reading, if I be not deceived. (That same framing of his style to an old rustic language[181] I dare not allow,* since neither Theocritus in Greek, Virgil in Latin, nor Sannazaro in Italian did affect it.) Besides these, I do not remember to have seen but few (to speak boldly) printed, that have poetical sinews in them: for proof whereof, let but

---

[177] The great artificer and inventor in classical mythology.

[178] The three ways in which oratory could be mastered: cf. *Rhet. Her.* 1. 2. 3, and Wilson, pp. 78–9.

[179] This basic distinction, between *res* (thought, subject-matter) and *verba* (language, expression), was taken over from Roman grammar by the rhetoricians (e.g. Cicero, *De or.* 3. 5. 19, 3. 31. 125); and by Horace (*Ars P.* 38–72, 310–11). Cf. Ascham, p. 141 n. 1.

[180] *Tristia* 4. 10. 26: 'Et quod tentabam [var.: 'conabar'] dicere, versus erat', 'And whatever I tried to say, turned into verse'. Sidney substitutes the future tense, as if giving a melancholy prognostic.

[181] Cf. E.K.'s justification of it, pp. 176–8. It is strange that Sidney should here invoke classical authority against Spenser, when Renaissance scholars recognized that Virgil's style in the *Eclogues* attempted to render a country dialect, appropriate to shepherds.

most of the verses be put in prose,[182] and then ask the meaning, and it will be found that one verse did but beget another, without ordering at the first what should be at the last; which becomes a confused mass of words, with a tingling* sound of rhyme, barely accompanied with reason.

Our tragedies and comedies (not without cause cried out against), observing rules neither of honest civility* nor skilful poetry, excepting *Gorboduc*[183] (again, I say, of those that I have seen), which notwithstanding, as it is full of stately speeches and well-sounding phrases, climbing to the height of Seneca's style, and as full of notable morality, which it doth most delightfully teach, and so obtain the very end of poesy, yet in truth it is very defectuous in the circumstances,* which grieveth me, because it might not remain as an exact model of all tragedies. For it is faulty both in place and time, the two necessary companions of all corporal actions. For where the stage should always represent but one place, and the uttermost time presupposed in it should be, both by Aristotle's precept[184] and common reason, but one day, there is both many days, and many places, inartificially* imagined.

But if it be so in *Gorboduc*, how much more in all the rest?[185] where you shall have Asia of the one side, and Afric of the other, and so many other under-kingdoms, that the player, when he cometh in, must ever begin with telling where he is, or else the tale will not be conceived. Now ye shall have three ladies walk to gather flowers: and then we must believe the stage to be a garden. By and by we hear news of shipwreck in the same place: and then we are to blame if we accept it not for a rock. Upon the back of that comes out a hideous monster with fire and smoke, and then the miserable beholders are bound to take it for a cave. While in the meantime two armies fly in, represented with four swords and bucklers, and then what hard heart will not receive it for a pitched field?

---

[182] Cf. Gascoigne, p. 166; Jonson's testimony (p. 534) that his schoolmaster Camden made him first write his Latin poetical exercises in prose; and North, p. 511.

[183] A Senecan tragedy by Thomas Sackville and Thomas Norton, the first English tragedy in blank verse, performed before Queen Elizabeth in 1561 and printed *c.*1570 under the title *Ferrex and Porrex*.

[184] Cf. *Poet.* 5. 1449[b]12 ff.: 'Tragedy endeavours to keep as far as possible within a single circuit of the sun, or something near that', unlike epic. Sidney's strictures about the 'correct' form or conventions of drama expresses neoclassic attitudes which later hardened into the supposedly binding rules concerning the three unities, recently introduced by Castelvetro in 1571 in his commentary on Aristotle's *Poetics* (cf. *LCPD*, pp. 309–10). Cf. also Scaliger, *Poetice* 3. 96, 6. 3.

[185] Cf. Whetstone, pp. 173–4, and Jonson, pp. 526–7.

Now, of time they are much more liberal, for ordinary it is that two young princes fall in love; after many traverses,* she is got with child, delivered of a fair boy; he is lost, groweth a man, falls in love, and is ready to get another child; and all this in two hours' space: which, how absurd it is in sense, even sense may imagine, and art hath taught, and all ancient examples justified, and at this day, the ordinary players in Italy will not err in. Yet will some bring in an example of *Eunuchus*[186] in Terence, that containeth matter of two days, yet far short of twenty years. True it is, and so was it to be played in two days, and so fitted to the time it set forth. And though Plautus[187] have in one place done amiss, let us hit with him, and not miss with him. But they will say: How then shall we set forth a story, which containeth both many places and many times? And do they not know that a tragedy is tied to the laws of poesy,[188] and not of history; not bound to follow the story, but, having liberty either to feign a quite new matter, or to frame the history to the most tragical conveniency?* Again, many things may be told which cannot be showed, if they know the difference betwixt reporting and representing. As, for example, I may speak (though I am here) of Peru, and in speech digress from that to the description of Calicut; but in action I cannot represent it without Pacolet's horse.[189] And so was the manner the ancients took, by some *nuncius** to recount things done in former time or other place.

Lastly, if they will represent an history, they must not (as Horace saith) begin *ab ovo*,[190] but they must come to the principal point of that one action which they will represent. By example this will be best expressed. I have a story of young Polydorus, delivered for safety's sake, with great riches, by his father Priam to Polymnestor, king of Thrace, in the Trojan war time. He, after some years, hearing the overthrow of Priam, for to make the treasure his own, murdereth the child. The body of the child is taken up by Hecuba. She, the same day, findeth a sleight to be revenged most cruelly of the tyrant. Where now

---

[186] But the action of that play is completed in one day. Sidney probably confuses it with Terence's *The Self-Tormentor*, which takes two days. Shepherd (*GKS*, p. 221) suggests that the word 'not' has been omitted before 'far short'.

[187] In *Captives*, which does not observe this 'rule' of time.

[188] Cf. Spenser's letter to Ralegh, p. 300.

[189] The flying horse of the enchanter Pacolet, in the late medieval romance *Valentine and Orson*, popular in the 16th cent.

[190] Cf. *Ars P*. 147, which criticizes the obvious starting-point 'from the egg' or very beginning, praising Homer for plunging 'in medias res', in the midst of events; also Scaliger, *Poetice* 3. 96. Sidney's example is Euripides' *Hecuba*.

would one of our tragedy writers begin, but with the delivery of the child? Then should he sail over into Thrace, and so spend I know not how many years, and travel numbers of places. But where doth Euripides? Even with the finding of the body, leaving the rest to be told by the spirit of Polydorus. This needs no further to be enlarged; the dullest wit may conceive it.

But besides these gross absurdities, how all their plays be neither right tragedies, nor right comedies, mingling kings and clowns, not because the matter so carrieth it, but thrust in the clown by head and shoulders, to play a part in majestical matters, with neither decency nor discretion,[191] so as neither the admiration and commiseration, nor the right sportfulness, is by their mongrel tragi-comedy obtained. I know Apuleius[192] did somewhat so, but that is a thing recounted with space of time, not represented in one moment; and I know the ancients have one or two examples of tragi-comedies, as Plautus hath *Amphitruo*.[193] But, if we mark them well, we shall find that they never, or very daintily,* match hornpipes and funerals. So falleth it out that, having indeed no right comedy, in that comical part of our tragedy, we have nothing but scurrility, unworthy of any chaste ears, or some extreme show of doltishness, indeed fit to lift up a loud laughter, and nothing else: where the whole tract* of a comedy should be full of delight, as the tragedy should be still maintained in a well-raised* admiration.

But our comedians* think there is no delight without laughter; which is very wrong, for though laughter may come with delight, yet cometh it not of delight, as though delight should be the cause of laughter; but well may one thing breed both together. Nay, rather in themselves they have, as it were, a kind of contrariety: for delight we scarcely do but in things that have a conveniency to ourselves or to the general nature; laughter almost ever cometh of things most disproportioned[194] to ourselves and nature. Delight hath a joy in it, either permanent or present. Laughter hath only a scornful tickling. For

---

[191] For similar strictures on indecorum cf. Whetstone, pp. 173–4.

[192] In his *Metamorphoses, or Golden Ass* (tr. W. Aldington, 1566), where the love story of Cupid and Psyche is introduced into the story of Charis' misfortunes.

[193] In the prologue (50 ff.) Plautus described *Amphitryon* as a tragi-comedy, arousing much critical discussion in the Renaissance: cf. Scaliger, *Poetice* 1. 7, and Fletcher, pp. 502–3.

[194] The classical theory of comedy, set out by Aristotle in *Poet.* 5 (cit. n. 107 above), and by Cicero in *De or.* 2. 58. 235–2. 70. 280 (itself deriving from Aristotle, *Eth. Nic.* 4. 8. 1128ᵃ5 ff.), held that the comic is based on ridicule, provoked by the exposition of shame or deformity. For Renaissance modifications of this theory (Castiglione, Castelvetro, Trissino), cf. *LCPD* index, s.v. 'comedy', 'comic' (p. 686) and *GKS*, pp. 223–5.

example, we are ravished with delight to see a fair woman, and yet are far from being moved to laughter. We laugh at deformed creatures, wherein certainly we cannot delight. We delight in good chances, we laugh at mischances; we delight to hear the happiness of our friends and country, at which he were worthy to be laughed at that would laugh. We shall, contrarily, laugh sometimes to find a matter quite mistaken and go down the hill against the bias,[195] in the mouth of some such men, as for the respect of them one shall be heartily sorry, he cannot choose but laugh; and so is rather pained than delighted with laughter. Yet deny I not but that they may go well together: for as in Alexander's picture well set out we delight without laughter, and in twenty mad antics[196] we laugh without delight; so in Hercules,[197] painted with his great beard and furious countenance, in woman's attire, spinning at Omphale's commandment, it breedeth both delight and laughter. For the representing of so strange a power in love procureth delight: and the scornfulness of the action stirreth laughter.

But I speak to this purpose, that all the end of the comical part be not upon such scornful matters as stir laughter only, but, mixed with it, that delightful teaching which is the end of poesy. And the great fault even in that point of laughter, and forbidden plainly by Aristotle,[198] is that they stir laughter in sinful things, which are rather execrable than ridiculous; or in miserable, which are rather to be pitied than scorned. For what is it to make folks gape at a wretched beggar and a beggarly clown; or, against law of hospitality, to jest at strangers, because they speak not English so well as we do? What do we learn? since it is certain

> nil habet infelix paupertas durius in se,
> quam quod ridiculos homines facit.[199]

But rather, a busy loving courtier and a heartless threatening Thraso; a self-wise-seeming schoolmaster;[200] an awry-transformed traveller:

---

[195] In bowls, when the slope of the ground counteracts the swerve which the bowler intended.

[196] Dances of madmen, considered a source of amusement in the 16th cent. and after.

[197] Hercules' infatuation with Queen Omphale, for whom he performed humiliating tasks, was commonly taken as a comic emblem of inversion.

[198] *Poet.* 5. 1449ᵃ32 ff.

[199] Juvenal, *Sat.* 3. 152–3: 'Of all the woes of luckless poverty none is harder to endure than this, that it exposes men to ridicule'.

[200] Cf. Rhombus, in Sidney's masque *The Lady of May*, and Holofernes in *Love's Labour's Lost*.

these if we saw walk in stage names, which we play naturally,* therein were delightful laughter, and teaching delightfulness: as in the other, the tragedies of Buchanan do justly bring forth a divine admiration. But I have lavished out too many words of this play matter. I do it because, as they are excelling parts of poesy, so is there none so much used in England, and none can be more pitifully abused; which, like an unmannerly daughter showing a bad education, causeth her mother poesy's honesty* to be called in question.

Other sort of poetry almost have we none, but that lyrical kind of songs and sonnets: which, Lord, if He gave us so good minds, how well it might be employed, and with how heavenly fruits, both private and public, in singing the praises of the immortal beauty, the immortal goodness of that God who giveth us hands to write and wits to conceive; of which we might well want words, but never matter; of which we could turn our eyes to nothing, but we should ever have new-budding occasions. But truly many of such writings as come under the banner of unresistible love, if I were a mistress, would never persuade me they were in love; so coldly they apply fiery speeches, as men that had rather read lovers' writings (and so caught up certain swelling phrases which hang together, like a man that once told me the wind was at north-west and by south, because he would be sure to name winds enough), than that in truth they feel those passions, which easily (as I think) may be betrayed* by that same forcibleness or *energeia*[201] (as the Greeks call it) of the writer. But let this be a sufficient though short note, that we miss the right use of the material* point of poesy.

Now, for the outside of it, which is words, or (as I may term it) diction,* it is even well worse. So is that honey-flowing matron eloquence apparelled, or rather disguised, in a courtesan-like painted affectation: one time with so far-fet words, they may seem monsters, but must seem strangers to any poor Englishman; another time with coursing of a letter,[202] as if they were bound to follow the method of a dictionary; another time with figures and flowers extremely winter-starved. But I would this fault were only peculiar to versifiers, and had not as large possession among prose-printers, and (which is to be

[201] On this term, describing a writer's effective power of representing the subject clearly (both in ideas and in words), cf. Puttenham, pp. 224–5 n. 59, and Scaliger, *Poetice* 3. 24, 26.

[202] Sidney echoes frequent warnings against excessive rhetoric, and the related faults of using strange or far-fetched words, 'coursing a letter', or excessive alliteration. Cf. Wilson, *Art*, ed. Medine, p. 193; E.K., p. 179, Puttenham, *Arte*, ed. Willcock and Walker, p. 174; Campion, p. 431.

marvelled) among many scholars, and (which is to be pitied) among some preachers. Truly I could wish, if at least I might be so bold to wish in a thing beyond the reach of my capacity, the diligent imitators[203] of Tully and Demosthenes (most worthy to be imitated) did not so much keep Nizolian paper-books of their figures and phrases, as by attentive translation* (as it were) devour them whole, and make them wholly theirs. For now they cast sugar and spice upon every dish that is served to the table, like those Indians,[204] not content to wear earrings at the fit and natural place of the ears, but they will thrust jewels through their nose and lips, because they will be sure to be fine.

Tully, when he was to drive out Catiline, as it were with a thunderbolt of eloquence, often used the figure of repetition, as *Vivit. Vivit? Immo in senatum venit, &c.*[205] Indeed, inflamed with a well-grounded rage, he would have his words (as it were) double out of his mouth, and so do that artificially which we see men in choler do naturally. And we, having noted the grace of those words, hale them in sometime to a familiar epistle, when it were too much choler to be choleric. How well store of *similiter cadences*[206] doth sound with the gravity of the pulpit, I would but invoke Demosthenes' soul to tell, who with a rare daintiness* useth them. Truly they have made me think of the sophister[207] that with too much sublety would prove two eggs three, and though he might be counted a sophister, had none for his labour. So these men bringing in such a kind of eloquence, well may they obtain an opinion of a seeming finesse,* but persuade few—which should be the end of their finesse.

[203] On the topic of *imitatio*, Sidney repeats Quintilian's recommendation of Demosthenes and Cicero as models (*Inst.* 10. 1. 105–12, 10. 2. 24–5; cf. Ascham, pp. 149–50). He shares the widespread disapproval of the excesses of Ciceronianism, with its narrow use of Cicero as an exclusive model, as in the *Thesaurus Ciceronianus* (1535) of Marius Nizolius, which attempted to limit Latin vocabulary to Cicero's own usage; and he follows the sound classical advice (as in Seneca, *Ep.* 84), that, like a bee producing honey, the imitator should fully digest his models in order to create something of his own. Cf. Bacon, pp. 458–9.

[204] According to early accounts of Brazil.

[205] Cicero, *Cat.* 1: 'O tempora, O mores! Senatus haec intellegit, consul videt; hic tamen vivit. Vivit? Immo vero etiam in senatum venit, . . .' This famous opening, regularly studied by Tudor schoolboys (cf. *IDR*, pp. 261–3, for King Edward VI's surviving notebook), was often cited as an instance of the rhetorical figure *epizeuxis*, by which (as Sidney allusively puts it), the words 'double out of his mouth'.

[206] On the figure *similiter cadentia*, the choice of words with similar endings, cf. Campion, p. 431, Hoskyns, p. 417.

[207] According to this traditional story, a 'sophister' or superficial logician tried to fool an unlearned man to believe that two eggs were three, claiming that here was one, there were two, and 1 plus 2 makes 3. But his would-be dupe ate both eggs, inviting the sophister to eat the third.

Now for similitudes in certain printed discourses, I think all herbarists, all stories of beasts, fowls, and fishes are rifled up,[208] that they may come in multitudes to wait upon any of our conceits; which certainly is as absurd a surfeit to the ears as is possible: for the force of a similitude not being to prove anything to a contrary disputer, but only to explain to a willing hearer; when that is done, the rest is a most tedious prattling, rather over-swaying the memory from the purpose whereto they were applied, than any whit informing the judgement, already either satisfied, or by similitudes not to be satisfied. For my part, I do not doubt, when Antonius and Crassus,[209] the great fore-fathers of Cicero in eloquence, the one (as Cicero testifieth of them) pretended not to know art, the other not to set by it, because with a plain sensibleness they might win credit of popular ears; which credit is the nearest step to persuasion; which persuasion is the chief mark* of Oratory—I do not doubt (I say) but that they used these knacks very sparingly; which, who doth generally use, any man may see doth dance to his own music, and so to be noted by the audience more careful to speak curiously* than truly.

Undoubtedly (at least to my opinion undoubtedly) I have found in diverse small learned courtiers a more sound style than in some professors of learning; of which I can guess no other cause but that the courtier, following that which by practice he findeth fittest to nature, therein (though he know it not) doth according to art, though not by art: where the other, using art to show art, and not hide art[210] (as in these cases he should do), flieth from nature, and indeed abuseth art.

But what? methinks I deserve to be pounded* for straying from poetry to oratory: but both have such an affinity in the wordish

---

[208] An attack on the style recently popularized by Lyly in *Euphues* (1578–9), which used ad nauseam similes drawn from what has been called the 'unnatural natural history' of Pliny. Cf. Falstaff's parody: 'For though the camomile, the more it is trodden on, the faster it grows, [yet] youth, the more it is wasted, the sooner it wears' (*1 Henry IV*, 2. 4. 399 ff.).

[209] The main speakers in *De oratore* are Antonius and Crassus, famous orators of a previous generation. Cicero ascribes to Antonius a contempt of 'art', or rhetorical theory (2. 7. 30 ff.), belied by his actual practice of it, and to Crassus 'the reputation of looking down upon learning' (2. 1. 4). In fact, just like Sidney's use of the modesty topos (or *sprezzatura*), both excelled in all branches of oratory (cf. *IDR*, pp. 30–5). To win 'credit' with the audience is the successful use of *ethos*, presenting the orator's own character in a favourable light: Aristotle, *Rh.* 1. 2. 1356ᵃ1–33; Cicero, *De or.* 2. 42. 178, 43. 182–4.

[210] Cf. Aristotle *Rh.* 3. 1. 1404ᵇ (*ALC*, p. 137); *Poet.* 24. 1460ᵇ1; Ovid, *Ars am.* 2. 313 ('Art's most effective when concealed'); Longinus, *On Sublimity* 17, 38 (*ALC*, pp. 481, 496); the old adage, ars est celare artem; and Puttenham, p. 292.

consideration,[211] that I think this digression will make my meaning receive the fuller understanding—which is not to take upon me to teach poets how they should do, but only, finding myself sick among the rest, to show some one or two spots of the common infection grown among the most part of writers; that, acknowledging ourselves somewhat awry, we may bend to the right use both of matter and manner: whereto our language[212] giveth us great occasion, being indeed capable of any excellent exercising of it. I know some will say it is a mingled language. And why not so much the better, taking the best of both the other? Another will say it wanteth grammar. Nay truly, it hath that praise, that it wanteth not grammar: for grammar it might have, but it needs it not; being so easy in itself, and so void of those cumbersome differences of cases, genders, moods, and tenses, which I think was a piece of the Tower of Babylon's curse, that a man should be put to school to learn his mother-tongue. But for the uttering sweetly and properly the conceits of the mind, which is the end of speech,[213] that hath it equally with any other tongue in the world; and is particularly happy in compositions* of two or three words together, near the Greek, far beyond the Latin: which is one of the greatest beauties can be in a language.

Now of versifying there are two sorts, the one ancient, the other modern: the ancient marked the quantity of each syllable, and according to that framed his verse; the modern observing only number (with some regard of the accent), the chief life of it standeth in that like sounding of the words, which we call rhyme.[214] Whether of these be the more excellent, would bear many speeches: the ancient (no doubt) more fit for music, both words and time[215] observing quantity, and more fit lively to express diverse passions, by the low or lofty sound of the well-weighed syllable. The latter likewise, with his rhyme, striketh a certain music to the ear; and, in fine, since it doth delight,

---

[211] That is, *lexis*, *elocutio*, or 'diction', as we should call it.

[212] Although Sidney expresses sharp criticisms of contemporary English literature he shares the Europe-wide promotion of the vernaculars against Greek and Latin; cf. R. F. Jones, *The Triumph of the English Language* (Stanford, Calif., 1953); E.K., pp. 177–9, Daniel, pp. 442–3.

[213] Cf. Wilson, p. 77, Hoskyns, pp. 399–400, Jonson, p. 574.

[214] For this distinction between 'verse', composed according to the rules of classical (quantitative) metrics, and 'rhyme', which used accentual metrics and (sometimes, but not always) rhyme, cf. Ascham, p. 157, Gascoigne, p. 165, Puttenham, pp. 215–6, Campion, pp. 430–1, Daniel, pp. 442–5. Further discussion in *GKS*, pp. 233–4.

[215] The Olney *Apology* reads 'tune' here, but 'time' is evidently the correct reading; cf. n. 23 above for Morley, and *GKS*, p. 234.

though by another way, it obtains the same purpose: there being in either sweetness, and wanting in neither majesty. Truly the English, before any vulgar language I know, is fit for both sorts: for, for the ancient, the Italian is so full of vowels that it must ever be cumbered with elisions; the Dutch[216] so, of the other side, with consonants, that they cannot yield the sweet* sliding* fit for a verse; the French in his whole language hath not one word that hath his accent in the last syllable saving two, called *antepenultima*; and little more hath the Spanish, and therefore very gracelessly may they use dactyls. The English is subject to none of these defects.

Now for rhyme,[217] though we do not observe quantity, yet we observe the accent very precisely, which other languages either cannot do, or will not do so absolutely. That *caesura*, or breathing place[218] in the midst of the verse, neither Italian nor Spanish have, the French and we never almost fail of. Lastly, even the very rhyme itself the Italian cannot put it in the last syllable, by the French named the masculine rhyme, but still in the next to the last, which the French call the female, or the next before that, which the Italian term *sdrucciola*.[219] The example of the former is *buono*: *suono*, of the *sdrucciola* is *femina*: *semina*. The French, of the other side, hath both the male, as *bon*: *son*, and the female, as *plaise*: *taise*, but the *sdrucciola* he hath not: where the English hath all three, as *due*: *true*, *father*: *rather*, *motion*: *potion*; with much more which might be said, but that I already find the triflingness of this discourse is much too much enlarged.

[PERORATION]

So that[220] since the ever-praiseworthy poesy is full of virtue-breeding delightfulness, and void of no gift that ought to be in the noble name

---

[216] The greater flexibility of English over 'Dutch' (that is, German) and other languages, was asserted by Sidney's rules for scansion, which he produced from a digest made for him by Thomas Drant, translator of Horace and advocate of classical metres. These are reprinted by William Ringler in *The Poems of Philip Sidney* (Oxford, 1962), pp. 389–93.

[217] Modern accentual verse in general.

[218] Cf. Gascoigne, pp. 168–9; Campion, pp. 435–6.

[219] This Italian term (meaning 'slippery') applies to rhymes in which there are several unstressed syllables after the last accent.

[220] As Shepherd notes (*GKS*, p. 235), the conclusion is tripartite, as recommended in the rhetorical handbooks (e.g. *Rhet. Her.* 2. 3. 47–2. 31. 50): here, a summing-up; an amplification invoking authorities; and an emotional appeal to engage the self-interest of the audience.

of learning; since the blames laid against it are either false or feeble; since the cause why it is not esteemed in England is the fault of poet-apes, not poets; since, lastly, our tongue is most fit to honour poesy, and to be honoured by poesy; I conjure you all that have had the evil luck to read this ink-wasting toy of mine, even in the name of the Nine Muses, no more to scorn the sacred mysteries of poesy; no more to laugh at the name of poets, as though they were next inheritors to fools; no more to jest at the reverent title of a rhymer; but to believe, with Aristotle, that they were the ancient treasurers of the Grecians' divinity;[221] to believe, with Bembus,[222] that they were first bringers-in of all civility; to believe, with Scaliger,[223] that no philosopher's precepts can sooner make you an honest man than the reading of Virgil; to believe, with Clauserus, the translator of Cornutus,[224] that it pleased the heavenly deity, by Hesiod and Homer, under the veil of fables, to give us all knowledge, logic, rhetoric, philosophy natural and moral, and *quid non?*; to believe, with me, that there are many mysteries contained in poetry,[225] which of purpose were written darkly, lest by profane wits it should be abused; to believe, with Landino,[226] that they are so beloved of the gods that whatsoever they write proceeds of a divine fury; lastly, to believe themselves, when they tell you they will make you immortal by their verses.

Thus doing, your name shall flourish in the printers' shops; thus doing, you shall be of kin to many a poetical preface; thus doing, you shall be most fair, most rich, most wise, most all; you shall dwell upon

[221] Aristotle refers to Hesiod and the other *theologoi*, that is, 'writers of theogonies' or 'mythologists', as we should put it (*Metaph.* 3. 4. 1000ª9). But Sidney seems to be drawing rather on Boccaccio's misreading, *De genealogia deorum* 14. 8: 'Aristotle . . . asserts that the first poets were theologians', and 15. 8: 'Aristotle himself avers that they were the first to ponder theology' (*Boccaccio on Poetry*, tr. Osgood, pp. 46, 122, 163).

[222] Pietro Bembo (1470–1547), influential humanist; the opinion ascribed to him was widely shared.

[223] Cf. *Poetice* 3. 19 (ed. Deitz, ii. 242–3).

[224] L. Annaeus Cornutus (1st cent. AD), a Stoic philosopher, teacher of Persius and Lucan. His fragmentary treatise *De natura deorum* was published in 1543 by the German humanist Conrad Clauser, whose preface Sidney summarizes.

[225] On the old tradition that a certain amount of obscurity is proper to high poetry see Chapman, pp. 392–4.

[226] Cristoforo Landino (1424–1504), the Florentine humanist and Neoplatonist, who discusses the divine fury in the prologue (sect. 7) to his edition of Dante's *Divina Commedia* (Florence, 1481). As Shepherd notes (*GKS*, p. 236) Sidney conveniently forgets that he has already rejected Plato's ascription of a 'divine force' to poetry (above, p. 376).

superlatives. Thus doing, though you be *libertino patre natus*, you shall suddenly grow *Herculea proles*,[227]

Si quid mea carmina possunt.[228]

Thus doing, your soul shall be placed with Dante's Beatrice, or Virgil's Anchises.[229] But if (fie of such a but) you be born so near the dull-making cataract of Nilus[230] that you cannot hear the planet-like music of poetry; if you have so earth-creeping a mind that it cannot lift itself up to look to the sky of poetry, or rather, by a certain rustical disdain, will become such a mome* as to be a Momus[231] of poetry; then, though I will not wish unto you the ass's ears of Midas, nor to be driven by a poet's verses, as Bubonax was, to hang himself, nor to be rhymed to death, as is said to be done in Ireland;[232] yet thus much curse I must send you, in the behalf of all poets, that while you live, you live in love, and never get favour for lacking skill of a sonnet; and, when you die, your memory die from the earth for want of an epitaph.

---

[227] 'Son of a freedman' (Horace, *Sat.* 1. 6. 6); and 'offspring of Hercules'.

[228] Virgil, *Aen.* 9. 446, 'If aught my verse avail, no day shall ever blot you from the memory of time': a passage promising the immortality of fame to the dead friends Nisus and Euryalus.

[229] In the *Divina Commedia* Beatrice inhabits Paradise; in the *Aeneid* 6. 679 ff. Aeneas finds his father Anchises in the Elysian Fields.

[230] Cf. Cicero, *De republica* 6. 18. 19, on the inhabitants of the region Catadupa, deafened by the Nile's cataracts, as types of humanity unable to hear the music of the spheres.

[231] The god of ridicule and fault-finding.

[232] Midas was awarded asses' ears for judging the music of Pan better than Apollo's (Ovid, *Met.* 11. 146 ff.); 'Bubonax' is Sidney's conflation of Bupalus, a sculptor who (according to Pliny, *Naturalis historia* 36. 5. 4) portrayed the ugly poet Hipponax, and was driven to suicide by his satirical verses. The Irish were reputed to use verse charms to rhyme either man or beast to death: cf. Campion, p. 430.

16

George Chapman,
The proper difficulty of poetry (1595)

GEORGE CHAPMAN (1559?–1634), poet, dramatist, and translator; nothing is known of his education. His poetry includes *The Shadow of Night* (1594), *Ovid's Banquet of Sense* and other poems (1595), and a completion of Marlowe's *Hero and Leander* (1598). For his Homer translations see p. 512. He also translated poetry by Petrarch (1612), Musaeus (1616), Hesiod (1618), and Juvenal.

TEXT. From *Ovids Banquet of Sence* (1595), the dedicatory epistle to Mathew Roydon (fl. 1580–1622), a minor poet who associated with Ralegh and William Warner; his poem on Sidney, 'An Elegie, or friends passion for his Astrophill', appeared in *The Phoenix Nest* (1593).

Chapman's defence of recondite, difficult poetry shows his consistent desire to appeal to an intellectual elite, scorning the clear and open communication with a wide audience recommended by rhetoric (e.g. *De or.* 1. 3. 12; *Inst.* 8. 1. 1 ff.). In annotating this text I have benefited from P. B. Bartlett (ed.), *The Poems of George Chapman* (New York and London, 1941), and the still unequalled study by F. E. Schoell, *Études sur l'Humanisme continental en Angleterre à la fin de la Renaissance* (Paris, 1926). See also G. Snare, 'Chapman's Ovid', *Studies in Philology* 75 (1978), 430–50.

[DEDICATION TO MATHEW ROYDEN]

Such is the wilfull poverty of judgments (sweet Mathew), wandering like passportless men[1] in contempt of the divine discipline of poesy, that a man may well fear to frequent their walks. The profane multitude I hate,[2] and only consecrate my strange* poems to these searching spirits whom learning hath made noble and nobility sacred; endeavouring that material oration, which you call *schema*;[3] varying

---

[1] Lacking passports, or permission to go abroad.

[2] 'Odi profanum vulgus': Horace, *Odes* 3. 1.

[3] As Schoell pointed out (p. 224), Chapman silently quotes from Ps.-Plutarch's essay 'De Homero', a standard definition of a rhetorical *schema* (*figura*): 'A figure is a form of speech varying from normal usage through some fashioning made either for beauty or usefulness' (cf. *Inst.* 9. 1. 11, etc.).

in some rare fiction* from popular custom, even for the pure sakes of
ornament and utility; this of Euripides exceeding sweetly relishing
with me, *Lentem coquens ne quisquam olentis addito.*[4]

But that poesy should be as perviall[5] as oratory, and plainness her
special ornament, were the plain way to barbarism, and to make the
ass run proud of his ears; to take away strength from lions, and give
camels horns.[6]

That *enargeia*,[7] or clearness of representation required in absolute*
poems, is not the perspicuous delivery of a low invention but high and
hearty invention expressed in most significant and unaffected phrase.
It serves not a skilful painter's turn to draw the figure of a face only
to make known who it represents, but he must limn,* give lustre,
shadow and heightening; which though ignorants will esteem spiced*
and too curious,* yet such as have the judicial* perspective will see it
hath motion, spirit and life.

There is no confection* made to last but it is admitted more cost
and skill than presently to be used simples;* and in my opinion, that
which being with a little endeavour searched, adds a kind of majesty
to poesy, is better than that which every cobbler may sing to his patch.

Obscurity in affection of words, and indigested conceits,* is pedantical and childish; but where it shroudeth itself in the heart of his
subject, uttered with fitness of figure and expressive epithets, with that
darkness will I still labour to be shadowed.[8] Rich minerals are digged
out of the bowels of the earth, not found in the superficies and dust
of it; charms made of unlearned characters are not consecrate by the

---

[4] A proverb recorded in Erasmus' *Adagia* (1. 7. 23) '*In lente unguentum*' ('Perfume on the
lentils'), quoting Aristotle (*De sensu* 443ᵇ30 f.): 'For there is much truth in the gibe levelled
at Euripides by Stratis, that when cooking lentils it is a mistake to add perfume' (*CWE* xxxii.
79–81).

[5] This adjective, meaning 'easily seen through', is idiosyncratic to Chapman. Rhetoricians
regularly put poetry and oratory on the same level, e.g. *De or.* 1. 16. 70, 3. 7. 27.

[6] Alluding to a fable by Aesop, in which the camel begged horns from Jove.

[7] For this concept in Greek rhetoric see the note to Puttenham, pp. 224–5.

[8] Although Chapman pushes the aesthetic of obscurity to the maximum, there were
precedents in classical moral philosophy for the principle that 'good things [such as temperance and justice] are difficult' (Plato, *Resp.* 4. 435c, 2. 364a; *Cratylus* 384a; Aristotle, *Eth.
Nic.* 2. 3. 1105ᵃ9). This idea was widened to include difficulty of language, as in Castiglione's
The Courtier (1528), defending writing which in its subtlety makes the reader exert himself,
and taste 'that pleasure which is had when we achieve difficult things' (1. 17; tr. C. S. Sin-
gleton (New York, 1959), p. 59). Many readers knew Erasmus' constantly expanding *Adagia*,
a collection of proverbs and sayings with long commentaries, as on *Difficilia quae pulchra*,
'Good things are difficult' (2. 1. 12) and *Sileni Alcibiades* (3. 3. 1), which applies the principle that things that look worthless on the outside can prove admirable to knowledge:

Muses which are divine artists, but by Euippe's daughters,[9] that challenged them with mere nature, whose breasts I doubt not had been well worthy commendation if their comparison had not turned them into pies.*

Thus (not affecting glory for mine own slight labours, but desirous others should be more worthily glorious; nor professing sacred poesy in any degree), I thought good to submit to your apt judgment. Acquainted long since with the true habit of poesy, and now since your labouring wits endeavour heaven-high thoughts of nature, you have actual means to sound the philosophical conceits that my new pen so seriously courteth. I know that empty and dark spirits will complain of palpable night; but those that beforehand have a radiant and light-bearing intellect will say they can pass through Corinna's garden[10] without the help of a lantern.

'The real truth of things is always most profoundly concealed, and cannot be detected easily or by many people'. Cf. *CWE* xxxiii. 22–4, xxxiv. 262–82; Schoell, pp. 58–60; Bartlett, pp. 422, 430; Sidney, pp. 353, 370. Dudley North, however, thought that '*difficilia quae pulchra* is to be understood of the attaining, and not the exercising of faculties' (p. 510).

[9] The Pierides (Ovid, *Met.* 5. 294 ff.). Euippe's nine daughters presumptuously challenged the Muses to a song-contest, and in punishment were metamorphosed into magpies, 'which can imitate any sound they please'.

[10] The garden of Ovid's fictitious mistress, in which the action of Chapman's poem is set.

Robert Southwell,
In praise of religious poetry (1595)

ROBERT SOUTHWELL (1561–95), English poet and Jesuit martyr. Born into a Catholic family, he was sent abroad to be educated, first at the Jesuit school, Douai, then at the Roman College. He entered the Society of Jesus in 1578, was ordained in 1584, and returned to England two years later as a priest on the English Mission, becoming chaplain to the Countess of Arundel. In June 1592 he was arrested, imprisoned in solitary confinement in the Tower, and on 21 February 1595 hanged and quartered at Tyburn for high treason.

TEXT. From *Saint Peter's Complaint, With other Poemes* (1595). This collection, probably assembled and edited by Southwell's friends, appeared immediately after his execution; a second, enlarged edition appeared within a month or so, and was reprinted in 1597 and 1599. In 1602 a third, enlarged edition appeared, including Southwell's most famous poem, 'The Burning Babe' (for Jonson's admiration of which, see p. 532), and a total of fifteen other editions followed by 1636. For an authoritative text and helpful commentary see James H. McDonald and Nancy Pollard Brown (eds.), *The Poems of Robert Southwell, S. J.* (Oxford, 1967).

THE AUTHOR TO HIS LOVING COUSIN

Poets, by abusing their talent, and making the follies and feignings of love the customary subject of their base endeavours, have so discredited this faculty that a poet, a lover, and a liar[1] are by many reckoned but three words of one signification. But the vanity of men cannot counterpoise the authority of God, who delivering many parts of scripture in verse, and by his apostle[2] willing us to exercise our devotion in hymns and spiritual sonnets, warranteth the art to be good, and the use allowable.* And therefore not only among the heathens,[3] whose gods were chiefly canonized by their poets, and their paynim*

---

[1] Cf. *A Midsummer Night's Dream* 5. 1. 7 f.: 'The lunatic, the lover, and the poet | Are of imagination all compact'. For the poet as liar cf. Sidney, pp. 369–70 and notes.
[2] Cf. Eph. 5: 19; Col. 3: 16; 1 Cor. 14: 26.
[3] The Greeks and Romans.

divinity oracled in verse; but even in the Old and New Testament, it hath been used by men of greatest piety, in matters of most devotion. Christ himself, by making a hymn[4] the conclusion of his last supper, and the prologue to the first pageant of his Passion, gave his spouse a method* to imitate, as in the office of the Church it appeareth; and to all men a pattern, to know the true use of this measured and footed[5] style.

But the devil, as he affecteth* deity and seeketh to have all the complements of divine honour applied to his service, so hath he among the rest possessed also most poets with his idle fancies. For in lieu of solemn and devout matter, to which in duty they owe their abilities, they now busy themselves in expressing such passions as only serve for testimonies to how unworthy affections they have wedded their wills. And because the best course to let them see the error of their works is to weave a new web in their own loom,[6] I have here laid a few coarse threads together to invite some skilfuller wits to go forward in the same, or to begin some finer piece wherein it may be seen how well verse and virtue suit together. Blame me not (good Cousin) though I send you a blameworthy present, in which the most that can commend it is the goodwill of the writer, neither art nor invention giving it any credit. If in me this be a fault, you cannot be faultless that did importune me to commit it, and therefore you must bear part of the penance when it shall please sharp censures* to impose it.

In the meantime, with many good wishes I send you these few ditties.* Add you the tunes, and let the mean,[7] I pray you, be still a part in all your music.

TO THE READER

Dear eye that dost peruse my muse's style,
With easy censure deem* of my delight:

---

[4] Cf. Matt. 26: 30; Mark 14: 26.

[5] That is, having regular form, composed of metrical feet.

[6] Southwell intends to use the methods of worldly love poetry for religious ends. As Nancy Brown has shown (edn. cit., pp. xviii, xcvi f., 124, 135 ff., etc.), many of Southwell's poems are in effect parodies of love poetry (in some cases of specific poems by Sir Edward Dyer), transferring the secular poet's longing for his lady, his sense of loss and despair, to the theme of spiritual love.

[7] Punning on the sense of 'mean' in music, 'a middle or intermediate part in a harmonized composition or performance, *esp.* the tenor and alto' (*SOED*); perhaps referring to Christ.

Give sobrest* count'nance leave sometime to smile,
And gravest wits to take a breathing flight;
Of mirth to make a trade may be a crime,   5
But tired spirits for mirth must have a time.

The lofty eagle soars not still* above,
High flights will force her from the wing to stoop,
And studious thoughts at times men must remove,*
Lest by excess before their time they droop.   10
In coarser studies 'tis a sweet repose,
With poet's pleasing vein to temper prose.

Profane conceits and feigning fits I fly,
Such lawless stuff doth lawless speeches fit:
With David verse to virtue I apply,   15
Whose measure best with measured words doth sit.
It is the sweetest note that man can sing,
When grace in virtue's key tunes nature's string.

18

John Hoskyns,
Sidney's *Arcadia* and the rhetoric of English
prose (*c.*1599)

JOHN HOSKYNS (1566–1638), lawyer and writer, was educated at Winchester, and New College Oxford, becoming a fellow in 1586 and taking his MA in 1592. He became MP for Hereford (1614), serjeant-at-law (1623), and a judge. In his *Brief Lives* John Aubrey records many anecdotes of 'his great wit', which sometimes got Hoskyns into trouble. A friend of Camden, Donne, and Selden, he was said to have helped revise the style both of Ralegh's *History of the World* and Ben Jonson's poems.

TEXT. Preserved in manuscript, British Library Harleian MS 4604. Modern editions: by Hoyt H. Hudson, *Directions for Speech and Style* (Princeton, 1935), most of whose suggested emendations I have accepted, and by Louise Brown Osborn, *The Life, Letters and Writings of John Hoskyns 1566–1638* (New Haven, 1937; Hamden, Conn., 1973).

Apparently written in order to instruct a young law-student of the Temple in the best modes of speech and writing, Hoskyns's *Directions* form a textbook in rhetoric which is both prescriptive and descriptive. The MS title-page indicates this double purpose:

To
{
Pronounce
Pen Letters
Vary
Amplify
Illustrate
}
Otherwise than ever any precepts
have been taught

Containing all the figures of Rhetoric and the Art of the best
English, exemplified, either all out of *Arcadia*, which it censureth,
or by Instances.
The matter whereof may benefit Conversation.
The quotations being taken out of Sir Philip Sidney's *Arcadia*, the first
edition in quarto . . .

Hoskyns gave his young protégé a copy of the 1590 edition of *Arcadia*, which he had profusely annotated: an *M* in the margin indicated a metaphor, *des* marked notable descriptions, and *dc* passages demonstrating poetic decorum. The student was intended to learn these and other rhetorical devices (Hoskyns lists some 40 tropes and figures) while reading, and then use them in his own writing. Hoskyns's treatment of this material is informal, fresh, and illuminating. Many of his comments reveal a profound understanding of the nature of rhetoric and its function in achieving expressivity.

The popularity of this little treatise can be seen by the frequency with which it was used (without acknowledgement): Ben Jonson transcribed parts of it in his *Timber*, a notebook probably not intended for publication, but which was printed posthumously in his *Works*, 1641 (see p. 558); Thomas Blount used most of it in his *Academy of Eloquence* (1654); and 'John Smith' (probably John Sergeaunt) took over many passages from Blount in *The Mysterie of Rhetorique Unvail'd* (1657).

For this edition I have adapted Hoskyns's quotations from Sidney to match the excellent edition by Victor Skretkowicz, *The Countess of Pembroke's Arcadia (The New Arcadia)* (Oxford, 1987), which commendably quotes all of Hoskyns's comments on individual stylistic devices. These page references are incorporated into the text following the quotation.

PREFACE

The conceits of the mind are pictures of things and the tongue is interpreter of those pictures.[1] The order of God's creatures in themselves is not only admirable and glorious, but eloquent; then he that could apprehend the consequence* of things, in their truth, and utter his apprehensions as truly were a right* orator. Therefore Cicero said much when he said, *dicere recte nemo potest, nisi qui prudenter intellegit*.[2]

The shame of speaking unskilfully were small if the tongue were only disgraced by it. But as the image of the king in a seal of wax, ill represented, is not so much a blemish to the wax or the signet that sealeth it as to the king whom it resembleth, so disordered speech is not so much injury to the lips which give it forth, or the thoughts which put it forth, as to the right proportion and coherence of things in themselves, so wrongfully expressed. Yet cannot his mind be

---

[1] A synthesis of Aristotle's influential account of language: 'spoken sounds are symbols of affections in the soul ... [which] are likenesses of actual things' (*De Interpretatione* 1. 16ᵃ2–8), with Horace, *Ars P.* 111: 'animi motus interprete lingua' ('Nature ... with the tongue for interpreter, proclaims the emotions of the soul'). There are also certain similarities, as both modern editors have shown (Hudson, pp. 54 ff., Osborn, pp. 262–3) with accounts of language given by Pierre de la Primaudaye in *L'Académie Françoise* (English translations, 1586 and 1594); but these ideas were widely disseminated.

[2] *Brut.* 6. 23: (but reading *bene*, not *recte*) 'For no one can be a good speaker who is not a sound thinker'.

thought in tune whose words do jar, nor his reason in frame whose
sentences are preposterous;* nor his fancy clear and perfect whose
utterance breaks itself into fragments and uncertainties. Were it an
honour to a prince to have the majesty of his embassage spoiled by a
careless ambassador? And is it not as great an indignity that an excellent conceit* and capacity* by the indiligence of an idle tongue should
be defaced? Careless speech doth not only discredit the personage of
the speaker but it doth discredit the opinion of his reason and judgment, it discrediteth the truth, force, and uniformity* of the matter
and substance. If it be so, then, in words which fly and escape censure,
and where one good phrase begs pardon for many incongruities and
faults, how shall he be thought wise whose penning* is thin and
shallow? How shall you look for wit* from him whose leisure and
whose head, assisted with the examination of his eyes, could yield you
no life and sharpness in his writing? . . .

FOR VARYING[3]

A *METAPHOR*, or translation,[4] is the friendly and neighbourly borrowing of one word to express a thing with more light and better note,*
though not so directly and properly as the natural name of the thing
meant would signify. As, 'feigned sighs': the nearest to feigning is
teaching an imitation of truth by art and endeavour; therefore Sir
Philip Sidney would not say 'unfeigned sighs', but 'untaught sighs'
(440). 'Desirous': now desire is a kind of thirst, and not much different from thirst is hunger, and therefore for 'swords desirous of blood'
he saith 'hungry of blood' (395), where you may note three degrees
of metaphors in the understanding: first, that the fitness of bloodshed
in a weapon usurps the name 'desirous', which is proper to a living
creature, and then that it proceedeth to 'thirst', and then to 'hunger'.
The rule of a metaphor is that it be not too bold nor too far-fetched.[5]
And though all metaphors go beyond the signification of things, yet
are they requisite to match the compassing sweetness of men's minds,
that are not content to fix themselves upon one thing but they must
wander into the confines; like the eye, that cannot choose but view the
whole knot when it beholds but one flower in a garden of purpose;*

---

[3] In rhetoric the term 'varying' covers several processes by which the writer achieved
variety and expressiveness.
[4] The Latin term for metaphor is *translatio*.
[5] Cf. Aristotle, *Rh.* 3. 3. 1406^b8; Henry Peacham, *The Garden of Rhetoric* (1593), p. 14.

or like an archer that, knowing his bow will overcast or carry too short, takes an aim on this side or beyond his mark.

Besides, a metaphor is pleasant because it enricheth our knowledge with two things at once, with the truth and with similitude;[6] as this: 'heads disinherited of their natural seigniories' (340), whereby we understand both beheading, and the government of the head over the body, as the heir hath over the lordship which he inheriteth. Of the same matter in another place: 'to divorce the fair marriage of the head and the body' (426), where besides the cutting off the head we understand the conjunction of head and body to resemble marriage. The like in 'concealing love', uttered by these words: 'to keep love close prisoner' (308); and in number of places in your book (which are all noted with this letter, *M*, in the margent).

An *ALLEGORY* is the continual following of a metaphor (which before I defined to be the translation of one word) and proportionable* through the sentence, or through many sentences; as, 'Philoclea was so environed with sweet rivers of clear virtue as could neither be battered nor undermined' (419), where Philoclea is expressed by the similitude of a castle, her nature (defence) by the natural fortification of a river about a castle, and the metaphor continues in the tempting her by force or craft, expressed by battering and undermining. Another:

But when that wish had once displayed his ensign in her mind, then followed whole squadrons of longings that so it might be, with a main battle of mislikings and repinings against their creation. (145–6)

'Ensigns', 'squadrons', 'main battle'—metaphors still derived from the same thing as at first, war.

As I said before that a metaphor might be too bold or too far-fetched, so I now remember that it may be too base; as, 'the tempest of judgement had broken the main mast of his will' (238), 'a goodly audience of sheep',[7] 'shoulders of friendship' (126), and suchlike too base; as in that speech, 'fritter of fraud and seething-pot of iniquity' (380), and they that say 'a red herring is a shoeing-horn to a pot of ale'. But they that speak of a scornful thing speak grossly. Therefore, to delight generally, take those terms from ingenious

---

[6] Cf. Peacham, ibid., p. 13.
[7] Cf. Thomas Wilson, *The Art of Rhetoric (1560)*, ed. Peter E. Medine (University Park, Pa., 1994), p. 192.

and several professions; from ingenious arts to please the learned,
and from several* arts to please the learned of all sorts; as from the
meteors, planets, and beasts in natural philosophy, from the
stars, spheres, and their motions in astronomy, from the better part of
husbandry,* from the politic government of cities, from navigation,
from military profession, from physic; but not out of the depth of
these mysteries. But ever (unless your purpose be to disgrace)[8] let the
word be taken from a thing of equal or greater dignity, as, speaking
of virtue, 'the sky of perfect virtue over clouded with sorrow'
(323), where he thought it unfit to stoop to any metaphor lower than
heaven. You may assure yourself of this observation, and all the rest,
if you but compare those places in your book noted with this note,
M; and in truth it is the best flower, growing most plentifully in
all *Arcadia*.

An emblem,[9] an allegory, a similitude, a fable, and a poet's tale differ
thus: an emblem is but the one part of the similitude, the other part
(viz., the application) expressed indifferently* and jointly in one sentence, with words some proper to the one part, some to the other; a
similitude hath two sentences, of several proper* terms compared; a
fable is a similitude acted by fiction in beasts, a poet's tale, for the most
part, by gods and men. In the former examples, paint a castle compassed with rivers and let the word be, '*Nec obsidione nec cuniculis*'
(neither by siege nor undermining): that is an emblem, the proper
terms of the one part. Lay* it as it is in Sir Philip Sidney: 'Philoclea's
virtue', the proper terms of the one part; 'environed', 'rivers', 'battered', 'undermined' (419), the terms of the other part; all these terms
in one sentence and it is an allegory. Let it be this:

There was a lamb in a castle, and an elephant and a fox besieged it. The
elephant would have assailed the castle, but he would not swim over the
river. The fox would make a hole in the earth to get under it, but he
feared the river would have sunk in upon him and drowned him.

Then is it a fable. Let Spenser tell you such a tale of a Faery Queen,
and Ovid of Diana, and then it is a poet's tale. But utter it thus in one
sentence:

---

[8] Aristotle, *Rh.* 3. 2. 1405ª10–28.

[9] The emblem consisted of three interrelated parts: a picture, a motto or 'word', and the
application, usually written in verse. See Rosemary Freeman, *The English Emblem Book*
(London, 1948).

Even as a castle compassed about with rivers cannot be battered or undermined,

and this in another:

Philoclea, defended round about with virtuous resolutions, could neither be forced nor surprised by deceit,

then it is a similitude in his own nature,—which is the ground of all emblems, allegories, fables, and fictions.

METONYMIA is an exchange of a name when one word comes in lieu of another, not for similitude, but for other natural affinity and coherence; as when the matter is used for that which thereof consisteth, as, 'I want silver', for 'money'; when the efficient* or author is used for the thing made, as, 'my blade is a right Sebastian',[10] for 'of Sebastian's making'; the thing containing for the thing or person contained, as, 'the city met the Queen', for 'the citizens'; the adjunct, property, quality, or badge for the subject of it, as, 'deserts are preferred', for 'men deserving'; give 'room to the coif', for 'the sergeant'. No doubt better examples of this sort are in *Arcadia* if I had leisure to look so low as where they are.

SYNECDOCHE is an exchange of the name of the part for the whole, or of the name of the whole for the part. There are two kinds of total comprehensions, as an entire body and a general name; as, 'Ay, my name is tossed and censured by many tongues', for 'many men', where the part of an entire body goes for the whole. Contrariwise, 'he carries a goldsmith's shop on his fingers', for 'rings'; 'he fell into the water and swallowed the Thames', for 'the water'. So the general name for the special: 'put up your weapon', for 'your dagger'; and the special for the particular, as, 'the Earl is gone into Ireland',[11] for 'Earl of Essex'; the particular for the special, as, 'I would willingly make you a Sir Philip Sidney', for 'an eloquent, learned, valiant gentleman'; one for many, as, 'the Spaniard, they say, comes against us', for 'the Spaniards', and such like, which, because they are easy, I have exemplified familiarly.* Both these figures serve well when you have mentioned a thing before, for variety in repetition; and you may well observe better instances in your reading than my interrupted thought can now meet with.

---

[10] A famous sword-maker in Toledo.
[11] Essex left for Ireland in Apr. 1599, returning in Sept. Cf. *Henry V*, 5 *prol.* 29–33.

CATACHRESIS (in English, abuse) is now grown in fashion—as most abuses are. It is somewhat more desperate than a metaphor. It is the expressing of one matter by the name of another which is incompatible with it, and sometimes clean contrary; as, 'I gave order to some servants of mine, whom I thought as apt for such charities as myself, to lead him out into the forest and there to kill him' (181), where 'charity' is used for 'cruelty' (but this may also be by the figure *ironia*); and the abuse of a word drawn from things far different, as,

A voice beautiful to his ears.　(69)
Neither in behaviour nor action accusing in himself any great trouble in mind.　(93)
Do you grudge me part of your sorrow?　(150)
Being thy sister in nature, I would I were not so far off a kin in fortune. (156)

This is a usual figure with the fine conversants* of our time, when they strain for an extraordinary phrase, as,

I am not guilty of those phrases.
I am in danger of preferment.
I have hardly escaped good fortune.
He threatens me a good turn,

all by contrary; and as he said that misliked a picture with a crooked nose, affirming 'the elbow of his nose to be disproportionable'.

The ears of men are not only delighted with store and exchange of divers words but feel great delight in repetition of the same; which, because it beginneth in the middle, and in the end, and in sundry correspondencies of each of their places, one to another, it happeneth, therefore, it hath purchased several names of figures; as a repetition of the same word or sound immediately or without interposition of any other is called EPIZEUXIS.

Oh let not, let not from you be poured upon me destruction.　(231)
Thou hast lived, for thy sake and by thy authority, to have Philoclea tormented. . . . Tormented! Tormented! Torment of my soul! Philoclea tormented?　(441)

This figure is not to be used but in passion.

ANADIPLOSIS is a repetition in the end of the former sentence and beginning of the next, as, 'Shall Erona die? Erona die? O heav'n,' etc. (201). And Cecropia's seducing speech:

You fear lest you should offend. Offend! And how know you that you should offend? Because she doth deny. Deny! Now, by my troth I could laugh, etc.   (402)

Why lived I, alas? Alas, why loved I? To die wretched! And to be the example of the heavens' hate! And hate, and spare not! For your worst blow is stricken.   (432)

And as no man is sick in thought upon one thing but for some vehemency* or distress, so in speech there is no repetition without importance.

CLIMAX is a kind of *anadiplosis* leading by degrees, and making the last word a step to the further meaning. If it be turned to an argument, it is a *sorites*:

A young man of great beauty, beautified with great honour, honoured by great valour, etc.   (450)

[You could not enjoy your goodness] without government, nor government without a magistrate, and no magistrate without obedience, and no obedience where every one upon his private passion may interpret the doings of the rulers.   (286)

Now to make it a *sorites*, or climbing argument, join the first and the last with an *ergo*, as, '*ergo*, you cannot enjoy your own goods where every man upon his private passion doth', etc. This in penned speech is too academical, but in discourse more passable and plausible.

Seeing, to like; and liking to love; and loving, straight to feel the most incident effects of love: to serve and preserve.   (301)

Deceived me, and through the deceit abused me, after the abuse forsaken me.   (240)

What doth better become wisdom than to discern what is worthy the loving? What more agreeable to goodness than to love it, so discerned; and what to greatness of heart than to be constant in it, once loved? (254)

The like, where the last word or some one word in the last sentence begets the next clause. This figure hath his time when you are well entered into discourse and have procured attention and mean to rise and amplify.

ANAPHORA is when many clauses have the like beginning:

But be not, be not most excellent lady, you that nature hath made to be the lodestar of comfort, be not the rock of shipwreck; you whom virtue hath made the princess of felicity, be not the minister of ruin; you whom my choice hath made the goddess of my safety. . . . (231)

This figure beats upon one thing to cause the quicker feeling in the audience, and to awake a sleepy or dull person.

EPISTROPHE is contrary to the former, when many clauses end with the same words:

Where the richness did invite the eyes, the fashion did entertain the eyes, and the device did teach the eyes the present misery of the presenter himself.   (334)
And all that day and night he did nothing but weep, 'Philoclea!'; sigh, 'Philoclea!'; and cry out, 'Philoclea!'   (433)
Either arm their lives or take away their lives.   (459)

This figure is rather of narration or instruction than emotion.

SYMPLOKE, or *COMPLEXIO*, is when several sentences have the same beginning and the same ending:

The most covetous man longs not to get riches out of a ground which can bear nothing. Why? Because it is impossible. The most ambitious wight vexeth not his wits to climb into heaven. Why? Because it is impossible.   (149)

This is the wantonest of repetitions, and is not to be used in matters too serious. You have an example of it in [my] fustian* speech about tobacco,[12] in derision of vain rhetoric.

EPANALEPSIS is the same in one sentence which *symploke* or *complexio* is in several sentences, as,

Severe to his servants, to his children severe,

or the same sound reiterated first and last in a sentence, as,

His superior in meat, in place his inferior.
In sorrow I was born, and must die in sorrow.
Unkindness moved me, and what can so trouble my courses or wrack my thoughts as unkindness?

---

[12] For this speech parodying vain rhetoric see Hudson edn., pp. 108–13.

This [is] a mild and sweet figure of much use, though, single and by itself, not usual in the *Arcadia* and therefore unnoted; but, 'she the overthrow of my desires and yet the recompense of my overthrow' (129); 'so as their strength failed them sooner than their skill, and yet their breath failed them sooner than their strength' (464).

EPANODOS is when the midst and the end, or the midst and the beginning are the same, as,

If there were any true pleasure in sleep and idleness, then no doubt the heathen philosophers would have placed some part of the felicity of their heathen gods in sleep and idleness.
Your diligence to speak well must be great, but you shall be abundantly recompensed for the greatness in the success, persuasion.
If I ever wish for the perfection of eloquence, it is for your instruction; and for your benefit I would wish I were eloquent.

This kind of repetition and the former (*epanalepsis*) are most easily admitted into discourse and are freest from the opinion of affectation, because words received at the beginning of many sentences or at both ends of the same are more notorious.*

ANTIMETABOLE, or *COMMUTATIO*, is a sentence inversed or turned back, as,

If any that either for the love of honour, or honour of his love.   (365)
That as you are child of a mother, so do your best to be mother of a child.   (332)
They misliked what themselves did, and yet still did what themselves misliked.   (415)
If before he languished because he could not obtain his desiring, he now lamented because he could not desire the obtaining.   (413–14)
Either not striving because he was contented, or contented because he would not strive.   (249)
Just to exercise his might, and mighty to perform his justice.   (363)

Our learned knight skipped often into this figure, as: 'Urania, the sweetest fairness and fairest sweetness' (4); 'as this place served us to think of those things, so those things serve as places to call to memory more excellent matters' (4); 'while she might prevent it she did not feel it, now she felt it when it was past preventing' (146); 'but with that, Dorus blushed; and Pamela smiled. And Dorus the more blushed at her smiling; and she the more smiled at his blushing' (173); 'judging the action by the minds, and not the minds by the action' (287). Yet he concealed the particularity of his affection by this, sometimes by not turning the words wholly back as they lay:

To account it not as a purse for treasure, but as a treasure itself, worthy to be pursed up in the purse of his own heart.   (355)
Men venture lives to conquer; she conquers lives without venturing. (356)
Showed such fury in his force, such stay in his fury,

which is rather *epanodos*. Sometimes the same sense must be in contrary words, as, 'Parthenia desired above all things to have Argalus; Argalus feared nothing but to miss Parthenia' (29), where 'fear to miss' is put instead of 'desire to have'.

Neither could you have thought so well of me if extremity of love had not made your judgment partial, nor you could have loved me so entirely if you had not been apt to make so great (though undeserved) judgements of me,   (50)

where he returns for 'extremity of love', 'loving entirely', and for 'partial judgment', 'great undeserved judgment'. And notwithstanding that this is a sharp and witty figure and shows out of the same words a pithy distinction of meaning, very convenient for schoolmen,* yet Mr. P.[13] did wrong to tire this poor figure by using it thirty times in one sermon. For use this, or any other point, unseasonably, it is as ridiculous as it was in the fustian oration: 'horsemill, mill-horse'[14] etc. But let discretion[15] be the greatest and general figure of figures.

PARONOMASIA is a pleasant touch* of the same letter, syllable, or word, with a different meaning; as, for the running upon the word 'more',

This very little is more than too much.

Sir Philip Sidney, in *Astrophel and Stella*[16] calls [it] the 'dictionary method' and the verses so made 'rhymes running in rattling rows',

[13] Thomas Playfere (1561?–1609), a Cambridge preacher much given to rhetorical word-play.
[14] Cf. Hudson edn., p. 112, and Wilson, *Art of Rhetoric*, ed. cit., p. 227.
[15] Cf. Bacon's Essay 'Of Discourse' (1597): 'Discretion of speech is more than eloquence . . .': *Francis Bacon*, ed. Brian Vickers (Oxford, 1996), p. 82.
[16] Sonnet 15, lines 5–6.

which is an example of it. There is a swinish poem made thereof in Latin, called *Pugna Porcorum*;[17] and L. Lloyd[18] in his youth tickled [it] in fashion of a poet's dictionary:

Hector, Hanno, Hannibal dead, Pompey, Pyrrhus spilled; Cyrus, Scipio, Caesar slain, and Alexander killed.

The author of *Albion's England*[19] hath set forth good invention too often in this attire. In those days Lyly,[20] the author of *Euphues*, seeing the dotage of the time upon this small ornament, invented varieties of it; for he disposed the agnominations[21] in as many fashions as repetitions are distinguished. By the author's rhetoric, sometimes the first word and the middle harped one upon another, sometimes the first and the last, sometimes in several* sentences, sometimes in one; and this with a measure, COMPAR,[22] a change* of contention, or contraries, and a device of a similitude, in those days made a gallant show. But Lyly himself hath outlived this style and breaks well from it.

An *AGNOMINATION* of some syllables is sometimes found in *Arcadia*, as,

Alas, what can saying make them believe whom seeing cannot persuade? (136)
And whilst he was followed by the valiantest, he made a way for the vilest. (344)
Who went away, repining but not repenting. (363)
His mind, and her merit. (430)

Not only Lyly, whose posy* at the beginning of his book was stamped with cognizance,* 'Commend it or amend it', but even with Dr.

[17] A poem of this name by the Flemish friar J. L. Placentius, published in 1530, consisted of 250 lines, every word beginning with the letter *p*.
[18] Ludowick Lloyd (fl. 1573–1610), a court official and minor poet, in 'An Epitaph upon the death of Sir Edward Saunders', in *The Paradyse of Daintie Devises* (1578).
[19] William Warner (*c*.1558–1609), whose versified history of England had several revised and enlarged editions between 1586 and 1606.
[20] John Lyly (1554?–1606), whose moralizing novel *Euphues* (1578, 1580; over thirty editions by 1617) achieved notoriety for its highly rhetorical prose style.
[21] A rhetorical figure involving the echoing of syllables and letters, resembling alliteration.
[22] Another name for *parison* (pp. 263–4), in which a series of clauses or sentences have the same syntactical structure, noun corresponding to noun, verb to verb, etc.

Matthew[23] this figure was of great accompt, and he lost no estimation by it:

Our paradise is a pair of dice, our alms-deeds are turned into all misdeeds, our praying into playing, our fasting into feasting.

But that kind of breaking words into another meaning is pretty to play with among gentlewomen, as, 'you will have but a bare gain of this bargain'; otherwise it will best become the tuftaffeta* orators to skip up and down the neighbourhood of these words that differ more in sense than in sound, tending nearer to metre than to matter; in whose mouth long may that phrase prosper, 'a man not only fit for the gown but for the gun, for the pen but for the pike, for the book but for the blade'!

See to what preferment* a figure may aspire if it once get in credit in a world that hath not much true rhetoric! That was the cause that Sir Philip Sidney would not have his style be much beholding to this kind of garnish. And of a truth, if the times gives itself too much to any one flourish, it makes it a toy* and bars a learned man's writings from it, lest it seem to come more of the general humor than the private judgment.

POLYPTOTON, or TRADUCTIO, is a repetition of words of the same lineage,* that differ only in termination, as,

Exceedingly sorry for Pamela, but exceedingly exceeding that exceedingness in fear for Philoclea.   (427)
By this faulty using of our faults.   (238)

Sometime the same word in several cases, as,

He was afraid to show his fear, but for very fear would have hid his fear lest it should discomfort others.   (338)

Sometime the same verb in several voices, as,

Forsaken of hope and forsaking comfort.   (430)

Sometime the same adjective in several comparisons:

Much might be said in my defence, much more for love, and most of all for that divine creature which hath joined me and love together. (74)

This is a good figure, and may be used with or without passion; but so as the use of it come from some choice and not from barrenness.

---

[23] Tobie Matthew (1546–1628), public orator of Oxford University (1569–72), who became Bishop of Durham (1595) and Archbishop of Canterbury (1606), was notorious for his rhetorical word-play.

TO AMPLIFY[24]

To amplify and illustrate are two the chiefest ornaments of eloquence, and gain of men's minds two the chiefest advantages, admiration* and belief. For how can you commend a thing more acceptably to our attention than by telling us it is extraordinary and by showing us that it is evident? There is no looking at a comet if it be either little or obscure, and we love and look on the sun above all stars for these two excellencies, his greatness, his clearness: such in speech is amplification and illustration.

We amplify five ways: by comparison, division, accumulation, intimation, and progression.

Comparison is either of things contrary, equal, or things different. . . .

In these two sorts of amplifying you may insert all figures as the passion of the matter shall serve, and for the proper season* and state of each figure look in the end of their particular treatises.

Division, the second way of amplification, which Bacon[25] in his fifth 'colour' took out of the rhetoricians: 'A way to amplify anything' (quoth he) 'is to break it and make an anatomy of it into several parts, and to examine it according to several circumstances.' He said true. It is like the show which peddlers make of their packs, when they display them; contrary to the German magnificence that serves in all the good meat in one dish. But whereas he says that this art of amplifying will betray itself in method and order, I think that it rather adorneth itself. For instead of saying, 'he put the whole town to the sword', let men reckon all ages and sorts and say:

He neither saved the young men, as pitying the unripe flower of their youth, nor the aged men, as respecting their gravity, nor children, as pardoning their weakness, nor women, as having compassion upon their sex; soldier, clergyman, citizen, armed or unarmed, resisting or submitting,—all within the town destroyed with the fury of that bloody execution.

Note that your divisions here are taken from age, profession, sex, habit, or behaviour, and so may be from all circumstances. This only

---

[24] In Renaissance, as in classical rhetoric, to 'amplify' a topic meant to increase its importance and emotional impact on the hearer or reader.

[25] Cf. 'Of the Colours of Good and Evil, a fragment', appended to Bacon's *Essays* (1597): Vickers, edn. cit., pp. 97–101.

trick made up Sir John Davies's *Poem of Dancing*:[26] all danceth, the heavens, the elements, men's minds, commonwealths, and so by parts all danceth. . . .

The third kind of amplification is accumulation, which is heaping up of many terms of praise or accusing, importing* but the same matter without descending to any part; and hath his due season after some argument or proof. Otherwise it is like a schoolmaster foaming out synonymies, or words of one meaning, and will sooner yield a conjecture of superfluity of words than of sufficiency of matter. But let us give some example. To amplify 'a sedition':

Tumults, mutinies, uproars, desperate conspiracies, wicked confederacies, furious commotions, traitorous rebellions, associations in villainy, distractions from allegiance, bloody garboils, and intestine massacres of the citizens.

But this example is somewhat too swelling. . . .

FIGURES SERVING FOR AMPLIFICATION

Here are figures that make a fair offer to set forth a matter better than it is.

The first of them in single words and phrases is HYPERBOLE, wherein I will give you some such examples as by my once reading long since I observed in *Arcadia*. Sometimes it expresseth a thing in the highest degree of possibility, beyond the truth, that it descending thence may find the truth; sometimes in flat impossibility,[27] that rather you may conceive the unspeakableness than the untruth of the relation.

Possibly: as, for 'an hypocritical host':

He gave as pleasing entertainment as the falsest heart could give him that he means the worst unto. (165)
As cruel a fight as eye did ever see or thought could reasonably imagine. (408)
Inquiry making their eyes, ears, and tongues serve for nothing else but that inquiry. (57)

---

[26] *Orchestra or a Poeme of Dancing* (1596). In a dedicatory sonnet Davies states that it took him only fifteen days to write this poem of over 900 lines.

[27] This classification of the degrees of hyperbole owes something to Demetrius, *On Style* 2. 124–5 (*ALC*, p. 196). The term 'unspeakableness' refers to the rhetorical figure *adynaton*, by which we claim that our message is beyond the power of words to convey. See E. R. Curtius, *European Literature and the Latin Middle Ages*, tr. W. R. Trask (New York, 1953), pp. 159–62, 'Inexpressibility Topoi'.

This is the uttermost that is possible, but in the frontiers of possibility:

Accustomed to use victory as an inheritance.   (413)

With more impossibility, thus:

Though a thousand deaths followed it, and every death were followed with a thousand shames.   (120)
The world sooner want occasions than he valour to go through them. (29)
Words and blows came so thick together as the one seemed lightning to the other's thunder.   (405)

Sometimes there is no certain quantity of a thing set, but plainly and ingeniously told, unenarrable,* as, 'have pity of him whose love went beyond the bounds of conceit—much more, of uttering' (322); and this figure is more credit to your wit than to your speech.

CORRECTIO, having used a word of sufficient force, yet pretending* a greater vehemence of meaning, refuseth it and supplies the place with a greater, as: 'I persuade you [not] to lose the hold of occasion whilst it may not only be taken, but offers, nay, sues to be taken' (358), where the first rising of the matter is upon 'not only, but also', then upon the correcting, 'nay'. . . . This figure is to be used when you would make the thing more credible itself than in the manner of your utterance. It is sometimes used upon passion, with an intent to amplify, as:

O you stars, if you do not succour me? No, no, you cannot help me!   (149)
O Parthenia—No more Parthenia! What art thou? What seest thou?   (378)

There are two contrary ways to these former, and both lead to amplification, but in dissembling sort. The first is IRONIA, which expresseth a thing by contrary, by show of exhortation when it dehorteth, as:

Yet a while, sleep a while, fold thine arms a while, etc., and so shall necessity overtake thee like a traveller, and poverty set upon thee like an armed man.[28]

. . . PARALEPSIS,[29] the second counterfeit of amplification is when you say you let pass that which notwithstanding you touch at full . . .

---

[28] Prov. 24: 33–4 (Geneva Bible).
[29] Known in Latin as *antiphrasis* (*Inst.* 9. 2. 47), but also *occupatio* and *praeteritio*.

There are other figures that fitly come in after amplification, or any great heat justly inflamed: interrogation and exclamation. *INTERROGA-TION*[30] is but a warm proposition, and therefore serves more fitly than a bare affirmation, which were but too gentle and harmless a speech; as, 'The credit of your behaviour is to cover imperfections and set forth your best parts,' better thus uttered: 'Is it not the chiefest credit of behaviour to set forth your good parts fairly, and cleanly to cover your imperfections?' . . .

It is very fit for a speech to many and indiscreet* hearers, and therefore much used in Pyrocles's oration to the seditious multitude, and then it may well be frequented* and iterated:

And I pray you, did the sun ever bring you a fruitful harvest but that it was more hot than pleasant? Have any of you children that be not sometimes cumbersome? Have any of you fathers that be not sometimes wearish? What, shall we curse the sun, hate our children, or disobey our fathers?   (286–7)

EXCLAMATION is not lawful but in extremity of emotion,[31] as Pyrocles, seeing the mild Philoclea innocently beheaded, cried out:

O tyrant heaven! Traitor earth! Blind providence! No justice? How is this done? How is this suffered? Hath this world a government? (431)

The like in the beginning of the second book of *Arcadia* in the person of Gynecia, tormented in mind:

'O sun . . . O you heavens . . . O deserts, deserts . . . O virtue . . . O imperfect proportion of reason, which can too much foresee, and too little prevent!   (119–20)

. . . *ACCLAMATION* is a sententious* clause of a discourse or report,* such as Daniel[32] in his poems concludes with perpetually. It is a general instruction; for every man commonly for his pains in reading any history of other men looks for some private use to himself, like a teller* who, in drawing great sums of other men's money,

---

[30] Aristotle, *Topics* 1. 4. 101^{b}13–32.

[31] That is, according to the laws of decorum, which taught that style should be made appropriate to the speaker, the occasion, and the genre: cf. Puttenham, p. 228.

[32] *Acclamatio* (*Inst.* 8. 5. 11), or the summing-up figure *epiphonema* (cf. E.K., p. 189, n. 61; Puttenham, pp. 264–5), was used by Daniel in *Musophilus* (1599) and by many Elizabethan poets. Sometimes marginal notes indicate an 'acclamation'.

challengeth somewhat in the pound for his own fee. It serves for amplification. . . .

Contrary to amplification is DIMINUTION, and descends by the same steps that amplification ascends by, and differs no otherwise than up-hill and down-hill; which is the same way, begun at several times. Yet some examples in your *Arcadia* give you to observe two ways of diminishing single terms; one, by denying the contrary, as, if you should say 'reasonable pleasant', Arcadian speech is 'not unpleasant' (152); 'hardly liked'—'not misliked' (192); 'not unfit' (161); 'not altogether unmodest' (267); 'not deny' (137); 'not disdained' (315). But why should I give examples of the most usual phrases in the English tongue? As, we say 'not the wisest man that I ever saw', for 'a man of small wisdom'. The second way is by denying the right use of the word but by error of some; as,

Those fantastical-minded people that children and musicians call lovers. (52)
This colour of mine, which she (in the deceivable style of affection) would entitle beautiful, (250)

. . . and such like. But the former fashion of diminution sometimes in ironical[33] sort goes for amplification; as, speaking of a great personage, 'no mean man', etc. This is an ordinary figure for all sorts of speeches. But these figures are but counterfeits of amplification.

THESE FIGURES FOLLOWING SERVE PROPERLY FOR AMPLIFICATION

SYNOECIOSIS is a composition of contraries, and by both words intimateth the meaning of neither precisely, but a moderation and mediocrity of both; as, 'bravery' and 'rags' are contrary, yet somewhat better than both is 'brave raggedness' (404). The like:

A wanton modesty, and an enticing soberness. (315)
And with that, she prettily smiled; which, mingled with her tears, a man could not tell whether it were a mourning pleasure or a delightful sorrow. (438)
It was an excellent pastime (to those that would delight in the play of virtue) with what a witty ignorance she would not understand. (455)

---

[33] The MS reads 'erroneous'; in his *Academy of Eloquence* Blount reads 'ironious' (Hudson, p. 85).

Impatient patient.   (237)
Absented presence.   (67)
Well-wishing spite and unkind carefulness.   (278)

And one contrary is affirmed to be in the other directly by making one the substantive, the other adjective, as above in the examples; or indirectly, as in these words following:

Seeking honour by dishonouring, and to build safety upon ruin. (412)
O foolish woman—and most miserably foolish, since wit makes thee foolish.   (359)
Captivity might seem to have authority over tyranny.   (363)

This is a fine course to stir admiration in the hearer, and make them think it a strange harmony which must be expressed in such discords; therefore this example shall conclude:

There was so perfect agreement in so mortal disagreement, like a music made of cunning discords.   (368)

This is an easy figure now in fashion, not like ever to be so usual.
    CONTENTIO[34] is contrary to the former. That was a composition of terms disagreeing; this is an opposition of them, as:

There was strength against nimbleness, rage against resolution, fury against virtue, confidence against courage, pride against nobleness. (463)
He is a swaggerer amongst quiet men, but a quiet man amongst swaggerers; earnest in idle things, idle in matters of earnestness,

where there is both *antimetabole* for the turning of sentences back, and *contentio* respecting the contrarieties of things meant thereby.

Could not look on, would not look off.   (229)
Neither the one hurt her nor the other help her.   (228)

    This figure Ascham[35] told Sturmius that he taught the Queen of England, and that she excels in practice of it; and indeed it is a

---

[34] Commonly known as *antithesis*. Cf. *Inst.* 9. 3. 81 f.
[35] Roger Ascham (see p. 140) was private tutor to Queen Elizabeth from 1548 to 1550. In this letter, dated 4 Apr. 1550, Ascham reports that 'she especially admires and strives for suitable metaphors and combinations of antitheses [*contrariorum collationes*] aptly matched and happily set in opposition' (cit. Hudson, p. 86).

figure fit to set forth a copious style. This figure serves much for amplification.

For comparison, COMPAR, or PARISON. Comparison is an even gait of sentences answering each other in measures interchangeably, such as in St Augustine[36] but often in Gregory the Divine; such as in the Bishop of W.[37] his books which he hath written in English, and many places of *Euphues*; but that St Augustine, Bilson, and Lyly do very much mingle this figure with *agnominatio* and *similiter cadens*.[38] It is a smooth and memorable* style for utterance, but in penning it must be used moderately and modestly. A touch of *agnomination* of the letter is tolerable with a *compar*, as in the first words of Philanax his speech,

If ever I could wish my faith untried and my counsel untrusted, (416)

and where there is a *similiter cadens*; but a more eminent falling alike in this:

My years are not so many but that one death may be able to conclude them, nor my faults so many but that one death may satisfy them. (420)

Without consonancy of fall or harping upon letter or syllable, and yet a *compar* because they say the words match each other in rank:

Save his grey hairs from rebuke, and his aged mind from despair, (227)

answer each other. Again:

Rather seek to obtain that constantly by courtesy which you can never, assuredly, enjoy by violence, (353)

verb to verb, adverb to adverb, and substantive to substantive.

[Loneliness] can neither warrant you from suspicion in others, nor defend you from melancholy in yourself. (82)

---

[36] His first career was as a rhetorician; he was celebrated for his rhetorical style: cf. Wilson, op. cit., p. 227. St Gregory of Nazianzus was also an accomplished prose stylist.

[37] Thomas Bilson (1547–1616), educated at Winchester and New College, was Master of Winchester (where he probably taught Hoskyns), and became Bishop in 1597. His sermons have several rhetorical features (passages quoted by Hudson, p. 88).

[38] The rhetorical figure *homoioptoton*, in which successive clauses end with words in identical cases. In English, an uninflected language, it usually refers to words ending with the same letter or syllable.

In some place there is a shorter *compar*, where substantive to substantive or word to word are joined, and yet without conjunction, which is *asyndeton*:

Her face with beauty, her head with wisdom, her eyes with majesty, her countenance with gracefulness, her lips with lovingness, her tongue with victory,   (139)

where many 'ands' are spared. Some places, only the conjunction is put in in the last in a *compar* of three; as,

Her wit indeed by youth, her affection by birth, and her sadness by her beauty.
A fair woman shall not only command without authority but persuade without speaking.   (356)

This is an excellent figure, in no place untimely if not too often. It fits well the even phrases and interpretations of an eloquent tongue that seems to be rich and wise, and to contain many parts (whereof each with a tedious man would make a sentence) [which] stick in the hearer's senses. Thereof I called it smooth and memorable. It hath been in request ever since the days of Isocrates, whose orations are full of them. This figure belongs more properly to that part of amplification called division than to accumulation.

SENTENTIA, if it be well used, is a figure—if ill and too much, it is a style; whereof none that writes humorously* or factiously* nowadays can be clear. For now there are such schisms of eloquence that it is enough for any ten years that all the bravest wits do imitate some one figure which a critic hath taught some great personage. So it may be within this two hundred years we shall go through the whole body of rhetoric. It is true that we study according to the predominance of courtly inclinations: whilst mathematics were in requests all our similitudes came from lines, circles, and angles; whilst moral philosophy is now a while spoken of, it is rudeness* not to be sententious. And for my part, I'll make one. I have used and outworn six several styles since I was first Fellow of New College, and am yet able to bear the fashion of [the] writing company. Let our age, therefore, only speak morally, and let the next age live morally.

It is very true that a sentence is a pearl in a discourse;[39] but is it a

---

[39] Hoskyns draws on Quintilian's account of *sententia* (*Inst*. 8. 5. 26–34), a passage used by Wilson (op. cit., p. 194) and by many other rhetoricians.

good discourse that is all pearl? It is like an eye in the body; but is it not monstrous to be all eyes? I take Cyclops to be as handsome a man as Argus. And if a sentence were as like to be an hand in the text as it is commonly noted with a hand in the margent, yet I should rather like the text that had no more hands than Hercules than that which had as many as Briareus. But these short-breathed gentlemen, these judicious minds, will show me in their works interrogations, agnominations, corrections, and all the figures of rhetoric: I yield to it; and yet will they show me nothing but sentences, unless there be some difference betwixt writing all in sentences and writing all sententiously. This is a sentence:

Man's experience is woman's best eyesight. (333)

There is small difference between a proposition and a question, if I forget not Aristotle, *1 Topica*.[40]

Since length of acquaintance, mutual secrecies, nor height of benefits could bind a savage heart. (264)

There is a sentence, and in it *asyndeton, zeugma*,[41] and metaphors.

Valuing money higher than equity, [he] felt that guiltlessness is not always with ease oppressed, (247)

where there is MEIOSIS,[42] 'not always with ease' for 'ever' and 'hardly'.

Who stands only upon defence stands upon no defence, (197)

with *synoeciosis* and *epanodos*.

Unlawful desires are punished after the effect of enjoying, but impossible desires are punished in the desire itself, (149)

a sentence with *distinctio* and *contentio*.

Love to a yielding heart is a king, but to a resisting is a tyrant, (108)

compar and *contentio*.

It is a foolish wittiness to speak more than one thinks, (93)

---

[40] The passage already referred to (n. 30).
[41] A figure in which a single word (often a verb) refers to other words in the same sentence, usually of disparate value: 'Doth sometimes counsel take, and sometimes tea'.
[42] A figure which diminishes or belittles.

synoeciosis. Neither is this sentence without a *compar*, and is a double sentence, as they call it:

To a heart fully resolute counsel is tedious, but reprehension is loathsome; and that there is nothing more terrible to a guilty heart than the eye of a respected friend.   (79)

There be also sentences particular to some men as well; as Amphialus, 'to whom abused kindness became spiteful rage' (397); 'fearfulness (contrary to all other vices) making Clinias think the better of another, the worse he found himself'; Euarchus 'making his life the example of his laws, his actions arising out of his deeds' (160–1). Which all may be taken for rule and commonplaces* by putting the general name for the special; as they say, drawing it *a thesi ad hypothesin*, from a position to a supposition.

These examples may make you believe that a sentence may be coursed* through the whole figure-book; and it shall appear in a set treatise that many figures may easily assemble in one clause, and any figure may sort with any: a slender reason to ground upon any one figure the frame and fashion of your whole style. In our profession there are not many (if two were many) whose speeches rely upon this figure; and in my judgment *sententia* is better for the bench than the bar.[43] Then of all others, why would the writers of these days imprison themselves in these maxims? It makes their style like *arena sine calce*,[44] as one saith of such a writer; and doth not he vouchsafe to use them that [called] them 'posies for rings'? If it be a matter of short direction for life and action, or notes for memory, I intend not to discredit this new trick. But otherwise, he that hath a long journey to walk in that pace is like a horse that overreacheth and yet goes slow. St Ambrose sanctifies this figure.[45]

TO ILLUSTRATE

Illustration consists in things or words; in the description of things living or dead; of living things, either reasonable, as of men and of personages and qualities; of unreasonable, as of horses, ships, islands, castles and such like.

[43] It is more appropriate for the judge to be sententious than the barrister pleading the case. Cf. *Inst.* 8. 5. 5.
[44] 'Sand without lime': the Emperor Caligula's judgement on Seneca's style, according to Suetonius (*Gaius Caligula* 53).
[45] His style is indeed notably sententious.

Men are described most excellently in *Arcadia*: Basilius, Plexirtus, Pyrocles, Musidorus, Anaxius, etc. But he that will truly set down a man in a figured story[46] must first learn truly to set down an humour, a passion, a virtue, a vice, and therein keeping decent* proportion add but names and knit together the accidents* and encounters.* The perfect expressing of all qualities is learned out of Aristotle's ten books of moral philosophy; but because, as Machiavel[47] saith, perfect virtue or perfect vice is not seen in our time, which altogether is humorous* and spurting,* therefore the understanding of Aristotle's *Rhetoric* is the directest means of skill to describe, to move, to appease, or to prevent* any emotion whatsoever; whereunto whosoever can fit his speech shall be truly eloquent. This was my opinion ever; and Sir Philip Sidney betrayed his knowledge in this book of Aristotle to me before ever I knew that he had translated any part of it. For I found the two first books Englished[48] by him in the hands of the noble studious Henry Wotton. But lately I think also that he had much help out of *Theophrasti Imagines*. For the web, as it were, of his story, he followed three: Heliodorus in Greek, Sannazarius' *Arcadia* in Italian, and *Diana* [by] de Montemayor[49] in Spanish.

But to our purpose—what personages and affections are set forth in *Arcadia*? For men: pleasant idle retiredness in King Basilius, and the dangerous end of it; unfortunate* valour in Plangus; courteous valour in Amphialus; proud valour in Anaxius (390–1); hospitality in Kalander; the mirror of true courage and friendship in Pyrocles and Musidorus; miserableness and ingratitude in Chremes (245–7); fear and fatal subtlety in Clinias (383–5); fear and rudeness, with ill-affected civility, in Dametas (110–17). And through the story, mutual virtuous love: in marriage, in Argalus and Parthenia (371–2); out of marriage,

---

[46] Cf. Horace, *Ars P.* 119–27.

[47] Cf. *Discourses on the First Ten Books of Livy* 1. 26: 'But men . . . know neither how to be entirely good or entirely bad'.

[48] If Sidney did indeed translate these first two books (which deal with the kinds of speeches, the main human emotions and character types, and the various topics), his translation has disappeared. Sir Henry Wotton (1568–1639) came from a distinguished family (his elder brother was a close friend of Sidney and is referred to in his *Defence*, p. 337), and was a notable collector of manuscripts.

[49] The *Ethical Characters* of Theophrastus (*c.*372–287 BC), one of Aristotle's leading pupils, are a classification of different psychological types, which helped create the vogue for character-writing in the early 17th cent. If this influence on Sidney seems unlikely, the other three models that Hoskyns suggests were indubitably important: the *Aethiopian Story* of Heliodorus, the *Arcadia* of Sannazaro, and the *Diana enamorada* of Jorge de Montemayor were all known to Sidney.

in Pyrocles and Philoclea, Musidorus and Pamela; true constant love unrespected in Plangus, and Helena (60–3); in the true Zelmane, inconstancy and envy (260–1); suspicion and tyranny in a king and his counsellors (175–6); generally false love in Pamphilus (237–40); and light* courage and credulity in Chremes' daughter; base dotage on a wife in Plangus' father. But in women: a mischievous seditious stomach in Cecropia (317–19); wise courage in Pamela; mild discretion* in Philoclea; Pamela's prayer (335–6); her discourse (359–63); squeamish cunning unworthiness in Artesia; respective* and restless dotage in Gynecia's love; proud ill-favoured sluttish simplicity in Mopsa.

Now in these persons is ever a steadfast decency* and uniform difference of manners observed, wherever you find them, and howsoever each interrupt the other's story and actions.

And for actions of persons, there are many, rarely* described: as a mutiny and fire in a ship (275); causes of an uproar (284–5, 290–3); the garboil (280–2); an armed skirmish (340–6); policy* and preparation (365–6); (but policy generally in all particular actions is noted in your book *pc*); managing a horse is described (153–4); tilting shows (94–104). Many other notable and lively portraits are, which I will not lay down to save you so sweet a labour as the reading of that which may make you eloquent and wise. Sir Philip Sidney's course was (besides reading Aristotle and Theophrastus) to imagine the thing present in his own brain[50] that his pen might the better present it to you. Whose example I would you durst follow till I pulled you back.

This have I written of illustration in conveyance* and well gaining of the substance of a treatise. Where evident and lively descriptions are in *Arcadia*, you have this note, *des*; where the person is aptly fitted with speech and action, *dc*: both these give light to the handling and grow into very pleasant acquaintance with the understanding and memory of the reader.

For special lights in every sentence, there are other sparks of figures. First, if there be any doubt or ambiguity in the words, it is better left out than distinguished; but if you are to answer any former speeches, you may disperse all clouds and remove all scruples with DISTINCTION. As, being charged that you have brought very light reasons, you may answer:

If by 'light' you mean 'clear', I am glad you do see them; if by 'light' you mean 'of no weight', I am sorry you do not feel them.

---

[50] Cf. Aristotle, *Poet.* 17. 1455ª22 ff.; and Sidney, p. 351.

So you may express yourself:

A man of hidden learning, hidden as well for the obscure and mean estate of his person as hidden for the unusual and intricate conceit of the matter.

But as ambiguity is not only in words but in matter, so both ways it is taken away by distinction. Sometimes it is in single words, as in these former ('light' and 'hidden'); sometimes in coherence of sentences, by relation of each word to each, or by reason of change of the pointing*—which is opened by utterance. You have many examples thereof in the *Courtier*, the second book of Cicero *De Oratore*,[51] and in Quintilian, where there is mention of *iocus ab ambiguo*. And you may satisfy yourself at full if you search but the margent of Erasmus'[52] *Apophthegms* where *ambigus* is written. . . .

Next follows DEFINITION, which is the shortest and truest exposition of the nature of anything. Hereof you have examples: of virtue and vice, in Aristotle's *Morals*; of passions, in his *Rhetoric*; both, in Thomas Aquinas' *Secunda*;[53] of many affections and perturbations, in *Tusculan Questions* and Cicero *De Finibus*. The general definition of virtue is this: *virtus est habitus rationi consentaneus*,[54] 'virtue is quality settled in reason'.

Fear is an apprehension of future harm.[55]
Thrift is a moderate and lawful increase of wealth by careful government of your own estate.
Compliment is performance of affected ceremonies in words, looks, or gesture,

where definition runs into division. Of seven or eight ways of definition, read Valerius's *Logic*.[56] But to be most perfectly*

---

[51] In bk. 2 of *Il Cortegiano* (1528) Castiglione borrowed many examples of witty sayings from *De or.* 2. 54. 216–71. 290.

[52] *Inst.* 6. 3. 47–58. Cf. e.g. Erasmus, *Apophthegmatum Opus* (Leyden 1544), in which marginal notes indicate anecdotes which turn upon verbal ambiguities, and Cicero, *De or.* 2. 61. 250–62. 254.

[53] In the *Summa Theologica* the first division of the second part (*Prima Secundae*) deals with the passions (*Quaestiones* 22–48), the virtues (49–70), and vices (71–89).

[54] A Latin version of the opening of Aristotle's definition, *Eth. Nic.* 2. 6. 1107^{a}1–2: 'Virtue is a state [concerned with choice, lying in a mean relative to us,] this being determined by reason . . .'.

[55] *Eth. Nic.* 3. 6. 1115^{a}8–10.

[56] The *Dialectica* (1564, etc.) by the Louvain scholar Cornelius Valerius.

instructed, read the sixth book of Aristotle's *Topica*. Your definitions
need not be strictly tied to the rules of logic, nor your divisions. . . .

Sometimes PARENTHESIS makes your discourse fair and more sensible;* as,

He, swelling in their humbleness (like a bubble swollen up with a small
breath, broken with a great), forgetting (or not knowing) humanity,
caused their heads to be struck off.   (176)
That what his wit could conceive (and his wit can conceive as far as
the limits of reason can stretch) was all directed to the setting forward
the suit of his friend.   (62)
Till the next morning (known to be a morning better by the hourglass
than by the day's clearness) having run fortune, etc.   (167)

And indeed all parentheses are in extremities, either graces or
disgraces to a speech. If they be long, they seem interruptions,
and therefore at the end of them there must be a retreat to the matter,
. . . as:

Assure thyself, most wicked woman, that has so plaguily a corrupted
mind as that thou canst not keep thy sickness to thyself, but must most
wickedly infect others, assure thyself, I say, etc.   (363) . . .

DIVISION is a severing of the whole into parts, as, of time, into
that past, present, and to come (which is rather a breaking than a
division); of magistrates, into supreme or subordinate, from their
order; of beasts or unreasonable creatures, into those of the air, water,
earth; love is either of beauty or virtue, from the object; study is
of liberal or mechanical sciences, from the subject. And so you
may divide as many ways as things may differ, as: by their beginnings, endings, properties, marks, effects, times, places, forms, and
persons in whom they are, and howsoever; whereof the proper treaty*
belongs to logic. And something is spoken thereof in the second way
of amplification. . . .

PERIPHRASIS AND *PARAPHRASIS*

There is in the best writers sometimes a vein of speech wherein
the vulgar conceits* are exceedingly pleased; for they admire this
most, that there is some excellency in it, and yet they themselves
suspect that it excels their admiration. In some examples I would
gladly discover the reason thereof. It cannot be but if either the

meaning or the words be obscure or unfamiliar unto a man's mind, that the speech so consisting should be much accepted; and yet it is impossible that there should be any extraordinary delight in ordinary words and plain meaning. How then shall we determine?* It is as it is in many dishes at our tables: our eyes and taste give them commendation, not for the substance but for the dressing* and service. What plainer meaning than 'sleep among thieves'? And verily, 'sleep', 'life', 'trust', are common English words. Yet it is not a common fashion of speech to say, 'trust a sleeping life among thieves' (244). In the same sense, 'when they had slept awhile' is ordinary; but 'when they had hearkened to the persuasion of sleep' (57) is extraordinary. Though all the words of it, by themselves, are most known and familiar, yet the bringing-in and fetch* of it is strange and admirable to the ignorant. We therefore call it PERIPHRASIS, or circumlocution, and it is much helped by metaphors; as before, 'inclined to sleep' is expressed by a metaphor taken from an orator, who moves and inclines by persuasion, and to be so moved it is 'to hearken'.

In this sort Sir Philip Sidney, being to speak his usual meanings, yet notwithstanding shunned usual phrases, as for 'it is absurd in my conceit', saith he: 'it hath great incongruity' (417). But let us have one bout more with our adversary, sleep. For 'having risen early', he saith: 'having striven with the sun's earliness' (260). Instead of 'Mopsa wept ill-favouredly': 'Mopsa disgraced weeping with her countenance' (316). Instead of saying, 'they that guarded Amphialus were killed themselves', it is said: 'seeking to save him, they lost the fortresses which nature placed them in' (344). Instead of 'Plangus' speech began to be suspected', it is said: 'Plangus' [actions] began to be translated into the language of suspicion' (219). And this of purpose did he write, to keep his style from baseness: as, being to name 'a thresher', he called him 'one of Ceres' servants' (345). Instead of 'his name was known to high and low', he saith that 'no prince could pretend height, not beggar lowness, to bar him from the sound thereof' (272). For 'old and young malcontents', he saith: 'such whom youthful age or youthful minds had filled with unlimited desires'. And this is by going *a concreto ad abstractum*,[57] and divers other ways.

If a short ordinary sense be oddly expressed by more words, it is *periphrasis*; but if by as many other, it is PARAPHRASIS, as 'many false oaths': 'plentiful perjury' (337); 'to make a great show of himself': 'to

---

[57] 'From the concrete to the abstract'.

make a muster of himself in the island' (382); for 'kill any married man': 'make his sword accursed by any widow' (379)—which is by consequence;[58] 'seeking by courtesy to undo him': 'making courtesy the outside of mischief' (317)—by similitude or metaphor. So, then, the course is: instead of any ordinary words importing* any trivial sense, to take the abstract, or some consequent, similitude, note, property, or effect, and thereby declare it. These two figures serve for illustration.

It is most convenient* sometimes for the bringing in of life and lustre to represent some unexpected strains* beside the tenor* of your tale, and act, as it were, your meaning; which is done either by feigning the presence or the discourse of some such persons as either are not at all or, if there be, yet speak not but by imagination. The first is by *apostrophe* or *prosopopoeia*.

APOSTROPHE is a turning of your speech to some new person, as to the people when your speech before was to the judge, to the defendant, to the adversary, to the witnesses, as:

And herein you witnesses are to consult with your own consciences and to enter into true examination of your memory. Did you mark his looks? Did you note his speeches? Did you truly observe the particular proceedings of the action?

To the people, thus:

Now let me entreat any man here present that thinks himself not exempted from misfortunes and privileged from all mischances, to imagine himself in my case and to undertake for my sake but some few thoughts of my distress.

Sometimes the occasion is to some quality, or thing, that yourself gives show of life to, as:

[Hope,] tell me, what canst thou hope for? . . . Love, be ashamed to be called love! Cruel hate, unspeakable hate is victorious over thee. (433)

But to animate and give life is *PROSOPOPOEIA*, as, to make dead men speak; as,

---

[58] A logical term (like 'consequent' below).

If your forefathers were now alive and saw you defacing so goodly a principality by them established, would they not say thus? (286)

Sir Philip Sidney gives meaning and speech to the needle, the cloth, and the silk (354–5); as learning, as a city, as death itself (340, 343, 377), is feigned to live and make a speech. . . .

19

Thomas Campion,
Classical metres suitable for English
poetry (1602)

THOMAS CAMPION (1567–1620), educated at Peterhouse Cambridge and Gray's Inn, began his career as a poet and composer by writing songs for Inns of Court revels. In 1601 he published *A Booke of Ayres*, in collaboration with the lutenist Philip Rosseter; four further collections were published, in 1613 and 1617, and two volumes of Latin epigrams. In the early 1600s he studied medicine at the University of Caen, and subsequently practised as a doctor in London, while continuing to write masques and other court entertainments.

TEXT. From *Observations in the Art of English Poesie. By Thomas Campion. Wherein it is demonstratively prooved, and by example confirmed, that the English toong will receive eight severall kinds of numbers, proper to it selfe, which are all in this booke set forth, and were never before this time by any man attempted* (London, 1602). Although not published until 1602, scholars have suggested that this treatise was actually written in 1591, during the main vogue for quantitative verse, when Campion was imitating Sidney's experiments. In the preface to his first *Booke of Ayres* Campion informed his readers that 'The Lyricke Poets among the Greekes and Latines were first inventers of Ayres, tying themselves strictly to the number and value of their silables, of which sort you shall find here onely one song in Saphicke verse; the rest are after the fascion of the time, eare-pleasing rimes without Arte'; which suggests that he had already abandoned quantitative verse. The work's dedicatee was Thomas Sackville (1536–1608), created Baron Buckhurst, who had been joint author (with Thomas Norton) of *Gorboduc* (1561: cf. Sidney, p. 381), and author of the *Induction* to *A Mirror for Magistrates* (1563). In annotating it I have benefited from the edition by Walter R. Davis, *The Works of Thomas Campion* (London, 1969). For Campion's debt to William Lilly's Latin grammar see J. K. Fenyo, 'Grammar and Music in Thomas Campion's *Observations in the Art of English Poesie*', *Studies in the Renaissance*, 17 (1970), 46–72, and for excellent studies of the whole issue see D. Attridge, *Well-Weighed Syllables: Elizabethan Verse in Classical Metres* (Cambridge, 1974), and J. Hollander, *Vision and Resonance: Two Senses of Poetic Form* (New York, 1975).

[DEDICATION TO THE LORD BUCKHURST, LORD HIGH
TREASURER OF ENGLAND]

In two things (right honourable) it is generally agreed that man excels
all other creatures, in reason and speech:[1] and in them by how much
one man surpasseth another, by so much the nearer he aspires to a
celestial essence.

Poesy in all kind of speaking is the chief beginner, and maintainer
of eloquence, not only helping the ear with the acquaintance of sweet
numbers,* but also raising the mind to a more high and lofty conceit.*
For this end have I studied to induce* a true form of versifying into
our language: for the vulgar and unartificial* custom of rhyming hath,
I know, deterred many excellent wits from the exercise of English
poesy. The observations which I have gathered for this purpose I
humbly present to your Lordship, as to the noblest judge of poesy, and
the most honourable protector of all industrious learning . . .

THE FIRST CHAPTER: ENTREATING OF NUMBERS
IN GENERAL

There is no writing too brief that, without obscurity, comprehends the
intent of the writer. These my late observations in English poesy I
have thus briefly gathered that they might prove the less troublesome
in perusing, and the more apt to be retained in memory. And I will
first generally handle the nature of numbers.

Number is *discreta quantitas*:[2] so that when we speak simply of
number, we intend* only the dissevered quantity. But when we speak
of a poem written in numbers, we consider not only the distinct
number of the syllables but also their value, which is contained in the
length or shortness of their sound. As in music we do not say a strain
of 'so many notes', but 'so many semibreves'[3] (though sometimes there
are no more notes than semibreves), so in a verse the numeration of
the syllables is not so much to be observed as their weight and due
proportion. In joining of words to harmony there is nothing more
offensive to the ear than to place a long syllable with a short note, or
a short syllable with a long note, though in the last the vowel often
bears it out.

---

[1] Cf. Cicero, *De or.* 1. 8. 32–3; *Inv. rhet.* 1. 4. 5; *Off.* 1. 16. 50; Wilson, p. 77; Sidney,
p. 367.
[2] 'Measured quantity': cf. Scaliger, *Poetice* 4. 1. 45.
[3] 'Whole notes; a metrical foot was to equal a whole note in time value' (ed. Davis).

The world is made by symmetry and proportion, and is in that respect compared to music, and music to poetry. For Terence says, speaking of poets, *artem qui tractant musicam*,[4] confounding* music and poesy together. What music can there be where there is no proportion observed? Learning first flourished in Greece, from thence it was derived unto the Romans, both diligent observers of the number and quantity of syllables, not in their verses only but likewise in their prose. Learning, after the declining of the Roman Empire, and the pollution of their language through the conquest of the Barbarians, lay most pitifully deformed till the time of Erasmus, Reuchlin,[5] Sir Thomas More, and other learned men of that age, who brought the Latin tongue again to light, redeeming it with much labour out of the hands of the illiterate monks and friars, as a scoffing book entitled *Epistolae obscurorum virorum*[6] may sufficiently testify. In those lack-learning times, and in barbarized Italy, began that vulgar and easy* kind of poesy which is now in use throughout most parts of Christendom, which we abusively call rhyme and metre, of *rithmus* and *metrum*,[7] of which I will now discourse.

THE SECOND CHAPTER: DECLARING THE UNAPTNESS OF RHYME IN POESY

I am not ignorant that whosoever shall by way of reprehension examine the imperfections of rhyme must encounter with many glorious* enemies, and those very expert and ready at their weapon, that can if need be *extempore* (as they say) rhyme a man to death.[8] Besides, there is grown a kind of prescription* in the use of rhyme, to forestall the right of true numbers,[9] as also the consent of many nations, against all which it may seem a thing almost impossible and vain to contend. All this and more can not yet deter me from a lawful defence of perfection, or make me any whit the sooner adhere to that which is lame and unbeseeming. For custom I allege* that ill uses are to be abolished, and that things naturally imperfect cannot be perfected by

---

[4] 'Who labour in the art of music': *Phormio*, prol. 17.

[5] Johann Reuchlin (1455–1522), a German humanist and celebrated Hebrew scholar.

[6] A series of satirical letters, mocking the pedantry of medieval theologians and friars, by Ulrich van Hutten and others, published in 1515 and 1516. See *Epistolae obscurorum virorum*, ed. and tr. F. G. Stokes (London, 1909).

[7] For these terms see Puttenham, p. 215 n. 45.

[8] Cf. Sidney, p. 391.

[9] Quantitative verse-forms; similarly 'numerous poesy' below.

use. Old customs, if they be better, why should they not be recalled, as the yet flourishing custom of numerous poesy used among the Romans and Grecians? But the unaptness of our tongues and the difficulty of imitation disheartens us; again, the facility and popularity of rhyme creates as many poets as a hot summer flies.

But let me now examine the nature of that which we call rhyme. By rhyme is understood that which ends in the like sound, so that verses in such manner composed yield but a continual repetition of that rhetorical figure which we term *similiter desinentia*,[10] and that, being but *figura verbi*, ought (as Tully and all other rhetoricians have judicially* observed) sparingly to be used, lest it should offend the ear with tedious affectation. Such was that absurd following of the letter amongst our English so much of late affected,* but now hissed out of Paul's Churchyard,[11] which foolish figurative repetition crept also into the Latin tongue, as it is manifest in the book of Ps called *praelia porcorum*, and another pamphlet all of Fs[12] which I have seen imprinted. But I will leave these follies to their own ruin, and return to the matter intended.

The ear is a rational sense and a chief judge of proportion; but in our kind of rhyming what proportion is there kept where there remains such a confused inequality of syllables? *Iambic* and *trochaic* feet, which are opposed by nature, are by all rhymers confounded;* nay, oftentimes they place instead of an *iambic* the foot *pyrrhichius*, consisting of two short syllables, curtailing their verse,[13] which they supply* in reading with a ridiculous and unapt drawing of their speech. As for example:

Was it my destiny, or dismal chance?

In this verse the two last syllables of the word 'destiny', being both short, and standing for a whole foot in the verse, cause the line to fall out shorter than it ought by nature. The like impure errors have in time of rudeness* been used in the Latin tongue, as the

[10] On *similiter desinens* (or *homoioteleuton*), cf. Quintilian, *Inst.* 9. 3. 77; Puttenham, p. 216; Sidney, p. 386. Cautions against overuse were frequent.

[11] The centre of London bookselling.

[12] On excessive alliteration cf. E.K., p. 179, Sidney, p. 385, and Hoskyns, p. 409, who also refers to this poem by Placentius; the pamphlet in *f*s has not been identified.

[13] 'Shortening the time value of the line: the line contains the requisite number of syllables, but its time value is thrown off by the substitution of a short syllable for a long' (ed. Davis). The *pyrrhichius* was a metrical foot composed of two short syllables, used in an ancient Greek war-dance, to music, performed in armour.

Carmina proverbialia[14] can witness, and many other such reverend baubles. But the noble Grecians and Romans, whose skilful monuments outlive barbarism, tied themselves to the strict observation of poetical numbers, so abandoning the childish titillation of rhyming that it was imputed a great error to Ovid for setting forth this one rhyming verse,

Quot caelum stellas tot habet tua Roma puellas.[15]

For the establishing of this argument, what better confirmation can be had then that of Sir Thomas More in his book of *Epigrams*, where he makes two sundry epitaphs[16] upon the death of a singing-man at Westminster, the one in learned numbers and disliked, the other in rude rhyme and highly extolled; so that he concludes, *tales lactucas talia labra petunt*, 'like lips like lettuce'.

But there is yet another fault in rhyme altogether intolerable, which is that it enforceth a man oftentimes to abjure* his matter* and extend a short conceit beyond all bounds of art. For in quatorzains, methinks, the poet handles his subject as tyrannically as Procrustes[17] the thief his prisoners, whom, when he had taken he used to cast upon a bed, which if they were too short to fill he would stretch them longer, if too long he would cut them shorter. Bring before me now any the most self-loved rhymer, and let me see if without blushing he be able to read his lame halting rhymes. Is there not a curse of nature laid upon such rude poesy, when the writer is himself ashamed of it, and the hearers in contempt call it rhyming and ballading? What divine in his sermon, or grave counsellor in his oration, will allege the testimony of a rhyme? But the divinity of the Romans and Grecians was all written in verse; and Aristotle, Galen, and the books of all the excellent philosophers are full of the testimonies of the old poets. By them was laid the foundation of all human wisdom, and from them the knowledge of all antiquity is derived. I will propound but one question, and so conclude this point. If the Italians, Frenchmen, and Spaniards, that with commendation have written in rhyme, were demanded whether they had rather the books they have published (if their tongue would

---

[14] A collection of rhyming proverbs often reprinted (e.g. London 1588), intended for young scholars, which Campion dismisses as a 'bauble' or trifling toy.

[15] *Ars am.* 1. 59: 'As many stars as has the sky, so many girls has your Rome'.

[16] For these epitaphs on Henry Abyngon (Master of the Children of the Royal Chapel at Westminster in the late 15th cent.) see More, *Latin Epigrams*, ed. L. Bradner and C. P. Lynch (Chicago, 1953), nos. 141–3.

[17] Jonson (p. 530) echoes this comment on the sonnet's constricting effect.

bear it) should remain as they are in rhyme, or be translated into the ancient numbers of the Greeks and Romans, would they not answer 'into numbers'? What honour were it then for our English language to be the first that after so many years of barbarism could second the perfection of the industrious Greeks and Romans? Which how it may be effected I will now proceed to demonstrate.

THE THIRD CHAPTER: OF OUR ENGLISH NUMBERS IN GENERAL

There are but three feet which generally distinguish the Greek and Latin verses, the *dactyl* consisting of one long syllable and two short, as *vivere*; the *trochee*, of one long and one short, as *vita*; and the *iambic* of one short and one long, as *amor*. The *spondee* of two long, the *tribrach* of three short, the *anapaestic* of two short and a long, are but as servants to the first. Divers other feet I know are by the grammarians cited, but to little purpose. The heroical* verse that is distinguished by the dactyl has been oftentimes attempted in our English tongue, but with passing pitiful success; and no wonder, seeing it is an attempt altogether against the nature of our language. For both the concourse* of our monosyllables make our verses unapt to slide,[18] and also, if we examine our polysyllables, we shall find few of them, by reason of their heaviness, willing to serve in place of a dactyl. Thence it is that the writers of English heroics do so often repeat Amyntas, Olympus, Avernus, Erinnys, and suchlike borrowed words, to supply* the defect of our hardly* entreated dactyl. I could in this place set down many ridiculous kinds of dactyls which they use, but that it is not my purpose here to incite men to laughter. If we therefore reject the dactyl as unfit for our use (which of necessity we are forced to do), there remain only the iambic foot, of which the iambic verse is framed, and the trochee, from which the trochaic numbers have their original.

Let us now then examine the property* of these two feet, and try if they consent* with the nature of our English syllables. And first for the iambics: they fall out so naturally in our tongue that if we examine our own writers, we shall find they unawares hit oftentimes upon the true iambic numbers, but always aim at them as far as their ear without

[18] That is, 'to allow an even flow of alternating vowels and consonants, thus avoiding the hiatus or "gaping" effect so disliked by rhetoricians since Isocrates' (ed. Davis).

the guidance of art can attain unto, as it shall hereafter more evidently appear. The trochaic foot, which is but an iambic turned over and over, must of force in like manner accord in proportion with our British syllables, and so produce an English trochaical verse. Then, having these two principal kinds of verses, we may easily out of them derive other forms, as the Latins and Greeks before us have done: whereof I will make plain demonstration, beginning at the iambic verse.

THE FOURTH CHAPTER: OF THE IAMBIC VERSE

I have observed, and so may any one that is either practiced in singing or has a natural ear able to time a song, that the Latin verses of six feet, as the heroic and iambic, or of five feet, as the trochaic, are in nature all of the same length of sound with our English verses of five feet. For either of them being timed with the hand, *quinque perficiunt tempora*, 'they fill up the quantity (as it were) of five semibreves'; as for example, if any man will prove* to time these verses[19] with his hand.

A pure iambic:

> *Suis et ipsa Roma viribus ruit.*

A licentiate iambic:

> *Ducunt volentes fata, nolentes trahunt.*

An heroic verse:

> *Tityre, tu patulae recubans sub tegmine fagi.*

A trochaic verse:

> *Nox est perpetua una dormienda.*

English iambics pure:

> The more secure, the more the stroke we feel
> Of unprevented harms; so gloomy storms
> Appear the sterner, if the day be clear.

The English iambic licentiate:

> Hark how these winds do murmur at thy flight.

[19] These quotations are from Horace, *Epode* 16. 2 ('and Rome through her own strength is falling'); Seneca, *Ep.* 107. 11 ('the fates lead the willing, and drag the unwilling'); Virgil, *Ecl.* 1. 1 ('you, Tityrus, lying in the shade of the spreading beech-tree'); and Catullus, 5. 6 ('we must sleep one perpetual night').

The English trochee:

> Still where Envy leaves, remorse doth enter.

The cause why these verses differing in feet yield the same length of sound, is by reason of some rests which either the necessity of the numbers or the heaviness of the syllables do beget. For we find in music that oftentimes the strains* of a song cannot be reduced to true number without some rests prefixed in the beginning and middle, as also at the close if need requires. Besides, our English monosyllables enforce many breathings,* which no doubt greatly lengthen a verse, so that it is no wonder if for these reasons our English verses of five feet hold pace with the Latins' of six.

The pure iambic in English needs small demonstration, because it consists simply of iambic feet; but our iambic licentiate[20] offers itself to a further consideration, for in the third and fifth place we must of force hold the iambic foot; in the first, second, and fourth place we may use a spondee or iambic, and sometimes a tribrach* or dactyl, but rarely an anapaestic foot, and that in the second or fourth place. But why an iambic in the third place? I answer, that the forepart of the verse may the gentlier slide into his dimeter,* as, for example sake, divide this verse:

> Hark how these winds do murmur at thy flight.

'Hark how these winds': there the voice naturally affects a rest; then 'murmur at thy flight': that is of itself a perfect* number, as I will declare in the next chapter; and therefore the other odd syllable between them ought to be short, lest the verse should hang too much between the natural pause of the verse and the dimeter following. The which dimeter, though it be naturally trochaical, yet it seems to have his original out of the iambic verse.

But the better to confirm and express these rules, I will set down a short poem in *licentiate iambics*, which may give more light to them that shall hereafter imitate these numbers.

> Go, numbers, boldly pass, stay not for aid
> Of shifting rhyme, that easy flatterer,
> Whose witchcraft can the ruder ears beguile.

---

[20] An accentual iambic which is 'licensed, allowed as free from rules', that is, having some permissible variations.

Let your smooth feet, inur'd to purer art,
True measures tread. What if your pace be slow,
And hops not like the Grecian elegies?
It is yet graceful, and well fits the state
Of words ill-breathed and not shap't to run.
Go then, but slowly, till your steps be firm;
Tell them that pity or perversely scorn
Poor English poesy as the slave to rhyme,
You are those lofty numbers that revive
Triumphs of princes and stern tragedies:
And learn henceforth t'attend those happy sprights
Whose bounding fury height and weight affects.
Assist their labour, and sit close to them,
Never to part away till for desert
Their brows with great Apollo's bays are hid.
He first taught number and true harmony;
Nor is the laurel his for rhyme bequeath'd.
Call him with numerous accents peis'd* by art,
He'll turn his glory from the sunny climes
The North-bred wits alone to patronise.
Let France their Bartas, Italy Tasso praise;
Phoebus shuns none but in their flight from him.

Though, as I said before, the natural breathing-place of our English iambic verse is in the last syllable of the second foot, as our trochee, after the manner of the Latin heroic and iambic, rests naturally in the first of the third foot, yet no man is tied altogether to observe this rule, but he may alter it, after the judgment of his ear, which poets, orators, and musicians of all men ought to have most excellent. . . .

These are those numbers which nature, in our English, destinates* to the tragic and heroic poem.[21] For the subject of them both being all one,* I see no impediment why one verse may not serve for them both, as it appears more plainly in the old comparison of the two Greek writers, when they say, *Homerus est Sophocles heroicus*, and again *Sophocles est Homerus tragicus;*[22] intimating that both Sophocles and Homer are the same in height* and subject, and differ only in the kind of their numbers.

---

[21] The two premier literary forms were tragedy and the epic. Cf. Sidney, pp. 363, 364–5, 381; Milton, pp. 593, 604.

[22] 'Homer is the epic Sophocles'; 'Sophocles is the tragic Homer'.

The iambic verse in like manner, being yet made a little more licentiate, that it may thereby the nearer imitate our common talk, will excellently serve for comedies . . .

THE SEVENTH CHAPTER: OF THE ENGLISH ELEGIAC[23] VERSE

The elegiac verses challenge* the next place, as being of all compound verses[24] the simplest. They are derived out of our own natural numbers, as near the imitation of the Greeks and Latins as our heavy syllables will permit. The first verse is a mere licentiate iambic; the second is framed of two united dimeters. In the first dimeter we are tied to make the first foot either a trochee or a spondee, the second a trochee, and the odd syllable of it always long. The second dimeter consists of two trochees (because it requires more swiftness than the first) and an odd syllable, which, being last, is ever common. I will give you example of Elegy . . . in this kind.

AN ELEGY

Constant to none, but ever false to me,
    Traitor still to love through thy faint desires,
Not hope of pity now nor vain redress
    Turns my griefs to tears and renew'd laments.
Too well thy empty vows and hollow thoughts
    Witness both thy wrongs and remorseless heart.
Rue not my sorrow, but blush at my name;
    Let thy bloody cheeks guilty thoughts betray.
My flames did truly burn, thine made a show,
    As fires painted are which no heat retain,
Or as the glossy *Pirop*[25] fains to blaze,
    But touched cold appears, and an earthy stone.
True colours deck thy cheeks, false foils thy breast,
    Frailer than thy light beauty is thy mind.
None canst thou long refuse, nor long affect,

---

[23] In Latin poetry the elegiac couplet was composed of a dactylic hexameter followed by a dactylic pentameter.

[24] Made up of different kinds of lines.

[25] Red bronze. Cf. Ovid, *Met.* 2. 2: 'clara micante auro flammesque imitante pyropo' ('bright with glittering gold and red bronze that simulates flames').

But turn'st fear with hopes, sorrow with delight,
Delaying, and deluding every way
   Those whose eyes are once with thy beauty chained.
Thrice happy man that entering first thy love
   Can so guide the straight reins of his desires,
That both he can regard thee and refrain:
   If graced, firm he stands, if not, easily falls.

THE EIGHTH CHAPTER: OF DITTIES* AND ODES

To descend orderly from the more simple numbers to them that are
more compounded, it is now time to handle such verses as are fit for
ditties or odes; which we may call lyrical, because they are apt to be
sung to an instrument, if they were adorned with convenient* notes.
Of that kind I will demonstrate three in this chapter. . . .

   The second kind consists of dimeter, whose first foot may either be
a spondee or a trochee. The two verses following are both of them
trochaical, and consist of four feet, the first of either of them being a
spondee or trochee, the other three only trochees. The fourth and last
verse is made of two trochees. The number is voluble,* and fit to
express any amorous conceit:

> Rose-cheeked Laura, come
> Sing thou smoothly with thy beauty's
> Silent music, either other
>   Sweetly gracing.
>
> Lovely forms do flow
> From consent divinely framed;
> Heav'n is music, and thy beauty's
>   Birth is heavenly.
>
> These dull notes we sing
> Discords need for helps to grace them;
> Only beauty purely loving
>   Knows no discord,
>
> But still moves delight,
> Like clear springs renewed by flowing,
> Ever perfect, ever in them-
>   selves eternal.

Thus have I briefly described eight several* kinds of English numbers, simple or compound. . . .

These numbers which by my long observation I have found agreeable with the nature of our syllables, I have set forth for the benefit of our language, which I presume the learned will not only imitate but also polish and amplify with their own inventions. Some ears accustomed altogether to the fatness* of rhyme may perhaps except* against the cadences of these numbers; but let any man judicially* examine them, and he shall find they close of themselves so perfectly that the help of rhyme were not only in them superfluous but also absurd. Moreover, that they agree with the nature of our English it is manifest, because they entertain so willingly our own British names, which the writers in English heroics could never aspire unto; and even our rhymers themselves have rather delighted in borrowed names than in their own, though much more apt and necessary. . . .

THE TENTH CHAPTER: OF THE QUANTITY OF ENGLISH SYLLABLES

The Greeks in the quantity of their syllables were far more licentious than the Latins, as Martial in his epigram of *Earinon* witnesseth, saying, *qui musas colimus severiores.*[26] But the English may very well challenge much more licence than either of them, by reason it stands chiefly upon monosyllables, which, in expressing with the voice, are of a heavy carriage, and for that cause the dactyl, tribrach, and anapaestic are not greatly missed in our verses. But above all, the accent of our words is diligently to be observed, for chiefly by the accent in any language the true value of the syllables is to be measured. Neither can I remember any impediment, except position, that can alter the accent of any syllable in our English verse. For though we accent the second of *Trumpington* short, yet is it naturally long, and so of necessity must be held of every composer. Wherefore the first rule that is to be observed is the nature of the accent, which we must ever follow.

The next rule is position, which makes every syllable long, whether the position happens in one or in two words, according to the manner of the Latins, wherein is to be noted that 'h' is no letter.

Position is when a vowel comes before two consonants, either in one

---

[26] *Epigrams* 9. 11. 17: 'We who cultivate severer Muses'.

or two words. In one, as in 'best', 'e' before 'st' makes the word 'best' long by position. In two words, as in 'settled love', 'e' before 'd' in the last syllable of the first word, and 'l' in the beginning of the second, makes 'led' in 'settled' long by position.

A vowel before a vowel is always short, as 'flying', 'dying', 'going', unless the accent alter it, in 'denying'.

The diphthong in the midst of a word is always long, as 'playing', 'deceiving'.

The synaloephas[27] or elisions in our tongue are either necessary to avoid the hollowness and gaping in our verse, as 'to' and 'the', 't'enchant', 'th'enchanter', or may be used at pleasure, as for 'let us' to say 'let's'; for 'we will', 'we'll'; for 'every', 'ev'ry'; for 'they are', 'they're'; for 'he is', 'he's'; for 'admired', 'admir'd'; and such like.

Also, because our English orthography (as the French) differs from our common pronunciation, we must esteem our syllables as we speak, not as we write; for the sound of them in a verse is to be valued, and not their letters, as for 'follow' we pronounce 'follo'; for 'perfect', 'perfet'; for 'little', 'littel'; for 'love-sick', 'love-sik'; for 'honour', 'honor'; for 'money', 'mony'; for 'dangerous', 'dangerus'; for 'ransome', 'ransum'; for 'though', 'tho'; and their like. . . .

These rules concerning the quantity of our English syllables I have disposed as they came next into my memory; others more method-ical, time and practice may produce. In the mean season, as the gram-marians leave many syllables to the authority of the poets, so do I likewise leave many to their judgments; and withal thus conclude, that there is no art begun and perfected at one enterprise.

---

[27] The contraction of two syllables into one; especially (in verse) the obscuration of a vowel at the end of a word when the word following begins with a vowel.

Samuel Daniel,
Classical metres unsuitable for English
poetry (*c*.1603)

SAMUEL DANIEL (1562–1619), son of a music master, was educated at Magdalen Hall Oxford. He worked for some years as a private tutor to William Herbert (who became Earl of Pembroke in 1601) and to Anne Clifford (daughter of the Earl of Cumberland). In 1607 he became one of the Queen's grooms of the privy chamber, and from 1615 to 1618 was inspector of the Children of the Queens' Revels at Bristol. His many poems included the sonnet collection *Delia*, and *The Complaint of Rosamond* (1592); *Musophilus, or A General Defence of Learning* (1599); *The Civil Wars* (1595, enlarged in 1609); *Works* (1601) and *Whole workes* (1623); together with a Senecan tragedy, *Cleopatra* (1594), and various masques and entertainments.

TEXT. From *A Defence of Ryme, Against a Pamphlet entituled: 'Observations in the Art of English Poetrie'. Wherein is demonstratively proved, that Ryme is the fittest harmonie of words that comportes with our Language* (London, *c*.1603). The work's addressee, William Herbert, third Earl of Pembroke (1580–1630), was the patron of Jonson, Massinger, and Inigo Jones. In 1623 the first folio of Shakespeare's works was dedicated to him as Lord Chamberlain and to his brother Philip.

TO WILLIAM HERBERT, EARL OF PEMBROKE

The general custom and use of rhyme in this kingdom, noble Lord, having been so long (as if from a grant of nature) held unquestionable, made me to imagine that it lay altogether out of the way of contradiction, and was become so natural as we should never have had a thought to cast it off into reproach, or be made to think that it ill became our language. But now I see, when there is opposition made to all things in the world by words,[1] we must now at length likewise fall to contend for words themselves, and make a question whether they be right or not. For we are told how that our measures* go wrong,

---

[1] So inverting the traditional teaching, that *verba* were subordinate to *res*—meaning both 'things' in the created universe, and the 'matter' or subject of a composition.

all rhyming is gross, vulgar, barbarous; which if it be so, we have lost much labour to no purpose; and, for mine own particular, I cannot but blame the fortune of the times and mine own genius, that cast me upon so wrong a course, drawn with the current of custom and an unexamined example. . . .

But yet now, upon the great discovery of these new measures, threatening to overthrow the whole state of rhyme in this kingdom, I must either stand out to defend or else be forced to forsake myself and give over all. And though irresolution and a self-distrust be the most apparent faults of my nature, and that the least check of reprehension, if it savour of reason, will as easily shake my resolution as any man's living, yet in this case, I know not how, I am grown more resolved, and, before I sink, willing to examine what those powers of judgement are that must bear me down and beat me off from the station of my profession, which by the law of nature I am set to defend; and the rather for that this detractor (whose commendable rhymes, albeit now himself an enemy to rhyme, have given heretofore to the world the best notice of his worth) is a man of fair parts and good reputation; and therefore the reproach forcibly cast from such a hand may throw down more at once than the labours of many shall in long time build up again. . . .

We could well have allowed of his numbers, had he not disgraced our rhyme, which both custom and nature doth most powerfully defend: custom that is before all law, nature that is above all art. Every language hath her proper number or measure fitted to use and delight, which custom, entertaining by the allowance of the ear, doth indenize* and make natural. All verse is but a frame of words confined within certain measure, differing from the ordinary speech, and introduced the better to express men's conceits, both for delight and memory. Which frame of words consisting of *rhythmus* or *metrum*,[2] number or measure, are disposed into diverse fashions, according to the humour of the composer and the set of the time. And these rhythms, as Aristotle[3] saith, are familiar amongst all nations, and *e naturali et sponte fusa compositione*, and they fall as naturally already in our language as ever art can make them, being such as the ear of itself doth marshall in their proper rooms. . . .

And for our rhyme (which is an excellency added to this work of measure, and a harmony far happier than any proportion antiquity

² For these terms cf. Puttenham, p. 215 and n. 45.
³ *Poet.* 4. 1448ᵇ20 ff., probably from an Italian commentary.

could ever show us) doth add more grace, and hath more of delight than
ever bare numbers, howsoever they can be forced to run in our slow language, can possibly yield. Which, whether it be derived of *rhythmus* or
of *romance*, which were songs the Bards and Druids about rhymes used,
and thereof were called *remensi*,[4] as some Italians hold, or howsoever, it
is likewise number and harmony of words, consisting of an agreeing
sound in the last syllables of several verses, giving both to the ear an
echo of a delightful report,* and to the memory a deeper impression of
what is delivered therein. For as Greek and Latin verse consists of the
number and quantity of syllables, so doth the English verse of measure
and accent.* And though it doth not strictly observe long and short
syllables, yet it most religiously respects the accent; and as the short and
the long make number, so the acute and grave accent yield harmony.
And harmony is likewise number; so that the English verse then hath
number, measure, and harmony in the best proportion of music.
Which, being more certain and more resounding, works that effect of
motion* with as happy success as either the Greek or Latin. And so
natural a melody is it, and so universal, as it seems to be generally borne
with all the nations of the world as an hereditary eloquence[5] proper to
all mankind. The universality argues the general power of it: for if the
barbarian use it, then it shows that it sways the affection of the barbarian; if civil nations practise it, it proves that it works upon the hearts of
civil nations; if all, then that it hath a power in nature on all. . . .

And such a force hath it in nature, or so made by nature, as the Latin
numbers, notwithstanding their excellency, seemed not sufficient to
satisfy the ear of the world thereunto accustomed, without this harmonical cadence; which made the most learned of all nations labour
with exceeding travail to bring those numbers likewise unto it; which
many did with that happiness, as neither their purity of tongue nor
their material contemplations are thereby any way disgraced, but
rather deserve to be reverenced of all grateful posterity with the due
regard of their worth. And for *Schola Salerna*, and those *Carmina
proverbialia*,[6] who finds not therein more precepts for use, concerning

---

[4] Daniel draws on Giraldi Cinthio's *Discorso intorno al comporre dei romanzi* (1554): 'there
is one who would derive this word from Remensi, others from Turpin . . . Since he was
Archbishop of Rheims (Remense), they maintain that these compositions have been called
Romances'; *Giraldo Cinthio on Romances*, tr. H. L. Snuggs (Lexington, Ky., 1968), p. 6.

[5] Cf. Sidney, pp. 338–40, Campion, p. 429.

[6] A book of medical rules in verse produced in 1100 by the 'School of Salerno', *Conser-
vandae bonae valetudinis praecepta*: cf. *ECE* ii. 13, 408. For the *Carmina proverbialia* cf.
Campion, p. 432.

diet, health, and conversation, than Cato, Theognis, or all the Greeks and Latins can show us in that kind of teaching? And that in so few words, both for delight to the ear and the hold of memory, as they are to be embraced of all modest readers that study to know and not to deprave.*

Methinks it is a strange imperfection that men should thus overrun the estimation of good things with so violent a censure, as though it must please none else because it likes not them. . . .

'Ill customs are to be left.'[7] I grant it; but I see not how that can be taken for an ill custom which nature hath thus ratified, all nations received, time so long confirmed, the effects such as it performs those offices of motion* for which it is employed; delighting the ear, stirring the heart, and satisfying the judgement in such sort as I doubt whether ever single numbers will do in our climate, if they show no more work of wonder than yet we see. And if ever they prove to become anything, it must be by the approbation of many ages that must give them their strength for any operation, as before the world will feel where the pulse, life, and enargy[8] lies; which now we are sure where to have in our rhymes, whose known frame hath those due stays for the mind, those encounters of touch as makes the motion certain,[9] though the variety be infinite.

Nor will the general sort for whom we write (the wise being above books) taste these laboured measures but as an orderly prose, when we have all done. For this kind acquaintance and continual familiarity, ever had betwixt our ear and this cadence, is grown to so intimate a friendship as it will now hardly ever be brought to miss it. For be the verse never so good, never so full, it seems not to satisfy nor breed that delight as when it is met and combined with a like sounding accent; which seems as the jointure* without which it hangs loose, and cannot subsist, but runs wildly on, like a tedious fancy without a close. Suffer then the world to enjoy that which it knows, and what it likes, seeing that whatsoever force of words doth move, delight, and sway the affections of men, in what Scythian[10] sort soever it be disposed or uttered, that is true number, measure, eloquence, and the perfection of speech. . . .

---

[7] Taking up Campion's argument: cf. p. 430.

[8] On this term cf. Puttenham, pp. 224–5 n. 59.

[9] The regular occurrence of rhymes in poetry gives it a steadiness of movement and helps understanding.

[10] The Scythians were a nomadic people inhabiting an ancient region extending over much of Europe and Asiatic Russia, who were also proverbial for savagery: cf. *King Lear* 1. 1. 116.

But could our adversary hereby set up the music of our times to a higher note of judgement and discretion, or could these new laws of words better our imperfections, it were a happy attempt; but when hereby we shall but as it were change prison, and put off these fetters to receive others, what have we gained? As good still to use rhyme and a little reason as neither rhyme nor reason, for no doubt, as idle wits will write in that kind as do now in this, imitation will after, though it break her neck. *Scribimus indocti doctique poemata passim.*[11] And this multitude of idle writers can be no disgrace to the good; for the same fortune in one proportion or other is proper in a like season to all states in their turn. . . .

For seeing it is matter that satisfies the judicial, appear it in what habit* it will, all these pretended proportions of words, howsoever placed, can be but words, and peradventure serve but to embroil our understanding. Whilst seeking to please our ear, we enthrall our judgement; to delight an exterior sense, we smooth up a weak confused sense, affecting sound to be unsound; and all to seem *servum pecus*,[12] only to imitate Greeks and Latins, whose felicity in this kind might be something to themselves, to whom their own *idiōma* was natural, but to us it can yield no other commodity than a sound. We admire them not for their smooth-gliding words, nor their measures, but for their inventions; which treasure, if it were to be found in Welsh and Irish, we should hold those languages in the same estimation; and they may thank their sword, that made their tongues so famous and universal as they are.

For to say truth, their verse is many times but a confused deliverer of their excellent conceits, whose scattered limbs we are fain to look out and join together, to discern the image of what they represent unto us. And even the Latins, who profess not to be so licentious* as the Greeks, show us many times examples, but of strange cruelty, in torturing and dismembering of words in the midst, or disjoining such as naturally should be married and march together by setting them as far asunder as they can possibly stand; that sometimes, unless the kind reader out of his own good nature will stay them up by their measure, they will fall down into flat prose, and sometimes are no other indeed in their natural sound. And then again, when you find them disobedient to their own laws, you must hold it to be *licentia poetica*,[13] and

---

[11] Horace, *Epist.* 2. 1. 117: 'but, skilled or unskilled, we scribble poetry, all alike'.

[12] Ibid. 1. 19. 19: 'O you mimics, you slavish herd!'

[13] On poetic licence see *De or.* 3. 38. 153, *Inst.* 10. 5. 4, *Ars P.* 9 f., and Gascoigne, p. 168.

so dispensable. The striving to show their changeable measures in the variety of their odes have been very painful* no doubt unto them, and forced them thus to disturb the quiet stream of their words, which by a natural succession otherwise desire to follow in their due course.

But such affliction doth laboursome curiosity* still lay upon our best delights (which ever must be made strange and variable), as if art were ordained to afflict nature, and that we could not go but in fetters. Every science, every profession, must be so wrapped up in unnecessary intrications, as if it were not to fashion but to confound* the understanding. . . .

And indeed, I have wished that there were not that multiplicity of rhymes as is used by many in sonnets, which yet we see in some so happily to succeed, and hath been so far from hindering their inventions as it hath begot conceit beyond expectation, and comparable to the best inventions of the world. For sure in an eminent spirit, whom nature hath fitted for that mystery, rhyme is no impediment[14] to his conceit, but rather gives him wings to mount, and carries him not out of his course but as it were beyond his power, to a far happier flight. All excellencies being sold us at the hard price of labour, it follows, where we bestow most thereof we buy the best success: and rhyme, being far more laborious than loose measures (whatsoever is objected) must needs, meeting with wit and industry, breed greater and worthier effects in our language. So that if our labours have wrought out a manumission from bondage, and that we go at liberty notwithstanding these ties, we are no longer the slaves of rhyme, but we make it a most excellent instrument to serve us. Nor is this certain limit observed in sonnets any tyrannical bounding of the conceit, but rather reducing it in *girum*[15] and a just form, neither too long for the shortest project nor too short for the longest, being but only employed for a present passion. For the body of our imagination being as an unformed chaos without fashion, without day, if by the divine power of the spirit it be wrought into an orb of order and form, is it not more pleasing to nature, that desires a certainty and comports not with that which is infinite, to have these closes,* rather than not to know where to end or how far to go, especially seeing our passions are often without measure? And we find the best of the Latins

[14] Cf. Spenser, *Shepheardes Calendar*, 'October', p. 187.
[15] Reducing it into a circle, the 'just form' or perfect shape, according to Renaissance beliefs; cf. 'an orb of order and form,' below.

many times either not concluding, or else otherwise in the end than they began.

Besides, is it not most delightful to see much excellently ordered in a small room, or little gallantly disposed and made to fill up a space of like capacity, in such sort that the one would not appear so beautiful in a larger circuit, nor the other do well in a less? Which often we find to be so, according to the powers of nature in the workman. And these limited proportions and rests of stanzas, consisting of six, seven, or eight lines, are of that happiness both for the disposition of the matter, the apt planting the sentence where it may best stand to hit, the certain close of delight with the full body of a just period well carried, is such as neither the Greeks or Latins ever attained unto. For their boundless running on often so confounds the reader that, having once lost himself, must either give off unsatisfied, or uncertainly cast back to retrieve the escaped sense, and to find way again into this matter.

Methinks we should not so soon yield our consents captive to the authority of antiquity unless we saw more reason; all our understandings are not to be built by the square* of Greece and Italy. We are the children of nature as well as they; we are not so placed out of the way of judgement but that the same sun of discretion* shineth upon us; we have our portion of the same virtues as well as of the same vices. . . . Time and the turn of things bring about these faculties according to the present estimation. . . . So that we must never rebel against use: *Quem penes arbitrium est et vis et norma loquendi.*[16]

It is not the observing of *trochaics*, nor their *iambics*, that will make our writings ought the wiser. All their poesy, all their philosophy is nothing unless we bring the discerning light of conceit with us to apply it to use.[17] It is not books but only that great book of the world and the all-overspreading grace of heaven that makes men truly judicial. . . . It is not the contexture of words but the effects of action that gives glory to the times. We find they had *mercurium in pectore*, though not in *lingua*;[18] and in all ages, though they were not Ciceronians,[19] they

---

[16] Horace, *Ars P.* 72: '[if Usage so will it,] in whose hand lies the judgement, the right and the rule of speech'.

[17] Cf. Gascoigne, pp. 162–3.

[18] 'They had eloquence in their hearts, if not on their tongues' (Mercury was the god of eloquence: cf. Jonson, p. 574).

[19] Here, simply scholars in rhetoric or philosophy. *Ars artium*: 'the art of arts'.

knew the art of men, which only is *ars artium*, the great gift of heaven, and the chief grace and glory on earth; they had the learning of government, and ordering their state; eloquence enough to show their judgements. . . .

There is but one learning, which *omnes gentes habent scriptum in cordibus suis*,[20] one and the selfsame spirit that worketh in all. We have but one body of justice, one body of wisdom throughout the whole world; which is but apparelled according to the fashion of every nation.

Eloquence and gay* words are not of the substance of wit; it is but the garnish of a nice* time, the ornaments that do but deck the house of a state. . . . Hunger is as well satisfied with meat served in pewter as silver. Discretion* is the best measure, the rightest foot in what habit soever it run. . . .

But had our adversary taught us by his own proceedings this way of perfection, and therein framed us a poem of that excellency as should have put down all, and been the masterpiece of these times, we should all have admired him. But to deprave* the present form of writing, and to bring us nothing but a few loose and uncharitable epigrams,[21] and yet would make us believe those numbers were come to raise the glory of our language, giveth us cause to suspect the performance, and to examine whether this new art *constat sibi*;[22] or *aliquid sit dictum quod non sit dictum prius.* . . .[23]

For what ado have we here? What strange precepts of art[24] about the framing of an iambic verse in our language? Which, when all is done, reaches not by a foot but falleth out to be the plain ancient verse, consisting of ten syllables or five feet, which hath ever been used amongst us time out of mind, and, for all this cunning and counterfeit name, can or will [not] be any other in nature than it hath been ever heretofore. And this new *dimeter* is but the half of this verse divided in two, and no other than the *caesura* or breathing place in the midst thereof, and therefore it had been as good to have put two lines

---

[20] 'All peoples have inscribed on their hearts'.

[21] Campion had included several of his epigrams to illustrate English trochaic verse (ch. 6), and elegiacs (ch. 7): *ECE* ii. 340–6.

[22] 'Is self-consistent'; cf. Horace, *Ars P.* 127: 'have it self-consistent'.

[23] 'Whether something is said which has not been said before': varying a sentence in Terence, sometimes cited in the *imitatio* debate as proof that originality was no longer possible: 'Nullum est iam dictum, quod non dictum sit prius' (*Eunuchus*, prol. 41): 'nothing can be said that has not been said before'.

[24] Daniel now attacks Campion's ch. 4: see p. 439.

in one, but only to make them seem diverse. Nay, it had been much better for the true English reading and pronouncing thereof, without violating the accent, which now our adversary hath herein most unkindly done. For, being as we are to sound it according to our English march,* we must make a rest, and raise the last syllable, which falls out very unnatural in 'desolate', 'funeral', 'Elizabeth', 'prodigal', and in all the rest, saving the monosyllables.

Then follows the English *trochaic*, which is said to be a simple verse, and so indeed it is, being without rhyme: having here no other grace than that in sound it runs like the known measure of our former ancient verse, ending (as we term it according to the French) in a feminine foot; saving that it is shorter by one syllable at the beginning, which is not much missed, by reason it falls full at the last. Next comes the *elegiac*, being the fourth kind, and that likewise is no other than our old accustomed measure of five feet. If there be any dif-ference, it must be made in the reading, and therein we must stand bound to stay where often we would not, and sometimes either break the accent or the due course of the word. And now for the other four kinds of numbers, which are to be employed for odes, they are either of the same measure, or such as have ever been familiarly used amongst us.

So that of all these eight several kinds of new promised numbers, you see what we have: only what was our own before, and the same but apparelled in foreign titles; which, had they come in their kind and natural attire of rhyme, we should never have suspected that they had affected* to be other, or sought to degenerate into strange manners. . . .

But see the power of nature; it is not all the artificial coverings of wit that can hide their native and original condition, which breaks out through the strongest bands of affectation and will be itself, do singularity what it can. And as for those imagined quantities of syllables, which have been ever held free and indifferent* in our lan-guage, who can enforce us to take knowledge of them, being *in nullius verba iurati*,[25] and owing fealty to no foreign invention? Especially in such a case where there is no necessity in nature, or that it imports* either the matter or form whether it be so or otherwise. But every versifier that well observes his work finds in our language, without

---

[25] Horace, *Epist.* 1. 1. 14: 'Nullius addictus iurare in verba magistri': 'I am not bound over to swear as any master dictates'.

all these unnecessary precepts, what numbers best fit the nature of her idiom, and the proper places destined to such accents as she will not let in to any other rooms than in those for which they were born. As for example, you cannot make this fall into the right sound of a verse:

> None thinks reward rendered worthy his worth,

unless you thus misplace the accent upon 'rendered' and 'worthy', contrary to the nature of these words. Which showeth that two feminine numbers (or *trochees*, if so you will call them) will not succeed in the third and fourth place of the verse. And so likewise in this case,

> Though death doth consume, yet virtue preserves,

it will not be a verse, though it hath the just syllables, without the same number in the second, and the altering of the fourth place in this sort:

> Though death doth ruin, virtue yet preserves.

Again, who knows not that we can not kindly* answer a feminine number with a masculine rhyme, or (if you will so term it) a *trochee* with a *spondee*, as 'weakness' with 'confess', 'nature' and 'endure', only for that thereby we shall wrong the accent, the chief lord and grave governor of numbers? Also you cannot in a verse of four feet place a *trochee* in the first without the like offence, as, 'Yearly out of his wat'ry cell'; for so you shall sound it 'Yearely', which is unnatural. And other such like observations usually occur, which nature and a judicial* ear of themselves teach us readily to avoid.

But now for whom hath our adversary taken all this pains? For the learned, or for the ignorant, or for himself, to show his own skill? If for the learned, it was to no purpose, for every grammarian in this land hath learned his *prosodia*, and already knows all this art of numbers. If for the ignorant, it was vain, for if they become versifiers, we are like to have lean numbers instead of fat* rhyme; and if Tully[26] would have his orator skilled in all the knowledges appertaining to God and man, what should they have who would be a degree above orators? Why then, it was to show his own skill, and what himself had observed; so he might well have done without doing wrong to the fame of the living, and wrong to England, in seeking to lay reproach upon her native ornaments, and to turn the fair stream and full course of

---

[26] Cicero, *De or.* 1. 6. 20.

her accents into the shallow current of a less uncertainty, clean out of the way of her known delight. . . .

But when after-times shall make a quest of inquiry,[27] to examine the best of this age, peradventure there will be found in the now contemned records of rhyme matter not unfitting the gravest divine and severest lawyer in this kingdom. But these things must have the date of antiquity to make them reverend and authentical. For ever in the collation* of writers men rather weigh their age than their merit. . . .

And let this make us look the better to our feet, the better to our matter, better to our manners. . . . and let this be the benefit we make by being oppugned, and the means to redeem back the good opinion vanity and idleness have suffered to be won from us; which nothing but substance and matter can effect. For *scribendi recte sapere est et principium et fons.*[28]

When we hear music, we must be in our ear in the outer room of sense, but when we entertain judgement, we retire into the cabinet and innermost withdrawing chamber of the soul. And it is but as music for the ear, *verba sequi fidibus modulanda Latinis*, but it is a work of power for the soul, *Numerosque modosque ediscere vitae.*[29] The most judicial and worthy spirits of this land are not so delicate,* or will owe so much to their ear as to rest upon the outside of words, and be entertained with sound; seeing that both number, measure, and rhyme is but as the ground or seat whereupon is raised the work that commends it, and which may be easily at the first found out by any shallow conceit . . .

But yet, notwithstanding all this which I have here delivered in the defence of rhyme, I am not so far in love with mine own mystery,[30] or will seem so froward* as to be against the reformation and the better settling these measures of ours. Wherein there be many things I could wish were more certain and better ordered, though myself dare not take upon me to be a teacher therein, having so much need to learn of others. And I must confess that to mine own ear those continual cadences of couplets used in long and continued poems are very tiresome and unpleasing, by reason that still, methinks, they run on with

---

[27] Cf. Florio, 'I in this search or quest of inquirie have spent most of my studies': Dedicatory epistle to his *Dictionary* (1598).

[28] Horace, *Ars P.* 309: 'Of good writing the source and fount is wisdom'.

[29] Horace, *Epist.* 2. 2. 141–3: '[In truth, it is profitable to cast aside toys and to learn wisdom; to leave to lads the sport that fits their age, and not] to search out words that will fit the music of the Latin lyre, but to master the rhythms and measures of a genuine life'.

[30] A learned trade or profession: here, poetry.

a sound of one nature, and a kind of certainty which stuffs the delight rather than entertains it. But yet, notwithstanding, I must not out of mine own daintiness* condemn this kind of writing, which peradventure to another may seem most delightful; and many worthy compositions we see to have passed with commendation in that kind. Besides, methinks, sometimes to beguile the ear with a running out and passing over the rhyme, as no bound to stay us in the line where the violence of the matter will break through, is rather graceful than otherwise. Wherein I find my Homer Lucan, as if he gloried to seem to have no bounds, albeit he were confined within his measures, to be in my conceit most happy. For so thereby they who care not for verse or rhyme may pass it over with taking notice thereof, and please themselves with a well measured prose. And I must confess my adversary hath wrought this much upon me, that I think a tragedy would indeed best comport with a blank verse and dispense with rhyme, saving in the *chorus*, or where a sentence* shall require a couplet. And to avoid this over-glutting the ear with that always certain and full encounter* of rhyme, I have essayed in some of my Epistles[31] to alter the usual place of meeting and to set it further off by one verse, to try how I could disuse mine own ear and to ease it of this continual burthen, which indeed seems to surcharge it a little too much. But as yet I cannot come to please myself therein, this alternate or cross rhyme holding still the best place in my affection.

Besides, to me this change of number in a poem of one nature fits not so well as to mix uncertainly feminine rhymes with masculine, which ever since I was warned of that deformity by my kind friend and countryman Master Hugh Samford, I have always so avoided it, as there are not above two couplets in that kind in all my poem of the Civil wars.[32] And I would willingly if I could have altered it in all the rest, holding feminine rhymes to be fittest for ditties,* and either to be set for certain, or else by themselves. But in these things, I say, I dare not take upon me to teach that they ought to be so, in respect myself holds them to be so, or that I think it right: for indeed there is no right in these things that are continually in a wandering motion, carried with the violence of uncertain likings, being but only the time that gives them their power.

[31] Such as 'To the Lord Henrie Howard' in *Certaine Epistles* (*Complete Works*, ed. A. B. Grosart, 5 vols. (London, 1885–96), i. 199 ff.).
[32] At this date Daniel had published *The first fowre bookes of the civile warres betweene the two houses of Lancaster and Yorke* (London, 1595); it was enlarged to eight books in 1609.

But the greatest hinderer to our proceedings and the reformation of our errors is this self-love, whereunto we versifiers are ever noted to be specially subject; a disease of all other the most dangerous and incurable, being once seated in the spirits, for which there is no cure but only by a spiritual remedy. . . . *Caecus amor sui;*[33] and though it would seem to see all without it, yet certainly it discerns but little within. For there is not the simplest writer that will ever tell himself he doth ill, but, as if he were the parasite only to soothe his own doings, persuades him that his lines can not but please others which so much delight himself: . . . And the more to show that he is so, we shall see him evermore in all places, and to all persons repeating his own compositions; and

Quem vero arripuit, tenet, occiditque legendo.[34]

Next to this deformity stands our affectation, wherein we always betray ourselves, to be both unkind and unnatural to our own native language in disguising or forging strange or unusual words, as if it were to make our verse seem another kind of speech out of the course of our usual practice; displacing our words, or inventing new only upon a singularity, when our own accustomed phrase, set in the due place, would express us more familiarly and to better delight than all this idle affectation of antiquity or novelty can ever do. And I cannot but wonder at the strange presumption of some men, that dare so audaciously adventure to introduce any whatsoever foreign words, be they never so strange, and of themselves, as it were, without a Parliament, without any consent or allowance, establish them as free-denizens in our language. But this is but a character of that perpetual revolution* which we see to be in all things that never remain the same: and we must herein be content to submit ourselves to the law of time, which in few years will make all that for which we now contend *Nothing.*

---

[33] Horace, *Odes* 1. 18. 14: 'blind self-love'.
[34] Horace, *Ars P.* 475: 'If he catches a man, he holds him fast and reads him to death'.

Ben Jonson,
Rhymes against rhyme (*c*.1603)

BEN JONSON (1572–1637), after Shakespeare the greatest dramatist of this period, was born in Westminster, the son of a minister, who died a month before Jonson's birth. (His mother subsequently married a master-bricklayer.) He was educated at Westminster School in the 1580s, where his teacher was William Camden, subsequently Headmaster and a distinguished scholar (see p. 534 and n. 40). Apprenticed as a bricklayer from 1589 on, Jonson joined the army in Flanders, probably in 1596. Writing for the theatrical entrepreneur Philip Henslowe by 1597, Jonson's career as a dramatist extended until 1633. Between 1603 and 1634 he also wrote many masques and entertainments for the court, and from 1616 was granted a pension as 'King's poet'.

TEXT. Poem 29 in *Underwoods*, first published in the two-volume *Works* (1640). Jonson expressed his views on the controversy over classical metre and vernacular rhymes again in 1619 (p. 528), registering his dissatisfaction with the arguments of both Campion (p. 428) and Daniel (p. 441). This brilliant poem repeats many of the classicists' negative accounts of rhyme, yet does so through rhyme itself, justifying its ability to transcend those limitations in the hands of a craftsman. In annotating it I have benefited from the great edition by C. H. Herford, P. and E. Simpson (eds.), *Ben Jonson*, 11 vols. (Oxford, 1925–52), who suggest that the poem 'may date from the Campion and Daniel controversy of 1602–3' (xi. 47); and William B. Hunter, Jr. (ed.), *The Complete Poetry of Ben Jonson* (New York, 1963).

A FIT OF RHYME AGAINST RHYME

Rhyme, the rack of finest wits,
That expresseth but by fits,[1]
True conceit,*
Spoiling senses of their treasure,

---

[1] Here, as in the title, Jonson may be punning on 'fit' as 'a sudden and transitory state of activity, inaction, etc.', as in 'fitfully' or spasmodically; and 'fit' as 'a part or section of a poem or song' (*SOED*).

Cozening judgement with a measure, 5
   But false weight.[2]
Wresting words from their true calling;
Propping verse, for fear of falling
   To the ground.
Jointing* syllables, drowning letters,[3] 10
Fastening vowels,[4] as with fetters
   They were bound!
Soon as lazy thou wert known,
All good poetry hence was flown,
   And art banish'd.[5] 15
For a thousand years together,
All Parnassus'[6] green did wither,
   And wit vanish'd.
Pegasus[7] did fly away,
At the wells[8] no muse did stay, 20
   But bewailed
So to see the fountain dry,
And Apollo's music die,
   All light failed!
Starveling* rhymes did fill the stage, 25
Not a poet in an age
   Worth crowning.
Not a work deserving bays,*
Nor a line deserving praise,
   Pallas[9] frowning. 30
Greek was free from rhyme's infection,
Happy Greek by this protection
   Was not spoiled,
Whilst the Latin, queen of tongues,

[2] Another pun, 'cozening' or cheating by giving true 'measure' (metre, rhythm) but 'false weight' (sense).
[3] Adding syllables, suppressing (or eliding) letters.
[4] Fixing the quality of vowels.
[5] The 'good poetry' (Greek and Latin) did not use rhyme, introduced in late classical Latin, 'a thousand years' earlier. Latin is 'not yet free', Jonson writes in a later stanza: but rhyme, although common in medieval poetry (especially church hymns), was very rare in neo-Latin.
[6] The mountain in central Greece sacred to Apollo and the muses; 'the hill' below.
[7] The Muses' winged horse; cf. Baldwin, p. 135 and n. 8.
[8] Hippocrene, the fountain on Mount Helicon from which poets derived inspiration.
[9] Pallas Athene, goddess of wisdom.

Is not yet free from rhyme's wrongs,   35
    But rests foiled.*
Scarce the hill again doth flourish,
Scarce the world a wit doth nourish,
    To restore
Phoebus to his crown again,   40
And the muses to their brain,
    As before.
Vulgar languages that want
Words, and sweetness, and be scant
    Of true measure,[10]   45
Tyrant rhyme hath so abused,
That they long since have refused
    Other caesure.[11]
He that first invented thee,
May his joints tormented be,   50
    Cramped forever;
Still may syllables jar with time,*
Still may reason war with rhyme,
    Resting never.
May his sense, when it would meet   55
The cold tumour* in his feet,
    Grow unsounder.
And his title be long fool,
That, in rearing such a school,
    Was the founder.   60

---

[10] European vernacular poetry used accentual, not quantitative scansion.
[11] The mid-line pause in classical verse; here opposed to the end-pauses created by rhyme.

Francis Bacon,
Imitatio and its excesses;
Poetry, rhetoric, and the imagination (1605)

FRANCIS BACON (1561–1626), the youngest son of Sir Nicholas Bacon (Lord Keeper to Queen Elizabeth), was educated at Trinity College Cambridge, and Gray's Inn. Deprived of an inheritance by his father's sudden death, he made a career in law and public service. He was an MP for over thirty years, and rose to become Solicitor General in 1607, Attorney-General in 1613, Lord Keeper in 1617, Lord Chancellor in 1618. He was created Baron Verulam in 1618, and in 1621 Viscount St Alban. But in that year an opposition group in Parliament accused him of bribery, and he was dismissed from office. In the intervals of public life he wrote many works of literature and philosophy: the *Essays* (1597, enlarged in 1612 and 1625), *The History of the Reign of King Henry the Seventh* (1622), the *Instauratio Magna* (1620), including the *Novum Organum* (two books only). Other works appeared posthumously.

TEXT. From *The Twoo Bookes of Francis Bacon. Of the proficience and advancement of Learning, divine and human* (1605). This work was the first public utterance of Bacon's plans for a renewal of knowledge, rejecting dead traditions and creating an ongoing exchange between observation and experiment in order to establish scientific laws. In Book One he defends learning from hostile criticisms, and then makes his own critique of those elements which block its advance. One of these is the over-cultivation of style at the expense of subject-matter (excerpt 1). Here his target is the excessive practice of *imitatio*, as shown in the veneration for Cicero's Latin style by some sixteenth century humanists (see Ascham, p. 156). In Book Two Bacon surveys the whole of human knowledge, redefining individual areas of inquiry and their relation to each other, and identifying those areas in which new research is needed. His discussion of the verbal arts (excerpt 2) results in a valuation of poetry and the imagination far more favourable than usual among Renaissance philosophers.

I

There be therefore chiefly three vanities in studies, whereby learning hath been most traduced.* For those things we do esteem vain, which are either false or frivolous, those which either have no truth or no use: and those persons we esteem vain, which are either credulous or curious;* and curiosity* is either in matter or words. So that in reason as well as in experience, there fall out to be these three distempers* (as I may term them) of learning; the first, fantastical* learning; the second, contentious* learning; and the last, delicate* learning; vain imaginations, vain altercations,* and vain affectations; and with the last I will begin.

Martin Luther,[1] conducted (no doubt) by an higher Providence, but in discourse of reason finding what a province* he had undertaken against the Bishop of Rome and the degenerate traditions of the church, and finding his own solitude, being no ways aided by the opinions of his own time, was enforced to awake all antiquity, and to call former times to his succours to make a party[2] against the present time; so that the ancient authors, both in divinity and in humanity, which had long time slept in libraries, began generally to be read and revolved. This by consequence did draw on a necessity of a more exquisite* travail* in the languages original wherein those authors did write, for the better understanding of those authors and the better advantage of pressing* and applying their words. And thereof grew again a delight in their manner of style and phrase, and an admiration of that kind of writing;[3] which was much furthered and precipitated by the enmity and opposition that the propounders of those (primitive* but seeming new) opinions had against the schoolmen;* who were generally of the contrary part, and whose writings were altogether in a differing style and form; taking liberty to coin and frame new terms of art to express their own sense and to avoid circuit of speech, without regard to the pureness,* pleasantness, and (as I may call it) lawfulness of the phrase or word. And again, because the great labour then was with the people (of whom the Pharisees were wont to say, '*Execrabilis ista turba, quae non novit legem*'),[4] for the winning and persuading of them, there grew of necessity in chief price* and

---

[1] Luther (1483–1546), founder of the Reformation, one side-effect of which was a revived study of Greek sources in order to define the original form of Christianity. Bacon is unusual in linking the Reformation with the revival of Greek and with the rejection of medieval scholastic philosophy, both of which were much wider Renaissance movements.

[2] To take sides against.

[3] The imitation of Cicero's prose-style, which reached the absurd stage of only using words or word-forms authorized by Cicero. Erasmus mocked it in his *Ciceronianus* (1528): cf. *CWE*, vol. xxvii, and Sidney (p. 386), attacking 'Nizolian paper books'.

[4] John 7:49: 'This multitude which knoweth not the law are accursed'. The Pharisees strictly observed the laws and rituals laid down by Moses.

request eloquence and variety of discourse, as the fittest and forciblest access into the capacity of the vulgar sort.[5]

So that these four causes concurring, the admiration of ancient authors, the hate of the schoolmen, the exact study of languages, and the efficacy of preaching, did bring in an affectionate[6] study of eloquence and copie* of speech, which then began to flourish. This grew speedily to an excess; for men began to hunt more after words than matter;[7] and more after the choiceness* of the phrase, and the round and clean composition of the sentence, and the sweet falling[8] of the clauses, and the varying and illustration of their works with tropes and figures, than after the weight of matter, worth of subject, soundness of argument, life of invention, or depth of judgment. Then grew the flowing and watery vein of Osorius,[9] the Portugal bishop, to be in price. Then did Sturmius[10] spend such infinite and curious pains upon Cicero the orator and Hermogenes the rhetorician, besides his own books of periods* and imitation and the like. Then did Carr of Cambridge, and Ascham,[11] with their lectures and writings, almost deify Cicero and Demosthenes, and allure all young men that were studious unto that delicate and polished kind of learning. Then did Erasmus take occasion to make the scoffing echo; '*Decem annos consumpsi in legendo Cicerone*', and the echo answered in Greek, '*one*', *Asine*.[12] Then grew the learning of the schoolmen to be utterly despised as barbarous. In sum, the whole inclination and bent of those times was rather towards copie than weight.

Here therefore is the first distemper of learning, when men study words and not matter: whereof though I have represented an example of late times, yet it hath been and will be '*secundum majus et minus*'[13]

---

[5] The common people, who could attend sermons but not read books.

[6] Zealous, devoted; but also 'affected'.

[7] All authorities on good writing and speaking urged that more attention be paid to the *res* or *sententia*, the 'matter' or meaning to be communicated, than to the *verba* embodying it.

[8] Polished and smooth sentence structure; symmetrical clauses marked by the rhetorical figures *similiter cadens* or *similiter desinens* (see pp. 216, 417).

[9] Jeronimo Osorio (1506–80), a theologian known as 'the Portuguese Cicero'.

[10] Johann Sturm (1507–89), head of the Strasbourg Gymnasium, who wrote influential commentaries on Cicero and Hermogenes, and published *De periodis* (1550) and *De imitatione oratoria* (1574).

[11] Nicholas Carr (1524–68) succeeded Sir John Cheke as the Cambridge Professor of Greek in 1547. Ascham (see p. 140) was a friend of both Osorius and Sturm.

[12] 'I have spent ten years reading Cicero'—'You ass!': from Erasmus' *Colloquy*, 'Echo'.

[13] 'To a greater or lesser degree'.

in all time. And how is it possible but this should have an operation to discredit learning, even with vulgar capacities, when they see learned men's works like the first letter of a patent or limned book;[14] which though it hath large flourishes, yet it is but a letter? It seems to me that Pygmalion's frenzy[15] is a good emblem or portraiture of this vanity: for words are but the images of matter;[16] and except they have life of reason and invention, to fall in love with them is all one* as to fall in love with a picture.

But yet notwithstanding it is a thing not hastily to be condemned, to clothe and adorn the obscurity even of philosophy itself with sensible* and plausible* elocution. For hereof we have great examples in Xenophon, Cicero, Seneca, Plutarch, and of Plato also in some degree; and hereof likewise there is great use; for surely to the severe* inquisition of truth, and the deep progress into philosophy, it is some hindrance; because it is too early satisfactory to the mind of man, and quencheth the desire of further search, before we come to a just period;[17] but then if a man be to have any use of such knowledge in civil occasions, of conference, counsel, persuasion, discourse,[18] or the like; then shall he find it prepared to his hands in those authors which write in that manner. But the excess of this is so justly contemptible that as Hercules, when he saw the image of Adonis, Venus' minion,* in a temple, said in disdain, '*Nil sacri es*',[19] so there is none of Hercules' followers in learning, that is, the more severe and laborious sort of inquirers into truth, but will despise those delicacies and affectations, as indeed capable of no divineness. And thus much of the first disease or distemper of learning.[20]

[14] The initial capital letter in official documents was 'limned' or illuminated with a drawing.

[15] In Ovid (*Met.* 10. 243) he deludedly fell in love with the statue he had made.

[16] A reminiscence of Aristotle's definition of language: cf. Hoskyns, p. 399.

[17] Satisfactory conclusion (to the inquiry).

[18] Situations in real life where the ability to express oneself is important, such as 'conference' (conversation), 'counsel' (formal advice-giving), 'persuasion' (oration), and 'discourse' (formal discussion of a topic in speech and writing).

[19] 'You're nothing sacred'; from Erasmus, *Adagia* 1. 8. 37, citing the scholiast on Theocritus 5. 21–2 (*CWE* xxxii. 143).

[20] The second disease of learning that Bacon diagnoses, seen in the excesses of medieval scholasticism, is to focus on a closed body of knowledge, resulting in uselessly elaborate exegesis and fruitless controversy; the third, seen in the occult arts, involves the uncritical acceptance of legends and mysteries, a symbiosis between 'delight in deceiving, and aptness to be deceived; imposture and credulity' (*Francis Bacon*, ed. Vickers, p. 142); cf. Jonson, p. 580.

2

The parts of human learning have reference to the three parts of man's understanding, which is the seat of learning: history to his memory, poesy to his imagination, and philosophy to his reason. . . .[21]

Poesy is a part of learning in measure* of words for the most part restrained, but in all other points extremely licensed,* and doth truly refer to the imagination; which, being not tied to the laws of matter, may at pleasure join that which nature hath severed, and sever that which nature hath joined, and so make unlawful matches and divorces of things: '*Pictoribus atque poetis*',[22] etc. It is taken in two senses, in respect of words or matter. In the first sense it is but a character of style, and belongeth to the arts of speech, and is not pertinent for the present. In the latter, it is (as hath been said) one of the principal portions of learning, and is nothing else but feigned history, which may be styled* as well in prose as in verse.[23]

The use of this feigned history hath been to give some shadow of satisfaction to the mind of man in those points wherein the nature of things doth deny it; the world being in proportion[24] inferior to the soul; by reason whereof there is agreeable to the spirit of man a more ample greatness, a more exact goodness, and a more absolute variety, than can be found in the nature of things. Therefore, because the acts or events of true history have not that magnitude which satisfieth the mind of man, poesy[25] feigneth acts and events greater and more heroical. Because true history propoundeth the successes* and issues of actions not so agreeable to the merits of virtue and vice, therefore poesy feigns them more just in retribution, and more according to revealed providence. Because true history representeth actions and events more ordinary and less interchanged, therefore poesy endueth them with more rareness, and more unexpected and alternative* variations. So as it appeareth that poesy serveth and conferreth to magnanimity,* morality, and to delectation.[26] And therefore it was ever

[21] Bacon was original in using the traditional division of the mental faculties, which goes back to Galen, to classify knowledge.

[22] Horace, *Ars P.* 9–10: 'Painters and poets [have always been able to take what liberties they would]'.

[23] Cf. Aristotle, *Poet.* 9. 1451ᵇ1 ff., and Sidney, pp. 347, 367.

[24] In terms of symmetry or harmony.

[25] Bacon again draws on Aristotle (*Poet.* 9. 1451ᵃ36 ff.) and Sidney, p. 343.

[26] That is, poetry transmits and encourages nobility of feeling, moral conduct, and pleasure. Cf. Sidney, pp. 346–7, 356, 365.

thought to have some participation of divineness, because it doth raise and erect* the mind, by submitting the shows* of things to the desires of the mind; whereas reason doth buckle* and bow the mind unto the nature of things. And we see that by these insinuations* and congruities with man's nature and pleasure, joined also with the agreement and consort* it hath with music, it hath had access* and estimation in rude times and barbarous regions, where other learning stood excluded.

The division of poesy which is aptest in the propriety thereof (besides those divisions which are common unto it with history, as feigned chronicles, feigned lives; and the appendices of history, as feigned epistles, feigned orations, and the rest) is into poesy narrative, representative, and allusive.[27] The narrative is a mere imitation of history, with the excesses before remembered; choosing for subject commonly wars and love, rarely state,* and sometimes pleasure or mirth. Representative is as a visible history, and is an image of actions as if they were present, as history is of actions in nature as they are, (that is) past. Allusive or parabolical[28] is a narration applied only to express some special purpose or conceit.* Which later kind of parabolical wisdom was much more in use in the ancient times, as by the fables of Aesop and the brief sentences of the Seven[29] and the use of hieroglyphics may appear. And the cause was, for that it was then of necessity to express any point or reason which was more sharp* or subtile* than the vulgar in that manner; because men in those times wanted* both variety of examples and subtlety of conceit: and as hieroglyphics were before letters, so parables were before arguments: and nevertheless now and at all times they do retain much life and vigour, because reason cannot be so sensible,* nor examples[30] so fit.

But there remaineth yet another use of poesy parabolical, opposite to that which we last mentioned, for that tendeth to demonstrate and illustrate* that which is taught or delivered, and this other to retire* and obscure it: that is when the secrets and mysteries of religion, policy,* or philosophy are involved* in fables or parables. Of this in

[27] Narrative poetry; drama; symbolic or allegorical poetry.

[28] In this form, as Bacon puts it elsewhere, 'ideas that are objects of the intellect are represented in forms that are objects of the sense'.

[29] The teaching of the 'seven wise men of Greece' was recorded in brief sayings. For the link between hieroglyphs and parabolical wisdom cf. Plutarch, *Mor.* 345 D ff.

[30] 'Rational utterance is not so easily understood; examples drawn from historical events are not so fitting'.

divine poesy[31] we see the use is authorized. In heathen poesy we see the exposition of fables doth fall out sometimes with great felicity; as in the fable that the giants being overthrown in their war against the gods, the Earth their mother in revenge thereof brought forth Fame:*

> *Illam Terra parens, ira irritata deorum,*
> *Extremam, ut perhibent, Coeo Enceladoque sororem*
> *Progenuit.*[32]

—expounded,* that when princes and monarchs have suppressed actual and open rebels, then the malignity of people (which is the mother of rebellion) doth bring forth libels and slanders and taxations* of the state, which is of the same kind with rebellion, but more feminine. So in the fable that the rest of the gods having conspired to bind Jupiter, Pallas called Briareus[33] with his hundred hands to his aid: expounded, that monarchies need not fear any curbing of their absoluteness by mighty subjects, as long as by wisdom they keep the hearts of the people, who will be sure to come in* on their side. So in the fable that Achilles was brought up under Chiron the centaur, who was part a man and part a beast: expounded ingeniously but corruptly by Machiavel,[34] that it belongeth to the education and discipline* of princes to know as well how to play the part of the lion in violence and the fox in guile, as of the man in virtue and justice. Nevertheless in many the like encounters,* I do rather think that the fable was first, and the exposition devised,* than that the moral was first, and thereupon the fable framed.* For I find it was an ancient vanity in Chrysippus,[35] that troubled himself with great contention to fasten the assertions of the Stoics upon the fictions of the ancient poets. But yet that all the fables and fictions of the poets were but pleasure and not figure,[36] I interpose no opinion. Surely of those poets which are now extant, even Homer himself (notwithstanding he was made a kind of scripture by

---

[31] Medieval commentators interpreted biblical texts on four levels: literal, allegorical, moral, anagogical. Cf. Harington, p. 309.

[32] *Aen.* 4. 178–80: 'Mother Earth, provoked to anger against the gods, brought forth last, as sister to Cœus and Enceladus'.

[33] But according to Homer (*Il.* 1. 396 ff.) it was Thetis who summoned Briareus (a mythical giant with a hundred arms and fifty heads) to free Zeus after the other Olympians had shackled him.

[34] According to Greek myth the centaur Chiron educated divine children and heroes, including Achilles and Asclepius. For Machiavelli see *The Prince*, ch. 18.

[35] A Stoic philosopher (b. 280 BC), mocked by Cicero (*De natura deorum* 1. 15. 38–41) for finding Stoic doctrines in the stories of the gods.

[36] 'Were but pleasing fictions, without a figurative meaning'.

the later schools of the Grecians),[37] yet I should without any difficulty pronounce that his fables had no such inwardness* in his own meaning; but what they might have upon a more original tradition, is not easy to affirm; for he was not the inventor of many of them.

In this third part of learning, which is poesy, I can report no deficience. For being as a plant that cometh of the lust of the earth, without a formal seed, it hath sprung up and spread abroad more than any other kind. But to ascribe unto it that which is due; for the expressing of affections, passions, corruptions, and customs, we are beholding to poets more than to the philosophers' works;[38] and for wit and eloquence not much less than to orators' harangues. . . .

Concerning speech and words, the consideration of them hath produced the science of grammar: for man still striveth to reintegrate himself in those benedictions, from which by his fault he hath been deprived; and as he hath striven against the first general curse by the invention of all other arts, so hath he sought to come forth of the second general curse[39] (which was the confusion of tongues) by the art of grammar: whereof the use in a mother tongue is small; in a foreign tongue more; but most in such foreign tongues as have ceased to be vulgar* tongues, and are turned only to learned tongues.[40] The duty of it is of two natures; the one popular,* which is for the speedy and perfect attaining languages, as well for intercourse of speech as for understanding of authors; the other philosophical, examining the power and nature of words as they are the footsteps and prints of reason: which kind of analogy between words and reason[41] is handled *sparsim,** brokenly, though I think it very worthy to be reduced* into a science by itself.

Unto grammar also belongeth, as an appendix, the consideration of the accidents* of words; which are measure, sound, and elevation or accent,[42] and the sweetness and harshness of them; whence have issued

[37] The allegorization of Homer began in the 4th cent. BC, but is especially associated with Neoplatonists working at Alexandria in the 2nd and 3rd cents. AD. In his commentaries on the *Republic* Proclus used allegorical interpretation to defend Homer from Plato's attacks.

[38] Like other Renaissance apologists for poetry, Bacon justifies it as a form of knowledge. Unlike them, he ranks it above philosophy for the insights it gives into human behaviour.

[39] The first 'general curse' resulted from Adam and Eve eating the forbidden fruit (Gen. 3: 1–24); the second was God's punishment for human arrogance in building the Tower of Babel (Gen. 11: 1–9).

[40] Languages learned from books (Greek, Latin).

[41] That is, the philosophy of language.

[42] These 'accessory qualities' of language include metre, intonation, and accent (the prominence given to particular syllables by stress or by pitch).

some curious observations in rhetoric, but chiefly poesy, as we consider it in respect of the verse and not of the argument: wherein though men in learned tongues do tie themselves to the ancient measures,[43] yet in modern languages it seemeth to me as free to make new measures of verses as of dances; for a dance is a measured pace, as a verse is measured speech. In these things the sense is better judge than the art:

> *Coena fercula nostrae*
> *Mallem convivis quam placuisse cocis.*[44]

And of the servile expressing antiquity[45] in an unlike and unfit subject, it is well said, '*Quod tempore antiquum videtur, id incongruitate est maxime novum*'. . . .[46]

Now we descend to that part which concerneth the illustration of tradition,[47] comprehended in that science which we call rhetoric, or art of eloquence; a science excellent, and excellently well laboured. For although in true value it is inferior to wisdom, as it is said by God[48] to Moses, when he disabled* himself from want of this faculty, 'Aaron shall be thy speaker, and thou shalt be to him as God'; yet with people it is the more mighty: for so Salomon saith, '*Sapiens corde appellabitur prudens, sed dulcis eloquio majora reperiet*',[49] signifying that profoundness of wisdom will help a man to a name or admiration, but that it is eloquence that prevaileth in an active life. And as to the labouring of it, the emulation of Aristotle with the rhetoricians of his time[50] and the experience of Cicero, hath made them in their works of Rhetorics exceed themselves. Again, the excellency of examples of eloquence in the orations of Demosthenes and Cicero added to the perfection of the precepts of eloquence, hath doubled the progression in this art; and therefore the deficiences which I shall note will rather be in some collections which may as handmaids attend the art than in the rules or use of the art itself.

---

[43] Classical metres: cf. Campion (p. 428) and Daniel (p. 441). Bacon endorses the moderns here.

[44] 'The dinner is for eating, and my wish is | That guests and not that cooks should like the dishes' (Martial, *Epigrams* 9. 81).

[45] The slavish imitation of classical models.

[46] 'There is nothing more new than an old thing that has ceased to fit'; untraced.

[47] 'The elucidation of discourse'; but 'illustration' also meant 'making more illustrious'.

[48] Exod. 4: 16.

[49] 'The wise in heart shall be called prudent but he that is eloquent shall attain greater things' (Prov. 16: 21).

[50] Cf. *De or.* 2. 38. 159; *Tusc.* 1. 4. 7; *Inst.* 3. 1. 14.

Notwithstanding, to stir the earth a little about the roots of this science, as we have done or the rest: The duty and office of rhetoric is to apply reason to imagination for the better moving of the will. For we see reason is disturbed in the administration* thereof by three means; by illaqueation* or sophism, which pertains to logic; by imagination or impression,* which pertains to rhetoric; and by passion or affection, which pertains to morality.* And as in negotiation with others men are wrought* by cunning, by importunity,* and by vehemency; so in this negotiation within ourselves men are undermined by inconsequences,[51] solicited and importuned by impressions or observations, and transported by passions. Neither is the nature of man so unfortunately built, as that those powers and arts should have force to disturb reason, and not to establish and advance it: for the end of logic is to teach a form of argument to secure reason, and not to entrap it; the end of morality is to procure the affections to obey reason, and not to invade it; the end of rhetoric is to fill the imagination to second reason, and not to oppress it: for these abuses of arts come in but *ex obliquo*,* for caution.

And therefore it was great injustice in Plato,[52] though springing out of a just hatred of the rhetoricians of his time, to esteem of rhetoric but as a voluptuary art, resembling it to cookery, that did mar wholesome meats, and help unwholesome by variety of sauces to the pleasure of the taste. For we see that speech is much more conversant in adorning that which is good than in colouring* that which is evil;[53] for there is no man but speaketh more honestly than he can do or think: and it was excellently noted by Thucydides[54] in Cleon, that because he used to hold on* the bad side in causes of estate, therefore he was ever inveighing against eloquence and good speech; knowing that no man can speak fair of courses sordid and base. And therefore as Plato[55] said elegantly, that 'virtue, if she could be seen, would move great love and affection'; so seeing that she cannot be shewed to the sense by corporal shape, the next degree is to shew her to the imagination in lively representation: for to shew her to reason only in subtilty of argument, was a thing ever derided in Chrysippus[56] and many

---

[51] 'Confused and deceived by fallacious arguments'.

[52] *Grg.* 462e ff. But see *IDR*, pp. 83–147.

[53] Cf. Aristotle, *Rh.* 1. 1. 1355ª22: 'Rhetoric is useful because things that are true and things that are just have a natural tendency to prevail over their opposites'.

[54] *History*, 3. 40, 42. 2.   [55] *Phdr.* 250d; Cicero, *Off.* 1. 5. 14.

[56] *Fin.* 4. 18 f.; *De or.* 2. 38. 159; *Tusc.* 2. 18. 42.

of the Stoics; who thought to thrust virtue upon men by sharp disputations and conclusions, which have no sympathy with the will of man.

Again, if the affections in themselves were pliant and obedient to reason, it were true there should be no great use of persuasions and insinuations[57] to the will, more than of naked proposition and proofs; but in regard of the continual mutinies and seditions of the affections,

> *Video meliora, proboque;*
> *Deteriora sequor:*[58]

reason would become captive and servile, if eloquence of persuasions did not practise* and win the imagination from the affection's part, and contract a confederacy* between the reason and imagination against the affections. For the affections themselves carry ever an appetite to good, as reason doth; the difference is, that 'the affection beholdeth merely the present; reason beholdeth the future and sum of time';[59] and therefore the present* filling the imagination more, reason is commonly vanquished; but after that force of eloquence and persuasion hath made things future and remote appear as present, then upon the revolt of the imagination reason prevaileth.

De prudentia sermonis privati.[60] We conclude therefore, that rhetoric can be no more charged with the colouring of the worse part,[61] than logic with sophistry, or morality with vice. For we know the doctrines of contraries are the same,[62] though the use be opposite. It appeareth also that logic differeth from rhetoric, not only as the fist from the palm,[63] the one close the other at large; but much more in this, that logic handleth reason exact and in truth, and rhetoric handleth it as it is planted in popular opinions and manners. And therefore Aristotle[64] doth wisely place rhetoric as between logic on the one side and moral

---

[57] Indirect arguments. In rhetoric *insinuatio* is used at the opening of a speech, to win the audience's goodwill.

[58] 'I see the better course and approve it, but I follow the worse': Medea's words in Ovid, *Met.* 7. 20.

[59] Aristotle, *De an.* 3. 10. 433^{b}5 ff.

[60] 'The wisdom of private discourse': a speech delivered to a small group, not a public assembly.

[61] Bacon echoes Aristotle's defence of rhetoric against Plato (*Rh.* 1. 1. 1355^{a}22 ff.), but gives it a greater ethical function.

[62] Aristotle, *Rh.* 1. 1. 1355^{a}30 ff.

[63] Traditionally, Zeno first compared logic to the fist (combative), rhetoric to the extended open palm (persuasive). Cf. *Fin.* 2. 6. 17; *Orat.* 32. 113; *Inst.* 2. 20. 7.

[64] *Rh.* 1. 2. 1356^{a}25 ff.

or civil knowledge on the other, as participating of both: for the proofs
and demonstrations of logic are toward all men indifferent* and the
same; but the proofs and persuasions of rhetoric ought to differ
according to the auditors:[65]

Orpheus in sylvis, inter delphinas Arion:[66]

which application, in perfection of idea, ought to extend so far, that
if a man should speak of the same thing to several persons, he should
speak to them all respectively* and several ways: though this politic
part of eloquence in private speech it is easy for the greatest orators
to want, whilst by the observing their well-graced forms of speech
they leese* the volubility of application:[67] and therefore it shall not be
amiss to recommend this to better inquiry. . . .

[65] *Rh*. 1. 2. 1356ᵃ14 ff.
[66] Virgil, *Ecl*. 7. 56: 'An Orpheus in the woods, an Arion among the dolphins'.
[67] That is, 'quickness in turning from one subject to another; versatility'.

Ben Jonson,
The moral function of poetry (1607)

BEN JONSON. See the headnote above (p. 454)

TEXT. From *Volpone, or The Fox* (1607); reprinted with alterations in the 1616 Folio. Jonson claimed in the verse prologue that 'five weeks fully penned it', namely in the spring of 1606, when it was first performed by the King's Men at the Globe. In the summers of 1606 and 1607 the company performed it at Oxford and Cambridge, and Jonson dedicated the Quarto edition of the play to 'the most noble and most equal sisters, the two famous Universities', of which he was an honorary MA. This dedicatory epistle may bear some marks of the so-called 'War of the Theatres', Jonson's quarrels with his fellow-dramatists Marston and Dekker, between 1599 and 1602 (briefly revived in 1606); but many of Jonson's utterances are part of his considered theory of drama. In annotating it I have benefited from C. H. Herford, P. and E. Simpson (eds.), *Ben Jonson*, 11 vols. (Oxford, 1925–52), abbreviated as *HS*, and from Gordon Campbell (ed.), *The Alchemist and other Plays* (Oxford, 1995).

. . . It is certain, nor can it with any forehead* be opposed, that the too much licence of poetasters* in this time hath much deformed their mistress; that every day, their manifold and manifest ignorance doth stick unnatural reproaches upon her. But for their petulancy,* it were an act of the greatest injustice either to let the learned suffer, or so divine a skill (which indeed should not be attempted with unclean hands) to fall under the least contempt. For if men will impartially, and not asquint,* look toward the offices* and function of a poet, they will easily conclude to themselves the impossibility of any man's being the good poet, without first being a good man.[1] He that is said to be able to inform* young men to all good disciplines, inflame grown men to all great virtues,[2] keep old men in their best and supreme state, or, as they decline to childhood, recover them to their first strength; that

---

[1] Cf. Strabo, *Geography* 1. 2. 5, as quoted, p. 64, n. 32.

[2] For the traditions that the poet 'forms' his readers' characters see Introduction, pp. 50 ff., and that his representation of virtue and vice should 'inflame' or inspire the reader to follow the one and avoid the other, cf. Cicero, *Arch.* 6. 14, Elyot, pp. 59–60, Surrey, p. 71, Sidney, p. 365, Heywood, p. 487, Massinger, pp. 550–1, and Milton, pp. 602–3.

comes forth the interpreter and arbiter of nature, a teacher of things divine no less than human, a master[3] in manners; and can alone (or with a few) effect the business of mankind: this, I take him, is no subject for pride and ignorance to exercise their railing rhetoric upon.

But it will here be hastily answered that the writers of these days are other things: that not only their manners, but their natures are inverted;* and nothing remaining with them of the dignity of poet but the abused name, which every scribe usurps; that now, especially in dramatic or (as they term it) stage-poetry, nothing but ribaldry, profanation, blasphemy, all licence of offence to God and man is practised. I dare not deny a great part of this (and am sorry, I dare not) because in some men's abortive features[4] (and would they had never boasted the light) it is over-true; but that all are embarked in this bold adventure for hell, is a most uncharitable thought, and, uttered, a more malicious slander. For my particular, I can (and from a most clear conscience) affirm that I have ever trembled to think toward the least profaneness; have loathed the use of such foul and unwashed bawdry as is now made the food of the scene. And howsoever I cannot escape, from some, the imputation of sharpness,* but that they will say I have taken a pride, or lust, to be bitter, and not my youngest infant but hath come into the world with all his teeth;[5] I would ask of these supercilious politics,* what nation, society, or general order, or state I have provoked? What public person? Whether I have not (in all these) preserved their dignity, as mine own person, safe? My works are read, allowed (I speak of those that are entirely mine);[6] look into them: what broad reproofs have I used? Where have I been particular? Where personal? Except to a mimic,* cheater, bawd, or buffoon, creatures (for their insolencies) worthy to be taxed?* Yet, to which of these so pointingly as he might not either ingenuously have confessed, or wisely dissembled his disease? But it is not rumour can make men guilty, much less entitle me to other men's crimes. I know that nothing

---

[3] This sentence summarizes passages in Antonio Minturno's *De poeta* (1559), pp. 8–9, 79, including his definition of the poet as 'vir bonus dicendi atque imitandi peritus', modelled on Cato's definition of the orator: cf. *Inst.* 12. 1. 1 ff. (cit. *CES* i. 221 and *HS* ix. 683).

[4] Other dramatists' prematurely published plays.

[5] Jonson's *Sejanus*, performed in 1605, was accused of being seditious. He had to defend himself before the Privy Council, and omitted his collaborator's contribution to the play before it was published.

[6] Plays were 'allowed' or licensed for performance by the Master of the Revels. Jonson got into trouble with three plays not 'entirely mine', that is, written collaboratively; in addition to *Sejanus*, he was imprisoned for his share in *The Isle of Dogs* and *Eastward Ho!*

can be so innocently writ or carried, but may be made obnoxious* to construction;* marry, whilst I bear mine innocence about me, I fear it not. Application is now grown a trade with many; and there are that profess to have a key for the deciphering of everything:[7] but let wise and noble persons take heed how they be too credulous, or give leave to these invading interpreters to be over-familiar with their fames,* who cunningly and often utter their own virulent malice under other men's simplest meanings.

As for those that will (by faults which charity hath raked* up, or common honesty concealed) make themselves a name with the multitude, or (to draw their rude and beastly claps)* care not whose living faces they entrench with their petulant styles:[8] may they do it without a rival, for me; I choose rather to live graved in obscurity, than share with them in so preposterous* a fame. Nor can I blame the wishes of those severe and wiser patriots,* who providing* the hurts these licentious spirits may do in a state, desire rather to see fools and devils, and those antique relics of barbarism retrieved, with all other ridiculous and exploded follies, than behold the wounds of private men, of princes, and nations. For, as Horace makes Trebatius speak, among these

Sibi quisque timet, quamquam est intactus, et odit.[9]

And men may justly impute such rages, if continued, to the writer, as his sports. The increase of which lust in liberty, together with the present trade of the stage, in all their misc'line interludes,[10] what learned or liberal* soul doth not already abhor? Where nothing but the filth of the time is uttered, and that with such impropriety of phrase, such plenty of solecisms, such dearth of sense, so bold prolepses,[11] so racked metaphors, with brothelry able to violate the ear of a pagan, and blasphemy to turn the blood of a Christian to water.

---

[7] Several dramatists complained that their fictitious characters and general satire had been wrongly identified with real-life people and events.

[8] That is, 'engrave with insolent styluses; a stylus could be used as an engraving tool and as an offensive weapon' (Campbell edn.).

[9] *Sat.* 2. 1. 23, which Jonson translated (*Poetaster* 3. 5. 41 f.): 'in satires each man, though untouched, complains | As he were hurt; and hates such biting strains'.

[10] The Latin term, *ludi miscelli*, 'a variety entertainment, with the suggestion of a medley, a hotchpotch' (*HS* ix. 685).

[11] Here not in the dominant sense of anticipating later events (cf. Puttenham, p. 239), but in the less familiar one of assigning an event or name too early a date; hence 'gross anachronisms'.

I cannot but be serious in a cause of this nature, wherein my fame
and the reputations of divers honest and learned are the question;
when a name, so full of authority, antiquity, and all great mark, is—
through their insolence—become the lowest scorn of the age; and
those men subject to the petulancy* of every vernaculous* orator, that
were wont to be the care of kings and happiest monarchs. This it is
that hath not only rapt* me to present indignation, but made me studious heretofore; and by all my actions to stand off from them; which
may most appear in this my latest work—which you, most learned
arbitresses, have seen, judged, and to my crown, approved—wherein
I have laboured, for their instruction and amendment, to reduce* not
only the ancient forms, but manners of the scene: the easiness, the
propriety, the innocence, and last the doctrine, which is the principal
end of poesy, to inform men in the best reason of living.[12] And though
my catastrophe may, in the strict rigour of comic law, meet with
censure,[13] as turning back to my promise, I desire the learned and
charitable critic to have so much faith in me to think it was done of
industry:* for with what ease I could have varied it nearer his scale*
(but that I fear to boast my own faculty) I could here insert. But my
special aim being to put the snaffle in their mouths, that cry out, we
never punish vice in our interludes, etc., I took the more liberty;
though not without some lines of example drawn even in the ancients
themselves, the goings-out of whose comedies are not always joyful,[14]
but oft-times the bawds, the servants, the rivals, yea, and the masters
are mulcted:* and fitly, it being the office of a comic poet to imitate
justice, and instruct to life, as well as purity of language, or stir up
gentle affections. To which I shall take the occasion elsewhere[15] to
speak.

For the present (most reverenced sisters) as I have cared to be
thankful for your affections past, and here made the understanding*
acquainted with some ground of your favours, let me not despair their
continuance, to the maturing of some worthier fruits: wherein, if my

---

[12] Cf. Aristophanes, *Frogs* 1008–10: *Aeschylus*: 'for a gift of what kind is it right to admire
any poet?' *Euripides*: 'For his expertise and his sound advice and because we improve by our
teaching | mankind's civic sense and their natures too' (*ALC*, p. 21).

[13] The ending of *Volpone* seems to break the general (Aristotelian-Ciceronian) rule that
comedy should 'sport with human follies, not with crimes' (cf. pp. 174, 362, 383).

[14] Cf. e.g. the ending of Plautus' *Miles gloriosus*, with the exposure of Pyrogopolinices.

[15] In his commentary on Horace's *Ars poetica*, which Jonson had announced in the epistle
to *Sejanus* (1605) as ready for publication (see Drummond, p. 535), but which perished in
the fire at his home in 1623.

muses be true to me, I shall raise the despised head of poetry again, and stripping her out of those rotten and base rags wherewith the times have adulterated her form, restore her to her primitive habit, feature,[16] and majesty, and render her worthy to be embraced and kissed of all the great and master-spirits of our world. As for the vile and slothful, who never affected* an act worthy of celebration, or are so inward with their own vicious natures as they worthily fear her, and think it a high point of policy to keep her in contempt with their declamatory and windy invectives: she shall out of just rage incite her servants (who are *genus irritabile*)[17] to spout ink in their faces, that shall eat farther than their marrow, into their fames; and not Cinnamus the barber[18] with his art shall be able to take out the brands, but they shall live, and be read, till the wretches die, as things worst deserving of themselves in chief, and then of all mankind.

[16] 'Her original clothing and appearance'.
[17] Cf. Horace, *Epist.* 2. 2. 102: '[poets are] an easily provoked breed'.
[18] Cf. Martial, *Epigrams* 6. 64. 24–6, on this Roman hairdresser and surgeon, famous for his ability to remove the scars which showed that his clients had been branded for a crime.

24

Thomas Heywood,
A defence of drama (*c*.1608)

THOMAS HEYWOOD (1573/4–1641) was educated at Emmanuel College
Cambridge, and began his theatrical career in London as an actor. He is first
mentioned in Henslowe's *Diary* in the autumn of 1596, but had probably been
one of the dramatists involved in revising Munday's *Sir Thomas More*
(*c*.1593). He worked as an actor and playwright for the Admiral's Men in the
late 1590s, thereafter with Worcester's Men, and in succession Queen Anne's,
until that company broke up in 1619. He claimed in 1633 'two hundred and
twenty [plays] in which I have had either an entire hand, or at least the
main finger'. His acknowledged compositions include *A Woman Killed with
Kindness* (1603), *If You Know not me, You Know Nobody* (1605), and *The Rape
of Lucrece* (1603–8). Two of the writers who contributed commendatory
verses to this treatise, Richard Perkins and Christopher Beeston, were fellow
actors and sharers in the Queen's company. John Taylor (1580–1653), 'the
water poet', was a friend of Heywood.

TEXT. From *An Apology for Actors. Containing three briefe Treatises. 1. Their
Antiquity. 2. Their ancient Dignity. 3. The true use of their quality* (London,
1612). E. K. Chambers dated the composition of this pamphlet to *c*.1607–8:
The Elizabethan Stage (Oxford, 1933), iv. 250. Even so, it comes long after the
major dispute over the theatre, sparked off by the Puritan Stephen Gosson's
*The School of Abuse. Conteining a pleasant invectiue against Poets, Pipers,
Plaiers, Jesters and such like Catterpillers of a Commonwelth* (1579), which pro-
voked Thomas Lodge's *Defence of Poetry, Music and Stage Plays* in the same
year, and at least ten other treatises over the next decade (*ECE* i. 61–3).
Heywood also wrote a now-lost treatise, *Lives of All the Poets*, begun *c*.1614.
His defence of drama follows traditional lines. See A. M. Clark, *Thomas
Heywood: Playwright and Miscellanist* (Oxford, 1931), and Jonas Barish, *The
Anti-theatrical Prejudice* (Berkeley, 1981).

TO MY GOOD FRIENDS AND FELLOWS THE CITY-ACTORS

Out of my busiest hours I have spared myself so much time as to
touch* some particulars concerning us, to approve our antiquity,
ancient dignity, and the true use of our quality.* That it hath been
ancient, we have derived it from more than two thousand years ago

successively to this age. That it hath been esteemed by the best and greatest, to omit all the noble patrons of the former world, I need allege no more than the royal and princely services in which we now live. That the use thereof is authentic, I have done my endeavour to instance by history and approve by authority. To excuse my ignorance in affecting no flourish* of eloquence to set a gloss upon my treatise, I have nothing to say for myself but this: a good face needs no painting, and a good cause no abetting. Some over-curious have too liberally taxed* us, and he (in my thoughts) is held worthy reproof whose ignorance cannot answer for itself. I hold it more honest for the guiltless to excuse than the envious to exclaim; and we may as freely out of our plainness answer, as they out of their perverseness object, instancing myself by famous Scaliger, learned Doctor Gager, Doctor Gentilis,[1] and others, whose opinions and approved arguments on our part I have in my brief discourse altogether omitted, because I am loath to be taxed in borrowing from others; and besides, their works, being extant to the world offer themselves freely to every man's perusal. I am professed adversary to none: I rather covet reconcilement than opposition, nor proceeds this my labour from any envy in me but rather to show them wherein they err. So, wishing you judicial* audiences, honest poets, and true gatherers,[2] I commit you all to the fullness of your best wishes.

Yours ever,
T.H.

---

[1] J. C. Scaliger, in his *Poetices libri septem* (1560), assembled a great deal of information about Greek and Roman drama, including attacks and defences. Heywood also refers to John Rainolds, *Th'ouerthrow of stage-plays, by the way of controversie betwixt D. Gager and D. Rainoldes. Whereunto are added certeine latine letters betwixt maister Rainoldes, and D. Gentilis* (1599, 1629). The participants in this controversy were all distinguished Oxford scholars: Dr John Rainolds (1549–1607) was both a leading authority on Aristotle, whose lectures were frequently reprinted, and a puritan theologian who vigorously attacked Catholicism. William Gager (1555–1622) was the author of several Latin dramas, including *Meleager. Tragoedia nova* (Oxford, 1592), *Ulysses Redux Tragoedia Nova* (Oxford, 1592), and additional scenes to Seneca's *Hippolytus* (1591). Dr Alberico Gentili (1552–1608), Regius Professor of Civil Law at Oxford from 1587, published in 1593 a commentary on a subsection of a title in the Justinian Code, *Commentatio ad l[egem] III prof[essoribus] et med[icis]*, which has been described as 'the best and most penetrating of the Latin treatises on poetry printed in England': see J. W. Binns, *Intellectual Culture in Elizabethan and Jacobean England: The Latin Writings of the Age* (Leeds, 1990), pp. 127–31, 141–8, 350–4. Gentili replied to Rainolds's attack on the stage in *De actoribus et spectatoribus fabularum non notandis disputatio*, the first of his *Disputationes duae* (Hanau, 1599).

[2] Reliable money-takers (who stood at the various theatre entries).

TO THE JUDICIAL READER

I have undertook a subject, courteous reader, not of sufficient countenance* to bolster itself by his own strength, and therefore have charitably reached it my hand to support it against any succeeding adversary. I could willingly have committed this work to some more able than myself, for the weaker the combatant he needeth the stronger arms; but in extremities* I hold it better to wear rusty armour than to go naked. Yet if these weak habiliments of war can but buckler* it from part of the rude buffets of our adversaries, I shall hold my pains sufficiently guerdoned.* My pen hath seldom appeared in press till now:[3] I have been ever too jealous* of mine own weakness willingly to thrust into the press; nor had I at this time but that a kind of necessity enjoined me to so sudden a business. I will neither show myself over-presumptuous in scorning thy favour, nor too importunate a beggar by too servilely entreating it. What thou art content to bestow upon my pains, I am content to accept: if good thoughts, they are all I desire; if good words, they are more than I deserve; if bad opinion, I am sorry I have incurred it; if evil language, I know not how I have merited it; if anything, I am pleased; if nothing, I am satisfied, contenting myself with this—I have done no more than (had I been called to account) showed what I could say in the defence of my own quality.

Thine,
T. Heywood,
Firma valent per se, nullumque Machaona querunt.[4]

TO THEM THAT ARE OPPOSITE TO THIS WORK

Come your detracting tongues, contest no more,
Leave off for shame to wound the actors' fame,
Seek rather their wrong'd credit to restore,
Your envy and detractions quite disclaim.
    You that have termed their sports lascivious, vile,   5
    Wishing good princes would them all exile,[5]

---

[3] At the time of writing Heywood's name had indeed only appeared on the title-pages of *A Woman Kilde with Kindnesse* (1607), *The Rape of Lucrece. A True Roman Tragedie* (1608). *The Golden Age* (1611) and *The Silver Age* (1612) soon followed.

[4] Ovid, *Ex Ponto* 3. 4. 7: 'Strong things have health of their own, and need no Machaon', or doctor.

[5] Cf. Plato, *Resp.* 10. 595a ff.

See here this question to the full disputed:
Heywood hath you and all your proofs confuted.

Would'st see an emperor and his council grave,
A noble soldier acted to the life,   10
A Roman tyrant, how he doth behave
Himself at home, abroad, in peace, in strife?
    Would'st see what's love, what's hate, what's foul
        excess,
    Or would'st a traitor in his kind express?
    Our Stagirites[6] can, by the poet's pen,   15
    Appear to you to be the self-same men.

What though a sort for spite, or want of wit,
Hate what the best allow, the most forbear,
What exercise can you desire more fit
Than stately stratagems to see and hear?   20
    What profit many may attain by plays,
    To the most critic eye this book displays.
    Brave men, brave acts, being bravely acted too,
    Makes, as men see things done, desire to do.

And did it nothing but in pleasing sort   25
Keep gallants from misspending of their time,
It might suffice; yet here is nobler sport,
Acts well contriv'd, good prose, and stately rhyme.
    To call to church Campanus[7] bells did make;
    Plays, dice and drink invite men to forsake.   30
    Their use being good, then use the actors well,
    Since ours all other nations far excel.

                                        Ar. Hopton

TO MY LOVING FRIEND AND FELLOW,
            THOMAS HEYWOOD

Thou that do'st rail at me for seeing a play,
How wouldst thou have me spend my idle hours?
Wouldst have me in a tavern drink all day,
Melt in the sun's heat, or walk out in showers?

---

[6] Aristotle was born at Stagira or Stagirus in Chalcidice; hence a 'Stagirite' is any philosopher or moralist.
[7] A person credited with inventing the bell.

Gape at the lottery from morn till even,   5
To hear whose mottos blanks have, and who prizes?[8]
To hazard all at dice (chance six or seven),[9]
To card or bowl? my humour this despises.

But thou wilt answer: 'None of these I need,
Yet my tired spirits must have recreation.   10
What shall I do that may retirement breed,
Or how refresh myself, and in what fashion?

'To drab,* to game, to drink, all these I hate:
Many enormous* things depend on these.
My faculties truly to recreate   15
With modest mirth, and myself best to please,

'Give me a play, that no distaste* can breed.
Prove thou a spider, and from flowers suck gall;
I'll, like a bee, take honey from a weed;[10]
For I was never puritanical.   20

'I love no public soothers, private scorners,
That rail 'gainst lechery, yet love a harlot:
When I drink, 'tis in sight and not in corners;
I am no open saint, and secret varlet.*

'Still, when I come to plays, I love to sit   25
That all may see me in a public place,
Even in the stage's front, and not to get
Into a nook, and hood-wink there my face'.

This is the difference: such would have men deem
Them what they are not; I am what I seem.   30

                                        Rich. Perkins

---

[8] Lotteries (established in England from 1567) used slips or small pieces of paper ('mottoes'), representing either prizes or blanks, which were drawn from a pitcher; cf. *Merchant of Venice* 1. 2. 32.

[9] In the dice game of 'hazard' (known to Chaucer), if the caster throws the number he has named (between 5 and 9) he wins; if he throws some other number, that is called his 'chance', and he goes on playing till either the main or the chance turns up.

[10] An ancient metaphor for selecting the improving parts of literature, ignoring other passages: cf. Plutarch, *Poetas* 12; St Basil, *Address to young men, on how to benefit from Greek literature* 4. 7; and Elyot, p. 67.

TO MY GOOD FRIEND AND FELLOW,
THOMAS HEYWOOD

Let others task* things honest, and to please
Some that pretend more strictness* than the rest
Exclaim on plays: know, I am none of these
That inly love what outly I detest.
Of all the modern pastimes I can find   5
To content me, of plays I make best use,
As most agreeing with a generous mind.
There see I virtue's crown, and sin's abuse.
Two hours well spent, and all their pastimes done,
What's good I follow, and what's bad I shun.   10

Christopher Beeston

TO MY APPROVED GOOD FRIEND
M. THOMAS HEYWOOD

Of thee, and thy Apology for plays,
I will not much speak in contempt or praise;
Yet in these following lines I'll show my mind
Of plays, and such as have 'gainst plays repined.*
A play's a brief epitome of time,   5
Where man may see his virtue or his crime
Laid open, either to their vice's shame
Or to their virtue's memorable fame.
A play's a true transparent crystal mirror,
To show good minds their mirth, the bad their terror;   10
Where stabbing, drabbing, dicing, drinking, swearing
Are all proclaimed unto the sight and hearing
In ugly shapes of heaven-abhorrèd sin,
Where men may see the mire they wallow in.
And well I know it makes the devil rage   15
To see his servants flouted on a stage—
A whore, a thief, a pandar, or a bawd,
A broker,* or a slave that lives by fraud;
An usurer, whose soul is in his chest,
Until in hell it comes to restless rest;   20
A fly-blown* gull,* that fain would be a gallant;
A ragamuffin* that hath spent his talent;

A self-wise fool, that sees his wits out-stripped,
Or any vice that feels it self but nipped,*
Either in Tragedy or Comedy,   25
In Moral, Pastoral, or History—
But straight the poison of their envious tongues
Breaks out in volleys of calumnious wrongs,
And then a tinker or a dray-man* swears
'I would the house were fired about their ears'.   30
Thus when a play nips Satan by the nose,
Straight all his vassals are the actor's foes.
—But fear not, man, let envy swell and burst,
Proceed, and let the devil do his worst.
For plays are good, or bad, as they are used,   35
And best inventions often are abused.

> *Yours ever,*
> John Taylor

THE AUTHOR TO HIS BOOK

The world's a theatre, the earth a stage,
Which God and nature doth with actors fill.†   †So compared
Kings have their entrance in due equipage,   by the Fathers.
And some their parts play well, and others ill.
The best no better are in this theatre,   5
Where every humour's fitted in his kind.[11]
This a true subject acts, and that a traitor,
The first applauded, and the last confined.
This plays an honest man, and that a knave,
A gentle person this, and he a clown.   10
One man is ragged, and another brave:
All men have parts, and each man acts his own.
She a chaste lady acteth all her life,
A wanton courtesan another plays;
This covets marriage love, that nuptial strife,   15
Both in continual action spend their days.
Some citizens, some soldiers born to adventer,
Shepherds, and sea-men. Then our play's begun

---

[11] Where each human type is presented appropriately.

When we are born, and to the world first enter,
And all find exits when their parts are done.   20
If then the world a theatre present,
As by the roundness[12] it appears most fit,
Built with starry galleries of high ascent,
In which Jehovah doth as spectator sit,[13]
And chief determiner* to applaud the best   25
And their endeavours crown with more than merit,
But by their evil actions dooms the rest
To end disgraced, whilst others praise inherit;
He that denies then theatres should be,
He may as well deny a world to me.[†]   †No theatre,   30
                                               no world.

Thomas Heywood

AN APOLOGY FOR ACTORS; AND FIRST
TOUCHING THEIR ANTIQUITY

Moved by the sundry exclamations of many seditious sectists* in this
age, who, in the fatness* and rankness* of a peaceable commonwealth
grow up like unsavoury tufts of grass, which, though outwardly
green and fresh to the eye, yet are they both unpleasant and
unprofitable, being too sour for food and too rank for fodder; these
men, like the ancient Germans, affecting no fashion but their own,
would draw other nations to be slovens like themselves, and undertaking to purify and reform the sacred bodies of the church and
commonweal (in the true use of both which they are altogether
ignorant), would but like artless physicians, for experiment sake,
rather minister pills to poison the whole body than cordials* to
preserve any, or the least part. Amongst many other things tolerated
in this peaceable and flourishing state, it hath pleased the high
and mighty princes of this land to limit the use of certain public
theatres,[14] which, since many of these over-curious heads have lavishly
and violently slandered, I hold it not amiss to lay open some few
antiquities to approve the true use of them, with arguments (not of

---

[12] Elizabethan theatres were approximately round, having eight or sixteen sides.

[13] Alluding to the ancient idea of the world as a theatre in which human affairs are
observed by (or from) 'the gods': cf. L. G. Christian, *Theatrum Mundi: The History of an
Idea* (New York and London, 1987).

[14] Civic authorities in England licensed and controlled theatres and other places of public
entertainment.

the least moment) which, according to the weakness of my spirit and infancy of my judgement, I will (by God's grace) commit to the eyes of all favourable and judicial readers, as well to satisfy the requests of some of our well-qualified favourers, as to stop the envious acclamations of those who challenge to themselves a privileged invective, and against all free estates a railing liberty. Loath am I (I protest), being the youngest and weakest of the nest wherein I was hatched, to soar this pitch before others of the same brood, more fledge,* and of better wing than myself. But though they whom more especially this task concerns, both for their ability in writing and sufficiency in judgement (as their works generally witness to the world) are content to over-slip so necessary a subject, and have left it as to me, the most unworthy, I thought it better to stammer out my mind than not to speak at all; to scribble down a mark in the stead of writing a name, and to stumble on the way rather than to stand still and not to proceed on so necessary a journey.

Nox erat, et somnus lassos submisit ocellos.[15] It was about that time of the night when darkness had already overspread the world, and a hushed and general silence possessed the face of the earth, and men's bodies, tired with the business of the day, betaking themselves to their best repose, their never-sleeping souls laboured in uncouth dreams and visions, when suddenly appeared to me the tragic Muse, *Melpomene*,

> *animosa Tragœdia:*[16]
> *et movit pictis innixa cothurnis*
> *densum caesarie terque quaterque caput.*[17]

Her hair rudely dishevelled, her chaplet* withered, her visage with tears stained, her brow furrowed, her eyes dejected, nay her whole complexion quite faded and altered; and, perusing her habit, I might behold the colour of her fresh robe (all crimson) breathed,[18] and with the envenomed juice of some profane spilt ink in every place stained. Nay more, her buskin of all the wonted jewels and ornaments utterly

[15] Ovid, *Am.* 3. 5. 1: 'One night when sleep on tired eyes weighed | [I had a dream and was afraid]' (tr. A. D. Melville).

[16] Ovid, *Am.* 3. 1. 35: 'Haughty Tragedy'.

[17] Ibid. 3. 1. 31 f.: (Tragedy): 'Standing in her embroidered buskins she moved thrice and four times her head thick with hair'. Buskins were thick-soled boots worn by tragic actors in the ancient Athenian theatre; subsequently used figuratively for the genre tragedy.

[18] Tarnished, contaminated: Tragedy's robe, as she later protests, has been 'blasted', blighted or damaged by the 'envenomed ink' of those who have slandered drama.

despoiled, about which, in manner of a garter I might behold these letters written in a plain and large character:

> Behold my tragic buskin rent and torn,
> Which kings and emperors in their times have worn.

This I no sooner had perused but suddenly I might perceive the enraged Muse cast up her scornful head, her eyeballs sparkle fire, and a sudden dash of disdain intermixed with rage purples her cheek. When, pacing with a majestic gait, and rousing up her fresh spirits with a lively and quaint action,[19] she began in these or the like words:

> *Grande sonant tragici, tragicos decet ira cothurnos.*[20]
> Am I Melpomene, the buskined Muse,
> That held in awe the tyrants of the world
> And played their lives in public theatres,
> Making them fear to sin, since fearless I   5
> Prepar'd to write their lives in crimson ink,
> And act their shames in eye of all the world?
> Have not I whipped Vice with a scourge of steel,
> Unmasked stern Murder, shamed lascivious Lust,
> Plucked off the vizor from grim Treason's face,   10
> And made the sun point at their ugly sins?
> Hath not this powerful hand tamed fiery Rage,[21]
> Killed poisonous Envy with her own keen darts,*
> Choked up the covetous mouth with molten gold,
> Burst the vast womb of eating Gluttony,   15
> And drowned the drunkard's gall in juice of grapes?
> I have showed Pride his picture on a stage,
> Laid ope the ugly shapes his steel glass* hid,
> And made him pass thence meekly. In those days   20
> When emperors with their presence graced my scenes,
> And thought none worthy to present themselves
> Save emperors, to delight ambassadors,
> Then did this garland flourish, then my robe
> Was of the deepest crimson, the best dye:
> *cura deum fuerant olim regumque poetæ,*   25

---

[19] Elegant, beautiful gestures.
[20] Ovid, *Rem. am.* 375: 'The tragic style is grand; rage suits its buskins'.
[21] The seven deadly sins are invoked.

præmiaque antiqui magna tulere chori.[22]
Who lodged then in the bosom of great kings
Save he that had a grave cothurnate* Muse?
A stately verse in an iambic style
Became a Cæsar's mouth. Oh! these were times   30
Fit for you bards to vent your golden rhymes.
Then did I tread on arras; cloth of tissue[23]
Hung round the fore-front of my stage; the pillars
That did support the roof of my large frame
Double-apparelled in pure Ophir[24] gold,   35
Whilst the round circle of my spacious orb
Was thronged with princes, dukes, and senators.
nunc ederæ sine honore iacent.[25]
But now's the iron age, and black-mouthed curs
Bark at the virtues of the former world.   40
Such with their breath have blasted my fresh robe,
Plucked at my flowery chaplet, toused* my tresses;
Nay, some who (for their baseness hissed and scorned)
The stage, as loathsome, hath long-since spewed out,
Have watched their time to cast envenomed ink   45
To stain my garments with. Oh! Seneca,
Thou tragic poet, had'st thou lived to see
This outrage done to sad Melpomene,
With such sharp lines thou would'st revenge my blot
As armed Ovid against Ibis wrote.[26]   50

With that in rage she left the place and I my dream, for at the instant
I awaked; when, having perused this vision over and over again in my
remembrance, I suddenly bethought me how many ancient poets, tragic
and comic, dying many ages ago, live still amongst us in their works:[27]
as, amongst the Greeks, Euripides, Menander, Sophocles, Eupolis,

---

[22] Ovid, *Ars am.* 3. 405–6: 'Poets once were the charge of rulers and kings, and the old choruses obtained great rewards'.

[23] Arras is a rich tapestry fabric, in which figures and scenes are woven in colours; cloth of tissue is a rich cloth, often interwoven with gold and silver.

[24] A biblical region (probably on the south-east coast of Arabia), famous for its fine gold: cf. 1 Kings 9: 28; 22: 48; Isa. 13: 12.

[25] Ovid, *Ars am.* 3. 411: 'Now the poets' bays lie without honour in the dust'.

[26] 'An elaborate curse-poem in elegiacs (perhaps AD 10 or 11) directed at an enemy whose identity is hidden under the name of a bird of unclean habits' (*OCD*).

[27] Such lists of ancient dramatists, known and obscure, were common in historical compilations, such as Scaliger's *Poetice*.

Aeschylus, Aristophanes, Apollodorus, Anaxandrides, Nicomachus, Alexis, Tereus, and others; so, among the Latins, Attilius, Actius, Melithus, Plautus, Terence, and others whom for brevity sake I omit.

> *hos ediscit, et hos arcto stipata theatro*
> *spectat Roma potens; habet hos, numeratque poetas.*[28]

These potent Rome acquires and holdeth dear,
And in their round theatres flocks to hear.

These, or any of these, had they lived in the afternoon of the world, as they died even in the morning, I assure myself would have left more memorable trophies of that learned Muse whom, in their golden numbers, they so richly adorned. And amongst our modern poets, who have been industrious in many an elaborate and ingenious poem, even they whose pens have had the greatest traffic* with the stage have been in the excuse of these Muses most forgetful. But, leaving these, lest I make too large a head to a small body and so misshape my subject, I will begin with the antiquity of acting comedies, tragedies, and histories. And first in the golden world.

In the first of the Olympiads,[29] amongst many other active exercises in which Hercules ever triumphed as victor, there was in his nonage presented unto him by his tutor, in the fashion of a history acted by the choice of the nobility of Greece, the worthy and memorable acts of his father Jupiter; which, being personated with lively and well spirited action, wrought such impression in his noble thoughts that in mere emulation of his father's valour (not at the behest of his step-dame Juno), he performed his twelve labours.[30] Him valiant Theseus followed, and Achilles, Theseus; which bred in them such haughty* and magnanimous attempts that every succeeding age hath recorded their worths unto fresh admiration. Aristotle, that prince of philosophers, whose books carry such credit even in these our universities that to say *ipse dixit* is a sufficient axiom,[31] he, having the tuition of

---

[28] Horace, *Epist.* 2. 1. 60–1: 'These authors mighty Rome learns by heart; these she views, when packed in her narrow theatre; these she counts as her muster-roll of poets . . .'.

[29] In modern usage an Olympiad is the period of four years between Olympic games; Heywood uses it to refer to the games themselves, also confusing myth (Hercules) and history.

[30] Heywood follows a variant source, rejecting the standard account of Hera's implacable enmity as the cause of Hercules' labours and other difficulties.

[31] The phrase '*ipse dixit*', 'he himself said it', used of Pythagoras by his followers, signifies 'an unproved assertion resting only on the authority of a speaker, a dogmatic statement' (*NSOED*), erroneously regarded as a 'sufficient axiom' or self-evident truth.

young Alexander, caused the destruction of Troy to be acted before his pupil, in which the valour of Achilles was so naturally expressed that it impressed the heart of Alexander in so much that all his succeeding actions were merely shaped after that pattern; and it may be imagined that had Achilles never lived Alexander had never conquered the whole world.

The like assertion may be made of that ever-renowned Roman Julius Cæsar, who, after the like representation of Alexander in the temple of Hercules, standing in Cádiz,[32] was never in any peace of thoughts till by his memorable exploits he had purchased to himself the name of Alexander, as Alexander till he thought himself of desert to be called Achilles; Achilles, Theseus; Theseus, till he had sufficiently imitated the acts of Hercules; and Hercules, till he held himself worthy to be called the son of Jupiter. Why should not the lives of these worthies, presented in these our days, effect the like wonders in the princes of our times, which can no way be so exquisitely* demonstrated nor so lively portrayed as by action? Oratory is a kind of speaking picture; therefore, may some say, is it not sufficient to discourse to the ears of princes the fame of these conquerors? Painting, likewise, is a dumb oratory;[33] therefore may we not as well, by some curious* Pygmalion, draw their conquests to work the like love in princes towards these worthies by showing them their pictures drawn to the life as it wrought on the poor painter to be enamoured of his own shadow? I answer this:

> nec magis expressi vultus per aenea signa,
> quam per vatis opus mores animique virorum
> clarorum apparent.—[34]

The visage is no better cut in brass,
Nor can the carver* so express the face,
As doth the poet's pen, whose arts surpass
To give men's lives and virtues their due grace.

[32] According to Suetonius (*Julius Caesar* 7), having seen a statue of Alexander the Great in the temple of Hercules, Caesar 'was overheard to sigh impatiently: vexed, it seems, that at an age when Alexander had already conquered the whole world, he himself had done nothing in the least epoch-making' (tr. R. Graves).

[33] Heywood applies to oratory an analogy originally made for poetry. Cf. Plutarch, *Poetas* 3; Horace, *Ars P.* 361; Sidney, pp. 345, 352.

[34] Horace, *Epist.* 2. 1. 248–50: 'and features are seen with no more truth, when moulded in statues of bronze, than are the manners and minds of famous heroes, when set forth in the poet's work'.

A description is only a shadow, received by the ear but not perceived by the eye; so lively portraiture is merely a form seen by the eye, but can neither show action, passion, motion, or any other gesture to move the spirits of the beholder to admiration. But to see a soldier shaped like a soldier, walk, speak, act like a soldier; to see a Hector all besmeared in blood, trampling upon the bulks* of kings; a Troilus returning from the field in the sight of his father Priam, as if man and horse, even from the steed's rough fetlocks to the plume on the champion's helmet, had been together plunged into a purple ocean; to see a Pompey ride in triumph, then a Cæsar conquer that Pompey; labouring Hannibal alive, hewing his passage through the Alps. To see as I have seen, Hercules[35] in his own shape, hunting the boar, knocking down the bull, taming the hart, fighting with Hydra, murdering Geryon, slaughtering Diomed, wounding the Stymphalides, killing the Centaurs, pashing* the lion, squeezing the dragon, dragging Cerberus in chains, and lastly, on his high pyramids writing *Nil ultra*— Oh, these were sights to make an Alexander!

To turn to our domestic histories: what English blood, seeing the person* of any bold Englishman presented, and doth not hug his fame and honey* at his valour, pursuing him in his enterprise with his best wishes, and as being wrapped in contemplation offers to him in his heart all prosperous performance, as if the personator were the man personated? So bewitching a thing is lively and well-spirited action[36] that it hath power to new-mould the hearts of the spectators and fashion them to the shape of any noble and notable attempt. What coward, to see his countryman valiant, would not be ashamed of his own cowardice? What English prince, should he behold the true portraiture of that famous King Edward the Third, foraging France, taking so great a king captive in his own country, quartering the English lions with the French flower-deluce,[37] and would not be

[35] Heywood mentions ten of the traditional labours here; he had represented them on-stage in *The Silver Age, Including . . . the birth of Hercules* (acted *c.*1610, pr. 1612) and *The Brazen Age* (acted *c.*1612, pr. 1613), of which Act 5 concluded *The Labours and death of Hercules. Nil ultra* ('no further') was the motto of Charles V, traditionally written on the 'Pillars of Hercules', which marked the outlet of the Mediterranean.

[36] *Actio*, or gesture, the last of the processes through which an orator created and performed a speech, was invoked by apologists to legitimize drama, since rhetoric was a respectable academic discipline.

[37] The anglicized form of 'fleur-de-lis', the royal arms of France, which could be 'quartered', in heraldic terms, by being added to the hereditary English arms of lions. Edward III and the Black Prince defeated the French at the battle of Poitiers in 1355, taking King John II of France prisoner.

suddenly inflamed with so royal a spectacle, being made apt and fit for the like achievement? So of Henry the Fifth . . .

To leave Italy and look back into Greece. The sages and princes of Grecia, who for the refinedness of their language were in such reputation through the world that all other tongues were esteemed barbarous, these that were the first understanders,* trained up their youthful nobility to be actors, debarring the base mechanics* so worthy employment, for none but the young heroes were admitted that practice, so to embolden them in the delivery of any foreign embassy. These wise men of Greece (so called by the Oracle) could by their industry find out no nearer or directer course to plant humanity and manners in the hearts of the multitude than to instruct them by moralized mysteries what vices to avoid, what virtues to embrace, what enormities* to abandon, what ordinances* to observe; whose lives, being for some special endowments in former times honoured, they should admire and follow; whose vicious actions, personated in some licentious liver,[38] they should despise and shun; which, borne out as well by the wisdom of the poet as supported by the worth of the actors, wrought such impression in the hearts of the plebe* that in short space they excelled in civility and government, insomuch that from them all the neighbour nations drew their patterns of humanity, as well in the establishing of their laws as the reformation of their manners. These Magi and Gymnosophistœ,[39] that lived (as I may say) in the childhood and infancy of the world, before it knew how to speak perfectly, thought even in those days that action* was the nearest way to plant understanding in the hearts of the ignorant.

'Yea, but', say some, 'you ought not to confound* the habits of either sex as to let your boys wear the attires of virgins', &c. To which I answer: the scriptures are not always to be expounded merely according to the letter—for in such estate stands our main sacramental controversy[40]—but they ought exactly to be conferred* with the purpose they handle. To do as the Sodomites did, use preposterous lusts in preposterous habits,[41] is in that text flatly and severely forbidden; nor can I imagine any man that hath in him any taste or relish of

---

[38] Someone who lives in a licentious way.

[39] Persian priests and Hindu ascetics; types of 'wise men'.

[40] Much of the Reformation dispute between the Protestant and the Catholic faiths concerned the eucharist, and whether the conversion of bread and wine into the body and blood of Christ was literal or symbolic.

[41] The inhabitants of Sodom and Gomorrah were destroyed for their depravity; cf. Gen. 18–19.

Christianity to be guilty of so abhorred a sin. Besides, it is not probable that plays were meant in that text, because we read not of any plays known, in that time that Deuteronomy[42] was writ, among the children of Israel. Nor do I hold it lawful to beguile the eyes of the world in confounding the shapes of either sex as to keep any youth in the habit of a virgin, or any virgin in the shape of a lad, to shroud them from the eyes of their fathers, tutors or protectors, or to any other sinister intent whatsoever. But, to see our youths attired in the habit of women, who knows not what their intents be? Who cannot distinguish them by their names, assuredly knowing they are but to represent such a lady at such a time appointed?

Do not the universities, the fountains and well-springs of all good arts, learning, and documents, admit the like in their colleges? and they (I assure myself) are not ignorant of their true use. In the time of my residence in Cambridge,[43] I have seen tragedies, comedies, histories, pastorals and shows publicly acted, in which the graduates of good place and reputation have been specially parted.* This is held necessary for the emboldening of their junior scholars, to arm them with audacity against they come to be employed in any public exercise, as in the reading of the dialectic, rhetoric, ethic, mathematic, the physic or metaphysic lectures. It teaches audacity to the bashful grammarian, being newly admitted into the private college, and after* matriculated and entered as a member of the university, and makes him a bold sophister[44] to argue *pro et contra*, to compose his syllogisms, categoric or hypothetic (simple or compound), to reason and frame a sufficient argument to prove his questions or to defend any *axioma*, to distinguish of any dilemma, and be able to moderate in any argumentation whatsoever.

To come to rhetoric: it not only emboldens a scholar to speak but instructs him to speak well, and with judgement to observe his commas, colons, and full points; his parentheses, his breathing spaces and distinctions; to keep a decorum in his countenance, neither to frown when he should smile nor to make unseemly and disguised faces

---

[42] Cf. Deut. 22: 5: 'The woman shall not wear that which pertaineth unto the man, neither shall a man put on woman's raiment: for all that do so, are abomination unto the Lord thy God'. Ever since Tertullian, this text had been used by enemies of the theatre to denounce actors impersonating women. Rainolds had just revived the charge, Gager rejected it.

[43] For the vigorous tradition of acting in Cambridge see Alan H. Nelson, *Early Cambridge Theatres: College, University, and Stages, 1464–1720* (Cambridge, 1994).

[44] A student in his second or third year at Cambridge, who had mastered the Arts course in logic; the following technicalities suggest that Heywood had also done so.

in the delivery of his words; not to stare with his eyes, draw awry
his mouth, confound* his voice in the hollow of his throat, or tear
his words hastily betwixt his teeth; neither to buffet his desk like a
mad man, nor stand in his place like a lifeless image, demurely plod-
ding, and without any smooth and formal motion. It instructs him
to fit his phrases to his action, and his action to his phrase, and his
pronunciation[45] to them both.

Tully, in his book *Ad Caium Herennium*,[46] requires five things in an
orator: invention, disposition, elocution, memory, and pronunciation.
Yet all are imperfect without the sixth, which is action, for be his
invention never so fluent and exquisite, his disposition and order never
so composed and formal, his eloquence and elaborate phrases never
so material and pithy, his memory never so firm and retentive, his pronunciation never so musical and plausive,* yet without a comely* and
elegant gesture, a gracious and a bewitching kind of action, a natural
and familiar motion of the head, the hand, the body, and a moderate
and fit countenance suitable to all the rest, I hold all the rest as nothing.
A delivery and sweet action is the gloss* and beauty of any discourse
that belongs to a scholar. And this is the action behoveful in any that
profess this quality, not to use any impudent or forced motion in any
part of the body, nor rough or other violent gesture; nor on the contrary to stand like a stiff starched man, but to qualify* every thing
according to the nature of the person personated. For in overacting
tricks, and toiling too much in the antic* habit of humours, men of
the ripest desert, greatest opinions, and best reputations may break
into the most violent absurdities. I take not upon me to teach but to
advise, for it becomes my juniority rather to be pupilled myself than
to instruct others.

To proceed, and to look into those men that profess themselves
adversaries to this quality, they are none of the gravest and most
ancient doctors of the academy but only a sort of find-faults, such as
interest their prodigal tongues in all men's affairs without respect.
These I have heard as liberally in their superficial censures tax the
exercises performed in their colleges as these acted on our public
stages, not looking into the true and direct* use of either, but
ambitiously preferring their own presumptuous humours before the
profound and authentical judgements of all the learned doctors of the

---

[45] The final stages of the orator's preparation involved *actio* and *pronuntiatio*, the effective utterance of his speech, with appropriate gesture.

[46] This anonymous treatise was still ascribed to Cicero at this time.

university. Thus you see that, touching the antiquity of actors and acting, they have not been new, lately begot by any upstart invention, but I have derived them from the first Olympiads, and I shall continue the use of them even till this present age. And so much touching their antiquity.

Pars superest coepti: pars est exhausta, laboris.[47]

OF ACTORS, AND THEIR ANCIENT DIGNITY
THE SECOND BOOK

. . . To omit all the doctors, zanies, pantaloons, harlequins,[48] in which the French, but especially the Italians have been excellent, and according to the occasion offered to do some right to our English actors,[49] as Knell, Bentley, Mills, Wilson, Cross, Lanham, and others: these, since I never saw them, as being before my time, I cannot (as an eye-witness of their desert) give them that applause which no doubt they worthily merit; yet by the report of many judicial auditors, their performances of many parts have been so absolute* that it were a kind of sin to drown their worths in Lethe, and not commit their almost forgotten names to eternity.

Here I must needs remember Tarleton,[50] in his time gracious with the queen his sovereign, and in the people's general applause, whom succeeded Will Kempe,[51] as well in the favour of her majesty as in the opinion and good thoughts of the general audience. Gabriel, Singer, Pope, Phillips, Sly,[52] all the right I can do them is but this, that though they be dead their deserts yet live in the remembrance of many. Among so many dead let me not forget one yet alive, in his time the

---

[47] Ovid, *Ars am.* 1. 771: 'Part of my enterprise remains, part is now finished'.

[48] Type-characters in the *commedia dell'arte*. Zany (Venetian form of Gianni or Giovanni): a servant acting as a clown, sometimes imitating his master's acts in a ludicrously awkward way; pantaloon: a Venetian character, a lean and foolish old man wearing spectacles and close-fitting breeches; harlequin: witty servant, who wore particoloured tights.

[49] Little is known about the actors in early Elizabethan drama; but cf. the alphabetical index in E. K. Chambers, *The Elizabethan Stage*, ii. 327–8, 303, 330, 349–50, 313, 328.

[50] Richard Tarleton (d. 1588), a famous comedian, was introduced to Queen Elizabeth through the Earl of Leicester, and became one of the Queen's Men (1583); cf. *Elizabethan Stage*, ii. 342–5. *Tarleton's Jests* (probably in print before 1600; first surviving edition, 1611) is supposedly biographical.

[51] Will Kempe was well known by 1590 for his clowning and jigs. From 1594 on he was a member of the Chamberlain's Men, and his name survives in the stage-directions to *Romeo and Juliet* and *Much Ado about Nothing*.

[52] Cf. *The Elizabethan Stage*, ii. 339–40, 334–5, 296–8, 340–1.

most worthy, famous Master Edward Alleyn.[53] To omit these, as also
such as for their divers imperfections may be thought insufficient for
the quality, actors should be men picked out,* personable,* according
to the parts they present. They should be rather scholars, that, though
they cannot speak well know how to speak, or else to have that volubility* that they can speak well though they understand not what; and
so both imperfections may by instructions be helped and amended.
But where a good tongue and a good conceit both fail, there can never
be good actor.

I also could wish that such as are condemned for their licentiousness might by a general consent be quite excluded our society. For, as
we are men that stand in the broad eye of the world, so should our
manners, gestures, and behaviours savour of such government* and
modesty to deserve the good thoughts and reports of all men, and to
abide the sharpest censures even of those that are the greatest opposites* to the quality. Many amongst us I know to be of substance, of
government, of sober lives and temperate carriages, house-keepers,
and contributory* to all duties enjoined them, equally with them that
are ranked with the most bountiful; and if amongst so many of sort*
there be any few degenerate from the rest in that good demeanour
which is both requisite and expected at their hands, let me entreat you
not to censure hardly* of all for the misdeeds of some, but rather to
excuse us, as Ovid doth the generality of women:

> *Parcit paucarum diffundere crimen in omnes:*
> *Spectetur meritis quæque puella suis.*[54]

> For some offenders, that perhaps are few,
> Spare in your thoughts to censure all the crew:
> Since every breast contains a sundry spirit,
> Let every one be censured as they merit.

Others there are of whom, should you ask my opinion, I must
refer you to this, *Consule theatrum.*[55] Here I might take fit opportunity
to reckon up all our English writers, and compare them with the

---

[53] Edward Alleyn (1566–1626), one of the leading tragic actors in the Elizabethan theatre,
who was with Worcester's players in 1583, thereafter with the Admiral's Men; his roles
included Faustuts, Tamburlaine, and Barabas in *The Jew of Malta*. He was stepson-in-law
of the impresario Philip Henslowe, and with his considerable fortune from the theatre and
property investments founded Dulwich College.

[54] Ovid, *Ars am.* 3. 9–10: 'Lay not a handful's crime on all the race, | But on its merits
judge each woman's case' (tr. Melville).

[55] 'Look to the theatre'.

Greek, French, Italian, and Latin poets, not only in their pastoral, historical, elegiacal, and heroical poems, but in their tragical and comical subjects. But it was my chance to happen on the like, learnedly done by an approved good scholar, in a book called *Wits Commonwealth*,[56] to which treatise I wholly refer you, returning to our present subject. . . .

OF ACTORS, AND THE TRUE USE OF THEIR QUALITY
THE THIRD BOOK

Tragedies and comedies, saith Donatus,[57] had their beginning *a rebus divinis*, from divine sacrifices. They differ thus: in comedies *turbulenta prima, tranquilla ultima*; in tragedies, *tranquilla prima, turbulenta ultima*: comedies begin in trouble and end in peace; tragedies begin in calms and end in tempest. . . . The definition of the comedy, according to the Latins: a discourse consisting of divers institutions,* comprehending civil and domestic things, in which is taught what in our lives and manners is to be followed, what to be avoided. The Greeks define it thus: *Kōmōdia estin idiōtikōn kai politikōn pragmatōn achin donos poroichēn*.[58] Cicero saith,[59] a comedy is the imitation of life, the glass of custom, and the image of truth. . . .

To proceed to the matter. First, playing* is an ornament to the city, which strangers of all nations repairing* hither report of in their countries, beholding them here with some admiration; for what variety of entertainment can there be in any city of Christendom more than in London? But some will say, this dish might be very well spared out of the banquet. To him I answer: Diogenes, that used to feed on roots, cannot relish a march-pane.* Secondly, our English tongue, which

---

[56] This treatise by Francis Meres, *Palladis Tamia. Wits Treasury being the second part of Wits Common Wealth* (1598), in which English writers are listed under various genres, juxtaposed with a list of Greek and Roman authors, was shown by D. C. Allen to have been plagiarized from J. Ravisius Textor's *Officina*: see his edition, *Francis Meres's treatise 'Poetrie'* (Urbana, Ill., 1933).

[57] Aelius Donatus, a grammarian of the 4th cent. AD, whose commentary on Terence was often reprinted in Renaissance editions, together with the fragmentary essay *De Comoedia et Tragoedia* by Evanthius, the source for the following definitions. For a translation of both texts, see A. Preminger, O. B. Hardison, Jr., and K. Kerrane (eds.), *Classical and Medieval Literary Criticism* (New York, 1974), pp. 299–309.

[58] 'Comedy is [a representation of] a portion of the actions of average men and citizens, which involves no danger'. Attributed to Aristotle's pupil, Theophrastus, this definition gained great currency from its inclusion in the late 4th cent. *Ars grammatica* of Diomedes.

[59] This often quoted saying was attributed to Cicero by Donatus.

hath been the most harsh, uneven, and broken language of the world, part Dutch, part Irish, Saxon, Scotch, Welsh, and indeed a galli-maufry of many but perfect in none, is now by this secondary means of playing continually refined, every writer striving in himself to add a new flourish* to it. So that in process, from the most rude and unpol-ished tongue it is grown to a most perfect and composed* language, and many excellent works and elaborate poems writ in the same, that many nations grow enamoured of our tongue, before despised. Neither sapphic, ionic, iambic, phaleutic, adonic, glyconic, hexameter, tetrameter, pentameter, asclepediac, choriambic, nor any other meas-ured verse[60] used among the Greeks, Latins, Italians, French, Dutch or Spanish writers, but may be expressed in English, be it blank verse or metre, in distichon or hexastichon,[61] or in what form or feet, or what number you can desire. Thus you see to what excellency our refined English is brought, that in these days we are ashamed of that euphony and eloquence which within these sixty years the best tongues in the land were proud to pronounce. Thirdly, plays have made the ignorant more apprehensive,* taught the unlearned the knowledge of many famous histories, instructed such as cannot read in the discovery* of all our English chronicles; and what man have you now of that weak capacity that cannot discourse of any notable thing recorded even from William the Conqueror, nay, from the landing of Brute, until this day, being possessed of their true use, for or* because plays are writ with this aim and carried with this method, to teach their subjects obedience to their king, to show the people the untimely ends of such as have moved tumults, commotions, and insurrections, to present them with the flourishing estate of such as live in obedi-ence, exhorting them to allegiance, dehorting them from all traitorous and felonious stratagems.

Omne genus scripti gravitate tragœdia vincit.[62]

If we present a tragedy, we include the fatal and abortive ends of such as commit notorious murders, which is aggravated* and acted with all the art that may be, to terrify men from the like abhorred practices. If we present a foreign history, the subject is so intended* that in the lives of Romans, Grecians or others, either the virtues of

---

[60] Classical verse was strictly quantitative, and so, despite Heywood's assurances, cannot be reproduced in English. Cf. Campion, p. 428, and Daniel, p. 441.

[61] A distichon is a two-line verse, or couplet; a hexastichon is a verse of six lines.

[62] Ovid, *Tristia* 2. 1. 381: 'In solemn grandeur tragedy's unrivalled'.

our countrymen are extolled or their vices reproved. As thus, by
the example of Cæsar to stir soldiers to valour and magnanimity;*
by the fall of Pompey, that no man trust in his own strength. We
present Alexander killing his friend in his rage, to reprove rashness;
Midas choked with his gold, to tax covetousness; Nero against
tyranny; Sardanapalus against luxury; Ninus against ambition, with
infinite others, by sundry instances either animating men to noble
attempts or attacking the consciences of the spectators, finding
themselves touched* in presenting the vices of others. If a moral, it
is to persuade men to humanity and good life, to instruct them in
civility and good manners, showing them the fruits of honesty and the
end of villainy.

> *versibus exponi tragicis res comica non vult.*[63]

Again Horace, *Arte Poetica*:

> *at vestri proavi Plautinos et numeros et*
> *laudavere sales.*[64]

If a comedy, it is pleasantly contrived with merry accidents, and
intermixed with apt and witty jests, to present before the prince at
certain times of solemnity, or else merrily fitted to the stage. And what
is then the subject of this harmless mirth? Either in the shape of
a clown to show others their slovenly and unhandsome behaviour,
that they may reform that simplicity* in themselves which others
make their sport, lest they happen to become the like subject of
general scorn to an auditory. Else it entreats of love, deriding foolish
inamorates who spend their ages, their spirits, nay themselves in the
servile and ridiculous employments of their mistresses. And these are
mingled with sportful accidents, to recreate such as of themselves are
wholly devoted to melancholy, which corrupts the blood, or to refresh
such weary spirits as are tired with labour or study, to moderate the
cares and heaviness of the mind, that they may return to their trades
and faculties* with more zeal and earnestness after some small, soft,
and pleasant retirement. Sometimes they discourse of pantaloons,
usurers that have unthrifty sons, which both the fathers and sons may
behold to their instructions; sometimes of courtesans, to divulge their
subtleties and snares in which young men may be entangled, showing

---

[63] Horace, *Ars P.* 89: 'A theme for comedy refuses to be set forth in verses of tragedy'.

[64] Ibid. 270–1: 'Yet your forefathers, you say, praised both the measures and the wit of
Plautus'.

them the means to avoid them.[65] If we present a pastoral we show the harmless love of shepherds, diversely moralized, distinguishing betwixt the craft of the city and the innocence of the sheep-cote. Briefly, there is neither tragedy, history, comedy, moral, or pastoral from which an infinite use cannot be gathered. I speak not in the defence of any lascivious shows, scurrilous jests, or scandalous invectives. If there be any such, I banish them quite from my patronage. Yet Horace, *Sermon I, satyr iv*, thus writes:

> *Eupolis atque Cratinus Aristophanesque poetæ,*
> *atque alii quorum comœdia prisca virorum est,*
> *si quis erat dignus describi, quod malus, aut fur,*
> *quod maechus foret, aut sicarius, aut alioqui*
> *famosus, multa cum libertate notabant.*[66]

'Eupolis, Cratinus, Aristophanes, and other comic poets in the time of Horace, with large scope and unbridled liberty, boldly and plainly scourged all abuses as in their ages were generally practiced, to the staining and blemishing of a fair and beautiful common-weal.' Likewise a learned gentleman[67] in his *Apology for Poetry* speaks thus: tragedies well-handled be a most worthy kind of poesy, comedies make men see and shame at their faults; and, proceeding further, amongst other university plays he remembers the tragedy of *Richard the Third*, acted in St John's in Cambridge so essentially* that had the tyrant Phalaris beheld his bloody proceedings it had mollified his heart, and made him relent at sight of his inhuman massacres. Further, he commends of comedies the Cambridge *Pedantius* and the Oxford *Bellum Grammaticale*; and, leaving them, passes on to our public plays, speaking liberally in their praise and what commendable use may be gathered of them. If you peruse *Margarita Poetica*[68] you may see what excellent uses and sentences he hath gathered out of *Terence* his *Andria*, *Eunuchus*, and the rest; likewise out of *Plautus* his *Amphitruo*, *Asinaria* . . . But I should tire myself to reckon the names of all French, Roman, German, Spanish, Italian, and English

---

[65] Cf. Elyot, pp. 65–6, and Massinger, pp. 552–3.

[66] Horace, *Sat.* 1. 4. 1–5: 'Eupolis and Cratinus and Aristophanes, true poets, and the other good men to whom Old Comedy belongs, if there was anyone deserving to be drawn as a rogue and thief, as a rake or cut-throat, or as scandalous in any way, set their mark upon him with great freedom'.

[67] Sir John Harington: above, p. 313.

[68] The *Margarita poetica* of Albertus von Eyb, first published in 1472, continued to be reprinted into the 17th cent.

poets, being in number infinite, and their labours extant to approve their worthiness.

Is thy mind noble, and wouldst thou be further stirred up to magnanimity?* Behold upon the stage thou mayest see Hercules, Achilles, Alexander, Cæsar, Alcibiades, Lysander, Sertorius, Hannibal, Antigonus, Philip of Macedon, Mithridates of Pontus, Pyrrhus of Epirus; Agesilaus among the Lacedemonians, Epaminondas amongst the Thebans; Scævola alone entering the armed tents of Porsenna, Horatius Cocles alone withstanding the whole army of the Etrurians; Leonidas of Sparta choosing a lion to lead a band of deer, rather than one deer to conduct an army of lions—with infinite others, in their own persons, qualities and shapes, animating thee with courage, deterring thee from cowardice. Hast thou of thy country well deserved? and art thou of thy labour evil requited? To associate* thee thou mayest see the valiant Roman Marcellus pursue Hannibal at Nola, conquering Syracuse, vanquishing the Gauls at Padua, and presently* (for his reward) banished his country into Greece. There thou mayest see Scipio Africanus, now triumphing for the conquest of all Africa, and immediately exiled the confines of Romania.[69] Art thou inclined to lust? behold the falls of the Tarquins in the rape of Lucrece, the guerdon of luxury in the death of Sardanapalus, Appius destroyed in the ravishing of Virginia, and the destruction of Troy in the lust of Helen.[70] Art thou proud? Our scene presents thee with the fall of Phaethon, Narcissus pining in the love of his shadow, ambitious Hamon, now calling himself a god, and by and by thrust headlong among the devils. We present men with the ugliness of their vices, to make them the more to abhor them; as the Persians use, who above all sins loathing drunkenness, accustomed in their solemn feasts to make their servants and captives extremely overcome with wine, and then call their children to view their nasty and loathsome behaviour, making them hate that sin in themselves which showed so gross and abominable in others. The like use may be gathered of the drunkards, so naturally imitated in our plays, to the applause of the actor, content

[69] Roman territory. Publius Cornelius Scipio Africanus the Elder (236–183 BC), a distinguished soldier and consul, was forced into exile by political opponents.

[70] Some of these subjects were treated by Heywood himself. His *The Rape of Lucrece* shows Tarquin's punishment; *The Iron Age* (1612–13) emphasizes Helen's guilt. In the next paragraph: the story of *Appius and Virginia* was dramatized by Webster and (perhaps) Heywood, sometime between 1608 and 1634. Heywood brought Diana on stage in *The Golden Age* (1611), Lucrece (as mentioned), and Jane Shore in *1 and 2 Edward IV* (1599). The Countess of Salisbury appears in Shakespeare (and others) *Edward III*, p. 325 above.

of the auditory, and reproving of the vice. Art thou covetous? go no further than Plautus, his comedy called Euclio.[71]

> *Dum fallax servus, durus pater, improba lena*
> *vivent et meretrix blanda, Menandros erit.*[72]

> While there's false servant, or obdurate sire,
> Sly bawd, smooth whore, Menander we'll admire.

To end in a word, art thou addicted to prodigality, envy, cruelty, perjury, flattery, or rage? Our scenes afford thee store of men to shape your lives by, who be frugal, loving, gentle, trusty, without soothing,* and in all things temperate. Wouldst thou be honourable, just, friendly, moderate, devout, merciful, and loving concord? Thou mayest see many of their fates and ruins who have been dishonourable, unjust, false, gluttonous, sacrilegious, bloody-minded, and brokers of dissension. Women, likewise, that are chaste are by us extolled and encouraged in their virtues, being instanced by Diana, Belphoebe, Matilda, Lucrece, and the Countess of Salisbury. The unchaste are by us showed their errors in the persons of Phryne, Lais, Thais, Flora; and amongst us, Rosamond and Mistress Shore. What can sooner print modesty in the souls of the wanton than by discovering unto them the monstrousness of their sin?

It follows, that we prove these exercises to have been the discoverers of many notorious murders, long concealed from the eyes of the world.[73] To omit all far-fetched instances, we will prove it by a domestic and home-born truth, which within these few years happened. At Lynn, in Norfolk, the then Earl of Sussex's players acting the old history of *Friar Francis*,[74] and presenting a woman who, insatiately doting on a young gentleman, the more securely to enjoy his affection mischievously and secretly murdered her husband, whose ghost haunted her; and at divers times, in her most solitary and private contemplations, in most horrid and fearful shapes appeared and stood before her. As this was acted, a towns-woman, till then of good estimation and report, finding her conscience at this presentment* extremely troubled, suddenly screeched and cried out, 'Oh! my husband, my husband! I see the ghost of my husband fiercely threat-

---

[71] The miserly old man in Plautus' *Aulularia* (the source of Molière's *L'Avare*).
[72] Ovid, *Am.* 1. 15. 17–18: 'as long as tricky slave, hard father, treacherous bawd, and wheedling harlot shall be found, Menander will endure'.
[73] Cf. *Hamlet* 2. 2. 596–606: 'I have heard | That guilty creatures sitting at a play . . .'.
[74] This title could also be *Fair Francis*.

ening and menacing me!' At which shrill and unexpected outcry the people about her, moved to a strange amazement, inquired the reason of her clamour; when presently, un-urged, she told them that seven years ago she, to be possessed of such a gentleman (meaning[75] him), had poisoned her husband, whose fearful image personated itself in the shape of that ghost. Whereupon the murderess was apprehended, before the justices further examined, and by her voluntary confession after condemned. That this is true, as well by the report of the actors as the records of the town, there are many eyewitnesses of this accident yet living vocally to confirm it. . . .

Another of the like wonder happened at Amsterdam in Holland. A company of our English comedians* (well known) travelling those countries, as they were before the burgers and other the chief inhabitants acting the last part of the *Four Sons of Aymon*, towards the last act of the history, where penitent Rinaldo like a common labourer lived in disguise, vowing as his last penance to labour and carry burdens to the structure of a goodly church there to be erected; whose diligence the labourers envying, since by reason of his stature and strength he did usually perfect* more work in a day than a dozen of the best (he working for his conscience, they for their lucres). Whereupon, by reason his industry had so much disparaged their living,* conspired among themselves to kill him, waiting some opportunity to find him asleep, which they might easily do, since the sorest labourers are the soundest sleepers, and industry is the best preparative to rest. Having spied their opportunity, they drove a nail into his temples, of which wound immediately he died. As the actors handled this, the audience might on a sudden understand* an out-cry and loud shriek in a remote gallery; and pressing about the place, they might perceive a woman of great gravity strangely amazed, who with a distracted and troubled brain oft sighed out these words: 'Oh, my husband, my husband!' The play without further interruption proceeded; the woman was to her own house conducted, without any apparent suspicion, every one conjecturing as their fancies led them. In this agony she some few days languished, and on a time, as certain of her well-disposed neighbours came to comfort her, one amongst the rest being church-warden: to him the sexton posts,* to tell him of a strange thing happening to him in the ripping up of a grave. 'See here' (quoth

---

[75] As A. H. Gilbert observes (*LCPD*, p. 564), with the sense 'indicating, setting forth'; cf. *A Midsummer Night's Dream* 5. 1. 322: 'And thus she means, videlicet'.

he) 'what I have found', and shows them a fair skull, with a great nail pierced quite through the brain-pan: 'But we cannot conjecture to whom it should belong, nor how long it hath lain in the earth, the grave being confused, and the flesh consumed.' At the report of this accident the woman, out of the trouble of her afflicted conscience, discovered a former murder; for twelve years ago, by driving that nail into that skull (being the head of her husband) she had treacherously slain him. This being publicly confessed, she was arraigned, condemned, adjudged, and burned.—But I draw my subject to greater length then I purposed; these therefore out of other infinites I have collected, both for their familiarness and lateness of memory.

Thus, our antiquity we have brought from the Grecians in the time of Hercules; from the Macedonians in the age of Alexander; from the Romans long before Julius Caesar; and since him, through the reigns of twenty-three emperors succeeding, even to Marcus Aurelius. After him they were supported by the Mantuans, Venetians, Valencians, Neapolitans, the Florentines, and others; since by the German princes, the Palsgrave, the Landsgrave, the dukes of Saxony, of Brunswick, &c. The cardinal at Brussels hath at this time in pay a company of our English comedians. The French king allows certain companies in Paris, Orleans, besides other cities; so doth the king of Spain in Seville, Madrid, and other provinces. But in no country they are of that eminence that ours are. So our most royal and ever-renowned sovereign hath licensed us in London; so did his predecessor, the thrice-virtuous virgin, Queen Elizabeth, and before her, her sister, Queen Mary, Edward the Sixth, and their father Henry the Eighth; and before these, in the tenth year of the reign of Edward the Fourth, Anno 1490. John Stow,[76] an ancient and grave chronicler, records—amongst other varieties[77] tending to the like effect—that a play was acted at a place called Skinners-well, fast by Clerkenwell, which continued eight days, and was of matter from Adam and Eve, the first creation of the world; the spectators were no worse than the royalty of England. And amongst other commendable exercises in this place the Company of the Skinners of London held certain yearly solemn plays; in place whereof, now in these latter days the wrestling and such other pastimes have been kept, and is still held about Bartholomewtide. Also, in the year 1390, the fourteenth year of the reign of Richard the Second, the 18 of July,

[76] See John Stow, *A Survey of London* (1603 edn.), ed. C. L. Kingsford, 2 vols. (Oxford, 1908), i. 15–16, for the following references to plays, interludes, and wrestling.
[77] Series of parallel instances.

were the like interludes recorded of at the same place, which continued three days together, the king and queen and nobility being there
present. Moreover, to this day in divers places of England there be
towns that hold the privilege of their fairs, and other charters by yearly
stage-plays, as at Manningtree in Suffolk, Kendall in the north, and
others. To let these pass, as things familiarly known to all men.

Now, to speak of some abuse lately crept into the quality, as an
inveighing against the state, the court, the law, the city, and their governments, with the particularizing of private men's humours yet alive,
noble-men, and others: I know it distastes many; neither do I any way
approve it, nor dare I by any means excuse it. The liberty which some
arrogate to themselves, committing their bitterness and liberal invectives against all estates to the mouths of children,[78] supposing their
juniority to be a privilege for any railing, be it never so violent, I could
advise all such to curb and limit this presumed liberty within the bands
of discretion and government. But wise and judicial censurers, before
whom such complaints shall at any time hereafter come, will not, I
hope, impute these abuses to any transgression in us, who have ever
been careful and provident to shun the like. I surcease to prosecute*
this any further, lest my good meaning be by some misconstrued; and
fearing likewise, lest with tediousness I tire the patience of the
favourable reader, here (though abruptly) I conclude my third and last
TREATISE.

stultitiam patiuntur opes, mihi parvula res est.[79]

---

[78] Referring to the Children of the Chapel, acting at the Blackfriars theatre, who performed *Cynthia's Revels* (1600) and *Poetaster* (1601), in which Jonson satirized the plays
and players of the public theatres, especially Marston and Dekker, setting off a noisy
controversy. Cf. *Hamlet* 2. 2. 330–58, ed. Harold Jenkins (London, 1982) and pp. 1–3, 255–7,
470–2 of that edition.

[79] Horace, *Epist.* 1. 18. 29 (adapted): 'Wealth allows of folly; my means are but trifling'.

John Fletcher,
On pastoral tragicomedy (*c*.1610)

JOHN FLETCHER (1579–1625) was educated at Benet (now Corpus Christi) College Cambridge, and had a prolific career as a dramatist. He wrote numerous plays with Francis Beaumont (*c*.1584–1616), innovating in tragicomedies displaying a pronounced emotionality, including *Philaster* (*c*.1609), *A King and no King* (1611), and *The Maid's Tragedy* (1611). He collaborated with Shakespeare on *The Two Noble Kinsmen* (1613) and *Henry VIII* (1613).

TEXT. From *The Faithful Sheperdess*, probably performed in 1608 and printed in 1610. Pastoral tragicomedy was a new genre in the Renaissance, introduced by two contrasting works, Torquato Tasso's lyrical *Aminta* (1581) and Giovanni Battista Guarini's more plot-based *Il Pastor Fido* (1590; 20 editions by 1602). Although pastoral elements figure in earlier English plays, such as *As You Like It* (1599), *The Maid's Metamorphosis* (anonymous, *c*.1600), and Samuel Daniel's *Queen's Arcadia* (1605), credit is due to Fletcher for writing the first fully pastoral tragicomedy in English. He consciously emulated Italian modes, as found in Guarini's *Compendio della poesia tragicomica* (1599–1601; excerpts in *LCPD*, pp. 504–33), and other theoretical works. See M. T. Herrick, *Tragicomedy: Its Origin and Development in Italy, France, and England* (Urbana, Ill., 1955).

TO THE READER

If you be not reasonably assured of your knowledge in this kind of poem, lay down the book or read this, which I would wish had been the prologue. It is a pastoral tragicomedy, which the people seeing when it was played, having ever had a singular gift in defining, concluded to be a play of country-hired shepherds,[1] in grey cloaks, with curtailed* dogs in strings, sometimes laughing together, and sometimes killing one another; and, missing Whitsun ales, cream, wassail

---

[1] Guarini had insisted on this point: cf. Herrick, *Tragicomedy*, p. 139, *LCPD*, p. 530.

and morris-dances,[2] began to be angry. In their error I would not have you fall, lest you incur their censure.

Understand therefore a pastoral to be a representation of shepherds and shepherdesses, with their actions and passions, which must be such as may agree with their natures, at least not exceeding former fictions and vulgar traditions. They are not to be adorned with any art but such improper ones as nature is said to bestow, as singing and poetry, or such as experience may teach them, as the virtues of herbs and fountains, the ordinary course of the sun, moon, and stars, and such like. But you are ever to remember shepherds to be such as all the ancient poets and modern of understanding have received them: that is, the owners of flocks, and not hirelings.[3]

A tragicomedy is not so called in respect of mirth and killing, but in respect it wants deaths, which is enough to make it no tragedy; yet brings some near it,[4] which is enough to make it no comedy, which must be a representation of familiar people, with such kind of trouble as no life be questioned. So that a god[5] is as lawful in this as in a tragedy, and mean people as in a comedy.

Thus much I hope will serve to justify my poem, and make you understand it; to teach you more for nothing, I do not know that I am in conscience bound.

---

[2] Traditional components of English holiday festivals. Cf. Perdita: 'Methinks I play as I have seen them do | In Whitsun pastorals' (*The Winter's Tale* 4. 4. 133 f.).

[3] That is, prosperous farmers, not day-labourers.

[4] This influential definition of tragicomedy, as a genre which 'wants', or lacks deaths, but includes some intermediate degree of danger, while drawing on contemporary theory, looks back to classical attempts to distinguish tragedy from comedy. Diomedes the grammarian (4th cent. AD) defined comedy as a 'treatment of private and civil station that is without danger to life' (*LCPD*, p. 508). Guarini's requirements for tragicomedy included '(1) great personages, (2) verisimilar (i.e. fictitious) plot, (3) emotions "with their edge abated", (4) tragic danger but not death, (5) moderate laughter, (6) feigned complications, (7) happy reversal of fortune, (8) "above all the comic order"' (Herrick, *Tragicomedy*, p. 263).

[5] The *deus ex machina*, sometimes used to resolve the plot-complication in classical drama.

26

Dudley North,
Against obscurity in love poetry (*c.*1610)

DUDLEY NORTH (1581–1666), third Baron North, succeeded to his title at the age of 19. After completing his education at Cambridge (without taking a degree), he divided his life between attendance at the court of King James, where he took an active part in jousts and masques, and his estate at Kirtling, Cambridgeshire. He discovered the springs at Tunbridge Wells, and publicized those at Epsom. An accomplished singer and performer on the treble viol, North wrote poetry and essays, and made several translations from the French. His grandson, Roger North, left an attractive memoir of him: see John Wilson (ed.), *Roger North on Music* (London, 1959). In criticizing contemporary styles in verse, including what is sometimes called 'Metaphysical' poetry, North restated the classical virtues of coherence and clarity. It is tantalizing not to know which poets he meant.

TEXT. From *A Forest of Varieties* (1645), a collection of poems, essays, letters, devotional meditations, and characters; reissued, with revisions, *as A Forest promiscuous of various Seasons' Productions* (1659). The Preface is entitled 'Concerning petty Poetry, made more generall in address then at the first'. In editing it I have benefited from L. A. Beaurline, 'Dudley North's Criticism of Metaphysical Poetry', *Huntington Library Quarterly*, 25 (1962), 299–313, and E. W. Tayler (ed.), *Literary Criticism of Seventeenth-Century England* (New York, 1967).

[DEDICATING HIS VOLUME OF POEMS TO
LADY MARY WROTH][1]

. . . My travail* ended with their first birth, and so I hope or wish the reader's may at the first reading. For if they be not plain and easy it is against my will, which as it wants strength to imitate so cannot approve the riddling humour lately affected by many, who think nothing good that is easy, nor anything becoming* passion that is not expressed with an hyperbole above reason. These tormentors of their

---

[1] Niece to Sir Philip Sidney, authoress of *The Countesse of Montgomerie's Urania* (1621), a close imitation of the *Arcadia*, and an active patroness of contemporary literature.

own and their readers' brains I leave to be admired in their high obscure flight, while myself will be happy if I can procure but a famil-iar delight to a superficial* reading. They affect* to shew more wit than love, and in truth so much that whilst they commend beyond reason, they shew that either they want reason to commend, or their subject to be commended. Like ill-ranging spaniels they spring figures,[2] and, ravished with their extravagant fancies, pursue them in long excursions, neglecting their true game and pretended affection. Be the matter or the discourser's capacity never so poor and mean, I ever affect a man that maketh right conclusions.[3] And for myself, I would rather be thought to want invention and knowledge than judge-ment and good consequence in what I utter.

The poetry of these times abounds in wit, high conceit, figure, and proportions; thin, light, and empty in matter and substance; like fine-coloured airy bubbles or quelque-choses,[4] much ostentation and little food. Conceits, similes, and allegories are good, so the matter be carried along in them, and not interrupted by them.[5] Venus is here[6] drawn by her doves, not serpents; and as I profess myself to want art[7] in all things, so in matters of love I think it may be best spared, as being an affection merely* natural, and where art is seldom comely* but authorised with a native disposition. Besides, verses of love are commonly made for women, whose chiefest beauty consists in being unsophisticated* by art, and are the more pleasing in conversation by possessing a free purity of unadulterated wit. And as we often see that those women that have bestowed on themselves the most art and costly dressing, nay many times that have the best proportion, are not yet the most winning, so in verses there is to be expressed a natural spirit and moving air* (or accent), more alluring and charming the affection than others of a far more rich, fair and curious* composition.

The world in all things is full of critics, that are sharp-sighted to reprehend, and will approve nothing but according to their own rule (many times out of square). But for my part I hold the same opinion of verses as of airs in music, or houses, that let them be delightful and pleasant to the first appearance, with conveniency* to the design; and

---

[2] Such poets 'flush out' rhetorical figures or conceits, pursuing them at the expense of the poem's coherence.

[3] Judgements arrived at by reasoning; properly conducted argument.

[4] 'Something dainty or elegant, but unsubstantial; a trifle' (*OED*).

[5] Provided that they continue the poem's argument, not interrupt it.

[6] That is, in love poetry.

[7] In the sense of 'technical training'.

for the fantasticated[8] rules of art, architecture, and proportion, let them observe them that list*—and commonly who most affects them most fails in the general delightfulness and use. Poetry is in truth a kind of music, the fable of Orpheus expressed as much. Music hath its anthems, pavanes, fantasies, galliards, corantos, airs, sarabands, toys, chromatiques, &c.[9] And verses have their hymns, tragedies, satires, heroics, sonnets, odes, songs, epigrams, distichs, and strong lines,[10] which are their chromatiques, and of themselves may be excellent in their art, but long dwelt upon grow harsh and distasteful. The commandments and preceptives* are none of the poetical parts of scripture.

Though I am no part of a scholar, yet thus much by casual opening of books I know, that Horace in matter of love hates difficulty; and though I believe it an imitation of his abrupt and harsh vein in his more serious pieces, that upon the worthiness of his name and matter hath debauched many from the formerly used, more open, familiar and pleasing manner of versifying, yet I find that even himself (howsoever either naturally or affectedly rugged,[11] except his lyric vein) when he uttereth his judgement, or prescribeth to others concerning measured compositions, no man is more frequent in recommendation of a round,* current,* clear and graceful delivery.[12] But what his moral, solid and satiric matter dispensed with is in slighter stuff intolerable. There shall you find the rough hands, but not the voice and substance; let them rather imitate his best than his worst. It cannot be good in limited lines, which are a purposed pause to the voice, to carry with a counter-time the period of the sense to the body of the next line;[13] much less to dismember an innocent word that every child

---

[8] Formed by the fancy or imagination, having no link with reality.

[9] This list of musical genres, vocal and instrumental, includes two rare terms: a 'toy' is 'a light, frivolous, or lively tune' (*NSOED*); a 'chromatic' is a melody including notes not belonging to the diatonic scale.

[10] In this list of literary genres 'heroic' poems are epics; a 'distich' is a pair of verse lines or couplet; 'strong lines' are compressed, sententious lines, with connotations of roughness or asperity, antithetic to smoothness. Cf. George Williamson, 'Strong lines', *English Studies*, 18 (1936), 152–9, repr. in his *Seventeenth Century Contexts* (London, 1960), pp. 120–32, and Hobbes, p. 615.

[11] 'Rough or harsh in sound' (*NSOED*).

[12] Cf. *Ars P.* 24–8, 445–50. 'The reference to "matter of love" is not taken from any specific passage in Horace but seems to be a description of the odes concerning love' (Beaurline).

[13] Lines of verse are 'limited' or given fixed limits by the choice of metre and stanza form, so that to carry the sense across the line-break sets up a 'counter-time', or opposed movement. Cf. Jonson, pp. 528–9 for the opposite view.

according to nature and use, in spelling would put together;[14] and words have a natural air,* accent, and quantity, whence to strain them is to rack* both them and the reader. Who will set himself to dance, or his horse to manage,[15] let him seek to observe good time, air, and fashion.

No man is fit for all things; whose genius was born for prose, let him write prose, rather than affecting verse to make such unnatural stuff as shall be good neither. I pity both in myself and others to see the best of our matter in one place so extremely pressed that it is a labour to discover it; and yet in another part of the same piece slight and superfluous stuff dilated at large.[16] A poet should raise light from smoke, not blow that which is light with him to carry but smoke to another. I am of his Majesty's mind,[17] that the best eloquence is to make ourselves clearly understood, and that to him who hath leisure there need no abbreviations. I had rather pay for a little more paper than to be put to the cost of my brain. The admirable inventions and matter of your unimitable uncle's[18] extant works flourish in applause of all, by a happy and familiar display of their beauties to the meanest, including withal such generosity of truly and profoundly extracted conceit* to the most inward life of whatsoever he expresseth that the strongest and clearest-seeing judgements may rest satisfied, yea transported in contemplation of the most lively and pleasing touches that a soul can apprehend or a pen distil. Yet somewhat more to authorize myself: Lipsius[19] upon perspicuity holds it the greatest misery in writing not only not to be understood, but to be understood with difficulty; and the sharpwitted Martial,[20] in contempt of the more formal and severe censurers and writers, professeth that he would have his verses need neither an Apollo nor grammarian;[21] and howsoever

[14] The practice of dividing a word in order to make a rhyme.

[15] The training of a horse in its paces.

[16] Two extremes in treating the subject-matter ('stuff', *res*): 'pressed' or compressed, 'dilated' or spun out at length.

[17] King James I, in *Basilicon doron* (Edinburgh, 1599; London, 1887 edn.), pp. 136, 141–2.

[18] Sir Philip Sidney, whose works were widely admired and imitated throughout the 17th cent.

[19] Justus Lipsius, *Epistolica institutio* (1590), ch. 8. For the virtue of *perspicuitas* cf. Wilson, p. 120, Gascoigne, p. 167, Jonson, p. 559, and Hobbes, p. 615.

[20] Cf. *Epigrams* 10. 59. 6: 'Hunc volo qui fiat non sine pane satur': '[I have no need of a reader too nice:] I want him who is not satisfied without bread'.

[21] *Epigrams* 10. 21. 3–6, reproving Sextus for writing poetry so difficult as to need an interpreter: 'your books do not require a reader, but an Apollo . . . On these terms let your books be praised by all means; let my poems, Sextus, please commentators [*grammaticis*]—

some may deny him to be exact, himself in his entertainments affects rather to please his guests than cooks.[22] Verses of love should be verses of pleasure, and to please in love, the smoother-faced the better.

I may be crabbed and rugged, but will never affect to be so, especially in verses whose true nature and use is to work a kind of a charm upon the mind, even with slightness of matter, by the well-wrought and exquisite harmony of their cadence and sound; there being to be transfused into verse sometimes such a natural spirit of magnanimity,* sometimes such a soft, wanton, and melting air of passion that the one shall never fail to affect a generous and heroic mind, nor the other to work a kind of tender and relenting disposition in a sensible[23] and well-natured constitution; neither of which shall easily be seen effected from a harsh and rude (though never so witty)* an expression. For as in persons, so in verses: some, let them mean never so lovingly, shall yet by their natural verjuice be ever out of the way of Bacchus and Venus.[24] But in point of obscurity, in some sort to excuse myself with others, I fear we all often unwillingly incur the error of it by thinking our meaning as open to others as to ourselves; when indeed the characters of our expression are fully supplied by our own understanding to ourselves, whilst to others they are lamely contracted and imperfect.

Thus much I have been bold to write, not only to excuse a poor mother wit, but somewhat to give a pass upon[25] their strange and uneasy habit,* who I doubt not but they will have many a gird at my easy and natural nakedness.—I mean those lofty dim-shooting archers, whom I wish to remember that he who shoots highest, shoots not ever nearest the mark; and he that may walk in the light, is to be suspected for choosing the dark. Now, Madam, I grant that all I can write (especially what these lines contain) is but vanity, and a most idle vanity; yet thus far I will excuse both the writing and the reading, that all the world is little better. We often condemn vain pleasures, and

so as to do without commentators'. In Roman schools the *grammaticus* taught grammar and elementary exposition of texts.

[22] Cf. *Epigrams* 9. 81. 3–4: '[Reader and hearer approve of my works, Aulus, but a certain poet says they are not polished.] I don't care much, for I should prefer the courses of my dinner to please guests rather than cooks.'

[23] Susceptible to feeling, sensitive.

[24] Those poets who naturally produce verjuice—'an acid liquour obtained from crab-apples, sour grapes, etc., formerly used in cooking and medicine' (*NSOED*)—cannot write love poetry. Cf. also 'Sine Cerere et Libero friget Venus', 'Without Ceres and Bacchus, Venus grows cold': Terence, *Eunuchus* 732.

[25] Have a pass at, criticize.

remember not that the most things the best of us most seriously do, have indeed no other end. For God being served and nature sustained, what fruit proceeds from our authority, learning, wealth, policy, and earnest intent to profit, but to satisfy our impulsive affections, which either propound to themselves a felicity whereof they fail in the possession, or seek to divert by such employments the dullness and otherwise obtruding miseries of their condition? Which, if you please to consider, you will the more excuse many pursuers of lawful and natural delights, and value those pleasures at the better rate which are most perdurable* and communicable. May the following wanton,* but as modest babes as their mother Venus could produce, though they cannot profit, yet afford some delight to that your worthy well-furnished mind, to which I wish all happiness that ever noble nature possessed, or can possess.

I must yet be so much longer, as to crave pardon for my unintended and I fear unpleasant length; it is the vice of writing to be endless. Thus hath my enmity to obscurity brought forth tediousness, yet not so much but that all this may be sooner read than some one passage of our night pieces[26] understood. They had need afford profitable stuff, who utter* it at so hard a rate. I wish your Ladyship's authority would so abate the price that our poorer abilities might hold trade without straining. And seeing I am upon the theme of verses, whither I mean not shortly to return, I humbly crave your favour after my fashion, disorderly to say thus much more, that howsoever some of the stricter* sort approve only of verses so close, useful, and substantially woven that there must be neither list,[27] looseness, nor the least superfluity of words: for my part, I am not of that strict order, nor ever yet saw it observed in any author. Nature hath mingled stalks with flowers, and husks with corn, and hath raised ornament from our excrementitial[28] hairs. Conceits and matter over-crushed afford commonly as little grace as pleasure, and to write all in abbreviations would take indeed less room, but much more time and trouble. A Geneva print[29] weakens the sight, nor is it good to hold your bow ever bent, or your horse straight reined. Sometimes amongst pithy and tough lines I think it not amiss to interpose one of an easy strain,

---

[26] Poetry composed at night, which may 'smell of the lamp', being too affected or pedantical; cf. 'lamp-oil' below.

[27] 'The selvage or edge of a cloth, usually of different material from the body of cloth' (*NSOED*).

[28] Growing out, excrescent.

[29] 'The kind of type used in the Geneva bibles' (*OED*): here, small print.

like resting places in lofty stairs, to ease the reader. Some fluency of
weak water helps the better in nourishment to convey what is more
solid. Lamp-oil yields no good savour, nor in salad nor verse. *Difficilia
quae pulchra*,[30] is to be understood of the attaining, and not the
exercising of faculties. You know how it is said of poems, that they
should be such *ut sibi quivis speret, idem sudet frustraque laboret
ausus idem*.[31]

Strong lines may be drawn on with cart-ropes, but the fairest have
generally an easy birth. It is rare for any thing to be well and hardly
performed. The French expression, *à delivre*,[32] implies as well perfectness as facility and dexterity. There may be employed such an
extraordinary (yet gentle) fineness of conceit, and conclusions so
designed, wrought, limned* and coloured, touches so bold, covert
allegories and subtleties so neat, transitions so easy, epithets so material,* metaphors and ambiguities so doubly fine, as shall be more
master-like than more sententious, sublime, abstruse, and strong-
appearing lines. Worth of matter and conception supposed, nothing
more commends a piece than terms well chosen, proper, lively, and
significant, with a free coming-on, and as free a close and conclusion.
Also a fair, clear and even through-carriage, with well-wrought joints
and connections, gives credit to the workman. I love as much a
great deal of force and depth couched in one word, as I hate little
in many.

We ordinarily write and speak the same things and notions, and to
the same purpose, but infinitely differ in the delivery and expression.
Some proceed in a stuttering confused obliquity, groping as in a mist
or darkness; some go more directly, and exhibit their ideas and conceptions with so clear and distinct a light, illustrations, instances,
demonstrations, enforcements and arguments so pertinent, perspicuous and concluding that the understanding and assent are captivated
beyond evasion or subterfuge. Sophistry and figures may appear fine
and witty, but prevail little upon the best judgements: reason must
convince the intellectual soul. May I write clearly and strongly rather
than finely and artificially; hence is the difference of elocution, hence
of persuasion, the one is light and airy, the other weighty and solid.

---

[30] 'The best things are difficult'. Cf. Chapman, p. 394.

[31] Horace, *Ars P*. 240–1: '[I shall make up my poem of known elements,] so that anyone
may hope to do the same, but he'll sweat and labour to no purpose when he ventures' (*ALC*,
p. 285).

[32] With ease, without encumbrance. 'Deliver', from the French, was used as an adjective
in this period, meaning 'free from impediments, agile'.

Most lovely and commanding is the beauty of a fair, ingenuous* and rich soul, fairly mounted and armed upon well-shaped and unanimously received virtue, goodness and reason. Verses are then good, when turned to prose they hold a fair and current sense,[33] and when translated into another language there is such mastery found in their conception by the advantage of what is genuine unto them, that there will be either more words or less conceit[34] and matter. The privilege they have over common phrase consists in the warranted becoming ornament of a lofty well-ordered spirit, and wantonness, such as shall make toys pass for jewels, and give to what of itself is precious an acquisite* lustre of workmanship beyond what prose can bear, and that in little room. Their voice is more constrained, and consequently more shrill and piercing. Nor is it in writing the least perfection (howsoever it hath found little observation) so to order and contract our expressions that one well-adapted word may run into and govern many of diverse and strong sense; for nothing gives more pleasure and satisfaction to a diligent, inquisitive, and judicious reader than much matter and conceit compendiously digested with sufficiency of perspicuity.

To conclude, lines of a far-fetched and laboured fancy, with allusions and curiosity,* and in similes of little more fruit or consequence than to ravish the reader into the writer's fine chameleon colours, and feed him with air,[35] I approve not so much as height and force of spirit sententiously and weightily exhibited. Wit needs not rack* itself where matter flows. Embroideries become not a rich stuff, and art is best expressed where it least appears. A strong wing is to be preferred before a painted, and good sense and matter elegantly delivered before extravagancy of fancy and conceit. Such unnatural impertinency serves rather to shadow* than illustrate, to overwhelm than set forth the subject; as well apposite as accurate writing is the author's glory.

---

[33] Cf. Jonson, p. 534.

[34] Here, as later in the paragraph, meaning 'thought', and put in apposition with 'matter', opposed to words (the *res/verba* distinction).

[35] The chameleon was thought to live on air alone.

27

George Chapman,
On translating and defending Homer
(1611, 1614)

GEORGE CHAPMAN. For Chapman's earlier poetry see above, p. 392. His career as a translator of Homer began in 1598 with the publication of *Seaven Bookes of the Iliads* (namely 1, 2, 7–11), rendered into rhyming couplets of fourteen syllables. In the same year he issued *Achilles Shield. Translated . . . out of his eighteenth booke of Iliades*, but now using rhymed decasyllabic verse. In 1608 he issued *Homer, Prince of Poets: Translated in twelve Bookes of his Iliads*, reusing his version of the earlier seven (with revisions) and adding five other books; finally, in 1611, *The Iliads of Homer* appeared, containing all twenty-four books. In 1614 the unsold sheets of this volume were bound up with a new translation of the *Odyssey* (in heroic couplets) to form *The Whole Works of Homer*.

TEXTS. (1) From *The Iliads of Homer Prince of Poets. Never before in any language truly translated. With a comment uppon some of his chiefe places; donne according to the Greeke* (1611). (2) From *The Whole Works of Homer* (1614), the dedicatory epistle (in verse and prose) to Robert Carr, Earl of Somerset, intended as a New Year's gift from the poet, who 'humbly celebrates this *New-Yeares Light* with discovery of that long hidden Relict, for whose presentment *Macedon* would have given a kingdome; *Homer reviv'd*'.

The two volumes of 1598 had included short prefaces, the second defending Homer from Scaliger's ranking of him below Virgil (both reprinted in *ECE* ii. 295–307). But for the 1611 volume Chapman prepared more extensive introductions, in prose and verse, of which I give a selection. As in the verse translations, in these prose texts Chapman displays (and partly acknowledges) a great debt to the Latin edition by Spondanus (Jean de Sponde), *Homeri quae extant omnia . . .* (Basel, 1583), which contains a parallel–column word-for-word translation into Latin (by Andreas Divus), and extensive commentaries by Spondanus. Chapman's borrowings from de Sponde and other contemporary scholars (Jean Scapula, Henri Estienne) were first shown by Frank L. Schoell, in *Études sur l'Humanisme continental en Angleterre à la fin de la Renaissance* (Paris, 1926), especially pp. 146–59, 162–77, still authoritative. In annotating these excerpts I have benefited from Schoell; Phyllis P. Bartlett (ed.), *The Poems of George Chapman* (New York and

London, 1941); Allardyce Nicoll (ed.), *Chapman's Homer*, 2 vols. (New York, 1956); and O. B. Hardison, Jr. (ed.), *English Literary Criticism: The Renaissance* (New York, 1963). See also G. de F. Lord, *Classical Presences in Seventeenth-Century English Poetry* (New Haven and London, 1987).

THE ILIAD

TO THE READER

[Chapman quotes classical testimonies[1] to Homer's supremacy as a poet]

Volumes of like praise I could heap on this,
    Of men more ancient and more learn'd than these;
But since true virtue enough lovely is
    With her own beauties, all the suffrages
Of others I omit; and would more fain
    That Homer for himself should be belov'd,   5
Who every sort of love-worth did contain.

    Which how I have in my conversion* prov'd
I must confess I hardly dare refer
    To reading judgements, since so generally   10
Custom hath made even th' ablest agents err
    In these translations. All so much apply
Their pains and cunnings word for word[2] to render
    Their patient authors, when they may as well
Make fish with fowl, camels with whales engender,
    Or their tongues' speech in other mouths compel.   15
For even as different a production
    Ask Greek and English, since, as they in sounds

Of translation, and the natural difference of dialects* necessarily to be observed in it.

---

[1] By Silius Italicus, Angelus Politianus, and Pliny; translated directly from the prefatory material in Spondanus' Homer, which also provides the first six lines of Chapman's own verse (Schoell, pp. 171–2; Nicoll, i. 663).

[2] A long critical tradition had attacked literal word-for-word versions, urging the translator to render the sense accurately while giving him freedom to find appropriate words: see F. M. Rener, *'Interpretatio': Language and Translation from Cicero to Tytler* (Amsterdam, 1989).

And letters shun one form and unison,
    So have their sense and elegancy bounds   20
In their distinguished* natures, and require
    Only a judgement to make both consent
In sense and elocution, and aspire
    As well to reach the spirit that was spent
In his example, as with art to pierce
    His grammar and etymology of words.[3]   25

Ironicè.
But as great clerks can write no English verse
    Because (alas! great clerks) English affords,
Say they, no height* nor copy*—a rude tongue[4]
    (Since 'tis their native)—but in Greek or Latin   30
Their writs* are rare,* for thence true poesy sprung—
    Though them (truth knows) they have but skill to
        chat-in
Compar'd with that they might say in their own,
    Since thither th' other's full soul cannot make
The ample transmigration to be shown
    In nature-loving poesy.[5] So the brake   35
That those translators stick in, that affect
    Their word-for-word traductions (where they lose
The free grace of their natural dialect
    And shame their authors with a forced glose)*   40
I laugh to see—and yet as much abhor

The neces-
sary
nearness of
translation
to the
example.
    More licence from the words than may express
Their full compression and make clear the author.
    From whose truth if you think my feet digress
Because I use needful periphrases,
    Read Valla, Hessus, that in Latin Prose   45

---

[3] Nicoll glosses: 'only a poet's judgment can hope to render the Greek lines effectively in English, aiming both to enter into the spirit of the original and to understand the individual meaning of its words' (i. 663).

[4] The marginal note—'Ironically'—draws attention to Chapman's mockery of orthodox scholarly opinion on the inferiority of the vernaculars. In his Preface to the *Seaven Bookes* (1598) Chapman had promised to provide his readers 'due praise of your mother tongue above all others, for Poesie' (*ECE* ii. 297). For other defences of English as a language eminently suitable for literature see Richard Carew, 'Epistle on the Excellency of the English Tongue' (*c.*1595–6), in *ECE* ii. 285–9. 4, and R. F. Jones, *The Triumph of the English Language* (Stanford, Calif., 1953).

[5] 'Since it is impossible for them to express themselves fully in an alien tongue' (Nicoll, i. 663.).

And verse convert him; read the Messines
   That into Tuscan turns him, and the glose
Grave Salel[6] makes in French as he translates—
   Which (for th' aforesaid reasons) all must do—   50
And see that my conversion much abates
   The licence they take, and more shows him too,[7]
Whose right not all those great learn'd men have done
   (In some main parts) that were his commenters.*
But (as the illustration of the sun   55
   Should be attempted by the erring stars)[8]
They fail'd to search his deep and treasurous heart.
   The cause was since they wanted the fit key

The
power of
nature
above art
in poesy.

Of Nature, in their down-right strength of art,[9]
   With poesy to open poesy—   60
Which in my poem of the mysteries[10]
   Reveal'd in Homer I will clearly prove,
Till whose near birth suspend your calumnies
   And far-wide imputations of self-love.
'Tis further from me than the worst that reads,   65
   Professing me the worst of all that write,
Yet what, in following one that bravely leads,
   The worst may show, let this proof hold the light.
But grant it clear: yet hath detraction got
   My blind side in the form my verse puts on[11]—   70
Much like a dung-hill mastiff that dares not
   Assault the man he barks at, but the stone
He throws at him takes in his eager jaws
   And spoils his teeth because they cannot spoil.
   The long verse[12] hath by proof receiv'd applause   75

---

[6] Laurentius Valla produced a Latin prose translation of Homer in 1474; Eobanus Hesse, one in Latin verse (1540). La Badessa Messanese translated the *Iliad* (bks. 1–5) into Italian (1546); Hugues Salel rendered the *Iliad* (bks. 1–10) into French (1555).

[7] 'Also reveals his spirit more accurately'.

[8] 'As if the wandering stars were to attempt to give light to the sun' (Nicoll, i. 664).

[9] 'Straightforward application of art (or rational learning)' (Nicoll, ibid.).

[10] Chapman never published this work.

[11] 'This, however, is to be understood—that my detractors rather attack the form of verse I use than my real accomplishments' (Nicoll, i. 664).

[12] In his Preface to *Achilles Shield* (1598) Chapman praised the fourteen-syllable line as the only suitable verse-form for Homer (*ECE* ii. 306–7). Jonson dismissed Chapman's use of it as 'but prose' (p. 529). For the *Odyssey* he changed to the decasyllabic couplet.

Beyond each other number, and the foil*
That squint-eye'd* envy takes is censur'd plain:
For this long poem asks this length of verse,
Which I myself ingenuously maintain
Too long our shorter authors to rehearse.   80
And for our tongue, that still is so impair'd
By travailing linguists,[13] I can prove it clear

Our
English
language
above all
others for
rhythmical
poesy.

That no tongue hath the Muses' utterance heard
For verse, and that sweet music to the ear
Struck out of rhyme, so naturally as this.   85
Our monosyllables so kindly fall
And meet, opposed in rhyme, as they did kiss;
French and Italian, most immetrical,[14]
Their many syllables in harsh collision
Fall as they break their necks, their bastard rhymes   90
Saluting as they justl'd in transition,
And set our teeth on edge, nor tunes nor times
Kept in their falls. And, methinks, their long words
Show in short verse as in a narrow place
Two opposites should meet with two-hand swords   95
Unwieldily, without or use or grace.

Thus having rid the rubs[15] and strew'd these flowers
In our thrice sacred Homer's English way,
What rests to make him yet more worthy yours?
To cite more praise of him were mere delay   100
To your glad searches for what those men found
That gave his praise, past all, so high a place;
Whose virtues were so many and so crowned
By all consents divine, that not to grace
Or add increase to them the world doth need   105
Another Homer but even to rehearse
And number them. They did so much exceed,
Men thought him not a man, but that his verse

---

[13] Nicoll suggests: 'which is so much injured by the foreign words introduced by Englishmen who have travelled abroad' (i. 664). Cf. Wilson, p. 120; Hobbes, p. 617.
[14] In the dedication to *Achilles Shield* (1598), Chapman had asserted the superiority of the English tongue as a vehicle for translation, over French, Italian, and Spanish. On monosyllables as a characteristic of English cf. *ECE* index, ii. 493. For the word 'rhythmical' in the marginal note, cf. Puttenham, pp. 215–6 n. 45.
[15] 'Dismissed the obstacles' (Nicoll, i. 664).

Some mere celestial nature did adorn;
    And all may well conclude it could not be   110
That for the place where any man was born,
    So long and mortally could disagree
So many nations as for Homer striv'd,
    Unless his spur in them had been divine.
Then end their strife and love him (thus reviv'd)   115
    As born in England; see him over-shine
All other-country poets, and trust this—
    That whose-soever Muse dares use her wing
When his Muse flies, she will be trussed* by his,
    And show as if a bernacle* should spring   120
Beneath an eagle. In none since was seen
    A soul so full of heaven as earth's in him. . . .

THE PREFACE

Of all books extant in all kinds, Homer is the first and best. No one before his, Josephus affirms, nor before him, saith Velleius Paterculus, was there any whom he imitated, nor after him any that could imitate him. And that poesy may be no cause of detraction from all the eminence we give him, Spondanus[16] (preferring it to all arts and sciences) unanswerably argues and proves. For to the glory of God and the singing of his glories (no man dares deny) man was chiefly made. And what art performs this chief end of man with so much excitation* and expression as poesy—Moses, David, Solomon, Job, Isaiah, Jeremiah, etc. chiefly using that to the end abovesaid? And since the excellence of it cannot be obtained by the labour and art of man (as all easily confess it), it must needs be acknowledged a divine infusion.* To prove which, in a word, this distich in my estimation serves something nearly:

    Great Poesy, blind Homer, makes all see
    Thee capable of all arts, none of thee.

[16] In the 'Prolegomena' to his edition, containing an essay '*De origine et dignitate poeticae*' and other pieces, which provide most of Chapman's material (Schoell, p. 172; Nicoll, i. 665).

For out of him, according to our most grave and judicial Plutarch,[17] are all arts deduced,* confirmed or illustrated. It is not therefore the world's vilifying of it that can make it vile, for so we might argue and blaspheme the most incomparably sacred. It is not of the world indeed, but (like truth) hides itself from it. Nor is there any such reality of wisdom's truth in all human excellence as in poets' fictions— that most vulgar and foolish receipt of poetical licence[18] being of all knowing men to be exploded (accepting it as if poets had a tale-telling privilege above others), no artist being so strictly and inextricably confined to all the laws of learning, wisdom and truth as a poet. For were not his fictions composed of the sinews and souls of all those, how could they defy fire, iron, and be combined with eternity? To all sciences, therefore, I must still (with our learned and ingenious Spondanus) prefer it, as having a perpetual commerce with the divine Majesty, embracing and illustrating all his most holy precepts and enjoying continual discourse with his thrice perfect and most comfortable spirit. And as the contemplative life is most worthily and divinely preferred by Plato to the active,[19] as much as the head to the foot, the eye to the hand, reason to sense, the soul to the body, the end itself to all things directed to the end, quiet to motion and eternity to time, so much prefer I divine poesy to all worldly wisdom. . . .

Poesy is the flower of the sun and disdains to open to the eye of a candle. So kings hide their treasures and counsels from the vulgar— *ne evilescant*, saith our Spondanus. We have example sacred enough that true poesy's humility, poverty and contempt are badges of divinity, not vanity. . . . I for my part shall ever esteem it much more manly and sacred in this harmless and pious study to sit till I sink into my grave than shine in your vainglorious bubbles and impieties—all your poor policies, wisdoms and their trappings at no more valuing than a musty nut.[20] And much less I weigh the frontless detractions of some stupid ignorants that, no more knowing me than their own beastly

---

[17] In addition to Plutarch's 'Life' of Homer, the Renaissance knew another essay *De Homero*, which modern scholarship ascribes to Pseudo-Plutarch.

[18] For this widely disseminated concept cf. *De or.* 3. 38. 153, *Ars P.* 9 f., *Inst.* 1. 8. 14, and J. T. Miller, *Poetic License* (New York, 1986).

[19] But Plato celebrates both philosophical activity and involvement in society—this being the whole point of *The Republic*.

[20] Spondanus is the source for most of this paragraph, down to 'musty nut' (*utiosa nuce*): Nicoll, i. 665.

ends, and I ever (to my knowledge) blest from their sight, whisper behind me vilifyings of my translation—out of the French affirming them, when both in French and all other languages but his own our with-all-skill-enriched poet is so poor and unpleasing that no man can discern from whence flowed his so generally-given eminence and admiration. And therefore (by any reasonable creature's conference of my slight comment and conversion)* it will easily appear how I shun them, and whether the original be my rule or not. In which he shall easily see I understand the understandings[21] of all other interpreters and commenters in places of his most depth, importance and rapture. In whose exposition and illustration if I abhor from the sense that others wrest and rack out of him, let my best detractor examine how the Greek word warrants me. . . .

If I fail in something, let my full performance in other some restore me—haste spurring me on with other necessities. For as at my conclusion I protest, so here at my entrance, less than fifteen weeks was the time in which all the last twelve books were entirely new translated—no conference had with any one living in all the novelties I presume I have found. Only some one or two places I have showed to my worthy and most learned friend, Master Harriot,[22] for his censure how much mine own weighed: whose judgement and knowledge in all kinds I know to be incomparable and bottomless—yea, to be admired as much as his most blameless life and the right sacred expense of his time is to be honoured and reverenced. Which affirmation of his clear unmatchedness in all manner of learning I make in contempt of that nasty objection often thrust upon me:—that he that will judge must know more than he of whom he judgeth, for so a man should know neither God nor himself. Another right learned, honest and entirely loved friend of mine, Master Robert Hughes,[23] I must needs put into my confessed conference touching Homer, though very little more than that I had with Master Harriot. Which two, I protest, are all, and preferred to all. Nor charge I their authorities with any allowance* of my general labour, but only of those one

---

[21] Nicoll judges that 'Chapman has here been misled by his prevailing love of puns' into asserting not merely that he knows others' interpretations of Homer, but that his own are superior.

[22] Thomas Harriot (1560–1621), distinguished linguist, mathematician, and astronomer. Chapman had addressed verses to him in *Achilles Shield*.

[23] Evidently belonging to the Harriot circle, and one of Chapman's long-standing friends.

or two places which for instances of my innovation, and how it showed to them, I imparted. If any tax* me for too much periphrasis or circumlocution in some places, let them read Laurentius Valla and Eobanus Hessus, who either use such shortness as cometh nothing home to Homer, or, where they shun that fault, are ten parts more paraphrastical than I.[24] . . .

And this one example I thought necessary to insert here to show my detractors that they have no reason to vilify my circumlocution sometimes, when their most approved Grecians, Homer's interpreters, generally hold him fit to be so converted. Yet how much I differ, and with what authority, let my impartial and judicial reader judge— always conceiving how pedantical and absurd an affectation it is in the interpretation of any author (much more of Homer) to turn him word for word, when (according to Horace[25] and other best lawgivers to translators) it is the part of every knowing and judicial* interpreter not to follow the number and order of words but the material things themselves, and sentences to weigh diligently, and to clothe and adorn them with words and such a style and form of oration as are most apt for the language into which they are converted. If I have not turned him in any place falsely (as all other his interpreters have in many and most of his chief places); if I have not left behind me any of his sentence,* elegancy, height, intention and invention; if in some few places (especially in my first edition, being done so long since and following the common tract)* I be something paraphrastical and faulty—is it justice in that poor fault (if they will needs have it so) to drown all the rest of my labour? . . .

If any further edition of these my silly* endeavours shall chance, I will mend what is amiss (God assisting me) and amplify my harsh comment to Homer's far more right and mine own earnest and ingenious love of him. . . . And so little I will respect malignity and so much encourage myself with mine own known strength, and what I find within me of comfort and confirmance (examining myself throughout with a far more jealous* and severe eye than my greatest enemy, imitating this:

---

[24] Chapman now quotes examples of other translations which also fail to render Homer line for line.—However, in his case (as Schoell demonstrated) the English text often differs substantially from the Greek, because Chapman versified material from the Latin editor's glosses and footnotes as if it were Homeric poetry.

[25] *Ars P.* 133–4, the oft-quoted lines: 'Nec verbum verbo curabis reddere | fidus interpres' ('. . . do not seek to render word for word as a slavish translator'.)

Judex ipse sui totum se explorat ad unguem, etc.)[26]—

that after these *Iliads* I will (God lending me life and any meanest means) with more labour than I have lost here and all unchecked alacrity dive through his *Odysses*. . . .

THE ODYSSEY

[DEDICATION TO ROBERT CARR, EARL OF SOMERSET][27]

. . . And that your Lordship may in his face take view of his mind, the first word of his *Iliads* is *menin*, wrath; the first word of his *Odysses*, *andra*, man: contracting in either word his each work's proposition.* In one, predominant perturbation: in the other, over-ruling wisdom; in one, the body's fervour* and fashion* of outward fortitude, to all possible height of heroical action: in the other, the mind's inward, constant, and unconquered empire, unbroken, unaltered with any most insolent and tyrannous infliction. To many most sovereign praises is this poem entitled, but to that grace in chief which sets on the crown both of poets and orators, *to ta mikra megalos, kai ta koina kainos*:[28] that is, *Parva magnè dicere; pervulgata novè, ieiuna plenè*: 'to speak things little, greatly; things common, rarely; things barren and empty, fruitfully and fully'.

The return of a man into his country is his whole scope and object; which in itself, your Lordship may well say, is jejune* and fruitless enough, affording nothing feastful, nothing magnificent. And yet even this doth the divine inspiration render vast, illustrious, and of miraculous composure.* And for this (my Lord) is this poem

---

[26] Ps.-Virgil, *De institutione viri boni* 3: 'as a judge he examines himself completely, down to the fingernails'.

[27] Robert Carr, Earl of Somerset (*c.*1592–1645), a favourite of King James I from 1603 to 1614 (when he was supplanted by George Villiers, afterwards Duke of Buckingham), experienced a dramatic rise to power. Having been a page on the King's arrival in England, 1603, he was knighted in 1607, and created successively Viscount Rochester (1611), private secretary to the King (1612), Earl of Somerset (1613), and Lord Chamberlain (1614). But his involvement with his wife in the imprisonment and poisoning of Sir Thomas Overbury (1613) led to his disgrace, imprisonment in the Tower for six years, and an inglorious end to his career.

[28] Cf. Plato, *Phdr.* 267a, Socrates' ironic praise of the rhetoricians Tisias and Gorgias, 'who could make trifles seem important and important points trifles [by the force of their language]'; Chapman, ignoring the irony (like most Renaissance readers of Plato), adds both a Latin and an English version.

preferred to his *Iliads*, for therein much magnificence, both of person and action, gives great aid to his industry, but in this are these helps exceeding sparing, or nothing; and yet is the structure so elaborate and pompous* that the poor plain groundwork (considered together) may seem the naturally rich womb to it, and produce* it needfully.

Much wondered at therefore, is the censure of Dionysius Longinus[29] (a man otherwise affirmed grave, and of elegant judgement), comparing Homer in his *Iliads* to the sun rising, in his *Odysses* to his descent or setting, or to the ocean robbed of his aesture,* many tributary floods and rivers of excellent ornament withheld from their observance—when this his work so far exceeds the ocean, with all his court and concourse, that all his sea is only a serviceable stream to it! Nor can it be compared to any one power to be named in nature, being an entirely well-sorted and digested confluence of all, where the most solid and grave is made as nimble and fluent as the most airy and fiery, the nimble and fluent as firm and well bounded as the most grave and solid. And (taking all together) of so tender impression,* and of such command to the voice of the Muse that they knock heaven with her breath, and discover their foundations as low as hell. Nor is this all-comprising poesy fantastic, or mere fictive, but the most material and doctrinal illations* of truth, both for all manly information of manners in the young, all prescription of justice, and even Christian piety in the most grave and high-governed. To illustrate both which, in both kinds, with all height of expression, the poet creates both a body and a soul in them. Wherein, if the body (being the letter or history)[30] seems fictive, and beyond possibility to bring into act, the sense, then, and allegory (which is the soul) is to be sought; which intends* a more eminent expressure of virtue for her loveliness, and of vice for her ugliness, in their several* effects, going beyond the life, than any art within life can possibly delineate.

Why, then, is fiction to this end so hateful to our true ignorants? Or why should a poor chronicler of a Lord Mayor's naked truth

---

[29] *On Sublimity*, ch. 11: 'Homer in the *Odyssey* may be compared to the setting sun: the size remains without the force . . . It is as though the ocean were withdrawing into itself, and flowing quietly in its own bed' (*ALC*, p. 471).

[30] That is, the narrative or story.

(that peradventure will last his year) include* more worth with our
modern wizards than Homer for his naked Ulysses, clad in eternal
fiction? But this proser Dionysius, and the rest of these grave and
reputatively learned (that dare undertake for their gravities the
headstrong censure of all things, and challenge the understanding of
these toys* in their childhoods, when even these childish vanities
retain deep and most necessary learning enough in them to make them
children in their ages, and teach them while they live) are not in these
absolutely divine infusions* allowed either voice or relish. For, *qui
poeticas ad fores accedit* etc. (says the Divine Philosopher), he that
knocks at the gates of the Muses *sine Musarum furore*[31] is neither to
be admitted entry nor a touch* at their thresholds, his opinion of entry
ridiculous, and his presumption impious. Nor must poets themselves
(might I a little insist on these contempts, not tempting too far your
Lordship's Ulyssean patience) presume to these doors without the
truly genuine and peculiar* induction,* there being in poesy a twofold
rapture (or alienation of soul, as the abovesaid teacher terms it): one,
insania, a disease of the mind and a mere madness, by which the
infected is thrust beneath all the degrees of humanity: *et ex homine,
Brutum quodammodo redditur*[32] (for which, poor poesy, in this diseased
and impostorous age, is so barbarously vilified). The other is *divinus
furor*, by which the sound and divinely healthful *supra hominis naturam
eregitur, et in Deum transit.*[33] One a perfection directly infused from
God; the other an infection obliquely and degenerately proceeding
from man.

Of the divine fury (my Lord) your Homer hath ever been both first
and last instance, being pronounced absolutely, *ton sophōtaton, kai ton
theiōtaton poiētēn;*[34] the most wise and most divine poet. Against

---

[31] 'Who comes to the portals of poetry . . . without the inspiration of the Muses' (tr.
Hardison); from the commentary on *Ion* by Marsilio Ficino (1433–99), Chapman's 'Divine
Philosopher' in his *Opera Omnia Divini Platonis* (1484). The term 'alienation of soul' (*alien-
atio mentis*), in Ficino's *argumentum*, describes an ecstatic process by which the intuitive
intelligence is liberated from the body and the other faculties (reason, sense, imagination),
ascending or returning to heaven. In this divine alienation (utterly different from the insan-
ity of pathological melancholics, who are reduced to the level of brutes), man 'is lifted above
his human nature, and passes over to or into God'.

[32] 'A brute is somehow made from a man' (tr. Hardison); from the *Ion* commentary.

[33] '. . . Is elevated above the nature of man and becomes God-like'; ibid.

[34] *Ion* 503b (slightly garbled): '[many excellent poets . . .] Homer, the wisest [Plato: 'best']
and most divine of all'.

whom, whosoever shall open his profane mouth may worthily receive answer, with this of his divine defender[35] (Empedocles, Heraclitus, Protagoras, Epicharmus, etc. being of Homer's part) *tis oun*,[36] 'who against such an army, and the general Homer, dares attempt the assault, but he must be reputed ridiculous?' And yet against this host, and this invincible commander, shall we have every *Besogne** and fool a leader.

Holding then in eternal contempt (my Lord) those short-lived bubbles, eternise your virtue and judgement with the Grecian monarch, esteeming not as the least of your New-year's presents

Homer (three thousand years dead) now reviv'd,
Even from that dull death that in life he liv'd,
When none conceited him, none understood
That so much life, in so much death as blood
Conveys about it, could mix. But when death   5
Drunk up the bloody mist that human breath
Pour'd round about him (poverty and spite
Thick'ning the hapless vapour), then truth's light
Glimmer'd about his poem, the pinch'd soul
(Amidst the mysteries it did enroll)   10
Brake powerfully abroad. And as we see
The sun all hid in clouds at length got free,
Through some forc'd covert, over all the ways
Near and beneath him, shoots his vented* rays
Far off, and sticks them in some little glade,   15
All woods, fields, rivers, left besides in shade:
So your Apollo, from that world of light,
Closed in his poem's body, shot to sight
Some few forced beams, which near him were not seen
(As in his life or country), fate and spleen   20
Clouding their radiance; which when death had clear'd
To far-off regions his free beams appear'd,
In which all stood and wondered, striving which
His birth and rapture should in right enrich.

---

[35] Plato, identified with Ion.
[36] 'Whosoever', the first word of the following (untraced) quotation, which Chapman translates.

Twelve Labours of your Thespian[37] Hercules,   25
I now present your Lordship; do but please
To lend life means till th'other twelve receive
Equal achievement . . .

---

[37] Chapman's ironic self-description, having been a 'tragedian' for many years before dedicating himself to translations.

28

Ben Jonson,
The faults of contemporary drama (1612)

BEN JONSON. See the headnote above, p. 454.

TEXT. From *Every Man In His Humour*, the revised (or 'English') version, as printed in the first Folio edition of Jonson's *Works* (1616). The first version of this comedy, in which the characters have Italian names, was performed by the Lord Chamberlain's Men in 1598, and printed as a separate Quarto in 1601. The play is known to have been revived at court in February 1605 by the King's Men (as the company was named after King James I's accession), and the wholesale rewriting of it may have taken place on that occasion; if not, then at some time between 1607 and 1612. The Prologue appears for the first time in the Folio, and some scholars have assigned it to the 1605 revision; but Gabriele Jackson, in her edition of the play for the Yale Ben Jonson (New Haven and London, 1969) argues persuasively (pp. 186 ff., 221 ff.) for a dating to 1612. In editing this text I have benefited from her edition and from C. H. Herford, P. and E. Simpson (eds.), *Ben Jonson*, 11 vols. (Oxford, 1925–52). The play is dedicated to William Camden, Jonson's master at Westminster School (see pp. 454, 534).

> Though need make many poets, and some such
> As art and nature have not better'd much;
> Yet ours, for want, hath not so loved the stage
> As he dare serve th'ill customs of the age:[1]
> Or purchase your delight at such a rate   5
> As, for it, he himself must justly hate.

---

[1] For similar criticisms of the 'ill customs' and improbabilities of popular drama (throughout Europe) cf. Whetstone, pp. 173–4, and Sidney, pp. 381–2. G. B. Jackson points out that Jonson's wording here is remarkably close to Thomas Shelton's translation of Cervantes' *Don Quixote*, printed in 1611–12 by William Stansby (who was printing Jonson's Folio at that time). In part 4, ch. 21, the village Canon attacks modern (Spanish) comedies: 'what greater absurdity can be in such a subject than to see a child come out in the first scene of the first act in his swaddling clouts, and issue in the second already grown a man, yea, a bearded man?' The Canon also attacks the authors of 'modern comedies', these 'notorious fopperies', for claiming that 'they must be such as they be for to please the people's humours, . . . therefore it is better for them to gain good money and means by many, than bare opinion or applause by a few'. Despising the reduction of comedy to 'a vendible merchandise', the Canon invokes Cicero's famous definition (as recorded by Donatus): 'the comedy, as Tully affirms, ought to be a mirror of men's life, a pattern of manners, and an image of truth'.

To make a child, now swaddled, to proceed
Man, and then shoot up, in one beard, and weed
Past threescore years: or, with three rusty swords,
And help of some few foot-and-half-foot words,   10
Fight over York and Lancaster's long wars:[2]
And in the tiring-house[3] bring wounds to scars.
He rather prays, you will be pleas'd to see
One such, today, as other plays should be.
Where neither Chorus wafts you o'er the seas;[4]   15
Nor creaking throne[5] comes down, the boys to please;
Nor nimble squib is seen, to make afear'd
The gentlewomen; nor roll'd bullet heard
To say, it thunders; nor tempestuous drum
Rumbles,[6] to tell you when the storm doth come,   20
But deeds, and language, such as men do use:
And persons, such as comedy would choose
When she would show an image of the times,
And sport with human follies, not with crimes.[7]
Except we make 'em such by loving still   25
Our popular errors, when we know they're ill.
I mean such errors, as you'll all confess
By laughing at them, they deserve no less:
Which when you heartily do, there's hope left then,
You, that have so grac'd monsters,[8] may like men.   30

[2] Jonson mocks the English history plays, including Shakespeare's cycle on the Wars of the Roses, acted between 1592 and 1600. Sidney had ridiculed the use of a few actors to represent whole armies (p. 381), as had Shakespeare in *Henry V* (4 Chorus 50). The 'foot-and-half-foot *words*' renders Horace's *ampullas et sesquipedalia verba* (*Ars P.* 139), which Jonson translated as 'Their bombard-phrase, and foote-and-halfe-foot words'. Accusations of bombast in Elizabethan drama were common, and easily made.

[3] The 'tiring [or 'attiring'] house' was the actors' dressing room.

[4] The Chorus (or *nuntius*) was a single character, one of whose functions was to alert the audience to major changes of scene, as in Heywood's *The Four Prentises of London* (*c.*1594), where the Chorus 'wafts' the audience to France, Italy, and Ireland, or in *Henry V*, where they are shuttled to and fro across the Channel.

[5] The Elizabethan public theatre sometimes used a throne descending from 'the heavens' (the roof over the stage, painted with the stars), to represent the descent of goddesses or angels, as in Act 4 of the *Tempest*, when 'Juno descends'.

[6] Jonson mocks the simple but effective off-stage sound-effects in Elizabethan drama: the 'squib' or firework used to represent thunder and lightning; the rolling of a cannonball over (an upper?) floor, or the use of a bass drum to imitate a storm.

[7] Blending definitions of comedy by Aristotle and Cicero: cf. Sidney's *Defence*, p. 362 n. 107; and p. 383 n. 194.

[8] Possibly a reference to Caliban in *The Tempest* (acted 1612); however, the opposition men/monster is basic to much polemical literature on the side of 'nature'.

29

William Drummond,
Ben Jonson's literary table-talk (1619)

WILLIAM DRUMMOND OF HAWTHORNDEN (1585–1649), Scottish
poet, educated at the High School and University of Edinbugh, studied
law at Bourges and Paris. On his father's death in 1610 became laird of
Hawthornden, thereafter devoting himself to poetry and mechanical experiments. His works include a lament on the death of Prince Henry, *Tears on the
Death of Moeliades* (1613); *Poems* (1614); *Forth Feasting* (1617); and *Flowers of
Sion* (1623). He invited Jonson to visit him in 1618–19: Jonson (who weighed
about 20 stone) walked from London to Scotland.

TEXT. First published in an abridged form in 1711, and in full as *Ben Ion-
soniana: informations by Ben Jonson to W. D. when he came to Scotland upon
foot, 1619. Certain informations and manners of Ben Jonson's to W. Drummond*
(1833). It is difficult to know how seriously to take some of Jonson's *obiter
dicta*, since Drummond (like Boswell to Dr Johnson) may have mischievously
provoked him by introducing topics calculated to irritate. Some of his personal judgements on contemporary poets reveal an animus or resentment
which contradicts Jonson's tributes to them elsewhere. I have chosen rather
those pronouncements which contain some literary judgement or evaluation.

In annotating these selections I have benefited from C. H. Herford, P. and
E. Simpson (eds.), *Ben Jonson*, 11 vols. (Oxford, 1925–1952), here abbre-
viated as *HS*; from George Parfitt (ed.), *Ben Jonson: The Complete Poems*
(Harmondsworth, Middx., 1975, 1980); and from E. W. Tayler (ed.),
Literary Criticism of Seventeenth-Century England (New York, 1967).

That he had an intention to perfect* an epic poem entitled *Herologia*,
of the worthies of his country, roused by fame, and was to dedicate it
to his country; it is all in couplets, for he detesteth all other rhymes.
Said he had written a discourse of poesy both against Campion and
Daniel,[1] especially this last, where he proves couplets to be the bravest*
sort of verses, especially when they are broken, like hexameters;[2] and

---

[1] See Campion (p. 428), Daniel (p. 441). Jonson's treatise is not extant, but see his brilliant 'Fit of Rhyme against Rhyme', p. 454.
[2] That is, 'broken' by having a pronounced caesura, so that the sense runs over the
line/rhyme ending, making some lines seem unusually long. This produces the character-
istically asymmetrical movement of Jonson's verse.

that cross-rhymes and stanzas (because the purpose* would lead him beyond eight lines to conclude) were all forced.*

He recommended to my reading Quintilian (who—he said—would tell me all the faults of my verses as if he had lived with me) and Horace; Plinius secundus' *Epistles*;[3] Tacitus, Juvenal, Martial; whose epigram '*Vitam quae faciunt beatiorem*'[4] etc., he hath translated.

His censure of the English poets was this, that Sidney did not keep a decorum[5] in making everyone speak as well as himself.

Spenser's stanzas pleased him not, nor his matter, the meaning of which allegory he had delivered in papers to Sir Walter Raleigh.[6] . . .

That Michael Drayton's *Poly-Olbion*[7] (if he had performed what he promised to write, the deeds of all the worthies) had been excellent; his long verses pleased him not.

That Sylvester's translation of Du Bartas was not well done, and that he wrote his verses before it, ere he understood to confer.* Nor that of Fairfax[8] his.

That the translations of Homer and Virgil in long Alexandrines[9] were but prose.

That John Harington's Ariosto, under all translations, was the worst. That when Sir John Harington desired him to tell the truth of

---

[3] Pliny the Younger (AD *c*.61–*c*.112), studied rhetoric under Quintilian, practised as a lawyer, and advanced from senator to consul. He published nine books of literary letters, carefully composed on rhetorical principles, which were models for later writers.

[4] *Epigrams* 10. 47, which Jonson translated, beginning 'The things that make the happier life, are these' (ed. Parfitt, pp. 352–3).

[5] Jonson makes the same criticism of Guarini (p. 530), and Sidney, Guarini, and Lucan (p. 535). The heroic characters in the *Arcadia* speak in a similar high style, but properly diversified according to context; the rustic characters, however, speak in a distinctly lower style, so that Jonson's later criticism of Dametas is hardly just.

[6] See p. 297. For a different verdict on Spenser see *Timber*, p. 573.

[7] Drayton's *Poly-olbion. Or a Chorographicall Description of Tracts, Rivers, Mountaines, Forests, and other Parts of this renowned Isle of Great Britaine, With intermixture of the most Remarquable Stories, Antiquities, Wonders, Rarityes, Pleasures, and Commodities of the same: digested in a Poem*, appeared in 1612, with notes by John Selden; part 2 in 1622. Early references to the poem by Drayton and others give no support to Jonson's account of its intended subject.

[8] Joshua Sylvester published his translation of Guillamme Du Bartas's *Semaine ou Creation du Monde* in 1605, for which Jonson wrote a laudatory poem (*Epigrams* 132). Now he admits that he is ignorant of French, and was unqualified to judge the translation. Fairfax's version of Tasso's *Gerusalemme Liberata*, *Godfrey of Bulloigne*, appeared in 1600.

[9] Jonson refers to Chapman's *Iliad* (see p. 512), and to its predecessors in using fourteeners: Thomas Phaer's version of the *Aeneid* (bks. 1–9, 1562), completed by Thomas Twyne in 1584; and Arthur Hall's *Ten Books of Homer's Iliades* (1581).

his epigrams, he answered him, that he loved not the truth, for they were narrations, and not epigrams.[10]

That Warner, since the king's coming to England, had marred all his *Albion's England*.[11]

That Donne's *Anniversary* was profane and full of blasphemies. That he told Mr Donne, if it had been written of the Virgin Mary it had been something; to which he answered, that he described the idea* of a woman,[12] and not as she was.

That Donne, for not keeping of accent,[13] deserved hanging. . . .

That Shakespeare wanted art.[14] . . .

His judgement of stranger poets was: that he thought not Bartas a poet but a verser,[15] because he wrote not fiction.

He cursed Petrarch for redacting verses to sonnets, which he said were alike that tyrant's bed,[16] where some who were too short were racked, others too long cut short.

That Guarini, in his *Pastor Fido*,[17] kept not decorum, in making shepherds speak as well as himself could.

---

[10] For Harington's *Orlando Furioso* see p. 302 and notes. Harington published three collections of *Epigrams* (1613; 1615; 1618), which do indeed lack the compression proper to that genre. See Jonson's more explicit criticism, p. 534.

[11] Periodically enlarged, William Warner's poem first appeared in 1586; the 4th edn. (1612) covered the early part of James I's reign.

[12] Donne's two 'Anniversaries', *An Anatomy of the World* (1611) and *The Progress of the Soule* (1612), were commissioned to commemorate the death of 15-year-old Elizabeth Drury, whom Donne had never met. He defended himself with the argument that he 'took such a person [*persona*], as might be capable of all I could say'.

[13] Donne's break with the conventions of metrical regularity was a creative innovation which other contemporaries admired: cf. Carew, p. 554.

[14] Cf. Ovid, *Am.* 1. 15. 20 (a roll-call of poets): 'Ennius arte carens' ('Ennius lacks art'). This negative judgement on Shakespeare will be revised in the poem written for the 1623 Folio (p. 539). In the Induction to *Bartholomew Fair* (1614) Jonson displayed his canons of literary correctness, announcing that he had 'observ'd a special decorum' in rendering the London scene, not including such features of romance as had been recently found in Shakespeare's late plays: 'If there be never a servant-monster i' the Fair who can help it, he says; nor a nest of antiques? He is loth to make Nature afraid in his plays, like those that beget tales, tempests, and such like drolleries, to mix his head with other men's heels . . .'.

[15] Quintilian described a contemporary as 'a better versifier than poet' (10. 1. 89). For the view that fiction, not verse, is the basic distinguishing mark of poetry cf. Aristotle, *Poet.* 9. 1451[b]27 ff., Elyot, p. 64, and Sidney, p. 347, 367.

[16] Procrustes, the legendary brigand of Eleusis, an enemy of Theseus, forced his victims to lie down on one of two beds, either stretching or amputating them to fit. For a similar comment on the constrictions of rhyme cf. Campion, p. 432. The image of Procrustes' bed for the sonnet derives from Stefano Guazzo and Claudio Tolomei (*HS* i. 155).

[17] Guarini's *Pastor Fido* (1585), an influential pastoral tragicomedy: cf. Fletcher, p. 502.

That Lucan,[18] taken in parts, was good, divided; read altogether, merited not the name of a poet. . . .

He esteemeth Donne the first poet in the world, in some things: his verses of the lost chain he hath by heart; and that passage of 'The Calm',[19] that dust and feathers do not stir, all was so quiet. Affirmeth Donne to have written all his best pieces ere he was twenty-five years old.

Sir Henry Wotton's verses of a happy life[20] he hath by heart, and a piece of Chapman's translation of the thirteen of the *Iliad*, which he thinketh well done.

That Donne said to him he wrote that epitaph on Prince Henry, 'Look to me, faith', to match Sir Ed. Herbert[21] in obscureness.

He hath by heart some verses of Spenser's *Calendar*,[22] about wine, between Colin and Percy.

The conceit of Donne's 'Transformation' or '*metempsychosis*',[23] was, that he sought the soul of that apple which Eva pulled, and thereafter made it the soul of a bitch, then of a she wolf, and so of a woman. His general purpose was to have brought in all the bodies of the heretics from the soul of Cain, and at last left it in the body of Calvin. Of this he never wrote but one sheet, and now, since he was made doctor, repenteth highly, and seeketh to destroy all his poems.

That Petronius, Plinius secundus, Tacitus, spoke best Latin; that Quintilian's 6, 7, 8 books[24] were not only to be read, but altogether

---

[18] M. Annaeus Lucanus (AD 39–65), whose unfinished epic *De Bello Civili* (sometimes known as the *Pharsalia*) was much admired for its pathos, sensationalism, and rhetorical high style. Quintilian described him as 'fiery and passionate and remarkable for the grandeur of his general reflexions, but . . . more suitable for imitation by the orator than by the poet' (*Inst.* 10. 1. 90). Jonson translated a speech from bk. 8 (ll. 484–95: ed. Parfitt, p. 353).

[19] Cf. *Elegy* 11, 'The Bracelet. Upon the loss of his Mistress' Chain, for which he made satisfaction', in *The Complete English Poems of John Donne*, ed. A. J. Smith (Harmondsworth, Middx., 1971), p. 251; and the verse-letter 'The Calm', ibid. p. 199.

[20] Sir Henry Wotton (1568–1639), poet and diplomat: for this poem, 'How happy is he born and taught', cf. *HS* i. 157.

[21] Smith edn., p. 253; Herbert's 'Elegy for the prince' (1612) was not published until 1665.

[22] Cf. p. 188 (for 'Colin' read 'Cuddy').

[23] This obscure work, *The Progress of the Soul*, dated 16 Aug. 1601, was first published in the posthumous edition of Donne's *Poems*, 1633 (*HS* i. 158 and ed. Smith, pp. 176, 502). Donne became DD in 1615, and other sources record his remorse for his youthful love poetry.

[24] But it is unlikely that anyone would recommend bk. 8 of the *Institutes*, which discusses style and the tropes, without adding bk. 9, an extensive discussion of the figures of thought and speech. The reference is surely mistaken.

digested. Juvenal, Persius, Horace, Martial, for delight; and so was Pindar. For health Hippocrates.[25] . . .

For a heroic poem, he said, there was no such ground as King Arthur's fiction; and that Sir P. Sidney had an intention to have transformed all his *Arcadia* to the stories of King Arthur.[26]

Particulars of the actions of other poets, and apophthegms. . . .

That in that paper Sir W. Raleigh had of the allegories of his *Faerie Queene*, by the blatant beast the puritans were understood; by the false Duessa[27] the Queen of Scots.

That Southwell[28] was hanged; yet so he had written that piece of his 'The burning babe', he would have been content to destroy many of his. . . .

That Donne himself, for not being understood, would perish.

That Sir W. Raleigh esteemed more of fame than conscience.

The best wits of England were employed for making of his *History*. Ben himself had written a piece to him of the Punic War, which he altered and set in his book. Sir W. hath written the life of Queen Elizabeth,[29] of which there is copies extant.

Sir P. Sidney had translated some of the Psalms, which went abroad under the name of the Countess of Pembroke.[30] . . .

Shakespeare, in a play, brought in a number of men saying they had suffered shipwreck in Bohemia, where there is no sea near[31] by some 100 miles. . . .

The Countess of Rutland was nothing inferior to her father, Sir P. Sidney, in poesy.[32] . . .

---

[25] Hippocrates (fl. 460 BC), the greatest medical writer of antiquity.

[26] There seems to be no other evidence for this assertion.

[27] This is evidently a different document to the one printed above, p. 297. Whatever its authority, these identifications are too narrowly historical. The Blatant Beast embodies calumny; Duessa represents both falsehood and the Catholic church, seen as the Whore of Babylon or Antichrist.

[28] See p. 395.

[29] Ralegh's *History of the World* (1614)—for which Jonson wrote a prefatory poem, 'The Mind of the Frontispiece to a Book' (*Underwoods* 24; ed. Parfitt, p. 161)—certainly included contributions from other scholars, although they are unidentified (*HS* i. 162). Ralegh's Life of Elizabeth has not survived.

[30] Sidney translated Psalms 1–43, his sister the remainder, as other contemporaries (including Donne) knew. They were not published until 1823.

[31] In Shakespeare's source, Greene's *Pandosto*, the King of Sicily 'provided a navie of ships, and sayled into Bohemia'. Cf. *The Winter's Tale* 3. 3. 1 f., where Antigonus' ship lands on the 'deserts of Bohemie', that is, a deserted region on the coast.

[32] Jonson paid her similar tributes in *Epigrams* 89 (ed. Parfitt, p. 59) and *Forest* 12 (ibid., pp. 111–13).

Owen is a poor pedantic schoolmaster, sweeping his living from the posteriors of little children, and hath nothing good in him, his epigrams[33] being mere narrations.

Chapman hath translated Musaeus[34] in his verses, like his Homer. . . .

Of his own life, education, birth, actions. His grandfather came from Carlisle, and he thought from Annandale to it; he served Henry VIII, and was a gentleman. His father lost all his estate under Queen Mary, having been cast in prison and forfeited; at last turned minister: so he was a minister's son. He himself was posthumous born, a month after his father's decease, brought up poorly, put to school by a friend (his master Camden);[35] after, taken from it and put to another craft (I think was to be a wright or bricklayer), which he could not endure. Then went he to the Low Countries, but returning soon, he betook himself to his wonted studies. In his service in the Low Countries he had, in the face of both the camps, killed an enemy and taken *opima spolia*[36] from him. And since his coming to England, being appealed to the fields, he had killed his adversary,[37] which had hurt him in the arm, and whose sword was ten inches longer than his; for the which he was imprisoned, and almost at the gallows. Then took he his religion by trust, of a priest who visited him in prison. Thereafter he was twelve years a papist.

He was Master of Arts in both the universities,[38] by their favour, not his study. . . .

He was delated* by Sir James Murray to the king for writing something against the Scots in a play, *Eastward Ho*, and voluntarily imprisoned[39] himself with Chapman and Marston, who had written it amongst them. The report was, that they should then have their

---

[33] John Owen (1560–1622), master of King Henry VIII Grammar School, Warwick, who enjoyed a European reputation for his Latin epigrams; the criticism is unfair.

[34] Chapman translated the *Divine Poem of Musaeus* (1616) into heroic couplets (like his *Odyssey*).

[35] The friend was probably Sir John Hoskyns (see p. 398); for Camden, see p. 534. Jonson left Westminster in 1589.

[36] 'Great spoils'; this may have been in 1596 (*HS* i. 6), after Jonson had finished his apprenticeship as a bricklayer.

[37] Gabriel Spencer, an actor who had been imprisoned with Jonson in 1597 for their involvement in the scandalous satirical comedy, *The Isle of Dogs*. Subsequently Jonson quarrelled with Spencer, and killed him in a duel in Hoxton Fields on 22 Sept. 1598. Jonson escaped the gallows by claiming benefit of clergy.

[38] The degrees were awarded *honoris causa*.

[39] Jonson and Chapman were imprisoned in 1605 for the unauthorized publication of *Eastward Ho!*, which offended King James with its mockery of the Scots (*HS* i. 190–200).

ears cut, and noses. After their delivery he banqueted all his friends; there was Camden, Selden[40] and others. At the midst of the feast his old mother drank to him, and shewed him a paper which she had (if the sentence had taken execution) to have mixed in the prison among his drink, which was full of lusty strong poison; and that she was no churl,* she told, she minded first to have drunk of it herself.

He hath consumed a whole night in lying looking to his great toe, about which he hath seen Tartars and Turks, Romans and Carthaginians, fight in his imagination. . . .

Sundry times he hath devoured his books, once sold them all for necessity. . . .

At his hither coming, Sir Francis Bacon[41] said to him, he loved not to see poesy go on other feet than poetical *dactylus* and *spondaius*. . . .

His opinion of verses.

That he wrote all his first in prose, for so his master Camden,[42] had learned him.

That verses stood by sense without either colours or accent;[43] which yet other times he denied. . . .

A great many epigrams were ill, because they expressed in the end, what should have been understood by what was said, as that of Sir John Davies.

Some loved running verses, *plus mihi complacet*.[44] . . .

---

[40] John Selden (1584–1614), the great jurist and a friend of Jonson, whose *Titles of Honour* (1614) was prefaced with a long celebratory poem by Jonson: *Underwoods* 14 (ed. Parfitt, pp. 147–9). William Camden (1551–1623), antiquarian and historian, became second master of Westminster School in 1575 and headmaster in 1593. Jonson hailed him in *Epigrams* 14 as 'Camden, most reverent head, to whom I owe | All that I am in arts, all that I know' (ed. Parfitt, p. 39).

[41] Jonson's esteem for Bacon is shown in *Timber*, below, pp. 565–7 and 580; also in his poem on Bacon's sixtieth birthday, 1621 (*Underwoods* 51; ed. Parfitt, p. 198). For Bacon's views on classical metres see pp. 464–5.

[42] Virgil largely draughted the *Aeneid* in prose, and versified it piece by piece, not necessarily in chronological sequence, according to the Donatus/Suetonius, *Life* (23). In his epic poem *Africa*, Petrarch versified whole periods of Livy. In *The Staple of News* (1626) Jonson versified passages from his prose masque, *News from the New World Discovered in the Moon* (1620), and from Seneca's *Epistulae morales*, which he had translated into prose in his notebook *Timber* (cf. *HS* i. 168; x. 265, 279, 280). Cf. also North, p. 511.

[43] That is, poetry must be judged purely on its argument, irrespective of style (the 'colours' of rhetoric) or versification ('accent'). Cf. also Gascoigne, pp. 162–3, and North, p. 511.

[44] Jonson opposes the views of Daniel, p. 452, who rejected 'those continual cadences of couplets' and preferred 'sometimes to beguile the ear with a running out and passing over

Of his works. . . .

He hath commented and translated Horace, *Art of Poesy*:[45] it is in dialogue ways; by Criticus he understandeth Dr Donne. The old book that goes about, *The Art of English Poesy*,[46] was done twenty years since, and kept long in writ as a secret.

He had an intention to have made a play like Plautus' *Amphitruo*, but left it off, for that he could never find two so like others[47] that he could persuade the spectators they were one. . . .

Of all his plays he never gained two hundred pounds. . . .

. . . In his *Sejanus* he hath translated a whole oration of Tacitus; the first four books of Tacitus ignorantly done in English. . . .[48]

Lucan, Sidney, Guarini, make every man speak as well as themselves, forgetting decorum; for Dametas sometimes speaks grave sentences.

He dissuaded me from poetry, for that she had beggared him, when he might have been a rich lawyer, physician, or merchant. . . .

He was better versed, and knew more in Greek and Latin, than all the poets in England, and quintessenceth their brains.[49]

Of all styles he loved most to be named honest, and hath of that an hundred letters so naming him. . . .

In his merry humour he was wont to name himself The Poet. . . .[50]

. . . He is a great lover and praiser of himself, a contemner and

the rhyme'. E. W. Tayler notes that 'the quotation from an anonymous epitaph on Lucan, famed for his end-stopped lines, should read: *plus mihi comma placet*, by which Jonson means to register his preference for the end-stopped line as against the excessively loose enjambment of "running verses"' (edn. cit., p. 89).

[45] In the Quarto dedication of *Sejanus* (1605) Jonson announced his intention to 'shortly' publish this preface, together with his translation of Horace's *Art of Poetry*. Jonson had apparently expanded the preface (including a defence of his *Bartholomew Fair*) by 1614, and put it into dialogue form, but it perished in the 1623 fire at his lodgings. His translation of the poem survives in two versions (ed. Parfitt, pp. 354–71).

[46] See p. 190. Internal evidence supports Jonson's claim that Puttenham wrote much of it long before its publication in 1589. Perhaps the 'twenty years since' refers to a composition date of 1569.

[47] Shakespeare, at any rate, was not deterred by this problem; in the *Comedy of Errors* he took over plot-elements from both Plautus' *Amphitruo* and *Menaechmi*, involving two sets of identical twins.

[48] The speech of Cremutius Cordus in *Sejanus* 3. 407–60, is translated from Tacitus, *Annals* 4. 34–5. Jonson dismisses R. Greneway's undistinguished translation, *The annales of Cornelius Tacitus* (1598).

[49] That is, Jonson claims to be unequalled in his knowledge of the Greek and Latin poets, whose work he 'refines or purifies down to its essence': a variation on the traditional metaphors for *imitatio* (see the Introduction, pp. 24–5).

[50] As Aristotle was traditionally called 'the philosopher', and Virgil 'the poet'.

scorner of others, given rather to lose a friend than a jest, jealous of every word and action of those about him (especially after drink, which is one of the elements in which he liveth), a dissembler* of ill parts which reign in him, a bragger of some good that he wanteth;* thinketh nothing well but what either he himself or some of his friends and countrymen hath said or done. He is passionately kind and angry, careless either to gain or keep; vindictive, but, if he be well answered, at himself.

For any religion, as being versed in both.[51] Interpreteth best sayings and deeds often to the worst. Oppressed with fantasy, which hath over-mastered his reason, a general disease in many poets. His inventions are smooth and easy; but above all he excelleth in a translation.

---

[51] Jonson converted to Roman Catholicism in 1598, while imprisoned for the murder of Gabriel Spencer. In 1606 he and his wife were formally charged as recusants, but Jonson only returned to the Protestant faith in 1610.

Ben Jonson,
A tribute to Shakespeare (1623)

BEN JONSON. See headnote above, p. 454.

TEXT. From *Mr. William Shakespeares Comedies, Histories, & Tragedies* (1623), the 'First Folio' edition of Shakespeare's works. Jonson had probably known Shakespeare since the early 1590s, and wrote at least six plays for his theatrical company, the Lord Chamberlain's Men (after 1603 known as the King's Men). Shakespeare acted in Jonson's *Every Man in his Humour* at the Curtain in 1598, and in *Sejanus* at court (or at the Globe) in 1603. For Jonson's many references to Shakespeare see J. Munro *et al.*, *The Shakespere Allusion-Book: A Collection of Allusions to Shakespere from 1591 to 1700*, ed. E. K. Chambers, 2 vols. (Oxford, 1932).

As Anthony Miller has shown ('Jonson's Praise of Shakespeare and Cicero's *De Oratore*, III.vii', *Notes and Queries*, NS 38 (1991), 82–3), in this celebrated memorial poem Jonson's comparison of Shakespeare with rival poets, grouped in threes, imitates a passage in which Cicero's persona, Crassus, introducing a discussion of the sources of rhetorical excellence, points out that within the conventional resources of any art a great variety of work can be produced: 'There is a single art of sculpture, in which eminence was obtained by Myron, Polyclitus and Lysippus, all of whom were different from one another . . . There is a single art and method of painting, and nevertheless there is an extreme dissimilarity between Zeuxis, Aglaphon and Apelles . . . And if this be surprising and nevertheless true in the case of what may be called the silent arts, how much more remarkable it is in oratory and in language . . . This can in the first instance be observed in the case of poetry, poets being the next of kin to orators; what a difference there is between Ennius, Pacuvius and Accius, and in Greek between Aeschylus, Sophocles and Euripides, although all of them win almost equal applause in their various styles of writing' (3. 7. 26–7). Jonson substitutes the name of Seneca for Ennius, and matches the three greatest classical tragic dramatists with the triad Lyly, Kyd, and Marlowe, adding another triad of comic dramatists, Aristophanes, Terence and Plautus. Miller suggests that Jonson's pithy characterizations of writers ('tart Aristophanes, | Neat Terence, witty Plautus') owes something to Cicero's assignment of individual stylistic qualities: 'Isocrates had grace of style [*suavitas*], Lysias precision [*subtilitas*], Hyperides penetration [*acumen*], Aeschines sonorousness [*sonitas*], Demosthenes force [*vis*]. . . . Africanus had weight [*gravitas*], Laelius smoothness [*lenitas*], Galba harshness [*asperitas*], Carbo a kind of flow and melody [*profluens*]: which of these in the old days was not eminent? And yet each eminent in his own particular style' (28). In Jonson's generous version, Shakespeare excels in all styles, and transcends all ages.

TO THE MEMORY OF MY BELOVED, THE AUTHOR MR WILLIAM SHAKESPEARE: AND WHAT HE HATH LEFT US

To draw no envy, Shakespeare, on thy name,
 Am I thus ample* to thy book, and fame:
While I confess thy writings to be such,
 As neither man, nor muse, can praise too much.
'Tis true, and all men's suffrage.* But these ways   5
 Were not the paths I meant unto thy praise:
For seeliest* ignorance on these may light,
 Which, when it sounds at best, but echoes right;[1]
Or blind affection, which doth ne'er advance
 The truth, but gropes, and urgeth all by chance;   10
Or crafty malice might pretend this praise,
 And think to ruin, where it seemed to raise.
These are, as some infamous bawd, or whore,
 Should praise a matron.* What could hurt her more?
But thou art proof against them, and indeed   15
 Above th' ill fortune of them, or the need.

I, therefore, will begin. Soul of the age!
 The applause! delight! the wonder of our stage!
My Shakespeare, rise; I will not lodge thee by
 Chaucer, or Spenser, or bid Beaumont lie   20
A little further, to make thee a room:[2]
 Thou art a monument, without a tomb,
And art alive still, while thy book doth live,
 And we have wits to read, and praise to give.
That I not mix* thee so, my brain excuses;   25
 I mean with great, but disproportion'd* Muses:
For, if I thought my judgement were of years,[3]

[1] 'At the best, uninformed judgements may echo sound ones'.
[2] A reference to the opening lines of the *Elegy on Shakespeare* by William Basse (d. 1653?), a poem known from several manuscript copies (see *The Shakespeare Allusion-Book*, i. 286–9): 'Renowned Spenser, lye a thought more nye | To learned Chaucer, and rare Beaumont lye | A little neerer Spenser, to make roome | For Shakespeare in your threefold, fowerfold Tombe.' Spenser, Chaucer, and Beaumont were all buried in Westminster Abbey. Shakespeare was buried in Stratford; a monument to him was only erected in the Abbey in 1740.
[3] Having a long enough perspective; 'of sufficient historical authority'.

I should commit* thee surely with thy peers,
And tell, how far thou didst our Lyly outshine,
Or sporting Kyd, or Marlowe's[4] mighty line. 30
And though thou hadst small Latin, and less Greek,[5]
From thence to honour thee, I would not seek
For names; but call forth thund'ring Aeschylus,
Euripides, and Sophocles to us,
Pacuvius, Accius,[6] him of Cordoba[7] dead, 35
To life again, to hear thy buskin tread,
And shake a stage. Or, when thy socks[8] were on,
Leave thee alone, for the comparison
Of all, that insolent Greece, or haughty Rome[9]
Sent forth, or since did from their ashes come. 40
Triumph, my Britain, thou hast one to show,
To whom all scenes of Europe homage owe.
He was not of an age, but for all time!
And all the Muses still were in their prime,
When like Apollo he came forth to warm 45
Our ears, or like a Mercury[10] to charm!
Nature herself was proud of his designs,
And joy'd to wear the dressing of his lines!
Which were so richly spun, and woven so fit,

[4] Jonson sets Shakespeare above his predecessors in drama: John Lyly (?1554–1606), writer of court comedies; Thomas Kyd (1558–95—'sporting' puns on Kid, meaning 'little goat', perhaps 'immature'), author of *The Spanish Tragedy* (1587); and Christopher Marlowe (1564–93), praised for his resonant blank verse.

[5] Here 'had'st' is the subjunctive: 'Even if you had had little scholarship'—which was not the case—'I would not seek to honour you by comparing you with classical poets, but would rather call them back to witness how far you excel them': a generous tribute. As J. E. Spingarn pointed out (*Literary Criticism in the Renaissance* (New York, 1924), p. 89n.), Jonson's 'small Latin, and less Greek' echoes Antonio Minturno's phrase, attacking those critics who 'per aventura sanno poco del Latino e pochissimo del Greco', and who affirm that Greek dramas were not divided into acts and scenes, like the Roman: cf. *L'Arte Poetica* (Venice, 1564; Munich, 1971), p. 158.

[6] Two tragic writers in early Rome, linked by Cicero, as above and *Orat.* 11. 36, also by Horace in *Epist.* 2. 1. 56.

[7] Seneca the Younger, born in Corduba, Spain, whose tragedies, both in Latin and in English translation (see above, p. 125), had a great influence on Elizabethan drama.

[8] The 'buskin' (Lat. *cothurnus*) was a thick-soled boot worn by tragic actors in the ancient Athenian theatre, and figuratively used refers to tragedy. The 'sock' (Lat. *soccus*) was a light shoe or slipper worn by comic actors; hence, comedy.

[9] Jonson models this pair of epithets on the elder Seneca's *Controversiae* 1, pref. 6, referring to 'insolenti Graeciae' ('the haughty Greeks'). He reused them to praise Francis Bacon: cf. p. 566.

[10] The Gods of music and enchantment. Mercury charmed Apollo with a lyre, after stealing his oxen.

As, since, she will vouchsafe* no other wit.   50
The merry Greek, tart Aristophanes,
 Neat Terence, witty Plautus, now not please;
But antiquated, and deserted lie
 As they were not of Nature's family.
Yet must I not give Nature all:[11] Thy Art,   55
 My gentle Shakespeare, must enjoy a part.
For though the Poet's matter, Nature be,
 His Art doth give the fashion.[12] And, that he,
Who casts to write a living line, must sweat,
 (Such as thine are) and strike the second heat   60
Upon the Muse's anvil: turn[13] the same,
 (And himself with it) that he thinks to frame;
Or for the laurel, he may gain a scorn,
 For a good Poet's made, as well as born.[14]
And so wert thou. Look how the father's face   65
 Lives in his issue, even so, the race
Of Shakespeare's mind, and manners brightly shines
 In his well turned, and true-filèd lines:
In each of which, he seems to shake a lance,[15]
 As brandish'd at the eyes of ignorance.   70
Sweet swan of Avon! What a sight it were
 To see thee in our waters yet appear,
And make those flights upon the banks of Thames,
 That so did take* Eliza, and our James!
But stay, I see thee in the hemisphere   75
 Advanc'd, and made a constellation[16] there!
Shine forth, thou star of Poets, and with rage,
 Or influence,[17] chide, or cheer the drooping stage;
Which, since thy flight from hence, hath mourned like night,
 And despairs day, but for thy volume's light.   80

[11] A reply to Francis Beaumont, whose poem to Jonson (*c.* 1615) professed to 'let slippe
. . . schollershippe, | And from all Learninge keepe these lines as cleere | As Shakespeares
best are, which . . . showe | How farr sometimes a mortal man may goe | By the dimme
light of Nature': cf. E.K. Chambers, *William Shakespear* (Oxford, 1930), ii. 224–5.
 [12] The poet's skills give his subject-matter 'fashion' or lasting form.
 [13] Jonson was fond of such metaphors describing poetry in terms of a craftsman working
wood or metal: cf. 'well turned' and 'true-filèd' a few lines later, and *Timber*, below, p. 585.
 [14] Challenging the old proverb (see Sidney, p. 379) 'Orator fit, Poeta nascitur' ('The orator
is made; the poet is born'). In Jonson's book the poet, too, is formed by 'art, imitation,
exercise' (*Rhet. Her.* 1. 2. 3). [15] Punning on Shakespeare's name, as he had on Kyd's.
 [16] That of Cygnus, constellation of the swan in the northern hemisphere. Jonson had
used this conceit in a prefatory poem to Hugh Holland in 1603 (*The Complete Poetry of Ben
Jonson*, ed. W. B. Hunter, Jr. (New York, 1963), pp. 341, 374).
 [17] Having elevated Shakespeare to the stars, Jonson now invokes the astrological belief in
their maleficent or beneficent effects.

John Ford,
Elegy on John Fletcher (*c*.1625)

JOHN FORD (1586–*c*.1640) was educated at Exeter College Oxford (leaving after one year), and at the Middle Temple, like other contemporaries turning from the law to drama and poetry (Beaumont, Campion, Sir John Davies, Marston). His earliest dramatic works were in collaboration with Dekker, Webster, and Rowley, achieving independence with *The Lovers' Melancholy* (1629), *'Tis Pity She's a Whore* (1633), and *Perkin Warbeck* (1634). Throughout his career Ford wrote poetry, including a number of memorial poems: both *Fames Memoriall* (1606) and *Funeral Teares* (1606) for the Duke of Devonshire; *A Funerall Elegye* (1612) for William Peter (published as 'by W.S.'); *A Memoriall, Offered to that man of virtue, Sir Thomas Overburie* (1616); and 'On the best of English Poets, Ben. Jonson, Deceased', in *Ionsonus Virbius* (1638). See *The Nondramatic Works of John Ford* (Binghamton, NY, 1991), ed. L. E. Stock, G. D. Monsarrat, J. M. Kennedy, D. Danielson; and, for the *Funerall Elegye* ascription, Brian Vickers, *Counterfeiting Shakespeare: The Politics of Attribution* (Cambridge University Press, forthcoming).

TEXT. From MS S4975 M1, in the William Andrews Clark Memorial Library, Los Angeles. In this miscellany of poetry, the poem is subscribed 'John Ford'. This text was discovered and added to the Ford canon by the late Jeremy Maule, in an unpublished essay. I have used his transcription, incorporating three suggested emendations, and modernizing spelling and punctuation; my single editorial intervention is at l. 104, reading 'o'er' for 'are'.

TO THE MEMORY OF THE LATE EXCELLENT POET
JOHN FLETCHER

> Here needs no marble to adorn this hearse,[1]
> Nor art of heralds, nor a flatt'ring verse:
> Nor mourners in their black, nor useless tears,
> Nor empty praises, nor the common fears
> Which greatness leaves behind it, to advance   5

---

[1] Cf. Ford's 'commendation' of Barnabe Barnes, *Four Bookes of Offices* (1606), beginning: 'Not to adorne, but to commend this Frame, . . . | Nor to commend, for this commends the same' (*Non-Dramatic Works*, p. 334).

The memory of waste and ignorance.
For thy deserts, while yet thou liv'st, foreseeing
This custom, blotted it quite out from being.
Instead of which thou didst prepare a room
For the virgins, who about thy tomb 10
Circling their wreaths of laurel, whilst the throng
Of the profane kept out, in sacred song
Culled from thine own strains—for but thine own,
All others wanted grace in thine alone;
The Muses wept and sung, which notes must be 15
Anthems from them, though elegies on thee.
Yet I'll not drop a tear, nor force a passion;
I will not coin a sigh, nor court the fashion
Of customary friendship, to betray
Thy loss to common errors. Every day, 20
In many months have many hundreds died,
And with them all they could call theirs, beside
The poor remembrance of their names, as soon
Forgotten as their funeral rites are done.
Nor didst thou find a nearer way to die 25
Than they, for as they do so dost thou lie
Confin'd in dust. The difference is, their graves
Are onely stuck'd with cypress' dreadful leaves,
Shadows of long oblivion, whilst from thine
Fresh laurel springs,[2] that everflow'ring sign 30
Of noble knowledge, by whose heavenly flame
The scholar grows immortal in her name.
    Hence comes it that I neither dare nor can
Mourn thy exchange of life: for being man
Thou couldst not shun thy end. We who survive 35
Are dead, not thou, for we are dead, alive,[3]
In all the faculties that dress the mind

---

[2] Cf. Ford's elegy for Jonson, ll. 9–10: '*Lawrell* and *Cypresse* else, had growne together, | And *withered* without *Memory* to either' (*Nondramatic Works*, p. 357).

[3] Ford often used this conceit, opposing life and death. Cf. *Funerall Elegye* 494 f.: 'his singlenesse was such. | So that he dyes but once, but doubly lives'; and 536 ff: 'Hee dy'de in life, yet in his death he lives'; and on Overbury, beginning: 'Once dead and twice alive; Death could not frame | A death, whose sting could kil him in his fame. | He might have liv'd, had not the life which gave | Life to his life, betraid him to his grave' (*Nondramatic Works*, p. 344). In his prose work *A Line of Life* (1620), Ford wrote that men who 'endeavour to live well, live with an expectation of death, and when they dye, dye to live, and live for ever' (ibid. 303).

Or inward senses trim, and so declined,
So miserable ignorant, so weak,
That we can boast no language now to speak. 40
The British, Roman, Danish, Saxon, French
Had patch'd an English barbarism;[4] to blanch*
Which gross confusion every age applied
Some help, by which our tongue was beautified,
Not perfited; till those high powers, by whom 45
England advanced to glory—like old Rome,[5]
Mighty in power and unmoved in station,
Could justly call her people now a nation—
Lent her a language, copious and refined,
By the grand master in his art designed 50
To this eternal fame, that from his pen
Men formed a language, and that language men.
A sacred pen, from whose wit-flowing strain
Rarely or never dropped a line in vain.
Whence to his fate this honour doth befall, 55
That who of his likes any, must like all;
So like, and so impartial to approve,
As not to dare to censure but to love;
Admire if imitation be allowed,
Of only imitation to be proud. 60
    For when his chaster Muse vouchsafes to sing
Sweet tunes of modest subjects, the wished spring
Presents no choristers whose pleasing throats
Could warble music in more serene notes
Than the quick marriage of his rich conceits, 65
Equalled by art to prove theirs Nature's slights.
When he to sportive pleasures of more youth
Had framed his numbers, love hath called that truth
Which custom hath styled fiction—nay, the chaste
His harmless mirth for lovers have embraced. 70
When to the stage he would address his song
Kings have vouchsafed attention, and as long

[4] Cf. Heywood, pp. 493–4.
[5] Cf. Ford's elegy for Jonson, ll. 14 ff.: 'Whose *Glory* hath fil'd up the *Booke* of *Fame*!', whose work 'addes this farre more, | 'Tis finish'd what unperfect was before. | The *Muses*, first in *Greece* begot, in *Rome* | Brought forth, our *best* of *Poets* hath cald home, | Nurst, taught, and planted here; that Thames now sings | The *Delphian Altars*, and the sacred *Springs*' (*Nondramatic Works*, p. 358).

As his sweet studies did enrich their ears
Princes with queens, and ladies with chief peers
Have listened and applauded, by their choice 75
Of judgements to conform* the general voice.
And here in pardon have thy merits found
A happy thrift, in being justly crowned
With more than common praise, that did'st reduce*
The stage from monsters[6] to familiar use 80
Of master words and credit, by which right
The court might learn to speak, the schools to write.
    I search too far the treasures of a mine
Not to be fathomed, lest my pen like thine
Could figure in so full a height 85
As it could miss nor glory, nor conceit.
Be silent therefore now, ye Under-elves,
Whose grace in writing is to praise yourselves
By reading in stol'n corners rhymes as stale
As your admirers are, who strong in ale 90
And foul tobacco roar in your defence,
Still without wit and ofter without sense.
Before you touch with an unhallowed hand
The virgin bay, be taught to understand
What 'tis to be a poet. Fix before 95
Your eyes this great example, and no more
Cherish your ignorance, which damns the age
With misbelief, and arms the times with rage
Against this sacred art. 'Tis known too well,
Too many write that know not how to spell,[7] 100
Straight abusing greatness and procuring
Restraint to such as daub* them, though alluring
Clerks, 'prentices, or chamber-maids to read
With admiration o'er mere scraps of reed.
Who scribble ballads, or would vent a play 105
Of gross impossibilities for a day;
Or he that can translate an amorous line

---

[6] As with the 'play | Of gross impossibilities' below (l. 106), Ford echoes the common sense of superiority that Jacobean and Caroline dramatists had over their primitive Elizabethan predecessors. Cf. Jonson, pp. 526–7.
[7] Cf. Ford's prefatory poem to Massinger's *Roman Actor* (1629), beginning: 'To write, is growne so common in our Time . . .' (*Nondramatic Works*, p. 350).

For ladies closets, and swears 'this is mine',
Is not a poet. Much diviner fires
Warms Phoebus' sons within. He that desires 110
Fame by desert, and be a poet known,
Must write like Fletcher, or he must be none.

Dignum laude virum Musa vetat mori.[8]

---

[8] Horace, *Odes* 4. 8. 28: "'Tis the Muse forbids the hero worthy of renown to perish'.

32

Philip Massinger,
A defence of drama (1626)

PHILIP MASSINGER (1583–1640) was probably educated at Salisbury Grammar School, and attended St Alban Hall Oxford in 1602–3, forced to leave when his father died. In 1613 he is next heard of collaborating on plays written for Henslowe. From 1616 to 1625 he wrote many plays together with John Fletcher, principal dramatist for the King's Men, becoming their chief dramatist from Fletcher's death until 1640, writing for both the Globe and Blackfriars theatres. Massinger is know to have written all or part of fifty-five plays, twenty-two of which are lost; of the remaining thirty-three, fifteen were his own work.

TEXT. From *The Roman Actor. A Tragaedie* (1629). Licensed for performance in October 1626, Massinger's dramatization of events in the life of the Roman emperor Domitian (AD 51–96) was the author's favourite work, 'the most perfect birth of my Minerva', as he described it in the dedication. The plot was based on Suetonius' biography—probably in Philemon Holland's translation (*The Historie of Twelve Caesars*, 1606), together with Tacitus, Juvenal, and other sources for the character of Paris, the emperor's favourite actor, who (according to Juvenal) captivated women with his performances, including—fatally for him—the empress Domitia. His defence of the theatre, a famous set-piece for actors in the eighteenth and nineteenth centuries, was based on classical and contemporary sources. As Sir Thomas Jay, one of the play's dedicatees, wrote in his prefatory poem:

> . . . when thy Paris pleades in the defence
> Of Actors, every grace, and excellence
> Of Argument for that subject, are by Thee
> Contracted in a sweet Epitome.

In annotating this selection I have benefited from the editions by A. H. Gilbert, *LCPD*, pp. 568–73; *The Plays and Poems of Philip Massinger*, ed. P. Edwards and C. Gibson, 5 vols. (Oxford, 1976); and *The Selected Plays of Philip Massinger*, ed. C. Gibson (Cambridge, 1978).

THE ROMAN ACTOR

[ACT I, SCENE I]

AESOPUS.[1] What do we act today?

LATINUS.   Agave's frenzy,
With Pentheus' bloody end.[2]

PARIS.   It skills* not what;
The times are dull, and all that we receive
Will hardly satisfy the day's expense.
The Greeks, to whom we owe the first invention,   5
Both of the buskined scene and humble sock,[3]
That reign in every noble family,
Declaim against us;[4] and our amphitheatre,
Great Pompey's work, that hath given full delight
Both to the eye and ear of fifty thousand[5]   10
Spectators in one day, as if it were
Some unknown desert, or great Rome unpeopled,
Is quite forsaken.

LATINUS.   Pleasures of worse natures
Are gladly entertained; and they that shun us
Practise, in private, sports the stews* would blush at.   15
A litter borne by eight Liburnian slaves,
To buy diseases from a glorious* strumpet,
The most censorious of our Roman gentry,
Nay, of the guarded robe,[6] the senators,
Esteem an easy purchase.

PARIS.   Yet grudge us
That with delight join profit,[7] and endeavour   20
To build their minds up fair, and on the stage
Decipher* to the life what honours wait
On good and glorious actions, and the shame

---

[1] A famous tragic actor, contemporary with Roscius and Cicero. Latinus was a celebrated mime and favourite of Domitian, for whom he acted as an informer.

[2] As dramatized by Euripides in *The Bacchae*. Juvenal, *Sat.* 7. 87, mentions an *Agave* which Statius was forced to sell to Paris.

[3] Cf. Horace, *Ars. P.* 275–81, Heywood, p. 482.

[4] Juvenal attacked Greek influence on Roman society in *Sat.* 3. 58 ff.

[5] Built by Pompey in 55 BC. Pliny (*Naturalis historia* 36. 24) estimated that it held 40,000 spectators.

[6] A toga with a broad purple border, worn by senators.

[7] Cf. Horace, *Ars P.* 343, and Sidney, pp. 345 ff.

That treads upon the heels of vice, the salary   25
   Of six sestertii.[8]
AESOPUS.   For the profits, Paris,
   And mercenary gain, they are things beneath us,
   Since while you hold your grace and power with Caesar,
   We from your bounty find a large supply,
   Nor can one thought of want ever approach us.   30
PARIS. Our aim is glory, and to leave our names
   To aftertimes.
LATINUS.   And would they give us leave,
   There ends all our ambition.
AESOPUS.   We have enemies,
   And great ones too, I fear. 'Tis given out lately
   The consul Aretinus, Caesar's spy,[9]   35
   Said at his table, ere a month expir'd,
   For being galled* in our last comedy
   He would silence us for ever.
PARIS.   I expect
   No favour from him; my strong Aventine[10] is
   That great Domitian, whom we oft have cheered   40
   In his most sullen moods, will once* return,
   Who can repair with ease the consul's ruins.
LATINUS. 'Tis frequent* in the city, he hath subdued
   The Catti, and the Daci, and ere long,
   The second time will enter Rome in triumph.   45
         Enter two LICTORS
PARIS. Jove hasten it!—With us?—I now believe
   The consul's threats, Aesopus.
1 LICTOR.   You are summoned
   T'appear today in Senate.
2 LICTOR.   And there to answer
   What shall be urged against you.
PARIS.   We obey you.
   Nay, droop not, fellows; innocence should be bold.   50
   We, that have personated in the scene
   The ancient heroes, and the falls of princes

---

[8] About a shilling, the price of admission to the Jacobean private theatres.

[9] Aretinus Clemens, an informer and favourite of Domitian, who commanded the Praetorian Guard, but was suspected of treason and executed.

[10] A potion of great strength.

With loud applause, being to act ourselves,
Must do it with undaunted confidence.
Whate'er our sentence be, think 'tis in sport;   55
And though condemned, let's hear it without sorrow,
As if we were to live again tomorrow.
1 LICTOR. 'Tis spoken like yourself. . . .

[ACT 1, SCENE 3]

ARETINUS. The purpose of this frequent* Senate
Is first to give thanks to the gods of Rome,
That for the propagation of the empire   5
Vouchsafe us one to govern it like themselves.
In height of courage, depth of understanding,
And all those virtues and remarkable graces
Which make a prince most eminent, our Domitian
Transcends the ancient Romans.   10

  .   .   .   .
                'Tis then most fit
That we (as to the father of our country,
Like thankful sons, stand bound to pay true service   25
For all those blessings that he showers upon us)
Should not connive, and see his government
Depraved and scandalised by meaner men,
That to his favour and indulgence owe
Themselves and being.
PARTHENIUS.   Now he points at us.   30
ARETINUS. Cite Paris, the tragedian.
PARTHENIUS.   Here.
ARETINUS.   Stand forth.
In thee, as being the chief of thy profession,
I do accuse the quality* of treason,
As libellers against the state and Caesar.
PARIS. Mere accusations are not proofs, my lord: 35
In what are we delinquents?
ARETINUS.   You are they
That search into the secrets of the time,
And, under feigned names, on the stage present
Actions not to be touched* at; and traduce
Persons of rank and quality of both sexes,   40

And, with satirical and bitter jests,
Make even the senators ridiculous
To the plebeians.
PARIS.   If I free not myself,
And, in myself, the rest of my profession
From these false imputations, and prove   45
That they make that a libel which the poet
Writ for a comedy,[11] so acted too,
It is but justice that we undergo
The heaviest censure.
ARETINUS.   Are you on the stage,
You talk so boldly?
PARIS.   The whole world being one,   50
This place is not exempted; and I am
So confident in the justice of our cause
That I could wish Caesar, in whose great name
All kings are comprehended, sat as judge
To hear our plea, and then determine* of us.   55
If to express* a man sold to his lusts,
Wasting the treasure of his time and fortunes
In wanton dalliance, and to what sad end
A wretch that's so given over does arrive at;
Deterring careless youth, by his example,[12]   60
From such licentious courses; laying open
The snares of bawds, and the consuming arts
Of prodigal strumpets, can deserve reproof;
Why are not all your golden principles,
Writ down by grave philosophers to instruct us   65
To choose fair virtue for our guide, not pleasure,[13]
Condemned unto the fire?
SURA.   There's spirit in this.
PARIS. Or if desire of honour was the base
On which the building of the Roman empire
Was raised up to this height; if to inflame[14]   70

---

[11] Jonson complained in *Epicoene* (1616) about malicious commentators who 'make a libel, which he [the dramatist] made a play'; cf. also the preface to Volpone (p. 471), on 'invading interpreters'.
[12] On the superior power of poetry to teach by example cf. Spenser, p. 299, Sidney, pp. 351–3.
[13] In classical and Renaissance moral philosophy *virtus* and *voluptas* are incompatible opposites.
[14] On the power of literature to 'inflame' its audience to virtue, cf. Introduction, pp. 50–5.

The noble youth with an ambitious heat
To endure the frosts of danger, nay, of death,
To be thought worthy the triumphal wreath
By glorious undertakings, may deserve
Reward or favour from the commonwealth;[15]   75
Actors may put in for as large a share
As all the sects of the philosophers.
They with cold precepts[16]—perhaps seldom read—
Deliver* what an honorable thing
The active virtue is; but does that fire   80
The blood, or swell the veins with emulation,
To be both good and great, equal to that
Which is presented on our theatres?
Let a good actor, in a lofty scene,
Show great Alcides[17] honoured in the sweat   85
Of his twelve labors; or a bold Camillus,[18]
Forbidding Rome to be redeemed with gold
From the insulting Gauls; or Scipio,[19]
After his victories, imposing tribute
On conquered Carthage; if done to the life,   90
As if they saw their dangers and their glories,
And did partake with them in their rewards,
All that have any spark of Roman in them,
The slothful arts laid by, contend to be
Like those they see presented.[20]

RUSTICUS.   He has put   95
The consuls to their whisper.

PARIS.   But 'tis urged
That we corrupt youth, and traduce superiors.
When do we bring a vice upon the stage,

---

[15] Edwards and Gibson (edn. cit.) compare Bodin, *Six Bookes of a Commonwealth* (tr. Knolles, 1606), 5. 4, justifying the 'desire of honour': 'I hold that there is nothing more necessary for youth (as Theophrastus said) the which doth inflame them with an honest ambition . . . never any commonwealth did bring forth such famous men, and so many, as Rome did' (pp. 586–7).

[16] Cf. Sidney, p. 351.

[17] Hercules.

[18] Roman general who defeated a Gallic invasion (387 BC), recovering the gold with which the Romans had bought peace.

[19] Scipio Africanus, famous for having carried the Second Punic War from Italy to Africa, defeated the Carthaginians in 202 BC.

[20] On the superior power of events presented to the eye, cf. Horace, *Ars P*. 179–82, and Heywood, pp. 486–7.

That does go off unpunished?[21] Do we teach,
By the success of wicked undertakings,   100
Others to tread in their forbidden steps?
We show no arts of Lydian panderism,
Corinthian poisons, Persian flatteries,
But mulcted* so in the conclusion that
Even those spectators that were so inclined   105
Go home changed men. And, for[22] traducing such
That are above us, publishing to the world
Their secret crimes, we are as innocent
As such as are born dumb. When we present
An heir that does conspire against the life   110
Of his dear parent, numbering every hour
He lives, as tedious to him; if there be,
Among the auditors, one whose conscience tells him
He is of the same mould, we cannot help it.
Or, bringing on the stage a loose adulteress,   115
That does maintain the riotous expense
Of him that feeds her greedy lust, yet suffers
The lawful pledges[23] of a former bed
To starve the while for hunger; if a matron,
However great in fortune, birth, or titles,   120
Guilty of such a foul unnatural sin,
Cry out, ''Tis writ by me',[24] we cannot help it.
Or, when a covetous man's expressed, whose wealth
Arithmetic cannot number, and whose lordships*
A falcon in one day cannot fly over;   125
Yet he so sordid in his mind, so griping,
As not to afford himself the necessaries
To maintain life;[25] if a patrician—
Though honoured with a consulship—find himself
Touched to the quick in this, we cannot help it.   130
Or, when we show a judge that is corrupt,

---

[21] Cf. Sidney, p. 356.   [22] As for.   [23] Legitimate children.
[24] 'Written about me'.
[25] Massinger inserts three plays within this play, the first of which (2. 1. 1–111, 161–70, 263–446) being *The Cure for Avarice*, a play (based on Horace, *Sat.* 2. 3. 108–26, 142–57) put on by Paris and his company at the request of Parthenius, in an attempt to cure his father Philargus, a rich miser, who grudges to spend money on clothes and food. The play failing in its goal, Domitian has Philargus hanged. The emperor subsequently executes Paris for his alleged affair with Domitia.

And will give up his sentence as he favours
The person, not the cause; saving the guilty,
If of his faction, and as oft condemning
The innocent, out of particular spleen;[26]   135
If any in this reverend assembly,
Nay, e'en yourself, my lord, that are the image
Of absent Caesar, feel something in your bosom
That puts you in remembrance of things past,
Or things intended, 'tis not in us to help it.   140
I have said, my lord; and now, as you find cause,
Or censure us or free us with applause.
LATINUS. Well pleaded, on my life! I never saw him
Act an orator's part before.
AESOPUS.   We might have given
Ten double fees to Regulus,[27] and yet   145
Our cause delivered worse.

---

[26] Partisan ill-will.   [27] A celebrated defence lawyer, and informer.

33

Thomas Carew,
Donne the renewer of English poetry (1633)

THOMAS CAREW (1595–1635) was educated at Merton College Oxford, and the Middle Temple. Between 1613 and 1616 he was employed as a secretary by Sir Dudley Carleton, English ambassador to Venice, and subsequently to the Netherlands. Dismissed for having written aspersions on his employer's character, Carew resumed his career in the employ of Sir Edward Herbert (later Lord Herbert of Cherbury) on his embassy to Paris in 1619, and subsequently gained various posts at the court of Charles I. As a poet, he was influenced by contemporary Italian models, notably Marino, and borrowed much from Donne and Jonson (whom he criticized in a poem, 'To Ben Jonson. Upon occasion of his Ode of defiance annext to his Play of *The New Inne*').

TEXT. From the elegies included in the first edition of Donne's verse, *Poems by J. D. with Elegies on the Authors Death* (1633). Donne died on 31 March 1631, his son publishing this collection, including the love poems written before Donne took holy orders, and which he subsequently regretted (see Jonson, p. 531). In annotating this text I have benefited from Rhodes Dunlop (ed.), *The Poems of Thomas Carew* (Oxford, 1949); Thomas Clayton (ed.), *Cavalier Poets* (Oxford, 1978); and A. C. Partridge (ed.), *The Tribe of Ben* (London, 1966).

AN ELEGY UPON THE DEATH OF THE DEAN OF PAUL'S,
DR. JOHN DONNE

Can we not force from widowed poetry,
Now thou art dead, great Donne, one elegy
To crown thy hearse? Why yet dare we not trust,
Though with unkneaded dough-baked prose,[1] thy dust,
Such as th' unscissored* churchman, from the flower   5
Of fading rhetoric, short-lived as his hour,

---

[1] Donne's poem *A Letter to the Lady Carey* includes a reference to the 'tasteless flat humility | In dough-baked man'; as we might say, 'half-baked', badly finished.

Dry as the sand that measures[2] it, should lay
Upon thy ashes on the funeral day?
Have we no voice, no tune? Didst thou dispense*
Through all our language both the words and sense?[3]   10
  'Tis a sad truth. The pulpit may her plain
And sober Christian precepts still retain;
Doctrines it may, and wholesome uses, frame,
Grave homilies and lectures; but the flame
Of thy brave soul—that shot such heat and light   15
As burnt our earth, and made our darkness bright,
Committed holy rapes upon our will,[4]
Did through the eye the melting heart distil,
And the deep knowledge of dark truths so teach,
As sense might judge what fancy could not reach—   20
Must be desired for ever. So the fire
That fills with spirit and heat the Delphic choir,[5]
Which, kindled first by thy Promethean breath,
Glowed here awhile, lies quenched now in thy death.
  The Muses' garden, with pedantic weeds   25
O'erspread, was purged* by thee; the lazy seeds
Of servile imitation thrown away,
And fresh invention[6] planted; thou didst pay
The debts of our penurious bankrupt age;
Licentious thefts, that make poetic rage   30
A mimic fury, when our souls must be
Possessed, or with Anacreon's ecstasy
Or Pindar's, not their own; the subtle cheat
Of sly exchanges, and the juggling feat
Of two-edged words,[7] or whatsoever wrong   35
By ours was done the Greek or Latin tongue,

---

[2] Preachers often took an hour-glass into the pulpit, to time their sermon.

[3] The traditional division of language into *verba* and *res* (or *significatio*).

[4] Carew imitates Donne's forceful style to describe the effect he had on his contemporaries.

[5] 'Pythia, the oracle, attended by five priests at Delphi, delivered her prophecies in hexameter verse' (Partridge).

[6] Carew is still using the traditional categories, *imitatio* and *inventio*, to attack the ineffectual copying of ancient models. Anacreon (6th cent. BC) was celebrated as poet of wine and love, in an elegant but hardly 'ecstatic' style.

[7] Perhaps referring to such stylistic faults as *amphibologia* or *ambiguitas* (*Rhet. Her.* 4. 53. 67), or to what Puttenham calls 'figures of sly exchange' (p. 241), such as *enallage* (Lat. *permutatio*).

Thou hast redeemed, and opened us a mine
Of rich and pregnant fancy; drawn a line
Of masculine expression,[8] which had good
Old Orpheus seen, or all the ancient brood   40
Our superstitious fools admire, and hold
Their lead more precious than thy burnished gold,[9]
Thou hadst been their exchequer,* and no more
They each in other's dust had raked for ore.
　　Thou shalt yield no precedence, but of time,   45
And the blind fate of language whose tuned chime[10]
More charms the outward sense; yet thou may'st claim
From so great disadvantage greater fame,
Since to the awe of thy imperious wit
Our stubborn language bends, made only fit   50
With her tough thick-ribbed hoops to gird about
Thy giant fancy, which had proved too stout
For their soft melting phrases.[11] As in time
They had the start, so did they cull the prime
Buds of invention many a hundred year,   55
And left the rifled fields, besides the fear
To touch their harvest; yet from those bare lands
Of what is purely thine thy only hands[12]
(And that thy smallest work) have gleanèd more
Than all those times and tongues could reap before.   60
　　But thou art gone, and thy strict laws will be
Too hard for libertines in poetry.[13]
They will repeal the goodly exiled train
Of gods and goddesses, which in thy just reign
Were banished nobler poems; now with these   65
The silenced tales o' th' *Metamorphoses*
Shall stuff their lines and swell the windy page,

---

[8] A common praise-category in Renaissance literary discussions; cf. also the term 'strong lines' in North, p. 506.

[9] Unlike lesser poets, Donne's *imitatio* became an *aemulatio*, transmuting lead to gold.

[10] Rhyme, the mark of modern vernacular poetry, seen by orthodox classicists as a 'disadvantage', compared to the precision of quantitative metres.

[11] Donne's powerful conceptions bent our unmalleable language.

[12] 'Your hands alone'.

[13] Clayton suggests a reference to 'the French *Libertin* poets', so called from their freethinking or non-orthodox beliefs. Partridge (more plausibly): poets 'who borrow from Ovid and ancient mythologies to bolster their invention, or supply their want of poetic sensibility'.

Till verse, refined by thee, in this last age
Turn ballad-rhyme, or those old idols be
Adored again with new apostasy.[14]   70
    O pardon me, that break with untuned verse
The reverend silence that attends thy hearse,
Whose awful solemn murmurs were to thee
More than these faint lines a loud elegy,
That did proclaim in a dumb eloquence   75
The death of all the arts, whose influence,
Grown feeble, in these panting numbers lies
Gasping short-winded accents,[15] and so dies:
So doth the swiftly turning wheel not stand
In th' instant we withdraw the moving hand,   80
But some small time maintain a faint weak course
By virtue of the first impulsive force;
And so, whilst I cast on thy funeral pile
Thy crown of bays,* oh, let it crack[16] awhile,
And spit disdain, till the devouring flashes   85
Suck all the moisture up, then turn to ashes.
    I will not draw thee envy to engross
All thy perfections,[17] or weep all our loss:
Those are too num'rous for an elegy,
And this too great to be expressed by me.   90
Though every pen should share a distinct part,
Yet art thou theme enough to tire all art;
Let others carve the rest; it shall suffice
I on thy tomb this epitaph incise:
    Here lies a king, that ruled as he thought fit   95
    The universal monarchy of wit;
    Here lie two flamens, and both those the best:
    Apollo's first, at last the true God's priest.[18]

[14] That is, poetry will revert to the level of street ballads, and the traditional mytho-
logical subject-matter, scorned by Donne, would be revived by 'apostate' poets, renouncing
their allegiance.

[15] Cf. Shakespeare, *1 Henry IV*, I. I. 3.

[16] Crackle in the flames, and perhaps 'wax sarcastic ("crack a joke")' (Clayton edn.).

[17] To list all Donne's gifts would arouse envy.

[18] A flamen was a Roman priest serving a particular god by kindling the sacrificial fire.
Donne was 'first' a poet, serving Apollo; 'at last' a Christian, serving God.

34

Ben Jonson
Notes on literature (*c.*1615–1635)

BEN JONSON. See above, p. 454.

TEXT. From *Timber: or discoveries made upon men and matter; as they have flowed out of his daily readings, or had their reflux to his peculiar notion of the times.* Published (posthumously) in *The Workes of Ben Jonson*, ii. (London, 1640–1). The running title in this edition is 'Explorata: or, Discoveries': Jonson's motto, which he inscribed on the books in his library, was '*Tanquam Explorator*' ('as a scout'), a phrase from Seneca (*Ep.* 2. 5). This collection is in effect a notebook, but as Jonson's slightly defensive subtitle indicates, it reflects his individual ('peculiar') notions, and the way in which his reading reflected ('reflux', a 'flowing back') his own experience of literature and life. It was obviously planned for publication in some form, and parts of it amount to a systematic treatment of some of the major topics in Renaissance literary theory: rhetoric, poetics, *imitatio*, style, ethics, tragedy and comedy. On the extent of Jonson's reading see D. McPherson, *Ben Jonson's Library and Marginalia: An Annotated Catalogue* (*Studies in Philology*, 'Texts and Studies', 71; Chapel Hill, NC, 1974).

In annotating these selections I have benefited from C. H. Herford, P. and E. Simpson (eds.), *Ben Jonson*, 11 vols. (Oxford, 1925–51), vol. viii for the text (pp. 555–649), vol. xi for the annotation (pp. 210–94), references abbreviated as *HS*; and from the compact edition by George Parfitt in *Ben Jonson, The Complete Poems* (Harmondsworth, Middx., 1975), pp. 373–458. In the notes I give line-references to Parfitt's edition (which differ from the Oxford text).

Jonson's title *Timber* is partly explained by the quotation on the title-page from Persius (*Satires* 4. 52): 'Tecum habila, ut noris quam sit curta supellex' ('Live in your own house, and recognize how poorly it is furnished'), and by a further quotation, as an epigraph to the work, from Caspar Gavartius' commentaries on Statius (1616), justifying the title *Sylvae* for Statius' lyrics: 'The fundamental material of facts and ideas, the word—so to speak—and called so as a result of the variety and multifarious nature of the contents. Exactly as we call a great number of trees growing at random a "wood", so the ancients used the word "wood" or "timber-trees" for those writings of theirs which had in them material on a range and diversity of things collected at random' (tr. Parfitt). Cicero

recommended the orator to collect 'silva rerum', a store of matter (*De or.* 3. 26. 103).

PERSPICUITAS ELEGANTIA[1]

A man should so deliver* himself to the nature of the subject whereof he speaks, that his hearer may take knowledge of his discipline* with some delight; and so apparel fair and good matter, that the studious of elegancy be not defrauded; redeem arts from their rough and braky* seats where they lay hid and overgrown with thorns, to a pure, open, and flowery light, where they may take the eye, and be taken by the hand. . . .

NON NIMIUM CREDENDUM ANTIQUITATI[2]

I know nothing can conduce more to letters than to examine the writings of the ancients, and not to rest in their sole authority, or take all upon trust from them; provided the plagues of judging and pronouncing against them be away: such as are envy, bitterness, precipitation,* impudence, and scurrile scoffing. For to all the observations of the ancients, we have our own experience; which, if we will use and apply, we have better means to pronounce. It is true they opened the gates and made the way, that went before us; but as guides, not commanders: *non domini nostri, sed duces fuere.*[3] Truth lies open to all; it is no man's several.* *Patet omnibus veritas, nondum est occupata. Multum ex illa etiam futuris relictum est.*[4]

CENSURA DE POETIS[5]

Nothing in our age, I have observed, is more preposterous* than the running judgements upon poetry and poets; when we shall hear those

[1] 'Clarity, elegance'; ll. 154 ff.: from Juan Luis Vives, *In libros de disciplinis praefatio* (1531). Vives (1492–1540), a friend of Erasmus and More, was a pioneer educationalist, very influential in England and other Northern Renaissance countries. His *De tradendis disciplinis*, tr. Foster Watson as *Vives: On Education* (Cambridge, 1913; Totowa, NJ, 1971), reiterated basic humanist principles for teaching literature. Jonson shortens and adapts these and other excerpts, redirecting them to his own purposes.

[2] 'Do not put too great a reliance on the ancients'; ll. 160 ff.: from Vives, ibid.

[3] 'They were not our masters, but our leaders'; Seneca, *Ep.* 33. 11.

[4] 'Much remains for those of the future'. Jonson has translated the preceding sentence as 'Truth lies open . . .'.

[5] 'Censure of poets'; ll. 728 ff. Apparently, Jonson's own composition.

things commended and cried up for the best writings which a man
would scarce vouchsafe* to wrap any wholesome drug in; he would
never light his tobacco[6] with them. And those men almost named for
miracles, who yet are so vile that if a man should go about to examine
and correct them, he must make all they have done but one blot. Their
good is so entangled with their bad, as forcibly one must draw on the
other's death with it. . . . But a man cannot imagine that thing so
foolish or rude but will find and enjoy an admirer; at least a reader or
spectator. The puppets are seen now in despite of the players;[7] Heath's
epigrams and the Sculler's poems[8] have their applause. There are
never wanting that dare prefer the worst preachers, the worst pleaders, the worst poets; not that the better have left to write or speak
better, but that they that hear them judge worse: *non illi pejus dicunt,
sed hi corruptius judicant.*[9] Nay, if it were put to the question of the
water-rhymer's works against Spenser's, I doubt not but they would
find more suffrages;* because the most favour common vices, out of
a prerogative the vulgar have to lose their judgements and like that
which is naught.

Poetry in this latter age hath proved but a mean mistress to such as
have wholly addicted themselves to her, or given their names up to her
family. They who have but saluted her on the by, and now and then
tendered their visits, she hath done much for, and advanced in the way
of their own professions—both the law, and the gospel[10]—beyond all
they could have hoped or done for themselves without her favour.
Wherein she doth emulate the judicious but preposterous bounty of
the time's grandees, who accumulate all they can upon the parasite or
freshman in their friendship, but think an old client or honest servant
bound by his place to write and starve.

Indeed, the multitude commend writers as they do fencers or
wrestlers,[11] who, if they come in robustiously,* and put for it with a

---

[6] Jokes about the uses to which one could put the paper on which poetry was written
were common in the Renaissance; cf. Jonson, *Epigrams* 3. 12.

[7] Popular taste sometimes put the puppet-shows on the same level as drama; cf. Jonson,
Alchemist 5. 1. 14.

[8] Two writers whom Jonson viewed with contempt: John Heath, author of *Two Centuries of Epigrammes* (1610), and John Taylor, a Thames waterman who called himself 'The
Water Poet' and published prolifically. He is the 'water-rhymer' of a few lines later, 'rhymer'
being for Jonson a category inferior to 'poet'.

[9] Translated in the previous sentence.

[10] Perhaps a mocking reference to Sir John Davies, Bishop Joseph Hall, and John Donne,
who all achieved more success through their professions than their poetry.

[11] This passage derives from Quintilian, *Inst.* 2. 12. 1–3.

deal of violence, are received for the braver fellows; when many times their own rudeness* is a cause of their disgrace, and a slight touch of their adversary gives all that boisterous force the foil. But in these things the unskilful are naturally deceived, and judging wholly by the bulk, think rude things greater than polished, and scattered more numerous than composed.[12] Nor think this only to be true in the sordid multitude, but the neater sort of our gallants; for all are the multitude, only they differ in clothes, not in judgement or understanding.

DE SHAKESPEARE NOSTRATI[13]

I remember the players have often mentioned it as an honour to Shakespeare, that in his writing, whatsoever he penned, he never blotted out line. My answer hath been, 'Would he had blotted a thousand'; which they thought a malevolent speech. I had not told posterity this but for their ignorance, who choose that circumstance to commend their friend by wherein he most faulted; and to justify mine own candour: for I loved the man, and do honour his memory, on this side idolatry, as much as any. He was, indeed, honest, and of an open and free nature; had an excellent fantasy, brave notions, and gentle expressions; wherein he flowed with that facility that sometime it was necessary he should be stopped. '*Sufflaminandus erat*',[14] as Augustus said of Haterius. His wit was in his own power; would the rule of it had been so too. Many times he fell into those things, could not escape laughter: as when he said in the person of Caesar, one speaking to him, 'Caesar, thou dost me wrong'; he replied, 'Caesar did never wrong,

[12] That is, 'value rough things more highly than those polished by art, and disorganized writing more than carefully-shaped'.

[13] 'Of our companion Shakespeare'; ll. 802 ff. Jonson refers to the preface by Heminges and Condell, Shakespeare's long-time fellow actors, to the First Folio (1623) of his works, in which they praised his facility in writing: 'His mind and hand went together: And what he thought, he uttered with that easiness, that wee have scarce received from him a blot in his papers'. By 'blot' they meant a heavily corrected manuscript; Jonson takes it to mean the necessary correcting or polishing one's work.

[14] M. Seneca, *Controv.* 4, pref. 7–11: 'Haterius used to let the public in to hear him declaim extempore . . . His speed of delivery was such as to become a fault. Hence that was a good remark of Augustus: "Haterius needs a brake"—he seemed to charge downhill rather than run. He was full of ideas as well as words . . . He had his talents under his own control—but the degree of their application he left to another's . . . in his anxiety to say nothing that was not elegant and brilliant, he often fell into expressions that could not escape derision . . . But he made up for his faults by his virtues, and provided more to praise than to forgive.'

but with just cause';[15] and such like: which were ridiculous. But he redeemed his vices with his virtues. There was ever more in him to be praised than to be pardoned.

INGENIORUM DISCRIMINA[16]

In the difference of wits I have observed there are many notes,* and it is a little mastery to know them: to discern what every nature, every disposition will bear; for before we sow our land we should plough it. There are no fewer forms of minds than of bodies amongst us. The variety is incredible, and therefore we must search. Some are fit to make divines, some poets, some lawyers, some physicians; some to be sent to the plough, and trades.

There is no doctrine will do good where nature is wanting. Some wits are swelling and high, others low and still, some hot and fiery, others cold and dull; one must have a bridle, the other a spur.

There be some[17] that are forward and bold, and these will do every little thing easily—I mean, that is hard by and next them: which they will utter, unretarded, without any shamefastness. These never perform much, but quickly. They are what they are on the sudden; they show presently, like grain that, scattered on the top of the ground, shoots up but takes no root, has a yellow blade, but the ear empty. They are wits of good promise at first, but there is an *ingenistitium*:[18] they stand still at sixteen, they get no higher.

You have others that labour only to ostentation, and are ever more busy about the colours and surface of a work, than in the matter and foundation: for that is hid, the other is seen.

Others,[19] that in composition are nothing but what is rough and broken: *quae per salebras altaque saxa cadunt.*[20] And if it would come gently, they trouble* it of purpose. They would not have it run without rubs,* as if that style were more strong and manly that struck

---

[15] Cf. *Julius Caesar* 3. 1. 47–8, where Caesar rejects Metellus Cimber's plea for the recall of his banished brother: 'Know, Caesar doth not wrong, nor without cause | Will he be satisfied.' Jonson's criticism overlooks the obvious sense of 'wrong' (meaning 'injury'), and ignores the rest of the sentence. But it is also possible that Shakespeare revised his text.

[16] 'Of the different kinds of personality'; ll. 828 ff.: from *Inst.* 2. 8. 1, 7–11, adapted.

[17] ll. 845–56: from *Inst.* 1. 3. 3–5.

[18] The marginal note translates: 'wit-stand'; that is, arrested intellectual development.

[19] ll. 875–81: from Seneca, *Ep.* 114. 15, 21.

[20] Martial, *Epigrams* 11. 90. 2: '[You approve of no verses that run smoothly,] but only of those that seem to leap over hills and crags'.

the ear with a kind of unevenness. These men err not by chance, but knowingly and willingly; they are like men that affect* a fashion by themselves, have some singularity in a ruff, cloak, or hatband; or their beards specially cut to provoke beholders, and set a mark upon themselves. They would be reprehended while they are looked on. And this vice, one that is in authority with the rest, loving, delivers over to them to be imitated; so that oft-times the faults which he fell into, the others seek for. This is the danger, when vice becomes a precedent.

Others[21] there are that have no composition* at all, but a kind of tuning and rhyming fall in what they write. It runs and slides and only makes a sound. Women's poets they are called, as you have women's tailors.

> They write a verse as smooth, as soft, as cream,
> In which there is not torrent, nor scarce stream.[22]

You may sound these wits, and find the depth of them, with your middle finger. They are cream-bowl, or but puddle-deep.

Some that turn over all books, and are equally searching in all papers, that write out of what they presently* find or meet, without choice: by which means it happens that what they have discredited and impugned in one work, they have before or after extolled[23] the same in another. Such are all the essayists, even their master Montaigne.[24] These, in all they write, confess still what books they have read last, and therein their own folly, so much, that they bring it to the stake[25] raw and undigested; not that the place did need it neither, but that they thought themselves furnished, and would vent* it. . . .

It[26] cannot but come to pass that these men who commonly seek to do more than enough may sometimes happen on something that is good and great, but very seldom; and when it comes, it doth not recompense the rest of their ill. For their jests and their sentences*— which they only and ambitiously seek for—stick out and are more

[21] From Seneca, *Ep.* 114. 18, 15.

[22] Unidentified; among the suggested 'women's poets' mocked here have been Daniel, Campion, and Middleton.

[23] So Quintilian criticized Didymus, a prolific author, who 'on one occasion objected to some story as being absurd, whereupon one of his own books was produced which contained the story in question' (1. 8. 20).

[24] Jonson despised the essay for its formlessness and consciously imperfect composition. Cf. Sir John Daw's opinion: 'Mere essayists! A few loose sentences and that's all' (*Epicoene* 2. 3. 46).

[25] Wager, as if risking a deposit. Essayists publish their work in an imperfect state.

[26] ll. 941–65: from *Inst.* 2. 11. 5–7; 2. 10. 13; 2. 12. 8.

eminent, because all is sordid and vile about them, as lights are more discerned in a thick darkness than a faint shadow. Now because they speak all they can, however unfitly, they are thought to have the greater copy;* where the learned use ever election and a mean,[27] they look back to what they intended at first, and make all an even and proportioned body.

The true artificer will not run away from nature, as he were afraid of her, or depart from life and the likeness of truth, but speak to the capacity of his hearers. And though his language differ from the vulgar somewhat, it shall not fly from all humanity, with the Tamerlanes and Tamerchams[28] of the late age, which had nothing in them but the scenical strutting and furious vociferation[29] to warrant them to the ignorant gapers.

He[30] knows it is his only art so to carry it, as none but artificers perceive it. In the meantime, perhaps, he is called barren, dull, lean, a poor writer, or by what contumelious* word can come into their cheeks, by these men, who without labour, judgement, knowledge, or almost sense, are received or preferred before him. He gratulates them and their fortune. Another age, or juster men, will acknowledge the virtues of his studies: his wisdom in dividing,[31] his subtlety in arguing, with what strength he doth inspire his readers; with what sweetness he strokes* them; in inveighing, what sharpness; in jest, what urbanity he uses. How he doth reign in men's affections; how invade, and break in upon them, and makes their minds like the thing he writes. Then in his elocution to behold what word is proper, which hath ornament, which height, what is beautifully translated,[32] where figures are fit, which gentle, which strong, to show the composition manly. And how he hath avoided faint, obscure, obscene, sordid, humble, improper, or effeminate phrase; which is not only praised of the most, but commended (which is worse), especially for that it is naught.

[27] That is, 'copy' or abundance of invention needs both 'election', or careful selection, and 'a meane', moderation or measure. Spingarn cites Scaliger, *Poetice* 5. 3, 'where the highest virtue of a poet is said to be *electio et sui fastidium*', and 6. 4, 'the life of all excellence lies in measure' (*CES* i. 221).

[28] Marlowe's *Tamburlaine* (published 1590, 1592) was famous for its spectacle and noise. One of its descendants, *Tamar Cam*, now lost, was acted by the Admiral's Men in 1596.

[29] For similar criticisms of a style of acting remote from real life cf. *Hamlet* 3. 2. 4–14.

[30] ll. 965–91: from *Inst.* 2. 12. 11–12; 2. 5. 8–10. Jonson's selection emphasizes the qualities that he most valued in a writer.

[31] The rhetorical technique of *partitio*, dividing a topic into its main parts. Other rhetorical skills are invoked: *movere*; *elocutio*; *electio verborum*; the virtues and vices of style.

[32] Figurative (the Latin for metaphor is *translatio*).

DOMINUS VERULAMIUS[33]

One, though he be excellent and the chief, is not to be imitated alone. For never no imitator ever grew up to his author; likeness is always on this side truth. Yet there happened in my time one noble speaker who was full of gravity in his speaking. His language, where he could spare or pass by a jest, was nobly censorious.* No man ever spoke more neatly, more pressly,* more weightily, or suffered less emptiness, less idleness, in what he uttered. No member* of his speech but consisted of the own graces: his hearers could not cough, or look aside from him, without loss. He commanded where he spoke, and had his judges angry and pleased at his devotion.* No man had their affections more in his power. The fear of every man that heard him was lest he should make an end.

SCRIPTORUM CATALOGUS[34]

Cicero is said to be the only wit* that the people of Rome had equalled to their empire: *ingenium par imperio.*[35] We have had many, and in their several ages—to take in but the former seculum*—Sir Thomas More, the elder Wyatt, Henry Earl of Surrey, Chaloner, Smith, Elyot, Bishop

[33] 'Lord Verulam': Francis Bacon, celebrated as a legal and parliamentary orator. Jonson's rehearsal of the standard classical warning against imitating only one model comes from the elder Seneca, *Controv.* 1, pref. 6: 'You should not imitate one man, however distinguished: for an imitator never comes up to the level of his model. This is the way it is; the copy always falls short of the reality' (cf. also *Inst.* 10. 2. 11, 24–6). Then Jonson takes over Seneca's praise of Cassius Severus: 'For . . . the dignity which he lacked in his life he possessed in plenty in his speech. So long as he steered clear of jokes, his oratory was worthy of a censor' (ibid. 3, pref. 4). 'His oratory was strong, polished, full of striking ideas; no-one was less tolerant of the superfluous in his pleading; there was no part that did not stand on its own feet, no place where the listener could afford to let his attention wander. Everything was vigorous and pointful. No-one was in more complete control of the emotions of his audience. . . . When he spoke, he was a king on his throne, so religiously did everyone do what they were told. When he required it, they were angry. Everyone was afraid, while he was speaking, in case he should stop' (3, pref. 2).

[34] 'List of writers'. Compare the similar catalogue in Puttenham, pp. 209 ff. The less familiar writers here are Sir Thomas Chaloner (1513–77), diplomat and translator of Erasmus' *Praise of Folly* (1549); Sir Thomas Smith, Secretary of State, Greek scholar and author of *De republica Anglorum* (1583); Bishop Stephen Gardiner (?1483–1558), chancellor under Mary and author of several (Catholic) religious tracts; Richard Hooker (1533–1600), author of *The Lawes of Ecclesiastical Politie* (1593–7; 1617); Robert Devereux (1566–1601), second Earl of Essex, Spenser's patron and a minor poet; Sir Henry Savile (1549–1622), translator of Tacitus (1580) and headmaster of Eton; Sir Edwin Sandys (1561–1629), parliamentarian and statesman, author of *Europae speculum* (1599); Thomas, Lord Egerton (?1540–1617), Lord Chancellor.

[35] Seneca, *Ep.* 1. 1, pref.

Gardiner, were for their times admirable; and the more, because they began eloquence with us. Sir Nicholas Bacon was singular, and almost alone, in the beginning of Queen Elizabeth's times. Sir Philip Sidney and Mr Hooker, in different matter, grew great masters of wit and language, and in whom all vigour of invention and strength of judgement met. The Earl of Essex, noble and high; and Sir Walter Raleigh, not to be contemned, either for judgement or style; Sir Henry Savile, grave, and truly lettered; Sir Edwin Sandys, excellent in both; Lord Egerton, the Chancellor, a grave and great orator, and best when he was provoked. But his learned and able (though unfortunate)* successor[36] is he who hath filled up all numbers, and performed that in our tongue which may be compared or preferred either to insolent Greece or haughty Rome. In short, within his view, and about his times, were all the wits born that could honour a language or help study. Now things daily fall: wits grow downward, and eloquence grows backward; so that he may be named and stand as the mark and *akmē* of our language.

DE AUGMENTIS SCIENTIARUM[37]

I have ever observed it to have been the office* of a wise patriot, among the greatest affairs of the state, to take care of the commonwealth of learning. For schools, they are the seminaries* of state; and nothing is worthier the study of a statesman than that part of the republic which we call the advancement of letters.* Witness the care of Julius Caesar, who in the heat of the civil war, writ his books of *Analogy*,[38] and dedicated them to Tully. This made the late Lord St Albans entitle his work *Novum Organum*; which though by the most of superficial

---

[36] Francis Bacon, Lord Chancellor from 1618 to 1621, dismissed from office by his political enemies on a charge of bribery. Jonson's praise of Bacon resumes his excerpt from the elder Seneca's *Controversiae*: 'Everything that Roman oratory has to set alongside or even above the haughty Greeks reached its peak in Cicero's day: all the geniuses who have brought brilliance to our subject were born then. Since, things have got daily worse. Perhaps this is due to . . . Fate, whose grim law is universal and everlasting—things that get to the top sink back to the bottom, faster than they rose' (1, pref. 6–7). By making Bacon the *akmē* (highest point) of English eloquence Jonson ranks him with Cicero, from whose pre-eminence Roman historians traced a long decline: cf. Ascham, p. 154. The phrase 'omnium numerum' occurs in Petronius, *Satyricon* 63 and 68, in the sense of 'achieved perfection'. Jonson also used Seneca's dismissal of the 'insolenti Graeciae' in his tribute to Shakespeare (p. 539).

[37] 'Of the growth of knowledge'; the title of the Latin translation (1623) of Bacon's *Two Bookes Of the proficience and advancement of Learning, divine and human* (1605). His *Novum Organum* was published in 1620, as part of his *Instauratio Magna*, a grandiose but uncompleted scheme for the rebirth of all knowledge.

[38] *De Analogia*, a lost work on the Latin language. Bacon praises it in the *Advancement* and elsewhere: cf. *Francis Bacon*, ed. B. Vickers (Oxford, 1996), p. 162.

men, who cannot get beyond the title of nominals,[39] it is not penetrated, nor understood, it really openeth all defects of learning
whatsoever, and is a book,

Qui longum noto scriptori porriget aevum.[40]

My conceit[41] of his person was never increased toward him by his
place or honours. But I have and do reverence him for the greatness
that was only proper to himself, in that he seemed to me ever, by his
work, one of the greatest men, and most worthy of admiration, that
had been in many ages. In his adversity I ever prayed that God would
give him strength; for greatness he could not want.* Neither could I
condole* in a word or syllable for him, as knowing no accident* could
do harm to virtue, but rather help to make it manifest.

DE CORRUPTELA MORUM[42]

There cannot be one colour of the mind, another of the wit. If the
mind be staid, grave, and composed, the wit is so; that vitiated,* the
other is blown and deflowered.* Do we not see, if the mind languish,
the members* are dull? Look upon an effeminate person: his very
gait confesseth him. If a man be fiery, his motion is so, if angry, 'tis
troubled and violent. So that we may conclude wheresoever manners
and fashions are corrupted, language is. It imitates the public riot.*
The excess of feasts and apparel are the notes of a sick state, and the
wantonness of language, of a sick mind. . . .

DE MALIGNITATE STUDENTIUM[43]

There be some men are born only to suck out the poison of books:
habent venenum pro victu; immo, pro deliciis. And such are they that

---

[39] The names of things, but not the realities.
[40] Horace, *Ars P.* 346: 'with honour make the far-known author live' (tr. Jonson).
[41] This tribute in fact derives, almost verbatim, from a letter (1 May 1621) written by Fr.
Fulgenzio Micanza, the Venetian patriot, to William Cavendish, first Earl of Devonshire.
His dispatches and letters are preserved at Chatsworth, with translations and annotations
by Thomas Hobbes, who had earlier been an amanuensis to Bacon, and who worked as tutor
and secretary to the Cavendish family (1608–28, 1631–7). Hobbes must have communicated
the letter to Jonson.
[42] 'Of the corruption of manners'; ll. 1172–84: from Seneca, *Ep.* 114. 3, 11, an essay on
style and its degeneration as a mirror of individual and social health.
[43] 'Of the malignity of the learned'; ll. 1259–80; source untraced. The Latin quotation
means: 'they have poison as a way of living; indeed as luxuries' (tr. Parfitt).

only relish the obscene and foul things in poets, which makes the profession taxed.* But by whom? Men that watch for it, and—had they
not had this hint*—are so unjust valuers of letters* as they think no
learning good but what brings in gain. It shows they themselves would
never have been of the professions they are, but for the profits
and fees.

But if another learning, well used, can instruct to good life, inform
manners,[44] no less persuade and lead men than they threaten and
compel, and have no reward, is it therefore the worse study? I could
never think the study of wisdom confined only to the philosopher, or
of piety to the divine, or of state* to the politic.* But that he which
can feign* a commonwealth, which is the poet, can govern it with
counsels, strengthen it with laws, correct it with judgements, inform
it with religion and morals, is all these. We do not require in him mere
elocution, or an excellent faculty in verse, but the exact knowledge of
all virtues and their contraries; with ability to render the one loved,
the other hated, by his proper embattling* them. The philosophers
did insolently, to challenge only to themselves that which the greatest
generals, and gravest counsellors never durst. For such had rather do
than promise the best things. . . .

POESIS ET PICTURA[45]

Poetry and picture are arts of a like nature, and both are busy about
imitation. It was excellently said of Plutarch, poetry was a speaking

---

[44] Cf. *Inst.* 1, pr.: 'My aim, then, is the education of the complete orator. The first essential for such one is that he should be a good man, and consequently we demand of him not
merely the possession of exceptional gifts of speech, but of all the excellences of character
as well. For I will not admit that the principles of upright and honourable living should
. . . be regarded as the peculiar concern of philosophy. The man who can really play his part
as a citizen and is capable of meeting the demands both of public and private business, the
man who can guide a state by his counsels, give it a firm basis by his legislation and purge
its vices by his decisions as a judge, is assuredly no other than the orator of our quest. . . .
[He will need] such virtues as courage, justice, self-control . . .'. Where rhetoric had previously included moral philosophy, Quintilian complains, now 'the task of forming character
and establishing rules of life' has been usurped by men claiming 'the sole possession of the
title of philosopher, a distinction which neither the greatest generals nor the most famous
statesmen and administrators have ever dared to claim for themselves. For they preferred
the performance to the promise of great deeds' (9–14). But orators 'frequently handle those
things which philosophy claims for its own. Who . . . does not speak of justice, equity, and
virtue?' (16).

[45] 'Of poetry and painting'. The famous saying of Simonides occurs in Plutarch, *Poetas*
3 (*Mor.* 17 F), and in *De gloria Athenensium* 3. 346 f.; cf. Sidney, pp. 345, 352.

picture, and picture a mute poesy. For they both invent, feign, and devise many things, and accommodate* all they invent to the use and service of nature. Yet of the two, the pen is more noble than the pencil; for that can speak to the understanding, the other, but to the sense. They both behold pleasure and profit as their common object; but should abstain from all base pleasures, lest they should err* from their end, and while they seek to better men's minds, destroy their manners. They both are born artificers, not made. Nature is more powerful in them than study.

DE PICTURA[46]

Whosoever loves not picture is injurious to truth, and all the wisdom of poetry. Picture is the invention of heaven: the most ancient, and most akin to nature. It is itself a silent work, and always of one and the same habit; yet it doth so enter and penetrate the inmost affection—being done by an excellent artificer—as sometimes it o'ercomes the power of speech and oratory. There are divers graces in it, so are there in the artificers. One excels in care, another in reason, a third in easiness, a fourth in nature and grace. Some have diligence and comeliness, but they want majesty. They can express a human form in all the graces, sweetness, and elegancy, but they miss the authority. They can hit nothing but smooth cheeks; they cannot express roughness or gravity. Others aspire to truth so much as they are rather lovers of likeness than beauty. Zeuxis and Parrhasius are said to be contemporaries; the first found out the reason of lights and shadows[47] in picture; the other more subtly examined the lines.

DE STILO[48]

In picture light is required no less than shadow; so in style, height as well as humbleness. But beware they be not too humble: as Pliny pronounced of Regulus' writings, you would think them written not on a child, but by a child. Many, out of their own obscene apprehensions,*

---

[46] 'Of painting'; ll. 1882 ff. Jonson's first sentence comes from Philostratus, *Imagines* 1; the rest is from *Inst.* 11. 3. 67; 12. 10. 6–9; and 12. 10. 4.

47 Two celebrated classical painters (5th cent. BC). The terms 'lights' and 'shadows' may refer to Pliny's use of *umbra* and *lumen* to denote background and foreground (*HS* xi. 258).

[48] 'Of style'; ll. 1905 ff.: from Pliny, *Epistulae* 3. 13. 4; 4. 7. 7.

refuse proper and fit words, as 'occupy',[49] 'nature', and the like; so the curious* industry in some, of having all alike good,[50] hath come nearer a vice than a virtue. . . .

DE STILO, ET OPTIMO SCRIBENDI GENERE[51]

For a man to write well, there are required three necessaries: to read the best authors, observe the best speakers, and much exercise of his own style. In style, to consider what ought to be written, and after what manner, he must first think and excogitate* his matter; then choose his words, and examine the weight of either. Then take care in placing and ranking both matter and words, that the composition be comely;* and to do this with diligence and often. No matter how slow the style be at first, so it be laboured,* and accurate; seek the best, and be not glad of the forward conceits* or first words that offer themselves to us, but judge of what we invent, and order what we approve.[52] Repeat often what we have formerly written; which beside that it helps the consequence,* and makes the juncture[53] better, it quickens the heat of imagination, that often cools in the time of setting down, and gives it new strength, as if it grew lustier by the going back. As we see in the contention of leaping, they jump farthest, that fetch their race largest;[54] or, as in throwing a dart or javelin, we force back our arms to make our loose* the stronger.

Yet if we have a fair gale of wind, I forbid not the steering out of our sail,[55] so the favour of the gale deceive us not. For all that we invent doth please us in the conception or birth, else we would never set it down. But the safest is to return to our judgement, and handle over again those things, the easiness of which might make them justly suspected. So did the best writers in their beginnings: they imposed upon

---

[49] Cf. Doll Tearsheet's comment on Pistol's self-description as 'Captain': 'A captain! God's light, these villains will make the word as odious as the word "occupy", which was an excellent good word before it was ill sorted' (2 *Henry IV*, 2. 4. 147 ff.).

[50] Excessive care ('curious' industry) to bring all parts of a composition to the same intensity is an offence against decorum.

[51] 'Of style, and the best way of learning to write'; ll. 2101 ff.: from *Inst*. 10. 3. 4–10. In the preceding pages, Jonson has quoted extensively from bk. 1, chs. 1–2, on children's education. *Stilum* in Latin also means pen: hence Jonson's 'how slow the style be at first . . .'.

[52] Having judiciously considered both *res* and *verba*, we must carefully arrange what we have chosen.

[53] The connection or transition between sections (*Inst*. 9. 4. 22, 32 ff.).

[54] That take the longest run-up.

[55] The writer can allow himself to be carried away by unexpected imaginative promptings, provided the basis has been properly laid.

themselves care and industry. They did nothing rashly. They obtained first to write well, and then custom made it easy and a habit. By little and little, their matter showed itself to 'em more plentifully; their words answered, their composition* followed, and all, as in a well-ordered family, presented itself in the place. So that the sum of all is: ready writing makes not good writing, but good writing brings on ready writing; yet when we think we have got the faculty,* it is even then good to resist it, as to give a horse a check sometimes with a bit, which doth not so much stop his course as stir his mettle. Again, whither a man's genius is best able to reach thither it should more and more contend, lift and dilate itself; as men of low stature raise themselves on their toes, and so oft-times get even, if not eminent.

Besides,[56] as it is fit for grown and able writers to stand of themselves, and work with their own strength, to trust and endeavour by their own faculties, so it is fit for the beginner and learner to study others and the best. For the mind and memory are more sharply exercised in comprehending another man's things than our own; and such as accustom themselves, and are familiar with the best authors, shall ever and anon find somewhat of them in themselves, and in the expression of their minds, even when they feel it not; be able to utter something like theirs, which hath an authority above their own. Nay, sometimes it is the reward of a man's study, the praise of quoting another man fitly: and though a man be more prone, and able for one kind of writing than another, yet he must exercise all. For as in an instrument, so in style, there must be a harmony and consent* of parts.

PRAECIPIENDI MODI[57]

I take this labour in teaching others, that they should not be always to be taught, and I would bring my precepts into practice; for rules are ever of less force and value than experiments. Yet with this purpose, rather to show the right way to those that come after, than to detect any that have slipped before by error; and I hope it will be more profitable: for men do more willingly listen, and with more favour, to precept than reprehension. Among divers opinions of an art (and most of them contrary in themselves) it is hard to make election;* and

---

[56] ll. 2153 ff.: are from *Inst.* 2. 7. 2–5; 2. 8. 12–15.

[57] 'Methods of teaching'. The word 'experiment' in this period usually meant 'experience'.

therefore, though a man cannot invent new things after so many, he may do a welcome work yet to help posterity to judge rightly of the old.

But[58] arts and precepts avail nothing, except nature be beneficial and aiding. And therefore these things are no more written to a dull disposition, than rules of husbandry* to a barren soil. No precepts will profit a fool, no more than beauty will the blind, or music the deaf.

As[59] we should take care that our style in writing be neither dry nor empty, we should look again it be not winding* or wanton* with far-fetched descriptions: either is a vice. But that is worse which proceeds out of want, than that which riots out of plenty. The remedy of fruitfulness is easy, but no labour will help the contrary. I will like and praise some things in a young writer, which yet if he continue in, I cannot but justly hate him for the same. There is a time to be given all things for maturity, and that even your country husbandman* can teach, who to a young plant will not put the pruning knife, because it seems to fear the iron, as not able to admit the scar. No more would I tell a green writer all his faults, lest I should make him grieve and faint, and at last despair. For nothing doth more hurt than to make him so afraid of all things as he can endeavour nothing. Therefore youth ought to be instructed betimes, and in the best things; for we hold* those longest we take soonest, as the first scent of a vessel lasts, and that tinct the wool first receives. Therefore a master should temper* his own powers, and descend to the other's infirmity.* If you pour a glut of water upon a bottle, it receives little of it; but with a funnel, and by degrees, you shall fill many of them, and spill little of your own; to their capacity they will all receive and be full.

And as it is fit to read the best authors to youth first, so let them be of the openest and clearest, as Livy before Sallust, Sidney before Donne. And beware of letting them taste Gower or Chaucer at first, lest falling too much in love with antiquity, and not apprehending the weight, they grow rough* and barren in language only.[60] When their judgements are firm and out of danger, let them read both the old and the new; but no less take heed that their new flowers and sweetness do not as much corrupt as the other's dryness and squalor,* if they choose

[58] ll. 2188 ff.: are from *Inst.* 1, pr. 26.

[59] ll. 2194 ff.: a tissue of excerpts from *Inst.* (2. 4. 3–14; 1. 1. 5; 1. 2. 27–8; 2. 5. 19–23) with omissions, freely adapted.

[60] For similar judgements on Donne's harshness and obscurity see the conversations with Drummond, pp. 530, 532.

not carefully. Spenser, in affecting the ancients, writ no language; yet I would have him read for his matter; but as Virgil read Ennius. The reading of Homer and Virgil is counselled by Quintilian[61] as the best way of informing* youth and confirming* man. For besides that the mind is raised with the height and sublimity of such a verse, it takes spirit from the greatness of the matter, and is tincted with the best things. Tragic and lyric poetry is good too, and comic with the best, if the manners of the reader be once in safety. In the Greek poets, as also in Plautus, we shall see the economy and disposition of poems better observed than in Terence and the later,[62] who thought the sole grace and virtue of their fable the sticking in of sentences,* as ours do the forcing in of jests. . . .

PRAECEPTA ELEMENTARIA[63]

It is not the passing through these learnings that hurts us, but the dwelling and sticking about them. To descend to those extreme anxieties and foolish cavils of grammarians, is able to break a wit in pieces, being a work of manifold misery and vainness, to be *elementarii senes.*[64] Yet even letters are, as it were, the bank of words, and restore themselves to an author as the pawns of language. But talking and eloquence are not the same: to speak, and to speak well, are two things. A fool may talk, but a wise man speaks, and out of the observation, knowledge, and use of things. Many writers perplex their readers and hearers with mere nonsense. Their writings need sunshine.

Pure[65] and neat language I love, yet plain and customary. A barbarous phrase hath often made me out of love with a good sense, and doubtful* writing hath racked me beyond my patience. The reason why a poet is said that he ought to have all knowledges is that he should not be ignorant of the most, especially of those he will handle. And indeed, when the attaining of them is possible, it were a sluggish and base thing to despair; for frequent imitation of anything becomes a habit quickly. If a man should prosecute as much as could be said of everything, his work would find no end.

---

[61] *Inst.* 1. 8. 5–9.
[62] The 'new' comedy of the Greeks.
[63] 'Elementary precepts'; ll. 2300 ff.
[64] Seneca, *Ep.* 36. 4: 'old men stuck in the rudiments of learning'.
[65] ll. 2315 ff.: from *Inst.* 8, pr. 23–5; 2. 21. 14; 1, pr. 25.

DE ORATIONIS DIGNITATE[66]

Speech is the only benefit man hath to express his excellency of mind above other creatures. It is the instrument of society. Therefore Mercury, who is the president of language, is called *deorum hominumque interpres.*[67] In all speech, words and sense are as the body and the soul. The sense is as the life and soul of language, without which all words are dead. Sense is wrought out of experience, the knowledge of human life and actions, or of the liberal arts, which the Greeks called *Enkyklon paideian.*[68] Words are the people's, yet there is a choice of them to be made; for *verborum delectus origo est eloquentiae.*[69] They are to be chosen according to the persons we make speak, or the things we speak of. Some are of the camp, some of the councilboard, some of the shop, some of the sheepcote, some of the pulpit, some of the bar, etc. And herein is seen their elegance and propriety, when we use them fitly and draw them forth to their just strength and nature by way of translation or metaphor. But in this translation we must only serve necessity (*nam temere nihil transfertur a prudenti*)[70] or commodity,* which is a kind of necessity: that is, when we either absolutely want* a word to express by, and that is necessity, or when we have not so fit a word, and that is commodity;* as when we avoid loss by it, and escape obsceneness, and gain in the grace and property,* which helps significance.

Metaphors far-fet* hinder to be understood; and affected, lose their grace. Or when the person fetcheth his translations from a wrong place: as if a privy councillor should at the table take his metaphor from a dicing house, or ordinary,* or a vintner's vault; or a justice of peace draw his similitudes from the mathematics; or a divine from a bawdy-house, or taverns; or a gentleman of Northamptonshire,

---

[66] 'Of the dignity of speech'; ll. 2328 ff.: from Vives, *De ratione dicendi* (Basel, 1537), bk. 1, introd., and chs. 1–2. For a modern translation see the Ph.D. diss. by J. F. Cooney, Ohio State Univ., 1996 (UMI order 67–6303), pp. 27, 30, 34–9.

[67] Cf. *Aen.* 4. 356: Mercury, bringing a message from Jove to Aeneas, is 'interpreter for gods and men'.

[68] The 'circle of education' or 'encyclopedia' originally constituting the seven liberal arts (*Inst.* 1. 10. 1).

[69] Vives cites Cicero, *Brut.* 72. 253 (quoting Julius Caesar's lost *De analogia*): 'the choice of words is the starting-point of eloquence', adapted by Jonson to read 'Delight in words is the origin of eloquence'. Jonson adds a marginal note: 'Of words, see Hor. De Art. Poetic. Quintil l. 8. Ludov. Vives pag. 6 & 7. Metaphora'. The passages from Quintilian are cited below. Cf. also Hoskyns, p. 400, and Hobbes, p. 617.

[70] 'The prudent man would never employ similitude without a motive' (Vives, tr. Cooney p. 38).

Warwickshire, or the Midland should fetch all his illustrations to his country neighbours from shipping, and tell them of the main sheet and the bowline.*

Metaphors[71] are thus many times deformed, as in him that said, *castratam morte Africani rempublicam*; and another, *stercus curiae Glauciam*; and *cana nive conspuit Alpes.* All attempts that are new in this kind are dangerous, and somewhat hard, before they be softened with use.

A man[72] coins not a new word without some peril, and less fruit: for if it happen to be received, the praise is but moderate; if refused, the scorn is assured. Yet we must adventure, for things at first hard and rough are by use made tender and gentle. It is an honest error that is committed, following great chiefs.

CONSUETUDO[73]

Custom is the most certain mistress of language, as the public stamp makes the current money. But we must not be too frequent with the mint, every day coining, nor fetch words from the extreme and utmost ages; since the chief virtue of a style is perspicuity,* and nothing so vicious* in it as to need an interpreter. Words borrowed of antiquity do lend a kind of majesty to style, and are not without their delight sometimes; for they have the authority of years, and out of their intermission[74] do win to themselves a kind of grace like newness. But the eldest of the present and newest of the past language is the best. For what was the ancient language, which some men so dote upon, but the ancient custom?

Yet when I name custom, I understand not the vulgar custom; for that were a precept no less dangerous to language than life, if we should speak or live after the manners of the vulgar; but that I call

---

[71] ll. 2371 ff.; Jonson supplements Vives from Vives' authority, Quintilian, *Inst.* 8. 6. 5–6; 14–17. Of the three offending metaphors quoted, two come from Cicero, who 'demonstrated [*De or.* 3. 41. 164] . . . how important it is to avoid grossness in metaphor, such as is revealed by the following examples, which he quotes:—"The state was gelded by the death of Africanus"; or "Glaucia, the excrement of the senate-house" '. The third is Quintilian's own instance that 'Metaphors may also be harsh, that is, far-fetched, as in phrases like "Jove with white snow the wintry Alps besprewed" '—a verse by the epic poet Furius, to which Horace also objected (*Sat.* 2. 5. 41).

[72] ll. 2377 ff.: from *Inst.* 1. 5. 71–2; 1. 6. 2.

[73] 'Custom': ll. 2385 ff., from *Inst.* 1. 6. 3, 39–41, 43–5. A marginal note reads *'Venustas'* (beauty, charm).

[74] The period when they were not in use.

custom of speech, which is the consent of the learned; as custom of life, which is the consent of the good. Virgil was most loving of antiquity; yet how rarely doth he insert *aquai*, and *pictai*![75] Lucretius is scabrous* and rough[76] in these: he seeks them, as some do Chaucerisms with us, which were better expunged and banished. Some words are to be culled out for ornament and colour, as we gather flowers to strew houses, or make garlands; but they are better when they grow to our style as in a meadow, where though the mere grass and greenness delights, yet the variety of flowers doth heighten and beautify. Marry, we must not play or riot too much with them, as in paronomasies, nor use too swelling* or ill-sounding words; *quae per salebras altaque saxa cadunt.*[77] It is true, there is no sound but shall find some lovers, as the bitterest confections* are grateful* to some palates.

Our composition[78] must be more accurate* in the beginning and end than in the midst, and in the end more than in the beginning; for through the midst the stream bears us. And this is attained by custom, more than care or diligence. We must express readily and fully, not profusely. There is difference between a liberal and a prodigal* hand. As it is a great point of art, when our matter requires it, to enlarge and veer out all sail;[79] so to take it in, and contract it, is of no less praise when the argument doth ask it: either of them hath their fitness in the place.

A good man always profits by his endeavour, by his help, yea, when he is absent; nay, when he is dead, by his example and memory. So good authors in their style.[80] A strict and succinct style is that where you can take away nothing without loss, and that loss to be manifest. The brief style is that which expresseth much in little. The concise style, which expresseth not enough, but leaves somewhat to be understood. The abrupt style, which hath many breaches,* and doth not seem to end, but fall. The congruent and harmonious fitting of parts in a sentence hath almost the fastening and force of knitting and

---

[75] *Inst.* 1. 7. 18, referring to these archaic genitives as used in *Aen.* 7. 464, 9. 26.

[76] Macrobius (*Saturnalia* 6. 3. 9) describes poetry in the age of Ennius as 'versus scabri'. For Jonson's dislike of archaicisms see n. 60 above.

[77] *Paronomasia* is a type of pun, playing on two words having a similar sound but a different meaning. For the quotation (from Martial) see n. 20 above.

[78] ll. 2424 ff.: from Vives, *De rat. dic.*, bk. 1.

[79] To gradually let out all sails.

[80] Jonson adds examples in the margin: for the 'succinct style' he instances Tacitus (Vives had cited Lysias); for 'the brief style' in the text he adds 'The laconic'; for the 'concise style' he cites Suetonius; and for the 'abrupt style' he cites Fabianus, a rhetorician who lived under Tiberius and Caligula, and whom Marcus Seneca castigated as obscure.

connection; as in stones well-squared, which will rise strong a great way without mortar.

PERIODI[81]

Periods are beautiful when they are not too long, for so they have their strength too, as in a pike or javelin. As we must take the care that our words and sense be clear, so if the obscurity happen through the hearer's or reader's want of understanding, I am not to answer for them, no more than for their not listening or marking:* I must neither find them ears nor mind. But a man cannot put a word so in sense but something about it will illustrate it, if the writer understand himself; for order helps much to perspicuity, as confusion hurts. *Rectitudo lucem adfert: obliquitas et circumductio offuscat.*[82]

We should therefore speak what we can the nearest way, so as we keep our gait, not leap; for too short may as well be not let into the memory, as too long not kept in. Whatsoever loseth the grace and clearness, converts into a riddle; the obscurity is marked, but not the value. That perisheth, and is passed by, like the pearl in the fable.[83] Our style should be like a skein of silk, to be carried and wound by the right thread, not ravelled and perplexed: then all is a knot, a heap.[84] There are words that do as much raise a style as others can depress it. Superlation* and overmuchness amplifies; it may be above faith, but never above a mean. . . . But there are hyperboles which will become one language, that will by no means admit another. As *eos esse Populi Romani exercitus, qui coelum possint perrumpere:*[85] who would say this with us, but a madman? Therefore we must consider in every tongue what is used, what received.

Quintilian[86] warns us that in no kind of translation, or metaphor, or allegory, we make a turn from what we began; as if we fetch the original of our metaphor from sea and billows, we end not in flames

---

[81] 'Sentences'; ll. 2453 ff.: from Vives, *De rat. dic.*, bk. 1.

[82] From Vives: 'A direct expression communicates light; twisted, ambiguous, and round-about ones confuse' (tr. Cooney, p. 71). A few lines below Jonson adds a marginal note: '*Obscuritas offundit tenebras*' ('obscurity encourages darkness').

[83] In Aesop's fable of the cock on the dunghill (Phaedrus, *Fabulae* 3. 12).

[84] I emend 'found' in the 1641 text to 'wound', restoring the coherence of a metaphor found elsewhere in Jonson (*HS* xi. 270); 'perplexed' means confused, pulled 'into a knot, or elfe-lock' as Jonson describes it elsewhere.

[85] A misquotation by Vives of the boast attributed to Caesar in *De bello hispaniensi* 42: 'Are they the armies of the Roman people which can burst the barriers of heaven?'

[86] *Inst.* 8. 6. 50; a warning against mixed metaphors.

and ashes: it is a most foul inconsequence. Neither must we draw out
our allegory too long, lest either we make ourselves obscure, or fall
into affectation, which is childish.

But[87] why do men depart at all from the right and natural ways of
speaking? Sometimes for necessity, when we are driven, or think it
fitter, to speak that in obscure words or by circumstance* which
uttered plainly would offend the hearers; or to avoid obsceneness; or
sometimes for pleasure and variety: as travellers turn out of the high-
way, drawn either by the commodity* of a footpath, or the delicacy or
freshness of the fields. And all this is called *eschēmatismenē*, or figured
language.

ORATIO IMAGO ANIMI[88]

Language most shows a man: speak, that I may see thee. It springs out
of the most retired and inmost parts of us, and is the image of the
parent of it, the mind. No glass renders a man's form or likeness so
true as his speech. Nay, it is likened to a man; and as we consider
feature and composition in a man, so words in language: in the greatness, aptness, sound, structure, and harmony of it. Some men are tall
and big, so some language is high and great. Then the words are
chosen, their sound ample, the composition full, the absolution plenteous,[89] and poured out, all grave, sinewy, and strong. Some are little
and dwarfs: so of speech, it is humble and low, the words poor and
flat, the members and periods thin and weak, without knitting or
number. The middle are of a just stature. There the language is plain
and pleasing,[90] even without stopping, round without swelling; all
well-turned, composed, elegant, and accurate. The vicious* language
is vast and gaping, swelling and irregular; when it contends to be high,
full of rock, mountain, and pointedness;* as it affects to be low, it is
abject and creeps, full of bogs and holes.

And according to their subject, these styles vary, and lose their
names: for that which is high and lofty, declaring excellent matter,

---

[87] ll. 2503 ff.: from Vives (tr. Cooney, p. 82), whose use of the Greek term for 'the figurative style' derives from *Inst.* (9. 1. 13).

[88] 'Speech is the image of the soul', a saying derived from Menander. Lines 2515 ff. are
from Vives, *De rat. dic.*, bk. 2, introd. (tr. Cooney, pp. 87 ff.). The injunction 'speak that I
may see thee' is recorded in Erasmus, *Apophthegmata* 3. 70.

[89] That is, 'the delivery free' (*HS* xi. 272); or 'the cadences rounded' (tr. Cooney, p. 89).
Jonson translates Vives ('*absolutiones fusae*') literally.

[90] Vives has *placida*, meaning 'calm', or 'easy'.

becomes vast and tumorous,* speaking of petty and inferior things; so that which was even and apt in a mean and plain subject, will appear most poor and humble in a high argument. Would you not laugh to meet a great councillor of state in a flat cap, with his trunk-hose and a hobby-horse cloak,[91] his gloves under his girdle, and yond haberdasher in a velvet gown, furred with sables? There is a certain latitude in these things, by which we find the degrees.

The next thing to the stature is the figure and feature in language: that is, whether it be round and straight, which consists of short and succinct periods, numerous* and polished; or square and firm, which is to have equal and strong parts everywhere answerable* and weighed.

The third is the skin and coat, which rests in the well-joining, cementing, and coagmentation of words:[92] when as it is smooth, gentle and sweet, like a table upon which you may run your finger without rubs, and your nail cannot find a joint; not horrid, rough, wrinkled, gaping, or chapped.

After these, the flesh, blood, and bones come in question. We say it is a fleshy style, when there is much periphrasis, and circuit of words;[93] and when with more than enough, it grows fat and corpulent: *arvina orationis*, full of suet and tallow. It hath blood and juice, when the words are proper and apt, their sound sweet, and the phrase neat and picked:* *oratio uncta, et bene pasta*. But where there is redundancy, both the blood and juice are faulty and vicious: *redundat sanguine, quae multo plus dicit, quam necesse est.*[94] Juice in language is somewhat less than blood; for if words be but becoming and signifying,* and the sense gentle, there is juice; but where that wanteth, the language is

---

[91] Jonson provides vivid English elaborations on Vives' bare term '*vestis*'. A 'trunk-hose' was a loose and baggy breeches, unsuitable dress for a councillor, as would be a 'hobby-horse' or long, billowing cloak covering the lower limbs.

[92] Namely, 'that grouping and joining of words which produces harmony or musicality' (tr. Cooney, p. 91). The margin adds the correct technical term, '*compositio*', the joining together of words, to be considered both from the aspect of euphony (avoiding ugly elisions or clumsy collisions of consonants), and syntax. Parfitt illustrates Jonson's analogy with a table by quoting Horace's *Ars poetica* 418, in Jonson's translation, a verse 'corrected to the nail': 'a metaphor from sculpture: the artist would use a finger nail to test the smoothness of the marble he had been working'.

[93] Latin, '*circuitus verborum*', or periphrasis.

[94] The Latin quotations are from Vives, respectively: 'An oration is bucolic [when it is made of rough words and common and country-like sentences . . .]. The blood and juice of an oration imply proper and apt words . . . full and sweet sound, clean diction . . . These features make the speech whole, well-nourished, and full of unction. When it has an excess of blood, the oration says much more than is necessary' (tr. Cooney, pp. 92–4). At the end: 'they have bones and sinews'.

thin, flagging, poor, starved, scarce covering the bone, and shows like stones in a sack. Some men, to avoid redundancy, run into that; and while they strive to have no ill blood or juice, they lose their good. There be some styles, again, that have not less blood, but less flesh and corpulence. These are bony and sinewy: *ossa habent, et nervos.*

NOTAE DOMINI SANCTI ALBANI DE DOCTRIN: INTEMPER[95]

It was well noted by the late Lord St Albans that the study of words is the first distemper* of learning; vain matter* the second; and a third distemper is deceit, or the likeness of truth: imposture held up by credulity. All these are the cobwebs of learning, and to let them grow in us is either sluttish* or foolish. Nothing is more ridiculous than to make an author a dictator, as the Schools have done Aristotle. The damage is infinite knowledge receives by it; for to many things a man should owe but a temporary belief, and a suspension of his own judgement, not an absolute resignation of himself, or a perpetual captivity. Let Aristotle and others have their dues, but if we can make farther discoveries of truth and fitness than they, why are we envied? Let us beware, while we strive to add, we do not diminish, or deface; we may improve, but not augment. By discrediting falsehood, truth grows in request.

We must not go about like men anguished and perplexed for vicious affectations of praise, but calmly study the separation* of opinions, find the errors have intervened, awake antiquity, call former times into question; but make no parties with the present, nor follow any fierce undertakers,* mingle no matter of doubtful credit with the simplicity* of truth, but gently stir the mould about the root of the question, and avoid all digladiations,* facility of credit, or superstitious* simplicity; seek the consonancy and concatenation* of truth; stoop only to point of necessity, and what leads to convenience. Then make exact animadversion* where style hath degenerated, where flourished and thrived in choiceness* of phrase, round and clean composition* of sentence, sweet falling of the clause, varying an illustration by tropes and figures, weight of matter, worth of subject, soundness of argument, life of invention, and depth of judgement. This is *monte potiri,*[96]

---

[95] 'Notes by Lord St Albans concerning the distempers of learning'. Lines 2588 ff. are a partial digest of Bacon's *Advancement of Learning*: see pp. 457–60, and *Francis Bacon*, ed. Vickers, pp. 138–44.

[96] Ovid, *Met.* 5. 254, referring to climbing Helicon.

to get the hill. For no perfect discovery can be made upon a flat or a level. . . .

DE POETICA[97]

We have spoken sufficiently of oratory: let us now make a diversion to poetry. Poetry, in the primogeniture, had many peccant* humours,* and is made to have more now through the levity and inconstancy of men's judgements. Whereas, indeed, it is the most prevailing eloquence, and of the most exalted charact.* Now the discredits and disgraces are many it hath received through men's study of depravation or calumny; their practice being to give it diminution of credit by lessening the professors' estimation,[98] and making the age afraid of their liberty; and the age is grown so tender of her fame, as she calls all writings *aspersions*.* That is the state-word, the phrase of court, Placentia[99] College, which some call Parasites' Place, the Inn of Ignorance. . . .

POETA—WHAT IS A POET?[100]

A poet is that which by the Greeks is called *kat' exochēn, ho Poiētēs*,[101] a maker or a feigner; his art, an art of imitation or feigning, expressing the life of man in fit measure, numbers, and harmony, according to Aristotle: from the word *poiein*, which signifies to make or feign.[102] Hence he is called a poet, not he which writeth in measure only, but that feigneth and formeth a fable,[103] and writes things like the truth. For the fable and fiction is (as it were) the form and soul of any poetical work or poem.

---

[97] 'Of Poetics'; ll. 2837 ff. No specific source known, but there are similarities to both Sidney's *Defence* and Bacon's *Advancement*.

[98] That is, 'the respect enjoyed by those who profess poetry'.

[99] A 'pleasance' or pleasure garden, such as the one built by Duke Humphrey at Greenwich.

[100] Jonson draws on the ancient distinction in literary criticism (going back to Varro and Plutarch) between *poeta*, *poema*, and *poesis* (cf. Spingarn, *CES* i. 226–7). It is found in Jacobus Pontanus, *Poeticarum institutionum libri III* (Ingoldstadt, 1594), as paraphrased by J. Buchler, Jonson's main source at ll. 2943 ff. below.

[101] 'The maker, par excellence'.

[102] Jonson cites Aristotle, *Poet.* 1. 1447ᵃ13 ff., perhaps through an intermediary, such as Scaliger's *Poetice*.

[103] Cf. Sidney, pp. 347, 367; Hobbes, p. 609.

POEMA—WHAT MEAN YOU BY A POEM?

A poem is not alone any work or composition of the poet's in many or few verses; but even one alone verse* sometimes makes a perfect poem. As when Aeneas hangs up and consecrates the arms of Abas with this inscription:

Aeneas haec de Danais victoribus arma,[104]

and calls it a poem, or *carmen*. Such are those in Martial:

Omnia, Castor, emis: sic fiet, ut omnia vendas,[105]

and

Pauper videri Cinna vult; et est pauper.[106]

So were Horace's odes called *Carmina*, his lyric songs. And Lucretius designs* a whole book in his sixth:

Quod in primo quoque carmine claret.[107]

And anciently all the oracles were called *carmina*; or whatever sentence* was expressed, were it much or little, it was called an epic, dramatic, lyric, elegiac, or epigrammatic poem.

POESIS[108]—BUT HOW DIFFERS A POEM FROM WHAT WE CALL POESY?

A poem, as I have told you, is the work of the poet, the end and fruit of his labour and study. Poesy is his skill or craft of making; the very fiction itself, the reason or form of the work. And these three voices differ, as the thing done, the doing, and the doer; the thing feigned, the feigning, and the feigner; so the poem, the poesy, and the poet. Now the poesy is the habit* or the art; nay, rather the queen of arts, which had her original from heaven, received thence from the Hebrews, and had in prime estimation with the Greeks,

---

[104] *Aen.* 3. 288: 'Aeneas hangs on these doors the arms won from Danaan conquerors'.
[105] Martial, *Epigrams* 7. 98: 'You buy everything, Castor; so the result will be that you sell everything.'
[106] Ibid. 8. 19: 'Cinna wishes to appear poor, and he is poor'.
[107] *De rerum natura* 6. 937: 'which is clearly shown in the beginning of my poem too'.
[108] ll. 2943 ff.: from Joannes Buchler, *Reformata poëseos institutio*, appended to his poetical dictionary, *Sacrarum Profanarumque Phrasium Poeticarum Thesaurus* (3rd edn. Cologne, 1607; five editions in London between 1624 and 1637, which describes itself as the thirteenth), ch. 6.

transmitted to the Latins and all nations that professed civility. The study of it (if we will trust Aristotle)[109] offers to mankind a certain rule and pattern of living well and happily, disposing us to all civil offices of society. If we will believe Tully,[110] it nourisheth and instructeth our youth, delights our age, adorns our prosperity, comforts our adversity, entertains us at home, keeps us company abroad, travels with us, watches, divides the times of our earnest* and sports, shares in our country recesses* and recreations, insomuch as the wisest and best learned have thought her the absolute mistress of manners and nearest of kin to virtue. And whereas they entitle philosophy to be a rigid and austere poesy, they have (on the contrary) styled poesy a dulcet and gentle philosophy, which leads on[111] and guides us by the hand to action with a ravishing delight and incredible sweetness.

But before we handle the kinds of poems, with their special differ-ences, or make court to the art itself as a mistress, I would lead you to the knowledge of our poet by a perfect information what he is or should be by nature, by exercise, by imitation, by study,[112] and so bring him down through the disciplines of grammar, logic, rhetoric, and the ethics, adding somewhat out of all peculiar to himself and worthy of your admittance or reception.

1. Ingenium[113]

First, we require in our poet or maker[114]—for that title our language affords him elegantly with the Greek—a goodness of natural wit. For[115] whereas all other arts consist of doctrine and precepts, the poet must be able by nature and instinct to pour out the treasure of his mind, and as Seneca[116] saith, *aliquando secundum Anacreontem insanire*

---

[109] Perhaps *Poet.* 9. 1451ᵇ5 f., or *Pol.* 7. 1336ᵃ30 ff.; or some Renaissance commentator on Aristotle.

[110] Cicero, *Arch.* 7. 16.

[111] Cf. Strabo, *Geography* 1. 2. 3: 'The ancients . . . regarded poetry as a sort of primary philosophy, which was supposed to introduce us to life from childhood, and teach us about character, emotion, and action in a pleasurable way. My own school, the Stoics, actually said that only the wise man could be a poet' (*ALC*, p. 300).

[112] The triad recommended to orators, 'theory, imitation, and practise' (*Rhet. Her.* 1. 2. 3).

[113] What Jonson calls 'natural wit'.

[114] Cf. Puttenham, p. 191, and Sidney, p. 342.

[115] ll. 2960 f.: from Cicero, *Arch.* 8. 18.

[116] ll. 2991 ff. (down to *nascitur*): from Seneca, *De tranquillitate animi* 17. 10–11.

jucundum esse:[117] by which he understands the poetical rapture. And according to that of Plato, *frustra poeticas fores sui compos pulsavit*; and of Aristotle, *nullum magnum ingenium sine mixtura dementiae fuit. Nec potest grande aliquid, et supra caeteros loqui, nisi mota mens.*[118] Then it riseth higher, as by a divine instinct, when it contemns* common and known conceptions. It utters somewhat above a mortal mouth. Then it gets aloft, and flies away with his rider, whither before it was doubtful to ascend. This the poets understood by their Helicon, Pegasus, or Parnassus; and this made Ovid to boast:

> *Est deus in nobis; agitante calescimus illo:*
> *Sedibus aetheriis spiritus ille venit.*[119]

And Lipsius, to affirm: *scio poetam neminem praestantem fuisse, sine parte quadam uberiore divinae aurae.*[120] And hence it is that the coming up of good poets (for I mind not *mediocres*, or *imos*) is so thin and rare among us. Every beggarly corporation affords the state a mayor or two bailiffs yearly; but *solus rex, aut poeta, non quotannis nascitur.*[121]

2. Exercitatio

To this perfection of nature in our poet we require exercise of those parts, and frequent. If his wit will not arrive suddenly at the dignity of the ancients, let him not yet fall out with it, quarrel, or be overhastily angry, offer to turn it away from study in a humour; but come to it again upon better cogitation, try another time with labour. If then it succeed not, cast not away the quills* yet, nor scratch the wainscot,*

---

[117] Seneca writes 'whether we believe with the Greek poet that "sometimes it is a pleasure also to rave"', not specifying Anacreon. Modern editors rather see an allusion to Menander (frg. 421), as echoed by Horace, 'dulce est desipere in loco' (*Odes* 4. 12. 28).

[118] This whole passage comes from Seneca: '[whether we believe . . .] with Plato that "the sane mind knocks in vain at the door of poetry" [*Phdr.* 245a], or with Aristotle that "no great genius has ever existed without some touch of madness"—be that as it may, the lofty utterance that rises above the attempts of others is impossible unless the mind is excited'. The reference to Aristotle is from the pseudo-Aristotelian *Problemata* 30. 1. 954ᵃ32 ff., and does not in fact refer to poetry.

[119] Jonson runs together two passages in Ovid beginning *est deus in nobis: Fasti* 6.5 ff.: 'There is a god within us; it is when he stirs that we burn'; and *Ars am.* 3. 549 f.: 'There is a god within us; and there are dealings with heaven. That inspiration comes from heavenly sources'. Cf. Spenser, p. 189 and n. 54.

[120] Lipsius, *Electorum liber* (Antwerp, 1580), 2. 17: 'I know there has never been a great poet who was without a more than ordinary share of divine inspiration' (tr. Parfitt).

[121] 'Only a king or a poet is not born every year' (Florus, Roman historian, 2nd cent. AD). In the previous sentence '*mediocres* or *imos*' means 'mediocrities or inferiors'.

beat not the poor desk, but bring all to the forge, and file again, turn it anew.[122] There is no statute law of the kingdom bids you be a poet against your will or the first quarter;[123] if it come in a year or two, it is well. The common rhymers pour forth verses, such as they are, extempore, but there never comes from them one sense worth the life of a day. A rhymer and a poet[124] are two things. It is said of the incomparable Virgil[125] that he brought forth his verses like a bear, and after formed them with licking. Scaliger[126] the father writes it of him, that he made a quantity of verses in the morning which afore night he reduced to a less number. But that which Valerius Maximus[127] hath left recorded of Euripides (the tragic poet)'s answer to Alcestis (another poet) is as memorable as modest: who, when it was told to Alcestis that Euripides had in three days brought forth but three verses, and those with some difficulty and throes, Alcestis glorying he could with ease have sent forth a hundred in the space, Euripides roundly replied, 'Like enough. But here is the difference: thy verses will not last those three days, mine will to all time.' Which was as to tell him he could not write a verse. I have met many of these rattles* that made a noise and buzzed. They had their hum, and no more. Indeed, things wrote with labour deserve so to be read, and will last their age.

3. Imitatio[128]

The third requisite in our poet or maker is imitation, to be able to convert the substance or riches of another poet to his own use. To make choice of one excellent man above the rest, and so to follow him till he grow very he, or so like him as the copy may be mistaken for the principal. Not as a creature that swallows what it takes

---

[122] Cf. Horace, *Sat.* 2. 3. 7 f.: (of the poet unable to write) 'In vain you blame the pen, and the innocent wall, begotten when gods and poets were angry, must suffer'; and *Ars P.* 441: 'Et male tornatos incudi reddere versus' ('and return the ill-shaped verses to the anvil').

[123] That is, in the first three months after you start.

[124] Cf. *Inst.* 10. 1. 89, and Jonson, p. 530 for this distinction.

[125] In the *Life* of Virgil by Suetonius/Donatus, ch. 1.

[126] Previous editors of Jonson have not found this remark in Scaliger's *Poetice*. It does occur, however, in Pontanus' *poeticarum institutionem libri III*, 3rd edn. (Ingolstadt, 1600), p. 51, giving as source the *Life of Virgil* jointly ascribed to Suetonius (his lost biographical collection *De viris illustribus*, or *De poetis*) and to the 4th-cent. grammarian Aelius Donatus (the teacher of St Jerome), ch. 22.

[127] *De dictis et factis memorabilibus* 3. 7. 11.

[128] ll. 3058 ff.: from Buchler, *Institutio poetica*, ch. 9.

in crude, raw, or indigested, but that feeds with an appetite, and
hath a stomach to concoct,* divide, and turn all into nourishment. Not
to imitate servilely (as Horace[129] saith) and catch at vices for virtue,
but to draw forth out of the best and choicest flowers, with the bee,
and turn all into honey:[130] work it into one relish* and savour, make
our imitation sweet, observe how the best writers have imitated, and
follow them: how Virgil and Statius have imitated Homer, how
Horace, Archilochus; how Alcaeus, and the other lyrics; and so of
the rest.

4. Lectio

But that which we especially require in him is an exactness of study
and multiplicity of reading, which maketh a full man,[131] not alone
enabling him to know the history or argument of a poem and to report
it, but so to master the matter and style as to show he knows how to
handle, place, or dispose of either with elegancy when need shall
be. And not think he can leap forth suddenly a poet by dreaming
he hath been in Parnassus, or having washed his lips (as they say)
in Helicon.[132] There goes more to his making than so: for to nature,
exercise, imitation, and study, art must be added, to make all these
perfect. And though these challenge to themselves much in the making
up of our maker, it is art only can lead him to perfection, and leave
him there in possession, as planted by her hand. It is the assertion
of Tully,[133] if to an excellent nature there happen an accession or
conformation* of learning and discipline, there will then remain
somewhat noble and singular. For as Simylus saith in Stobaeus,[134]
[. . .] 'without art, nature can never be perfect; and without nature,
art can claim no being'.

---

[129] *Ars P.* 131–5: '[The poet may imitate themes treated by others, and will succeed] if
you do not seek to render word for word as a slavish translator, and if in your copying you
do not follow too closely'.

[130] Cf. Seneca, *Ep.* 84. 3–6, Introduction, pp. 24–5 and Elyot, p. 67.

[131] Cf. Bacon, Essay 'Of Studies': 'Reading maketh a full man; conference, a ready man;
and writing, an exact man' (ed. Vickers, p. 439).

[132] Persius, prol. to *Satires* 1–3: 'I never soused my lips at the Nag's Spring; never, that
I can remember, did I dream on the two-topped Parnassus, that I should thus come forth
suddenly as a poet'. For the myth of Hippocrene, source of inspiration to poets, struck out
on Mount Helicon by the hoof of Pegasus, cf. Baldwin, p. 135 and n. 81.

[133] Cicero, *Arch.* 7. 15.

[134] From Stobaeus, *Florilegium*, via Pontanus, *Poeticarum institutionum libri III* (1594),
p. 2: cf. Spingarn, *CES* i. 228.

But our poet must beware that his study be not only to learn of himself, for he that shall affect to do that confesseth his ever having a fool to his master. He must read many, but ever the best and choicest. Those that can teach him anything, he must ever account his masters, and reverence: among whom Horace, and he that taught him, Aristotle, deserve to be the first in estimation.

Aristotle[135] was the first accurate critic and truest judge, nay, the greatest philosopher the world ever had, for he noted the vices of all knowledges in all creatures, and out of many men's perfections in a science he formed still one art. So he taught us two offices* together, how we ought to judge rightly of others, and what we ought to imitate specially in ourselves. But all this in vain without a natural wit, and a poetical nature in chief. For no man, so soon as he knows this or reads it, shall be able to write the better, but as he is adapted to it by nature, he shall grow the perfect writer. He must have civil prudence* and eloquence, and that whole not taken up by snatches or pieces, in sentences or remnants when he will handle business or carry counsels, as if he came then out of the declaimers' gallery, or shadow,[136] but furnished out of the body of the state, which commonly is the school of men.

The poet is the nearest borderer upon the orator, and expresseth all his virtues, though he be tied more to numbers;* is his equal in ornament, and above him in his strengths.[137] And of the kind, the comic comes nearest, because in moving the minds of men and stirring of affections—in which oratory shows and especially approves her eminence—he chiefly excels. What figure of a body was Lysippus ever able to form with his graver,* or Apelles[138] to paint with his pencil,* as the comedy to life expresseth so many and various affections of the mind? There shall the spectator see some insulting with joy, others fretting with melancholy, raging with anger, mad with love, boiling with avarice, undone with riot,* tortured with expectation, consumed

---

[135] ll. 3110 ff.: from Daniel Heinsius, *De tragoediae constitutione* (Leyden, 1611), ch. 1. See the translation by P. R. Sellin and J. J. McManamon, *On Plot in Tragedy* (Northridge, Calif., 1971), pp. 7–8.

[136] Heinsius (and so Jonson) alludes to the common complaint by Roman rhetoricians (notably Tacitus and Quintilian) about boys, who have learned to speak in the protected surroundings of the rhetors' schools for declamation, and are quite unprepared when they leave its shadows for the harsh sun of the open arena, where real orators contend.

[137] Translated from Cicero, *De or.* 1. 16. 70. Note the rhetorical sense of 'move' (*movere*) in the following sentence.

[138] As Horace records (*Epist.* 2. 1. 239 ff.), Alexander the Great forbade any other worker in bronze than Lysippus or any other painter than Apelles to represent him.

with fear; no perturbation in common life but the orator finds an example of it in the scene. . . .

I[139] am not of that opinion to conclude* a poet's liberty within the narrow limits of laws which either the grammarians or philosophers prescribe. For before they found out those laws there were many excellent poets that fulfilled them; amongst whom none more perfect than Sophocles, who lived a little before Aristotle. Which of the Greeklings durst ever give precepts to Demosthenes? or to Pericles, whom the age surnamed 'heavenly', because he seemed to thunder and lighten with his language?[140] or to Alcibiades,[141] who had rather nature for his guide than art for his master?

But whatsoever nature at any time dictated to the most happy, or long exercise to the most laborious, that the wisdom and learning of Aristotle hath brought into an art, because he understood the causes of things; and what other men did by chance or custom, he doth by reason; and not only found out the way not to err, but the short way we should take not to err. . . .

To judge[142] of poets is only the faculty of poets; and not all poets, but the best. *Nemo infelicius de poetis judicavit, quam qui de poetis scripsit.* But some will say critics are a kind of tinkers, that make more faults than they mend ordinarily. See their diseases, and those of grammarians. It is true, many bodies are the worse for the meddling with; and the multitude of physicians hath destroyed many sound patients with their wrong practice.

But[143] the office of a true critic or censor is not to throw by* a letter anywhere, or damn an innocent syllable, but lay the words together, and amend them; judge sincerely of the author and his matter, which is the sign of solid and perfect learning in a man. Such was Horace,

---

[139] ll. 3161 ff.: from Heinsius, *De tragoediae constitutione*, book 1 (a passage immediately before the praise of Aristotle).

[140] Cf. Aristophanes, *Acharnians* 530–1: 'Then in his wrath Olympian Pericles lightened and thundered and threw Greece into turmoil, making laws worded like drinking songs . . .'.

[141] Judged by Demosthenes (*Contra Meidian* 561) to be 'the most gifted speaker of his time', although he never studied at any rhetoric school.

[142] ll. 3189 f.: from J. J. Scaliger, *Confutatio Fabulae Burdonum* (in *Opuscula*, 1612), including the remark about the Italian critic Lilius Gyraldus: 'No one judged the poets more infelicitously than he who wrote *Of Poets*'. For the common idea that only poets should judge poetry, cf. *Rhet. Her.* 4. 2. 3 (laymen cannot properly judge either good orations or poems), and Spingarn, *CES* i. 229.

[143] ll. 3198 ff.: from Heinsius, *Ad Horatii de Plauto & Terentio iudicium, Dissertatio*, prefixed to his edition of Terence (1618).

an author of much civility, and—if any one among the heathen can be—the best master both of virtue and wisdom; an excellent and true judge upon cause and reason: not because he thought so, but because he knew so, out of use and experience. . . .

35

John Milton,
The making of a Christian poet (1641–1644)

JOHN MILTON (1608–74), the last great poet of the English Renaissance, was educated at St Paul's School (*c.*1620–4, under Alexander Gill), and at Christ's College Cambridge (1625–32). After six years spent at his father's house in the country, where he gave himself up 'with the most complete leisure to reading through the Greek and Latin writers'—a period in which he published *Comus. A masque* (1637), and *Lycidas* (1638)—he spent most of 1638–9 in Italy, being accepted into the Svogliati academy in Florence, and meeting many Italian writers and musicians (including Dati, Frescobaldi, and the imprisoned Galileo). In 1640 he began tutoring private pupils in London, and became involved in controversies on behalf of the Puritans against the Church of England, publishing a series of tracts, including *Areopagitica* (1644). In 1649 the Council of State appointed him Secretary for the Foreign Tongues, with the duty of writing official defences of Cromwell's policies. Imprisoned in 1659, after the defeat of the Parliamentarians, he was allowed to resume private life, publishing *Paradise Lost* in 1667, *Paradise Regained* and *Samson Agonistes* in 1671.

TEXTS. (1) From *The Reason of Church-government Urg'd against Prelaty* (1641), the second book. This is the fourth and longest of the five pamphlets Milton wrote in 1641–2 against the Anglican bishops. In attacking them he also felt the need to justify his actions, as a poet taking part in public controversy. This results in the following autobiographical passage, which describes his self-education as a poet, and argues that all writers have a duty to work *pro bono publico*, and thus cannot shun political engagement.

(2) From *An Apology Against a Pamphlet call'd A Modest Confutation of the Animadversions upon the Remonstrant against Smectymnuus* (1642). This is the last of Milton's antiprelatical pamphlets, part of a long-drawn-out controversy between Bishop Joseph Hall and five Puritan divines, calling themselves 'Smectymnus' from the initials of their names. Like the classical orator declaring his *ethos* or good character, Milton adds another autobiographical passage describing his sense of his own vocation as a Christian poet.

(3) From *Of Education. To Master Samuel Hartlib* (1644). Hartlib (*c.*1600–62), born in Prussia, the son of a Polish merchant and an English

mother, moved to England in 1628 and spent over thirty years tirelessly pro-
moting schemes for the reform of education and religion. His 'office of
address' became an intellectual clearing-house for writers throughout Europe.
At his invitation Milton set down his ideas for reforming education, in which
poetry and rhetoric play the climactic role in training the good citizen and
the Christian poet.

In editing these texts I have benefited from the great Yale edition of the
Complete Prose Works of John Milton, ed. D. M. Wolfe *et al.*, 8 vols. (New
Haven and London, 1953–82), abbreviated *CPM*.

I

. . . I should not choose this manner of writing [polemic, in prose],
wherein knowing myself inferior to myself, led by the genial[1] power
of nature to another task, I have the use, as I may account it, but of
my left hand. . . . For although a poet, soaring in the high region of
his fancies with his garland and singing robes about him, might
without apology speak more of himself[2] than I mean to do, yet for me
sitting here below in the cool element of prose, a mortal thing among
many readers of no empyreal conceit,[3] to venture* and divulge unusual things of myself, I shall petition to the gentler sort, it may not
be envy* to me.

I must say, therefore, that after I had from my first years by the
ceaseless diligence and care of my father (whom God recompense)
been exercised to the tongues[4] and some sciences,* as my age would
suffer, by sundry masters and teachers both at home and at the schools,
it was found that whether aught was imposed me by them that had
the overlooking, or betaken to of mine own choice in English or other
tongue, prosing or versing, but chiefly this latter, the style, by certain
vital signs it had, was likely to live. But much latelier in the private
academies of Italy, whither I was favoured to resort—perceiving that
some trifles which I had in memory, composed at under twenty or
thereabout (for the manner is that everyone must give some proof of
his wit and reading there) met with acceptance above what was looked
for, and other things which I had shifted* in scarcity of books and

---

[1] The gifts of nature, or general disposition.

[2] In classical rhetoric such self-revelations were used to establish the orator's good character and secure the audience's goodwill. Milton gave them a higher role: 'I conceav'd my
selfe to be not as mine own person, but as a member incorporate into that truth whereof I
was perswaded' (*CPM* i. 871).

[3] Sublime or elevated concepts.

[4] Milton knew Greek, Latin, Hebrew, French, Italian.

conveniences to patch up amongst them, were received with written encomiums, which the Italian is not forward to bestow on men of this side the Alps—I began thus far to assent both to them and diverse of my friends here at home, and not less to an inward prompting[5] which now grew daily upon me, that by labour and intent* study (which I take to be my portion in this life) joined with the strong propensity of nature, I might perhaps leave something so written to aftertimes, as they should not willingly let it die.

These thoughts at once possessed me, and these other; that if I were certain to write as men buy leases, for three lives[6] and downward, there ought no regard be sooner had than to God's glory, by the honour and instruction of my country. For which cause, and not only for that I knew it would be hard to arrive at the second rank among the Latins, I applied myself to that resolution which Ariosto followed against the persuasions of Bembo,[7] to fix all the industry and art I could unite to the adorning of my native tongue; not to make verbal curiosities* the end, that were a toilsome vanity, but to be an interpreter and relater[8] of the best and sagest things[9] among mine own citizens throughout this island in the mother dialect. That what the greatest and choicest wits of Athens, Rome, or modern Italy, and those Hebrews of old did for their country, I, in my proportion, with this over and above of being a Christian,[10] might do for mine; not caring to be once named abroad, though perhaps I could attain to that, but content with these British islands as my world; whose fortune hath hitherto been that if the Athenians, as some[11] say made their small deeds great and

---

[5] A divine inspiration to poetry.

[6] A lease that remains 'in force during the life of the longest liver of three specified persons'—not the lasting fame that a serious poet would aspire to.

[7] In 1642 Milton had been reading Sir John Harington's translation of Ariosto's *Orlando Furioso* (see p. 302), in the 'Life' attached to which it is recorded that Ariosto was determined 'to make some Poem, finding his strength to serve him to it, and though he could have accomplished it very wel in Latine, yet he chose rather his native tongue, . . . for when Bembo would have disswaded him from writing Italian, alledging that he should winne more praise by writing Latine: his answere was, that he had rather be one of the principal & chiefe Tuscan writers, than scarce the second or third among the Latins': *Orlando Furioso*, ed. R. McNulty (Oxford, 1972), p. 571.

[8] That is, one who teaches through God-given insight, as opposed to a mere story-teller.

[9] Milton echoes the standard belief in the primacy of thought or subject-matter (*res*) over verbal expression. Cf. Ascham, pp. 141–3, Gascoigne, p. 163; Sidney, p. 380; Daniel, p. 441; Bacon, p. 459; Carew, p. 555; Jonson, pp. 559, 570.

[10] So having a truer and stronger inspiration.

[11] Sallust, *Bellum Catilinae* 7. 2–4. The opening section of this history praises action on behalf of the state.

renowned by their eloquent writers, England hath had her noble
achievements made small by the unskilful handling of monks and
mechanics.[12]

Time serves not now, and perhaps I might seem too profuse to give
any certain account of what the mind at home in the spacious circuits
of her musing hath liberty to propose[13] to herself, though of highest
hope and hardest attempting; whether that epic form whereof the two
poems of Homer and those other two of Virgil and Tasso are a
diffuse,* and the book of Job a brief model; or whether the rules of
Aristotle herein are strictly to be kept, or nature to be followed, which
in them that know art and use judgement, is no transgression but an
enriching of art;[14] and lastly, what king or knight before the conquest
might be chosen in whom to lay the pattern[15] of a Christian hero. And
as Tasso gave to a prince of Italy[16] his choice whether he would
command him to write of Godfrey's expedition against the Infidels,
or Belisarius against the Goths, or Charlemain against the Lombards;
if to the instinct of nature and the emboldening of art aught may be
trusted, and that there be nothing adverse in our climate or the fate
of this age, it haply would be no rashness, from an equal diligence and
inclination, to present the like order in our own ancient stories. Or
whether those dramatic constitutions,[17] wherein Sophocles and
Euripides reign, shall be found more doctrinal* and exemplary to a
nation, the scripture also affords us a divine pastoral drama in the
Song of Solomon, consisting of two persons and a double chorus,
as Origen[18] rightly judges. And the Apocalypse of St John is the

[12] Milton (expressing the usual Protestant scorn for the Catholic Middle Ages) dismisses
monastic culture as that of illiterate hand workers.

[13] In the MS preserved at Trinity College Cambridge Milton jotted down (probably in
1641–2) outlines and notes of subjects for tragedies on Old and New Testament and British
themes (*CPM* viii. 539–96).

[14] Like many classical and Renaissance writers, Milton believed that 'art'—literary
theory, usually prescriptive—was only a systematization of nature.

[15] Milton, like Sidney, Spenser, and most Renaissance critics, believed that poets should
choose exemplary heroes.

[16] Alfonso II of Ferrara, Duke from 1559 to 1597, who is said to have preferred the story
of Godfrey of Bouillon (1058–1100) and the First Crusade.

[17] 'A constitution of a law, decree, or enactment. The word is used because tragedy
is intended to teach' (*CPM* i. 814 n.). Milton's introductory 'Or whether' reflects the
Renaissance belief that the teachings of epic differed from those of tragedy: cf. Tasso, in
LCPD, p. 503.

[18] An ascetic theologian (AD 185–254), in his *In Canticum Canticorum Prologus*, which
Milton knew from the *Operum theologicorum exegeticorum* (1628) of David Pareus (*CPM* i.
815 n.).

majestic image of a high and stately tragedy, shutting up* and intermingling her solemn scenes and acts with a sevenfold chorus of hal-
lelujahs and harping symphonies; and this my opinion the grave
authority of Pareus, commenting that book, is sufficient to confirm.

Or if occasion shall lead to imitate those magnific* odes and hymns
wherein Pindar and Callimachus are in most things worthy, some
others in their frame judicious, in their matter[19] most an end faulty.
But those frequent songs[20] throughout the law and prophets beyond
all these, not in their divine argument alone, but in the very critical*
art of composition, may be easily made appear over all the kinds of
lyric poesy to be incomparable. These abilities,[21] wheresoever they be
found, are the inspired gift of God rarely bestowed, but yet to some
(though most abuse) in every nation, and are of power beside the office
of a pulpit, to inbreed and cherish in a great people the seeds of virtue
and public civility;* to allay* the perturbations of the mind and set
the affections in right tune; to celebrate in glorious and lofty hymns
the throne and equipage of God's almightiness, and what He works
and what He suffers to be wrought with high providence in His
church; to sing the victorious agonies of martyrs and saints, the deeds
and triumphs of just and pious nations doing valiantly through faith
against the enemies of Christ; to deplore* the general relapses of kingdoms and states from justice and God's true worship.

Lastly, whatsover in religion is holy and sublime, in virtue amiable*
or grave, whatsoever[22] hath passion or admiration* in all the changes
of that which is called fortune from without, or the wily subtleties*
and refluxes of man's thoughts from within, all these things with a
solid and treatable smoothness[23] to paint out and describe. Teaching
over the whole book of sanctity and virtue through all the instances

[19] Distinguishing the structure of an ode (which in Pindar's case obeyed complex rules,
not universally understood) from its subject-matter.

[20] On the Bible as poetry cf. Sidney, pp. 341–2, 345, on the 'songs' and 'hymns' of
Solomon, Moses, and Debora, echoed by Harington (p. 311).

[21] Milton, blending sacred and secular theories of poetry as inspiration, lists five functions of the *vates* or serious national poet: (1) to inculcate virtue by precept (and by example:
see p. 595 and n. 24); (2) to temper and moderate the passions (as in Aristotle's notion of
catharsis: *Poet.* 6. 1449^{b}27 f.); (3) to praise the glory of God; (4) to celebrate the deeds of
Christians, in both suffering and in victory; (5) to deplore the relapses of England, which
Milton saw as his special task (*CPM* i. 816 n.). For similarities with Tasso cf. *LCPD*,
pp. 476, 488.

[22] Cf. Phil. 4: 8: 'Finally, brethren, whatsoever things are true, whatsoever things are
honest . . . just . . . pure . . . lovely . . . of good report: if there be any virtue, and if there
be any praise, think on these things'.

[23] Qualities of language, involving truth, deliberation, and a consistently wrought style.

of example, with such delight[24] to those especially of soft and delicious* temper who will not so much as look upon Truth herself, unless
they see her elegantly dressed, that whereas the paths of honesty and
good life appear now rugged and difficult, though they be indeed easy
and pleasant, they would then appear to all men both easy and pleasant, though they were rugged and difficult indeed. And what a benefit
this would be to our youth and gentry may be soon guessed by what
we know of the corruption and bane* which they suck in daily from
the writings and interludes[25] of libidinous and ignorant poetasters,*
who, having scarce ever heard of that which is the main consistence*
of a true poem, the choice of such persons as they ought to introduce,
and what is moral and decent* to each one, do for the most part lap*
up vicious principles in sweet pills[26] to be swallowed down, and make
the taste of virtuous documents* harsh and sour.

But because the spirit of man cannot demean itself lively[27] in this
body without some recreating intermission of labour and serious
things, it were happy for the commonwealth if our magistrates, as in
those famous governments of old,[28] would take into their care, not
only the deciding of our contentious lawcases and brawls, but the
managing of our public sports and festival pastimes, that they might
be, not such as were authorized[29] a while since, the provocations of
drunkenness and lust, but such as may inure and harden our bodies
by martial exercises to all warlike skill and performance, and may civ-
ilize, adorn, and make discreet our minds by the learned and affable
meeting of frequent academies, and the procurement of wise and
artful recitations sweetened with eloquent and graceful enticements to
the love and practice of justice, temperance, and fortitude,[30] instructing and bettering the nation at all opportunities, that the call of
wisdom and virtue may be heard everywhere, as Solomon[31] saith: 'She

[24] This notion that poetry teaches by delightful examples is central to Sidney's *Defence*
(see Introduction, pp. 12–18) and to many Renaissance treatises: cf. *LCPD*, pp. 316, 399–40,
and index, s.vv. 'delight', 'example', 'instruction'.

[25] A contemptuous term for popular drama.

[26] The opposite of correct practice, by which poetry was a 'sweet medicine' inclining the
reader towards virtue. Cf. Sidney, p. 358 and n. 89.

[27] Maintain mental health, by the interchange of work and pastime.

[28] As in ancient Greece, in the Olympian and other games, which encouraged athletics
as a part of education, and included contests in music, poetry, and oratory.

[29] By Charles 1 in 1633, a declaration known as the *Book of Sports*, declaring 'May-
games, Whitsun-ales, and morris-dances' lawful, so arousing the Puritans' anger.

[30] Three of the four cardinal virtues (omitting prudence); cf. Wilson, pp. 85–6, and
Cicero, *Off.* 1. 6. 18 ff.

[31] Prov. 1: 20–1 and 8: 2.

crieth without, she uttereth her voice in the streets, in the top of high places, in the chief concourse, and in the openings of the gates'. Whether this may not be, not only in pulpits, but after another persuasive method, at set and solemn panegyries;* in theatres, porches,* or what other place or way may win most upon the people to receive at once both recreation and instruction,[32] let them in authority consult.

The thing which I had to say, and those intentions which have lived within me ever since I could conceive myself anything worth to my country, I return to crave excuse that urgent reason hath plucked from me by an abortive and foredated[33] discovery. And the accomplishment of them lies not but in a power above man's to promise; but that none hath by more studious ways endeavoured, and with more unwearied spirit that none shall, that I dare almost aver of myself as far as life and free leisure will extend; and that the land had once enfranchised herself from this impertinent* yoke of prelaty, under whose inquisitorious and tyrannical duncery no free and splendid* wit can flourish. Neither do I think it shame to covenant with any knowing reader, that for some few years yet I may go on trust with him toward the payment of what I am now indebted, as being a work not to be raised from the heat of youth, or the vapours of wine, like that which flows at waste from the pen of some vulgar amorist, or the trencher fury of a rhyming parasite,[34] nor to be obtained by the invocation of Dame Memory and her Siren daughters,[35] but by devout prayer to that eternal Spirit who can enrich with all utterance and knowledge, and sends out his seraphim[36] with the hallowed fire of his altar, to touch and purify the lips of whom he pleases. To this must be added industrious and select reading,

[32] Joining *delectare* (poetry) and *docere* (religious instruction, from the pulpit), to produce a more 'persuasive' method.

[33] Milton did not feel ready to embark on his great work, the more 'urgent reason' being his controversy with the bishops. Earlier in this pamphlet he averred that 'if I hunted after praise by the ostentation of wit and learning, I should not write thus out of my own season, when I have neither yet completed to my mind the full circle of my private studies; . . . or were I ready to my wishes, it were a folly to commit any thing elaborately composed to the careless and interrupted listening of these tumultuous times' (*CPM* i. 807).

[34] Debased forms of poetry, the 'lascivious' popular literature which had been denounced by the Puritans in the London Petition of Dec. 1640, and the corrupt praises written by poets dependent on a patron for meals (on a 'trencher' or plate) and gifts.

[35] Milton confuses Memory, the mother of the Muses, with the sirens described by Plato (*Resp.* 10. 617–18), one of whom sits on each of the eight spheres.

[36] Cf. Isa. 6: 1–7, where God sends down a seraph with 'a live coal in his hands' to purify unclean lips.

steady observation, insight into all seemly and generous* arts and affairs. . . .

2

I had my time, readers, as others have who have good learning bestowed upon them, to be sent to those places where, the opinion was, it might be soonest attained; and as the manner is, was not unstudied in those authors which are most commended. Whereof some were grave orators and historians, whose matter methought I loved indeed, but as my age then was,[37] so I understood them; others were the smooth elegiac poets,[38] whereof the schools are not scarce, whom both for the pleasing sound of their numerous* writing, which in imitation I found most easy and most agreeable to nature's part in me, and for their matter, which what it is there be few who know not, I was so allured to read that no recreation came to me better welcome. For that it was then those years with me which are excused though they be least severe, I may be saved the labour to remember ye. Whence having observed them to account it the chief glory of their wit, in that they were ablest to judge, to praise, and by that could esteem themselves worthiest to love those high perfections which under one or other name they took to celebrate, I thought with myself by every instinct and presage* of nature, which is not wont to be false, that what emboldened them to this task, might with such diligence as they used embolden me; and that what judgement, wit, or elegance was my share, would herein best appear, and best value itself, by how much more wisely, and with more love of virtue I should choose (let rude ears be absent)[39] the object of not unlike praises. For albeit these thoughts to some will seem virtuous and commendable, to others only pardonable, to a third sort perhaps idle; yet the mentioning of them now will end in serious.*

Nor blame it, readers, in those years to propose to themselves such a reward as the noblest dispositions above other things in this life have sometimes preferred: whereof not to be sensible* when good and fair in one person meet, argues both a gross and shallow judgement, and withal an ungentle and swainish breast. For by the firm settling of these persuasions I became, to my best memory, so much a proficient that, if I found those authors anywhere speaking unworthy things of

---

[37] Cf. 1 Cor. 13: 11, 'When I was a child, I spoke as a child, I understood as a child . . .'.
[38] Milton was particularly attracted to Ovid.
[39] Cf. Virgil, *Aen.* 6. 258, 'procul o, procul este, profani' ('Away! away! unhallowed ones!').

themselves or unchaste of those names which before they had extolled, this effect it wrought with me, from that time forward their art I still applauded, but the men I deplored; and above them all, preferred the two famous renowners[40] of Beatrice and Laura, who never write but honour of them to whom they devote their verse, displaying sublime and pure thoughts, without transgression. And long it was not after, when I was confirmed in this opinion that he who would not be frustrate of his hope to write well hereafter in laudable things, ought himself to be a true poem,[41] that is, a composition and pattern of the best and honourablest things; not presuming to sing high praises of heroic men, or famous cities, unless he have in himself the experience and the practice of all that which is praiseworthy. These reasonings, together with a certain niceness* of nature, an honest haughtiness and self-esteem either of what I was, or what I might be (which let envy call pride), and lastly that modesty whereof, though not in the title-page, yet here I may be excused to make some beseeming profession; all these uniting the supply of their natural aid together, kept me still above those low descents of mind beneath which he must deject and plunge himself that can agree to saleable and unlawful prostitutions.

Next (for hear me out now, readers, that I may tell ye whether my younger feet wandered), I betook me among those lofty fables and romances, which recount in solemn cantos[42] the deeds of knighthood founded by our victorious kings, and from hence had in renown over all Christendom. There I read it in the oath of every knight, that he should defend to the expense of his best blood, or of his life if it so befell him, the honour and chastity of virgin or matron; from whence even then I learned what a noble virtue chastity sure must be, to the defence of which so many worthies, by such a dear* adventure of themselves, had sworn. And if I found in the story afterward any of them, by word or deed, breaking that oath, I judged it the same fault of the poet as that which is attributed to Homer,[43] to have written indecent things of the gods. Only this my mind gave me, that every free* and gentle spirit, without that oath, ought to be born a knight, nor needed to expect the gilt spur, or the laying of a sword upon his shoulder,[44] to stir him up both by his counsel and his arm to secure and protect the weakness of any attempted* chastity. So that even those

---

[40] Dante and Petrarch.   [41] Cf. Strabo, *Geography* 1. 2. 5, apud Elyot, p. 64 n. 32.
[42] Such as the *Faerie Queene*; cf. p. 297.
[43] By Plato, *Resp.* 2. 377d ff. (*ALC*, pp. 51 ff.).   [44] Attributes of knighthood.

books which to many others have been the fuel of wantonness* and loose living, I cannot think how, unless by divine indulgence, proved to me so many incitements, as you have heard, to the love and steadfast observation of that virtue which abhors the society of bordelloes.

Thus, from the laureate* fraternity of poets, riper years and the ceaseless round of study and reading led me to the shady spaces of philosophy, but chiefly to the divine volumes of Plato and his equal,* Xenophon.[45] Where, if I should tell ye what I learnt of chastity and love (I mean that which is truly so, whose charming cup is only virtue, which she bears in her hand to those who are worthy—the rest are cheated with a thick intoxicating potion which a certain sorceress,[46] the abuser of love's name, carries about), and how the first and chiefest office* of love begins and ends in the soul, producing those happy twins of her divine generation,[47] knowledge and virtue—with such abstracted* sublimities as these, it might be worth your listening, readers, as I may one day hope to have ye in a still time, when there shall be no chiding; not in these noises, the adversary, as you know, barking at the door. . . .

3

I will not resist, therefore, whatever it is either of divine or human obligement that you[48] lay upon me; but will forthwith set down in writing, as you request me, that voluntary idea, which hath long in silence presented itself to me, of a better education, in extent and comprehension far more large, and yet of time far shorter and of attainment far more certain, than hath been yet in practice. Brief I shall endeavour to be; for that which I have to say assuredly this nation hath extreme need should be done sooner than spoken. To tell you, therefore, that I have benefited herein among old renowned authors I shall spare; and to search what many modern Januas and Didactics[49]

[45] Author both of the *Memorabilia* of Socrates and the *Cyropaedia*, an idealized romance highly prized in the Renaissance: cf. Spenser, p. 299, Sidney, pp. 347, 353–5.

[46] Probably Circe, as described in *Comus*, ll. 45–52.

[47] Cf. Plato, *Symposium* 209a.

[48] Samuel Hartlib, who invited Milton to write this treatise.

[49] Titles of works by the Moravian educational reformer John Amos Comenius (1592–1670), a close associate of Hartlib, who visited England in 1641–2. The *Janua Linguarum Reserata* (1631), speedily translated into English (7 editions between 1631 and 1643), outlined a method of teaching languages and important facts by a series of sentences grouped into topics. The *Didactica Magna* was partially translated by Hartlib in *A Reformation of Schools* (1642).

more than ever I shall read have projected, my inclination leads me
not. But if you can accept of these few observations which have
flowered off,* and are, as it were, the burnishing* of many contemplative years altogether spent in the search of religious and civil
knowledge, and such as pleased you so well in the relating, I here give
you them to dispose of.

The end, then, of learning is, to repair the ruins of our first
parents[50] by regaining to know God aright, and out of that knowledge
to love him, to imitate him, to be like him, as we may the nearest, by
possessing our souls of true virtue, which, being united to the heavenly grace of faith, makes up the highest perfection. But because our
understanding cannot in this body found itself but on sensible* things,
nor arrive so clearly to the knowledge of God and things invisible as
by orderly conning over* the visible and inferior creature, the same
method is necessarily to be followed in all discreet* teaching.

And seeing every nation affords not experience and tradition
enough for all kind of learning, therefore we are chiefly taught the
languages of those people who have at any time been most industrious
after wisdom; so that language is but the instrument conveying to us
things useful to be known. And though a linguist should pride himself
to have all the tongues that Babel cleft the world into, yet if he have
not studied the solid things in them as well as the words and lexicons,[51]
he were nothing so much to be esteemed a learned man as any yeoman
or tradesman[52] competently wise in his mother-dialect only. . . .

And for the usual method of teaching arts, I deem it to be an old
error of universities, not yet well recovered from the scholastic grossness of barbarous ages, that, instead of beginning with arts most easy

[50] Milton takes literally the biblical notion of human corruption following the Fall (Ps.
14: 1–3; Rom. 3: 23), and shares the contemporary view of its severe consequences for nature
and human learning: cf. Vickers (ed.), *Francis Bacon*, pp. 109, 123, 564 ff.

[51] Milton reiterates the traditional dichotomy, by which the subject-matter (*res*) is more
important than whatever words we clothe it in (n. 9 above). Cf. Dionysius of Halicarnassus, *De compositio verborum* 1: 'The study of any kind of speech involves, one may say, two
kinds of exercise, one concerning thought and the other concerning words. The former
touches more on that department of rhetoric which deals with content, the latter on that
which deals with language'; young men may have ability with *verba*, but a mastery of *res*
only comes with maturity (*ALC*, p. 322), also Erasmus, *De ratione studii ac legendi interpre-
tandique auctores* (1512): 'knowledge as a whole seems to be of two kinds, of things and of
words. Knowledge of words comes earlier'—as a child learns language-skills—'but that of
things is the more important' (*CWE* xxiv. 666). Cf. Bacon, p. 459, and Milton's reference at
the end of the next paragraph to time mis-spent in 'learning mere words'.

[52] Those engaged in farming or trade, who, although not knowing languages, would be
familiar with the real world.

(and those be such as are most obvious to the sense), they present their young unmatriculated novices at first coming with the most intellective abstractions of logic and metaphysics;[53] so that they, having but newly left those grammatic flats and shallows where they stuck unreasonably to learn a few words with lamentable construction, and now on the sudden transported under another climate,[54] to be tossed and turmoiled with their unballasted wits in fathomless and unquiet deeps of controversy, do, for the most part, grow into hatred and contempt of learning, mocked and deluded all this while with ragged notions and babblements,[55] while they expected worthy and delightful knowledge; till poverty or youthful years call them importunately their several ways, and hasten them, with the sway of friends, either to an ambitious and mercenary, or ignorantly zealous divinity:[56] some allured to the trade of law,[57] grounding their purposes not on the prudent* and heavenly contemplation of justice and equity, which was never taught them, but on the promising and pleasing thoughts of litigious terms, fat contentions, and flowing fees. Others betake them to state affairs with souls so unprincipled in virtue and true generous breeding, that flattery, and court shifts,* and tyrannous aphorisms[58] appear to them the highest points of wisdom, instilling their barren hearts with a conscientious slavery, if, as I rather think, it be not feigned. Others, lastly, of a more delicious* and airy* spirit, retire themselves, knowing no better, to the enjoyments of ease and luxury, living out their days in feast and jollity; which, indeed, is the wisest and safest course of all these, unless they were with more integrity undertaken. And these are the errors, and these are the fruits of misspending our prime youth at the schools and universities, as we do, either in learning mere words, or such things chiefly as were better unlearnt. . . .

---

[53] Echoing Bacon's diagnosis of the bad effects of premature exposure to these difficult and abstract disciplines: cf. Vickers (ed.), *Francis Bacon*, pp. 119, 173. Milton's uses of the words 'metaphysics' and 'metaphysical' are always pejorative.

[54] In the literal sense (from the Greek *klima*, slope of ground, zone), a region of the earth, defined in purely topographical terms.

[55] For Milton, these were all characteristics of the medieval scholastic disputation.

[56] Milton often criticized the English clergy for these defects (*CPM* ii. 375 n.).

[57] Milton had a low estimate of the law as a profession, seeing it as interested not in justice but in 'litigious terms'—that is, the periods during which courts are in session, where 'contentions' or disputes brought fat fees.

[58] Perhaps the aphorisms associated in the Renaissance with Tacitus and Machiavelli, in the 'reason of state' tradition, which put pragmatic self-preservation above ethical principle.

I call, therefore, a complete and generous[59] education, that which fits a man to perform justly, skilfully, and magnanimously all the offices,* both private and public, of peace and war. And how all this may be done between twelve and one-and-twenty, less time[60] than is now bestowed in pure trifling at grammar and sophistry, is to be thus ordered: . . .

For their studies: first, they should begin with the chief and necessary rules of some good grammar, either that now used,[61] or any better; and while this is doing, their speech is to be fashioned to a distinct and clear pronunciation, as near as may be to the Italian, especially in the vowels. For we Englishmen, being far northerly, do not open our mouths in the cold air wide enough to grace a southern tongue, but are observed by all other nations to speak exceeding close and inward; so that to smatter Latin with an English mouth is as ill hearing as law French.

Next, to make them expert in the usefullest points of grammar, and withal to season them and win them early to the love of virtue[62] and true labour, ere any flattering seducement or vain principle seize them wandering, some easy and delightful book of education should be read to them, whereof the Greeks have store, as Cebes, Plutarch, and other Socratic discourses;[63] but in Latin we have none of classic authority extant, except the two or three first books of Quintilian[64] and some select pieces elsewhere.

But here the main skill and groundwork will be to temper* them such lectures and explanations upon every opportunity, as may lead and draw them in willing obedience, inflamed with the study* of

---

[59] Appropriate to one of noble birth or spirit (Lat. *generosus*, of good or noble birth). In several places Milton's language shows that this treatise is intended to train future leaders (*CPM* ii. 378–9 nn.).

[60] Renaissance education normally lasted fourteen years: seven for the grammar school, four for the BA, three for the MA. Starting later, Milton would reduce the curriculum to nine years; and the building concerned 'should be at once both School and University, not needing a remove to any other house of Schollership . . .' (*CPM* ii. 380).

[61] The Latin grammar by William Lily was the only authorized manual.

[62] Renaissance grammar teaching included elementary texts on manners and morals, such as the *Carmen de Moribus*, and Cato's *Distichs*. Milton recommends more exalted models.

[63] The *Pinax* or *Table of Cebes* was an allegorical dialogue on how happiness could be attained by practising the virtues. By Plutarch is probably meant the opening essay in the *Moralia*, 'On the Education of Children'. The 'Socratic discourses' could be those by Plato, or by Xenophon in his *Memorabilia*.

[64] The first two books of the *Institutio oratoria* give a humane description of education, which is to be adapted to the capacities of individual pupils, and based on encouragement, not force.

learning and the admiration of virtue,[65] stirred up with high hopes of living to be brave men and worthy patriots, dear to God and famous to all ages: that they may despise and scorn all their childish and ill-taught qualities, to delight in manly and liberal* exercises; which he who hath the art and proper eloquence to catch them with, what with mild and effectual persuasions, and what with the intimation of some fear, if need be, but chiefly by his own example, might in a short space gain them to an incredible diligence and courage, infusing into their young breasts such an ingenuous and noble ardour as would not fail to make many of them renowned and matchless men. . . .

By this time[66] years and good general precepts will have furnished them more distinctly with that act of reason which in ethics is called *prohairesis*,[67] that they may with some judgment contemplate upon moral good and evil. Then will be required a special reinforcement of constant and sound indoctrinating to set them right and firm, instructing them more amply in the knowledge of virtue and the hatred of vice, while their young and pliant affections are led through all the moral works of Plato, Xenophon, Cicero, Plutarch, Laertius, and those Locrian remnants;[68] but still to be reduced in their rightward studies, wherewith they close the day's work, under the determinate sentence[69] of David or Solomon, or the evangels and apostolic scriptures.

Being perfect in the knowledge of personal duty, they may then begin the study of economics.[70] And either now or before this they

[65] Cf. Cicero, *Arch.* 6. 14, Elyot, pp. 57–8, Sidney, p. 365, Jonson, pp. 469–70.

[66] After 3–4 years' study; boys would be aged 15 to 16. In the section omitted here Milton outlines a curriculum including arithmetic, geometry, astronomy, religion and scripture, Latin writers on agriculture, the use of globes and maps, beginning Greek (so that students can read classical works on biology, botany, physics, engineering, medicine, and geography), trigonometry, architecture, military fortification, meteorology, human anatomy, gardening, agriculture, pharmacy, and navigation. Once this knowledge of nature and the human arts has been acquired, 'those poets which are now counted most hard, will be both facil and pleasant'—such as Hesiod, Theocritus, Aratus, Oppian, Lucretius, Manilius, 'and the rurall part of Virgil' (*CPM* ii. 385–96).

[67] Choice. Cf. *Eth. Nic.* 2. 6. 1106[b]36, 3. 2–3. 1111[b]5 ff., where Aristotle defines it as a voluntary action based on reasoning.

[68] The standard texts in the study of moral philosophy: Plato's *Apology* and selected dialogues; Xenophon's *Apology for Socrates*, *Memorabilia*, and *Cyropaideia*; Cicero's *De officiis*; Plutarch's *Moralia*; Diogenes Laertius' *Lives and Opinions of Eminent Philosophers*; and the treatise *On the Soul of the World and Nature*, formerly attributed to Timaeus of Locri.

[69] Led back to the scriptural authorities which 'determine' or settle all questions.

[70] The management of a household (Greek *oikos*), with all that this implied. The closing reference to Sophocles' *Trachiniae* and Euripides' *Alcestis* picks out two tragedies in which a devoted wife plays a prominent role.

may have easily learned at any odd hour the Italian tongue. And soon after, but with wariness and good antidote, it would be wholesome enough to let them taste some choice comedies, Greek, Latin, or Italian; those tragedies also that treat of household matters, as *Trachiniae*, *Alcestis*, and the like.

The next move must be to the study of politics;[71] to know the beginning, end, and reasons of political societies, that they may not, in a dangerous fit* of the commonwealth, be such poor shaken uncertain reeds, of such a tottering conscience as many of our great councillors have lately shown themselves, but steadfast pillars of the state. After this they are to dive into the grounds of law and legal justice, delivered first and with best warrant by Moses, and, as far as human prudence can be trusted, in those extolled remains of Grecian law-givers, Lycurgus, Solon, Zaleucus, Charondas;[72] and thence to all the Roman edicts and tables, with their Justinian;[73] and so down to the Saxon and common laws of England and the statutes.

Sundays also and every evening may now be understandingly spent in the highest matters of theology and church history, ancient and modern: and ere this time at a set hour the Hebrew tongue might have been gained, that the Scriptures may be now read in their own original; whereto it would be no impossibility to add the Chaldee[74] and the Syrian dialect.

When all these employments are well conquered,[75] then will the choice histories, heroic poems, and Attic tragedies of stateliest and most regal argument, with all the famous political orations, offer themselves; which, if they were not only read, but some of them got by memory, and solemnly pronounced with right accent and grace as might be taught, would endue them even with the spirit and vigour of Demosthenes or Cicero, Euripides or Sophocles.

And now, lastly, will be the time to read with them those organic

---

[71] All things pertaining to citizens (Greek *politikos*).

[72] The ancient Greek legal codes referred to here were not extant in Milton's time, and were known only from later reports.

[73] The *Twelve Tables* were the first Roman code of laws (*c*.450 BC); the *Institutiones* and other legal works prepared under the direction of Justinian, Emperor of the East (AD 527–65), codified the Roman civil law for all Europe.

[74] Aramaic, the Semitic dialect in which portions of the Bible are preserved.

[75] It is instructive to note the four genres that Milton postpones to this late stage of education: history, epic, tragedy, and political orations. The authors recommended are Herodotus, Thucydides, Sallust, and perhaps Livy; Homer and Virgil; Sophocles and Euripides; Demosthenes and Cicero. These had formed the canon of the *studia humanitatis* since the 15th cent.

arts[76] which enable men to discourse and write perspicuously, elegantly, and according to the fitted style[77] of lofty, mean or lowly. Logic, therefore, so much as is useful, is to be referred to this due place, with all her well-couched heads and topics, until it be time to open her contracted palm[78] into a graceful and ornate rhetoric taught out of the rule of Plato, Aristotle, Phalereus, Cicero, Hermogenes, Longinus.[79]

To which poetry would be made subsequent, or, indeed, rather precedent, as being less subtile and fine, but more simple, sensuous, and passionate;[80] I mean not here the prosody of a verse, which they could not but have hit on before among the rudiments of grammar, but that sublime art which in Aristotle's *Poetics*, in Horace, and the Italian commentaries of Castelvetro, Tasso, Mazzoni,[81] and others, teaches what the laws are of a true epic poem, what of a dramatic, what of a lyric, what decorum is, which is the grand masterpiece to observe. This would make them soon perceive what despicable

---

[76] As Vives defined them, 'certain arts, such as grammar and dialectic, are only instruments of others, and for that reason are called by the Greeks *organa* [tools]', cit. *CPM* ii. 401 n.

[77] The appropriate style, adapted to the subject-matter. Cf. *Rhet. Her.* 4. 8. 11–12. 17; Wilson, p. 123; Puttenham, pp. 227 ff., 285 ff.; Whetsone, pp. 173–4; E.K., p. 176.

[78] The comparison of dialectic to the closed fist (representing argument tightly addressed to the subject), and rhetoric to the open palm (persuasively appealing to the audience for agreement) goes back to Zeno, as recorded by Cicero, *Fin.* 2. 6 and Quintilian, *Inst.* 2. 20. 7. Milton issued his own *Art of Logic* in 1672 (*CPM* viii. 139–407).

[79] This list of authorities on rhetoric includes Plato, surprisingly enough—but the full animus to Athenian oratory expressed in the *Gorgias* and *Phaedrus* has only been appreciated recently (cf. *IDR*, pp. 83–147); Aristotle and Cicero are to be expected; Hermogenes of Tarsus (born *c.* AD 150) wrote several rhetorical works, including *Peri ideōn*, on the 'ideas' or various kinds of style, which Milton knew; his reference to 'Phalereus', however, confuses the orator Demetrius Phalereus (born *c.*350 BC) with the Demetrius who wrote a book *On Style* in the 1st cent. AD; 'Longinus', to whom was attributed the treatise *Peri hupsous* (*On Sublimity*), was just becoming known at this time: cf. Chapman, pp. 522–3.

[80] Milton argues that poetry is less 'subtile' than rhetoric (*subtilis* is the word used by Cicero and Quintilian to describe the lowest level of style), but more straightforward, affecting the senses more directly, and stirring the emotions more powerfully. For Milton, as for Sidney and other Renaissance theorists, poetry is simply a higher form of rhetoric, and its study is still prescriptive, directed at practitioners.

[81] The Italian theorists were certainly used by earlier English critics (e.g. Sidney and Harington), but Milton is the first to give them equal standing with the classics. Ludovico Castelvetro (1505–71) produced an influential translation and commentary on Aristotle's *Poetics* in 1570; Giacomo Mazzoni (1548–98) wrote two discourses *Della Difesa della Commedia di Dante* (1572, enlarged in 1587); while Torquato Tasso (1544–95) issued *Discorsi Dell'Arte Poetica, et in particolare del Poema Heroico* in 1587, enlarged into *Discorsi del Poema Eroica* (1594). Excerpts from all three critics are in *LCPD*, pp. 304–57, 358–403, 466–503.

creatures our common rhymers and play-writers be; and show them what religious, what glorious and magnificent use might be made of poetry, both in divine and human things.

From hence, and not till now, will be the right season of forming them to be able writers and composers in every excellent matter, when they shall be thus fraught* with an universal insight into things:[82] or whether they be to speak in parliament or council, honour and attention would be waiting on their lips. There would then appear in pulpits other visages, other gestures, and stuff otherwise wrought than we now sit under, ofttimes to as great a trial of our patience as any other that they preach to us.

These are the studies wherein our noble and our gentle youth ought to bestow their time in a disciplinary way from twelve to one-and-twenty, unless they rely more upon their ancestors dead than upon themselves living. In which methodical course it so is supposed they must proceed by the steady pace of learning onward, as at convenient times for memory's sake to retire back into the middle ward, and sometimes into the rear of what they have been taught, until they have confirmed and solidly united the whole body of their perfected knowledge, like the last embattling[83] of a Roman legion.

[82] Milton reaffirms the traditional belief that a wide knowledge of the *res* or subject-matter is the prerequisite for any poet (or orator).

[83] Setting in battle array, having all their knowledge 'ready for action'; cf. Jonson's use of the word, p. 568.

36

Thomas Hobbes,
On epic poetry (1650 and 1675)

THOMAS HOBBES (1588–1679) was educated at Magdalen Hall Oxford, and spent most of the years 1608 to 1637 as a tutor to two noble families, the Cliftons and the Cavendishes (the Earls of Devonshire), during which he undertook three continental tours. When the Long Parliament assembled in 1640 he fled to Paris, where he made many friends among the exiled royalists, and became mathematics tutor to the Prince of Wales, the future Charles II. The publication of his *Leviathan* in 1651 aroused such a furore that he was forced to return to England in 1652, making his peace with Cromwell, and subsequently being granted a pension by the restored King. In addition to his great abilities in mathematics and natural philosophy, Hobbes was an outstanding Greek scholar: in 1629 he published a translation of Thucydides, in 1635 an abbreviated translation of Aristotle's *Rhetoric*, *A Briefe of the Art of Rhetorique*, and in his seventies he produced verse translations of Homer: the *Iliad* (1675), *Odyssey* (1676).

Sir William D'Avenant (1606–68), a successful dramatist in the 1620s and 1630s, appointed Poet Laureate in 1638, fought bravely on the royalist side during the civil war. He lived in exile in Paris from 1646, writing his epic poem *Gondibert* (1651), and (as he recorded in 'The Author's Preface to his much honour'd friend, Mr. Hobbes'), the philosopher had 'done me the honour to allow this Poem a daylie examination as it was writing'. On his return to England he was imprisoned in the Tower from 1650 to 1652. D'Avenant reopened the Drury Lane Theatre in 1658, becoming Master of the Revels in 1660. He was influential in establishing a new taste for opera, and in reviving the plays of Shakespeare (in adaptations).

TEXTS. (1) D'Avenant published his preface to *Gondibert* separately, as *A Discourse upon Gondibert, An Heroick Poem, written by Sʳ William D'Avenant: With an Answer to it by Mʳ Hobbs* (Paris, 1650), both being reprinted the following year, prefixed to the poem itself. D'Avenant's long and diffuse preface draws much from contemporary French discussions of epic and heroic romance, anticipating the new heroic drama of Dryden and Howard, while Hobbes restates older classical and Renaissance ideas.

(2) The preface to *Homer's Odysses, Translated by Tho. Hobbes of Malmsbury* (London, 1675): 'To the Reader, concerning The Vertues of an Heroique Poem'.

In annotating these texts I have benefited from Joel Spingarn's pioneering anthology, *CES* ii. 331–3, and from D. F. Gladish's edition of *Gondibert* (Oxford, 1971). For other aspects of Hobbes's literary theories cf. *Leviathan*, book 1 ch. 2, 'Of Imagination', ch. 4, 'Of Speech', and ch. 8, on 'The Vertues called intellectual' (that is, wit, fancy, and judgement); C. D. Thorpe, *The Aesthetic Theory of Thomas Hobbes* (Ann Arbor, 1940); J. T. Harwood (ed.), *The Rhetorics of Thomas Hobbes and Bernard Lamy* (Carbondale, Ill., 1986); Quentin Skinner, *Reason and Rhetoric in the Philosophy of Hobbes* (Cambridge, 1996).

THE ANSWER OF MR HOBBES TO SIR WILL. D'AVENANT'S PREFACE BEFORE *GONDIBERT*

Sir, If to commend your poem I should only say, in general terms, that in choice of your argument, the disposition of the parts, the maintenance of the characters of your persons, the dignity and vigour of your expression, you have performed all the parts of various experience, ready memory, clear judgement, swift and well-governed fancy, though it were enough for the truth, it were too little for the weight and credit of my testimony. For I lie open to two exceptions,* one of an incompetent, the other of a corrupted witness. Incompetent, because I am not a poet; and corrupted with the honour done me by your preface. The former obliges me to say something (by the way) of the nature and differences of poesy.

As philosophers have divided the universe (their subject) into three regions, celestial, aerial, and terrestrial, so the poets (whose work it is, by imitating human life in delightful and measured lines, to avert men from vice and incline them to virtuous and honourable actions)[1] have lodged themselves in the three regions of mankind: court, city, and country, correspondent in some proportion to those three regions of the world. For there is in princes and men of conspicuous* power (anciently called heroes) a lustre* and influence upon the rest of men, resembling that of the heavens; and an insincereness, inconstancy, and troublesome humour of those that dwell in populous cities, like the mobility, blustering, and impurity of the air; and a plainness, and (though dull) yet a nutritive faculty in rural people that endures a comparison with the earth they labour.

From hence have proceeded three sorts of poesy, heroic, scom-

---

[1] A typically Renaissance fusion of Aristotelian and Horatian theories. Cf. Introduction, pp. 15–18, 53–4, Elyot, pp. 62–4, Sidney, p. 345.

matic,[2] and pastoral. Every one of these is distinguished again in the manner of representation, which sometimes is narrative, wherein the poet himself relateth,* and sometimes dramatic, as when the persons are every one adorned[3] and brought upon the theatre to speak and act their own parts. There is, therefore, neither more nor less than six sorts of poesy. For the heroic poem narrative (such as is yours) is called an epic poem; the heroic poem dramatic is tragedy; the scommatic narrative is satire, dramatic is comedy; the pastoral narrative is called simply pastoral (anciently bucolic); the same dramatic, pastoral comedy. The figure* therefore of an epic poem and of a tragedy ought to be the same, for they differ no more but in that they are pronounced by one or many persons. Which I insert to justify the figure of yours, consisting of five books divided into songs, or cantos, as five acts divided into scenes has ever been the approved figure of a tragedy.[4]

They that take for poesy whatsoever is writ in verse[5] will think this division imperfect, and call in sonnets, epigrams, eclogues, and the like pieces (which are but essays, and parts of an entire poem), and reckon Empedocles and Lucretius (natural philosophers) for poets, and the moral precepts of Phocylides, Theognis,[6] and the quatrains of Pybrach,[7] and the history of Lucan, and others of that kind amongst poems; bestowing on such writers for honour the name of poets rather than of historians or philosophers. But the subject of a poem is the manners of men, not natural causes; manners presented, not dictated; and manners feigned (as the name of poesy imports) not found in men. They that give entrance to fictions writ in prose err not so much, but they err. For poesy requireth delightfulness, not only of fiction but of style; in which, if prose contend with verse it is with disadvantage and (as it were) on foot against the strength and wings of Pegasus.

---

[2] Gibing or scoffing; appropriate to satire.

[3] That is, 'when characters are individually formed' or 'embellished'.

[4] The convention of dramas being divided into five acts goes back to Donatus, and was applied to non-dramatic forms in 17th-cent. romances and histories (Gladish, edn. cit., pp. 290–1). However, D'Avenant only completed the first three books.

[5] In *Poet.* 1. 1447[b]11–24 Aristotle denied that verse is the defining mark of poetry: 'Homer and Empedocles have really nothing in common apart from their metre; so that, if the one is to be called a poet, the other should be termed a physicist rather than a poet'; cf. Elyot, p. 64, Sidney, pp. 347, 367.

[6] Both poets lived in the 6th cent. BC, and their fragmentary work includes moralizing passages.

[7] Gui du Faur, Sieur de Pibrac (1529–84), jurist and poet. His *Tetrastika*, or quatrains on marriage (1574) were translated by Joshua Sylvester in *Bartas his divine weekes and workes* . . . (1605; 1619), using the *Gondibert* stanza.

For verse amongst the Greeks was appropriated anciently to the service of their gods,[8] and was the holy style; the style of the oracles; the style of the laws; and the style of men that publicly recommended to their gods the vows and thanks of the people, which was done in their holy songs called hymns; and the composers of them were called prophets and priests before the name of poet was known. When afterwards the majesty of that style was observed, the poets chose it as best becoming their high invention. And for the antiquity of verse, it is greater than the antiquity of letters. For it is certain, Cadmus was the first that (from Phoenicia, a country that neighboureth Judea) brought the use of letters into Greece. But the service of the gods, and the laws (which by measured sounds were easily committed to the memory) had been long time in use before the arrival of Cadmus there.

There is, besides the grace of style, another cause why the ancient poets chose to write in measured language, which is this. Their poems were made at first with intention to have them sung, as well epic as dramatic (which custom hath been long time laid aside, but began to be revived, in part, of late years in Italy)[9] and could not be made commensurable to the voice or instruments in prose, the ways and motions whereof are so uncertain and undistinguished (like the way and motion of a ship in the sea) as not only to discompose the best composers but also to disappoint sometimes the most attentive reader, and put him to hunt counter for the sense.[10] It was therefore necessary for poets in those times to write in verse.

The verse which the Greeks and Latins (considering the nature of their own languages) found by experience most grave, and for an epic poem most decent,* was their hexameter; a verse limited not only in the length of the line but also in the quantity of the syllables. Instead of which we use the line of ten syllables, recompensing the neglect of their quantity with the diligence* of rhyme. And this measure is so proper for a heroic poem as without some loss of gravity and dignity it was never changed. A longer is not far from ill prose, and a shorter is a kind of whisking (you know), like the unlacing[11] rather than the

---

[8] Cf. Puttenham, pp. 194–5, Sidney, pp. 341–2, 345, and Milton, pp. 593–5.

[9] Hobbes travelled to Italy in 1636, visiting Galileo in Florence, where the first monodies and operas had been composed in the 1590s by Giulio Caccini and Jacopo Peri.

[10] Seek in the wrong direction; cf. North, p. 506.

[11] 'Whisking' means 'a light sweeping motion'; 'unlacing' can mean 'undoing the laces of armour, clothing, etc.', and so (presumably) depriving the Muse of her dignity.

singing of a Muse. In an epigram or a sonnet a man may vary his measures, and seek glory from a needless difficulty, as he that contrived
verses into the forms of an organ, a hatchet, an egg, an altar, and a
pair of wings.[12] But in so great and noble a work as is an epic poem,
for a man to obstruct his own way with unprofitable difficulties is great
imprudence. So likewise to choose a needless and difficult correspondence of rhyme is but a difficult toy,* and forces a man sometimes for
the stopping of a chink to say somewhat he did never think.[13] I cannot
therefore but very much approve your stanza, wherein the syllables in
every verse are ten, and the rhyme alternate.[14]

For the choice of your subject, you have sufficiently justified yourself in your preface. But because I have observed in Virgil, that the
honour done to Aeneas and his companions has so bright a reflection
upon Augustus Caesar, and other great Romans of that time, as a man
may suspect him not constantly possessed with the noble spirit of
those his heroes, and believe you are not acquainted with any great
man of the race of Gondibert, I add to your justification the purity of
your purpose, in having no other motive of your labour but to adorn
virtue, and procure her lovers, than which there cannot be a worthier
design, and more becoming noble poesy.

In that you make so small account of the example of almost all the
approved poets, ancient and modern, who thought fit in the beginning, and sometimes also in the progress of their poems, to invoke a
Muse or some other deity that should dictate to them or assist them
in their writings, they that take not the laws of art from any reason of
their own, but from the fashion of precedent times, will perhaps
accuse your singularity. For my part, I neither subscribe to their accusation nor yet condemn that heathen custom, otherwise than as accessory to their false religion. For their poets were their divines; had the
name of prophets; exercised amongst the people a kind of spiritual
authority; would be thought to speak by a divine spirit; have their

---

[12] For English examples of the *technopaegnion* or 'pattern poem' cf. Puttenham, ed. Willcock and Walker, bk. 2, ch. 11 (pp. 91–101), also *ECE* ii. 95–105, and Ascham, p. 159. Hobbes
may be referring to George Herbert's *The Temple* (1633), which includes 'The Altar' and
'Easter Wings'. For the classical models see A. Holden (ed.), *Greek Pastoral Poetry . . . The
Pattern Poems* (Harmondsworth, Middx., 1974).

[13] An over-elaborate rhyme sceme is a nuisance; Hobbes rhymes, to make his point.

[14] Hobbes approves of *Gondibert*'s verse and stanza-form (iambic pentameters, quatrains
rhyming *abab*), which D'Avenant had justified in his preface (Gladish edn., p. 17). Dryden
accepted quatrains as appropriate for heroic verse in the preface to his *Annus Mirabilis*
(1667).

works which they writ in verse (the divine style) pass for the word of God, and not of man; and to be hearkened to with reverence. Do not our divines (excepting the style) do the same, and by us that are of the same religion cannot justly be reprehended for it?

Besides, in the use of the spiritual calling of divines there is danger sometimes to be feared from want of skill, such as is reported of unskilful conjurers,[15] that mistaking the rites and ceremonious points of their art call up such spirits as they cannot at their pleasure allay again, by whom storms are raised that overthrow buildings, and are the cause of miserable wrecks at sea. Unskilful divines do oftentimes the like: for when they call unseasonably for zeal there appears a spirit of cruelty; and by the like error, instead of truth they raise discord; instead of wisdom, fraud; instead of reformation, tumult; and controversy instead of religion.[16] Whereas in the heathen poets, at least in those whose works have lasted to the time we are in, there are none of those indiscretions* to be found that tended to subversion or disturbance of the commonwealths wherein they lived. But why a Christian should think it an ornament to his poem, either to profane the true God or invoke a false one, I can imagine no cause but a reasonless imitation of custom; of a foolish custom; by which a man, enabled to speak wisely from the principles of nature and his own meditation, loves rather to be thought to speak by inspiration, like a bagpipe.

Time and education begets experience; experience begets memory; memory begets judgement, and fancy; judgement begets the strength and structure; and fancy begets the ornaments of a poem.[17] The ancients therefore fabled not absurdly in making memory the mother of the Muses.[18] For memory is the world (though not really, yet so as in a looking glass) in which the judgement, the severer sister, busieth herself in a grave and rigid examination of all the parts

---

[15] Cf. D'Avenant's preface (Gladish, p. 19).

[16] Hobbes assigned the cause of the English civil wars sometimes to religious dissension, sometimes to mis-used political eloquence.

[17] An instance of the rhetorical figure *gradatio* or *climax*: cf. Hoskyns, p. 260. In *Leviathan* (1. 8) Hobbes divides 'natural wit' into 'celerity of imagining (that is, swift succession of one thought to another)' or 'fancy' (imagination), and 'steady direction to some approved end' or judgement. Fancy excels at observing similitudes, judgement observes differences and dissimilitudes. 'In a good poem . . . both judgement and fancy are required; but the fancy must be more eminent, because they please for the extravagancy; but they ought not to please by indiscretion'; ed. R. Tuck (Cambridge, 1991), pp. 50–1.

[18] Mnemosyne, a daughter of Uranus and Ge, was goddess of memory and mother of the Muses; cf. Hesiod, *Theogony* 53–74; Ovid, *Met.* 6. 103 ff.

of nature, and in registering by letters their order, causes, uses, differences, and resemblances; whereby the fancy, when any work of
art is to be performed, finds her materials at hand and prepared
for use, and needs no more than a swift motion over them, that what
she wants, and is there to be had, may not lie too long unespied.
So that when she seemeth to fly from one Indies to the other, and
from heaven to earth, and to penetrate into the hardest matter,
and obscurest places, into the future, and into herself, and all this in
a point of time, the voyage is not very great, her self being all
she seeks; and her wonderful celerity consisteth not so much in motion
as in copious imagery discreetly* ordered, and perfectly registered
in the memory; which most men under the name of philosophy
have a glimpse of, and is pretended to by many that, grossly mistaking her, embrace contention in her place. But so far forth as the fancy
of man has traced the ways of true philosophy, so far it hath produced
very marvellous effects to the benefit of mankind. All that is beautiful or defensible* in building; or marvellous in engines and instruments of motion; whatsoever commodity* men receive from
the observation of the heavens, from the description of the earth,
from the account of time, from walking on the seas;[19] and whatsoever
distinguisheth the civility of Europe from the barbarity of the
American savages, is the workmanship of fancy, but guided by the
precepts of true philosophy. But where these precepts fail, as they
have hitherto failed in the doctrine of moral virtue, there the architect (fancy) must take the philosopher's part upon herself. He therefore that undertakes a heroic poem (which is to exhibit a venerable
and amiable image of heroic virtue) must not only be the poet, to place
and connect, but also the philosopher, to furnish and square* his
matter: that is, to make both body and soul, colour and shadow of his
poem out of his own store; which how well you have performed I am
now considering. . . .

To show the reader in what place he shall find every excellent
picture of virtue you have drawn, is too long. And to show him one
is to prejudice the rest; yet I cannot forbear to point him to the description of love in the person of Birtha, in the seventh canto of the second
book.[20] There has nothing been said of that subject neither by the
ancient nor modern poets comparable to it. Poets are painters:[21] I

---

[19] One of the miracles of Christ; cf. Matt. 14: 24 ff.
[20] Cf. *Gondibert*, edn. cit., pp. 169 ff.
[21] Cf. Plutarch, *Poetas* 3, and Sidney, pp. 345, 352.

would fain see another painter draw so true, perfect, and natural a love to the life, and make use of nothing but pure lines, without the help of any the least uncomely shadow, as you have done. But let it be read as a piece by itself, for in the most equal height of the whole the eminence of parts is lost.

There are some that are not pleased with fiction unless it be bold; not only to exceed the work, but also the possibility of nature. They would have impenetrable armours, enchanted castles, invulnerable bodies, iron men, flying horses, and a thousand other such things, which are easily feigned by them that dare.[22] Against such I defend you (without assenting to those that condemn either Homer or Virgil) by dissenting only from those that think the beauty of a poem consisteth in the exorbitancy* of the fiction. For as truth is the bound of historical, so the resemblance of truth is the utmost limit of poetical liberty. In old time amongst the heathen such strange fictions, and metamorphoses, were not so remote from the articles of their faith as they are now from ours, and therefore were not so unpleasant. Beyond the actual works of nature a poet may now go; but beyond the conceived possibility of nature, never. I can allow a geographer to make, in the sea, a fish or a ship which by the scale of his map would be two or three hundred miles long, and think it done for ornament, because it is done without the precincts of his undertaking; but when he paints an elephant so, I presently apprehend it as ignorance, and a plain confession of *terra incognita*.

As the description of great men and great actions is the constant design of a poet, so the descriptions of worthy circumstances are necessary accessions to a poem, and being well performed are the jewels and most precious ornaments of poesy. Such in Virgil are the funeral games of Anchises, the duel of Aeneas and Turnus, etc.; and such in yours are the hunting, the battle, the city mourning, the funeral, the house of Astragon, the library, and the temple, equal to his, or those of Homer whom he imitated.

There remains now no more to be considered but the expression, in which consisteth the countenance and colour of a beautiful Muse, and is given her by the poet out of his own provision, or is borrowed from others. That which he hath of his own is nothing but experience and knowledge of nature, and specially human nature, and is the true

----

[22] Deriving from Aristotle (*Poet.* 24. 1460ᵃ12), Renaissance literary theory evolved a special justification for 'marvellous' beings or incidents in tragedy, epic, and romance.

and natural colour. But that which is taken out of books (the ordinary boxes of counterfeit complexion)[23] shows well or ill as it hath more or less resemblance with the natural, and are not to be used (without examination) unadvisedly. For in him that professes* the imitation of nature (as all poets do) what greater fault can there be than to betray an ignorance of nature in his poem—especially having a liberty allowed him, if he meet with anything he cannot master, to leave it out?

That which giveth a poem the truth and natural colour consisteth in two things, which are: to know well, that is, to have images of nature in the memory distinct and clear; and to know much. A sign of the first is perspicuity, property, and decency,[24] which delight all sorts of men, either by instructing the ignorant or soothing* the learned in their knowledge. A sign of the latter is novelty of expression, and pleaseth by excitation of the mind; for novelty causeth admiration, and admiration curiosity, which is a delightful appetite of knowledge.[25]

There be so many words in use at this day in the English tongue, that though of *magnifique* sound, yet (like the windy blisters of a troubled water) have no sense at all; and so many others that lose their meaning by being ill coupled, that it is a hard matter to avoid them; for having been obtruded upon youth in the schools by such as make it, I think, their business there (as 'tis expressed by the best poet)

With terms to charm the weak and pose the wise,[26]

they grow up with them, and, gaining reputation with the ignorant, are not easily shaken off.

To this palpable darkness* I may also add the ambitious obscurity of expressing more than is perfectly conceived, or perfect conception in fewer words than it requires. Which expressions, though they have had the honour to be called strong lines,[27] are indeed no better than riddles, and not only to the reader, but also after a little time to the writer himself, dark* and troublesome.

---

[23] This mocking comparison with the superficiality of cosmetics devalues the long-established practice of *imitatio*, using an existing literary work as a model to be emulated.

[24] Hobbes emphasizes important traditional literary values: *perspicuitas, proprietas, decorum*.

[25] Cf. Aristotle, *Metaph*. 1. 980ᵃ22: 'All men by nature desire to know', and 982ᵇ12 ff.: 'it is owing to their wonder that men both now begin and at first began to philosophize'; similarly *Rh*. 1. 11. 1371ᵃ31–ᵇ10.

[26] *Gondibert*, bk. 2, canto 5, stanza 44 (p. 156).   [27] Cf. Dudley North, p. 506.

To the property* of expression I refer that clearness of memory by which a poet, when he hath once introduced any person whatsoever speaking in his poem, maintaineth in him to the end the same character he gave him in the beginning.[28] The variation whereof is a change of pace that argues the poet tired.[29]

Of the indecencies* of a heroic poem the most remarkable are those that show disproportion* either between the persons and their actions, or between the manners of the poet and the poem. Of the first kind is the uncomeliness* of representing in great persons the inhuman vice of cruelty, or the sordid vice of lust and drunkenness. To such parts as those the ancient approved poets thought it fit to suborn,* not the persons of men but of monsters and beastly giants, such as Polyphemus, Cacus, and the centaurs.[30] For it is supposed a Muse, when she is invoked to sing a song of that nature, should maidenly advise the poet to set such persons to sing their own vices upon the stage; for it is not so unseemly in a tragedy. Of the same kind it is to represent scurrility or any action or language that moveth much laughter. The delight of an epic poem consisteth not in mirth, but admiration.[31] Mirth and laughter is proper to comedy and satire. Great persons that have their minds employed on great designs have not leisure enough to laugh, and are pleased with the contemplation of their own power and virtues; so as they need not the infirmities and vices of other men to recommend themselves to their own favour by comparison, as all men do when they laugh. Of the second kind, where the disproportion is between the poet and the persons of his poem, one is in the dialect of the inferior sort of people, which is always different from the language of the court. Another is to derive the illustration of anything from such metaphors or comparisons as cannot come into men's thoughts but by mean* conversation, and experience of humble or evil arts, which the persons of an epic poem cannot be thought acquainted with.[32]

---

[28] Cf. Horace, *Ars P*. 124 ff.: 'if you are putting something untried on the stage and venturing to shape a new character, let it be maintained to the end as it began and be true to itself' (*ALC*, p. 282).

[29] A metaphor from horse-riding.

[30] Polyphemus is a character in Homer's *Odyssey* (9. 105–566); Cacus figures in the *Aeneid* (8. 184–270); the centaurs in Ovid's *Metamorphoses* (12. 210 ff.).

[31] The inclusion of *admiratio* (wonder or amazement) as one of the poet's goals was the work of Italian Renaissance critics, such as Robortello and Minturno; cf. Sidney, p. 363.

[32] D'Avenant had claimed a poet's right to use technical terms from 'any science, as well mechanicall, as liberall' (edn. cit., p. 22), but Hobbes reaffirms the classical belief that a writer should use a generally available and 'decent' vocabulary: cf. Wilson, p. 120.

From knowing much, proceedeth the admirable variety and novelty of metaphors and similitudes, which are not possibly to be lighted on in the compass of a narrow knowledge.[33] And the want whereof compelleth a writer to expressions that are either defaced by time or sullied with vulgar or long use. For the phrases of poesy, as the airs* of music, with often hearing become insipid,* the reader having no more sense of their force than our flesh is sensible* of the bones that sustain it. As the sense we have of bodies consisteth in change and variety of impression, so also does the sense of language in the variety and changeable use of words. I mean not in the affectation of words newly brought home from travel, but in new (and withal significant) translation to our purposes of those that be already received, and in far-fetched (but withal apt, instructive, and comely) similitudes.[34]

Having thus (I hope) avoided the first exception* against the incompetency of my judgement, I am but little moved with the second, which is of being bribed by the honour you have done me by attributing in your preface somewhat to my judgement. For I have used your judgement no less in many things of mine, which coming to light will thereby appear the better. And so you have your bribe again.

Having thus made way for the admission of my testimony, I give it briefly thus: I never yet saw poem that had so much shape of art, health of morality, and vigour and beauty of expression as this of yours. And but for the clamour of the multitude, that hide their envy of the present under a reverence of antiquity, I should say further that it would last as long as either the *Aeneid* or *Iliad*, but for one disadvantage; and the disadvantage is this: the languages of the Greeks and Romans, by their colonies and conquests, have put off flesh and blood, and are become immutable, which none of the modern tongues are like to be.[35] I honour antiquity, but that which is commonly called old time is young time.[36] The glory of antiquity is due not to the dead, but to the aged. . . .

---

[33] Cf. Aristotle, *Poet.* 3. 1459ᵃ5: 'by far the most important is to be good at metaphor. For this is the only thing that cannot be learned from anyone else, and it is a sign of natural genius, as to be good at metaphor is to perceive resemblances' (*ALC*, p. 122).

[34] Hobbes shows a traditional suspicion of neologisms, preferring the vocabulary to be enlarged by the use of metaphor ('translation'; Lat. *translatio*) and similes, which should not be too 'far-fetched': cf. Hoskyns, p. 400, and Jonson, p. 574.

[35] Scepticism as to whether the modern languages would last as long as Greek or Latin was another traditional response, found already in Montaigne and Bacon.

[36] Cf. Bacon, *Advancement of Learning*, bk. 1: 'Antiquity deserveth that reverence, that men should make a stand thereupon, and discover what is the best way; but when the discovery is well taken, then to make progression. And to speak truly, *Antiquitas saeculi*

I believe (sir) you have seen a curious kind of perspective,[37] where he that looks through a short hollow pipe upon a picture containing diverse figures, sees none of those that are there painted but some one person made up of their parts, conveyed to the eye by the artificial* cutting of a glass. I find in my imagination an effect not unlike it from your poem. The virtues you distribute there amongst so many noble persons[38] represent (in the reading) the image but of one man's virtue to my fancy, which is your own; and that so deeply imprinted as to stay forever there, and govern all the rest of my thoughts and affections. . . .

TO THE READER, CONCERNING THE VIRTUES OF AN HEROIC POEM

The virtues required in an heroic poem, and indeed in all writings published, are comprehended all in this one word, discretion.* And discretion consisteth in this, that every part of the poem be conducing, and in good order placed, to the end and design of the poet. And the design is not only to profit, but also to delight the reader.[39] By profit I intend not here any accession of wealth, either to the poet or to the reader; but accession of prudence, justice, fortitude, by the example of such great and noble persons as he introduceth speaking, or describeth acting. For all men love to behold, though not to practise, virtue. So that at last the work of an heroic poet is no more but to furnish an ingenuous reader (when his leisure abounds) with the diversion of an honest and delightful story, whether true or feigned.

But because there be many men called critics, and wits, and virtuosi,[40] that are accustomed to censure the poets, and most of them

---

juventus mundi ['What we call antiquity is the youth of the world']. These times are the ancient times, when the world is ancient, and not those which we account ancient . . . by a computation backward from ourselves': *Francis Bacon*, ed. B. Vickers (Oxford, 1996), pp. 144–5.

[37] An optical device producing some special or fantastic effect, e.g. by distortion of images.

[38] In some Renaissance theories of epic and romance, virtues and vices were supposed to be systematically divided up among the characters: cf. Introduction, p. 52.

[39] Cf. Horace, *Ars P*. 334–5.

[40] A 'wit' in this period was 'a person of great mental ability'; a 'virtuoso' (a word first recorded in 1651, according to *OED*) was someone with 'a special interest in, or taste for, the fine arts'. Hobbes is not necessarily being depreciatory.

of divers judgments: how is it possible (you'll say) to please them all? Yes, very well; if the poem be as it should be. For men can judge what's good, that know not what is best. For he that can judge what is best, must have considered all those things (though they be almost innumerable) that concur to make the reading of an heroic poem pleasant. Whereof I'll name as many as shall come into my mind.

And they are contained, first, in the choice of words; secondly, in the construction; thirdly, in the contrivance* of the story or fiction; fourthly, in the elevation of the fancy; fifthly, in the justice and impartiality of the poet; sixthly, in the clearness of descriptions; seventhly, in the amplitude of the subject.

And to begin with words, the first indiscretion is the use of such words as to the readers of poesy (which are commonly persons of the best quality) are not sufficiently known. For the work of an heroic poem is to raise admiration,* principally, for three virtues: valour, beauty, and love; to the reading whereof women no less than men have a just pretence,* though their skill in language be not so universal. And therefore foreign words, till by long use they become vulgar, are unintelligible to them. Also the names of instruments and tools of artificers, and words of art,[41] though spoken by a hero. He may delight in the arts themselves, and have skill in some of them; but his glory lies not in that, but in courage, nobility, and other virtues of nature, or in the command he has over other men. Nor does Homer in any part of his poem attribute any praise to Achilles, or any blame to Alexander, for that they had both learnt to play upon the guitar. The character of words that become a hero are property and significancy, but without both the malice and lasciviousness of a satire.

Another virtue of an heroic poem is the perspicuity and the facility* of construction, and consisteth in a natural contexture of the words, so as not to discover* the labour but the natural ability of the poet; and this is usually called a good style. For the order of words, when placed as they ought to be, carries a light before it whereby a man may foresee the length of his period, as a torch in the night shows a man the stops and unevenness in his way. But when placed unnaturally, the reader will often find unexpected checks, and be forced to go back and hunt for the sense, and suffer such unease as in a coach a man unexpectedly finds in passing over a furrow. And though the laws

---

[41] Technical terms, which Hobbes would exclude from polite literature: cf. n. 32 above.

of verse (which have bound the Greeks and Latins to number of feet
and quantity of syllables, and the English and other nations to number
of syllables and rhyme) put great constraint upon the natural course
of language, yet the poet, having the liberty to depart from what is
obstinate, and to choose somewhat else that is more obedient to such
laws and no less fit for his purpose, shall not be, neither by the measure nor by the necessity of rhyme, excused; though a translation
often may.

A third virtue lies in the contrivance. For there is difference
between a poem and a history in prose. For a history is wholly related*
by the writer; but in a heroic poem the narration is, a great part of it,
put upon some of the persons introduced by the poet. So Homer
begins not his *Iliad* with the injury done to Paris, but makes it related
by Menelaus,[42] and very briefly, as a thing notorious;* nor begins he
his *Odyssey* with the departure of Ulysses from Troy, but makes
Ulysses[43] himself relate the same to Alcinous, in the midst of his
poem; which I think much more pleasant and ingenious than a too
precise* and close following of the time.

A fourth is in the elevation of fancy, which is generally taken for the
greatest praise of heroic poetry; and is so, when governed by discretion. For men more generally affect* and admire fancy than they do
either judgment, or reason, or memory, or any other intellectual virtue;
and for the pleasantness of it, give to it alone the name of wit, accounting reason and judgment but for a dull entertainment.[44] For in fancy
consisteth the sublimity of a poet, which is that poetical fury[45] which
the readers for the most part call for. It flies abroad swiftly to fetch in
both matter and words; but if there be not discretion at home to distinguish which are fit to be used and which not, which decent* and
which undecent for persons, times, and places, their delight and grace
is lost. But if they be discreetly* used, they are greater ornaments of a
poem by much than any other. A metaphor also (which is a comparison
contracted into a word)[46] is not unpleasant; but when they are sharp
and extraordinary, they are not fit for an heroic poet, nor for a public
consultation, but only for an accusation or defence at the bar.

---

⁴² *Il*. 3. 97 ff.   ⁴³ *Od*. 8. 492 ff., 11. 505 ff.

⁴⁴ Cf. p. 612 above, n. 17, for Hobbes's definition of these terms.

⁴⁵ The idea of a *furor poeticus*, an inspiration proper to poetry, derives ultimately from
the (ironic) link between poetry and *mania* in Plato's *Ion* 533 c ff., rejected by Aristotle (*Poet.*
17. 1455ᵃ32 f.), but accepted by many Renaissance critics. Cf. Elyot, p. 64, Puttenham,
pp. 192–3, E.K., pp. 183, 189, Sidney, pp. 341, 346, 390, and *LCPD*, pp. 117–18, 693.

⁴⁶ Cf. Quintilian, *Inst*. 8. 6. 8.

A fifth lies in the justice and impartiality of the poet, and belongeth as well to history as to poetry. For both the poet and the historian writeth only (or should do) matter of fact. And as far as the truth of fact can defame a man, so far they are allowed to blemish the reputation of persons. But to do the same upon report, or by inference, is below the dignity not only of a hero but of a man. For neither a poet nor an historian ought to make himself an absolute master of any man's good name. None of the emperors of Rome whom Tacitus or any other writer hath condemned was ever subject to the judgment of any of them, nor were they ever heard to plead for themselves, which are things that ought to be antecedent to condemnation. Nor was, I think, Epicurus the philosopher (who is transmitted to us by the Stoics for a man of evil and voluptuous life) ever called, convented,* and lawfully convicted, as all men ought to be before they be defamed. Therefore 'tis a very great fault in a poet to speak evil of any man in their writings historical.

A sixth virtue consists in the perfection and curiosity* of descriptions, which the ancient writers of eloquence called icons,[47] that is images. And an image is always a part, or rather the ground of a poetical comparison. As, for example, when Virgil would set before our eyes the fall of Troy, he describes perhaps the whole labour of many men together in the felling of some great tree, and with how much ado it fell. This is the image. To which if you but add these words, 'So fell Troy', you have the comparison entire; the grace whereof lieth in the lightsomeness,* and is but the description of all, even of the minutest, parts of the thing described; that not only they that stand far off but also they that stand near, and look upon it with the oldest spectacles of a critic, may approve it. For poet is a painter, and should paint actions to the understanding with the most decent words, as painters do persons and bodies with the choicest colours to the eye; which, if not done nicely, will not be worthy to be placed in a cabinet.

The seventh virtue, which, lying in the amplitude of the subject, is nothing but variety, and a thing without which a whole poem would be no pleasanter than an epigram, or one good verse; nor a picture of a hundred figures better than any one of them asunder, if drawn with equal art. And these are the virtues which ought especially to be looked upon by the critics, in the comparing of the poets, Homer with

---

[47] Cf. Puttenham, pp. 276–7 and nn. 191, 195. The term enters rhetoric relatively late, in the younger Pliny (1st cent. AD) and in the *Eikones* of Philostratus (2nd cent. AD).

Virgil, or Virgil with Lucan. For these only, for their excellency, I have read or heard compared.

If the comparison be grounded upon the first and second virtues, which consist in known words and style unforced, they are all excellent in their own language, though perhaps the Latin than the Greek is apter to dispose itself into an hexameter verse, as having both fewer monosyllables and fewer polysyllables. And this may make the Latin verse appear more grave and equal, which is taken for a kind of majesty; though in truth there be no majesty in words but then when they seem to proceed from an high and weighty employment of the mind. But neither Homer, nor Virgil, nor Lucan, nor any poet writing commendably, though not excellently, was ever charged much with unknown words or great constraint of style, as being a fault proper to translators, when they hold themselves too superstitiously to the author's words.

In the third virtue, which is contrivance, there is no doubt but Homer excels them all. For their poems, except the introduction of their gods, are but so many histories in verse; whereas Homer has woven so many histories together as contain the whole learning of his time (which the Greeks called *Cyclopædia*), and furnished both the Greek and Latin stages with all the plots and arguments of the tragedies.

The fourth virtue, which is the height of fancy, is almost proper to Lucan,[48] and so admirable in him that no heroic poem raises such admiration* of the poet as his hath done, though not so great admiration of the persons he introduceth. And though it be the mark of a great wit* yet it is fitter for a rhetorician than a poet, and rebelleth often against discretion, as when he says,

Victrix causa Diis placuit, sed victa Catoni;[49]

that is,

> The side that won, the gods approved the most,
> But Cato better liked the side that lost.

—than which nothing could be spoken more gloriously to the exaltation of a man, nor more disgracefully to the depression of the gods.

---

[48] Marcus Annaeus Lucanus (AD 39–65), whose *De bello civili* (sometimes misnamed *Pharsalia*), in ten books, recounts the war between Caesar and Pompey. Sometimes criticized for his overwrought style, Lucan's epic remained popular in the 17th cent.

[49] *De bello civili.* 1. 128.

Homer indeed maketh some gods for the Greeks, and some for the Trojans, but always makes Jupiter impartial; and never prefers the judgment of a man before that of Jupiter, much less before the judgment of all the gods together.

The fifth virtue, which is the justice and impartiality of a poet, is very eminent in Homer and Virgil, but the contrary in Lucan. Lucan shows himself openly in the Pompeian faction, inveighing against Caesar throughout his poem, like Cicero against Catiline or Mark Antony, and is therefore justly reckoned by Quintilian[50] as a rhetorician rather than a poet. And a great part of the delight of his readers proceedeth from the pleasure which too many men take to hear great persons censured. But Homer and Virgil (especially Homer) do everywhere what they can to preserve the reputation of their heroes.

If we compare Homer and Virgil by the sixth virtue, which is the clearness of images or descriptions, it is manifest that Homer ought to be preferred, though Virgil himself were to be the judge.[51] For there are very few images in Virgil besides those which he hath translated out of Homer; so that Virgil's images are Homer's praises. But what if he have added something to it of his own? Though he have, yet it is no addition of praise, because 'tis easy. But he hath some images which are not in Homer, and better than his. It may be so; and so may other poets have which never durst compare themselves with Homer. Two or three fine sayings are not enough to make a wit. But where is that image of his better done by him than Homer, of those that have been done by them both? Yes, Eustathius (as Mr. Ogilby[52] hath observed) where they both describe the falling of a tree, prefers Virgil's description. But Eustathius is in that, I think, mistaken. The place of Homer is in the fourth of the *Iliad*,[53] the sense whereof is this:

> As when a man hath felled a poplar tree
> Tall, straight, and smooth, with all the fair boughs on;

---

[50] Cf. *Inst*. 10. 1. 90.

[51] Hobbes is consciously disagreeing with J. C. Scaliger, who devoted a long chapter (5. 3) of his *Poetices libri septem* (1561) to a comparison in which Virgil was elevated at the expense of Homer.

[52] Eustathius (12th cent. AD), a Byzantine cleric and scholar, wrote a vast compilation, *Commentaries on Homer's Iliad and Odyssey*, which preserves much material drawn from the old scholia and the lost writings of earlier scholars and lexicographers (*OCD*). John Ogilby (1600–76) published translations of Homer: *Iliad* (1660), *Odyssey* (1665), which were ridiculed by Dryden and Pope.

[53] *Il*. 4. 473–89. Hobbes adds his own translations.

> Of which he means a coach-wheel made shall be,
> And leaves it on the bank to dry i' th' sun:
> So lay the comely Simoisius,
> Slain by great Ajax, son of Telamon.

It is manifest that in this place Homer intended no more than to show how comely the body of Simoisius appeared as he lay dead upon the bank of Scamander, straight and tall, with a fair head of hair, and like a straight and high poplar with the boughs still on; and not at all to describe the manner of his falling, which, when a man is wounded through the breast, as he was with a spear, is always sudden.

The description of how a great tree falleth, when many men together hew it down, is in the second of Virgil's *Aeneids*.[54] The sense of it, with the comparison, is in English this;

> And Troy, methought, then sunk in fire and smoke,
> And overturnèd was in every part:
> As when upon the mountain an old oak
> Is hewn about with keen steel to the heart,
> And plied by swains with many heavy blows,
> It nods and every way it threatens round,
> Till overcome with many wounds, it bows,
> And leisurely at last comes to the ground.

And here again it is evident that Virgil meant to compare the manner how Troy after many battles, and after the losses of many cities, [was] conquered by the many nations under Agamemnon in a long war, and thereby weakened, and at last overthrown, with a great tree hewn round about, and then falling by little and little, leisurely.

So that neither these two descriptions nor the two comparisons can be compared together. The image of a man lying on the ground is one thing; the image of falling, especially of a kingdom, is another. This therefore gives no advantage to Virgil over Homer. 'Tis true that this description of the felling and falling of a tree is exceedingly graceful. But is it therefore more than Homer could have done if need had been? Or is there no description in Homer of somewhat else as good as this? Yes, and in many of our English poets now alive. If it then be lawful for Julius Scaliger[55] to say that if Jupiter would have described the fall of a tree he could not have mended* this of Virgil, it will be lawful

---

[54] *Aen.* 2. 624–31.
[55] *Poetice* 5. 3: 'Non si ipse Iupiter poeta fiat, melius loquatur' (1561 edn., p. 231).

for me to repeat an old epigram of Antipater,[56] to the like purpose, in favour of Homer:

> The writer of the famous Trojan war,
> And of Ulysses' life, O Jove, make known,
> Who, whence he was; for thine the verses are,
> And he would have us think they are his own.

The seventh and last commendation of an heroic poem consisteth in amplitude and variety; and in this Homer exceedeth Virgil very much, and that not by superfluity of words but by plenty of heroic matter, and multitude of descriptions and comparisons (whereof Virgil hath translated but a small part into his *Aeneids*), such as are the images of shipwrecks, battles, single combats, beauty, passions of the mind, sacrifices, entertainments and other things, whereof Virgil (abating what he borrows of Homer) has scarce the twentieth part. It is no wonder therefore if all the ancient learned men both of Greece and Rome have given the first place in poetry to Homer. It is rather strange that two or three, and of late time, and but learners of the Greek tongue, should dare to contradict so many competent judges both of language and discretion.

But howsoever I defend Homer, I aim not thereby at any reflection upon the following translation. Why then did I write it? Because I had nothing else to do. Why publish it? Because I thought it might take off* my adversaries from showing their folly upon my more serious writings,[57] and set them upon my verses to show their wisdom. But why without annotations? Because I had no hope to do it better than is already done by Mr. Ogilby.

---

[56] This epigram (wrongly ascribed to Antipater) can be found in the Planudean Anthology (Spingarn).

[57] Hobbes's unorthodox views aroused enormous hostility: cf. S. I. Mintz, *The Hunting of Leviathan: Seventeenth Century Reactions to the Materialism and Moral Philosophy of Hobbes* (Cambridge, 1962).

FURTHER READING

A. ANTHOLOGIES OF CRITICISM

GEBERT, C. (ed.), *An Anthology of Elizabethan Dedications and Prefaces* (Philadelphia, 1933).

GILBERT, A. H. (ed.), *Literary Criticism: Plato to Dryden* (New York, 1940; repr. Detroit, 1962, 1964).

GOYET, F. (ed.), *Traités de Poétique et de Rhétorique de la Renaissance (Sébillet, Aneau, Peletier, Fouquelin, Ronsard)* (Paris, 1990).

HARDISON, O. B., Jr. (ed.), *English Literary Criticism: The Renaissance* (New York, 1963).

PREMINGER, A., HARDISON, O. B., Jr., and KERRANE, K. (eds.), *Classical and Medieval Literary Criticism: Translations and Interpretations* (New York, 1974).

RUSSELL, D. A., and WINTERBOTTOM, M. (eds.), *Ancient Literary Criticism: The Principal Texts in New Translations* (Oxford, 1972).

SMITH, G. GREGORY (ed.), *Elizabethan Critical Essays*, 2 vols. (Oxford, 1904; repr. 1964).

SPINGARN, J. E. (ed.), *Critical Essays of the Seventeenth Century*, 3 vols. (Oxford, 1908; repr. 1957).

TAYLER, E. W. (ed.), *Literary Criticism of Seventeenth-Century England* (New York, 1967).

WEINBERG, B. (ed.), *Critical Prefaces of the French Renaissance* (Evanston, Ill. 1950).

——(ed.), *Trattati di Poetica e Retorica del Cinquecento*, 4 vols. (Bari, 1970–1974).

B. PRIMARY LITERATURE

ROGER ASCHAM, *The Scholemaster*, ed. R. J. Schoeck (Don Mills, Ontario, 1966).

FRANCIS BACON, *Francis Bacon*, ed. B. Vickers (Oxford and New York, 1996), the Oxford Authors series.

JOACHIM DU BELLAY, *La Deffence et Illustration de la Langue Francoyse*, ed. H. Chamard (Paris, 1948; repr. 1970).

GIOVANNI BOCCACCIO, *Boccaccio On Poetry: Being the Preface and the Fourteenth and Fifteenth Books of Boccaccio's* Genealogia Deorum Gentilium, ed. C. G. Osgood (Princeton, 1930; repr. Indianapolis and New York, 1956).

HENRY PEACHAM, *Henry Peachams 'The Garden of Eloquence'* (*1593*), ed. B.-M. Koll (Frankfurt am Main, Bern, New York, 1996).

GEORGE PUTTENHAM, *The Arte of English Poesie*, ed. G. D. Willcock and A. Walker (Cambridge, 1936; repr. 1970).

JULIUS CAESAR SCALIGER, *Poetices libri septem. Sieben Bücher über die Dichtkunst*, Books 1–4, ed. and German tr. L. Deitz, 3 vols. (Stuttgart–Bad Cannstatt, 1994–5).

PHILIP SIDNEY, *An Apology for Poetry or The Defence of Poesy*, ed. G. Shepherd (London, 1965; repr. Manchester, 1973).

——*Miscellaneous Prose of Sir Philip Sidney*, ed. K. Duncan-Jones and J. van Dorsten (Oxford, 1973).

JOANNES SUSENBROTUS, *Epitome Troporum ac Schematum*, ed. and tr. J. X. Brennan. Ph.D. diss., University of Illinois, 1953 (University Microfilms order no. 6921).

JUAN LUIS VIVES, *Vives: On Education: A Translation of the* De Tradendis Disciplinis *of Juan Luis Vives*, ed. F. Watson (Cambridge, 1913; repr. Totowa, NJ, 1971).

——*De Ratione Dicendi*, tr. J. F. Cooney, Ph.D. diss., Ohio State University, 1996 (Univ. Microfilms order no. 67-6303).

THOMAS WILSON, *The Art of Rhetoric* (*1560*), ed. P. E. Medine (University Park, Pa., 1994).

C. SECONDARY LITERATURE

AGUZZI, D. L., 'Allegory in the Heroic Poetry of the Renaissance', Ph.D. diss., Columbia University, NY, 1959 (Univ. Microfilms order no. Mic. 59-6993).

ATTRIDGE, D., *Well-Weighed Syllables: Elizabethan Verse in Classical Metres* (Cambridge, 1974).

BINNS, J. W., *Intellectual Culture in Elizabethan and Jacobean England: The Latin Writings of the Age* (Leeds, 1990).

BOLGAR, R. R., *The Classical Heritage and its Beneficiaries: From the Carolingian Age to the End of the Renaissance* (Cambridge and New York, 1954; repr. New York, 1964).

DORAN, M., *Endeavors of Art: A Study of Form in Elizabethan Drama* (Madison, 1954; repr. 1964).

HATHAWAY, B., *The Age of Criticism: The Late Renaissance in Italy* (Ithaca, NY, 1962).

——*Marvels and Commonplaces: Renaissance Literary Criticism* (New York, 1968).

HERRICK, M. T., *Comic Theory in the Sixteenth Century* (Urbana, Ill., 1950; repr. 1964).

——*Tragicomedy: Its Origin and Development in Italy, France, and England* (Urbana, Ill., 1955; repr. 1962).

HOLLANDER, J., *Vision and Resonance: Two Senses of Poetic Form* (New York, 1975).

JONES, E., *The Origins of Shakespeare* (Oxford, 1977).

KENNEDY, G. A. (ed.), *The Cambridge History of Literary Criticism, i: Classical Criticism* (Cambridge and New York, 1989; repr. 1993).

MYRICK, K. O., *Sir Philip Sidney as a Literary Craftsman* (Cambridge, Mass., 1935).

NELSON, W., *Fact or Fiction: The Dilemma of the Renaissance Storyteller* (Cambridge, Mass., 1973).

NORTON, G. (ed.), *The Cambridge History of Literary Criticism, iii: The Renascence* (Cambridge, 1999).

RUSSELL, D. A., *Criticism in Antiquity* (London, 1981).

SCOTT, I., *Controversies over the Imitation of Cicero in the Renaissance: With Translations of Letters between Pietro Bembo and Gianfrancesco Pico 'On Imitation' and a Translation of Desiderius Erasmus, The Ciceronian (Ciceronianus)* (New York, 1910; repr. Davis, Calif., 1991).

SPINGARN, J. E., *A History of Literary Criticism in the Renaissance* (New York, 1899; repr. 1924; 1963, with an introd. by B. Weinberg).

SWEETING, E. J., *Early Tudor Criticism: Linguistic & Literary* (Oxford, 1940).

VICKERS, BRIAN, *In Defence of Rhetoric* (Oxford, 1988; rev. edn., 1997).

——'Rhetoric and Poetics', in C. B. Schmitt and Q. Skinner (eds.), *The Cambridge History of Renaissance Philosophy* (Cambridge and New York, 1988), 715–45.

WEINBERG, B., *A History of Literary Criticism in the Italian Renaissance*, 2 vols (Chicago, 1961, 1974).

WEST, D., and WOODMAN, T. (eds.), *Creative Imitation and Latin Literature* (Cambridge and New York, 1979).

WHITE, H. O., *Plagiarism and Imitation During the English Renaissance: A Study in Critical Distinctions* (Cambridge, Mass., 1935; repr. New York, 1965, 1973).

WIMSATT, W. K., Jr., and BROOKS, C., *Literary Criticism: A Short History* (New York, 1957; repr. 1966).

GLOSSARY

abase, lower, minimize
abdicated, disinherited
abject, something cast off, despised, rejected
abjure, renounce, abandon
above the nock, exceeding just proportion
absolute, finished, complete, consummate
abstract, summary, epitome
abstracted, withdrawn from the contemplation of present objects
abuse (n.), deceit, imposture; improper usage
abuse (vb.), deceive
abusion, improper usage (*catachresis*)
accent, rhythmical stress
access, acceptance
accident, event
accidents, changes of word forms, to express number, case, etc.
accommodate, adapt
accord, reconcile
accountable, able to be computed
accumulate, heap up on, give to
accurate, careful
acquisite, acquired
act, record of things done
adamant, stone of impregnable hardness
adminiculation, corroboration, support
administration, control
admiration, wonder, amazement, reverence
advance, put forward; praise
advertisement, admonition, instruction
advouterer, adulterer
advouterous, adulterous
aesture, turbulence, boiling
affect (n.), emotion, mood; partiality; mental or physical disposition

affect (vb.), desire, strive for; like to practise, profess; admire
affection, passion, emotion; prejudice
affections, dispositions
affects, passions, emotions
affy, trust, confide
afore, previously
after, afterwards, subsequently
against, towards
aggravate, magnify, increase the gravity of (something evil, an offence, etc.)
agnition, recognition
air, manner, style; tune, melody
airy, vain, superficial
all, just; as if
all one, the same as
allay, moderate; purge
allege, affirm; cite, quote
alley, walk or passage in a garden or park
allow, praise, approve
allowable, appropriate, acceptable
allowance, praise, approval; acknowledgement
allowed, approved
almost, indeed
altercation, controversy
alternative, alternating
ambage, roundabout or indirect modes of speech
amendable, capable of correction
American, American Indian
amiable, worthy of being loved
ample, copious; treating of matters at full length
amplification, expansion of subject-matter; intensification
anatomy, dissection
angel, gold coin
animadversion, censure, rebuke

annealed, toughened by heat; made more protective
answerable, appropriate, decorous
answering, corresponding
antic, grotesque, bizarre
apace, quickly
apertly, openly, evidently
apparent, visible; probable, likely
appassionate, inflame with passion
apprehension, conception, understanding
apprehensive, pertaining to perception by the intellect or senses; discerning
arbour, tree bower
architector, architect
arrearing, reverse direction
artificial, made by art; skilful
artist, master of any liberal art; educated person
aspersion, calumniation, defamation
asquint, suspicious, critical
associate, accompany
assoil, explanation, solution
assuaged, diminished, moderated
assubtiling, refining
attempt, tempt, assault
autodidaktoi, self-taught persons
available, valid
avoid, depart from; make void, invalidate

bait (vb.), to give food and drink to an animal, especially on a journey
ban, curse, anathematize
band, binding quality; cohesion
bane, poison, harm
bar, tribunal
barbarousness, lack of literary culture
bare, mere, simple
bate, contention, strife
bays, laurel wreath, the poet's crown
bear, put up with
beau semblant, fine appearances
becoming, fitting, suitable
behight, promise, vow

behither, on this side of
beholding, indebted
belie, misrepresent
belike, probably, perhaps
bent, act of bending; aim, intent
bernacle, wild goose
Besogne, Bezonian; worthless fellow
betray, constitute evidence or a symptom of
bewray, divulge, reveal
bias, bulge
bidding base, singing competition
bide, remain, continue
blanch, palliate by misrepresentation
blaze, depict, proclaim
blazing, adorning with heraldic devices
blockam, over-indulgent, satiating
boisterous, savage, truculent
bolsterer, supporter, accomplice
bolt out, search, sift
bowline, rope used to hold a sail closer to the wind
braid, creation, composition
braky, rough, thorny
brave (adj.), splendid, showy
brave (vb.), to defy
braveness, excellence, superiority
bravery, ostentation, bravado
bravest, best, finest
breaches, elisions, compactings
breathing, pause for breath; caesura in verse-line.
brimly, clearly, distinctly
brise, bruise, impress
brocage, pimping
broker, pimp, bawd
bruit, rumour
bruited, famous
buckle, bend
buckler (vb.), to shield
bulk, body, belly, trunk
burden, refrain
burnishing, burnished appearance, polish
busy, meddlesome, importunate
but, merely

by, in respect of
by-accident, subsidiary event

cabinet, private chamber
cacemphaton, obscene expression
cadence, measured movement of
    sounds; the falling of the voice;
    rhyme
caesure, caesura
caitiff, base
camp, military existence
can, know how
cankered, malignant, spiteful
cantabanqui, itinerant singers
capacity, mental or intellectual power
carcass, living body
care, worry
cark, care, anxiety
carol, joyful hymn
carver, sculptor
cast (n.), contrivance, trick
cast (vb.), to find guilty, convict
casts, plans, plots
casualty, chance
censorious, severe, befitting a
    censor
censure, judgement
ceremonies, sacred objects
chafe, anger
chainshot, cannon balls linked by
    chain
challenge, claim
change (n.), exchange, variation
change (vb.), to exchange
changeling, a child secretly
    substituted for another in
    infancy
chaplet, wreath of flowers for the
    head
charact, mark, sign (of worth)
chase, run
cheap, cheaply
check, rebuke, reprove
choiceness, selectness, special
    excellence
churl, niggard; low-bred person
circumstance, circumlocution;
    subordinate matter or detail

circumstances, the adjuncts of
    action (e.g. time, place)
civility, good citizenship; correct
    behaviour
claps, applause
clatter (vb.), chatter, tattle
claw (vb.), flatter, fawn upon
cleanly, properly, decently
cleped, called
clerk, literate person, scholar
clerkly, scholarly
clip, cut, shorten
close, conclusion of a composition, or
    rhyme
cloudy, doubtful, uncertain
clout (vb.), to patch, adapt
cognizance, crest, badge
collation, comparison
collection, summary
colour (n.), rhetorical device;
    ornament of style or diction
colour (vb.), present in a favourable
    light
coloured, specious; glossed over
come in, join, side with
comedian, actor
comeliness, decorum
comely, appropriate; observing
    decorum
comfit, sweet
commenter, commentator
commit, connect, compare
commodity, advantage, benefit
commonplace, category in logic and
    rhetoric
compact, made up of, composed of
compass (n.), measure, proportion
compass (vb.), to achieve
compassion, sympathy
complexion, combination of
    qualities, physical constitution
composed, composite, complete
composition, the arrangement of
    words into clauses and sentences
compositions, compounds
composure, composition
comprehended, included, contained
compt, reckon, estimate

con over, study, get to know
con thank, express gratitude
concatenation, linking, connection
conceit, idea, thought, mental
conception; invention
conclude, restrict
concluding, finally proving
concoct, digest
concord, agreement, harmony; rhyme
concourse, confluence, concurrence
condescend, yield, defer
condole, grieve over, lament
confection, medicinal preparation
confederacy, union
confer, compare (e.g. a translation
with its original); evaluate
conference, comparison, collation
confirm, sanction; establish more
firmly
conform, confirm
conformation, adaptation
confound, confuse
confusion, discomfiture, ruin
conned, known, understood
consent (n.), harmony, concord
consent (vb.), be in accord or
harmony
consequence, a logical sequence,
inference
consequent, the second part of a
conditional proposition
consistence, coherence
consort, fellowship
conspicuous, remarkable, noteworthy
conspire, agree, concur
construction, misinterpretation
contemn, despise, scorn
contemplation, theorizing
contentious, quarrelsome
contributory, contributing, taking
part
contrivance, design, plotting
contumelious, insulting,
contemptuous
convenience, agreement, congruity,
propriety
conveniency, propriety, congruity,
appropriateness

convenient, apt, appropriate
conveniently, suitably, appropriately
convented, convened
conversant, conversationalist
conversation, behaviour, mode of
life
conversion, translation
convert, translate
conveyance, communication,
transmission; expression, style
copie, fullness of expression
copious, abundant
copy, copiousness, abundance
cordial, medicine to stimulate the
circulation and invigorate
corps, body, living person
corslet, piece of armour
cothurnate, wearing buskins; in
tragic style
couched, placed, arranged
countenance, credit, repute
counterfeit, represented, portrayed
countries, counties, regions
courage, disposition, spirits; sexual
vigour, passion
course, normal process
coursed, pursued, reiterated
courting, residing at court; acting the
courtier
critical, exercising careful judgement
crowder, fiddler, minstrel
cuckoo-spell, Cuckoo's repetitive call
cumbersome, obstructive,
interfering
cunning (adj.), skilful,
knowledgeable
cunning (n.), knowledge, skill,
dexterity
curiosities, whims, fancies
curiosity, undue subtlety, affectation,
fastidiousness
curious, fastidious, over-elaborate;
noteworthy, skilful
curiously, exquisitely
current, smoothly flowing
currentness, easy, flowing movement
curry-favell, one who solicits favour
by flattery

curst, malignant
curtailed, with tail cut short

daintily, rarely, sparingly
daintiness, fastidiousness, good taste
dainty, delightful, precious
dapper, pretty
dark, obscure
darkness, obscurity
dart, arrow
daub, paint crudely or inartistically
deal, considerable quantity
dear, hard, severe, costly
debar, prohibit, exclude
debase, depreciate, belittle
decency, appropriateness, decorum
decent, appropriate (of style to
    subject-matter)
decipher, depict
deduce, derive, draw from its source
deem, pronounce judgement
defensible, safe, capable of being
    defended
deflowered, deprived of flowers,
    lacking invention
delated, informed against
delicacy, delight, pleasantness
delicate, affected; delightful, pleasant
delicious, sensuous, voluptuous
deliver, expound; address
deliverer, transmitter
delivery, setting forth in words
demesne, dominion, power
deplore, lament, bewail
deprave, vilify, disparage
deprehend, seize, comprehend
derring-do, chivalric adventure
design (vb.), to designate
despiteful, contemptuous, disdainful
destinate, intended for; decreed
determinate, decided, settled on
determination, authoritative
    opinion, settlement
determine, come to a judicial
    decision; decide
determiner, judge
detriment, loss, damage
device, design, composition

devised, invented
devotion, dedication
dialect, language
diction, choice of words
diffuse, lengthy
digladiation, wrangling, argument
diligence, careful attention
dimeter, a verse line of two measures
direct, immediate
director, person giving advice or
    instruction
disable, disparage, belittle
disallow, disapprove
disciplinable, amenable to
    instruction
discipline, subject, learning;
    instruction, education
discover, display, reveal, expound
discovery, disclosure
discreet, judicious; appropriate,
    fitting
discretion, judgement, decorum
dispense, give out (as sole source)
disport, pastime
disproportioned, inappropriate
disputative, belonging to scholarly
    disputations
dissections, the products of
    dissection
dissembler, concealer
distaste, dislike, repugnance
distemper, disease, disorder
distinguished, distinct
ditty, short simple song
divers, various, sundry, several
diversities, distinctions
doctrinable, instructive
doctrinal, instructive, didactic
document, teaching, instruction,
    warning
dotage, folly
double (vb.), to repeat, reiterate
doubt, fear, dread
doubted, dreaded; doughty
doubtful, ambiguous
doubtfulness, ambiguity
drab (vb.), to associate with
    prostitutes, whores

dray-man, brewer's cart-driver
dread, dreaded
dressing, preparation
dricksy, timber having decayed spots hidden by healthy wood
dusked, obscured

ear, grain; harvest
earnest (n.), work, serious occupation
easiness, indulgence, laziness
easy, lazy; obtained with little effort
effectual, efficacious; earnest, urgent
efficacy, power to produce effects
efficient, cause of an effect
eft, afterwards
eftsoons, soon after, forthwith
either, each
eke, moreover, also
elect, chosen by God for salvation
election, choice
embattling, setting in battle array
enable, strengthen
encounter, instance; meeting, answer; manner, behaviour
encounterer, adversary; contrary, opposite
enforce, strengthen, reinforce
engine, contrivance, artifice
enormity, crime, transgression
enormous, outrageous, wicked
entertainment, manner of behaviour
entry, opening words
envy, odium, disrespect
equal, contemporary
equipage, equipment, retinue
ere, ever, at all
erect, inspire, embolden
err, wander
erst, until recently
esbastement, pastime, sport
essence, existence
essential, having an essence; really existing
essentially, according to its true essence
estate, national affairs

estranged, absent from his normal dwelling
ex obliquo, obliquely
except, object
exception, objection
exchequer, treasury
excitation, stimulation, arousal
excogitate, carefully consider
exercise, activity, customary practice
exorable, able to be moved by entreaty
exorbitancy, extravagance, excessiveness
exornation, ornamentation, adornment
expound, interpret
express, depict (on stage)
exquisite, painstaking; carefully chosen; excellent; affected
exquisitely, discriminatingly
extent, size, dimension
extenuation, mitigation
extreme (n.), severity, harsh penalty
extremities, state of urgency, crisis; carried to extremes

facility, fluency; easiness
fact, evil or wrongful action, crime
factious, quarrelsome
faculty, trade, occupation; ability, aptitude
fame, reputation; rumour
familiar, close acquaintance
familiarly, informally
fantastical, capricious, fanciful
fantasticalness, eccentricity, whimsicality
fantasy, imagination
far-fet, obscure, far-fetched
fashion, form
fast, firm
fat, rich, fertile
fatness, richness, abundance
fautor, partisan, abetter
featly, gracefully, neatly
fee, reward, punishment

feign, imaginatively create; disguise, conceal

felicity, appropriateness in invention or expression

fell, ruthless

fervour, ardour, intense feeling

fetch, act of fetching; contrivance, trick

fiction, fashioning, making

figure, form, shape

figuring, expressing, representing

finesse, refinement, delicacy

fit (n.), outbreak of fever or madness; part of a composition (poetry, music)

fit (vb.), to suit

fitty, fitting, suitable

fledge, able to fly, mature

fleeting, fickle, easily distracted

flourish, embellishment

flower off, produce, yield

fly-blown, broke, penniless

foil, repulse, defeat

foiled, frustrated, baffled

fon, foolish man

fond, uneducated, foolish

fondly, foolishly

fondness, foolishness, folly

for or, because

for the nonce, for a particular occasion; deliberately

force (vb.), to compel, constrain

forced, strained

fore-backwardly, starting at the wrong end

foregoing, precedent

forehead, assurance

formal, in outward form; well-formed, regular

forsooth, indeed

forthink, repent of

for-thy, for that

founder, supporter, patron

framed, constructed

frank, free, open, not practising concealment

fraught, equipped, supplied

free, generous

frequent, common talk; crowded

frequent (vb.), use habitually or repeatedly

frizzled, curled

from, away from

froward, unfavourable, perverse

furniture, materials, equipment; preparation, mental cultivation

fustian, inappropriately lofty language; bombast

gall, sore produced by chafing

gallantness, splendour, excellence

galled, mocked

gather, deduce, infer

gay, bright, showy

geason, rare, scarce

geld, castrate, emasculate

generous, magnanimous

gentile, pagan, heathen

gest, deed, exploit

get, beget, conceive

giants, race of beings who fought against the gods

gin, tool, instrument

glass, mirror

glorious, haughty

glose, gloss, expanding the translation

gloss, lustre, shine

good-fellow, boon companion; thief

got, begot; born

government, control, conduct

graff (n.), graft

graff (vb.), to plant, implant

grashing, gnashing

grateful, pleasing, acceptable

graver, engraver's tool, a burin

great, big

grief, harm, damage

groat, silver coin, worth fourpence

gross, obvious, easy to understand

grossly, plainly, obviously

ground, cause

groundsill, foundation

grudge (vb.), to grumble, complain

guards, ornamental borders, trimmings
guerdon, reward
gull, dupe, fool

habit, dress, garment
hackneyman, one who keeps horses for hire
halt, proceed lamely
han, have
hand, in, captive
hap, luck, fortune
hardiness, rudeness, audacity
hardly, forcibly; harshly
haughty, of exalted style, imposing; obscure
headiness, headstrongness
heal, health
heap, a great deal
hebrician, Hebrew scholar
heedily, carefully, attentively
height, high style; dignity, forcefulness
heresies, practices contrary to accepted doctrine
heroical, epic, poetry dealing with heroes and their deeds
hint, chance, opportunity
hold, retain; correspond, apply
hold on, support, side with
honest (vb.), to honour
honesty, honour, chastity
honey (vb.), to respond warmly
hugger mugger, secrecy, concealment
humanity, humanities; *studia humanitatis*
humorous, whimsical, capricious
humour, state, condition
husband (vb.), to take care of
husbandman, farmer
husbandry, management of a household; agriculture, farming

idea, ideal
idle, leisured
ill-affected, badly chosen
illaqueation, entangling in argument

illation, inference, deduction
illecebrous, attractive, exciting
ill-favoured, displeasing, disagreeable
ill-pleased, pleased by evil sights
illustrate, exemplify
imaginative, unreal, imaginary
immutation, change, alteration
imp (vb.), to graft, implant
impeachment, injury, damage
impertinency, inappropriateness, incongruity
impertinent, not belonging
implicative, a statement implying more than is expressed
import, signify, denote, imply
importunity, persistence
impression, pressure, influence
inartificially, inartistically
include, contain, comprise
incommodity, disadvantage, discomfort
incongruent, unsuitable, inappropriate
inconvenience, unsuitableness, impropriety
indecency, indecorum
indecent, inappropriate
indenize, naturalize; accept as a citizen
indifferent, impartial, neutral
indifferently, equally, impartially
indiscreet, inappropriate, injudicious
indiscretion, imprudence, transgression
indite, compose (a poem, etc.)
inditing, ability to speak or write
induce, introduce
induction, initiation, introduction
industry, of, intentionally
infirmity, lack of power, knowledge
inform, to shape, mould, form
infusion, pouring in, transfusion
ingenuous, noble, innocently frank
ingram, ignorant
inkhorn, pedantic; learned or bookish language
insinuate, introduce indirectly

insinuation, intertwining, connection
insipid, dull, flat
insolent, bold, swelling
instalment, installation
instinct, instilment
institution, instruction
intend, design, mean; attend to;
    intensify
intendant, meaning, signification
intendment, understanding;
    signification; design, intention
intent (adj.), intensive, assiduous
intent (n.), opinion, judgment;
    meaning
interlacing, intermingling
interview, inspection
inured, accustomed, familiar
inveigle, beguile, deceive, ensnare
inversion, transposition, reversal
invert, transpose, reverse
involved, enfolded
inwardness, hidden sense

jealous, protective, watchful;
    suspicious, mistrustful
jejune, meagre, unsatisfying
jointing, disjointing
jointure, junction, joint
judicial, judicious

kind, nature
kindly, characteristic, appropriate;
    according to nature
knit up, fasten, fix

laboured, ploughed, tilled; carefully
    considered
languishment, apathy caused by love
lap, wrap
lapping-up, wrapping together,
    conclusion
largely, generally, fully
laureate, worthy of the Muses'
    crown
law, allowance
lay (vb.), to express, couch
leasing, lie, falsehood
leese, lose
legendary, collection of legends

leman, lover
letters, literature
lewd, untaught, ignorant
liberal, fit for a gentleman;
    unprejudiced, open-minded
licensed, free
licentious, deviating freely from
    grammatical or literary
    correctness
liggen, lie
light, promiscuous, wanton; trivial,
    facetious
lightness, wantonness; frivolity
lightsomeness, radiance, brightness
limn, paint, portray, depict.
limned, depicted, portrayed
line and level, criterion, measure of
    excellence
lineage, lineal descent
list (vb.), to care, like, please
living, method of gaining one's
    livelihood
loose, discharge (of an arrow)
loosely, laxly, without restraint
lordship, estate
love-lay, love song
lower, lour, frown, scoul
luminous, bright
lustre, glory, splendour
lusty, physically vigorous
lyric, lyric poet

magnanimity, great courage,
    loftiness of thought or purpose
magnanimous, nobly valiant, of
    high courage
magnific, exalted, sublime; serving to
    magnify, eulogistic
majordomo, chief official of a
    princely household
maker, poet
making, writing poetry
manhood, physical strength, violence
mannerly, becomingly
manners, moral conduct
manured, cultivated
march, manner
marches, border regions

marchpane, marzipan
mark (n.), aim, target; unit of
  currency
mark (vb.), to pay due attention
marked, noticed
marmoset, ape, monkey
material, relevant, pertinent;
  concerning subject-matter
matron, respectable married woman
matter, subject-matter (*res*)
mean, unskilled, mediocre; inferior,
  vulgar
measure, poetic metre
mechanic, artisan, manual worker
meeken, lessen the violence of, tame
meet, suitable
member, part, section
members, bodily parts; genitals
memorable, easy to remember
mend, correct, improve
merely, entirely, purely
metaphysic, metaphysician,
  philosopher concerned with the
  first principles of things
method, mode of procedure
miller's round, rustic dance
mimic, actor; imitator
mind (vb.), to plan, intend
minion, servile agent, slave
ministry, provision, supply
mix, confuse
mome, blockhead, fool
monomachy, single combat; duel
mood, mode, form
morality, moral philosophy; moral
  sense, application
most, mostly
motion, emotion
mought, must
mulct, to punish, penalize
mystery, handicraft, trade
mystical, allegorical

narrowly, closely
naturally, in nature, real life
naught (adj.), immoral, licentious
naught (n.), wickedness, evil
naughtiness, wickedness

naughty, morally bad, wicked
ne, nor
necessity, being inevitably fixed
nesh, tender, delicate
next, nearest
nice, pampered, spoiled; minute, fine
nicely, fastidiously, fussily
niceness, modesty; fastidiousness
nip (n.), rebuke, reproof
nip (vb.), to rebuke, reprove
nock, above the, beyond measure
nonce, for the, expressly; for a
  particular purpose
note (n.), distinctive characteristic;
  distinction, excellence
note (vb.), to denote, indicate
notorious, conspicuous, obvious
numbers, metrical feet; verses;
  metrics
numbrous, metrical, measured
numerosity, rhythmical quality
numerous, rhythmic, harmonious
nuncius, messenger

obnoxious, liable or exposed to harm
obtestation, entreaty, supplication
occupy, make use of
odds, difference, disparity
of, from (the resources of)
of course, customarily
office, duty, function, occupation
once, shortly
one, the same; identical
opening, exposition; unfolding of a
  case
opposite, antagonist, opponent
or . . . or, either . . . or
ordinance, decree, injunction
ordinary, public eating-place
oriental, resplendent
otherwise, different
overlaid, overrun

painful, laborious, painstaking;
  difficult
painfulness, painstakingness
palmer, pilgrim
panegyries, solemn public assemblies

pardie, certainly, indeed

part (vb.), to assign a dramatic part or character

part stakes, share resources

particularity, particular point

pash, to strike violently, smash

pass, consider, care; depend; overlook, neglect; surpass

passement, decorative trimming of gold lace

passion, property, attribute

passport, password

patriot, fellow-countryman

paunch, stomach

pavilion, tent, canopy

paynim, pagan, heathen

pease, pea

peccadilia, small faults

peccant, unhealthy, corrupt

peculiar (adj.), proper, specific

peculiar (n.), own property

peeler, plunderer, thief

peevish, capricious, silly, perverse

peis'd, weighed

pelting, mean, insignificant, trifling

pencil, brush

penning, style

pensiful, thoughtful, pensive

percase, perhaps

perdurable, permanent, imperishable

perfect, complete

period, sentence, unit

person, personage, character

personable, pleasing in appearance and manner

perspicuity, clarity

Perusine, Peruvian

perverse, wicked, incorrect

petulancy, rudeness, insolence

Phoebus' race, the sun's course; a day

phrase, expressive resource

physic, medicine

picked, carefully arranged; adorned, ornate

picked out, distinguished, selected

pie, magpie

piece (vb.), to mend, insert

plausible, praiseworthy, commendable

plausive, pleasing, deserving applause

playing, acting

pleader, advocate

pleasance, frivolous delight(s)

plebe, plebeian, working class

plight, condition

poetaster, paltry or inferior poet

point (n.), part, element; period, full stop

point (vb.), to allude to

pointedness, jaggedness

pointing, punctuation

policy, politics, state affairs; prudent or expedient conduct

politic, sly, scheming person; politician

pompous, magnificent, splendid

popinjay, parrot

popular, used by the public

porch, side-chapel of a church

portrait (vb.), to portray

post (vb.), to hurry, make haste

posy, a short motto, often in verse, inscribed within a ring

pounded, placed in a pound for stray cattle

practice, practical skill, performance

practise, conspire

preceptive, precept, instruction

precipitation, over-hasty judgement

precise, strict in observing rules

prefer, promote

preferment, promotion, advancement

pregnant, full of ideas, inventive

premiss, previous statement or proposition from which another is inferred

preposterous, inverted, disordered; contrary to nature or reason

presage, prediction, portent

prescription, ancient custom

present, immediate considerations

presently, immediately

presentment, theatrical representation
presly, concisely
pressing, emphasizing
pretence, claim
pretend, signify, mean
pretext, reason, motive
prevent, anticipate; cut off beforehand
price, value
primitive, ancient
principals, the main feathers in each wing
privity, secrecy, privacy
privy, surreptitious, covert
process, course of a narrative
procure, to raise revenue through fines
prodigal, recklessly wasteful
produce, extend in length
profess, avow, lay claim to
proper, appropriate, according to decorum; admirable
property, propriety
propise, proper, suitable
propone, propose
proportionable, appropriate, suitable
proposition, theme, topic
prosecute, pursue, investigate
prove, test
providing, foreseeing
province, sphere of action
provocation, incitement, sexual desire
prudence, practical wisdom
prudent, wise, discerning
pureness, purity
purge, prune; clear up
purpose, subject-matter; design, planning

quaint, ingenious, cunning
qualify, modify, adapt, regulate
quality, profession, esp. acting
questionable, arguable
questionist, a habitual or professed questioner, spec. in theological matters

quick, alive
quill, pen
quodlibet, any question proposed as an exercise in argument

rack, torture, strain
ragamuffin, person in ragged dirty clothes
rage, move violently, with fury
railing, abusive, jesting
raked up, covered over
rakehelly, rascally, degraded
rampire, rampart, defence
rankness, over-luxuriance, grossness
rapt, transported, inspired
rare, fine
rarely, excellently, remarkably
rate, measure of intensity; proportion, standard
rattle, chatterer; trivial person
ravening, ravenous, voracious
rebated, rabbeted: having a groove or channel to receive the edge or tongue of another piece
recess, retreat, holiday
recited, listed, itemized
recoursing, returning
recreative, refreshing
reduce, restore to its original state; bring to order, subdue; set down
reduced, organized, collected
regal, small, portable organ
regiment, rule, government
regular, according to rules or principles
relate, narrate, recount
relation, connection, correspondence; narration
relieve, help, assist
relieved, freed from restraint
religious, scrupulous
relish, consistent taste
remembered, mentioned, referred to
remove, put away
rencounter, contest, esp. in wit or argument
repair, resort, visit; restore, redeem
repine, to complain

report (n.), testimony, narrative; response (one musical note or part answering another)
report (vb.), to refer
reported, re-echoed
reporter, gossip, rumour-monger
repugn, resist, object
repugnancy, contradiction, inconsistency
resound, return a response or answer; echo
respect, consideration
respective, attentive, undeviating
respectively, according to the person addressed
rest, find a subject
resumption, recapitulation, summary
retire, conceal; return, recapitulate
reveal, disclose, communicate
revolution, rotation, mutation
right, true, accurate
rigour, severity, harshness
ring, company of dancers
riot, dissolute or wasteful living
rive, split, shatter
robustious, violent, aggressive
Roman, Catholic
rough, lacking refinement, unpolished
round, smooth, uninterrupted, unified; direct, blunt
roundly, fluently; quickly
roundness, smoothness, regularity; bluntness
routs, bands, companies
rub, unevenness
rude, rough, crude
rudeness, simple 'rustic' utterance; ignorance, lack of culture
running, smooth, easily flowing

saccaged, sacked, plundered
sad, gloomy
saker, falcon
sauce (vb.), to prepare, dress (food)
saw, saying, maxim
scabrous, harsh, rough

scale, standard of estimation
scan, climb; analyse or judge verse
scene, theatre
scholastical, academic, pedantic
school, university
schoolmen, academic teachers, scholastic philosophers
science, knowledge acquired by study
scilicet, namely
scope, a mark for aiming at
season, right, appropriate time
sectist, member of a schismatical sect
seculum, age, generation
seeliest, simplest, most ingenuous
seemly, appropriate, fitting, suitable
seen, informed, learned
semblably, similarly
seminaries, seed-plots, sources of knowledge
sensible, perceptible by the senses; having a sense; conscious, aware
sensual, pertaining to the senses or sensation
sentence (n.), meaning, significance; moral reflection; notable saying or maxim; verdict
sentence (vb.), to pass judgement on, assess
sententiousness, fullness of meaning
separation, division, disagreement
serious, in, seriously
several (adj.), separate
several (n.), private possession
severally, separately, singly
severe, strict, exacting
severed, separated
shadow (vb.), to picture, represent; obscure, darken
shadowing, shading
sharp, acute
sharpness, outspoken satire
sheddeth, evaporates, disperses
shift (n.), trick, stratagem; change of place
shift (vb.), to manage, contrive
shining, splendour
shore, cleave, tear
show, appearance

shrew, bad-tempered wife
shrewd, harmful; mischievous, naughty
shriking, shriek, shrill cry
shrill, high-pitched, emphatic
shutting up, concluding
shyttle, contemptible
signifying, meaningful
sike, such
silly, weak, defenceless; unsophisticated, plain
simple, medicine composed of only one constituent, e.g. a single herb or plant
simplicity, naivety, stupidity; unpretentiousness
singularity, eccentricity, peculiarity
situation, positioning, location
skill (vb.), to matter
skoser, horse dealer
sleight, artful device
sliding, flowing
slipper, smooth, easily articulated
sluttish, slovenly
smally, very little
smatch (vb.), to smack of
snapshare, a share or portion obtained as an extra emolument
snudge, miser, skinflint
sobrest, most serious
solace, entertainment, recreation
soothing, flattery
sorrow, physical pain, suffering
sort, the same kind or class
sort (vb.), accord with, befit
sot (vb.), to besot, render foolish
sound (vb.), signify, imply
sovereign, superior
sparsim, dispersedly
speciality, special or particular point, detail
spice, incentive towards
spiced, delicate, over-scrupulous
spirits, animating powers
spleen, source of bad temper
splendid, illustrious, distinguished
spoil, property seized in war, pillaging

spoiling, destructive
sportingly, playfully
sprite, spirit, mind, courage
spurting, unpredictable
squalor, roughness
square (n.), implement for measuring or setting out right angles
square (vb.), to arrange, render appropriate
squint-eyed, suspicious, envious
squire, square (used by carpenters)
staff, stanza, verse
stand upon, depend on
stare, starling
starveling, meagre, scanty
state, national affairs; politics, statesmanship; estate; condition
staves, stanzas
steel glass, metal-backed mirror
stew, brothel
stick, disagree, hold a contrary opinion
still, always
stir, movement
stomach, spite, animosity
stomaching, enduring, putting up with
stone, precious stone
store, stock; supply
story, history
stounds, blows of battle
strain (n.), sequence of words or music, melody
strain (vb.), afflict
strained, uttered in song
straitly, strictly, severely
strange, unknown, unfamiliar
stratagematic, skilled in military strategy
strictness, moral rigour
stroke (vb.), soothe, flather
study, zeal, eagerness (Lat. *studium*)
styled, written; called
suborn, to furnish, equip, adorn
subtile, intricate, abstruse
subtlety, subtle argument; cunning
subverted, demolished, razed to the ground

success, outcome; result of an action
suffrage, vote, approval, consensus
sugared, sweet; refined
suggestion, temptation
suit, succession
summed, fledged
supererogation, doing more than is needed
superficial, superficies, surface
superlation, hyperbole
superstitious, excessive, superfluous
supply, complete, fill up
surclose, conclusion
surmounter, superior
surquidrous, arrogant, haughty
swarm, crowd densely, proliferate
sweet, melodious, harmonious
swelling, pompous, inflated
symphony, harmony

table, board on which a picture is painted
tablet, notebook, sketchbook
take, impress, capture
take off, divert, distract
task (vb.), to reprove, accuse of wrongdoing
tax (vb.), to criticize, reproach
taxation, censure
taxed, censured
teller, cashier
temper (n.), type, make
temper (vb.), to mix, blend; adapt (to someone's needs); modify
temperament, blending, mixture
tempered, balanced
tenor, continuous course; taughtness; general sense or meaning
tenths, a tenth part (or tithe) of one's annual produce or income, to be given to the church
terminant, termination
terms, manner of speaking
tho, then
through-beholding, thorough consideration
throw by, reject; put aside decisively
tickle, changeable, capricious

time, unit of measure, esp. in music
tingling, tinkling
title, recognized right to possession
to that, as to that
touch (n.), brief contact; stroke of wit, satire
touch (vb.), to censure, criticize; discuss
toused, dishevelled
tow, fibre of flax or hemp
toy, trivial thing
toying, flirting, dallying
tract, course, treatment
tradition, treatment, discussion; teaching
traduce, slander, discredit, misrepresent
traffic, trade, business
trait, stroke of the pen or pencil
translation, appropriation, transference; metaphor
transport, transfer
travail, study; pains of childbirth, labour
travailed, learned, experienced
traverse (n.), impediment, obstacle; dispute; cross-purposes
traverse (vb.), to deny (an allegation) in pleading
treaty, treatment, discussion
trencher, plate, platter
tribrach, a metrical foot consisting of three short syllables
trouble (vb.), to disturb
trow, believe, think
trump, trumpet; celebration, praise
trunk, hearing
truss (vb.), (of a bird of prey): to seize or clutch the prey in its talons
tuftaffeta, florid, bombastic, over-dressed
tumorous, bombastic
tumour, swelling
tun, large cask or barrel
tunable, tuneful, harmonious
turken, alter
turn, translate; word differently

twifallowed, repeated ploughing-up of land for sowing
twight, twitched, touched

unartificial, unskilful
uncomeliness, indecorum, impropriety
underlay, an additional piece placed beneath something
understand, perceive, hear
understander, person having knowledge
understanding, knowledgeable reader
undertaker, whoever undertakes a task
unegally, irregularly
unelected, unchosen
unenarrable, incapable of being expressed
unfortunate, unlucky, unhappy
unfurnish, deprive
ungirt, not drawn together
ungratefully, unkindly
uniformity, consistency
unmustered, unenlisted
unscissored, with uncut hair; untonsured
unsophisticated, unspoiled
unstaid, undecided; unregulated
untuned, unrhythmical
uplandish, outlandish, foreign
ure, use, effect
utmost, outermost
utter, offer for sale
utterance, gesture

vail, lower, in sign of submission
vain, useless, fruitless
varlet, rogue, rascal
vaunted, highly praised
vehemency, powerful or excessive passion
vein, characteristic style of expression
vent, sell, emit
venture, risk, hazard
vernaculous, ill-bred, scurrilous

verse, line (of poetry)
versicle, short verse
very, real, genuine
viciosity, vice, corruption of language
vicious, incorrect, deformed
videl., videlicet, 'namely'
virtue, manliness, courage
vitiated, corrupted, faulty
vix, hardly, scarcely
voice, word; entry in a dictionary
volubility, fluency in utterance
voluble, moving rapidly; easily moved; fluent
vouchsafe, permit, condescend; acknowledge
vulgar, vernacular

wade, advance (in discussion)
wainscot, wood panelling lining a room
wait on, escort; distinguish
walk, extended discourse
wan, won
want (n.), lack, omission, deficiency; poverty
want (vb.), lack
wanton (adj.), lascivious, lewd
wanton (vb.), flourish profusely, luxuriate
wantonest, most impetuous, unrestrained
ware, vigilant, cautious
warely, vigilantly, cautiously
wax, grow, become
ween, think, suppose
weet, know
well-raised, exalted
where, whereas
wield, have at command
wight, person
windball, inflatable ball, used in games
winding, indirect, full of circumlocutions
wink at, overlook, disregard
wis, know
wit, intellect; learned, talented person

without, unless

wittily, intelligently, cleverly

wittiness, ingenuity, intelligence

witty, ingenious, clever

wood, extreme, irascible

woodwose, savage, wild man of the
woods

words of art, technical terms

wote, know

would, want, wish (to do
something)

wrested, forced, strained

writ, writing

wrought, influenced

yielding, admitting

zodiac, circle; closed extent

INDEX OF NAMES

Note: Boldface figures indicate writings by the author concerned

INDEX OF TOPICS